# Portrait of an Artist

*For Mitchell "Micky" Wolfson, Jr.*

# ACKNOWLEDGEMENTS

We would like to thank:

Ruth Artmonsky
Nicholas Bagshawe
John Barkes
Louise Bawden
Philip Beck
Jonathan Black
Charles Beddington
Katrin Bellinger
Robin Birley
Rosalind & Prudence Bliss
Quentin and Susan Bone
George Breeze
David Buckman
Elizabeth Bulkeley
Michael Campbell
Zeynep Can
David Capps
Hermione & Francis Carline
Gill Clarke
Eleanor Christie-Chatterley
Edward Cheney
Andrew Cormack
Jackie Cundall
Sasha & Bonamy Devas
Daniel Dullaway
Ro Dunbar
Michael Edwards
Andrew Ellis
Nicholas Finney
Sarah Flynn
James Folley
Andy Friend
Carole Froude-Durix
Gerrish Fine Art
Mike Goldmark
Lucinda Gosling
Nicolas Granger-Taylor
Chloe Gunn
Diana Gunton
Sarah Guthrie
Jonathan Guthrie
Charlotte Halliday
Craig Hamilton
Geoff Hassell of artbiogs.co.uk
Mary Haynes
Beverley Heywood
Jenny Heywood
Matthew Hilton
Niall Hobhouse
Dr. Libby Horner
Martin Humphreys
Robert Imhoff
Shaun Kenny
Elaine Kilmurray
Ömer M. Koç
Simon Lawrence
Zoe Leclerc
David & Sophie Leighton
Adrian Lewis
Eva Liss
Todd Longstaffe-Gowan
Pauline Lucas
Joanna Lumley
Rupert Maas
Steven Maisel
Simon Martin
Jon McLeod
Robert Meyrick
Harry Moore-Gwyn
Conor Mullan
Jon McLeod
Professor Kenneth McConkey
Catherine & John Monnington
Victoria & Susannah Nathanson
John Noot
Richard Ormond
John Parsloe
Alan Powers
Jeffrey S. Reznick
Sir Simon Robey
Aishah Sanders
Ian Sanders
Robin Shaw
Fizz Shawal
Kathleen Simon
Daniel Simon
Robin Simon
Peyton Skipwith
Caspar Sloan
Iain & Barendina Smedley
Richard Sorrell
Mark Sorrell
Julia Sorrell
Stuart Southall
Anthony Thompson
Richard Thompson
David Thomson
Charles Tolkien-Gillett.
Anne Ullmann
David Wade
Jack Wakefield
Grant Waters
Stephen Whittle
Denys Wilcox
Malcolm Yorke

We would particularly like to thank Christopher Campbell-Howes for his assistance

Many of the works featured in this publication have been sold to public collections and to private collectors over the last three decades.
We are indebted to their unfailing support in making this project possible.





Fuller acknowledgements can be found in our individual online entries.

First published in 2021 by LISS LLEWELLYN

ISBN : 978-1-9993145-4-5





Photography: Glynn Clarkson, Pierre Emmanuel Coste & Petra van der Wal

Design and Typesetting by David Maes
Printed by Zenith Media, August 2021

# Portrait of an Artist

Edited by Sacha Llewellyn & Paul Liss

LAING ART GALLERY

30TH ANNIVERSARY LISS LLEWELLYN ESTABLISHED 1991

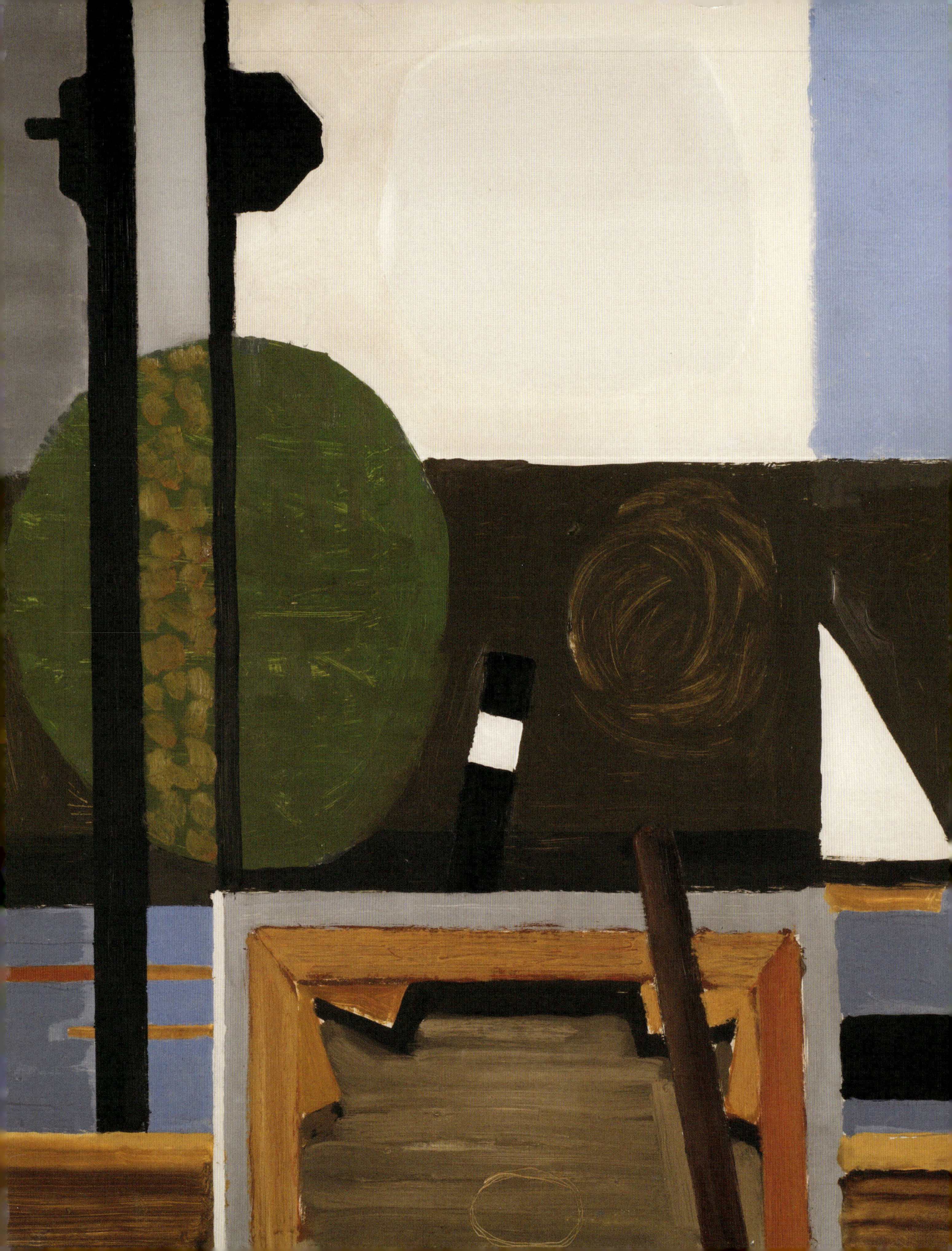

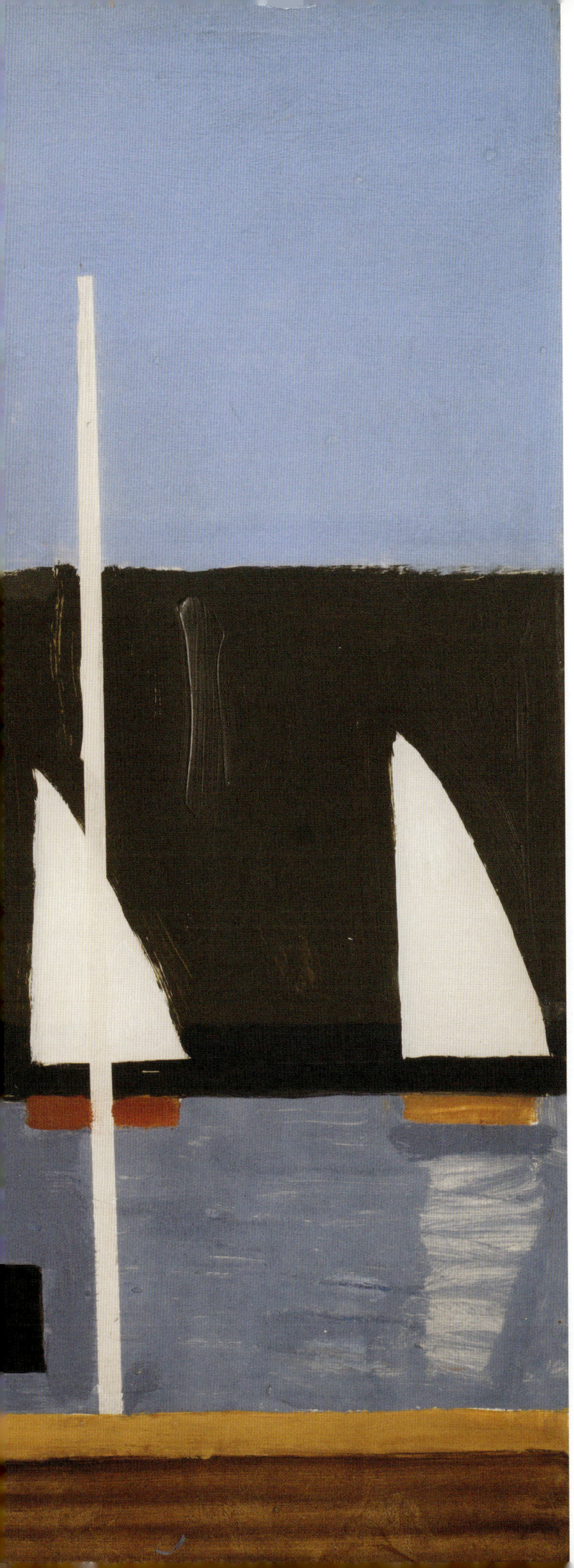

# Contents

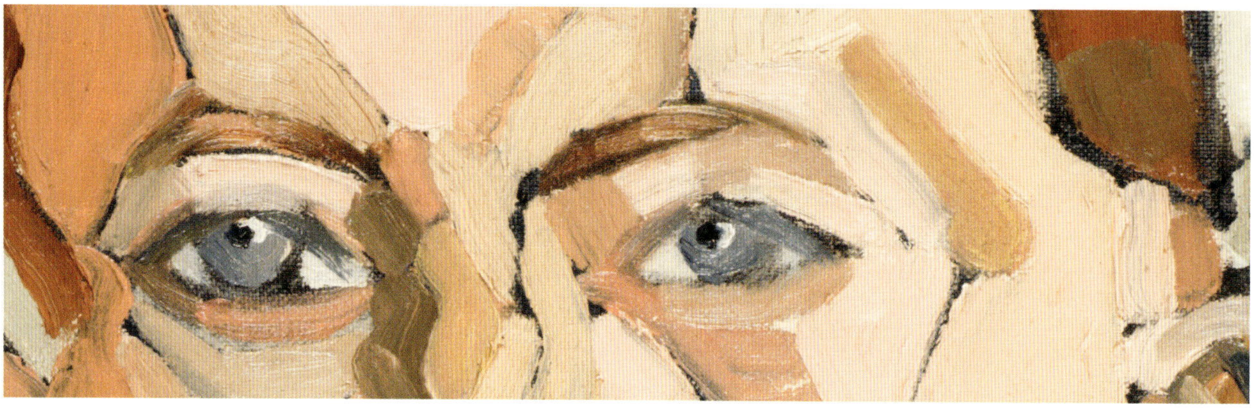

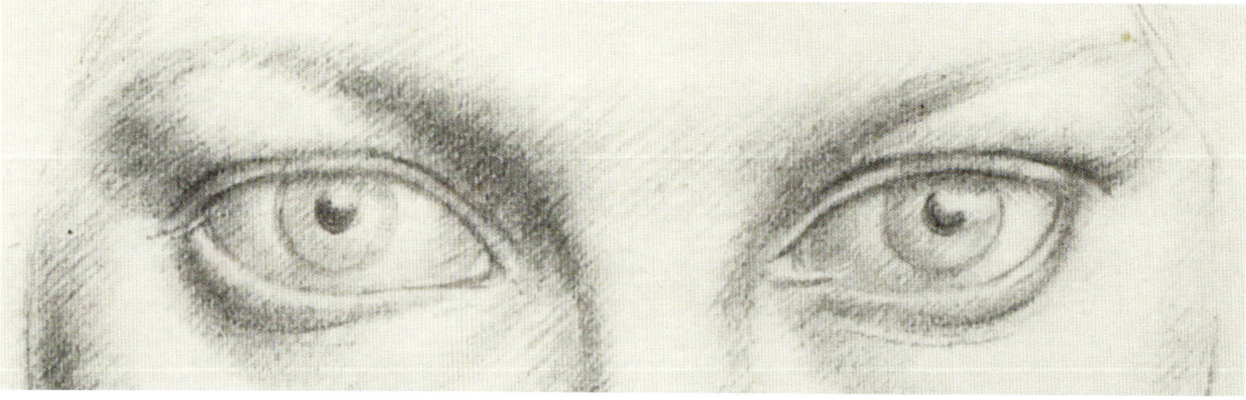

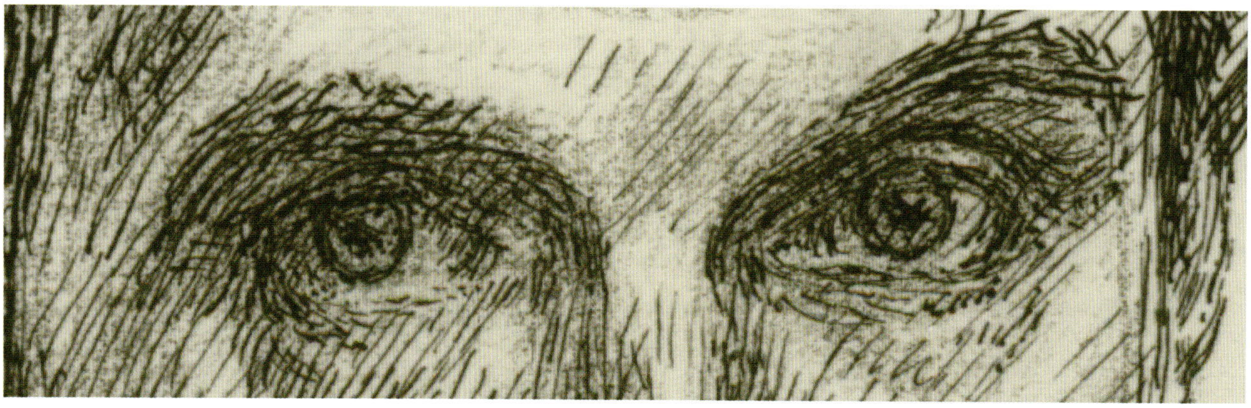

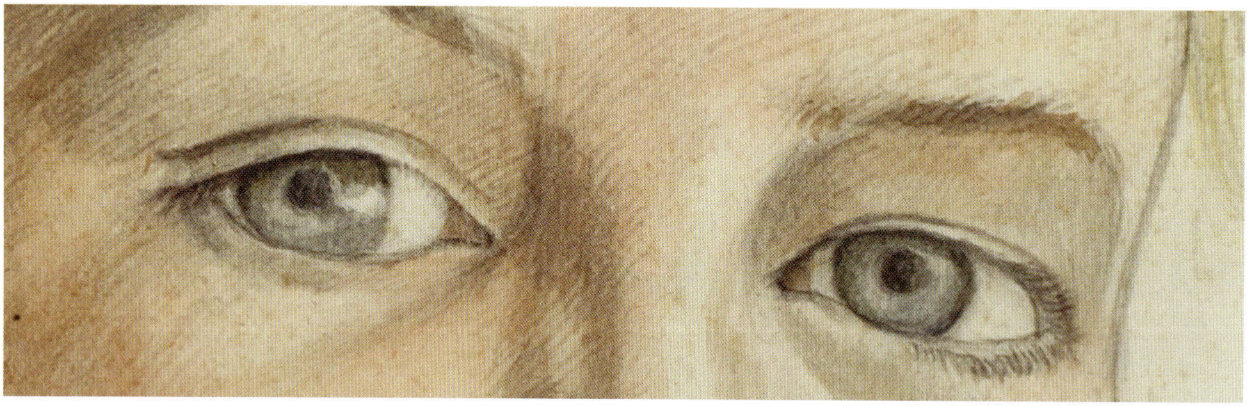

# Venue Statement

Unusual amongst British regional galleries, the Laing Art Gallery was gifted to the people of Newcastle without a collection of its own. Alexander Laing was not a connoisseur or collector, and when he wrote to the Newcastle Corporation in 1900 offering to provide the building, he was confident '...that by the liberality of the inhabitants it would soon be supplied with pictures and statuary for the encouragement and development of British Art'.

Precisely as Laing had anticipated, the intervening 120 years have seen the Gallery, through a series of gifts, bequests and purchases, accumulate one of the finest regional collections of fine and decorative art in the country. Changing displays highlight various aspects of the collection, and it is invigorating to be working with Liss Llewellyn once again on an exhibition that draws upon some of its strongest elements of 19th and 20th Century British art.

*Portrait of an Artist* offers an opportunity to step into the inner world of the artist, bringing the lives and image of those who existed behind the canvas to the forefront. Thanks to their years of working directly with artists' studios and an eye for the deceptively revealing, Liss Llewellyn have brought together a collection of works that expose something intensely personal about those who created them. The exhibition is a varied account of how these artists viewed and lived in their worlds, from the direct gaze of a self-portrait to an intimate moment between artist and sitter. It records the quiet interiors of artists' studios and homes that will resonate with many of us following the past year, as well as the creative process that is often so mysterious to viewers.

That some of the Laing's most popular works, by Sir William Orpen, Duncan Grant, Malcolm Drummond, and John Singer Sargent, have been used to complement the exhibition is especially fitting. We are also glad that *Portrait of an Artist* echoes the Gallery's aim to redress the imbalance in representation of women artists, by depicting those including Winifred Knights, Clare Leighton, Barbara Jones, Mary Adshead, Edith Granger-Taylor and Evelyn Dunbar as complex individuals and accomplished artists in their own right. We hope that together this collection of works by over 130 artists will provide insight into their practice, as well as an enticing glimpse of how artists see themselves.

Julie Milne, Chief Curator, Art Galleries

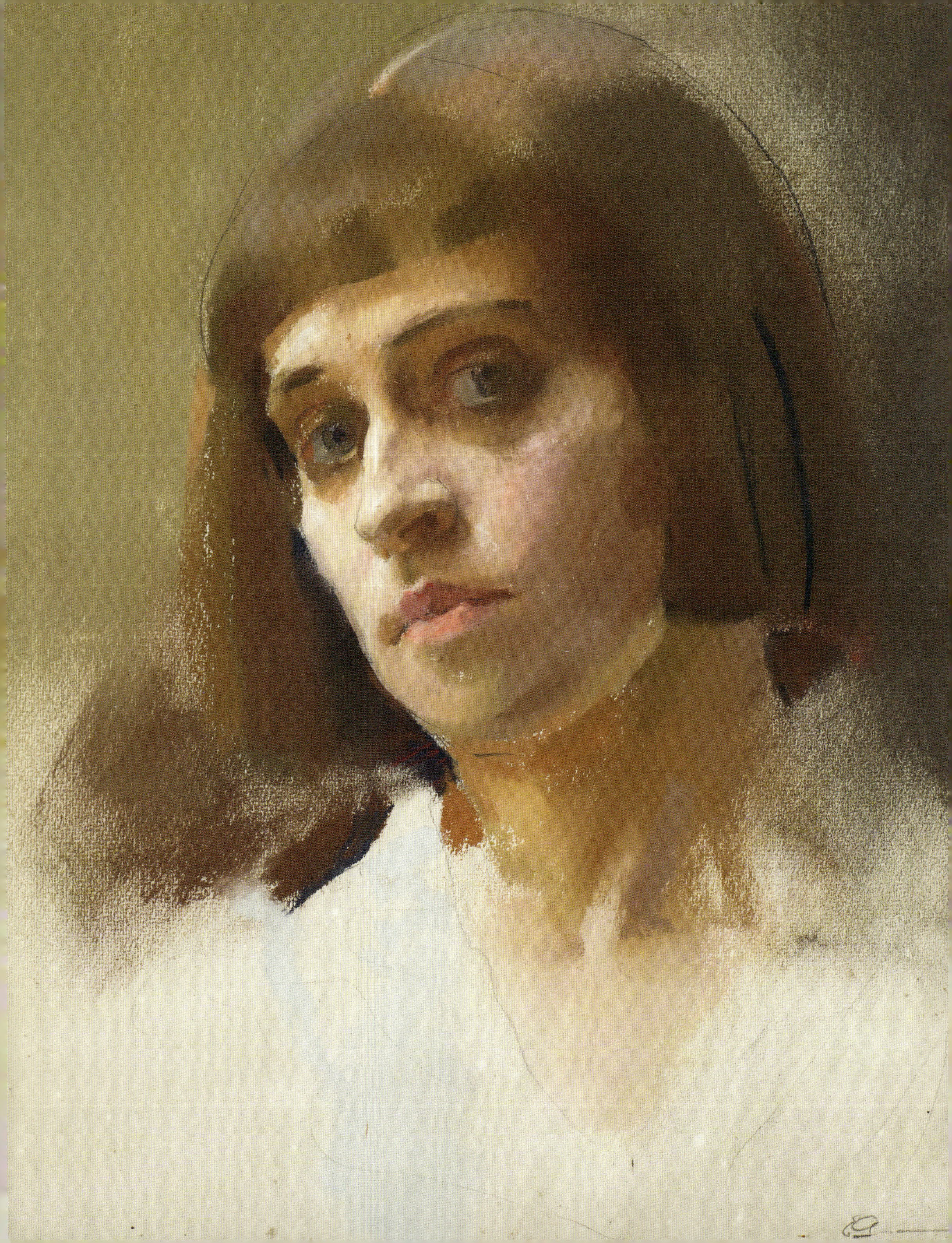

# Foreword

*'I think that every picture you make, every drawing you make, is a self-portrait. If they have anything in them at all, anything real, they must reflect something that comes from within.'*
Albert Houthuesen

This publication, and the exhibition that accompanies it, explore the theme of how artists portray themselves. The art of self-portraiture, with its rich history in Western Art stretching back to the time of Dürer, is at the heart of this project. But artists also frequently served as models in their own compositions – sometimes of necessity (they were short of a model or the money to pay for one) and sometimes because they wanted to position themselves as a participant in a particular narrative. Brangwyn painted himself taking the weight of the cross for Jesus, and Ziegler, going a step further, became Christ on the cross himself. Who can forget the haunting image of Winifred Knights as the central protagonist in her outstandingly original version of the deluge story?

Founded in 1991, Liss Llewellyn is celebrating its 30th anniversary. During the last three decades over twenty monographic publications, alongside themed publications on women artists, on war or religious art, have come to fruition. Of all of these productions *Portrait of an Artist* has been the longest in gestation. Haunting images of Evelyn Dunbar, Winifred Knights, Alan Sorrell, Robert Austin, Thomas Monnington, Kenneth Rowntree, Stanley Lewis, Karl Hagedorn, and Hugh Arthur Finney, first discovered in their studios, are presented in a new context.

Whether spontaneous works on paper or more formal compositions, it is hoped that these images have in common the power to transport the viewer momentarily back into the artist's milieu and the moment of creation. Here we can revel in the self-gaze of an artist, or the *frisson* that suggests the artist was in love with his or her subject.

This publication is limited exclusively to British artists and within a date range from the last quarter of the 19th to the last decade of the 20th century. The 385 works reproduced are organised into 5 sections: *Working Space, The Artist's Entourage, Artists by Artists, Self-portraits,* and *Allegories of Creation.* The content of each theme is explained in an introductory note which precedes each section with fuller entries for each work on the Liss Llewellyn website. All but 13 of the 385 images featured in this publication (**12**, **14**, **34**, **102**, **137**, **156**, **158**, **231**, **236**, **291**, **298**, **301**, **328**) are, or have been, owned by, or consigned to Liss Llewellyn at some point in the last three decades. During this period many have been sold to national and international public collections and to private collectors. We are indebted to their unfailing support for making this project possible.

We are delighted to be working for a second time this year with the Laing Art Gallery and we are immensely grateful to them for offering a home to this wonderful selection of images, which includes four masterpieces from their own collection, (**12**,**14**,**156**, **236**).

*Paul Liss*

1 **Edith Granger-Taylor** (1887-1958), *Self-portrait*, 1914, signed with monogram and dated, pastel on paper, 14 x 10 in. (36 x 25.5 cm).

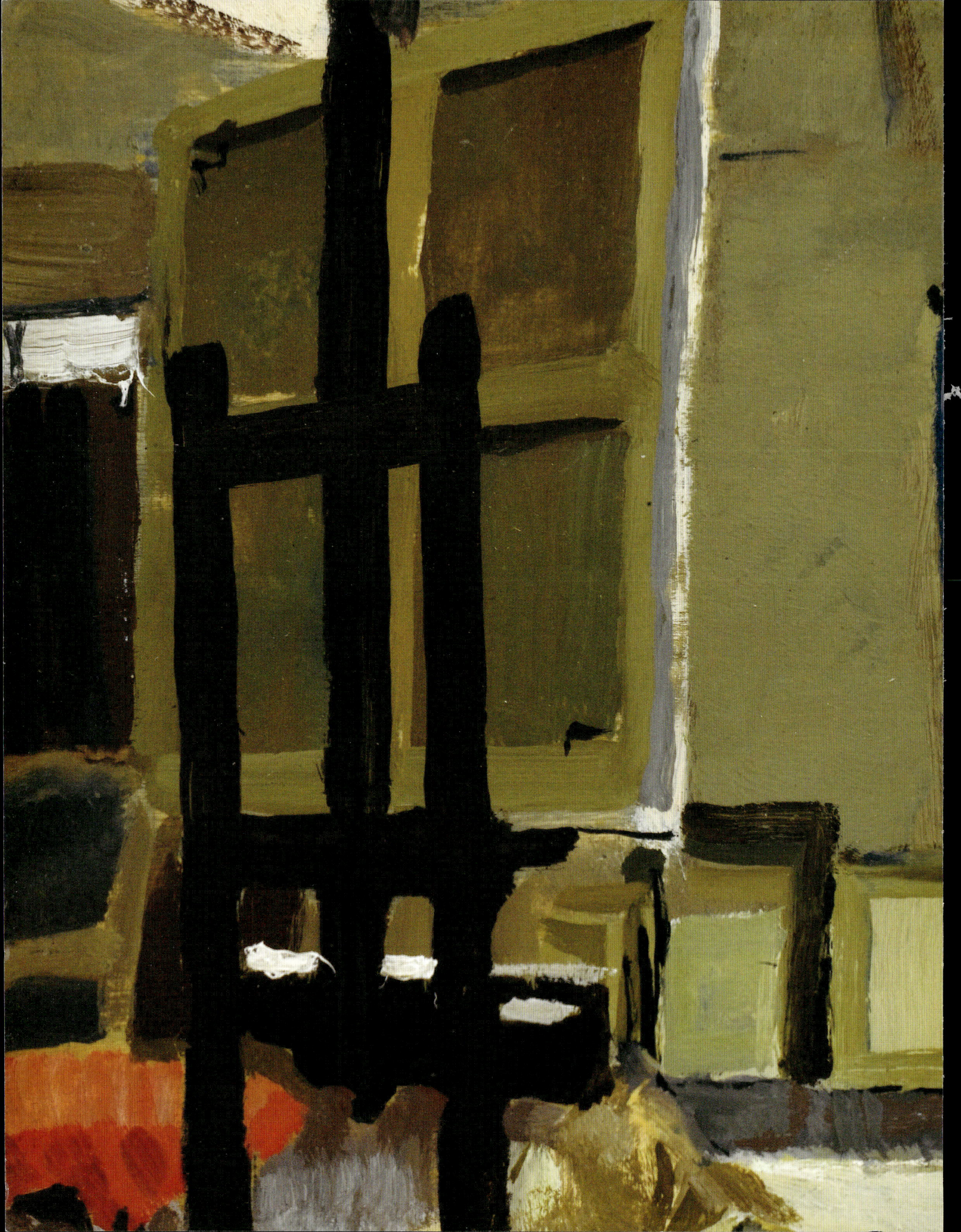

# WORKING SPACE

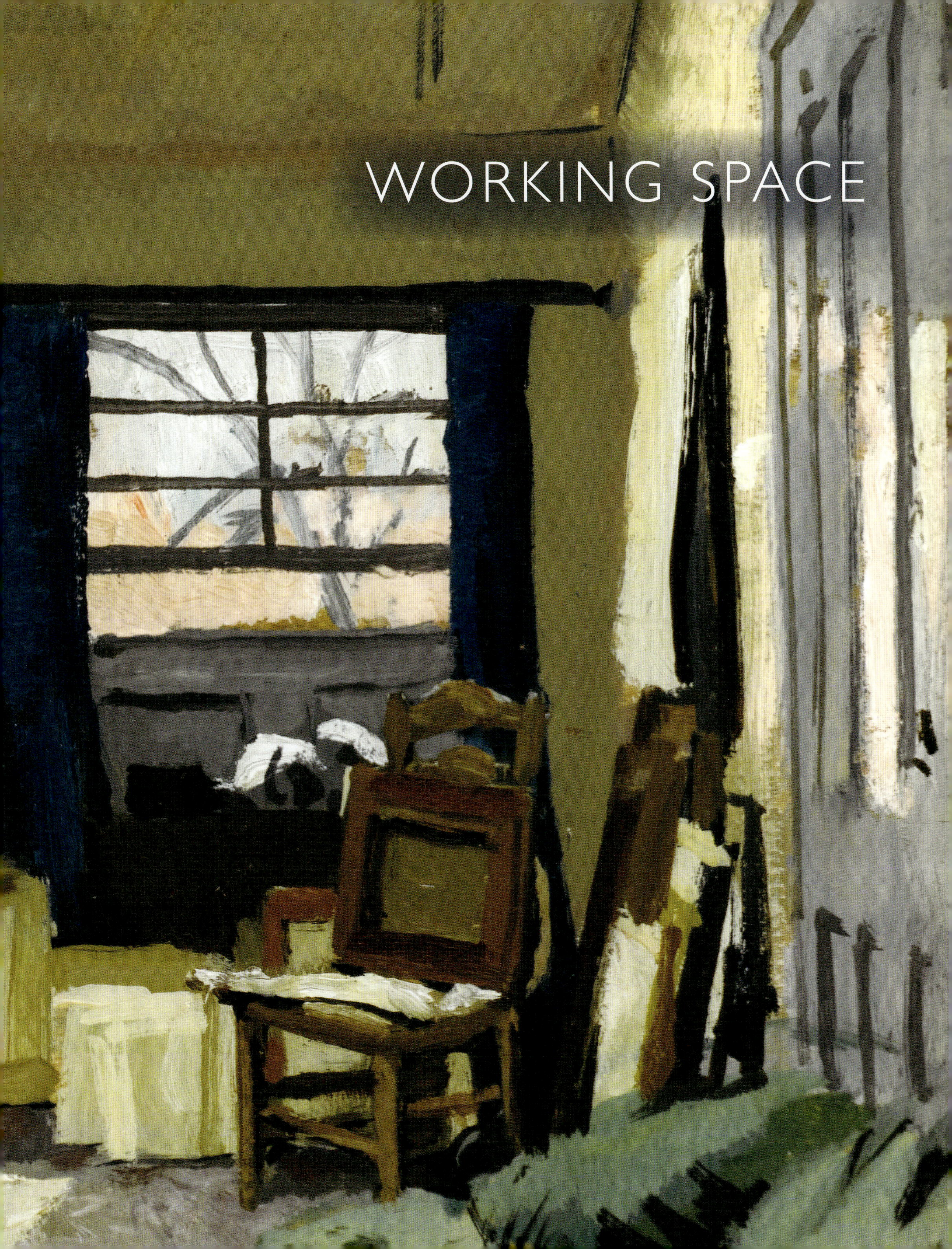

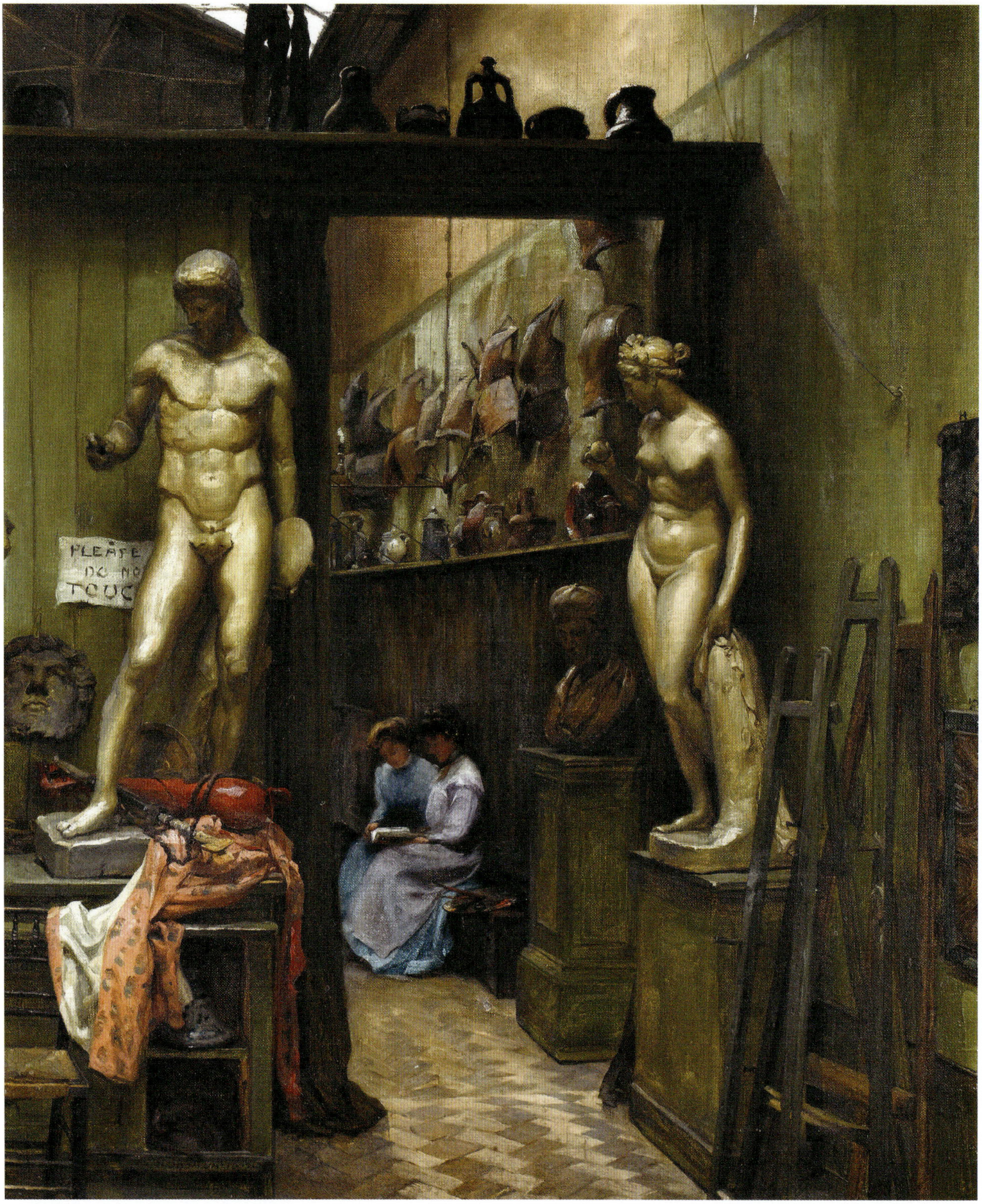


**2 Nellie Joshua** (1877-1960), *Heatherley's Art School*, c.1900,
oil on canvas, 24 x 18 in. (61 x 45.7 cm.)

Heatherley's, founded in 1845, is one of the oldest independent art schools in London and was the first to admit women to the life room on equal terms with men. In Joshua's highly observed work she depicts the school's large collection of historical dress, ceramics and armour which formed a costume studio for the use of students. One of the two students depicted – both wearing matching painting smocks in hues of blue – is likely to be a self-portrait.

# Working Space

*'The airless studios grow stifling. Kick the door open – the hum of life turns into a roar.'*
Feliks Topolski

*Working Space* explores different artistic milieux – from the art school, with its life rooms and plaster casts, to the artist's studio – the inner chambers where ideas are conceived and translated into form.

In search of the perfect space – or out of necessity – most artists moved studios several times during their careers. This was especially true of art students whose circumstances were often precarious.

Many artists – especially women – had to work where space was available. Percy Shakespeare's bedroom doubled as his studio. Frances Richards and Tirzah Garwood worked from kitchen tables, a factor that obliged them to limit their output to small scale work. A pen & ink drawing by Evelyn Dunbar shows the artist and her mother Florence, also a painter, in the 'snug', where peeling apples and painting might be concurrent activities.

Some artists sought spaces that facilitated solitude and the essential ingredients of light and volume. Thomas Monnington and Winifred Knights worked out of a converted barn on the Leyswood Estate. Robert Austin, Albert de Belleroche and Alan Sorrell all worked from converted chapels. More fortunate artists, such as Frank Brangwyn and Harry Bush, eventually had large purpose-built studio spaces, with north-facing windows, ideal for avoiding direct sunlight and for creating even tones throughout the day. Other artists, such as Gilbert Spencer, Charles Mahoney and John McKenzie worked from sheds in their gardens.

Outside these interior spaces lay the world beyond. Glimpsed through windows, these compositions define the artist's own relationship to indoor and outdoor spaces. Formal painting which took place in the studio was often preceded by painting *en plein air*, as for instance Mahoney, on painting trips to Pevensey, Cundall on his numerous tours of Europe, Rowntree with his serial views from Putney Bridge, and Frederick Austin from Chiswick Mall where his brother's home, Lingard House, looked onto the Thames.

The tokens of artistic practice collected around the cluttered corners of studios – from paint boxes to pots of brushes, mattresses to mahl sticks, or abandoned slippers to china ornaments also form part of this first section. Beyond the studio door artists recorded the spaces that defined the wider context in which they lived: bedrooms, kitchens, corridors or dining rooms. It is remarkable how often artists made paintings of the all-essential fire grate for warmth, the Aga for tea breaks.

In Barbara Jones' painting of the entrance hall of her Hampstead home, a self-portrait hangs by a full-size stuffed grizzly bear who welcomes guests (and by implication the viewer). For many artists, like Barbara Jones, working space lay somewhere between the physical confines of the studio walls and the unlimited realms of the imagination.

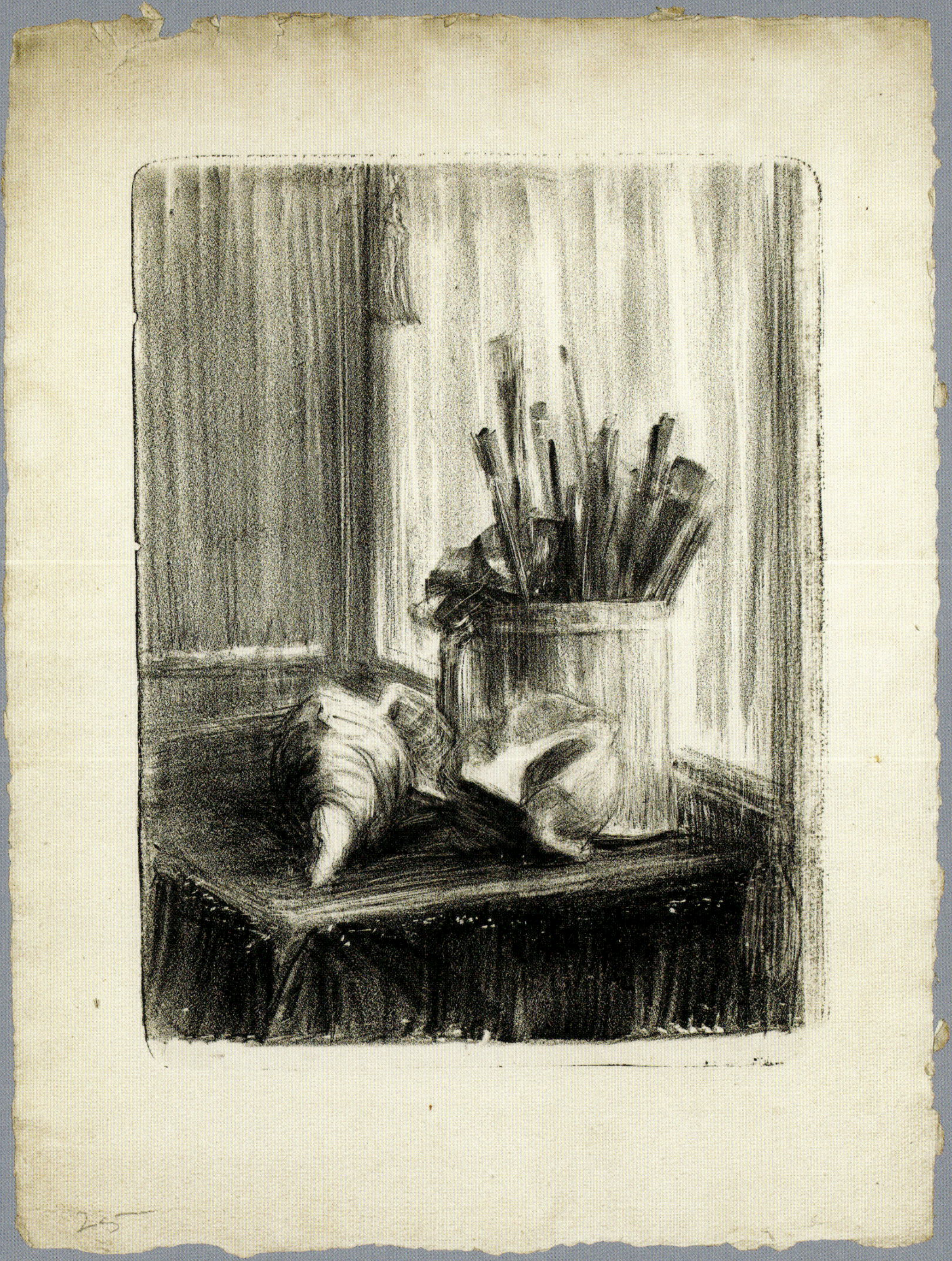

**3 Albert de Belleroche** (1864-1944), *Still Life with Paint Brushes*,
lithograph on paper, 25 ½ x 19 ¾ in. (65 x 50 cm).

Assemblages of objects lying around an artist's studio – paint brushes, pots, natural history objects, fabrics – often formed the subject of still lifes, though the chance arrangement of a composition was rarely as casual as it appeared.

**4 Charles H.H. Burleigh** (1869-1956), *Still Life in the Artist's Studio*,
oil on canvas, 29 x 23 ¼ in. (74 x 59 cm).

In Burleigh's studio view an easel is visible at the edge of the composition, with objects laid out in front, ready to be painted – a view of the terraced houses of the artist's native Hove is visible beyond, seen through half-drawn curtains.

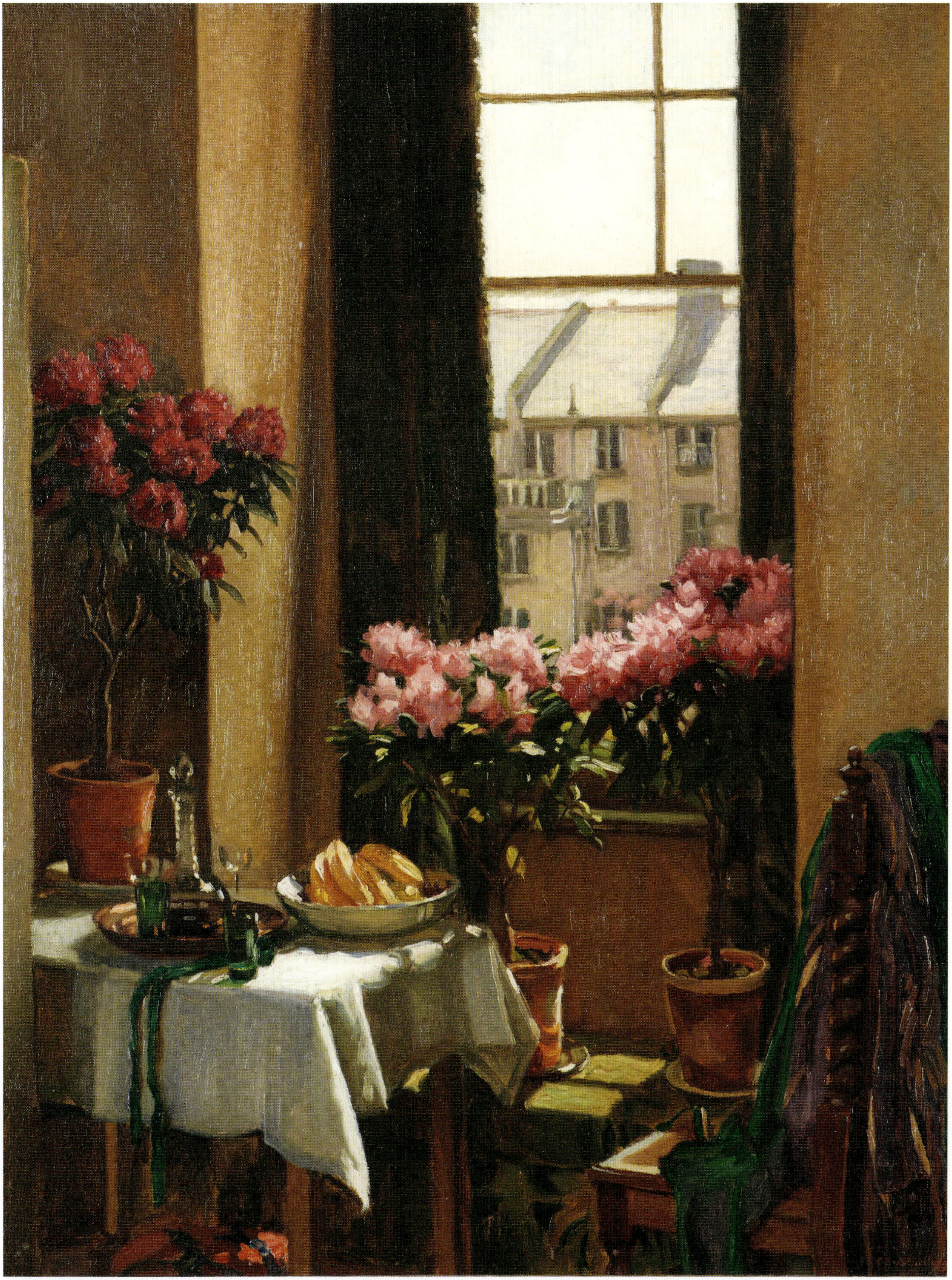

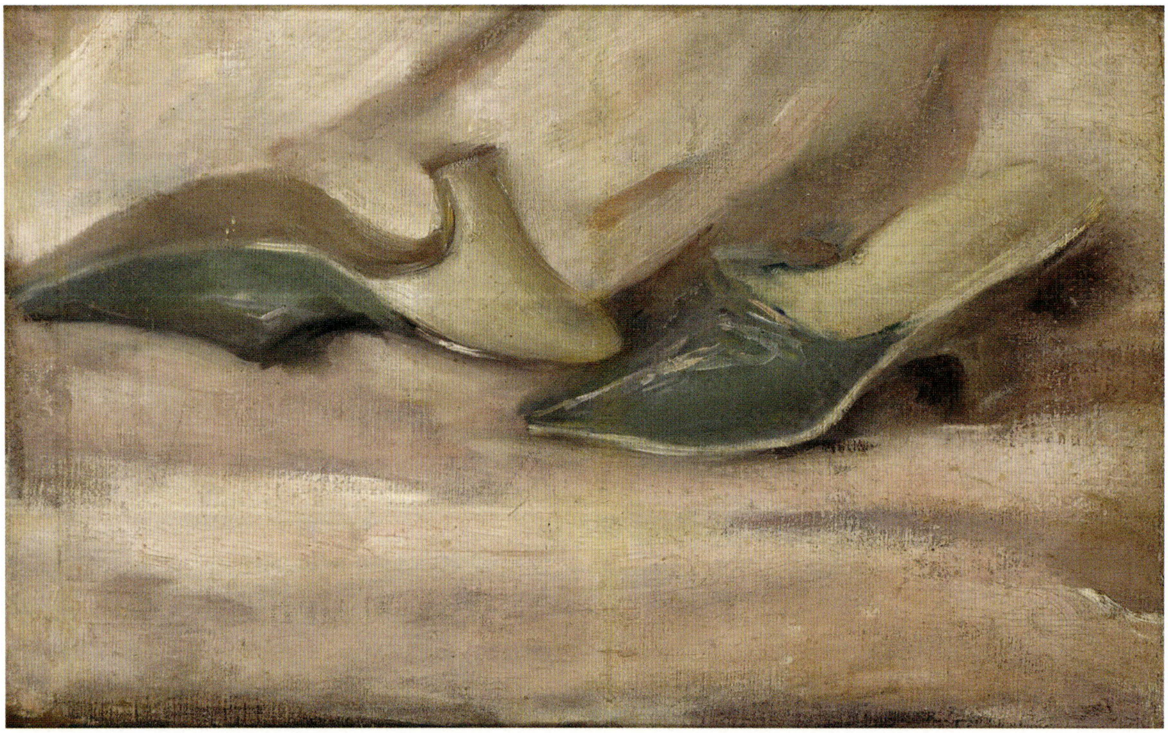

**5 Albert de Belleroche** (1864-1944), *Discarded Slippers*, c.1890, oil on canvas, 11 ¾ x 16 in. (30 x 40.4 cm).

Artists' studios contained numerous props – these discarded slippers would have been worn by one of Belleroche's models. The more formal *Les deux petits pots* shows a corner of the artist's Montmartre studio with the two treasured oriental pots in which he kept his paint brushes.

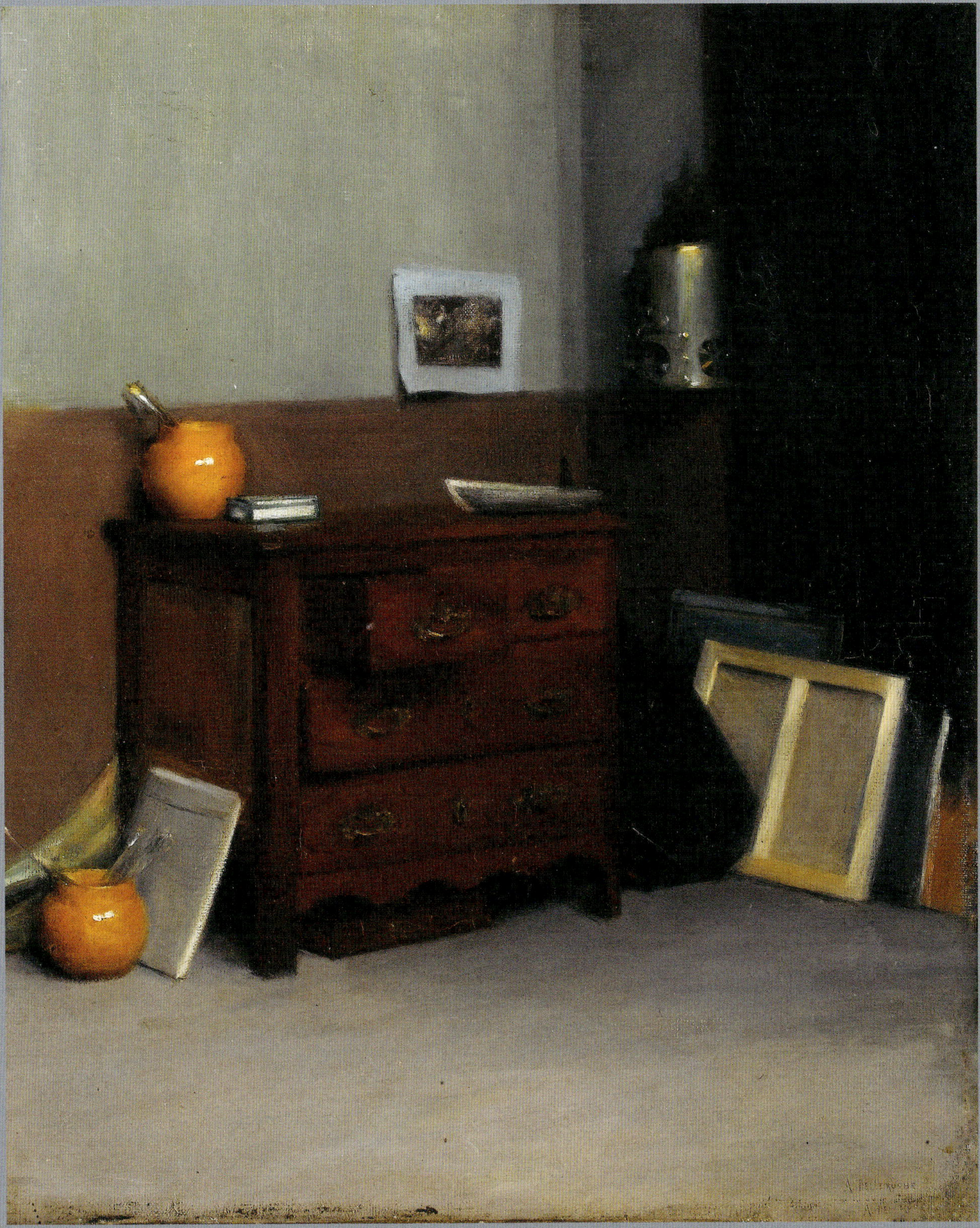

**6 Albert de Belleroche** (1864-1944), *Les deux petits pots (Les pots jaunes)*, c.1889, signed, oil on canvas, 18 ¼ × 15 in. (46.5 × 38.5 cm).

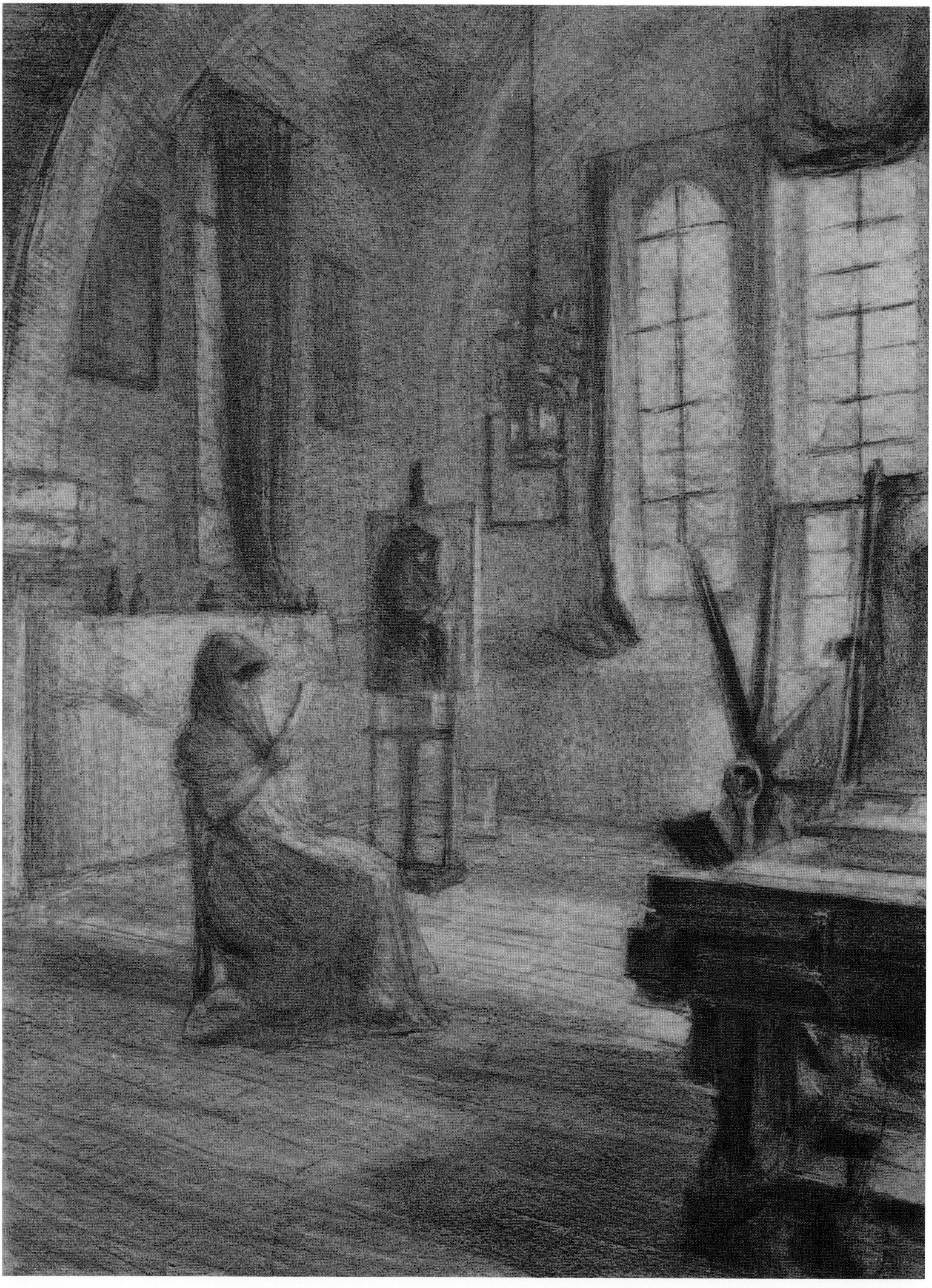

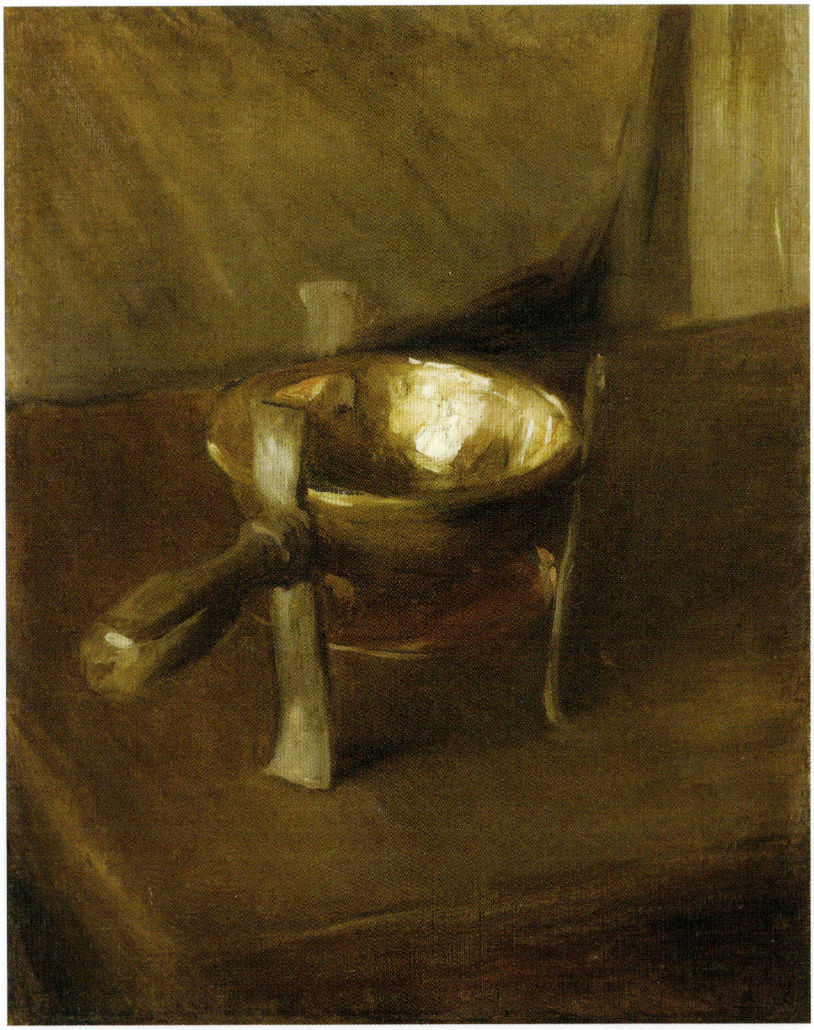

**8 Albert de Belleroche** (1864-1944), *Still life with Crucible*, c.1890, signed on reverse, oil on canvas (P. Aprin, Paris), 19 x 15 ½ in. (48.2 x 39.5 cm).

The crucible shown would have been kept in the artist's studio for the purpose of heating raw pigments to make and blend colours.

**7 Albert de Belleroche** (1864-1944), *The Artist's Studio, La Vieille Chapelle, La Boissiere, Châteaudun*, c.1909, lithograph on paper, 26 x 18 ¼ in. (66 x 46.5 cm).

Belleroche rented La Vieille Chapelle, at La Boissière, in order to spend weekends working away from Paris. As a printmaker he was unusual in insisting on printing his own lithographs and La Boissière housed his large Le Mercier lithographic press.

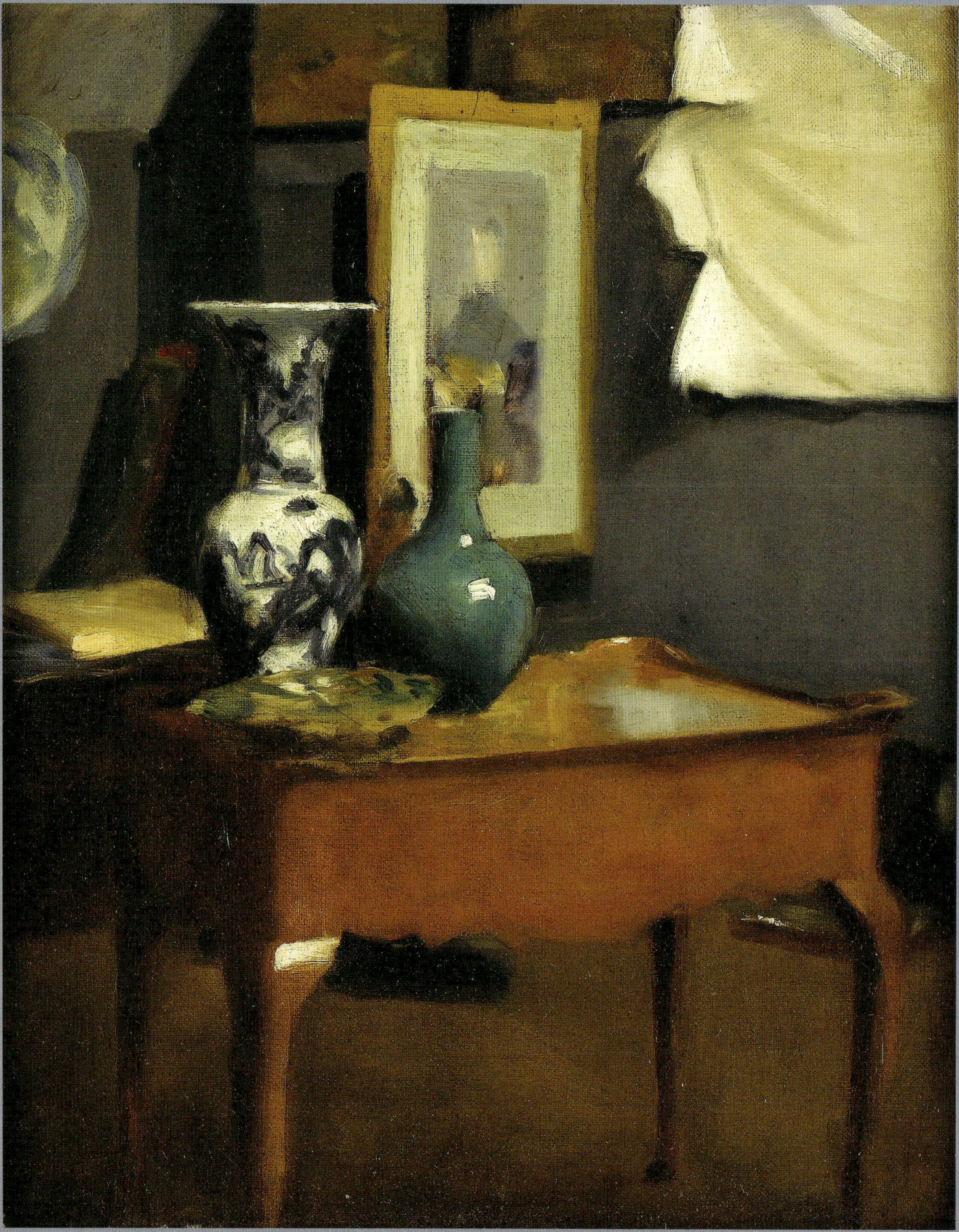

**9 Albert de Belleroche** (1864-1944), *Le Secretaire Louis XVI*,
oil on canvas, 18 ¼ × 15 ¼ in. (46.5 × 38.5 cm).

The *mise-en-scène* in this studio scene shows a variety of the artist's favourite props, with various paintings in different stages of completion, including a piece of unstretched canvas, in the background. Of Belleroche's still lifes Frank Brangwyn commented: "… he had carried the tradition of Chardin a step further and it is not surprising that Degas thought so highly of these works."

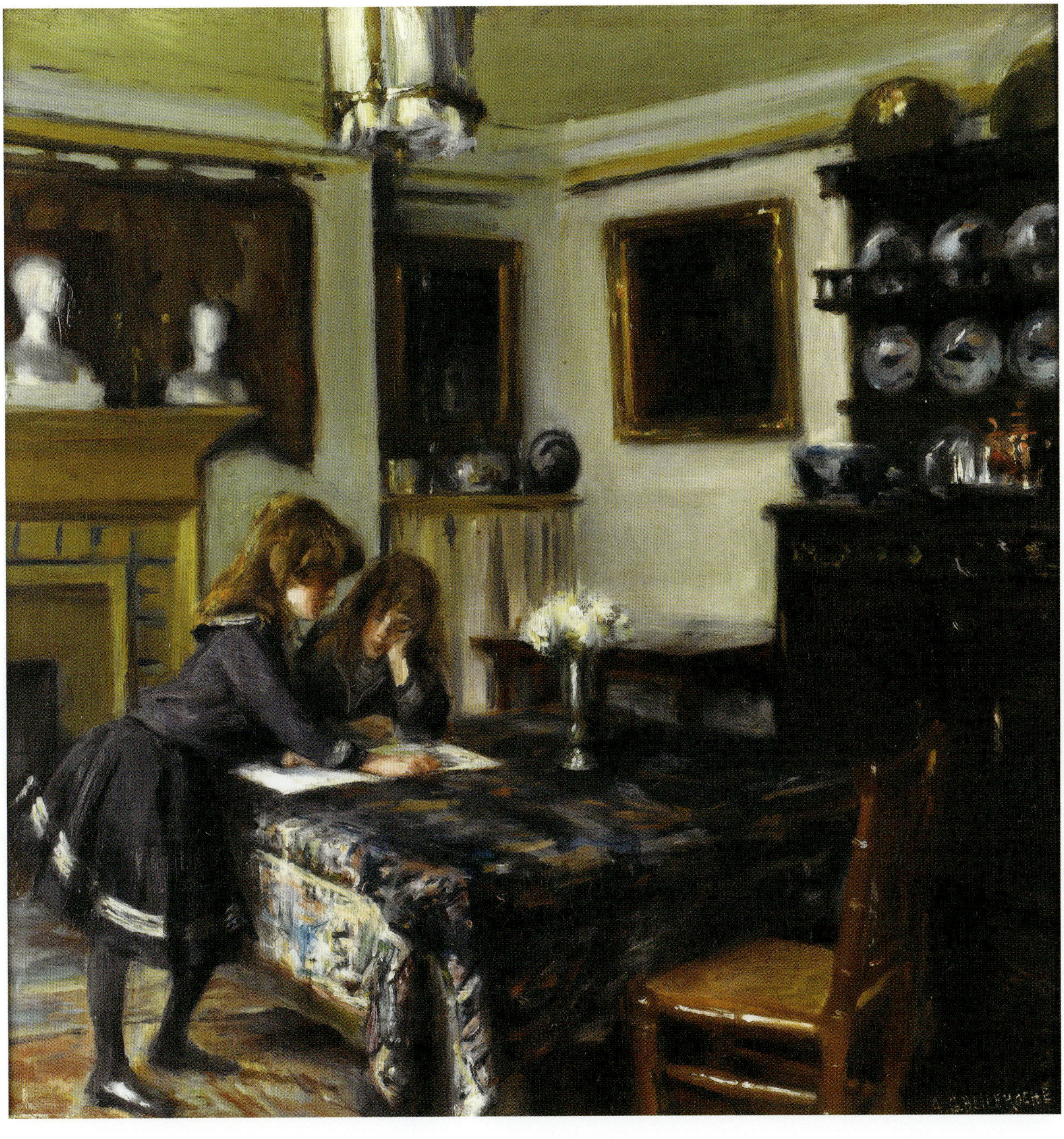

**10 Albert de Belleroche** (1864-1944), *The Dining Room of John Singer Sargent*, c.1884, signed, oil on canvas, 17 ¼ x 16 ¾ in. (43.5 x 42.5 cm).

Belleroche maintained several studios in both Paris and London at different points in his career, some of which he shared with his friend the celebrated American Impressionist John Singer Sargent. Sargent moved into the ground-floor studio at 33 Tite Street in 1886. Belleroche and Sargent painted almost identical views of the room – the latter's version, 'My Dining-Room', is now at Smith College Museum of Art, Northampton, Massachusetts.

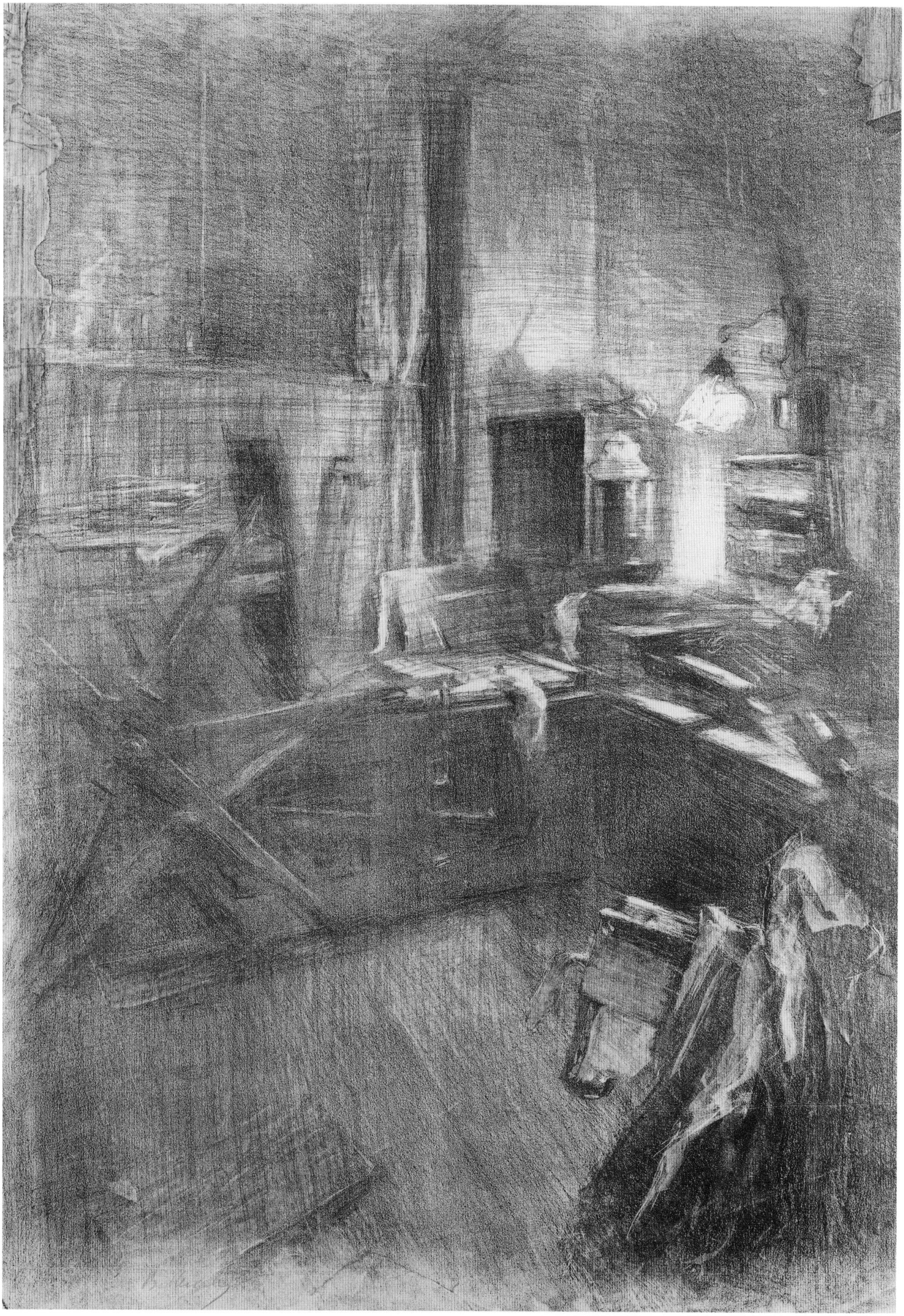

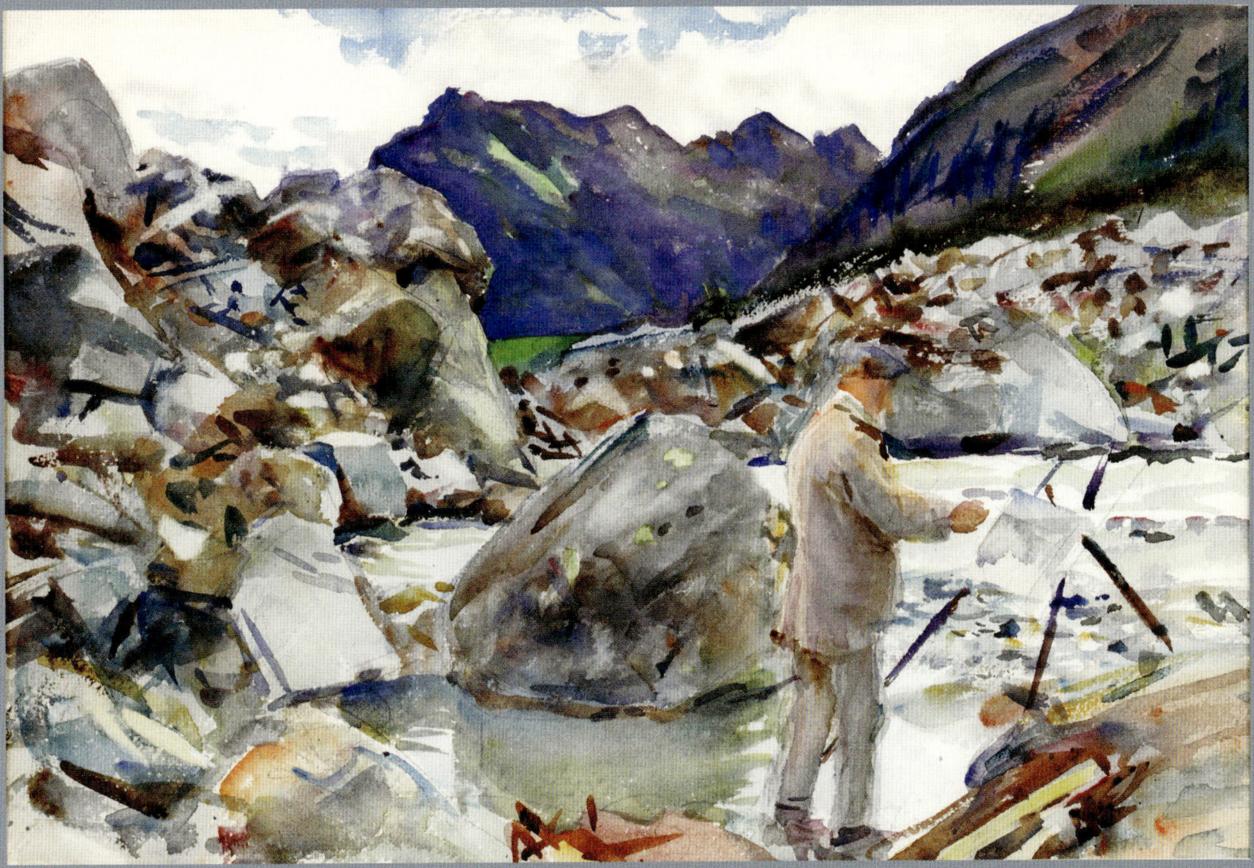

**12 John Singer Sargent** (1856-1925), *A Glacier Stream in the Alps*, 1904,
pencil and watercolour on paper, 15 ½ x 21 in. (39.4 x 53.2 cm). Collection: Laing Art Gallery.

John Singer Sargent painted many landscape watercolours during sketching holidays in the Alps. He was often accompanied by friends and fellow artists. Sargent was fascinated by light on water. The bright colours of this scene (which portrays the artist Ambrogio Raffele at work) are made more brilliant by the contrast with the white paper showing through the lattice of brushmarks. Opaque white watercolour reinforces the effect in places. Sargent was influenced by the vibrant colour and separate paint marks used by French painters such as Monet.

**11 Albert de Belleroche** (1864-1944), *L'Atelier, Hampstead*, c.1912, signed,
lithograph, working proof with some alterations in lithographic crayon, 25 x 18 ¾ in. (63.5 x 47.5 cm).

In 1912 the recently married Belleroche moved from Paris to London to set up a family home in West Hampstead.

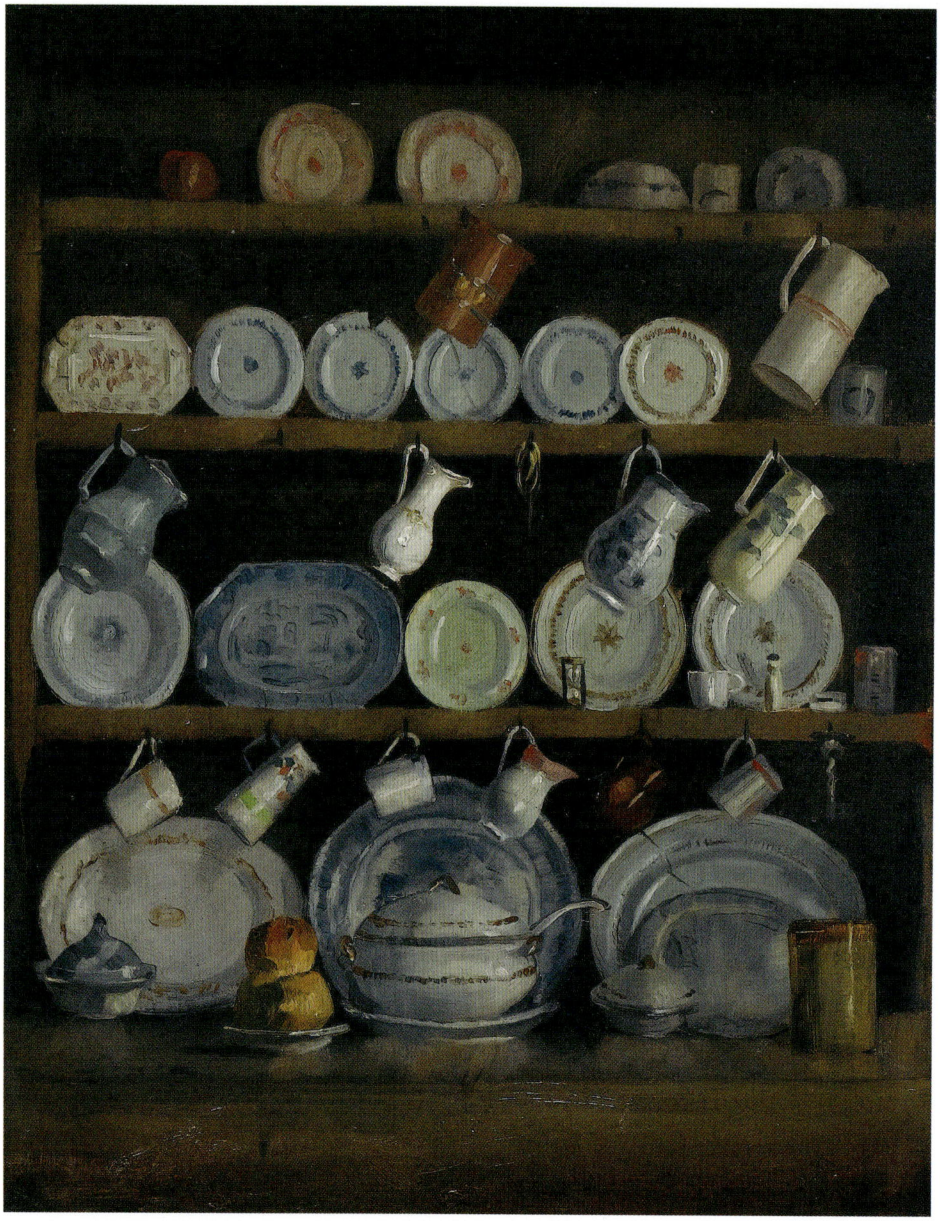

**13 Harold Harvey** (1886-1966), *The Kitchen Dresser*, c.1920,
oil on canvas, 16 x 12 ¾ in. (40.7 x 32.4 cm).

**14 Malcolm Drummond** (1880-1945), *19 Fitzroy Street* (Walter Richard Sickert's studio), 1912-14,
oil on canvas, 28 x 20 in. (71 x 50.8 cm). Collection: Laing Art Gallery.

Malcolm Drummond has painted three fellow artists (Manson, Gore and Ginner) of the Camden Town Group, which was formed in 1911. They are in their Fitzroy Street studio in London, where they held showings of their work. They concentrated on painting ordinary scenes from town and suburban life. This unconventional back view is characteristic of their approach. The strong shapes and bright colour of this picture were influenced by French Post-Impressionist art.

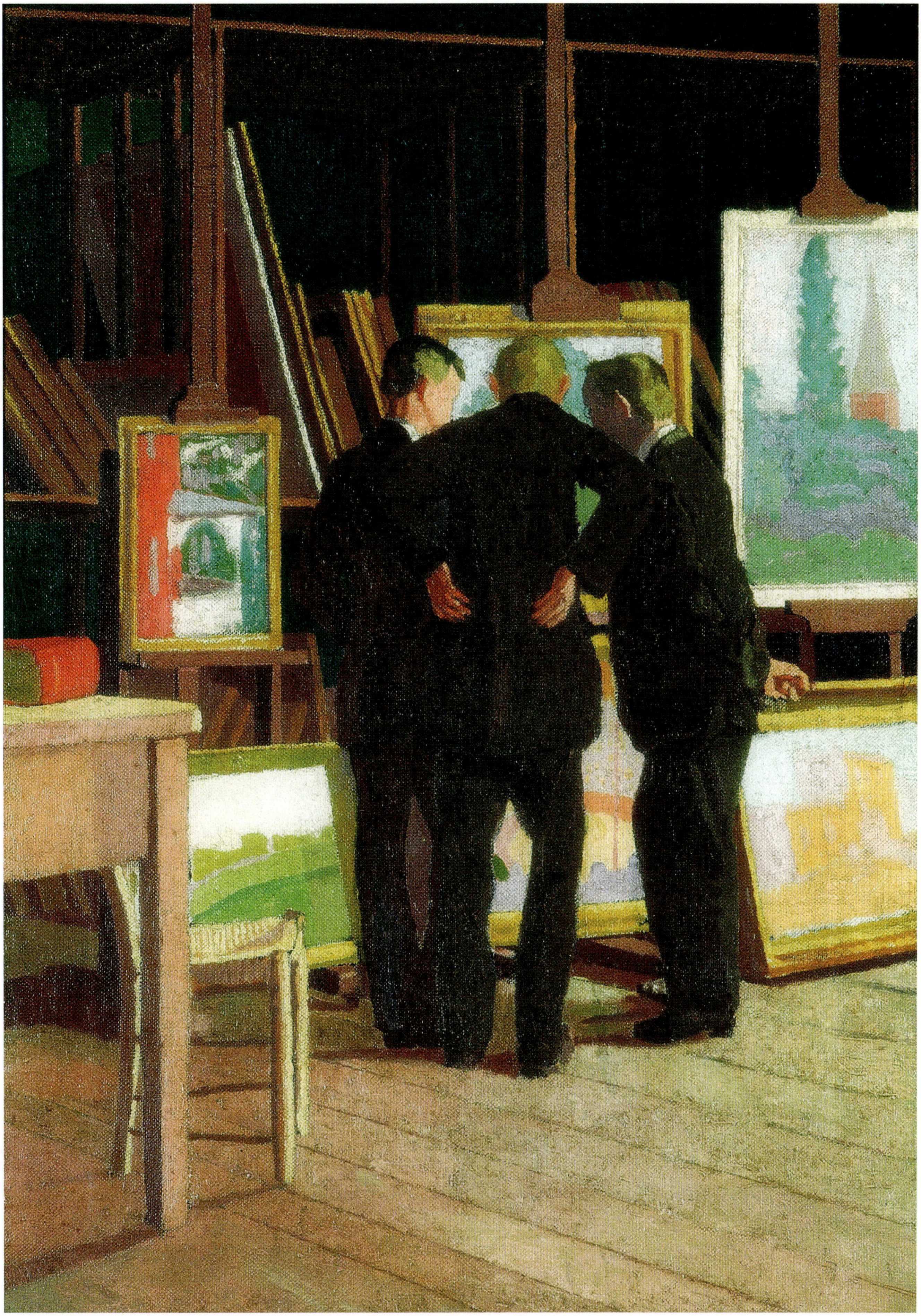

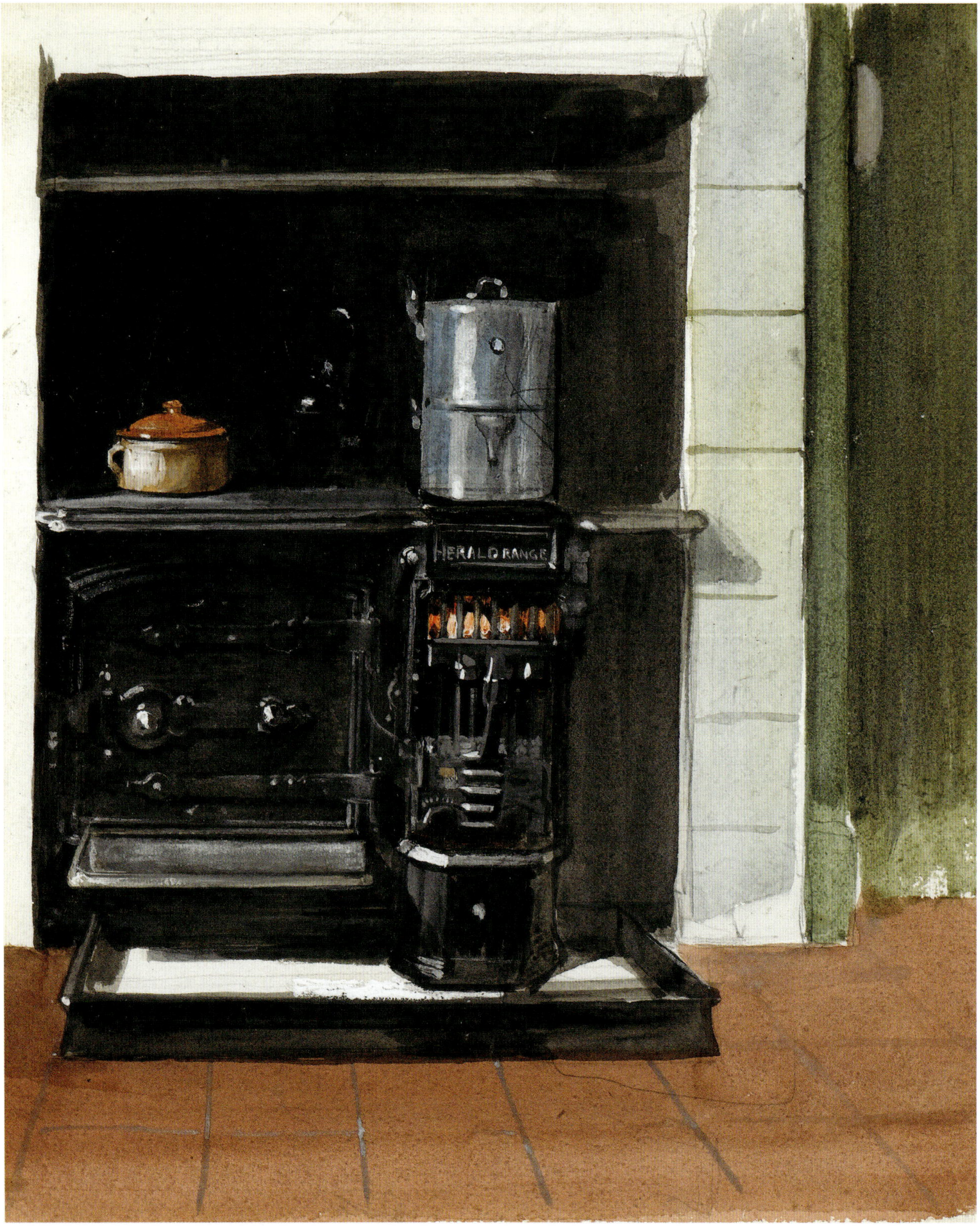


**15 Margaret Gere** (1878-1965), *The Kitchen Range*, c.1910, titled on a label to reverse, watercolour on paper, 10 x 9 in. (25.4 x 23 cm).

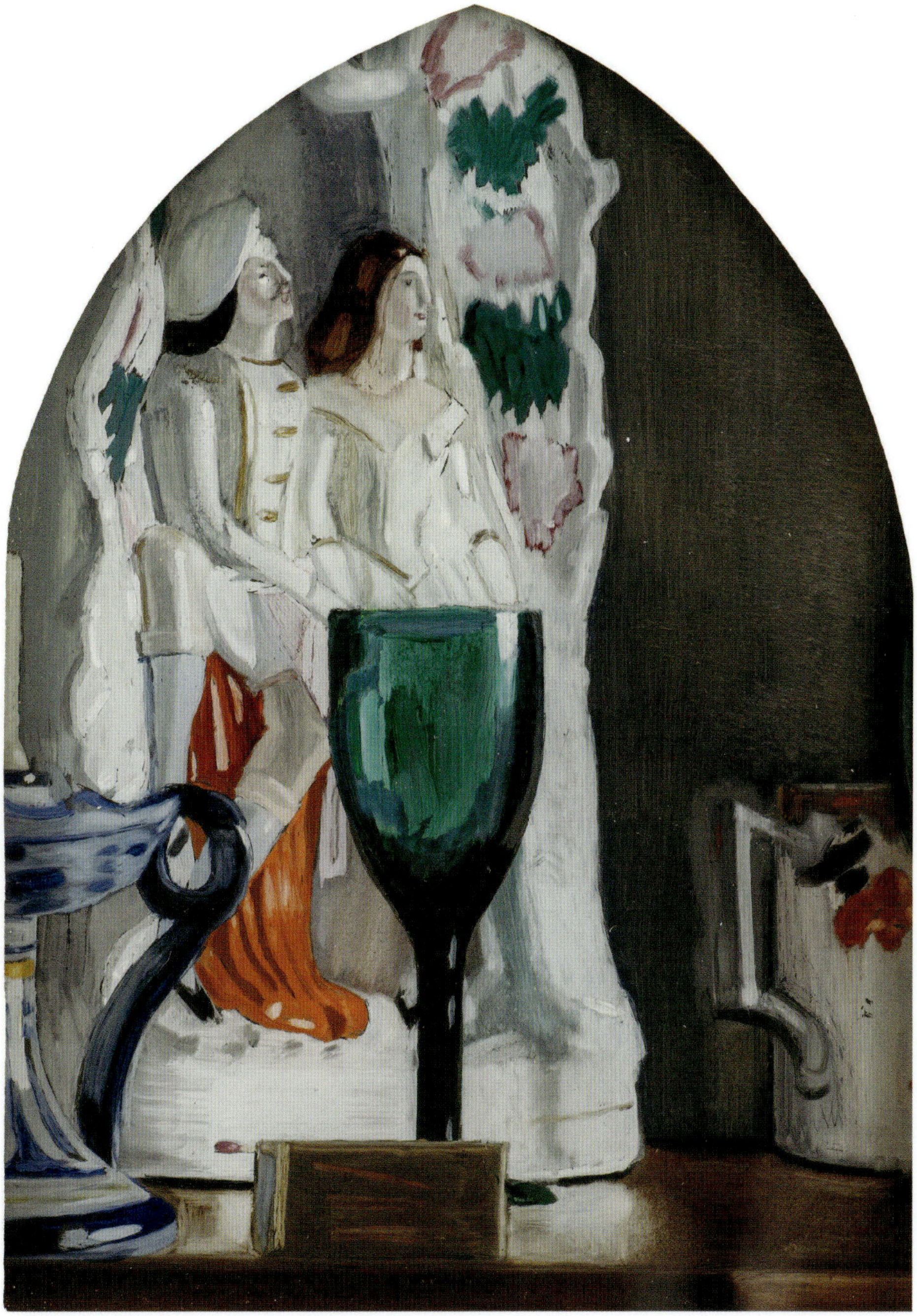

**16 Margaret Gere** (1878-1965), *The Staffordshire Ornament*, c.1910, oil on glass, 6 ¾ x 4 ¾ in. (17 x 12.3 cm).

Margaret Gere and her sister Edith were known as 'the masterful Miss Geres'. Although a versatile artist, of figure scenes, portraits, and landscapes, Gere's domestic interiors are amongst her most engaging works, offering an intimate account of her artistic vision.

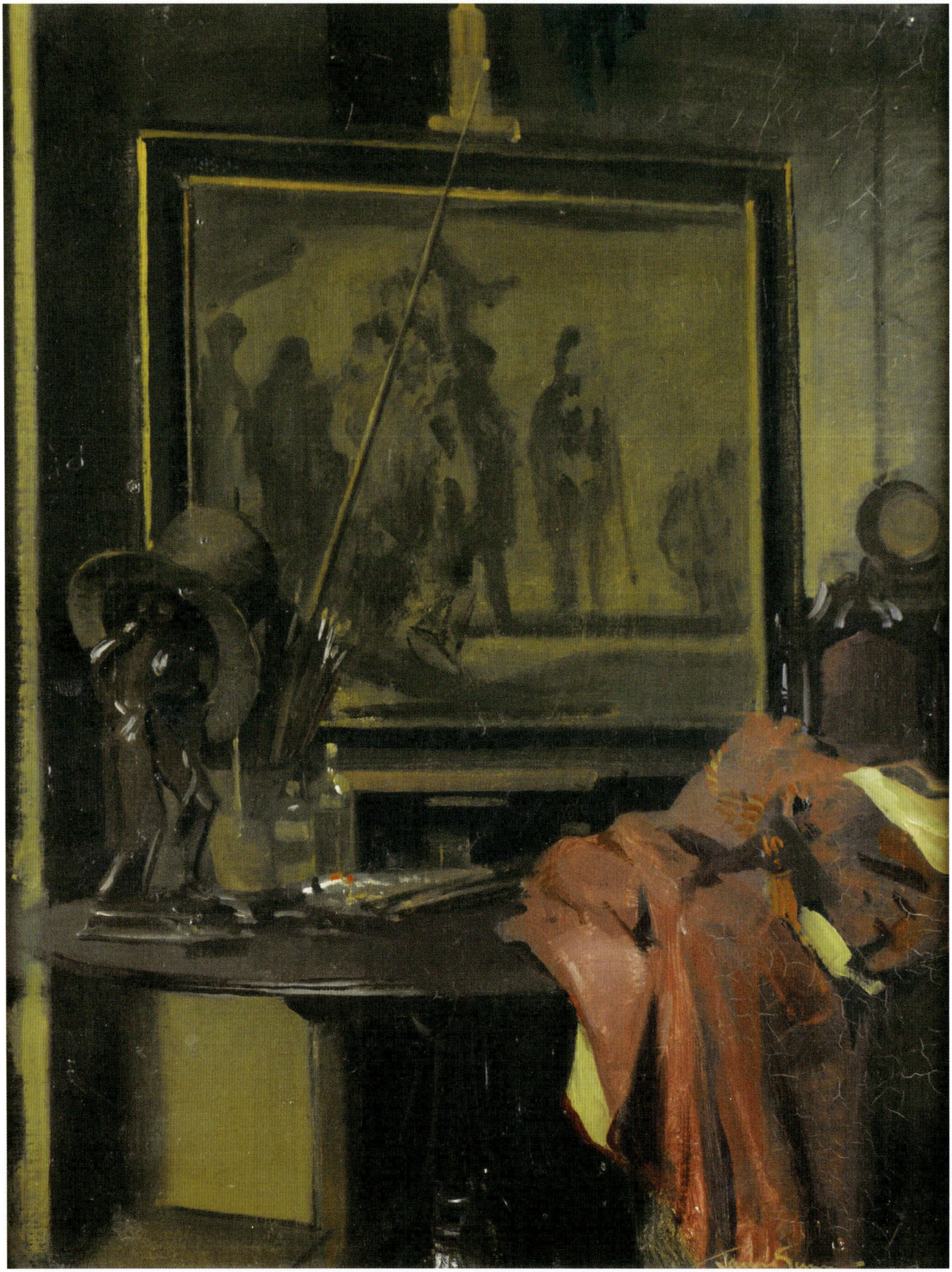

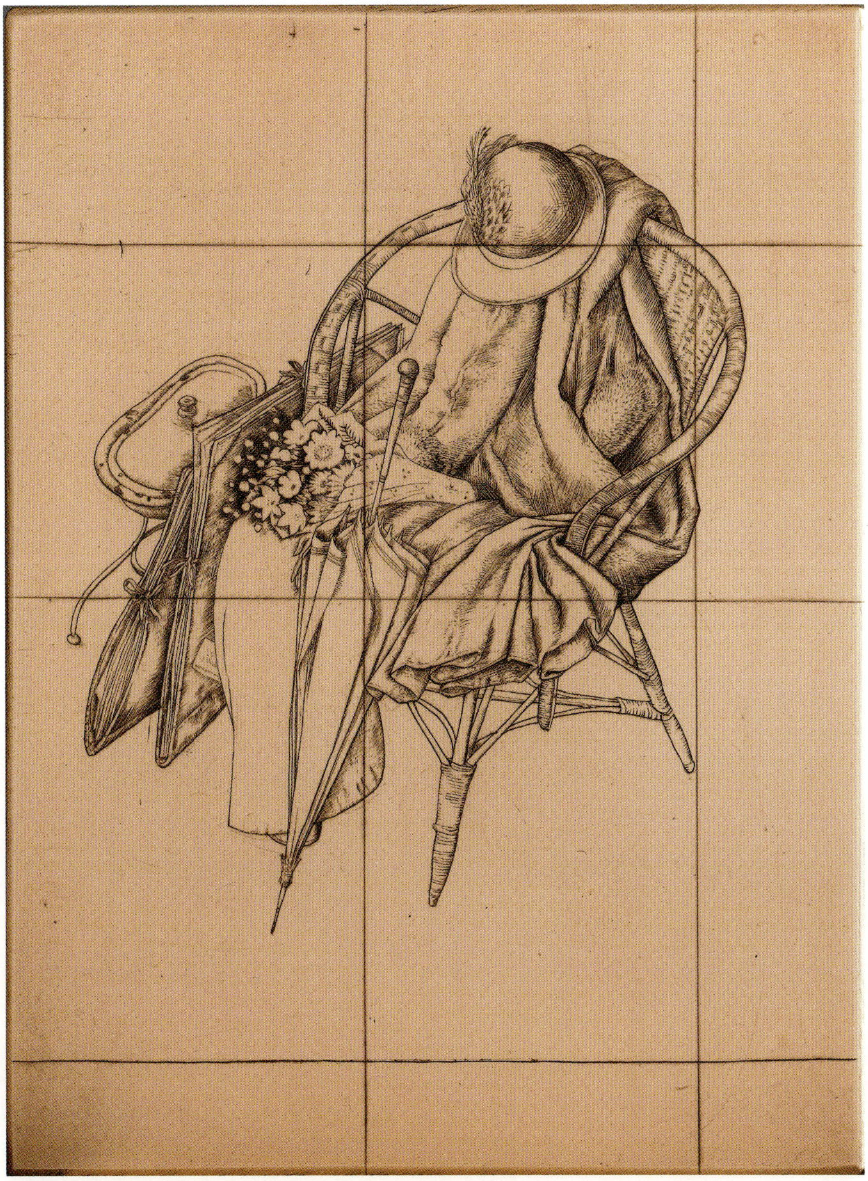

**18 Robert Austin** (1895-1973), *Souvenir of Paris*, mid 1920s,
line engraving, original copper plate (cancelled), 5 ¼ x 4 ½ in. (14.6 x 11.5 cm).

In the mid-1920s, as a Rome Scholar, Austin passed through Paris whilst travelling to the British School at Rome by train. In 1924 he married Ada (May) Harrison with whom he collaborated on *Some Tuscan Cities* (London, 1924) and it is tempting to imagine that this souvenir – the artist is represented by the two portfolios which lean towards the bouquet of flowers, feathered hat and fur trimmed coat – recalls their courtship.

**17 Sir Herbert James Gunn** (1893-1964), *Interior Scene, Memories of James Pryde*, c.1915-16, signed,
oil on board, 18 ½ x 14 ½ in. (46.5 x 36.5 cm).

James Gunn (**302**) and James Pryde shared a studio in London. As well as paying homage to Pryde in this '*chaos decoratif*' Gunn demonstrates his ability as a skilled artist, setting on a pedestal table the tools of his trade (palette, brushes and maulstick), alongside the top hat of his fellow artist Pryde. As Kenneth McConkey has observed, 'Piling up studio impedimenta into a large, jumbled still-life provided an instant test-piece for the nineteenth century painter – it was a genre that might typically include an exotic costume, a sword or piece of armour, a lay figure or statuette, and maybe, a discarded hat. The purpose of this '*chaos decoratif*' was to demonstrate the painter's abilities to prospective clients. It was a kind of badge or shop-sign'.

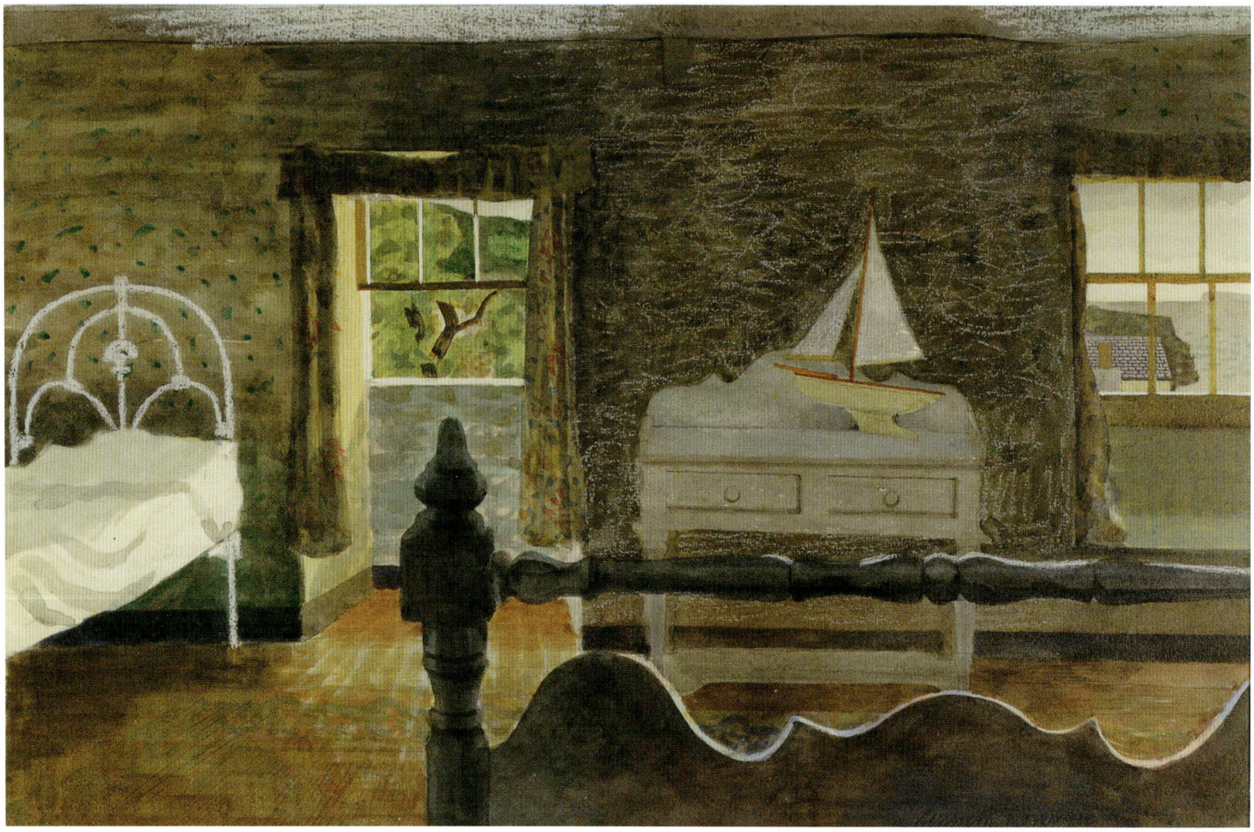

**19 Kenneth Rowntree** (1915-1997), *Holiday bedroom, LIttle Haven, Pembokeshire,* c.1950, watercolour on paper, 21 ¼ x 27 ¼ in. (54 x 69.3 cm).

Working from holiday rooms, attics, studios or bedrooms, artists ideally sought north-facing windows, avoiding direct sunlight and the resulting variation of effects on tone and colour.

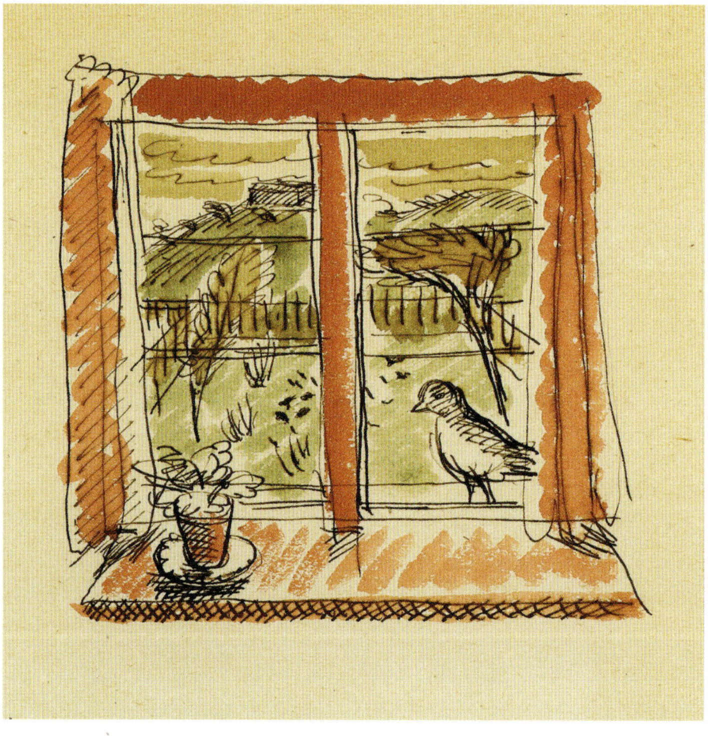

**20 Charles Mahoney** (1903-1968),
*Window Sill with Flower Pot and Bird,*
pencil, pen & ink and watercolour on paper,
15 ½ x 11 in. (39.4 x 28 cm).

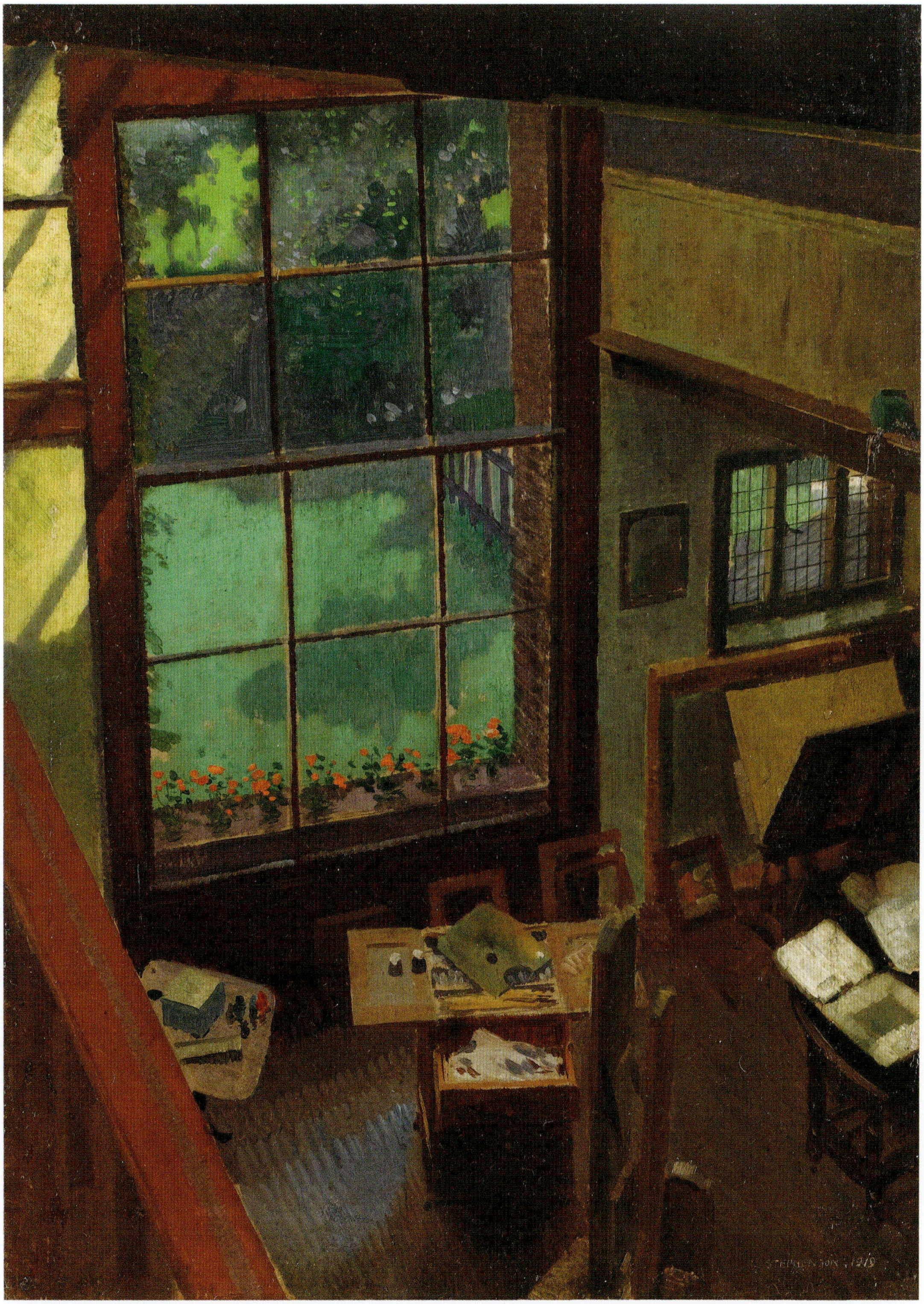

**21 John Cecil Stephenson** (1889-1965), *The Artist's Studio, (Mall Studios, 6 Tasker Road, Hampstead)*, 1919,
signed and dated in sgraffito, signed in pencil on the reverse,
oil on panel, 16 x 11 ¾ in. (40.5 x 30 cm).

During Stephenson's 46 years at the Mall Studios other residents included Herbert Read (who christened it 'the gentle nest of artists'), John Skeaping, Barbara Hepworth, Ben Nicholson and Henry Moore. Additionally, distinguished visiting artists included Mondrian, Calder and László Moholy-Nagy.

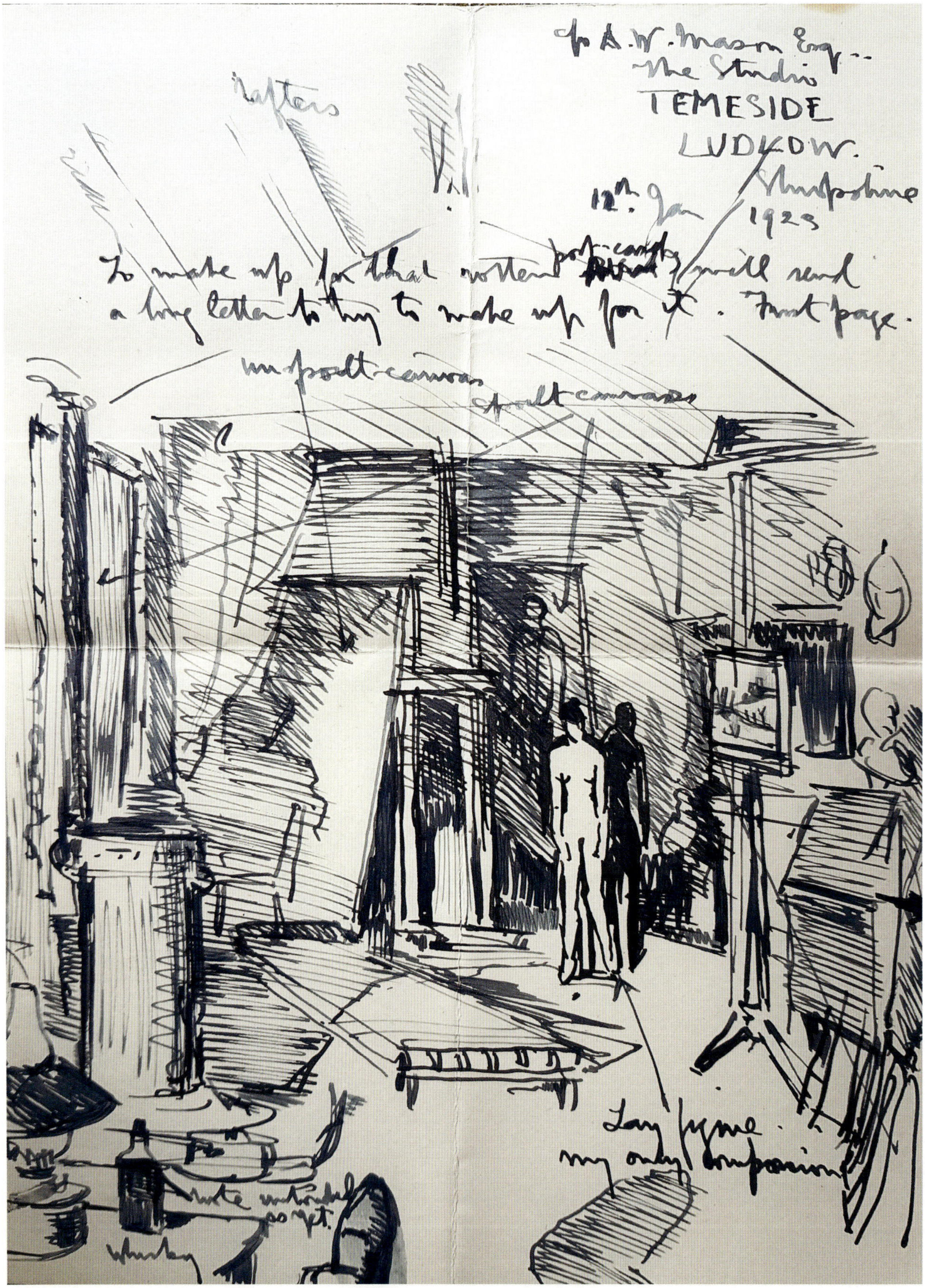

c/o A.W. Mason Esq.
The Studio
TEMESIDE
LUDLOW.
Shropshire
12th Jan
1923
rafters
To make up for that rotten post-card I will send a long letter to try to make up for it. First page.
unspoilt canvas
spoilt canvas
Lay figure.
my only companion
Whisky

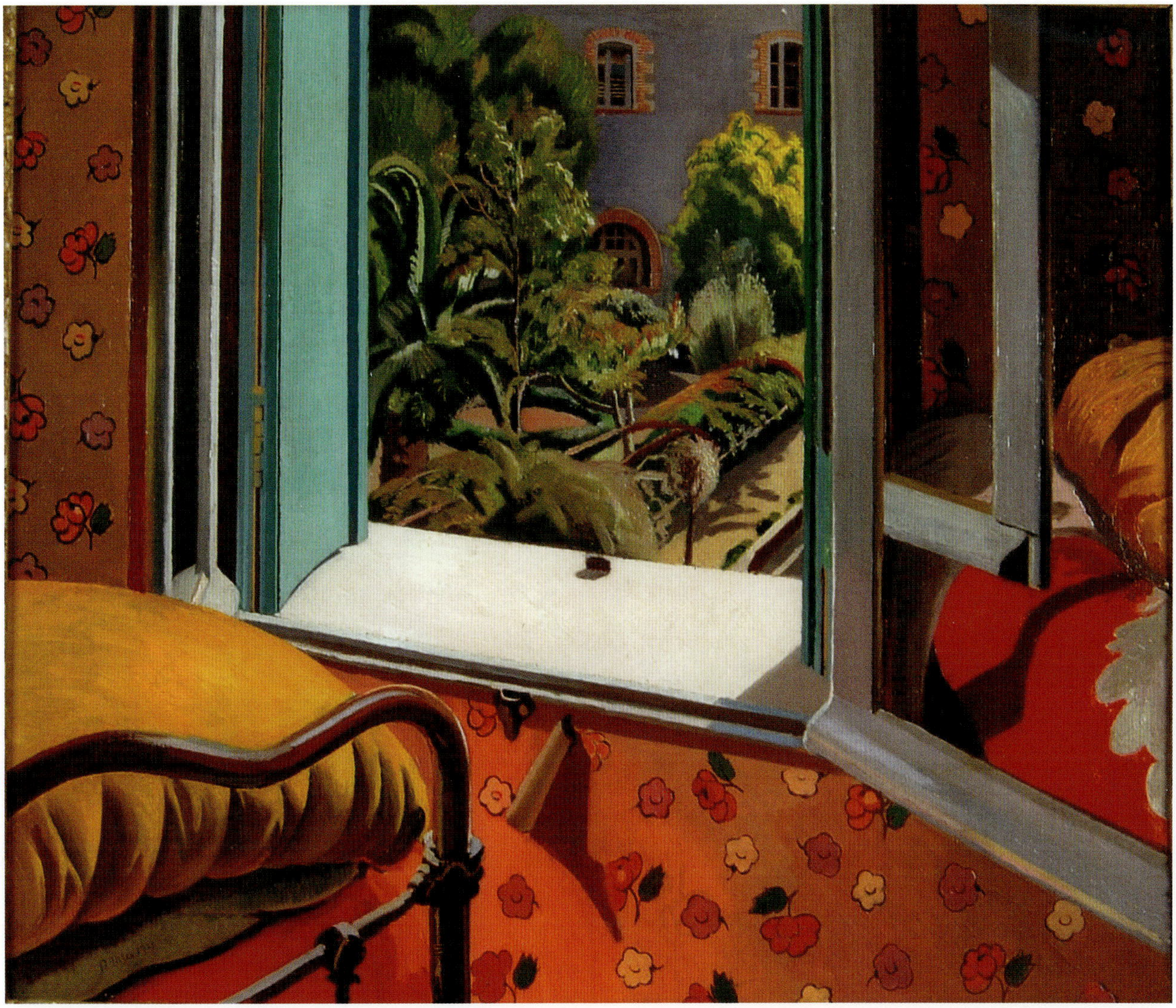

**23 Rudolph Ihlee** (1883-1968), *My Window, Collioure*, 1925, signed and dated, oil on canvas, 25 x 30 in. (63.5 x 76.2 cm).

Celebrated for its bright, Mediterranean palette – evident in the view from Ihlee's light-filled bedroom – Collioure was a centre of artistic activity. Among the many artists it attracted in the first half of the 20th century were André Derain, Georges Braque, Henri Matisse, Pablo Picasso, Charles Rennie Mackintosh and Tsuguharu Fujita.

**22 Charles Cundall** (1890-1971), Arnold Mason's Ludlow studio, an illustrated letter, 12 January 1923, signed and extensively inscribed, pen & ink on paper, 9 x 7 in. (23 x 17.5 cm).

Arnold Mason rented, as a studio, The Old Mill, Temeside, Ludlow, at the end of WW1 (**164**). He lent it to a variety of artist friends including Winifred Knights and Charles Cundall, the author of this humourous letter.

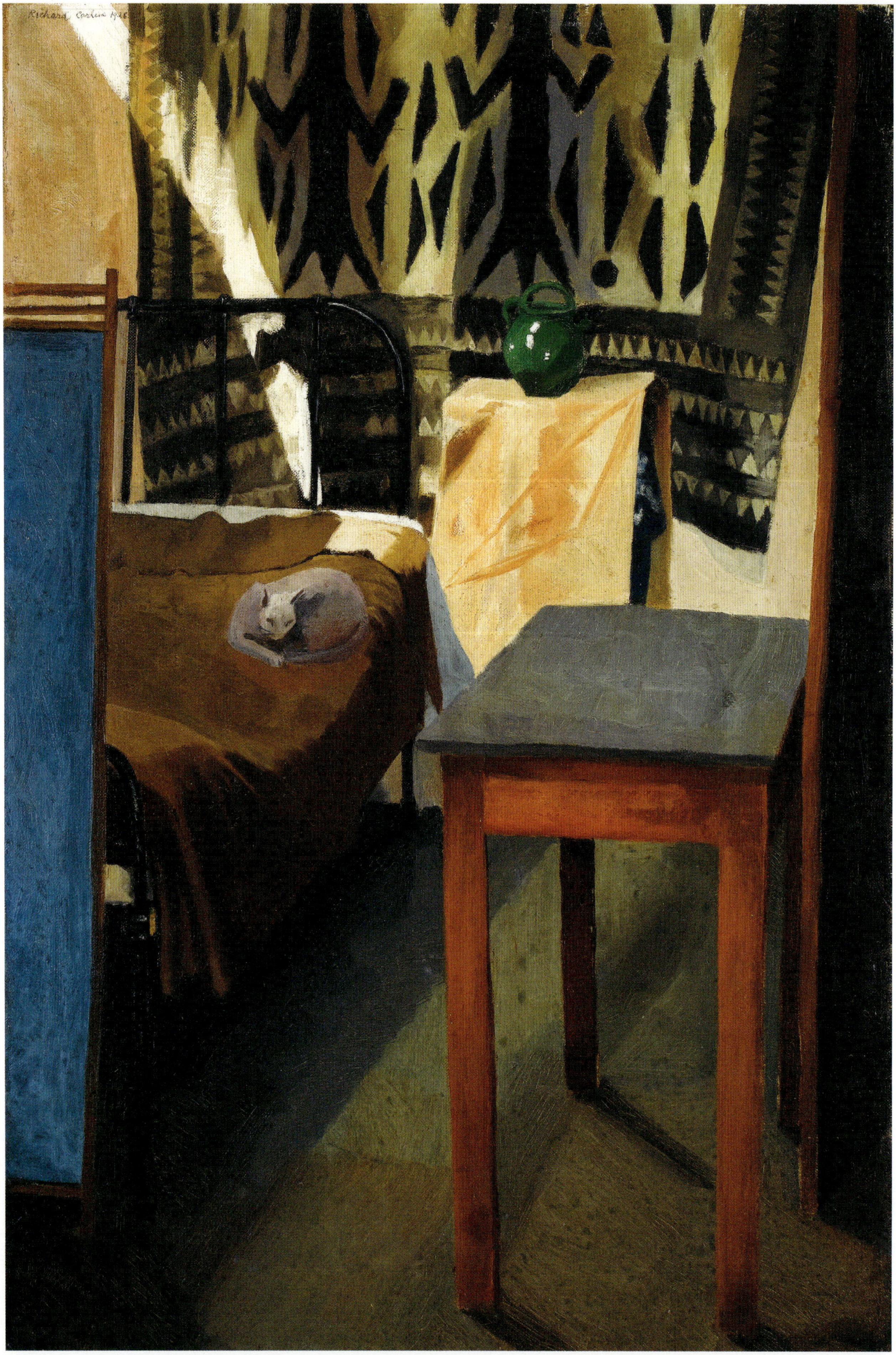
Richard Carline

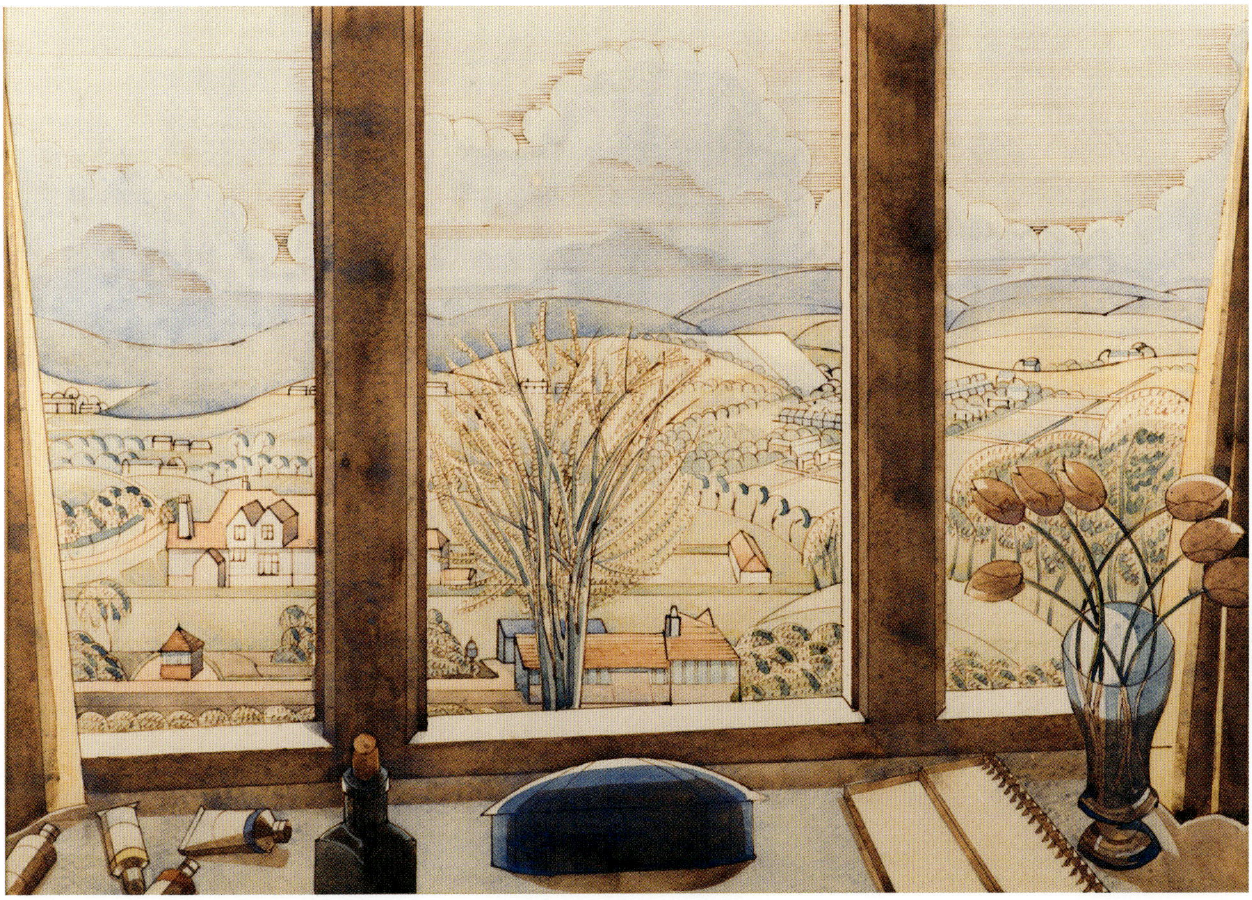

**25 Karl Hagedorn** (1889-1969), *Buxton from Westbourne,* mid-1920s, inscribed with title, pencil, pen & ink and watercolour on paper, 14 ½ x 20 ½ in. (36.5 x 52 cm).

Karl Hagedorn lived in Buxton from 1922 to 1927. This view is from his studio window. Tubes of paint, ink and a sketch pad are set out ready to capture the scene framed through the window.

**24 Richard Carline** (1896-1980), *Studio Interior,* 1926, signed and dated, oil on canvas, 29 x 20 in. (74 x 51 cm).

Dated 1926, when Richard Carline was at 47 Downshire Hill in Hampstead, his bedroom/studio includes a screen, an iron bed, a washstand, a work table, a cat and a drape with an Aztec pattern, which blocks out the daylight.

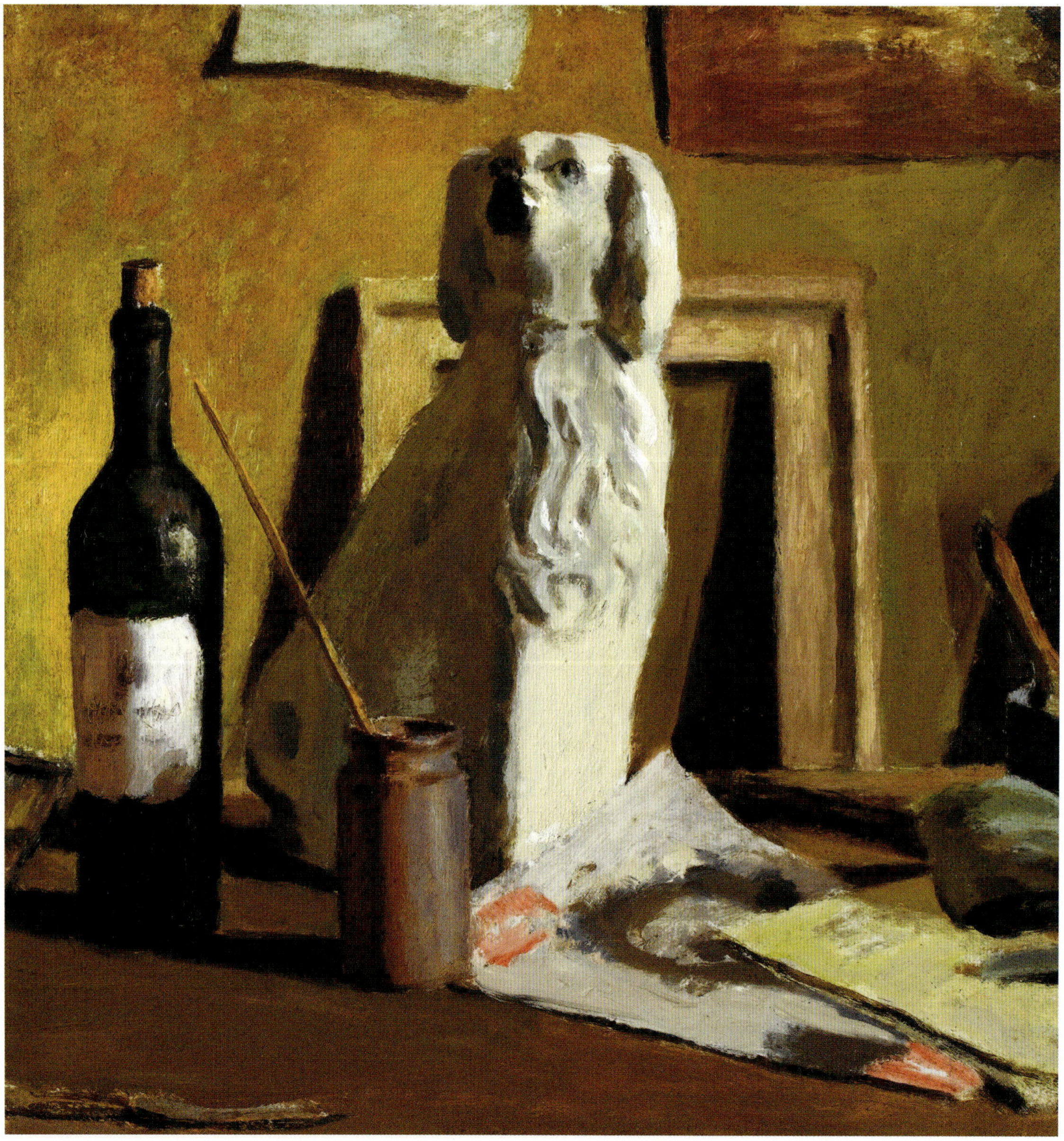

**26 Evan Charlton** (1904-1984), *Still Life with Staffordshire Dog*, oil on board, 18 ¾ x 18 in. (47.6 x 45.7 cm).

Objects in the artist's studio frequently became the inspiration for still lifes – although sometimes arranged formally they were more often than not the product of chance: plain walls, animated through the play of light and shade, form a lively backdrop to the loosely pinned sketches that adorn them. Against this background, three dimensional objects – a Staffordshire dog, discarded clothes – become the central focus.

**27 Victor Hume Moody** (1896-1990), *A Corner of the Artist's Studio*, c.1930, signed, oil on canvas board, 16 x 12 in. (40.6 x 30.5 cm).

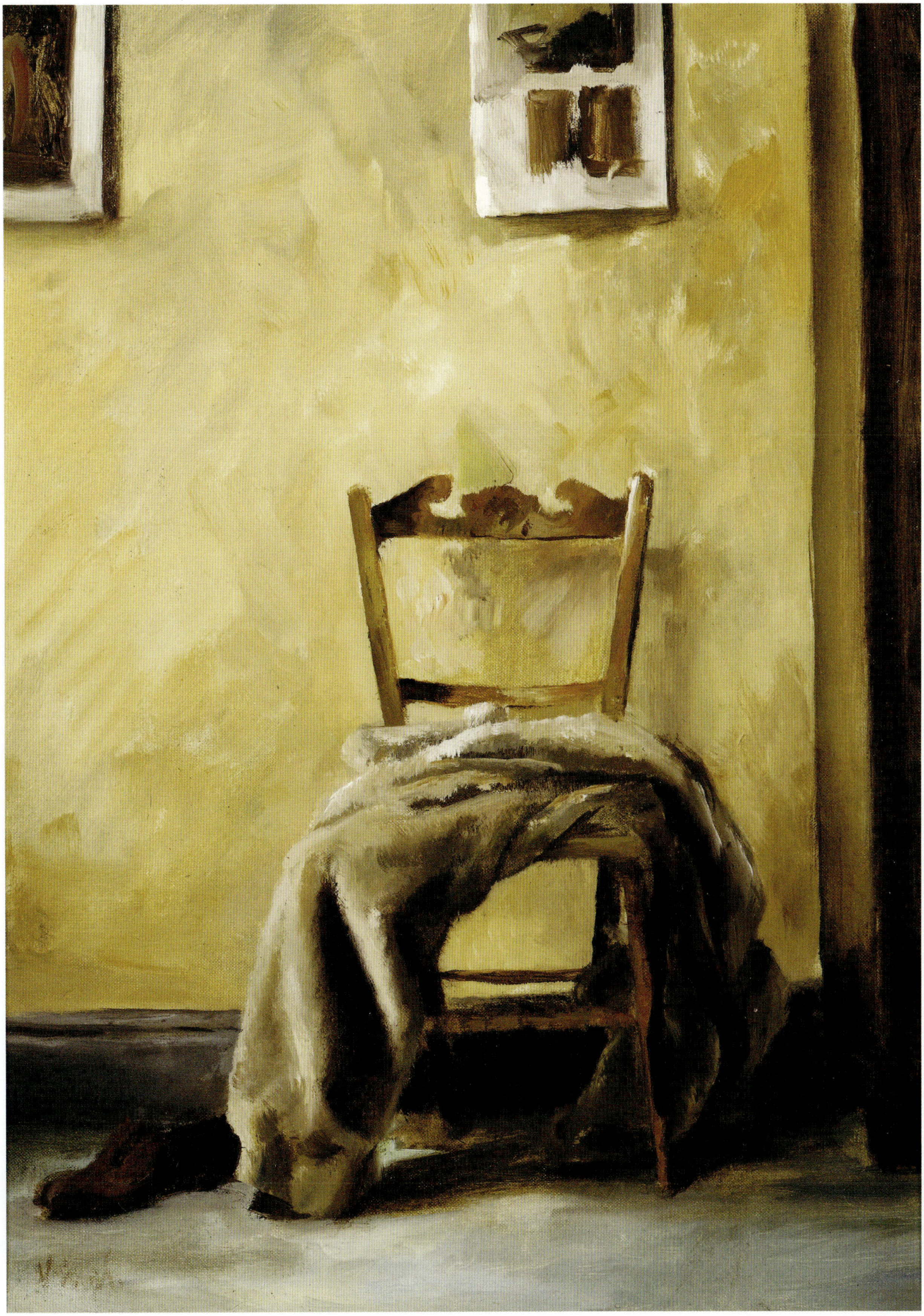

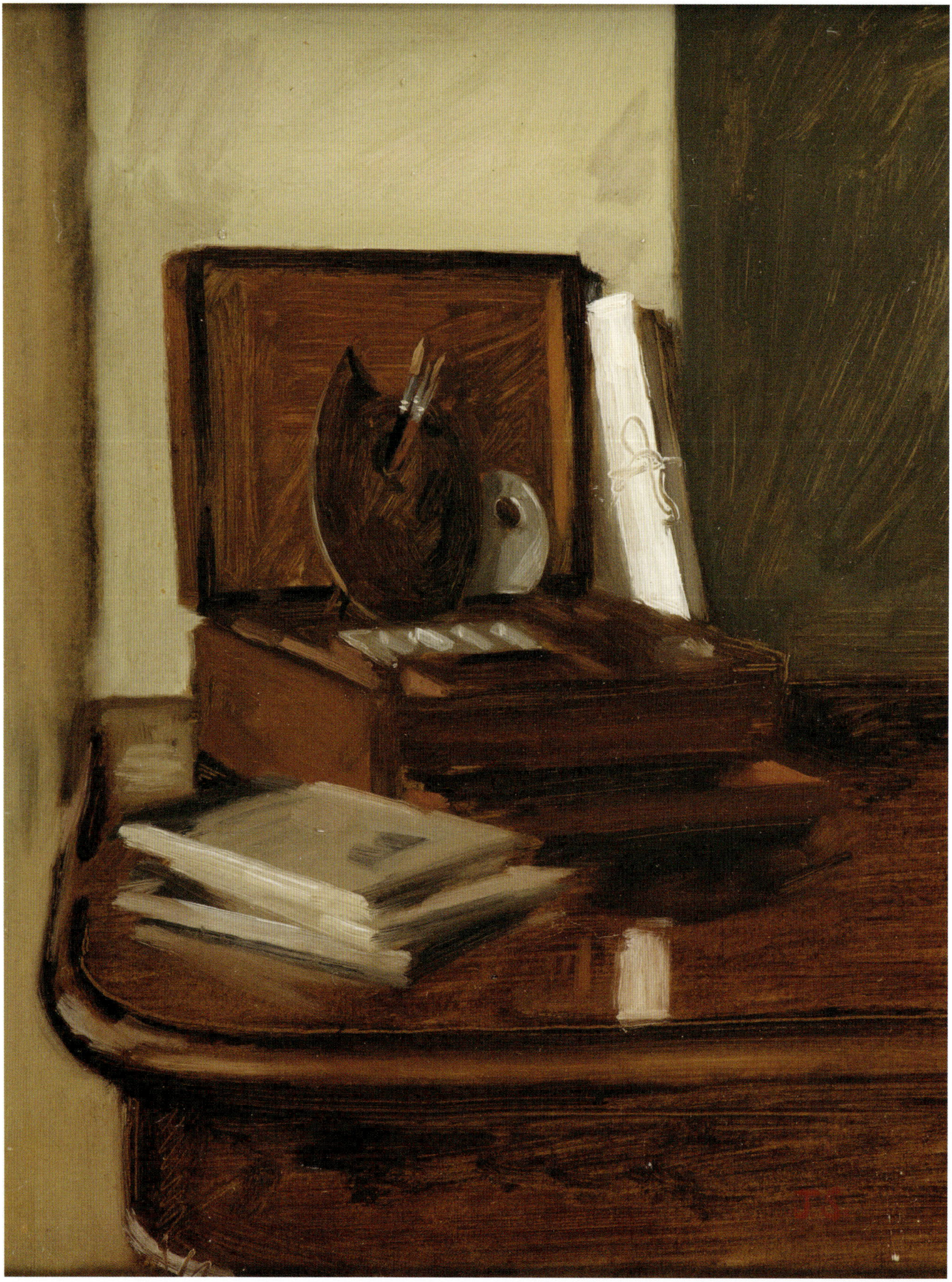

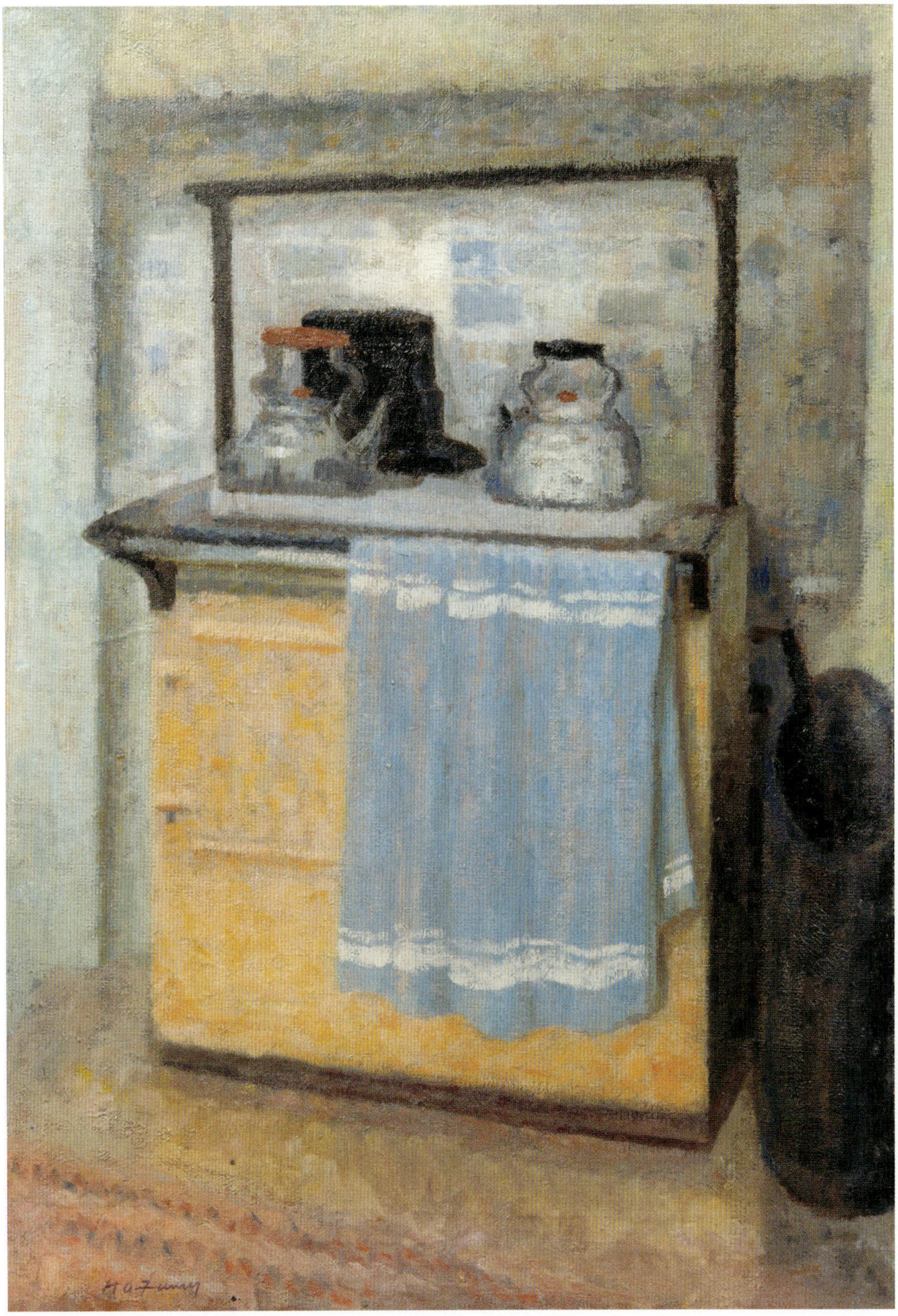

**29 Hubert Arthur Finney** (1905-1991), *Aga with Two Kettles and Blue Towel*, signed, c.1930, oil on canvas, 29 ½ x 21 in. (75 x 53.5 cm).

In his memoir Finney spoke of his passion for drawing as something that was always with him, and his continuous sense of awakening to the beauty found in even the most familiar of surroundings. (**310, 311, 324**)

**28 John Sergeant** (1937- 2010), *The Paint Box*, titled on label to reverse, oil on board, 9 ¼ x 7 ¼ in. (23.5 x18.3 cm).

Writing in Sergeant's obituary, Peyton Skipwith noted that the artist 'regarded colour as an intrusive and unnecessary distraction, though he did allow himself the occasional indulgence when the subject, such as a stylish pair of 1940s red shoes, or the eyelet on a luggage-tag, dictated'.

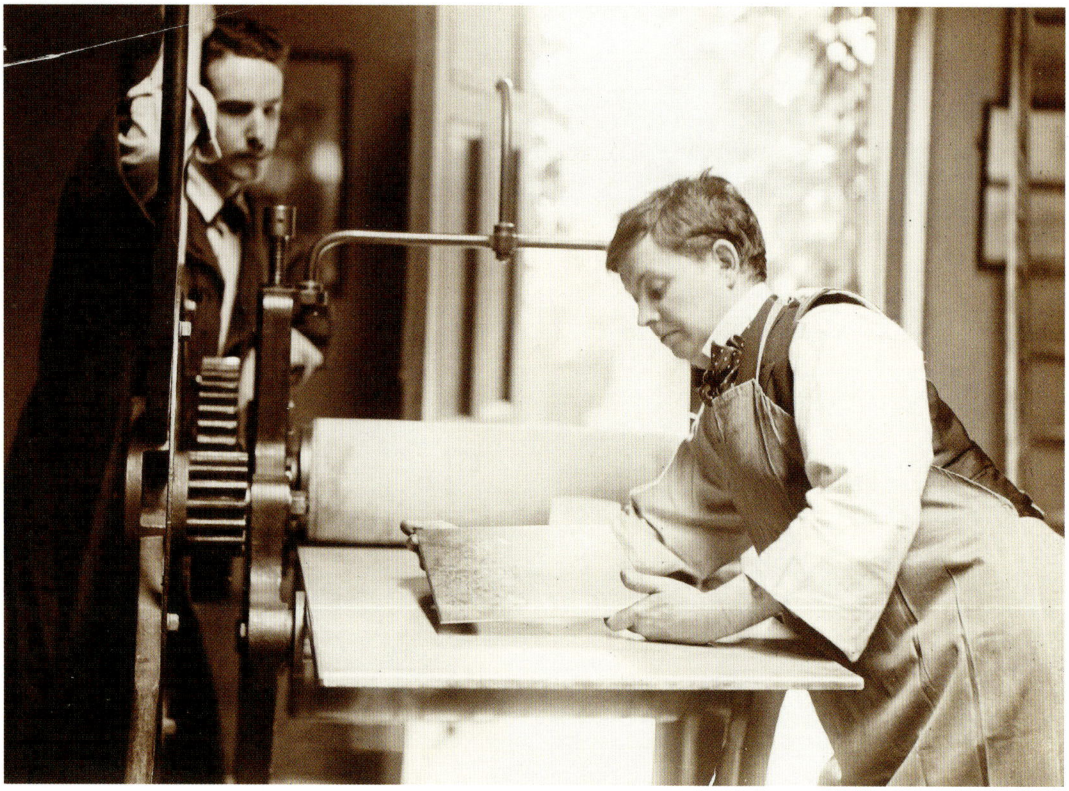

**30 Paul Laib** (1869-1958), Brangwyn and his assistant Edward Trumbull at the etching press, Temple Lodge Studio, c 1911, inscribed verso: 'FB & Trumbull',
photograph, 5 ¾ x 8 in. (15 x 20.3 cm).

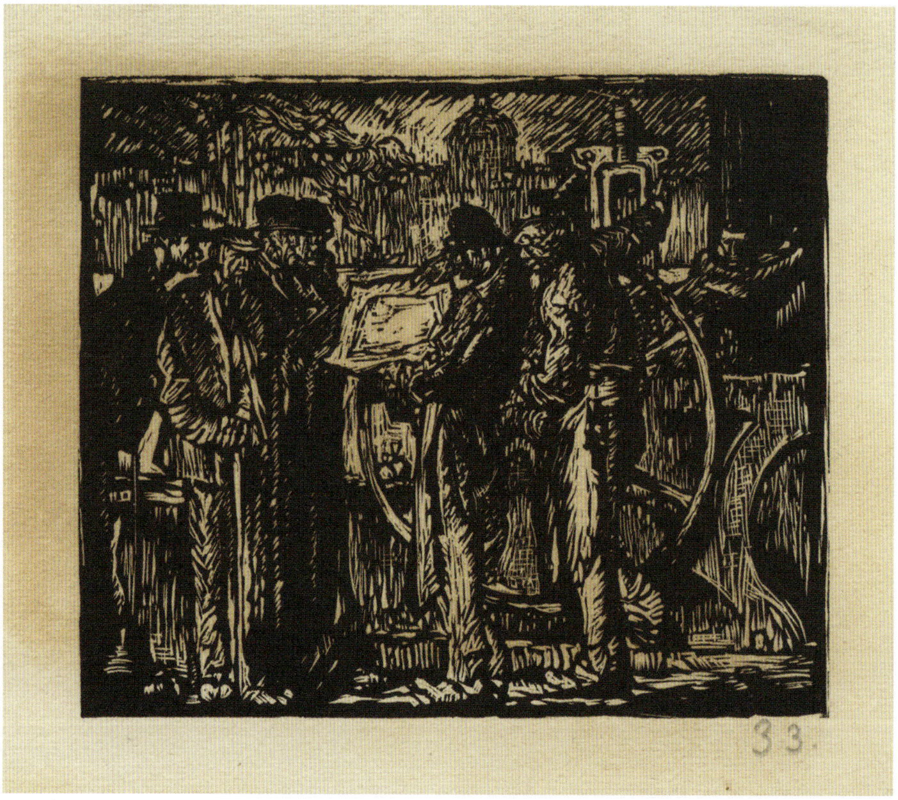


**31 Frank Brangwyn** (1867-1956),
*The Printers*, 1919 (V-1474)
woodcut, on tinted paper
image size: 4 ¼ x 5 in. (11 x 13 cm).

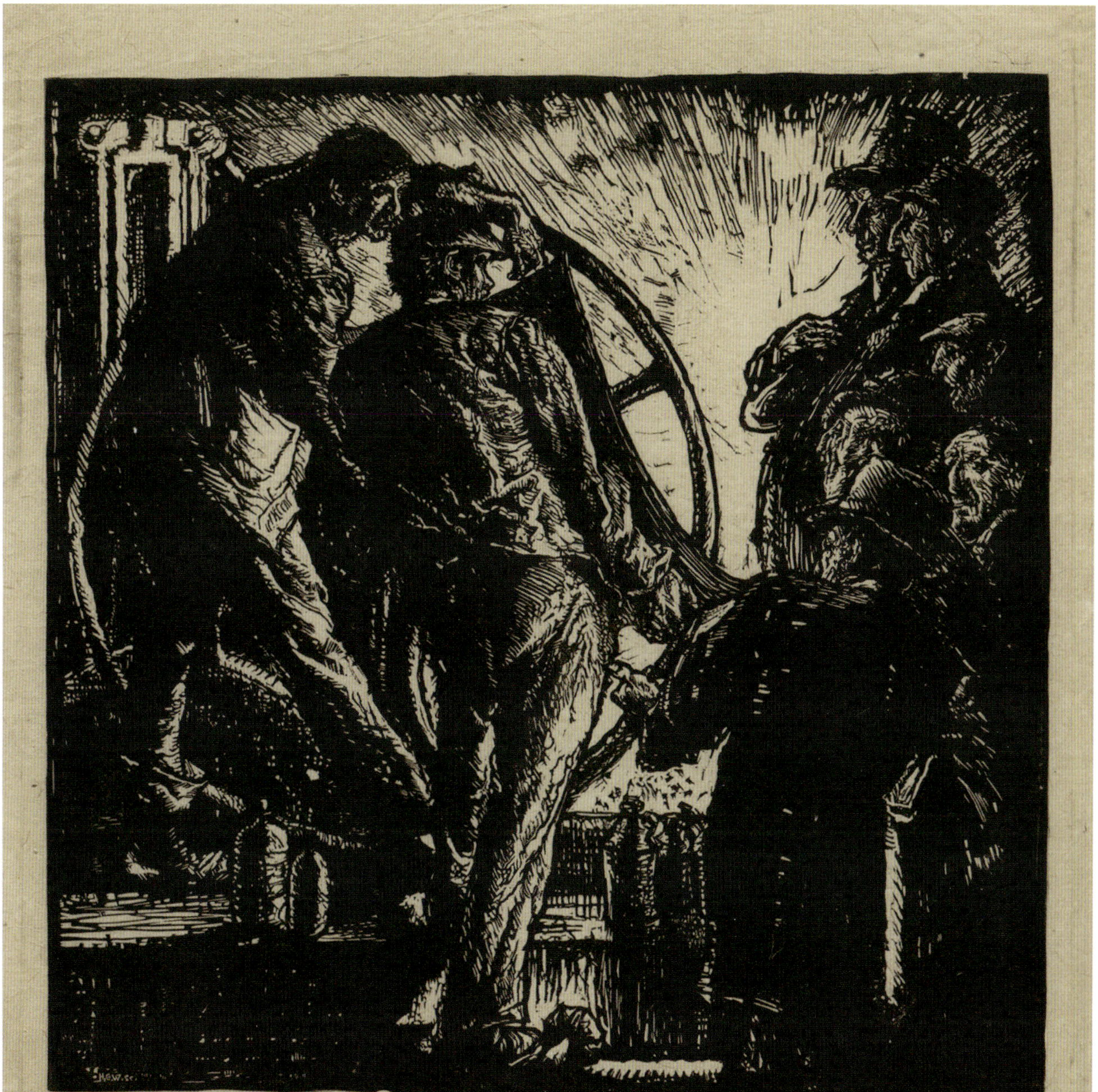


**32 Frank Brangwyn** (1867-1956), *The Printers*, c.1912, signed in pencil, inscribed to William Belleroche, woodcut, unique proof, 9 x 10 in. (22 x 25 cm).

Frank Brangwyn produced over 373 wood engravings and woodcuts between 1899 and 1935, including 71 bookplates and a large number of book illustrations and head and tail pieces. Brangwyn liked to oversee the printing process himself and owned his own etching press, a subject he was naturally drawn to.

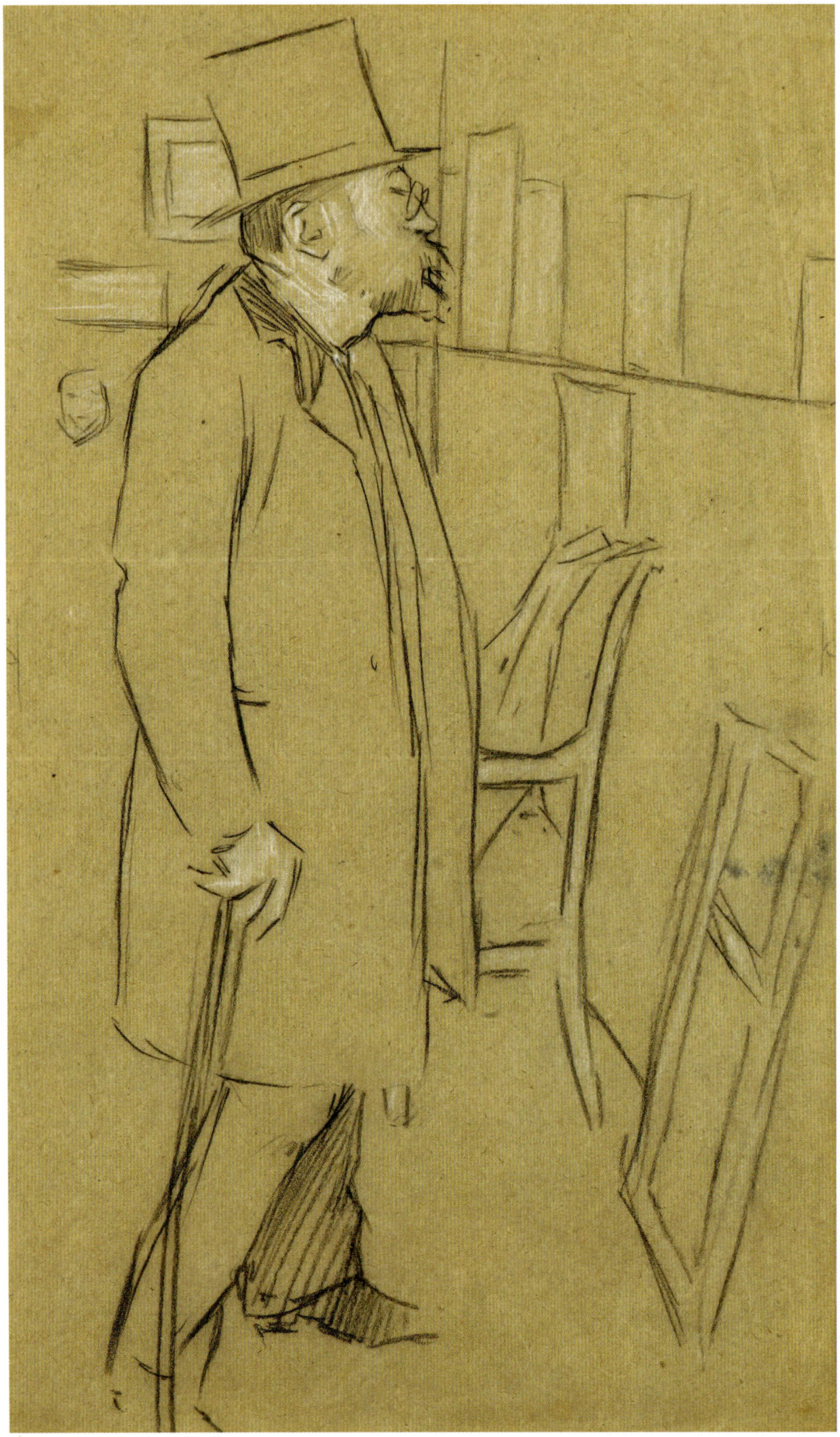

**33 William Rothenstein** (1872-1945), *The Connoisseur* (possibly a Portrait of Mons. Julien), c.1890, charcoal on paper, 14 ¼ x 8 ¾ in. (36 x 22 cm).
Collection: Santa Barbara Museum of Art, gift of Peyton Skipwith in honour of Will & Mary Richeson.

The Connoisseur was a frequent visitor to artists' studios. Often a collector, as well as a critic, he would assume the privilege of seeing – and giving his opinion on – an artist's most recent productions.

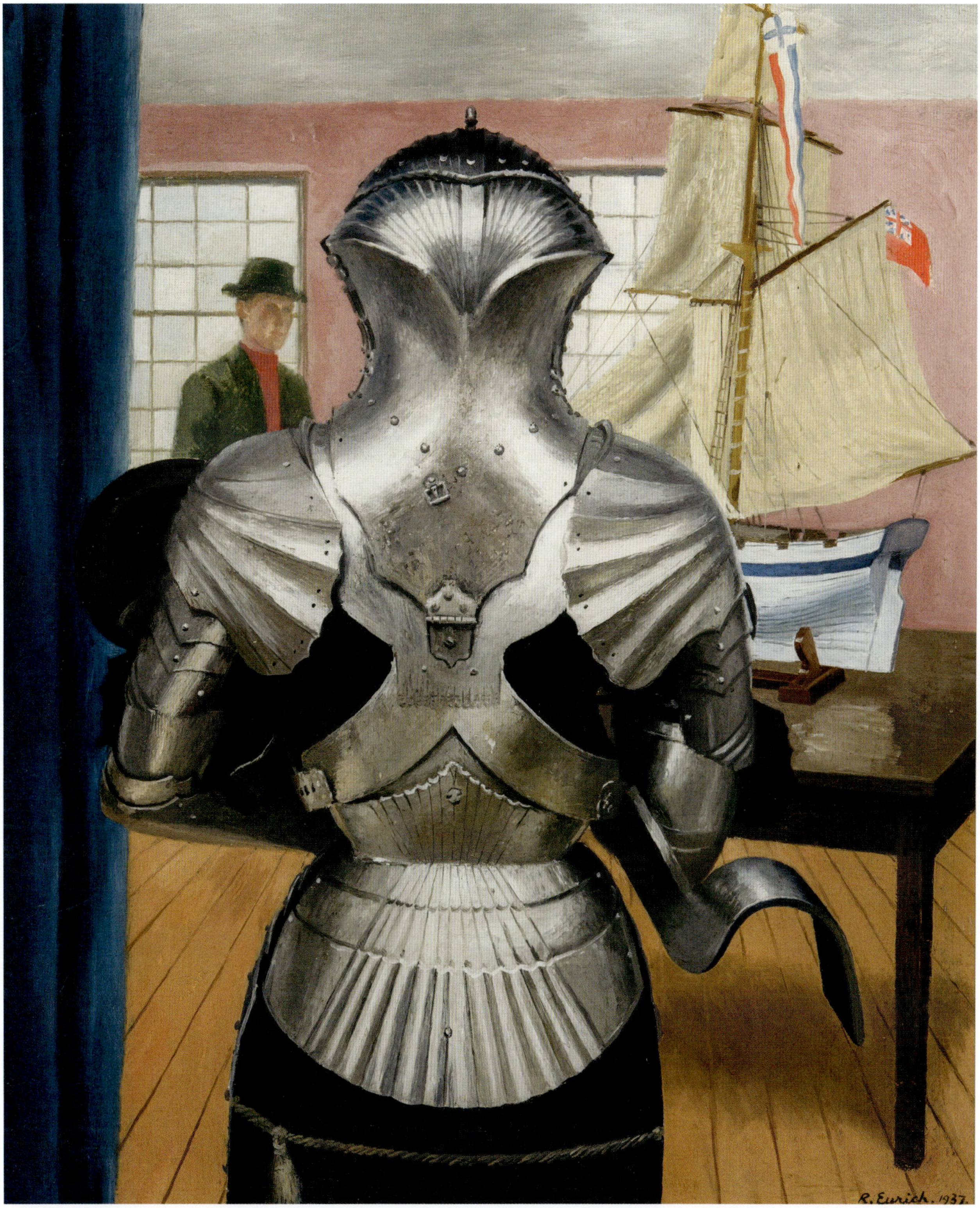


**34 Richard Eurich** (1903-1992), *In the Museum*, 1937, signed and dated, oil on panel, 20 x 17 in. (51 x 43 cm). Photo by Paul Carter © Richard Eurich Paintings.

'The subject matter,' according to Peyton Skipwith, 'is enigmatic. Dominated by the back of the exquisitely observed suit of armour placed slightly off centre, the viewer's eye navigates this either to right or left into the interior of a room, bare except for a wooden table supporting the large, fully rigged model of a 17th/18th century Royal Navy cutter, and the slightly diffident figure of a be-hatted man.'

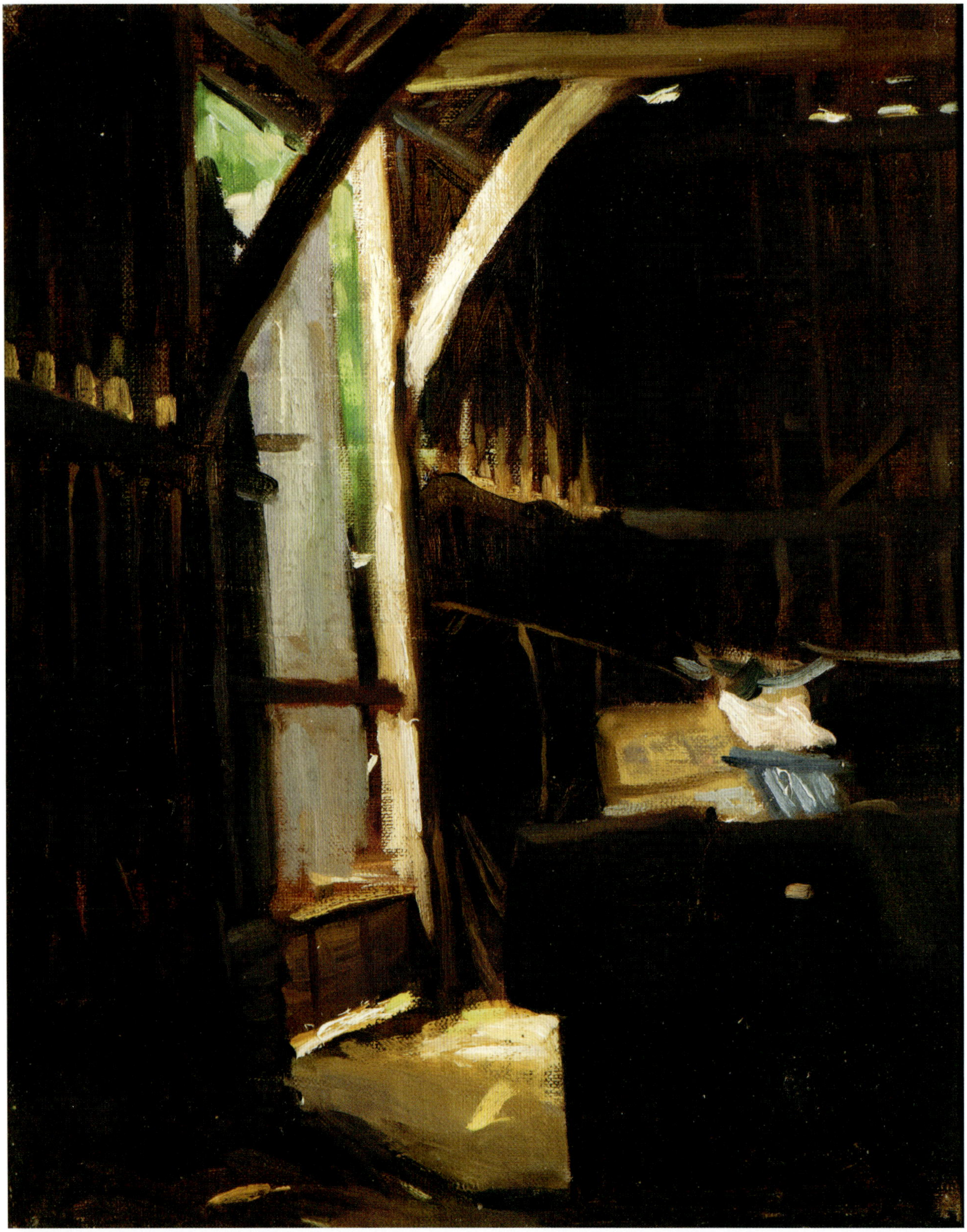

**35 Percy Jowett** (1892-1955), *Barn Interior*,
oil on canvas 12 ¾ x 10 ¼ in. (32.5 x 26 cm).

Jowett frequently worked in situ – this timber barn serving briefly as an impromptu studio.

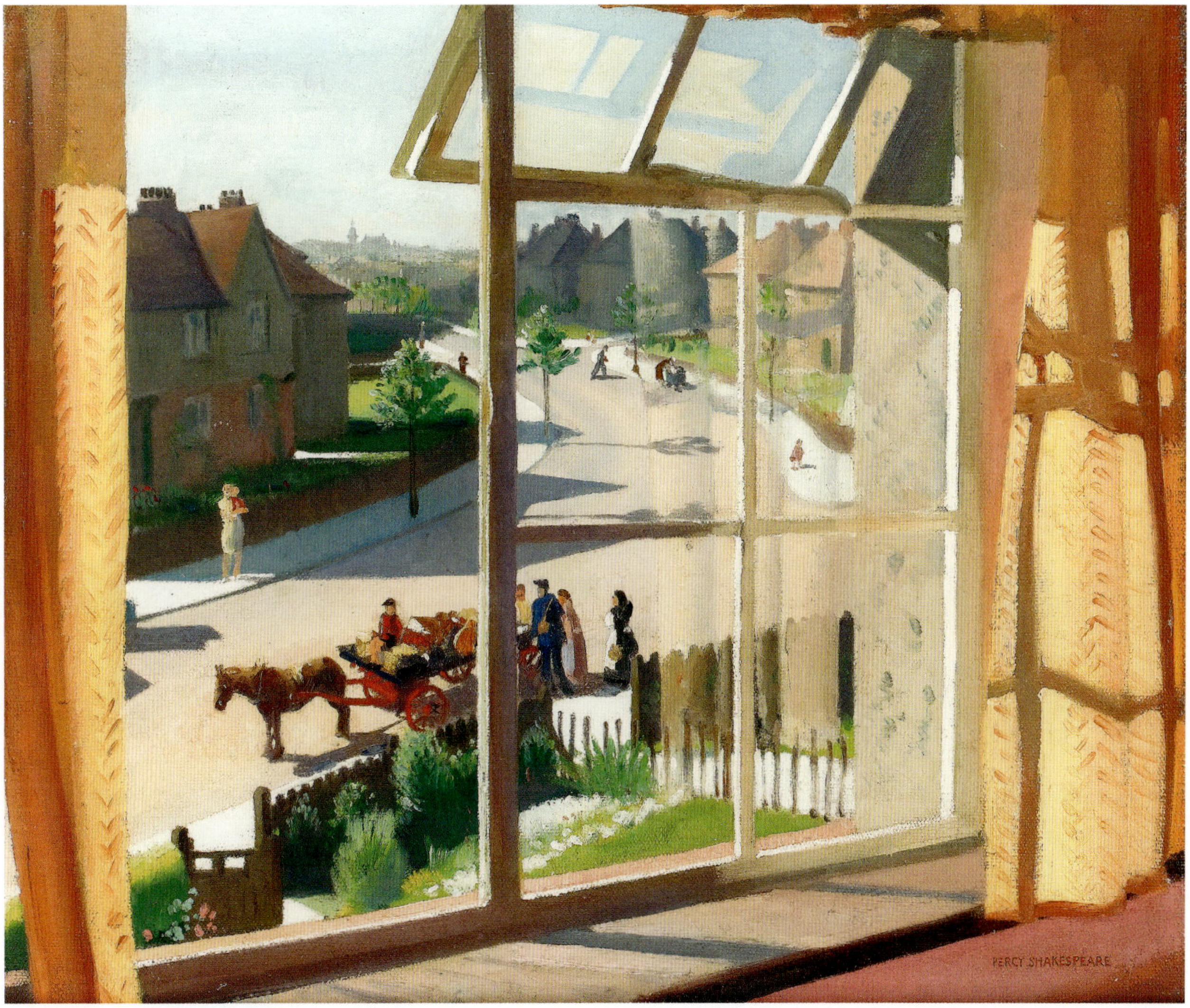


**36 Percy Shakespeare** (1906-1943), *View From the Artist's Bedroom*, signed, oil on canvas, 20 ½ x 24 ½ in. (52 x 62 cm).

Mr and Mrs Shakespeare and their eight children were re-housed from the Dudley slums to Wren's Nest, a green oasis in the industrial Black Country, in the late 1920s. The bedroom shown here, which Percy shared with one of his three brothers, also doubled as his studio and served as the setting for his striking self-portrait, *Morning Exercise*, 1934 (**309**).

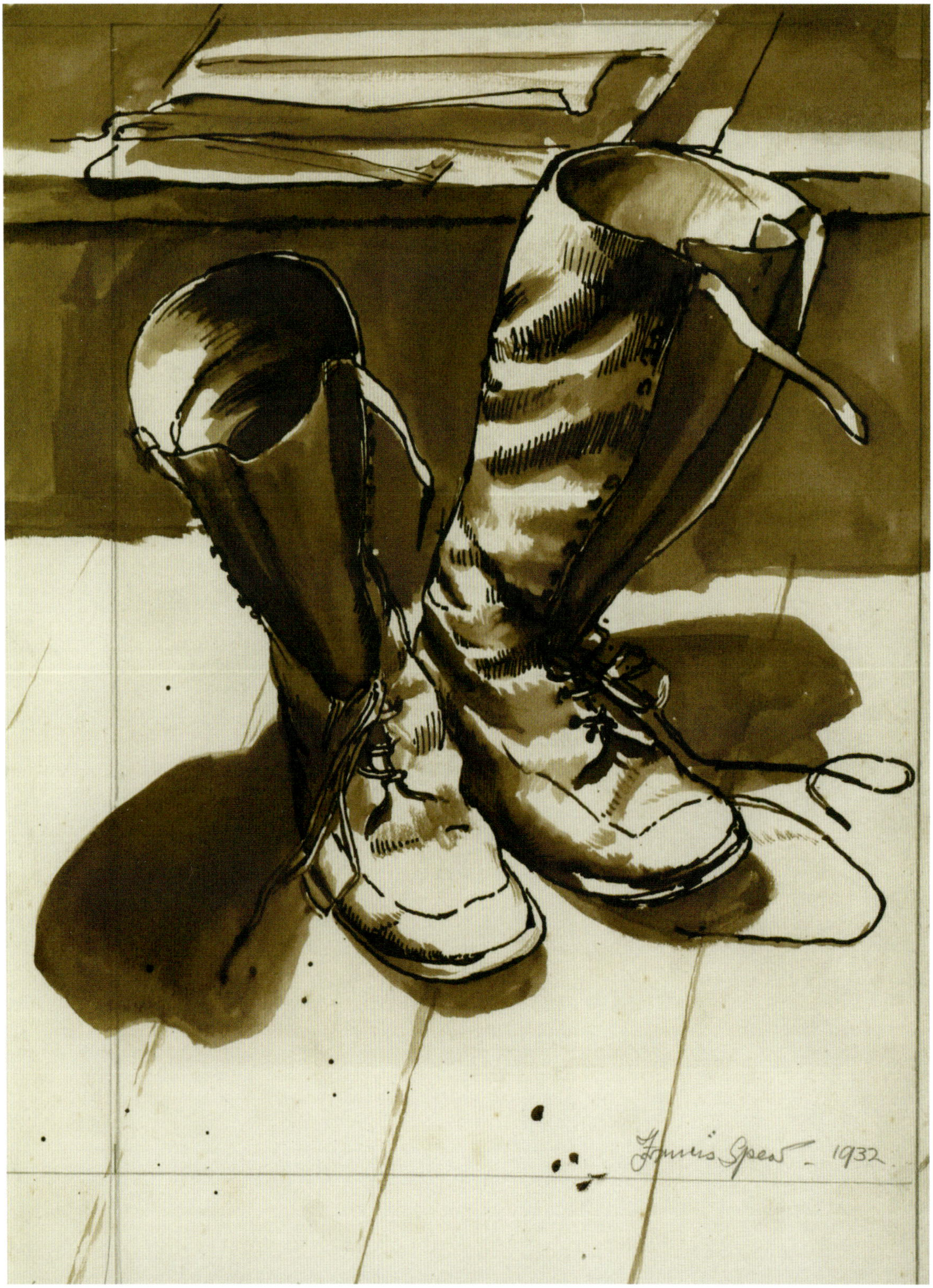


**37 Francis Spear** (1902-1979), *The Artist's Boots*, 1932, signed and dated, pen & ink on paper, 12 ½ x 9 ½ in. (32 x 24 cm).

Objects found in corners of his studio – discarded boots, shoes, hats, sheaves of drawing paper – were favoured subjects for Spear. His penchant for returning to the same themes led his fellow students to call him 'Haystacks Spear' on account of the fact that he produced so many landscape compositions with the same motif. (**273**, **274**)

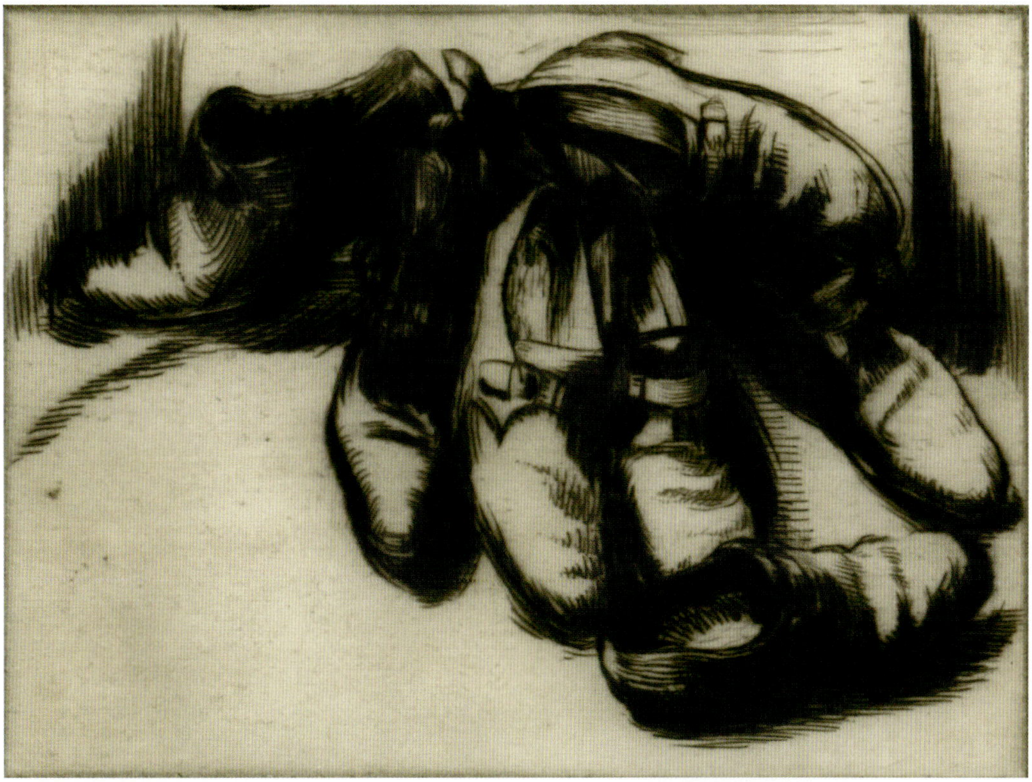

**38 Francis Spear** (1902-1979), *Discarded Shoes*, c. 1925,
etching on paper, 4 x 5 ½ in. (10.2 x 13.5 cm).

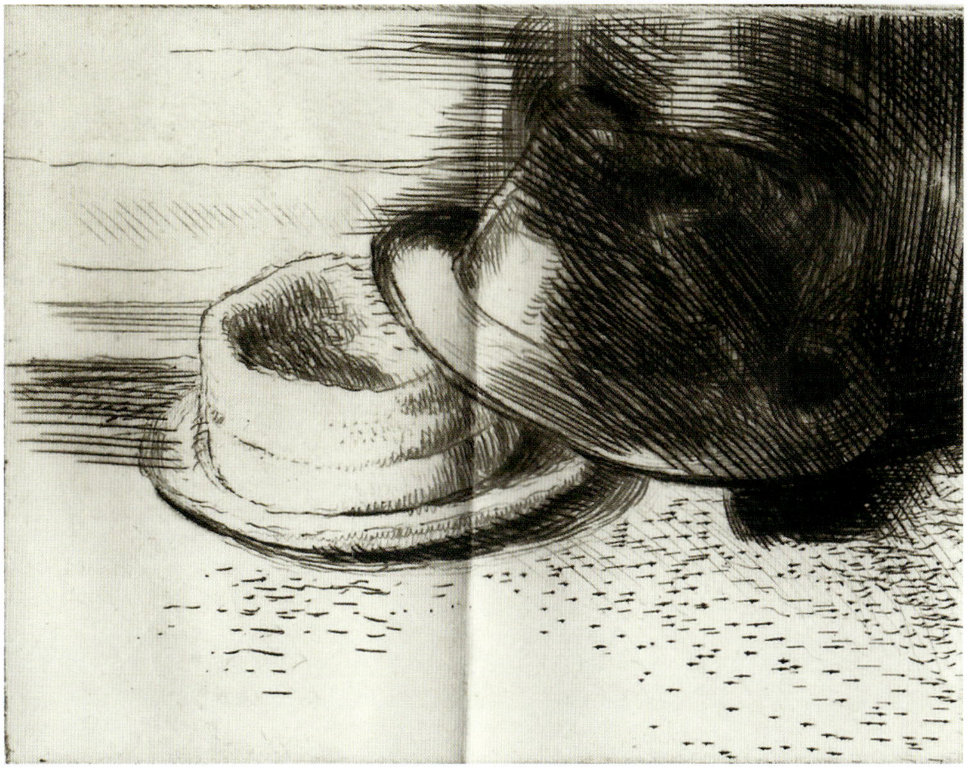

**39 Francis Spear** (1902-1979), *Hats*, early 1920,
etching on paper, 6 x 7 in. (15.2 x 17.8 cm).

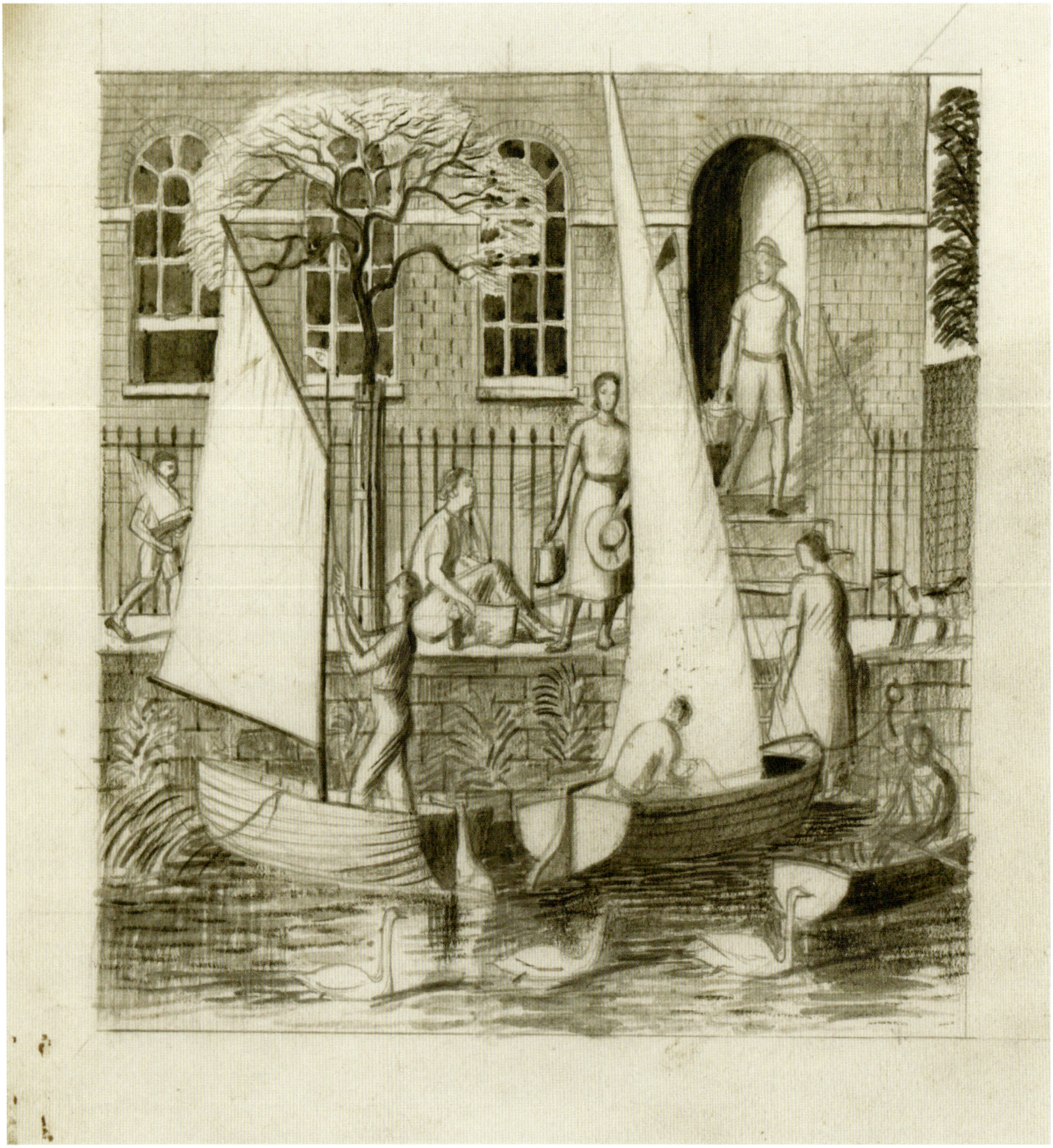

**40 Frederick Austin** (1902-1990), *Boats at Chiswick Mall*,
pencil, black chalk and wash on paper, 5 ½ x 5 ¼ in. (14 x 13.5 cm).

Robert Sargent Austin, Frederick's brother, moved to Chiswick Mall in 1931. A boat moored nearby facilitated sketching trips along the Thames.

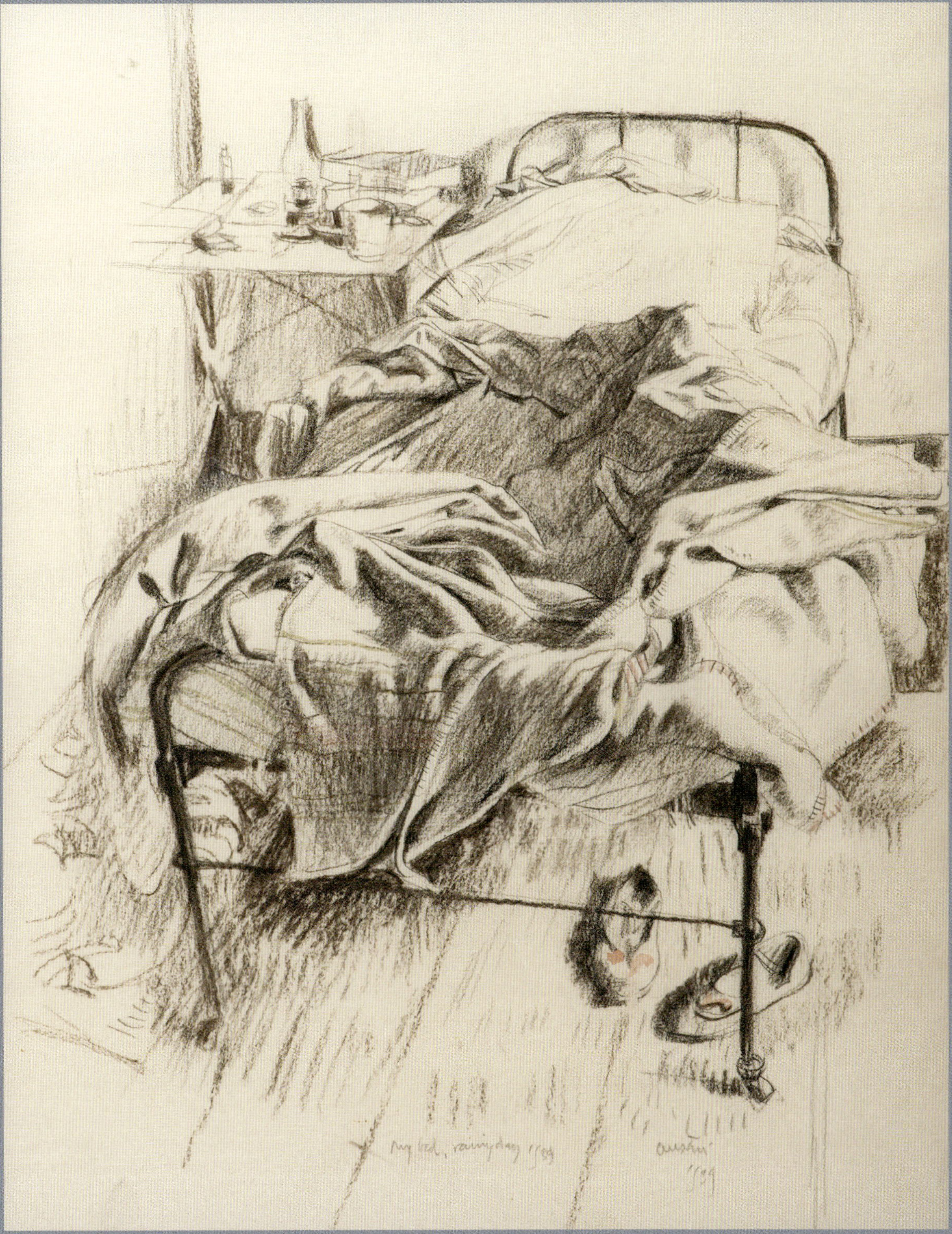

**41 Robert Austin** (1895-1973), *My Bed, Rainy Day,* 1939, signed, dated and inscribed with title, pencil, crayon, highlights in pink and green watercolour on paper, 18.3 x 12.2 in. (46.5 x 31 cm).

The artist's bedroom depicted at Lingard House was on the upper storey of the 18th century brick town house to which the Austin family moved in 1931. With windows on opposite sides of the room, Robert Austin was able to create a north-facing studio, while also profiting from views of the Thames to the south. He found an endless source of inspiration in the domestic and family routine which formed the backdrop to his work.

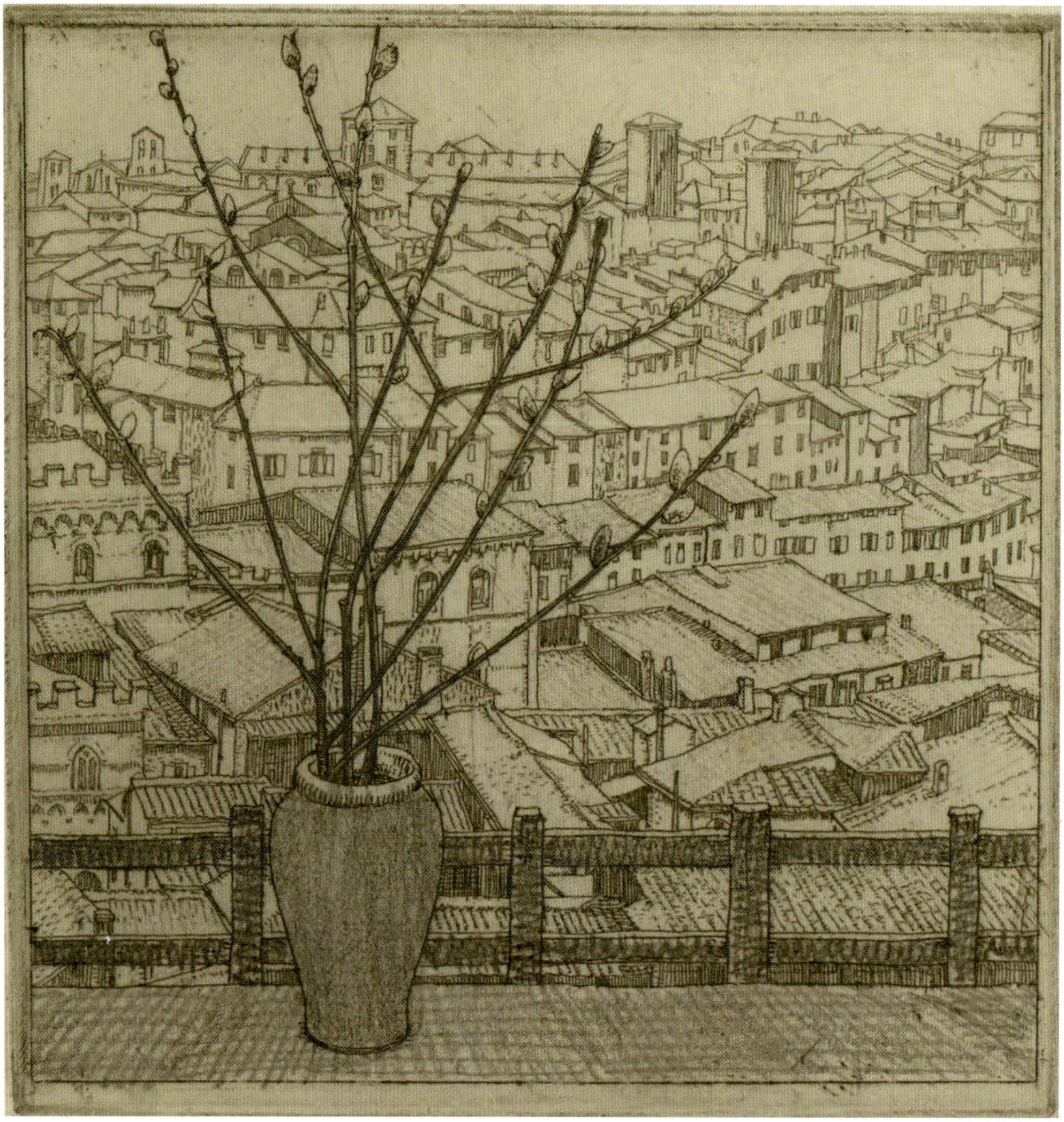

**42 Robert Austin** (1895-1973), *Siena, Evening*, 1923, inscribed in pencil 1st State, pencil over a line engraving, 4 ½ x 4 ¼ in.(11.5 x 10.8 cm).

A view on to an exterior space, framed by a window, offered a practical alternative for travelling artists when a dedicated studio space was not available. Throughout Austin's career exterior views from quirky angles were a frequent and favourite device. In *Modern Masters of Etching*, Salaman described *Siena, Evening*, as made up of … 'the roofs of the happy-hearted city decoratively observed from the point of view of a flower-pot on a window ledge'.

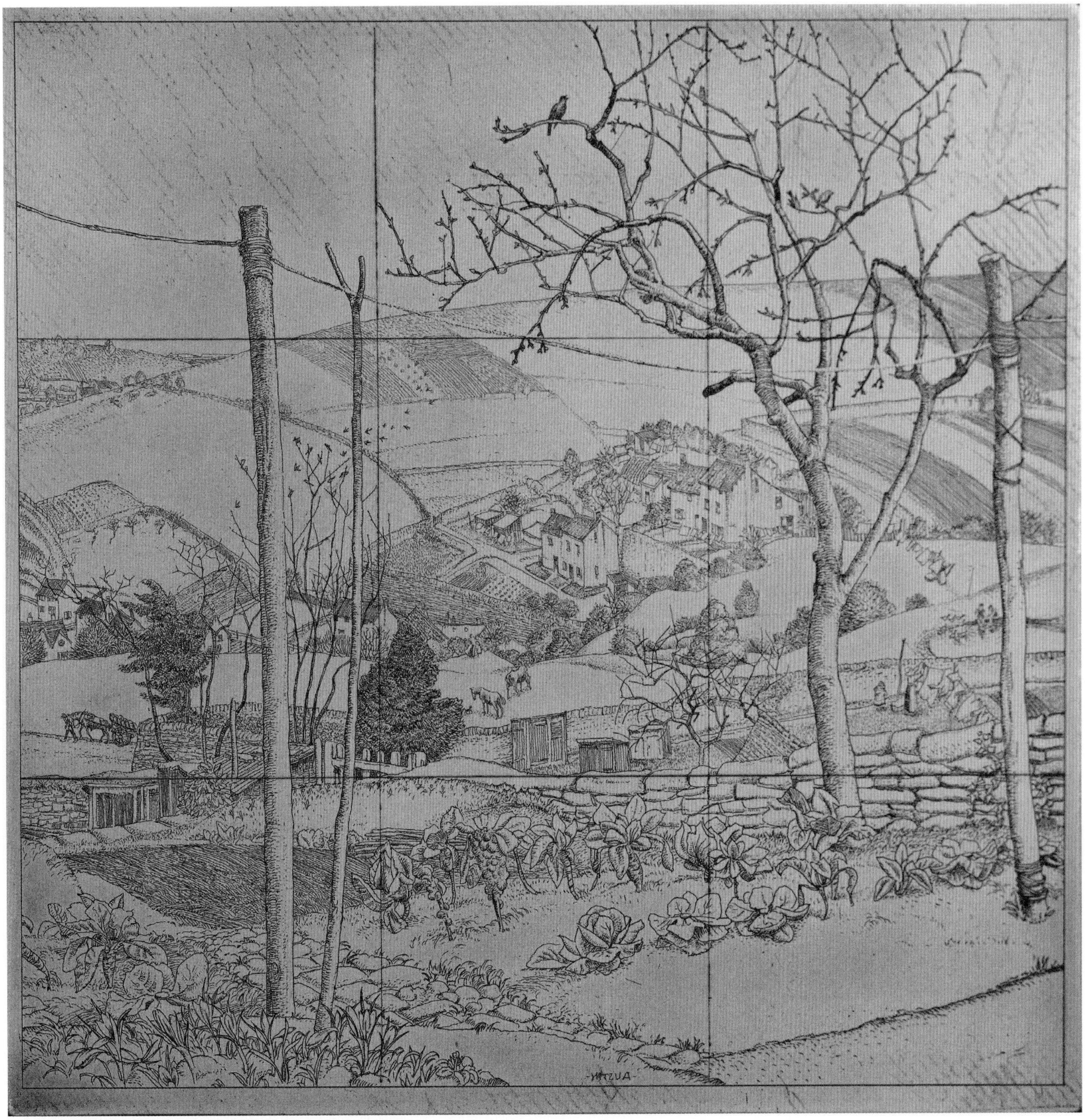

**43 Robert Austin** (1895-1973), *Early Spring, Gloucestershire*, 1922, (C.D. 30), original etched copper plate (cancelled), 7 x 7 ½ in. (17.5 x 19 cm).

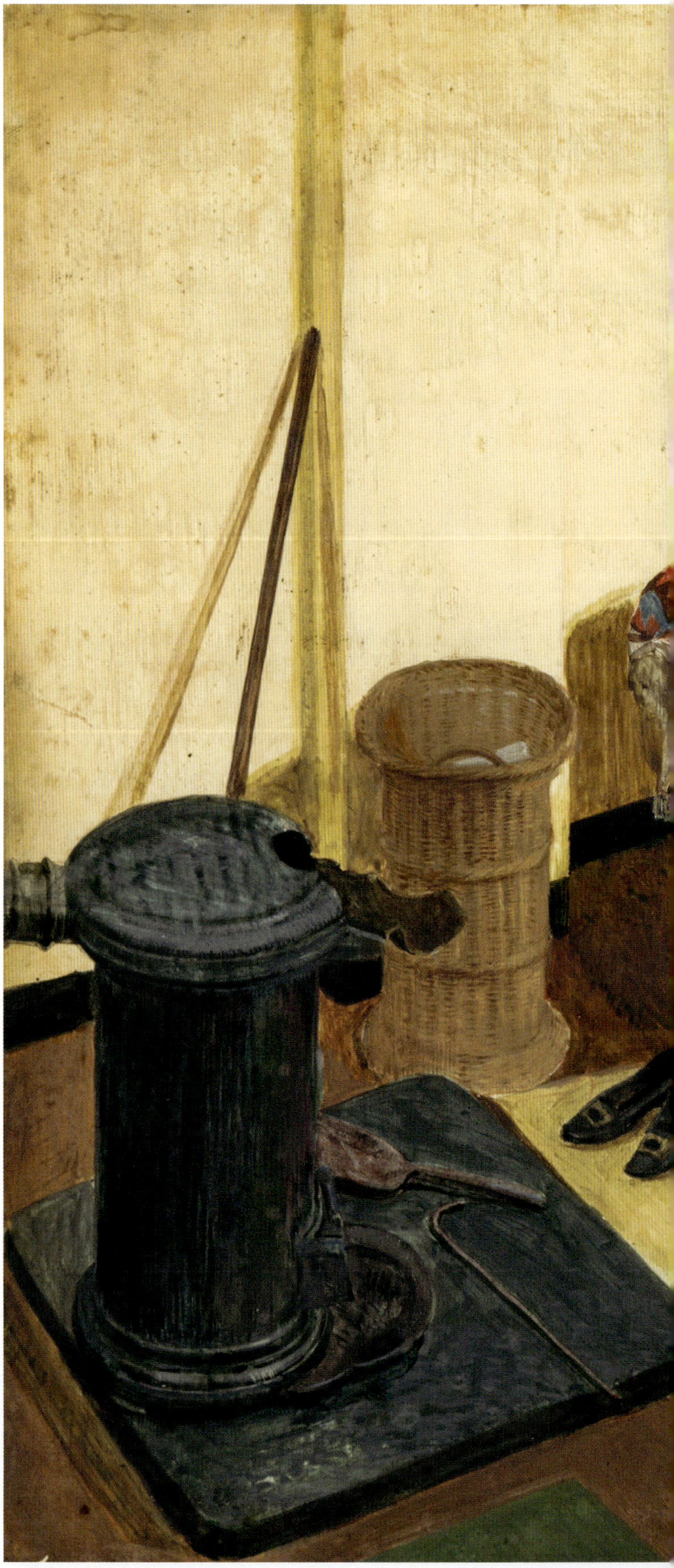

**44 Leon Underwood** (1890-1975), *Cecile on the Sofa*, 1920,
signed and dated,
tempera on panel, 11 ½ x 15 ¼ in. (29.5 x 38.5 cm).

1920 was a pivotal year for Leon Underwood. Having served during WW1 as a Captain in the Camouflage Section of the Royal Engineers, he then attended the Slade School of Art for a year's refresher course and won a British Prix de Rome scholarship. He taught a life drawing class at the Royal College of Art from 1920 until 1923 – when he resigned to travel on painting trips to Paris and Iceland. The setting for this painting is possibly the Hammersmith studio from where Underwood ran, intermittently until 1938, Brook Green School of Art. (**108**)

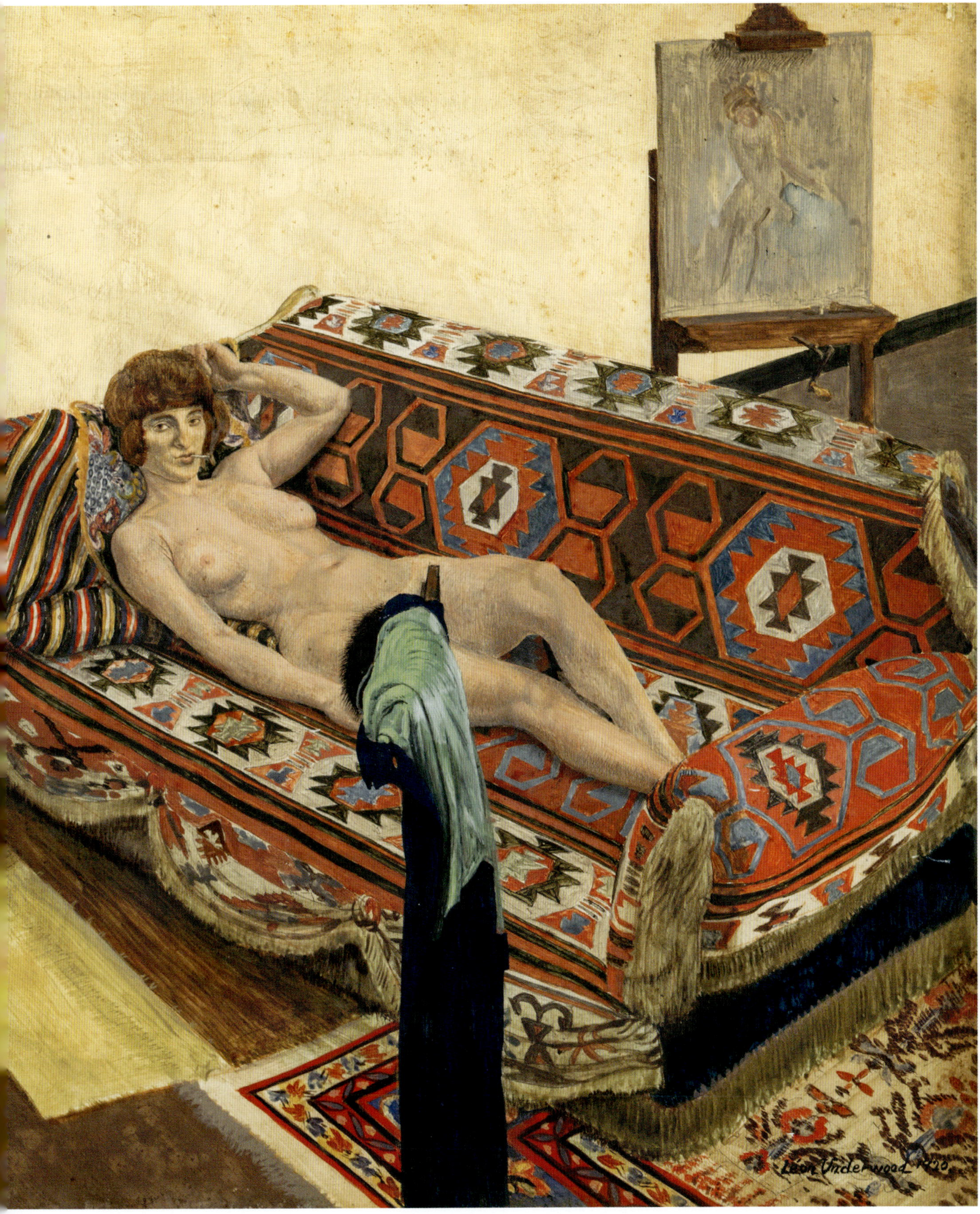
Leon Underwood

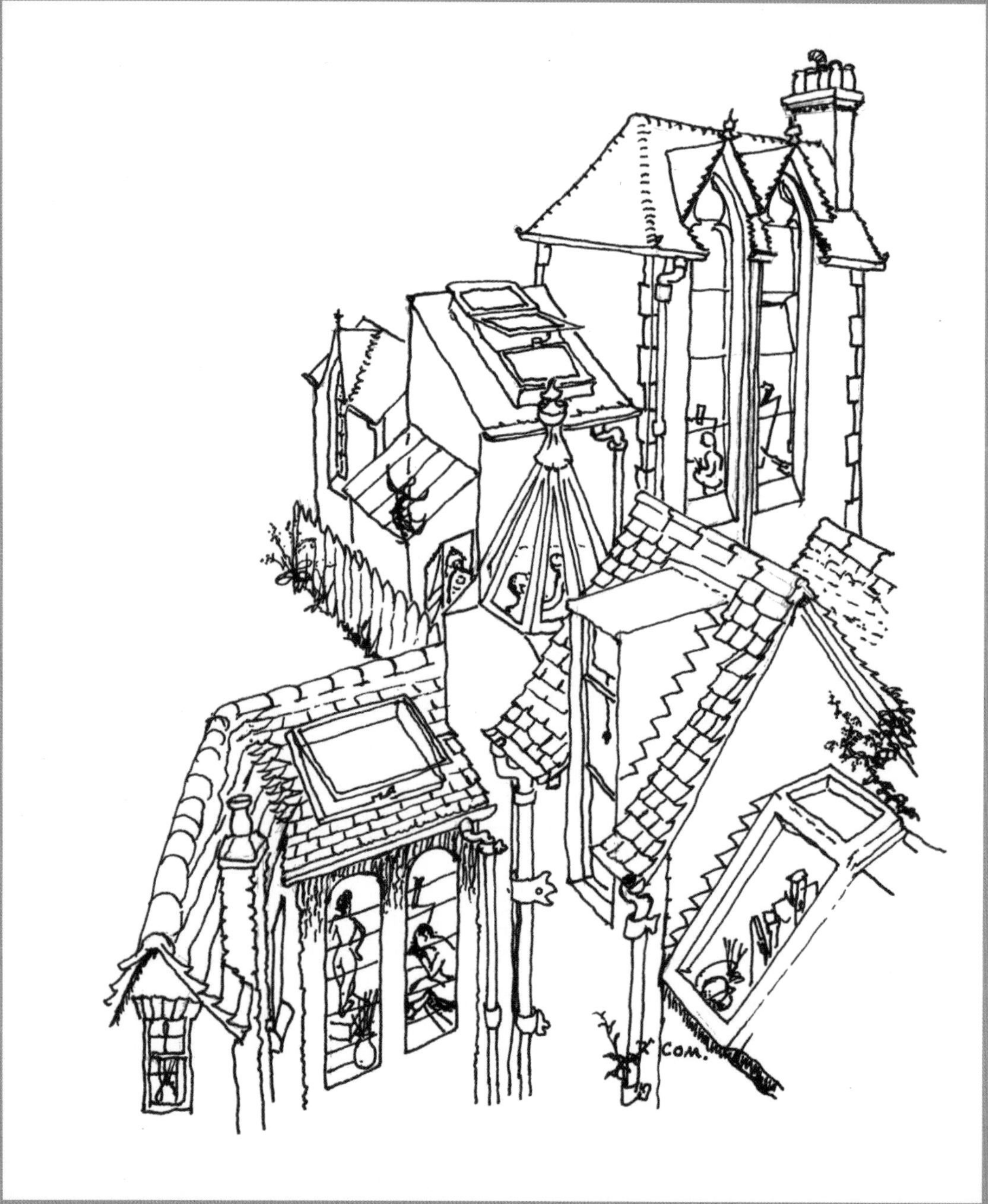


**45 Catherine Olive Moody** (1920-2009), *The Malvern Art School*, c.1980, signed, pen & ink on paper, 10 x 8 ¾ in. (25.5 x 22 cm).

This drawing was intended as an illustration for Catherine Moody's book *Painter's Workshop: An Exploration of the Studio* (published 1982) and shows the Malvern Art School with art classes in progress. Moody (**234**) was head of the school from 1962-80.

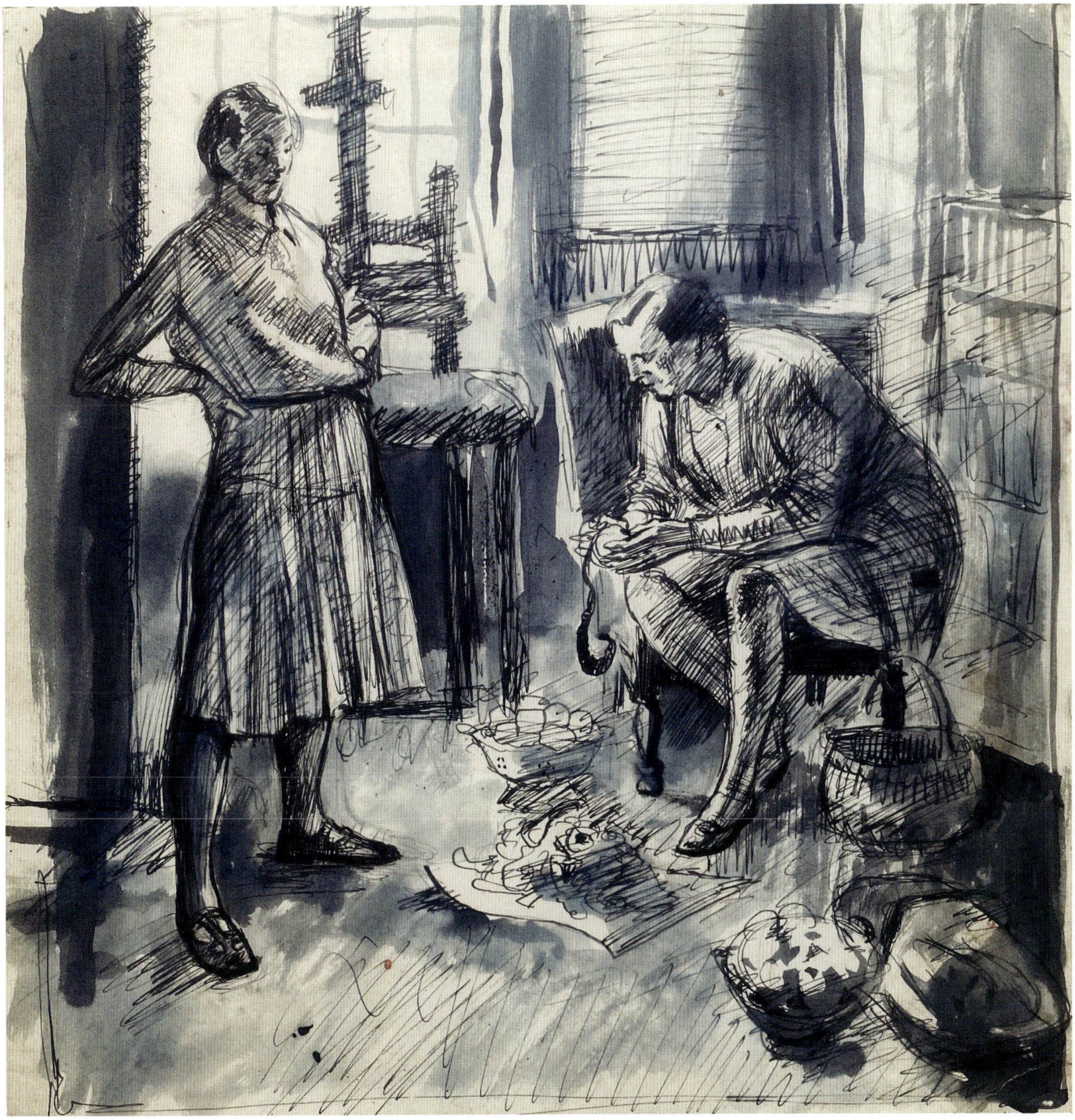

**46 Evelyn Dunbar** (1906-1960), *The Artist and Her Mother in the 'Snug'*, pen & ink on paper, 13 x 13 in. (33 x 33 cm).

The 'snug' was a sort of all-purpose fore-kitchen at 244 High Street, the family home of the Dunbars from 1913 to 1924. Florence, Evelyn's mother, is peeling apples, watched by her 15-year-old daughter. The easel in the background is Florence's and the 'snug' served as Florence's studio, as well as for multiple other tasks.

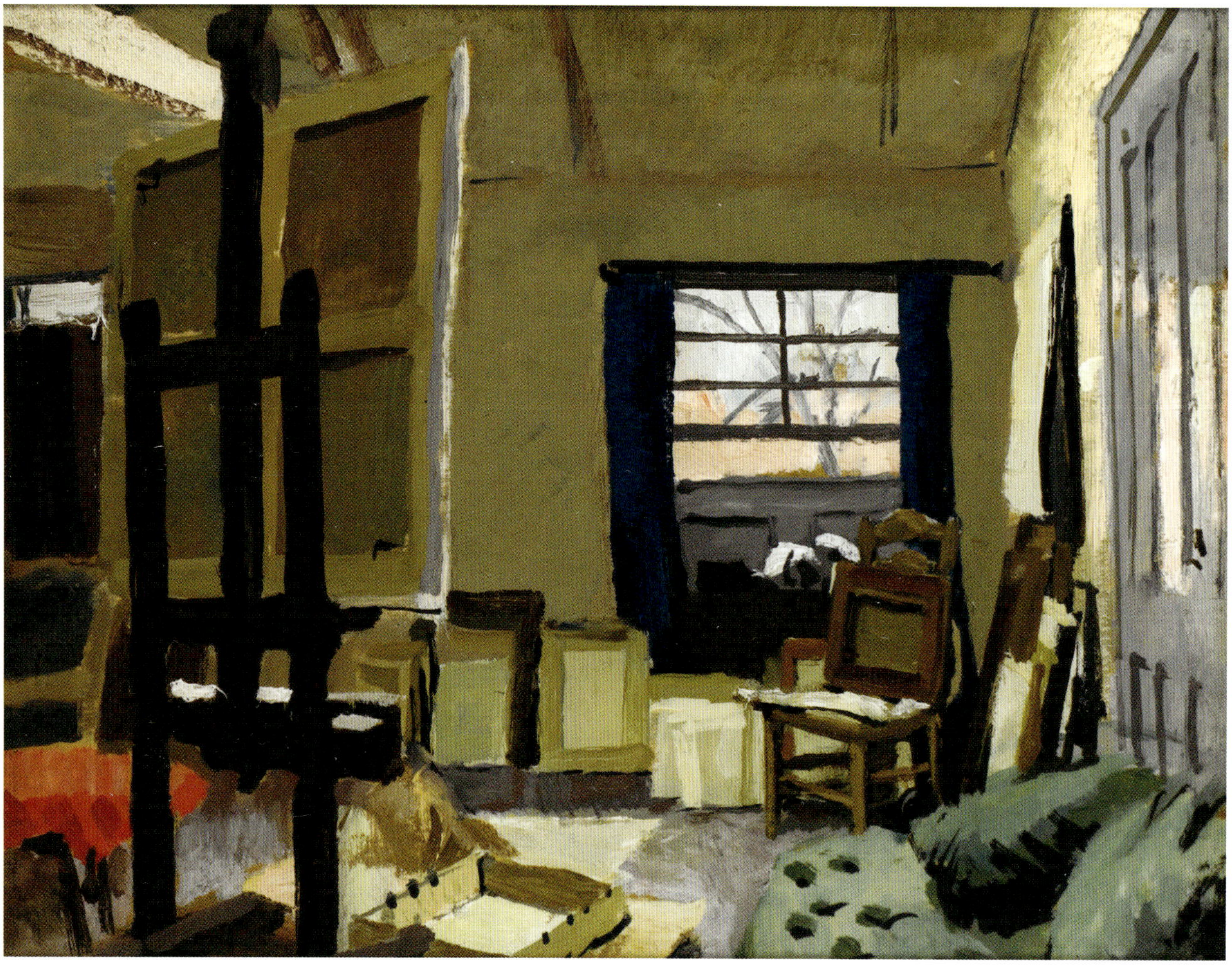

**47 Stephen Bone** (1904-1958), *The Artist's Studio, Haverstock Hill, London*, c.1938, oil on panel, 11 x 14 in. (27.9 x 35.6 cm).

Bone's panels were painted in just a few hours of intense concentration and testify to his painterly skill and sure sense of colour. The rapidity with which he produced work can be seen from the large number of stacked canvases against the back wall. (**227**)

**48 Catherine Olive Moody** (1920-2009), *Studio Lighting*, c.1982,
inscribed 'Studio lighting – A tall North window zone of light',
inscribed on reverse: 'Drawing by Catherine Moody Lorne Lodge1, Sling Lane, Malvern, Worcs, WR14 2TU',
'Illustration to Painters Workshop CH XIX – The Studio'
pen & ink on paper, 15 ¼ x 9 ¼ in. (38.7 x 23.5 cm).

First teaching at the Manchester College of Art and then Head of Malvern School of Art, 1962-80, Catherine Moody (**234**) was fascinated by the artist's working space. This drawing, used to illustrate her book *The Painter's Workshop: An Exploration of the Studio* (published 1982), shows the ideal space needed for a correctly proportioned portrait studio.

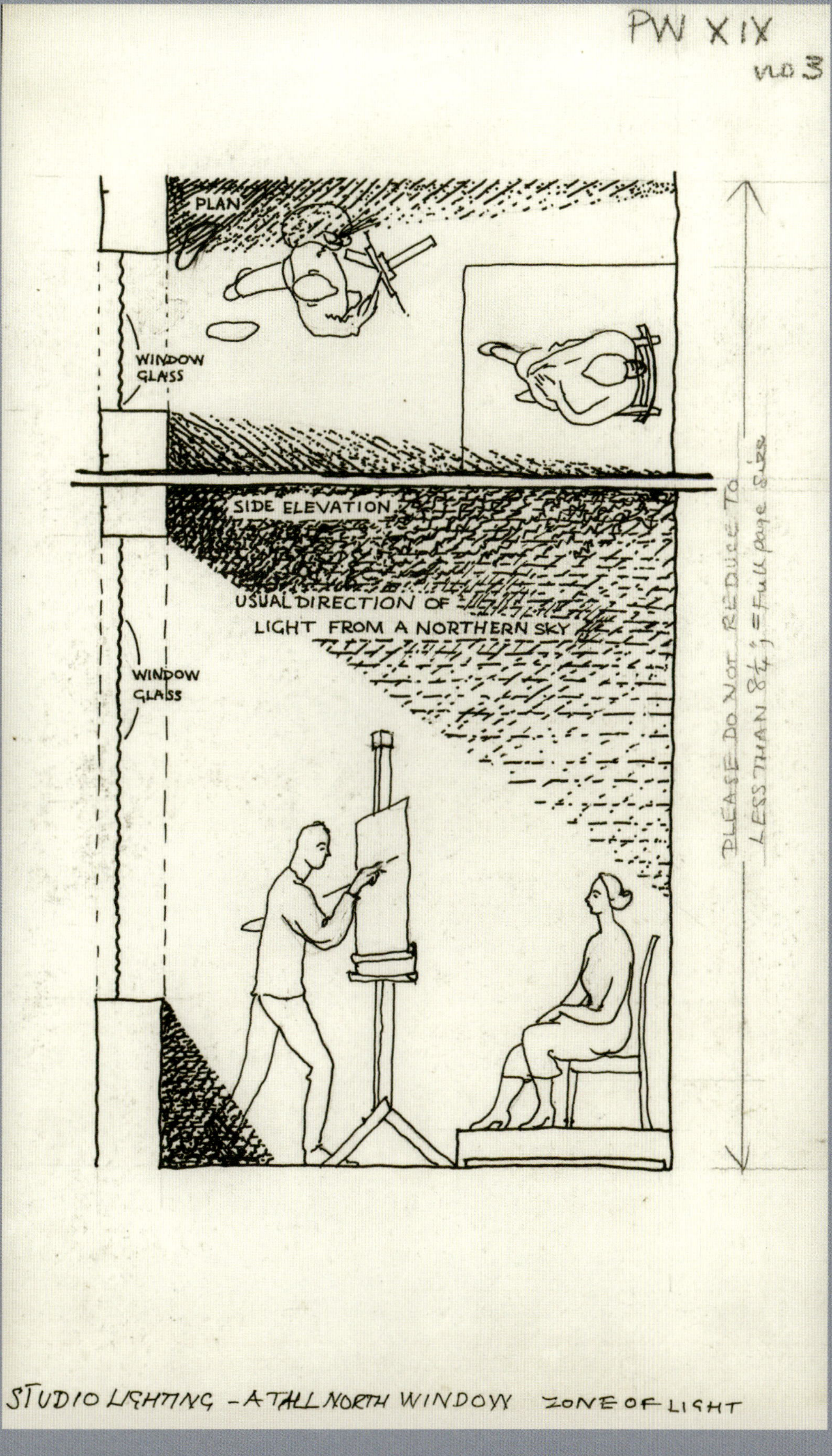
PW XIX
PLAN
WINDOW GLASS
SIDE ELEVATION
USUAL DIRECTION OF LIGHT FROM A NORTHERN SKY
WINDOW GLASS
PLEASE DO NOT REDUCE TO LESS THAN 8¼" = Full page size
STUDIO LIGHTING - A TALL NORTH WINDOW ZONE OF LIGHT

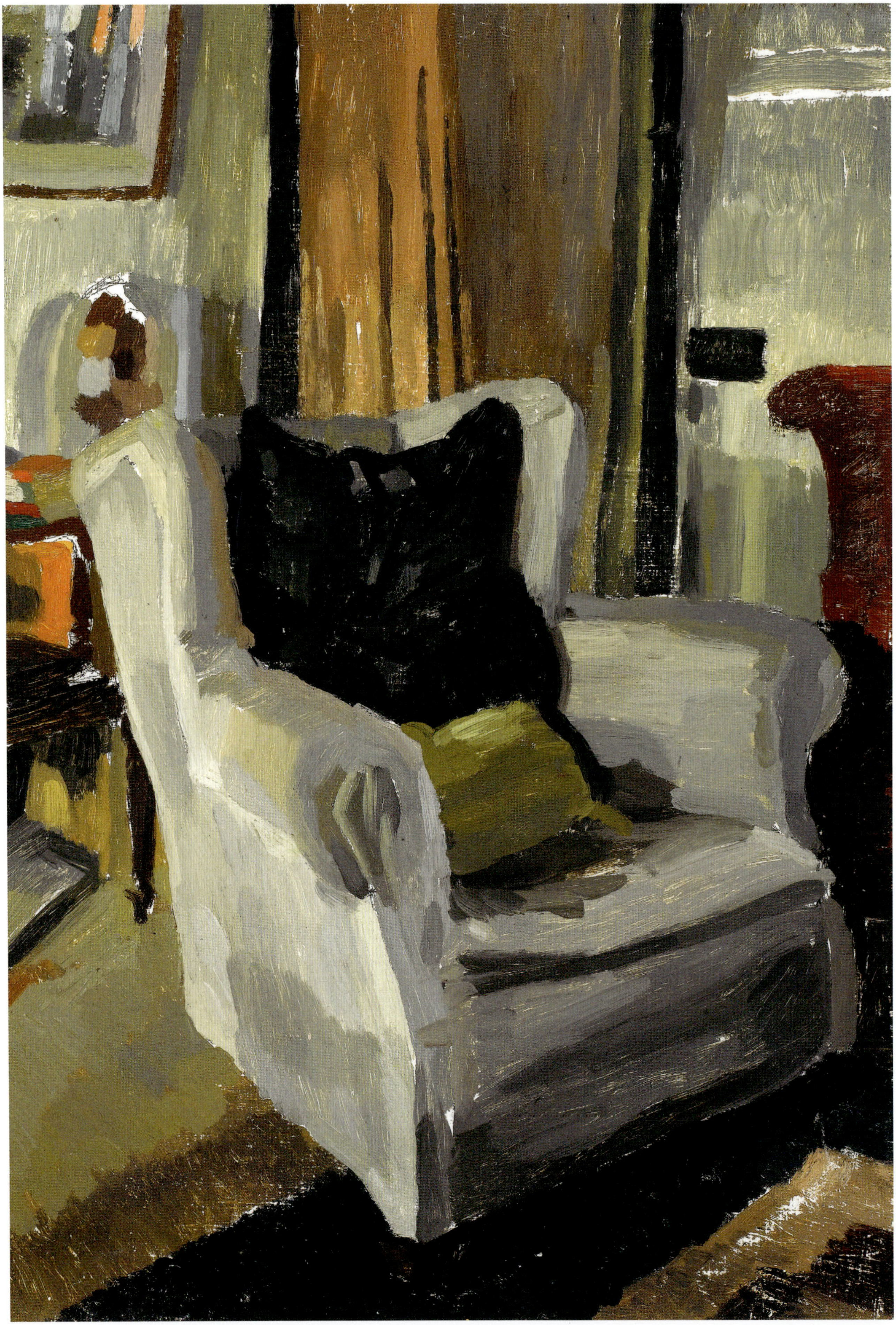

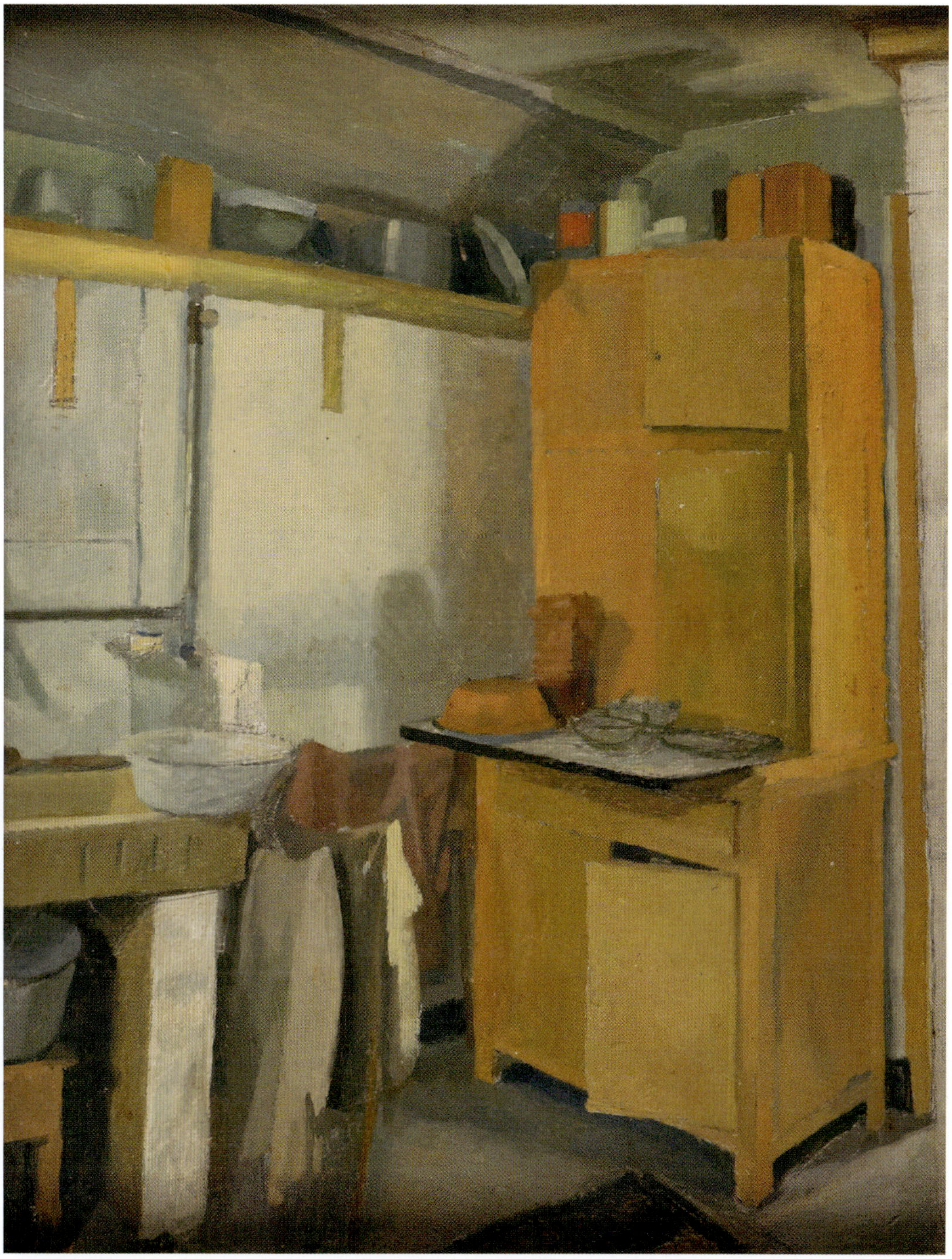

**50 Charles Mahoney** (1903-1968), *Kitchen at Oak Cottage*, c.1937,
oil on canvas, 18 x 14 in. (45.7 x 35.5 cm).

During his years as a student Mahoney lodged at a succession of addresses – an inconvenience that his recurrent ill health coupled with financial hardship and unscrupulous landlords did little to relieve. It was against this background that Oak Cottage, his home from 1937, came to represent such permanence in his life and art. The cottage was too small for a studio so, weather allowing, Mahoney worked from a shed in the garden, or inside the cottage when it was too cold.

**49 Charles Mahoney** (1903-1968), *The Artist's Chair, (Interior Oak Cottage)*, c.1937,
oil on panel, 17 ¼ x 12 in. (43.8 x 30.5 cm).

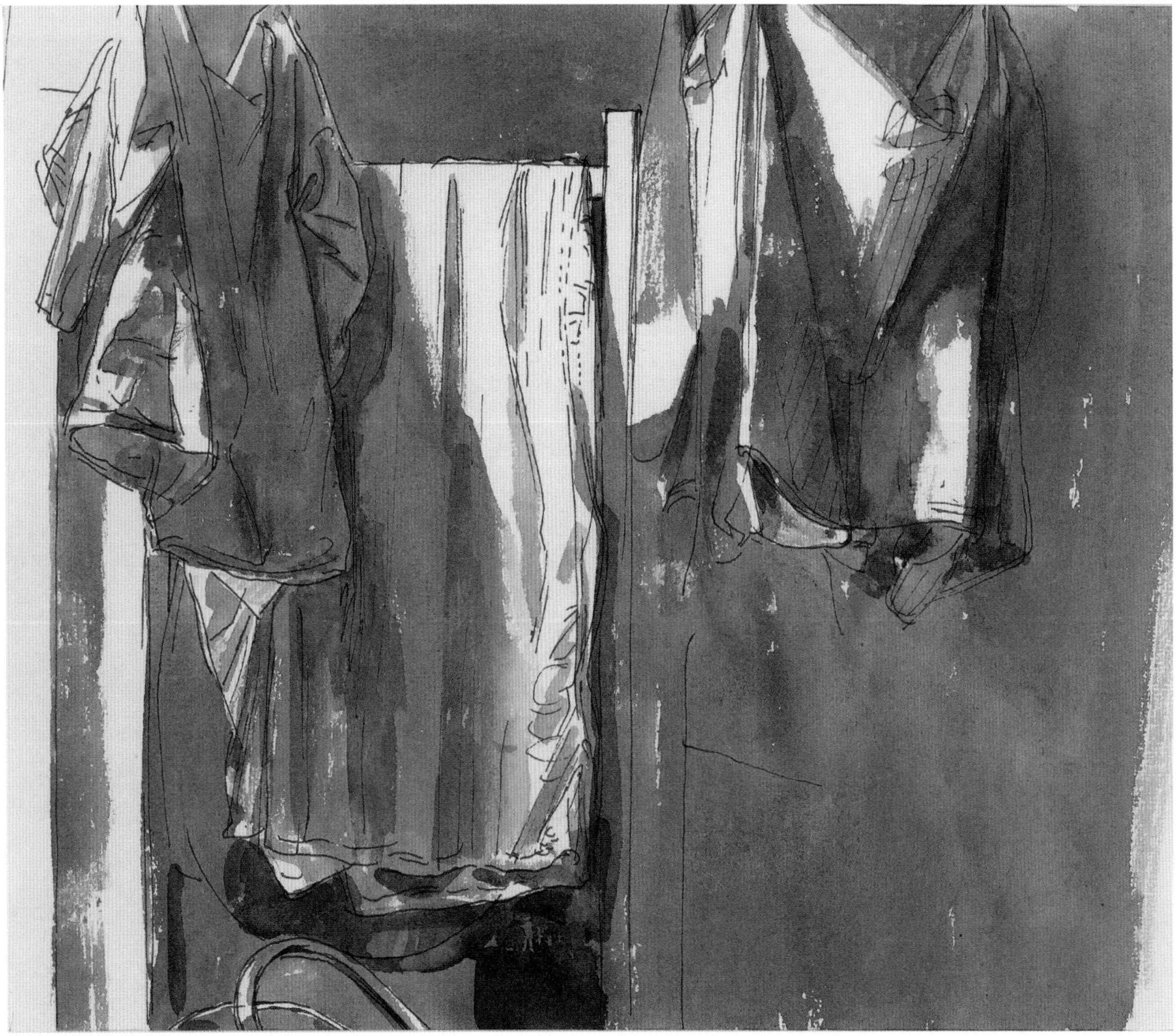

**51 Charles Mahoney** (1903-1968), *Washing Hanging to Dry*, c.1941,
pen & ink and wash on paper, 11.6 x 13 ¾ in. (29.5 x 35 cm).

Late in 1940 the Royal College of Art was evacuated to Ambleside in the Lake District. Mahoney and Percy Horton were amongst the staff. The students were housed in two hotels, men at the Queens and women at The Salutation. Mahoney was Resident Master in charge at the men's hostel.

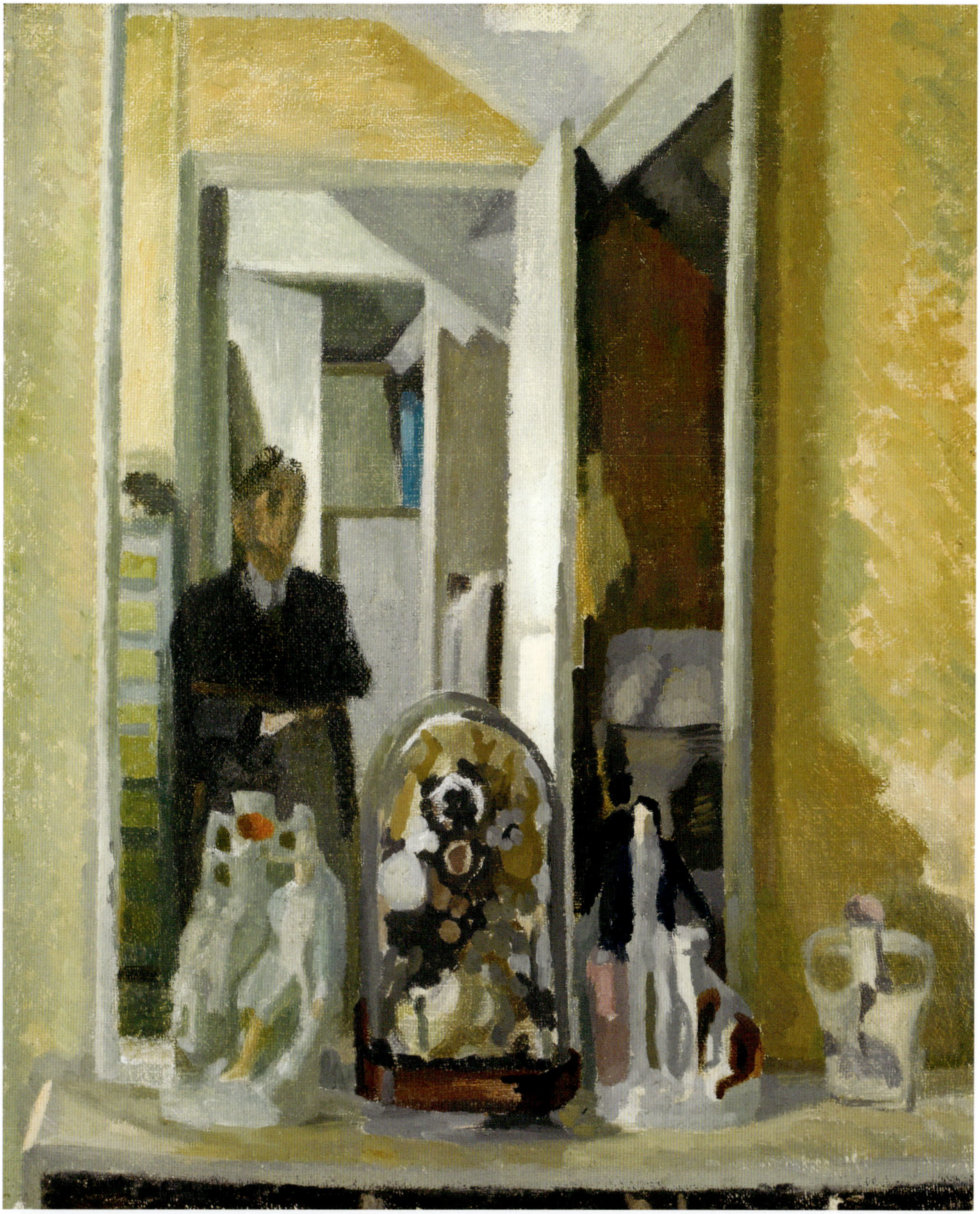

**52 Charles Mahoney** (1903-1968), *Self-portrait, Ambleside*, 1941
oil on canvas, 24 ¼ x 20 ¼ in. (61.3 X 51.2 cm).

Whilst at Ambleside, Mahoney became engaged to Dorothy Bishop, a calligraphy tutor from the Design School of the RCA. They were married in September 1941. The ornaments on the mantelpiece are souvenirs from the newlyweds' honeymoon in Edinburgh.

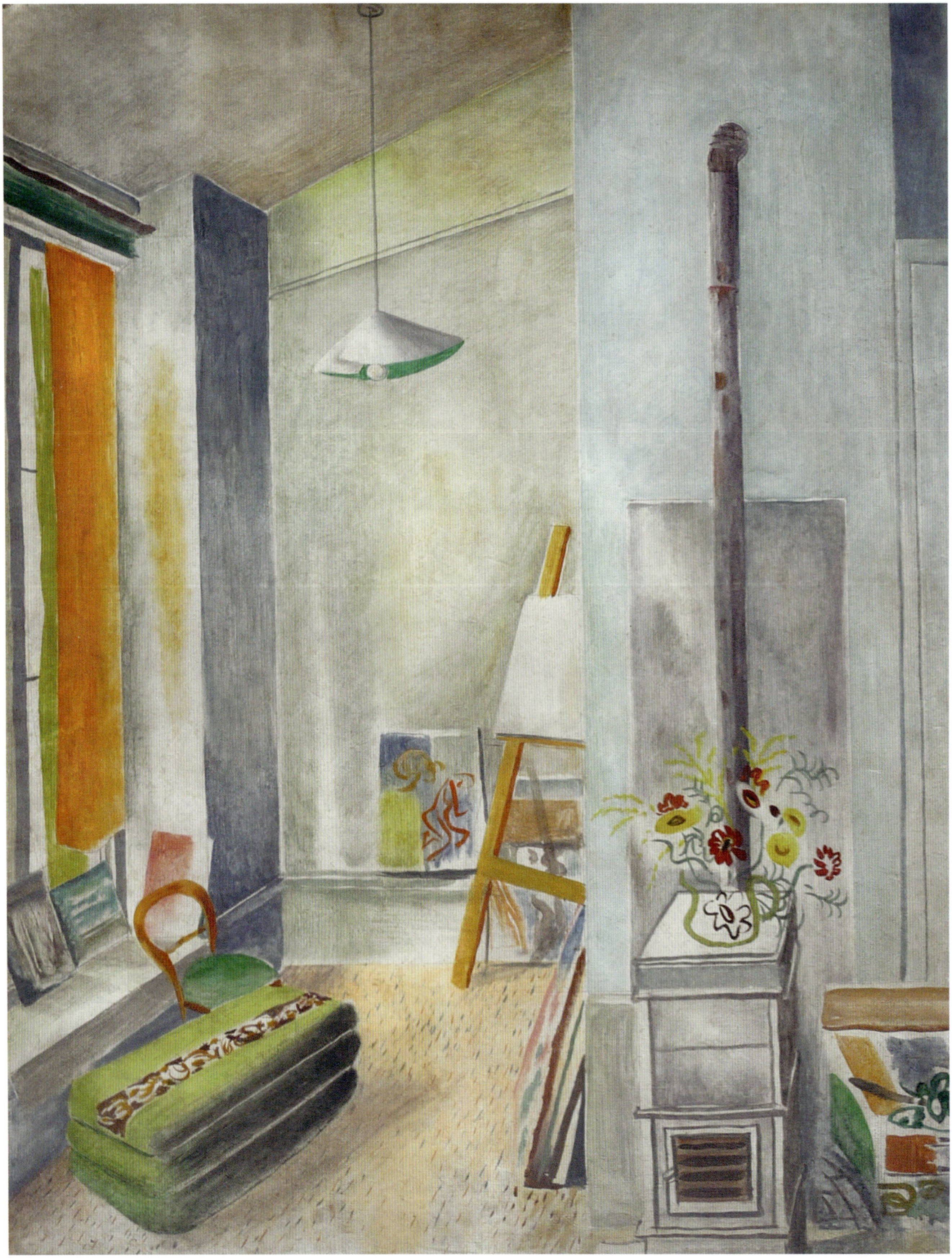

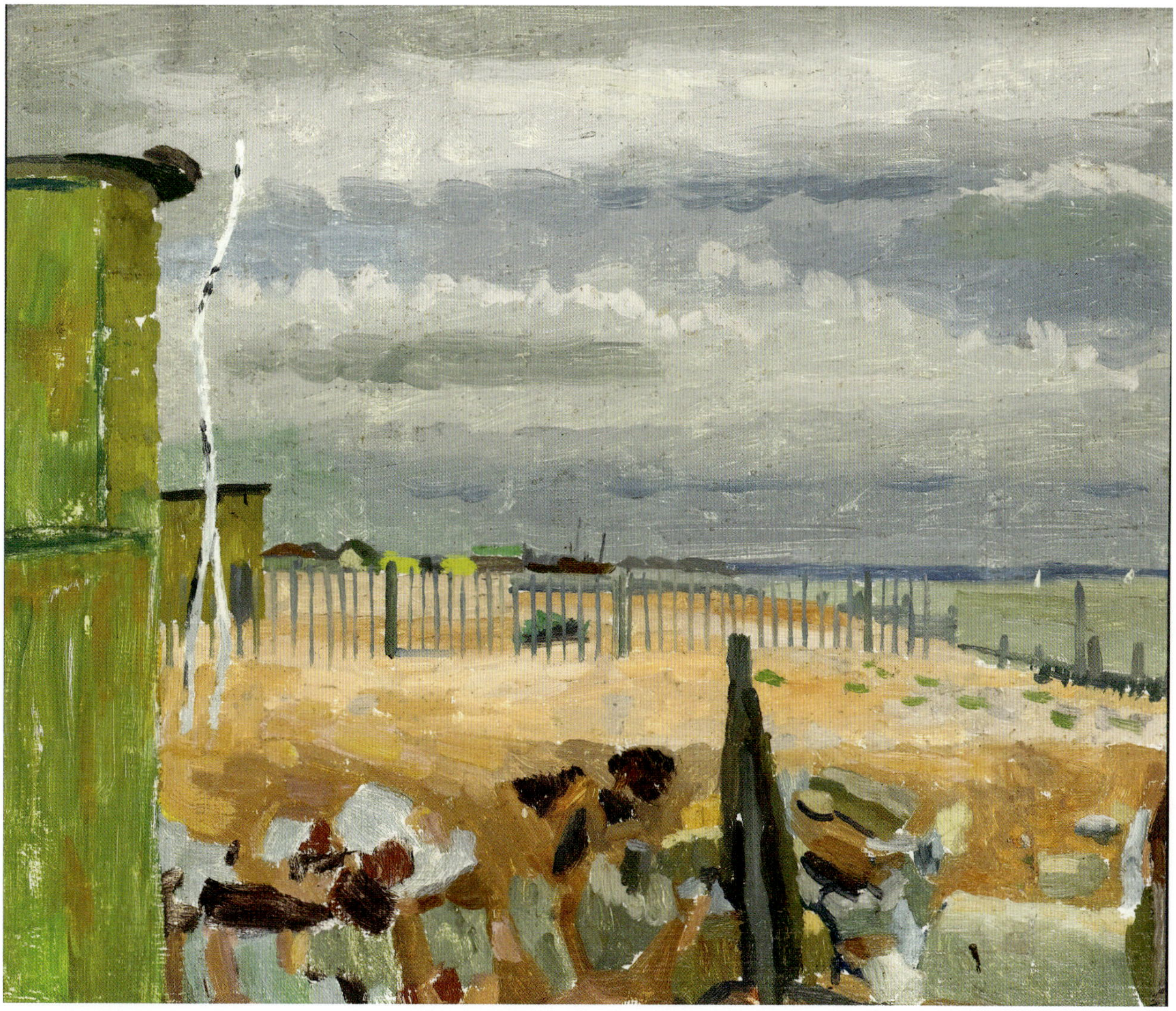

**54 Charles Mahoney** (1903-1968), *Caravan at Pevensey*, signed with initials, dated '58
oil on board, 11 × 14 ¾ in. (28 × 37.5 cm).

On the right-hand side of this beachscape an ex-workman's caravan belonging to Mahoney's friend, the sculptor Mark Batten, is visible. Mahoney rented a small beach house on the shingle at Pevensey Bay next door to the caravan, painting *en plein air* as much as the weather allowed.

**53 Mary Adshead** (1904-1995), *Studio Interior,* c.1930,
mixed media on board, 36 ¼ × 28 ½ in (92 × 72.4 cm).

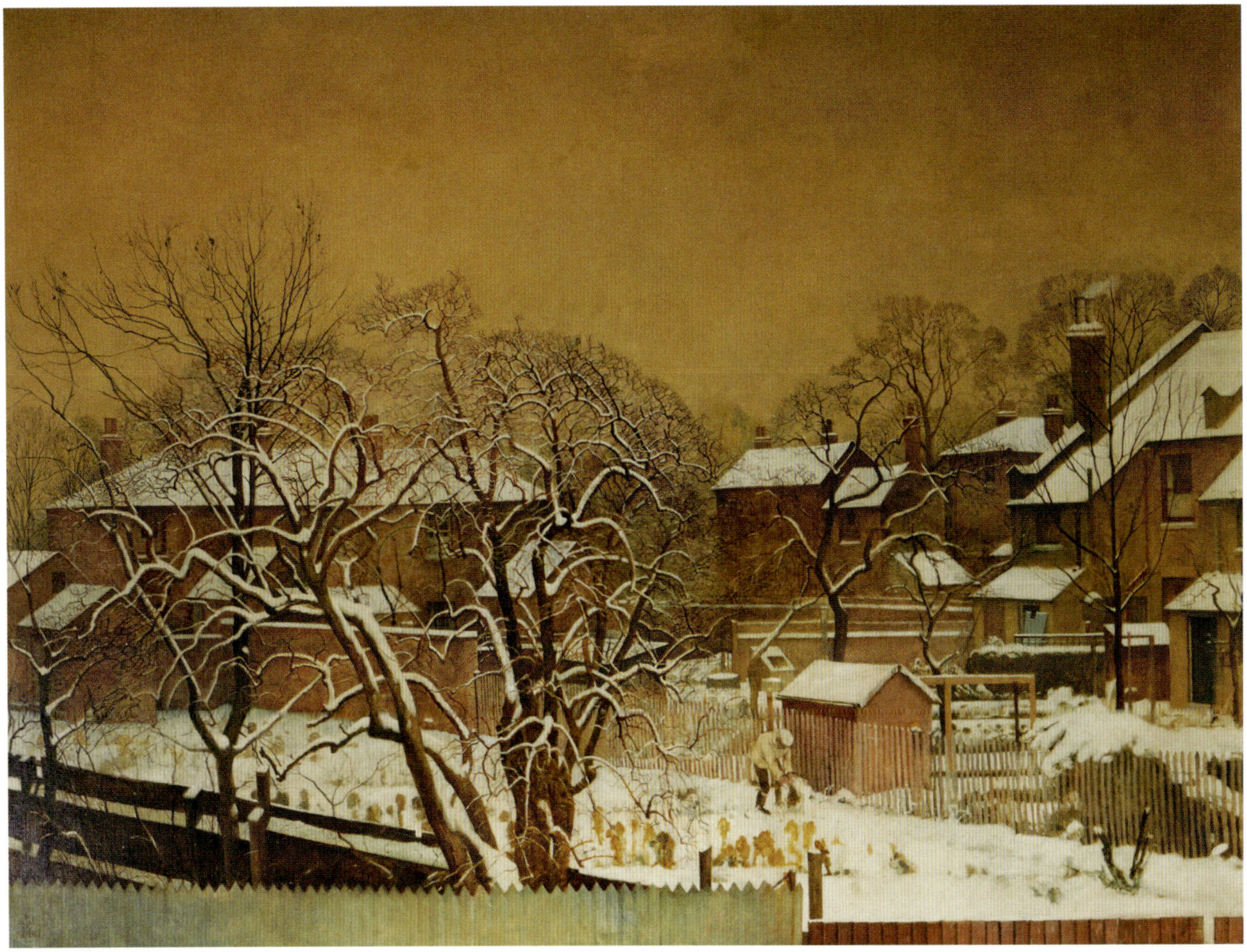

**55 Harry Bush** (1883-1957), *Snowfall in the Suburbs – A View from the Artist's House*, 1940, signed with monogram and dated, oil on canvas, 29 ¾ x 40 in. (75 x 101.6 cm).

Harry Bush and the artist Noel Laura Nisbet (1887-1956), whom he married in 1910, lived in a semi-detached house in Queensland Avenue, Merton Park, SW19, from 1914 until their deaths. The house, a gift from Noel's father, included custom-built studios in an extra top floor story. While Noel's work featured imagined scenes (often for book illustrations), over the years Bush regularly depicted the suburban back gardens seen from his studio. His favourite pear tree became a *leitmotif* in many of his works through which he was able to capture the passing seasons.

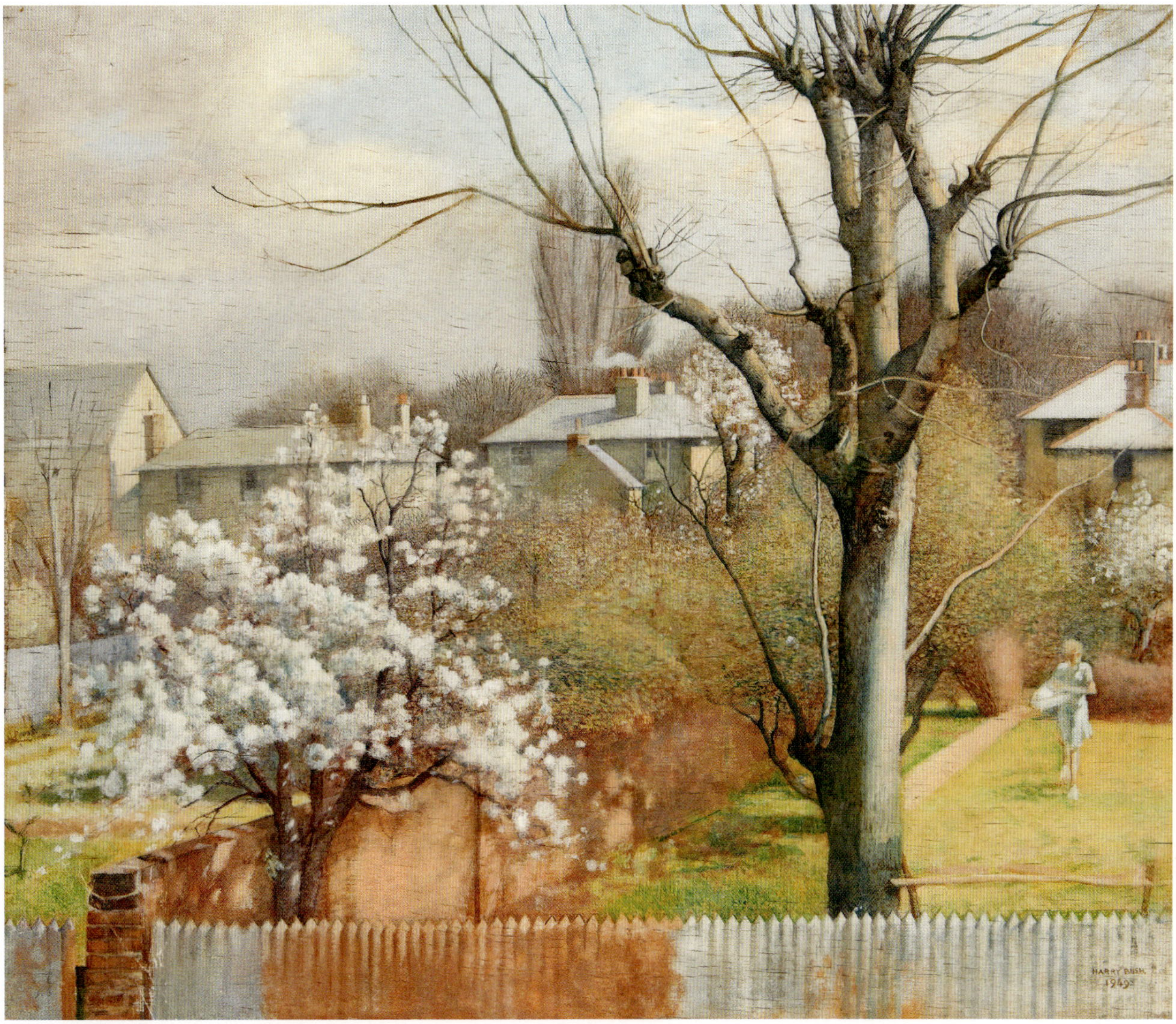

**56 Harry Bush** (1883-1957), *Spring Landscape, Merton*, 1949, signed and dated, oil on panel, 17 ½ x 20 ¾ in. (44.6 x 53 cm).

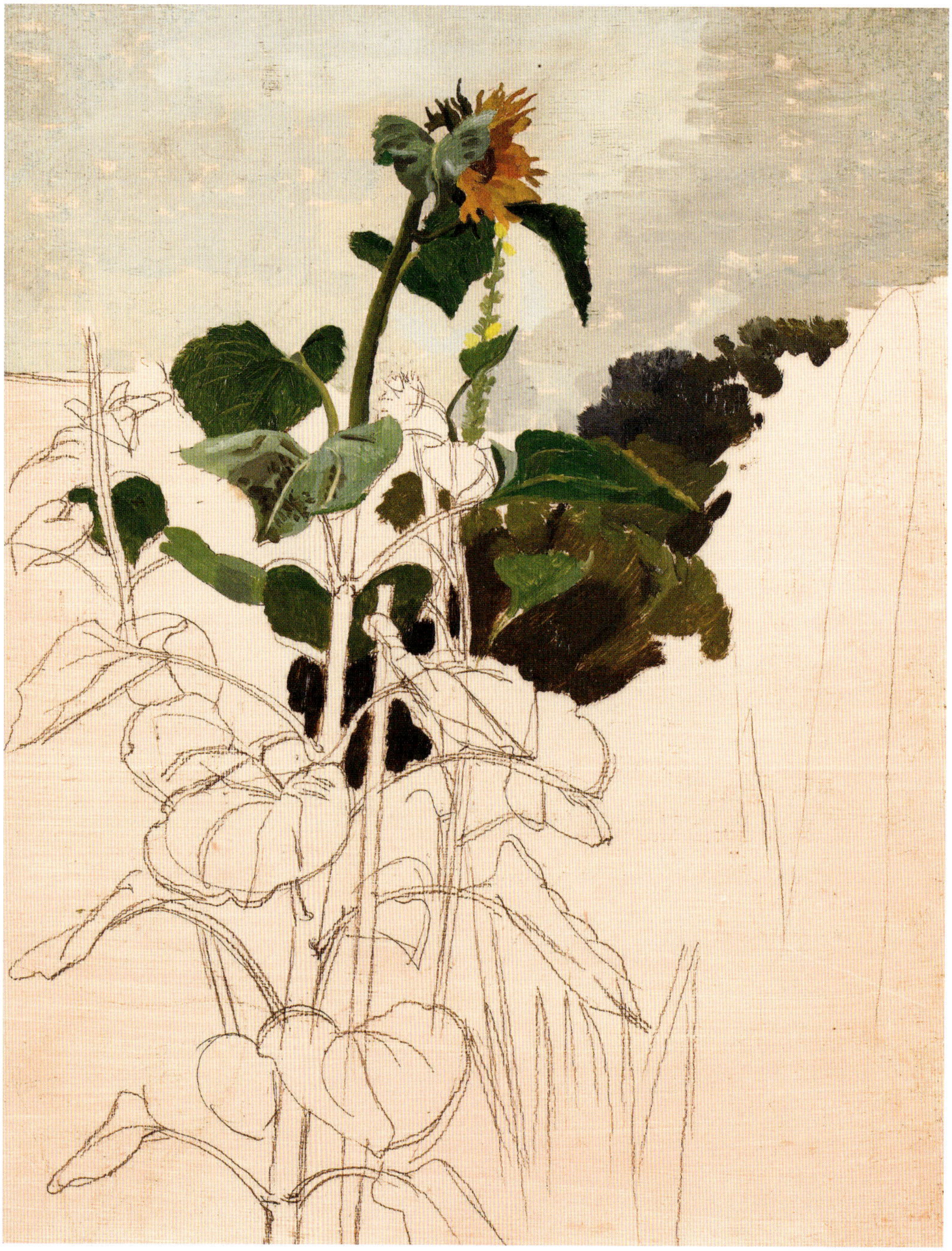

**57 Charles Mahoney** (1903-1968), *Study of a Sunflower,* late 1940s,
oil over pencil on board, prepared with a pink gesso ground, 15 x 12 in. (38 x 30.5 cm).

This composition shows sunflowers in the artist's back garden, as seen from his studio (a shed). Mahoney's unbridled enthusiasm for plants was shared with Edward Bawden, Evelyn Dunbar, Geoffrey Rhoades and John Nash, all of whom swapped cuttings with each other by post. (**157**, **198**, **218**, **314**)

**58 Stephen Bone** (1904-1958), *Christmas Tree,*
oil on board, 16 x 12 in. (40.6 x 30.5 cm).

This still life is likely to have been painted at Haverstock Hill, Hampstead, where Steven Bone and Mary Adshead moved in 1938. (**47**) Artists frequently made their own Christmas decorations and exchanged with each other hand-made Christmas cards.

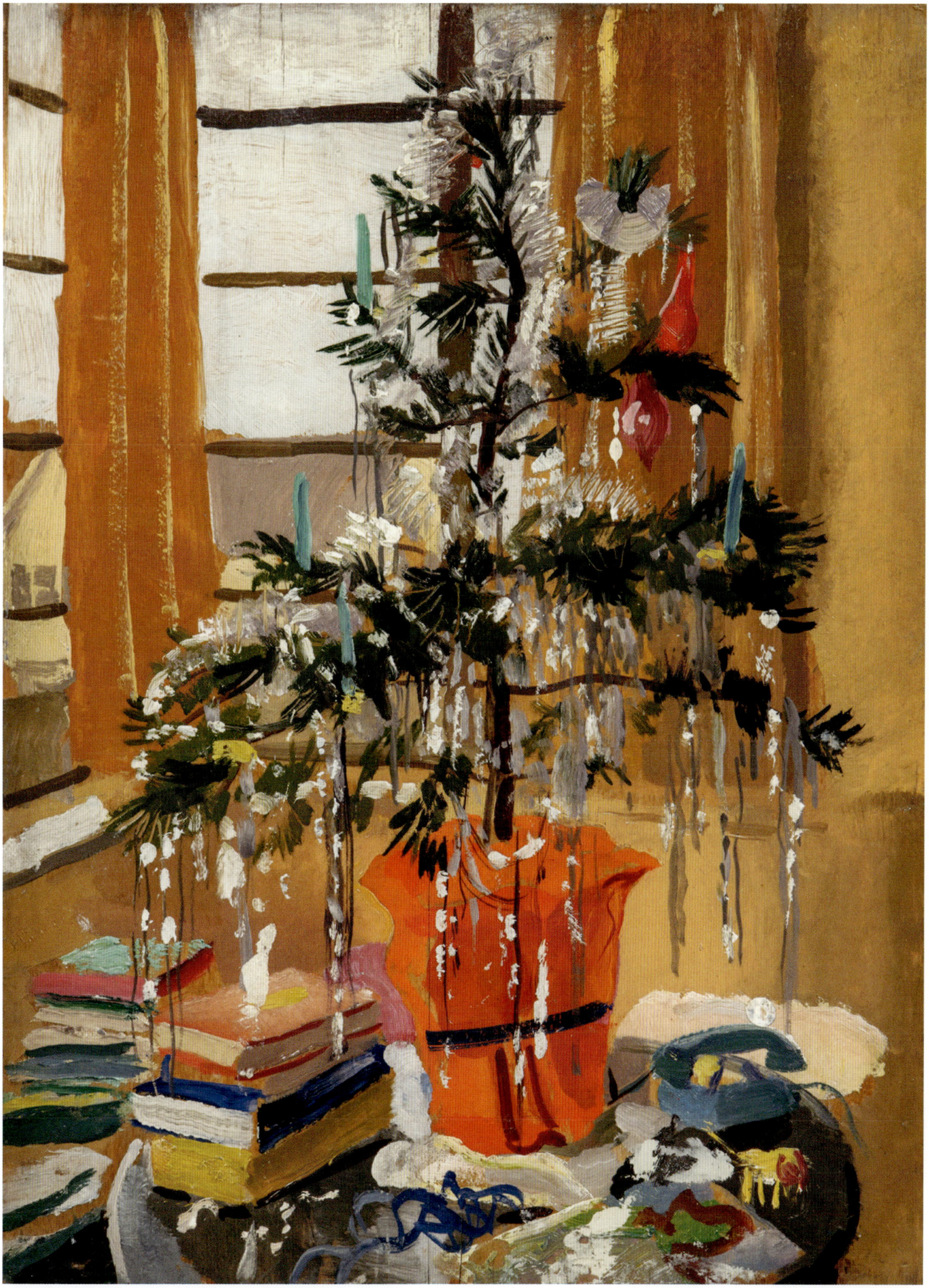

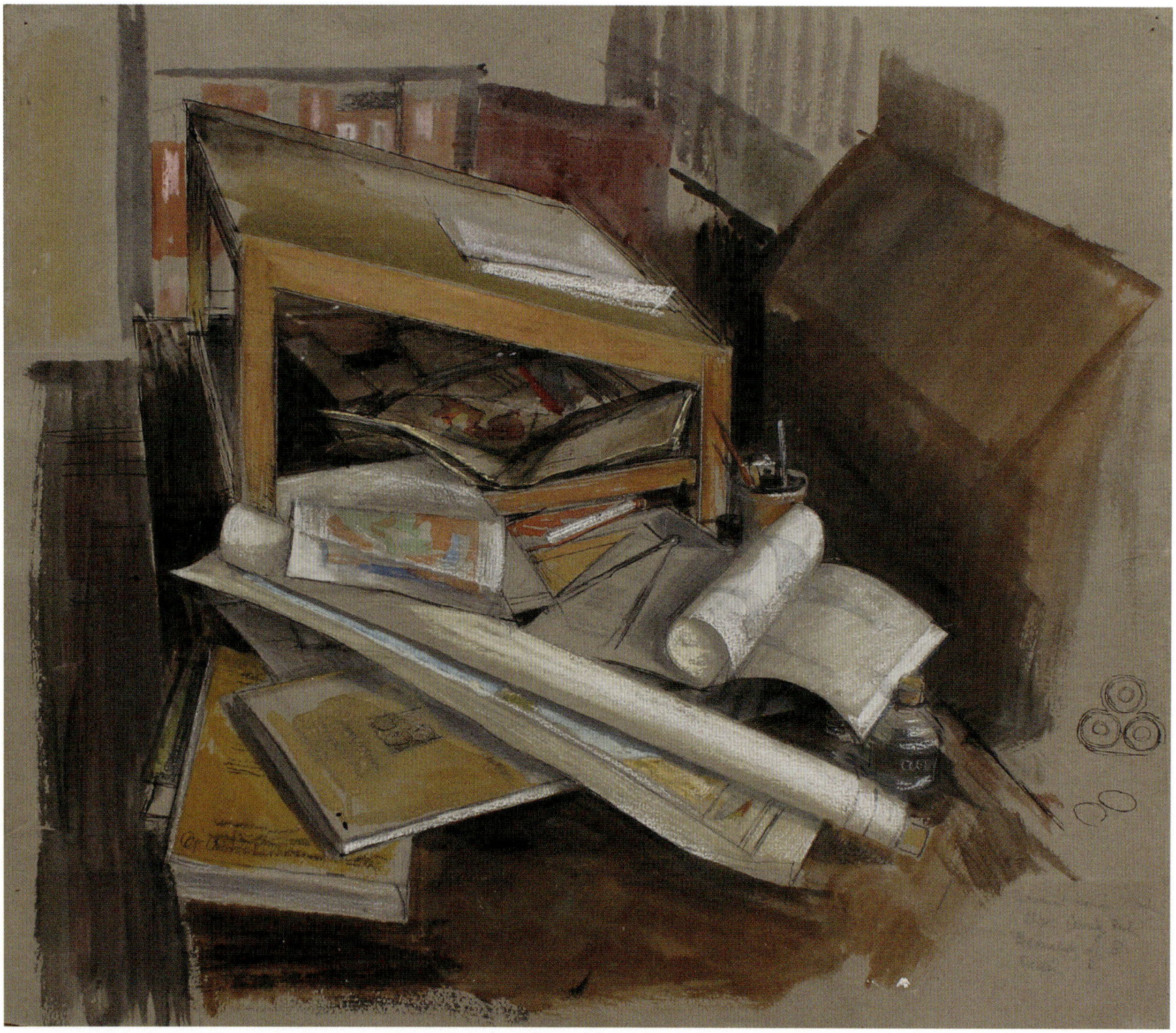

**59 Alan Sorrell** (1904-1974), *Corner of the Artist's Studio*, inscribed 'journal . . .', c.1946, watercolour with white highlights on paper, 12 ½ x 15 ¼ in. (32 x 38.5 cm).

Sorrell took evident pleasure in the details of the jumbled objects that he used as a background to his portrait of the distinguished archaeologist Sir Cyril Fox.

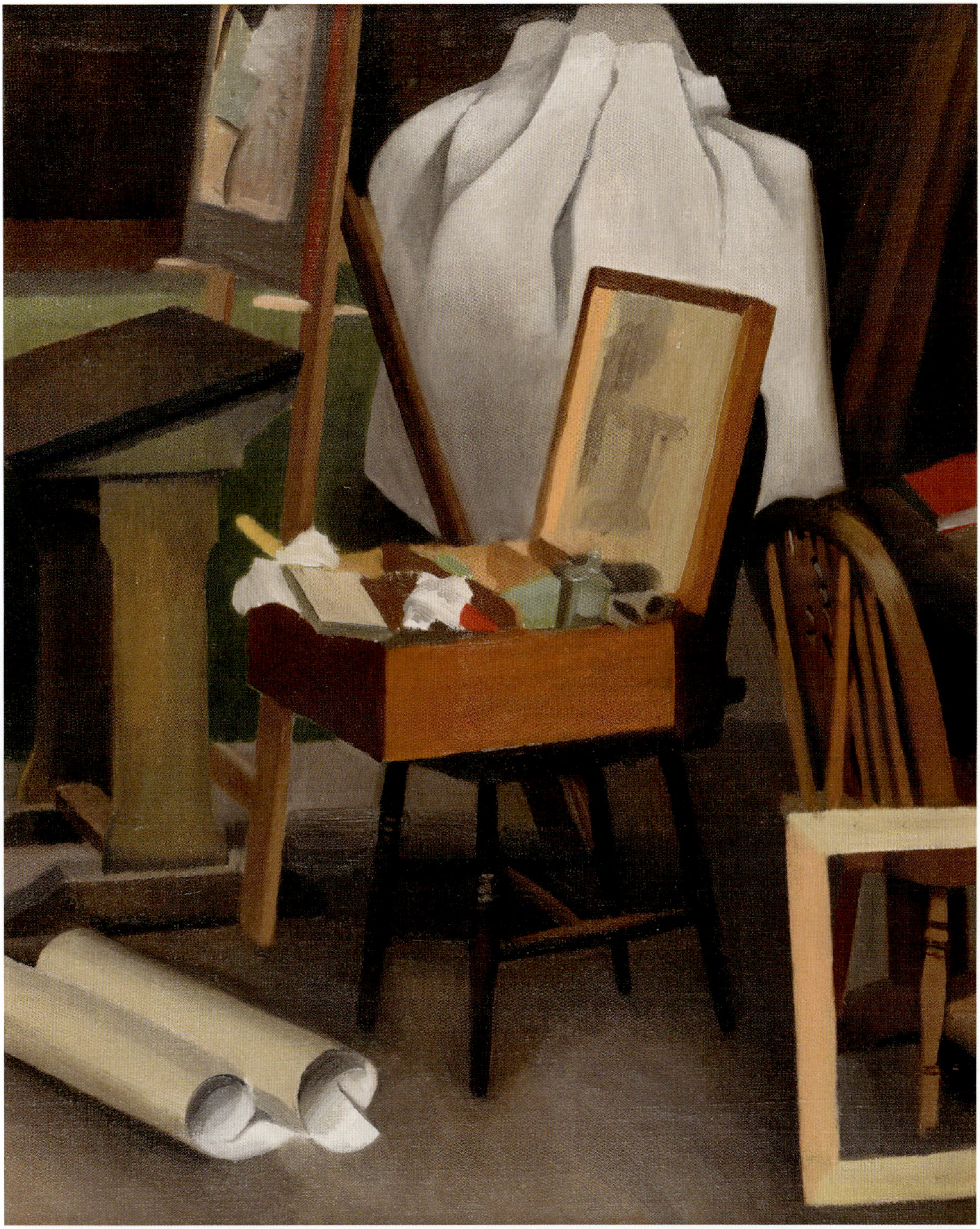

**60 Phoebe Willetts-Dickinson** (1917-1978), *Corner of the Artist's Studio with Paintbox on a Windsor Chair*, oil on canvas, 19 ½ x 16 in. (49.5 x 40.6 cm).

Ad hoc use of a Windsor chair supporting a paintbox, plus a lectern alongside (which might logically have been used for the transfer of drawings to the canvas on the easel above) suggest a makeshift studio in student lodgings.

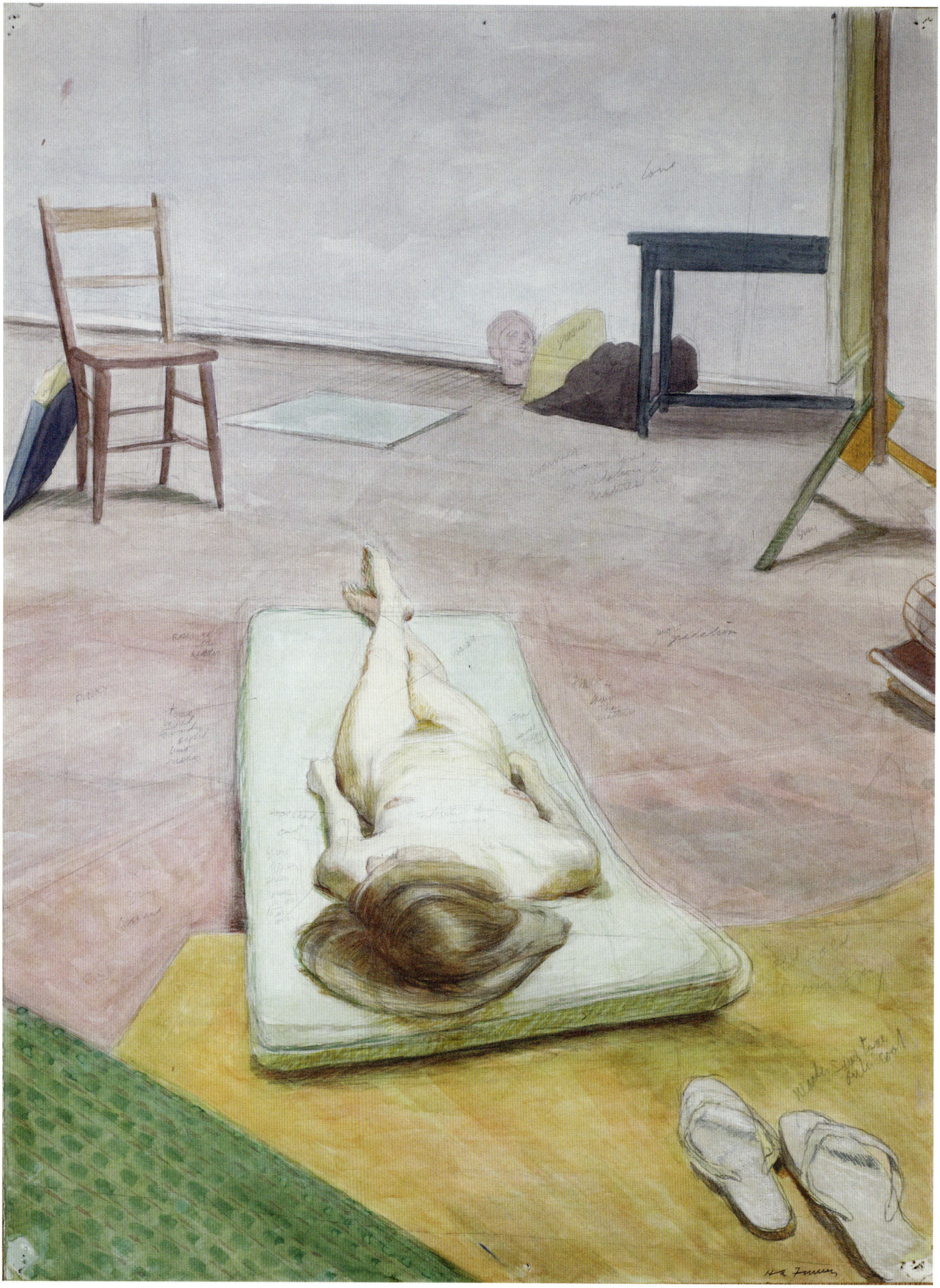

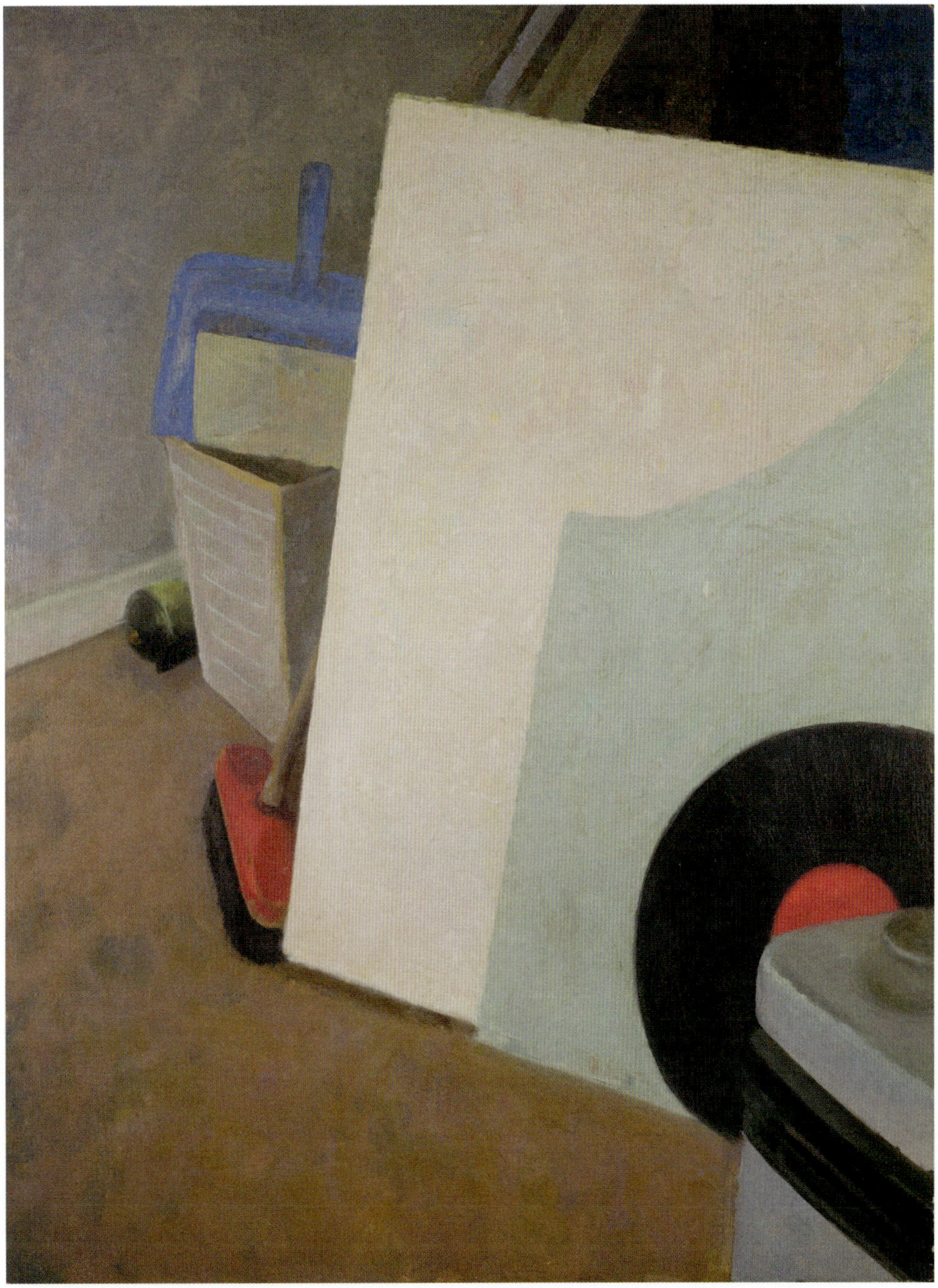

**62 Hubert Arthur Finney** (1905-1991), *Still Life of a Corner of the Artist's Studio with a Broomstick*, oil on board, 28 x 21 in. (71.5 x 53.5 cm).

Tools of domesticity, languishing in the corner of a room, are here elevated to form an attractive semi-abstract composition. (**310**, **311**, **324**)

**61 Hubert Arthur Finney** (1905-1991), *The Artist's Model in the Studio*, signed, inscribed with colour notes, watercolour on paper, 20 x 15 in. (50.8 x 38.1 cm).

In this composition the artist's model is surrounded by studio trappings: an electric heater to keep her warm, a canvas on an easel, discarded slippers, rugs, a plaster cast, a work table and chair, a portfolio and sketching board.

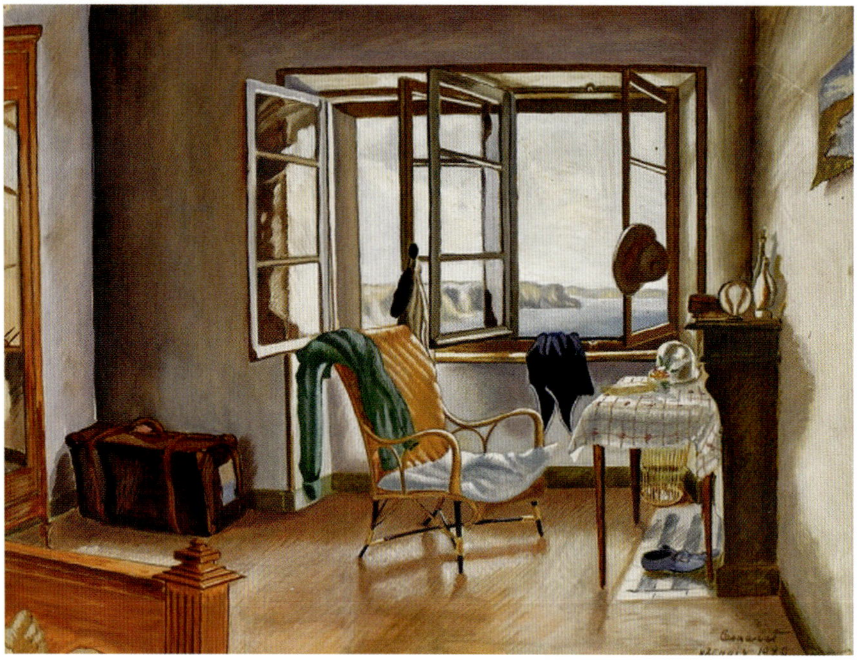

**63 Nadia Benois** (1896-1974), *The Artist's Hotel Room, Camaret-sur-Mer, Brittany,* 1920, signed and dated, oil on paper, 15 x 19 ¾ in. (38 x 50 cm).

Although there are no obvious signs of painting activity in this hotel room, pinned to the wall and just visible in the top right-hand corner is a landscape painting of a coastal view similar to the one that floats invitingly beyond wide open windows. Camaret-sur-Mer – a small fishing village at the westernmost tip of Brittany – was popular with artists for its luminous and picturesque coastline.

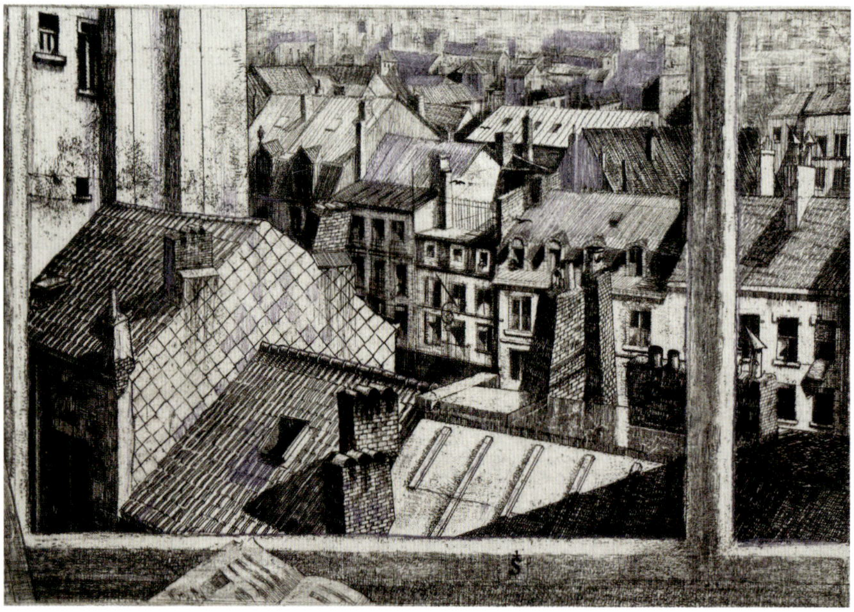

**64 Erik Smith** (1914-1972), *Rooftop View, Paris*, c. 1938, etching with blue pen and ink highlights, working proof, 7 ¼ x 10 ¾ in. (18 x 27 cm).

The cheapest accommodation in cities such as Paris were in the *chambres de bonne* on the top floors. For artists not only did these have the best light conditions, which made them ideal for studios, but also the best vantage points, perfect for observing changing weather conditions and capturing the ever-changing panorama of Metropolitan life.

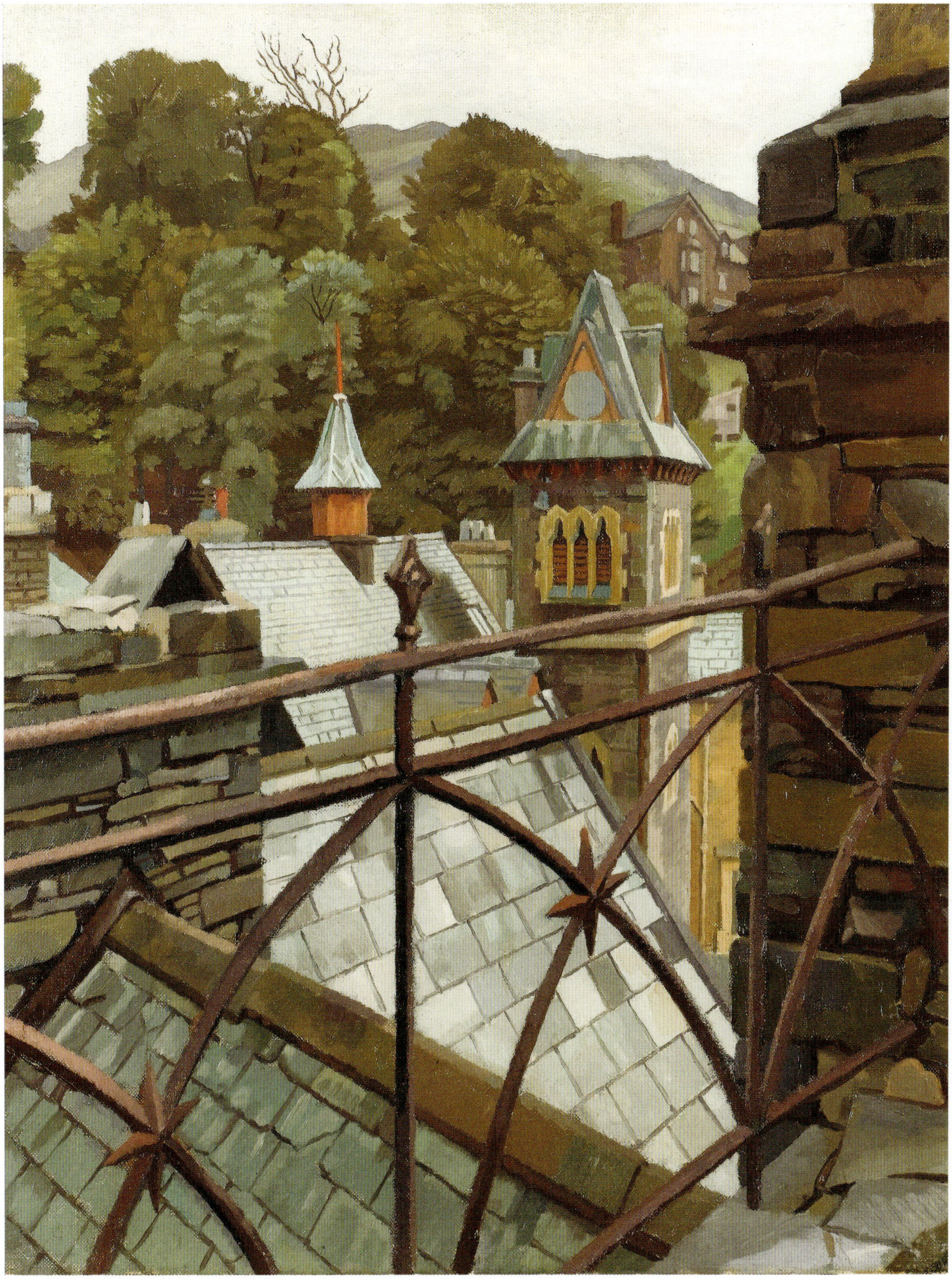

**65 Charles Mahoney** (1903-1968), *Ambleside, View from the Library Roof,* c.1942, oil on canvas, 18 x 14 in. (45.7 x 35.6 cm).

In late 1940 the Royal College of Art was evacuated to Ambleside in the Lake District. Along with other male staff, Mahoney was accommodated at the Queens Hotel where studios were set up in the spare attic spaces with spectacular roof top views. This composition demonstrates Mahoney's fondness for Victorian Gothic buildings, a taste which, like much that appealed to his eye, was unfashionable at the time.

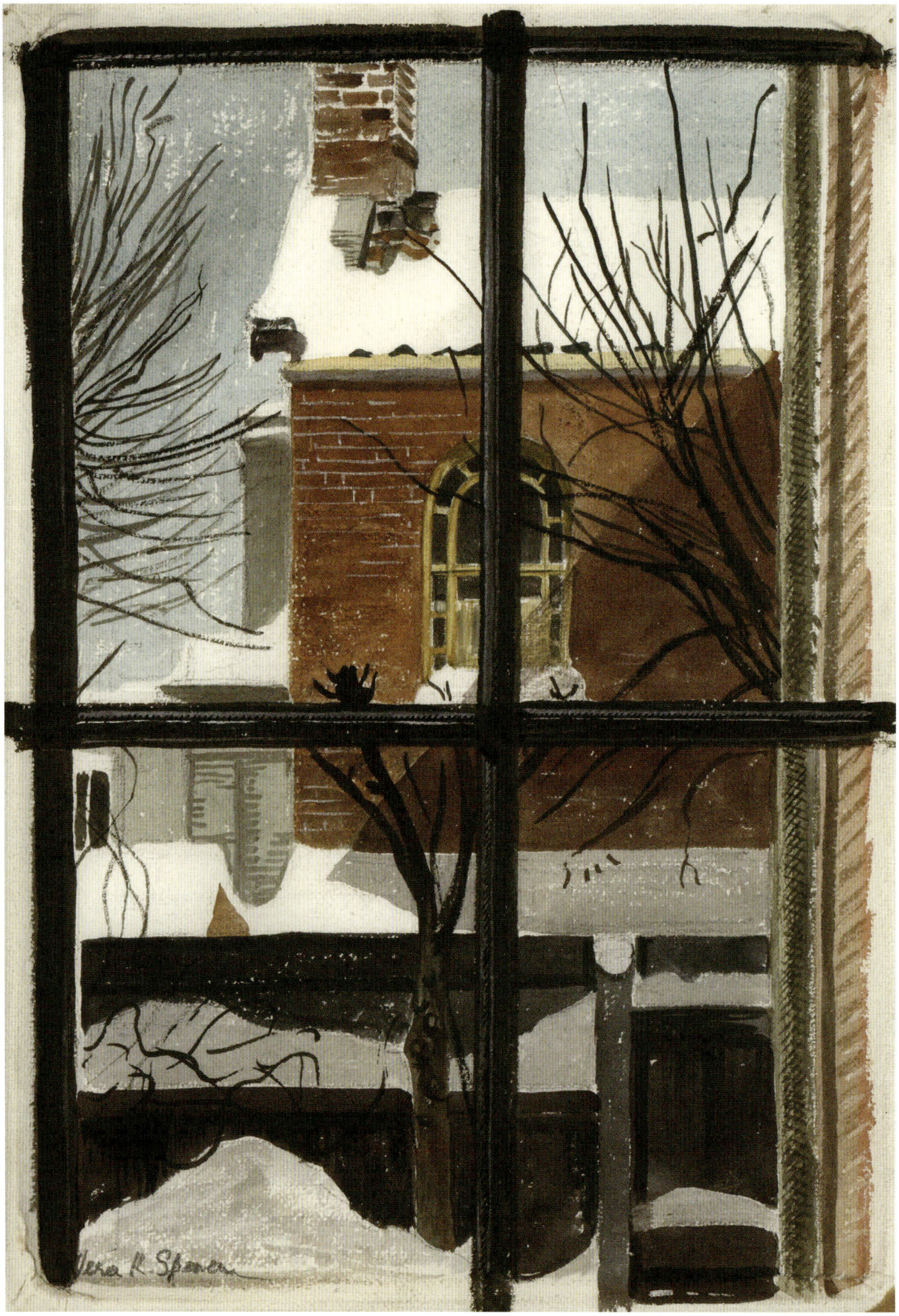


**66 Vera Spencer** (1926-2021), *View Through a Window – Winter*, c. 1948, signed, watercolour on paper, 15 x 11 in. (38 x 27.7 cm).

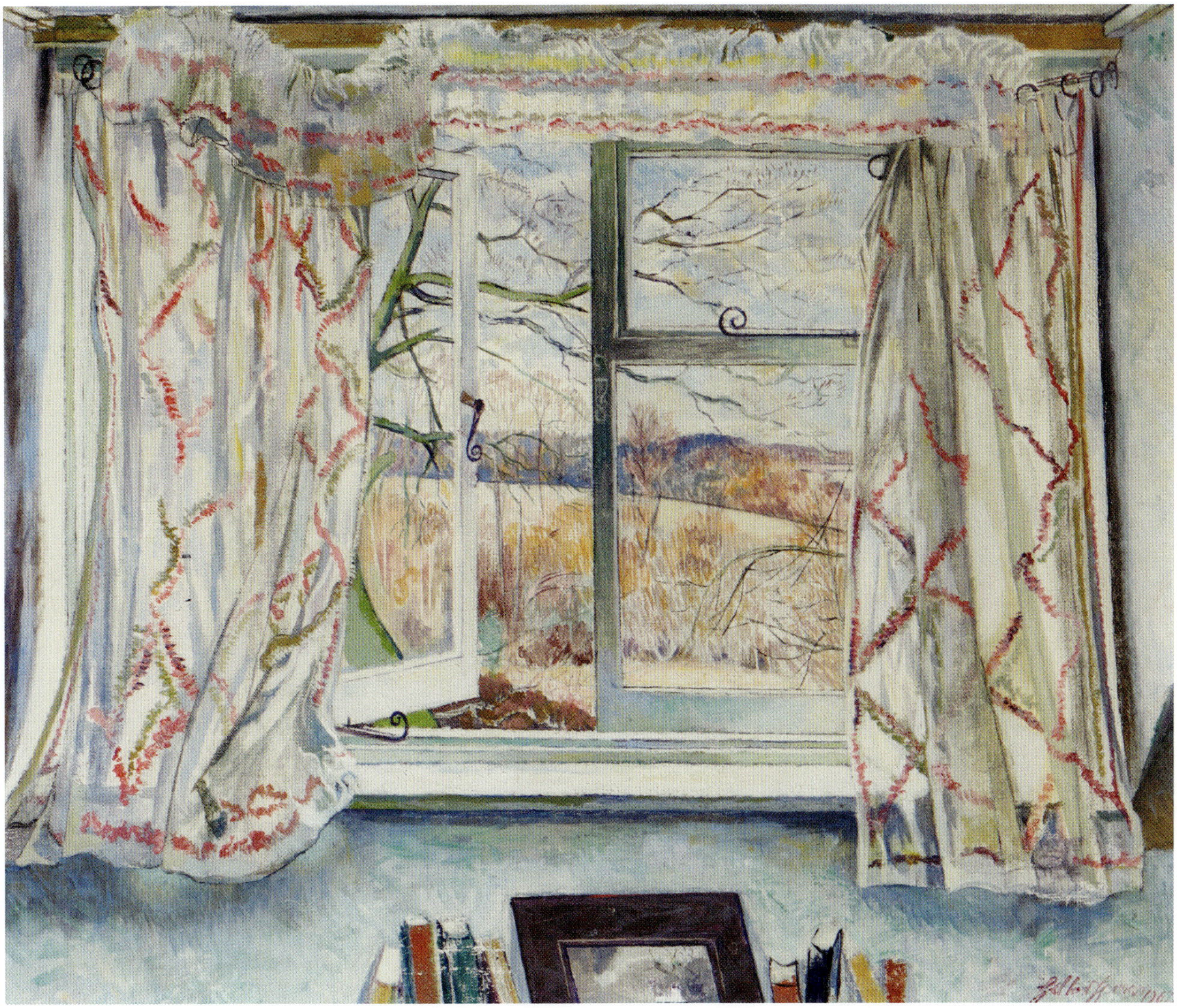

**67 Gilbert Spencer** (1892-1979), *Candlewick Curtains,* 1967, signed and dated, oil on canvas, 20 x 24 in. (50.5 x 61 cm).

Tree Cottage, Upper Basildon, Berkshire was where Gilbert and Ursula Spencer stayed between 1936 and 1970. In his autobiography, *Memoirs of a Painter* (1974), Spencer recalled: 'When I entered it for the first time, I hated it so much that I knocked it about, and messed it up to get it more in sympathy with my feelings for painting in odd corners, or bedrooms, indoors. The fact is I am no "studio" artist and never have been.' Spencer normally worked outdoors, but, in winter, would paint from his cottage windows or what he called his 'little Colt studio' in the garden. (**325**)

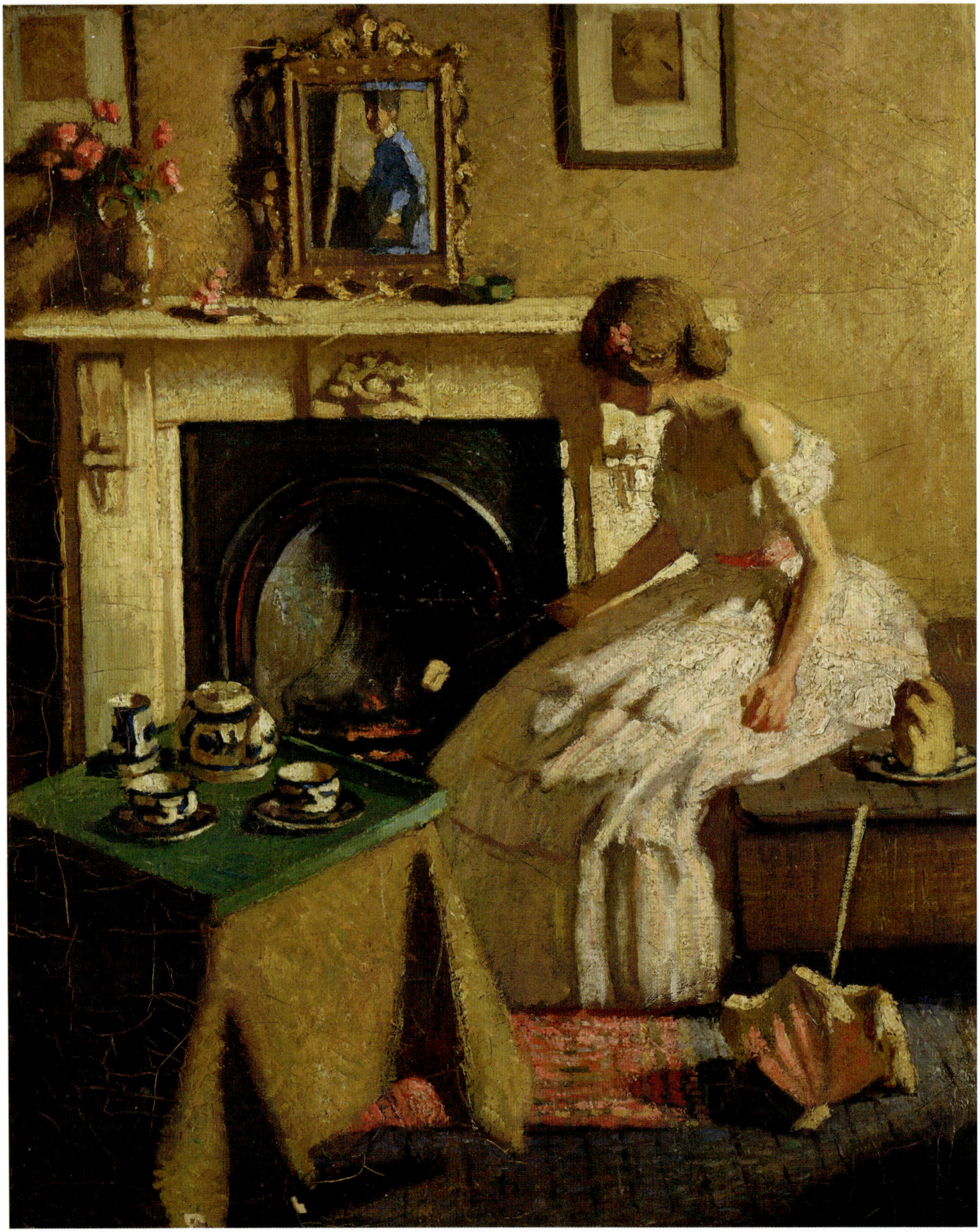

**68 Sydney Noel Simmons** (1881-1916), *The Artist's Sitting Room* (with self-portrait in a mirror), c.1905, oil on canvas, 20 x 24 in. (50.8 x 60.9 cm).

Sydney Noel Simmons typically painted Edwardian interiors which owe much to Tonks and Orpen – for instance in the mirror reflecting the artist and back wall parallel to the picture plane.

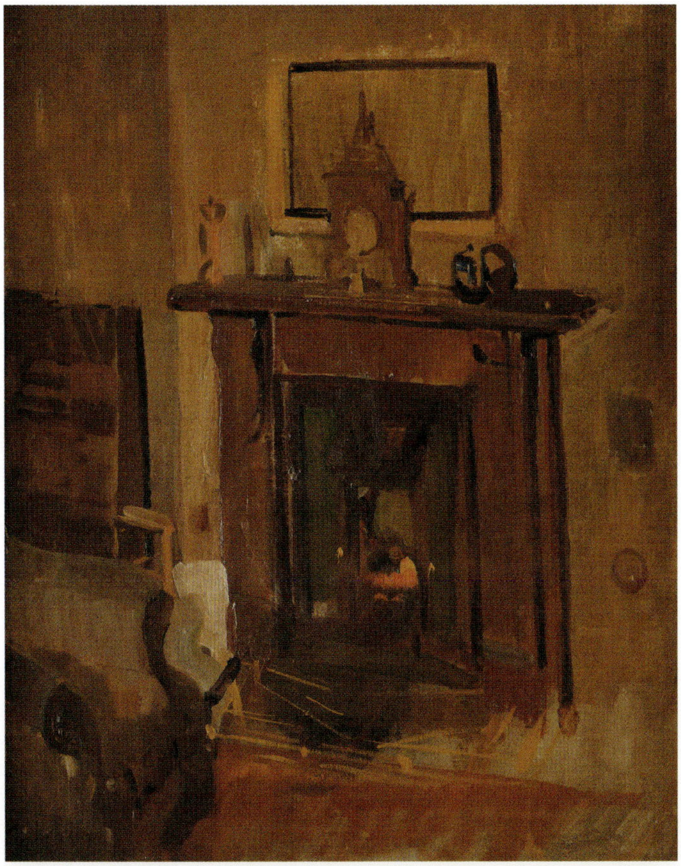

**69 Hilda Carline** (1889-1950),
*The Sitting Room at 3 Park Crescent, Oxford,* c.1910,
oil on canvas, 20 ½ x 16 in. (52.1 x 40.6 cm).

Jonathan Black has suggested that this shows the sitting room at 3 Park Crescent, Oxford where the Carlines lived from 1904 to early 1916.

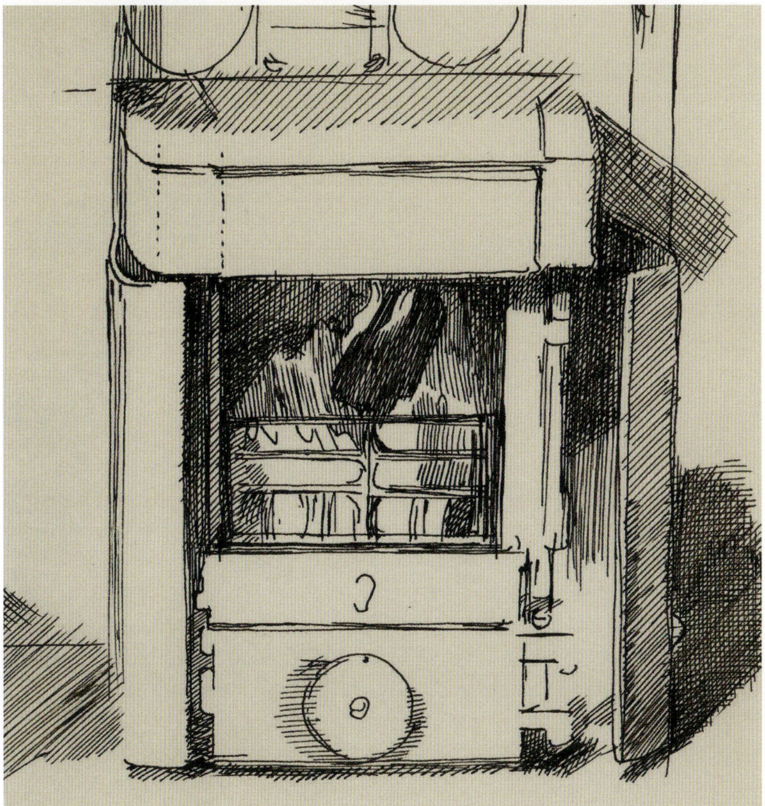

**70 Charles Mahoney** (1903-1968),
*Woodburner*, c.1940,
ink on paper, 6 ¾ x 6 ¼ in. (17.5 x 16 cm).

This pen and ink sketch probably shows the woodburner at Oak Cottage, the artist's house. (**49**, **50**)

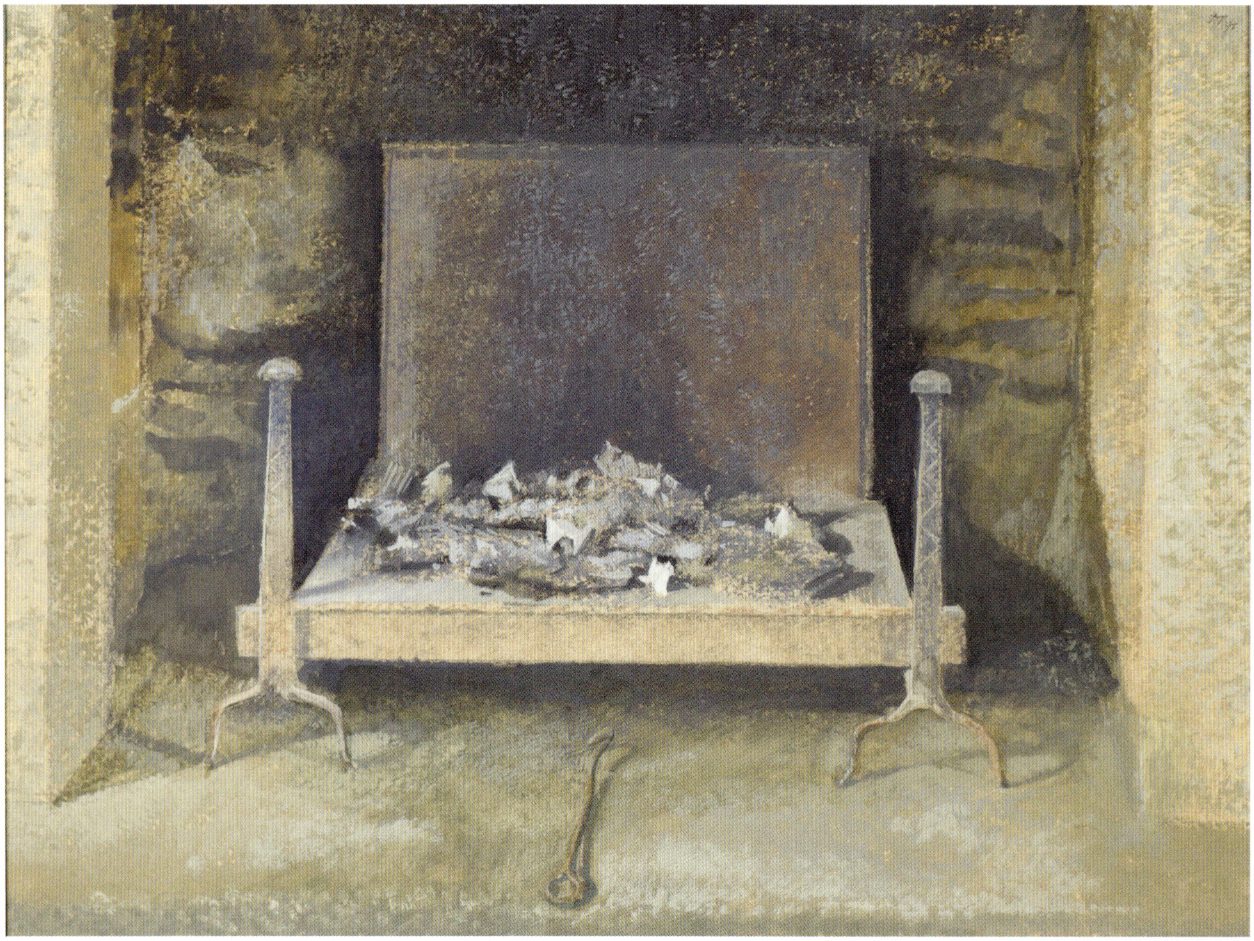

**71 David Tindle** (b. 1932), *Fireplace*, 1997, signed with initials, dated, gouache on paper, 11 x 14 ½ in. (28 x 36.8 cm).

Studios were frequently unheated – other than by open fire grates or wood burners. These motifs occur with surprising frequency in artists' compositions. The painting of flames and ashes, both as a technical challenge, and for their obvious narrative potential, offered an added attraction for artists. (**306**)

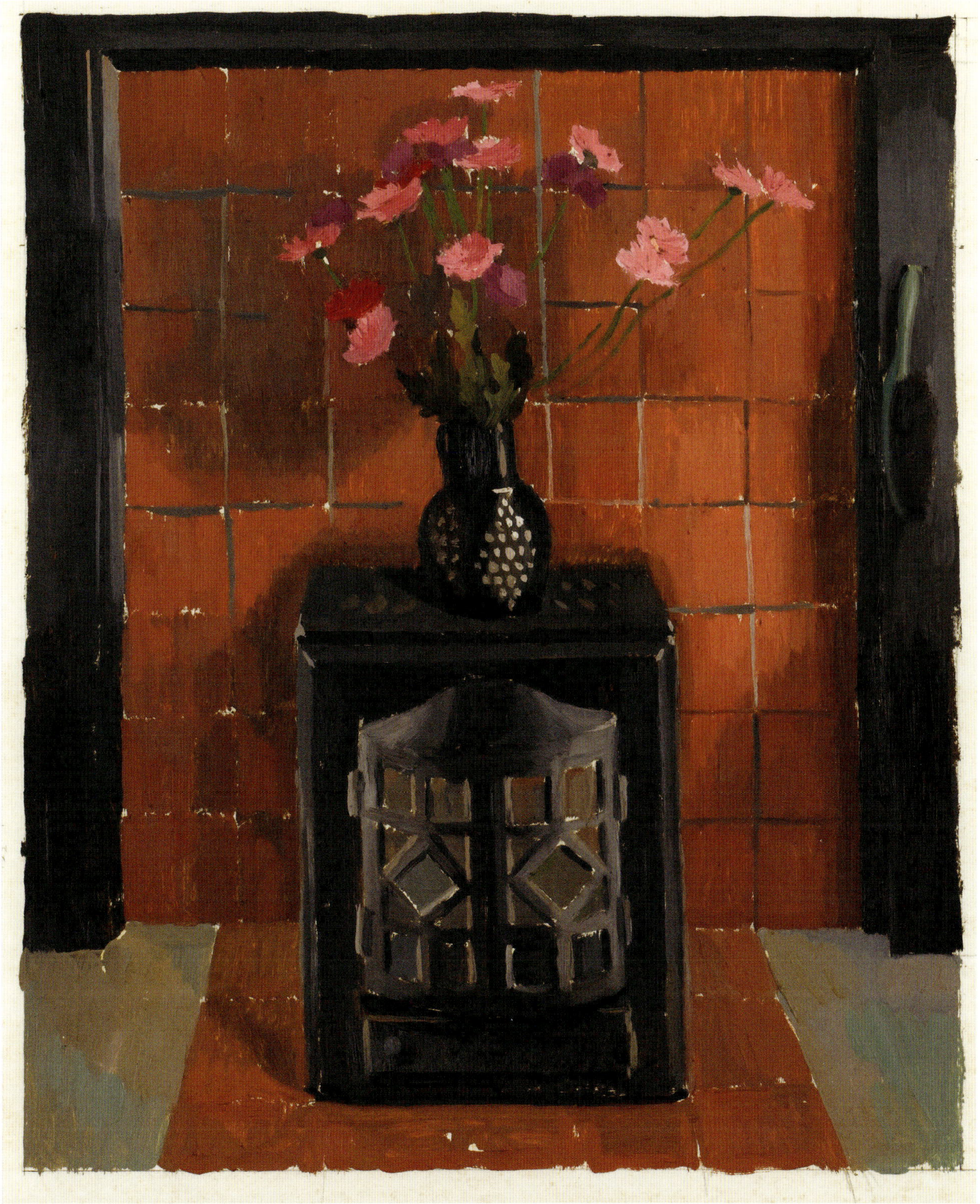

**72 Charles Mahoney** (1903-1968), *Woodburner with Cosmos in a Vase,*
oil on paper, 14 ¾ x 12 in. (37.5 x 30.5 cm).

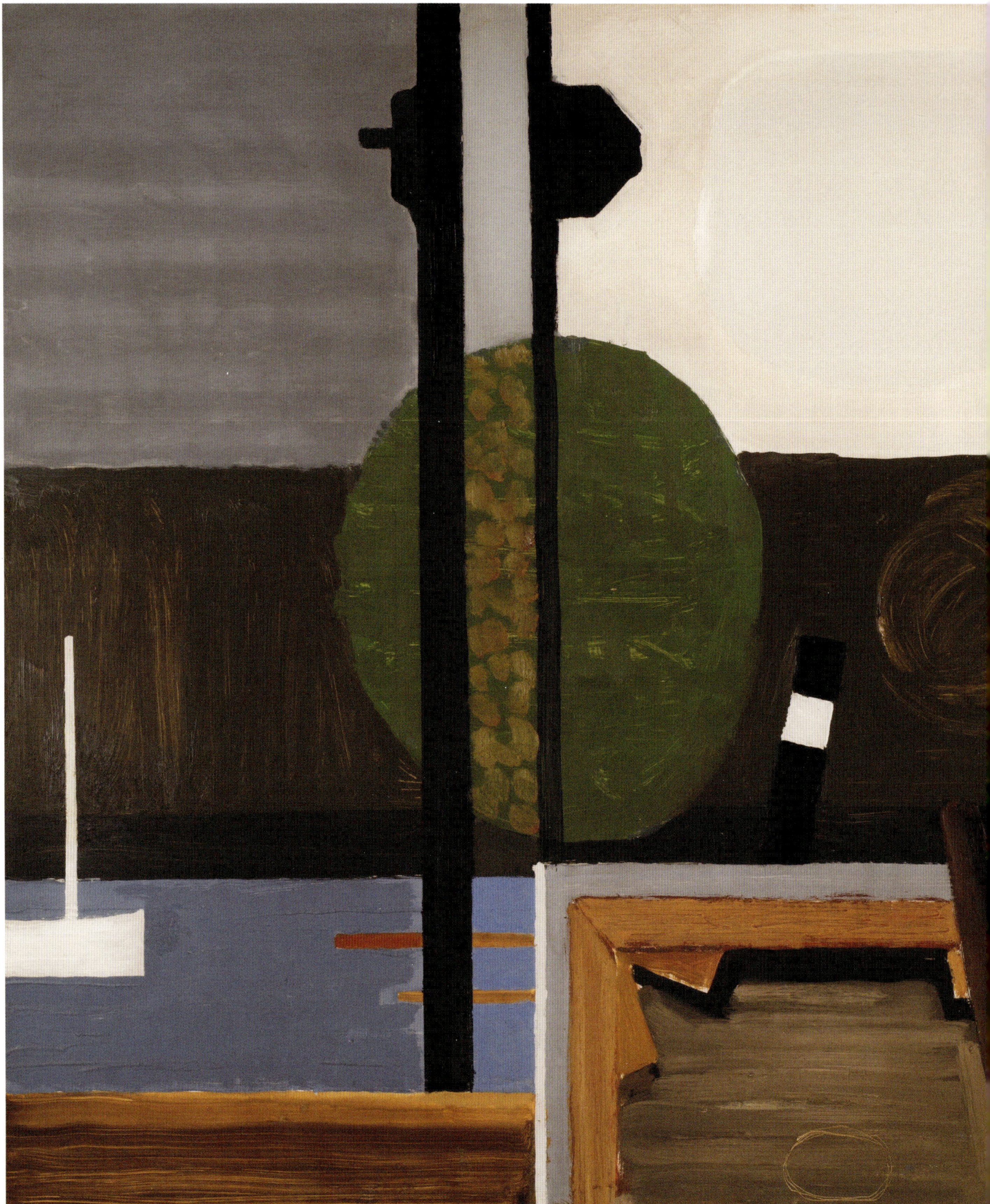

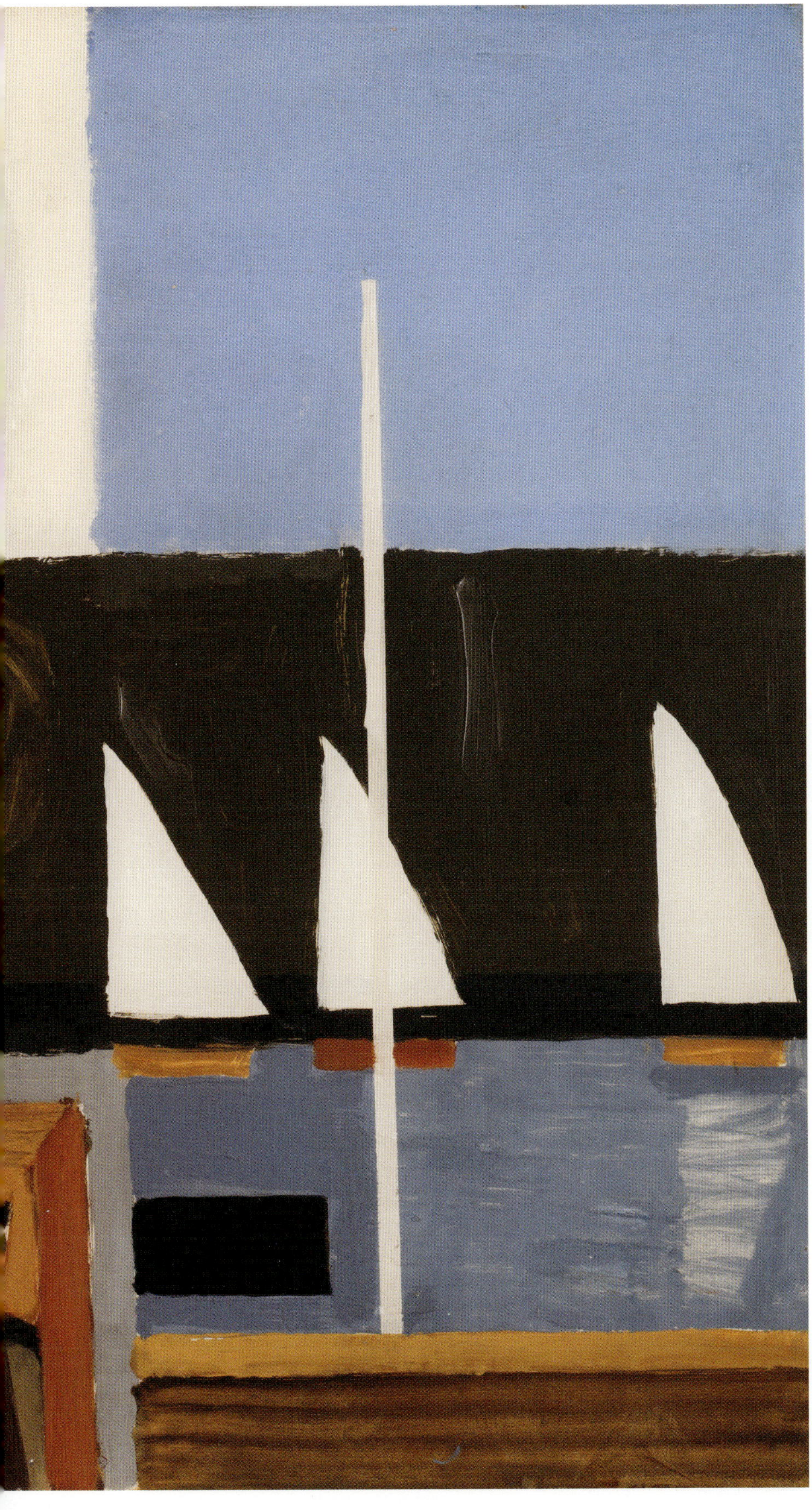

**73 Kenneth Rowntree** (1915-1997),
*View from the Studio (Putney)*, c. 1959,
oil on panel, 25 x 36 in. (63.5 x 91.2 cm).

Diana Rowntree, the artist's wife, recalled, 'We found a house on the Thames, upstream of Putney Bridge, and turned the attic into a studio. Its comfort permanently slowed Kenneth's working speed from the swift tempo demanded by one-day forays into distant landscapes.' The Thames provided Rowntree with a steady stream of subjects – views from his window, paintings of Putney Reach, and night time scenes. (**298**)

74

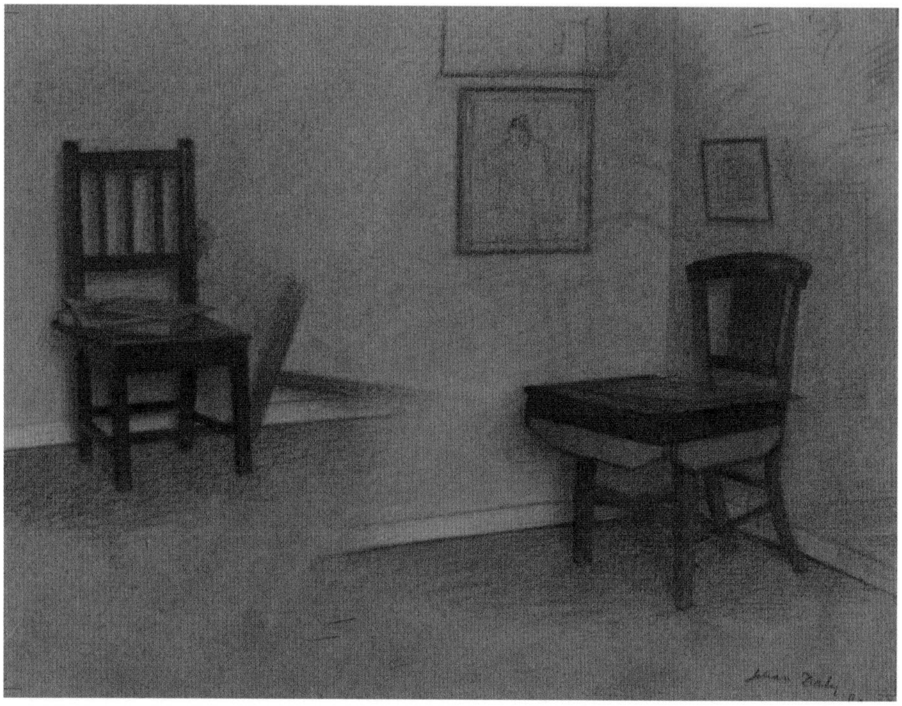

75

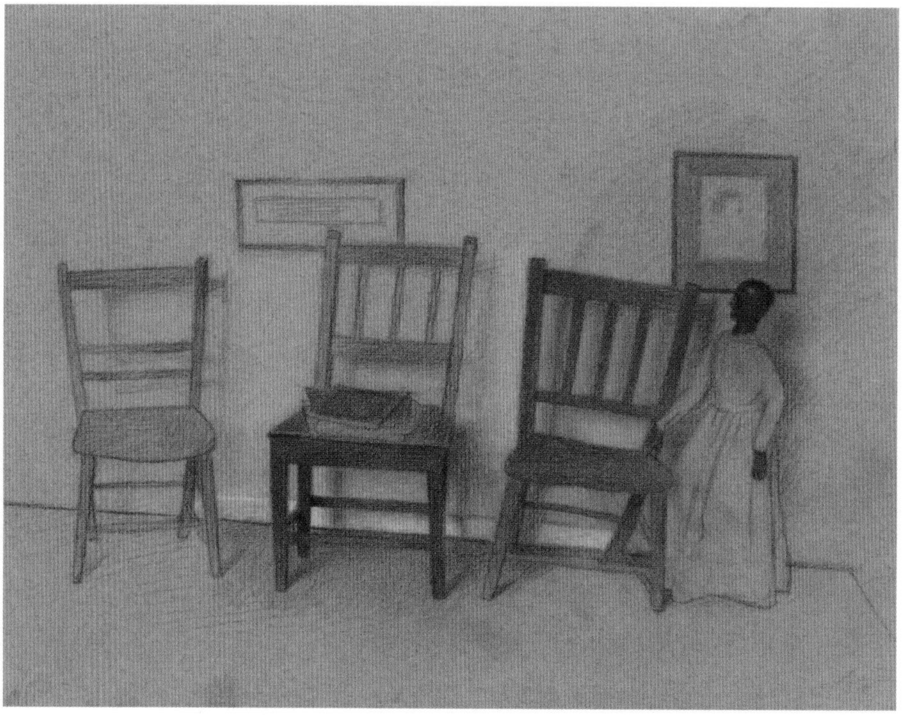

**Jehan Daly** (1918-2001),
**74** *A Corner of the Studio*, 1989,
signed and dated,
pastel on blue paper,
8 ¼ x 10 ½ in. (21 x 26.5 cm).

**75** *A Corner of the Studio with Lay Figure and Three Chairs*, c.1989,
pastel on blue paper,
9 x 11 ¾ in. (23 x 30 cm).

Despite being one of the most brilliant draughtsmen of his generation – fellow artist John Ward compared his immaculate pastels to those of the 18th-century Swiss master Jean Etienne Liotard – Daly wasn't interested in public recognition and was reluctant to exhibit. Nothing pleased him more than drawing his studio, for his pleasure, showing its simple contents: a lay figure, a set square, a pile of sketch books, a solander box, or an array of country chairs.

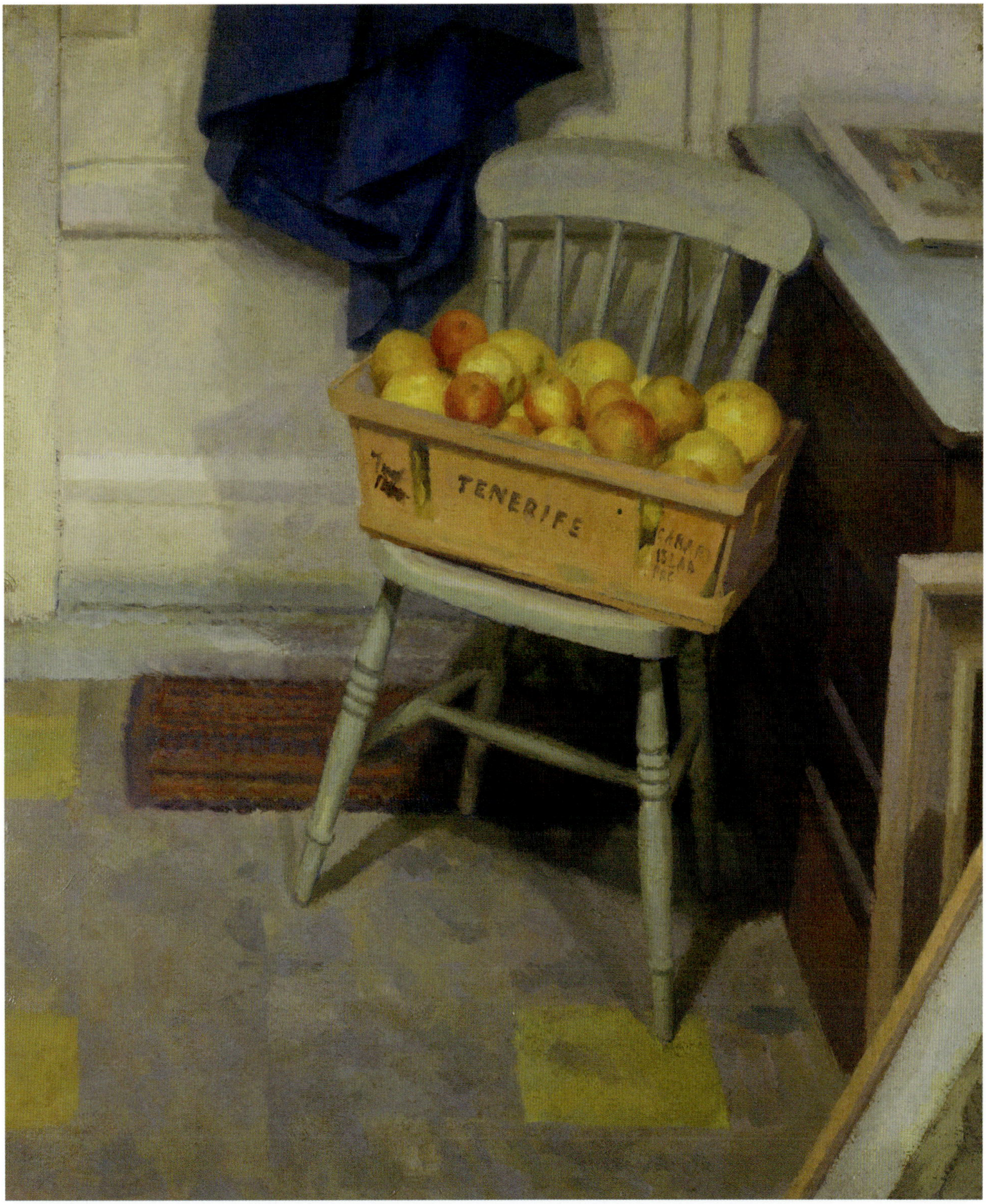


**76 Hubert Arthur Finney** (1905-1991), *Tenerife Crate with Apples on a Wooden Chair*, 1930s,
oil on panel, 24 x 20 in. (60.8 x 50.8 cm).

The pictures in the upright racks jutting out from the foreground clearly identify this space as the artist's studio. The crate of apples on a farmhouse slatback chair, which partially block both the doorway and the plan chest, are presumably temporarily placed as such for the purpose of this still life composition. (**310**, **311**, **324**)

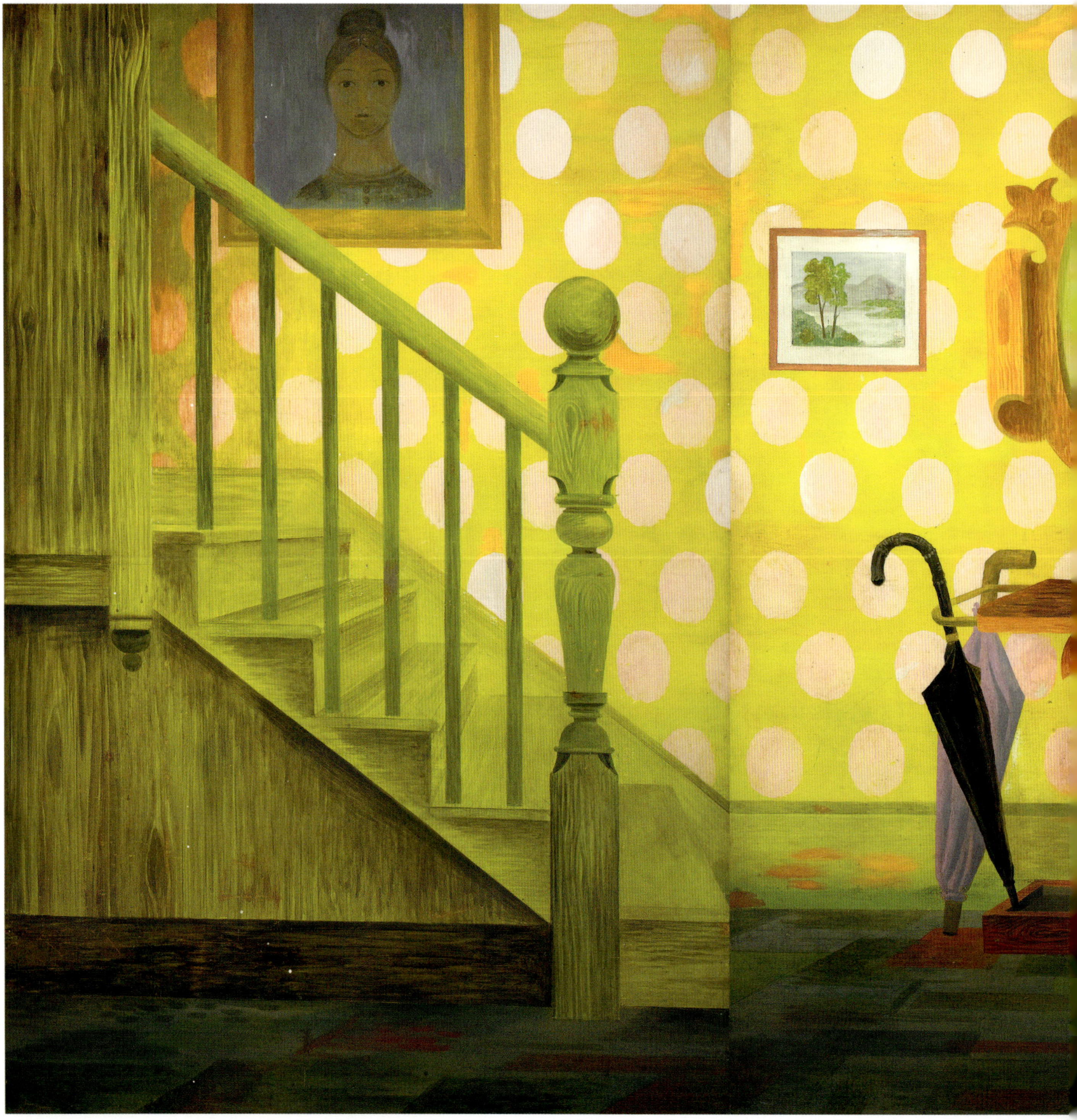

**77 Barbara Jones** (1912-1978), *Out in the Hall*, 1960,
oil and wax, 3 panels, 72 x 144 in. (183 x 365.8 cm).

The setting for *Out in the Hall* is the artist's Hampstead home, 2 Well Walk, which was filled with a lifetime's collection of eccentric objects, many of which found their way into her paintings. A self portrait can be seen above the banister, though on first sight the stuffed full-size grizzly bear, (who welcomes guests, and by implication the viewer) is more noticeable.

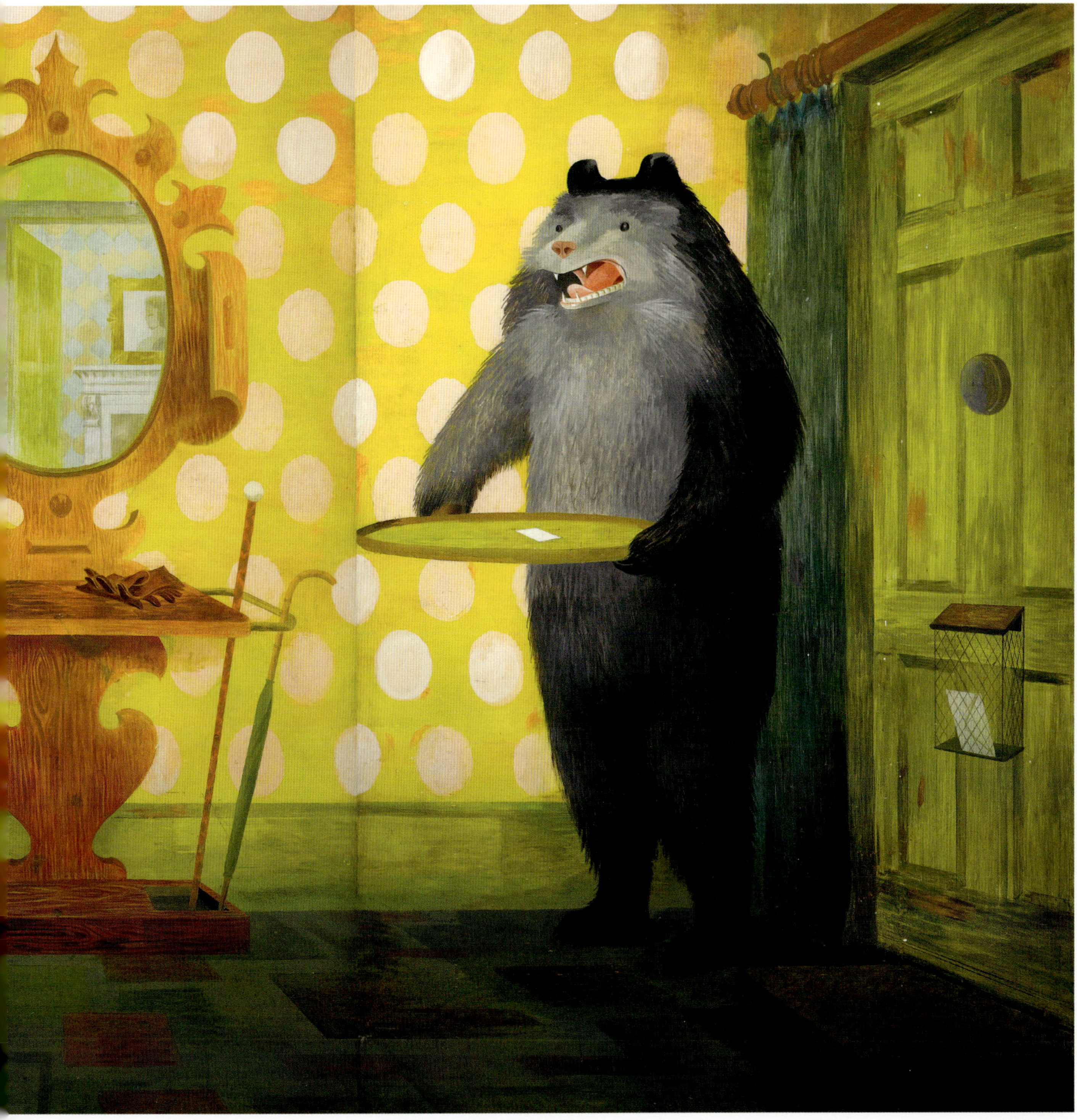

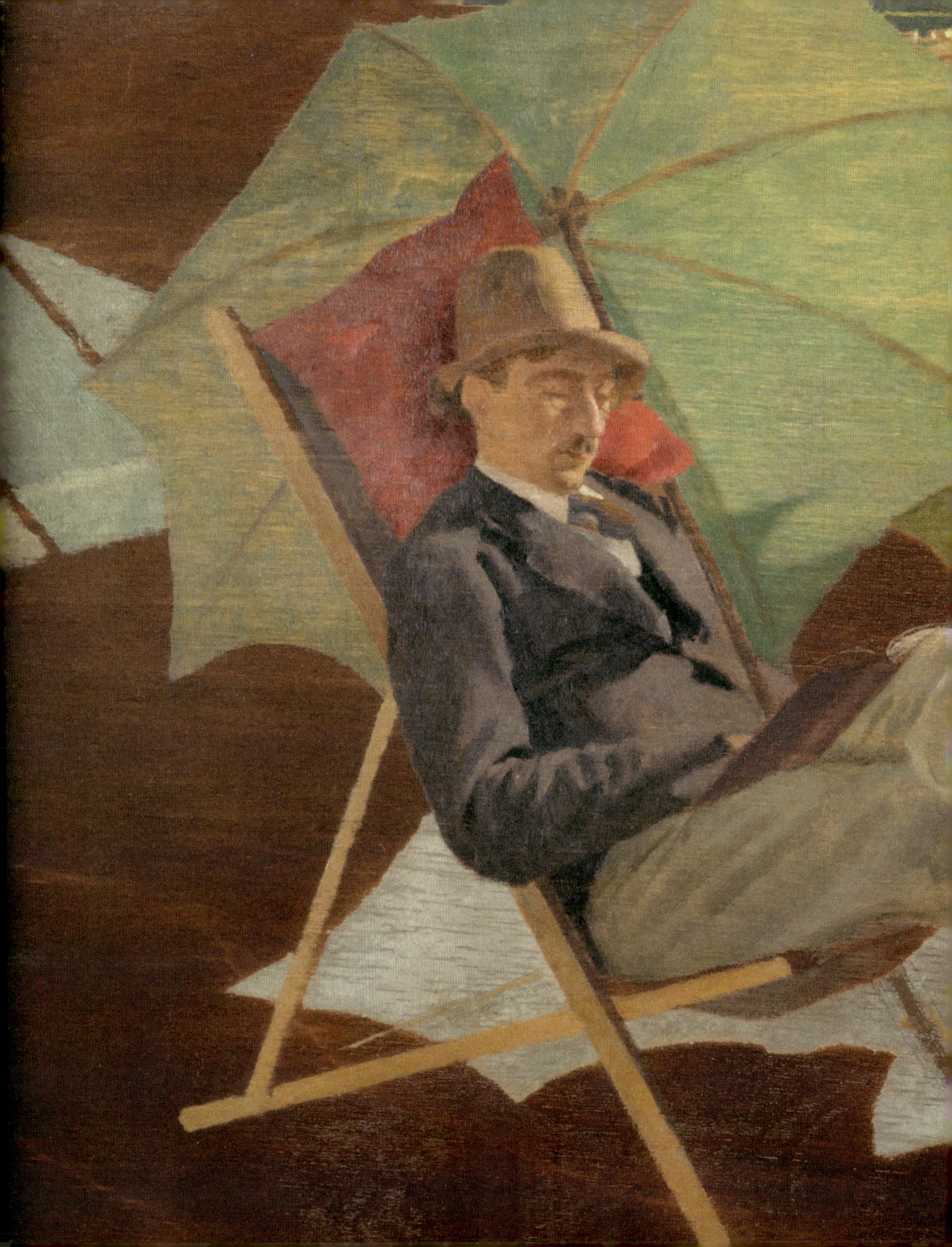

# THE ARTIST'S ENTOURAGE

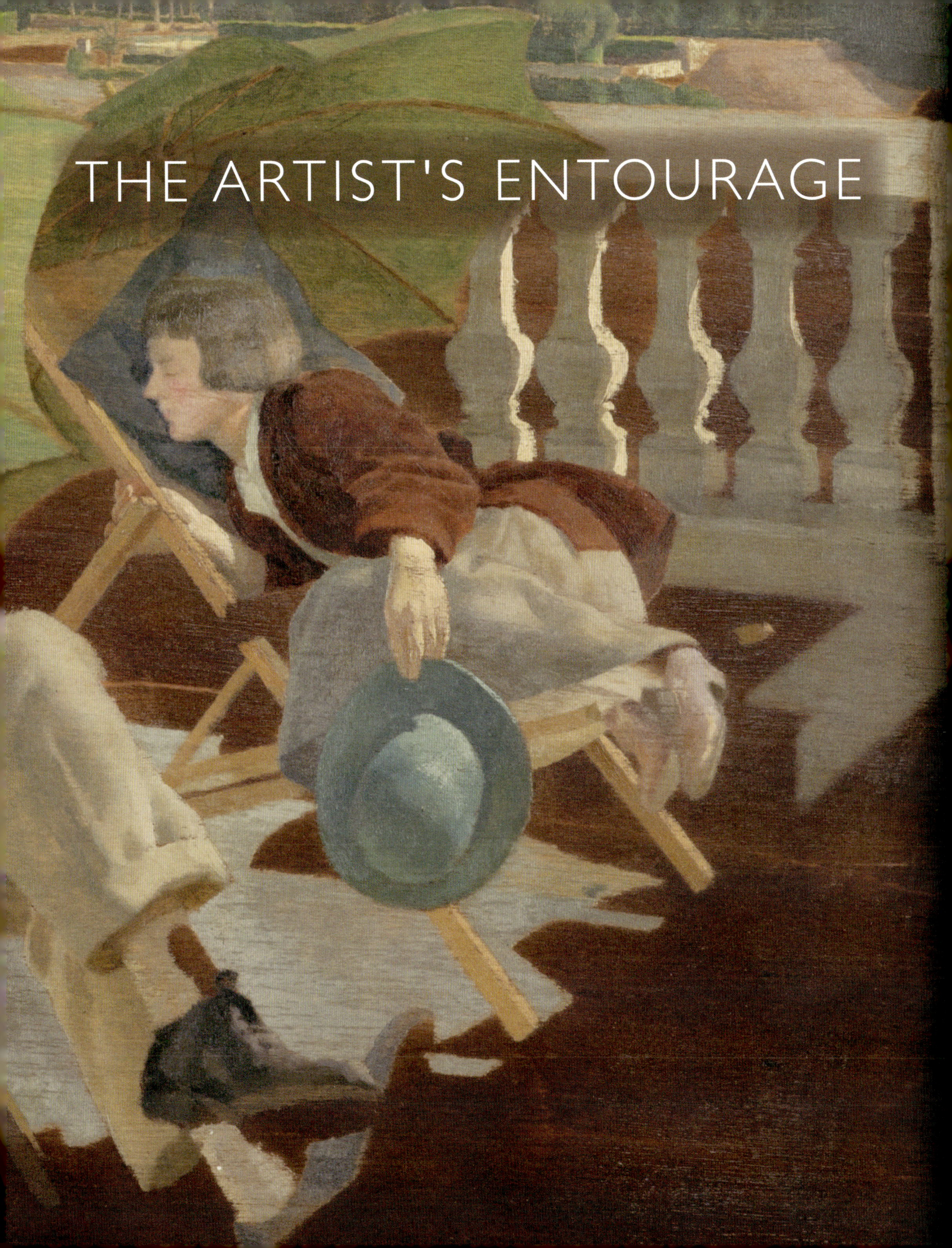

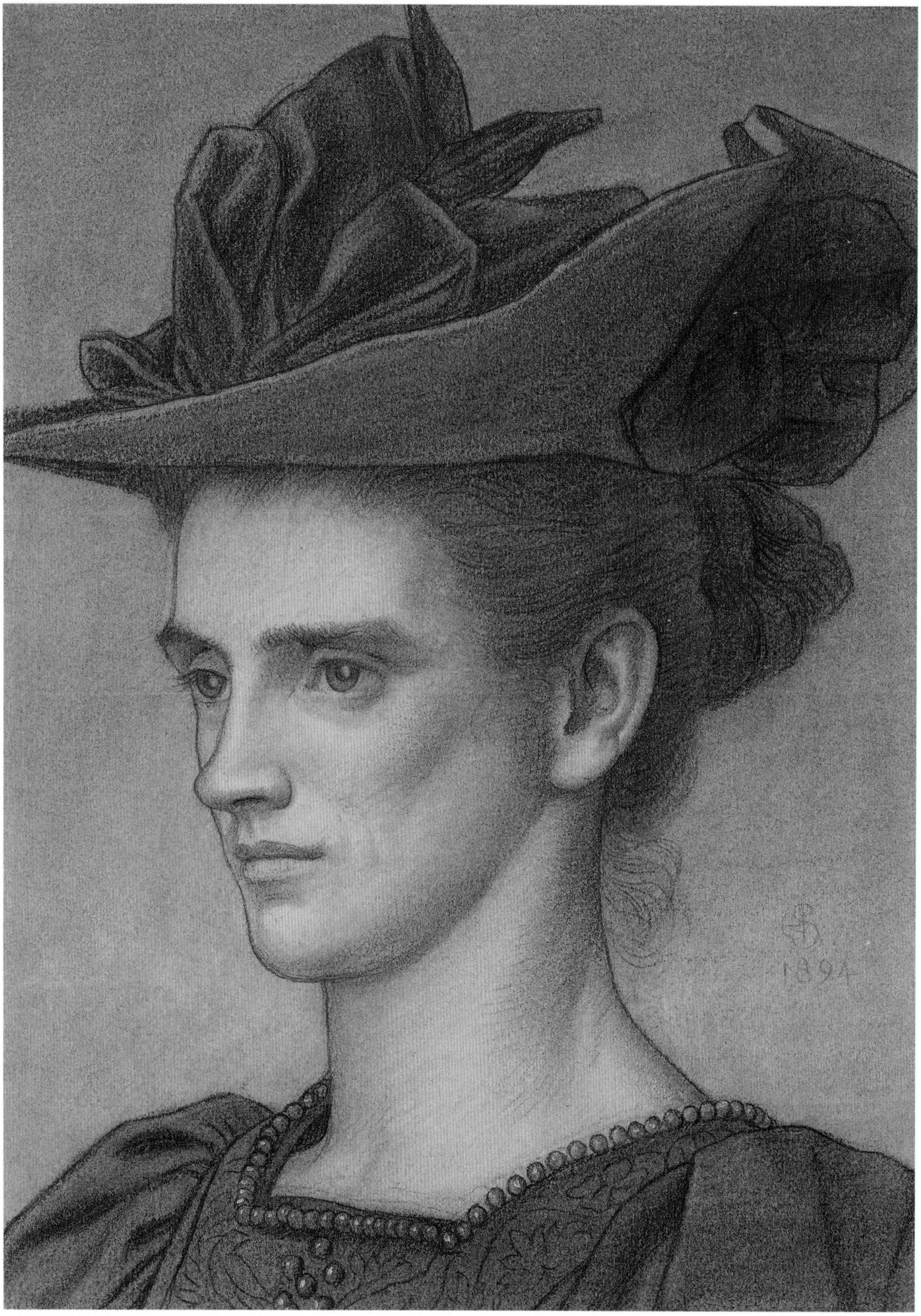


**78 Joseph Southall** (1861-1944), *Anna Elizabeth Baker* (study for *The Coral Necklace*), c.1894, monogrammed and dated, red chalk heightened with white, 10 x 7 ¼ in. (25.5 x 18.4 cm).

This is a study for the portrait of Anna Elizabeth Baker which Joseph Southall painted in tempera on panel in 1895. Southall and Baker were to marry in 1903, having delayed for years out of a sense of propriety because they were first cousins. She appears in many of Southall's pictures including his celebrated double portrait *The Agate*, 1911 (**245**).

# The Artist's Entourage

*'Every portrait that is painted with feeling is a portrait of the artist, not of the sitter. The sitter is merely the accident, the occasion. It is not he who is revealed by the painter; it is rather the painter who, on the coloured canvas, reveals himself.'*

Oscar Wilde, *The Picture of Dorian Gray*, 1890

Beyond the studio spaces with their accumulated inanimate objects, that were so often the subject of artist's compositions, the artist's milieu was inhabited by models and muses, wives and husbands, friends and children: the artist's entourage. That artists often had a more liberal outlook and bohemian values is not entirely inaccurate: there were at times fairly fluid lines within the artist's inner circle – models frequently became lovers, leading to marriage or children, and sometimes both.

The French phrase *sous le charme* – the sense that an artist is falling under the spell of his or her subject – explains so poignantly the *frisson* that is apparent in many works. The pencil portrait of Winifred Knights by Colin Gill (cover image) reveals that he was beguiled by her. Knights reciprocated in kind, producing a remarkably sensitive portrait of Gill. The tenderness of Frederick Austin's portrait of his wife on the return from their honeymoon is palpable. When Barnett Freedman fell in love with Claudia Guercio, he offered his future father-in-law a portrait of her, inscribed 'To Mr. V. Guercio, From Barnett Freedman, London, April 1926'. Other portraits of future wives are included by James Fitton and Ray Jones. Sir Gerald Kelly painted his wife Jane over fifty times. Charles Mahoney and Evelyn Dunbar, during their short-lived but intense courtship, took on the respective roles of Adam and Eve in the garden of Eden. Southall waited 8 years before marrying Anna Elizabeth Baker – having delayed out of a sense of propriety because they were first cousins.

Models *à la toilette* – washing, and brushing their hair, especially at night when the challenge of painting artificial light could be used to create exciting compositions – was a recurrent theme for artists like Belleroche, Austin, Souter and Fitton. In the best of their works there is a quality of intense regard, of intimacy, that elevates these compositions above the realm of merely banal observation.

In addition to partners and lovers as subjects, children appear time and time again in the oeuvre of artists. There are moments of tender observation – nursing mothers and mothers putting children to bed – that appear so frequently in the work of artists like Austin and Finney, that they became a staple of their artistic production. In these subjects artists found readily available models, though not always static or willing. Artists' children were often reluctant to pose – visibly so in the case of the resplendent Charlotte Halliday, though her likeness was easier to capture when watching *Children's Hour* with her brother. Beloved pets were also favourite subjects for artists – the names of Brangwyn's dogs, (Roger and Jock), Dunbar's (Laddie, Felbridge and Paul) and Austin's (Ling of Lingard) are as known to us as are Joseph Southall's and Fyffe Christie's splendidly named cats, Dante and Carmen.

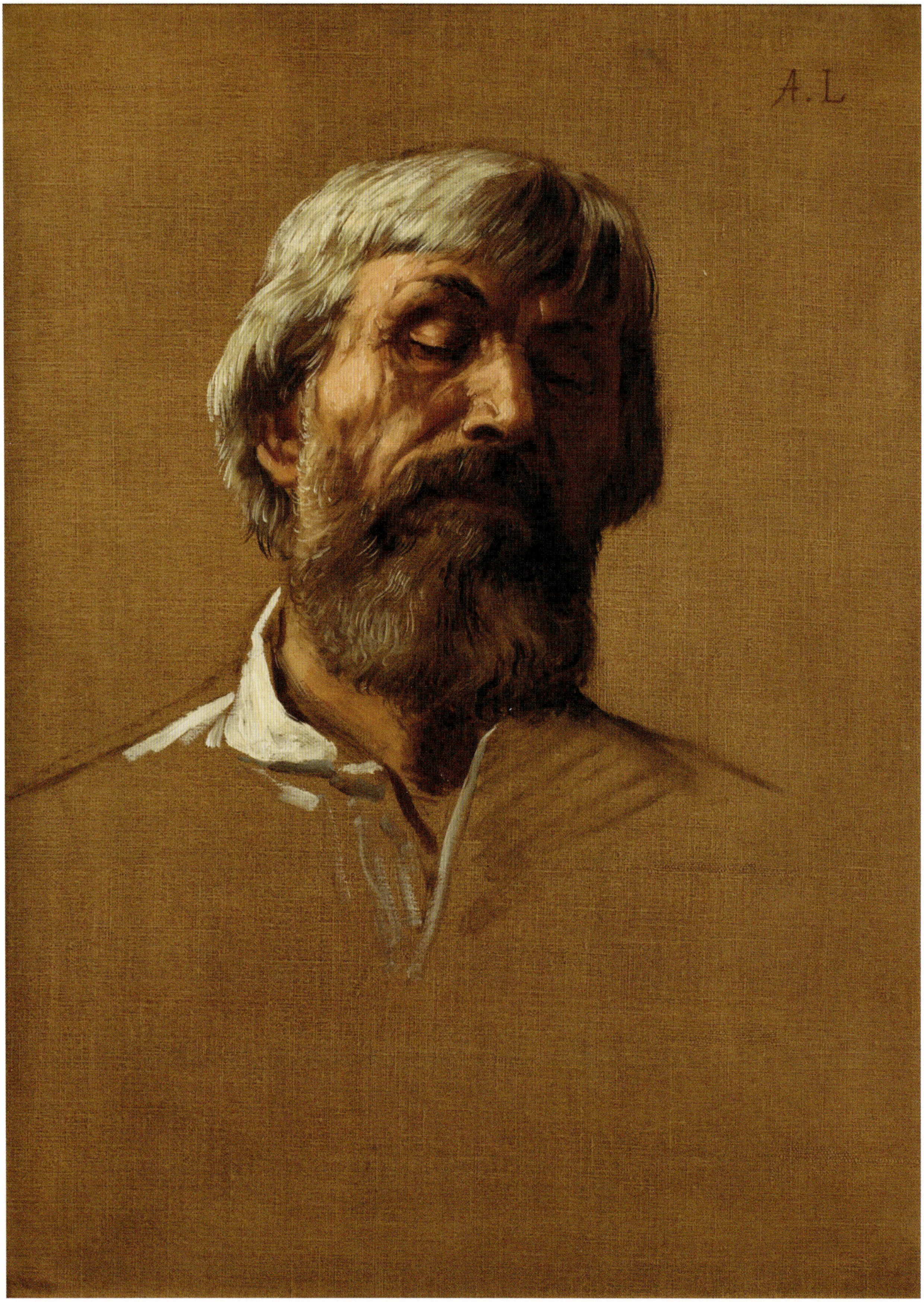
A.L

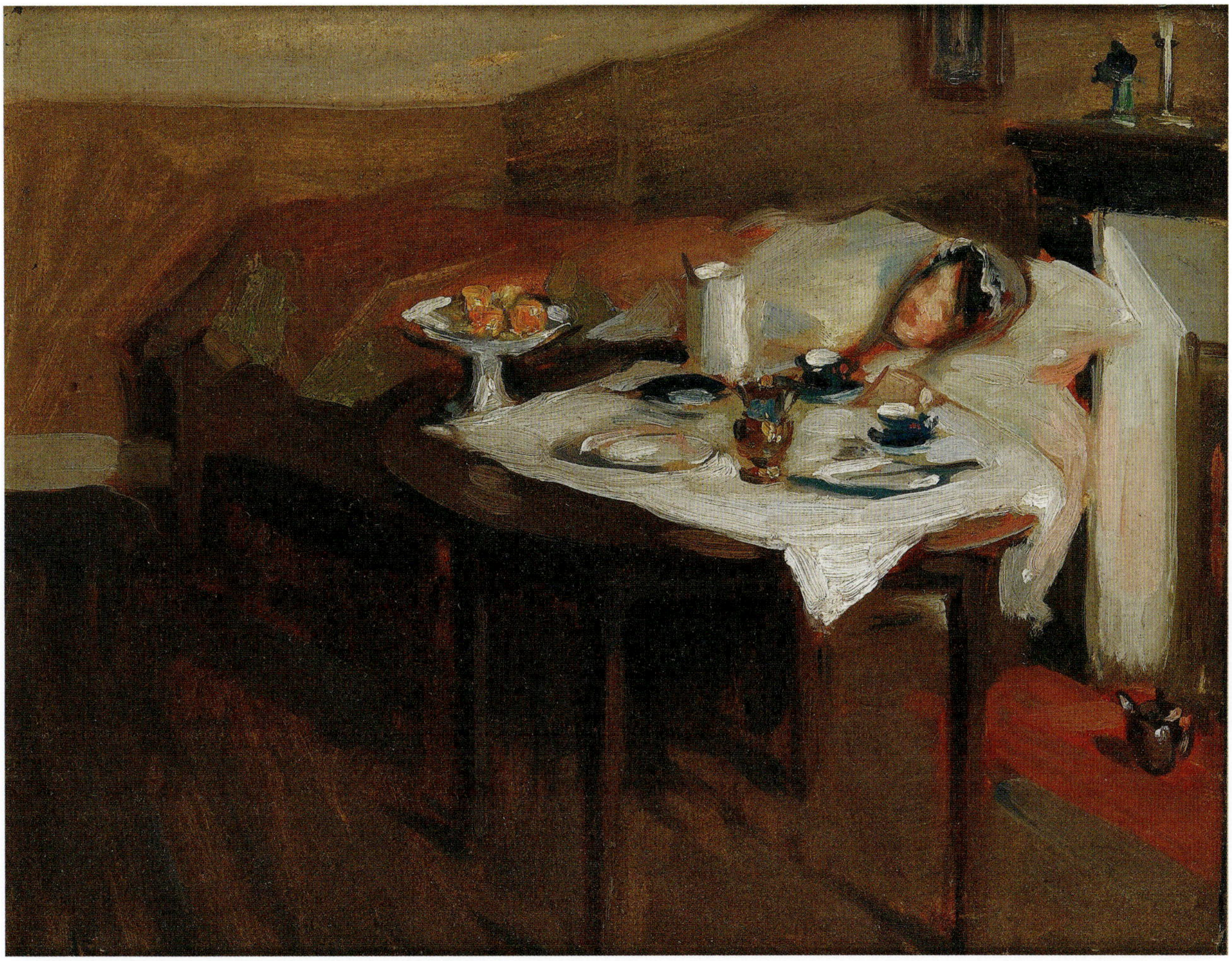

**80 Alexander Jamieson** (1873-1937), *The Artist's Wife, Biddy Macdonald,* c.1907, oil on board, 10 ½ x 13 ¼ in. (26.7 x 33.6 cm).

This painting dates to around 1907 when Jamieson married Gertrude Macdonald (known as Biddy), who was also an artist. With the breakfast he had just set out for her to wake up to, and the teapot warming by the fire, this rapidly painted panel records a moment of tender domesticity.

**79 Alphonse Legros** (1837-1911), *Head Study*, c.1880, signed with initials, oil on canvas, 22 ½ x 17 in. (57.2 x 43.2 cm).

According to a formula favoured by Legros, for his teaching demonstrations at the Slade School of Fine Art, this *Head Study* would have been rapidly painted, with an emphasis placed on the rendering of sitter's personality. At the Slade there were annual prizes for Head Painting and it was considered one of the three main disciplines along with the painting of Figures and Compositions.

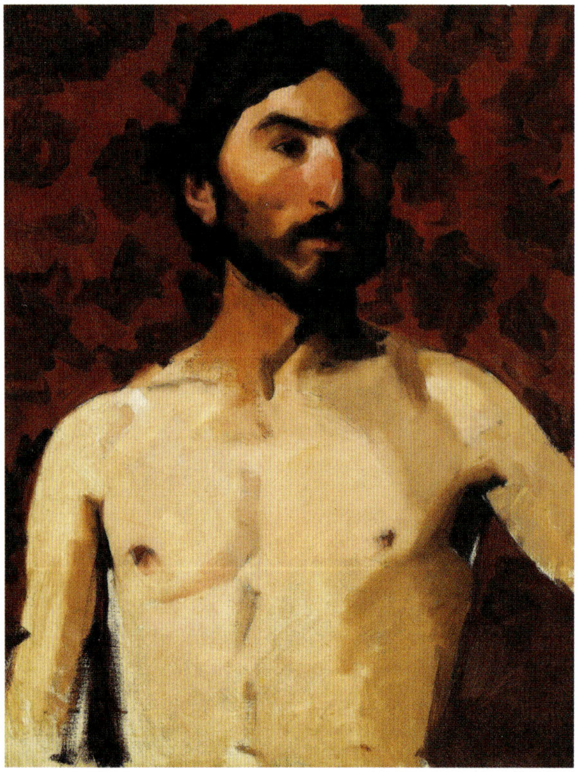

81

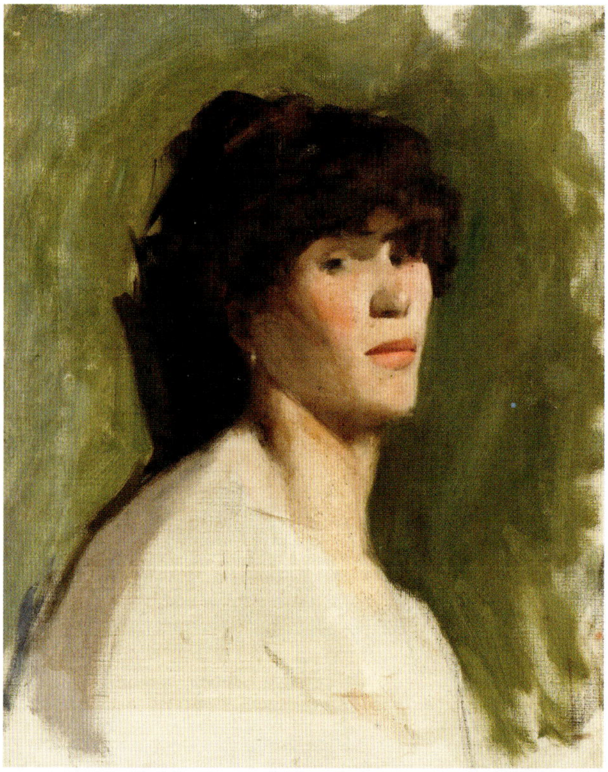

82

**Albert de Belleroche** (1864-1944),

**81** *Life Study*, c.1880, signed on reverse,
oil on canvas, 24 x 18 ½ in. (61 x 47 cm).

**82** *Portrait of a woman*, c.1885, signed on the reverse,
oil on canvas (stamped Paul Foinet), 20 x 16 in. (51 x 41 cm).

Praising one of Albert de Belleroche's paintings of a life model, Brangwyn wrote: That, in my opinion, is one of the finest examples of flesh painting that I have ever seen; it is not paint but real flesh'. Theses life studies by Albert de Belleroche date to his period of training under Carolus-Duran (1837-1917). The palette used, with subtle modulated flesh tones set against rich and contrasting background colours, especially dark reds, are typical of Carolus-Duran's signature portraits of the Belle Epoch. It was during this period that Belleroche met John Singer Sargent, who was to become a life long friend, and with whom he shared studios in Paris and London.

**83 Albert de Belleroche** (1864-1944), *Life Study in Silhouette*, 1890s,
oil on canvas, 30 x 20 in. (76 x 51 cm).

The model is believed to have been a participant in the *village nègre*, a popular – although nowadays unthinkable – feature of colonial exhibitions in Paris in the period 1870-1900. The device of painting in silhouette was frequently used by Henri Toulouse Lautrec, with whom Belleroche was especially acquainted through Lili Grenier, a favourite model of both artists.

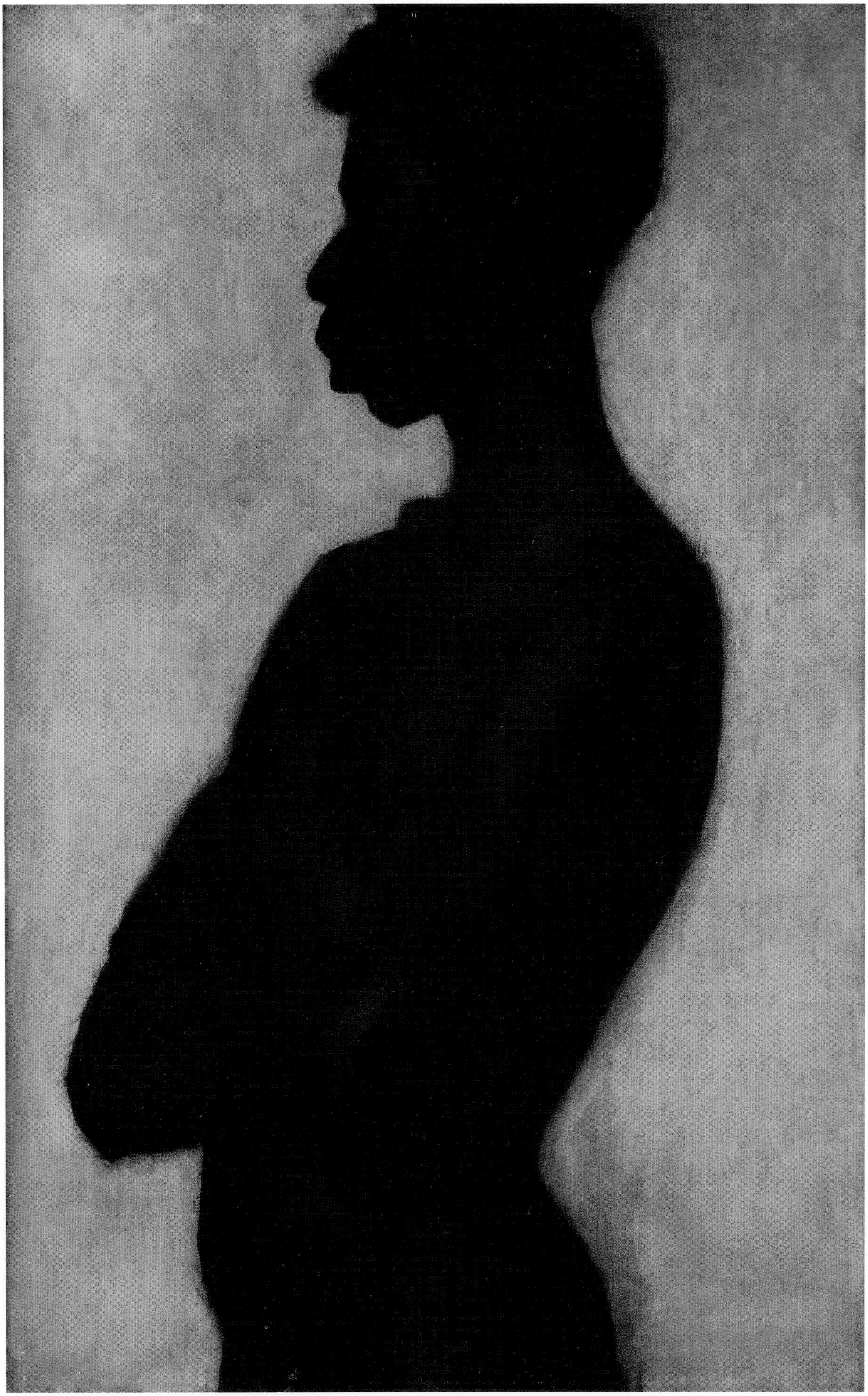

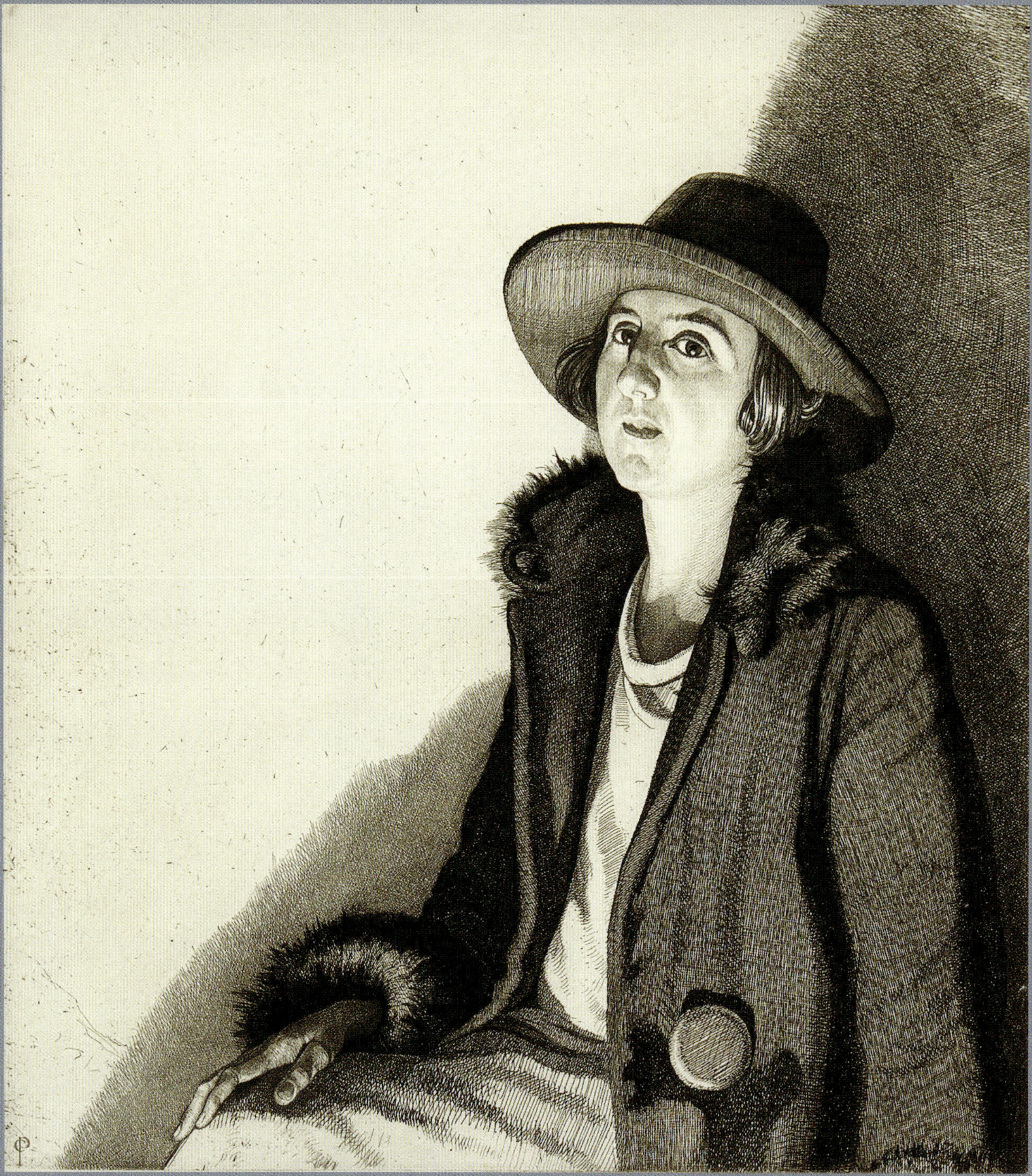

**84 Raymond Ray-Jones** (1886-1942), *Lamp-light (E.I.P)*, mid-1920s, signed in pencil, original printed label to verso, etching, plate size: 8 x 7 in. (20.3 x 18.2 cm).

The model is Effie Irene Pearce, whom Ray Jones married in 1926. (**250**)

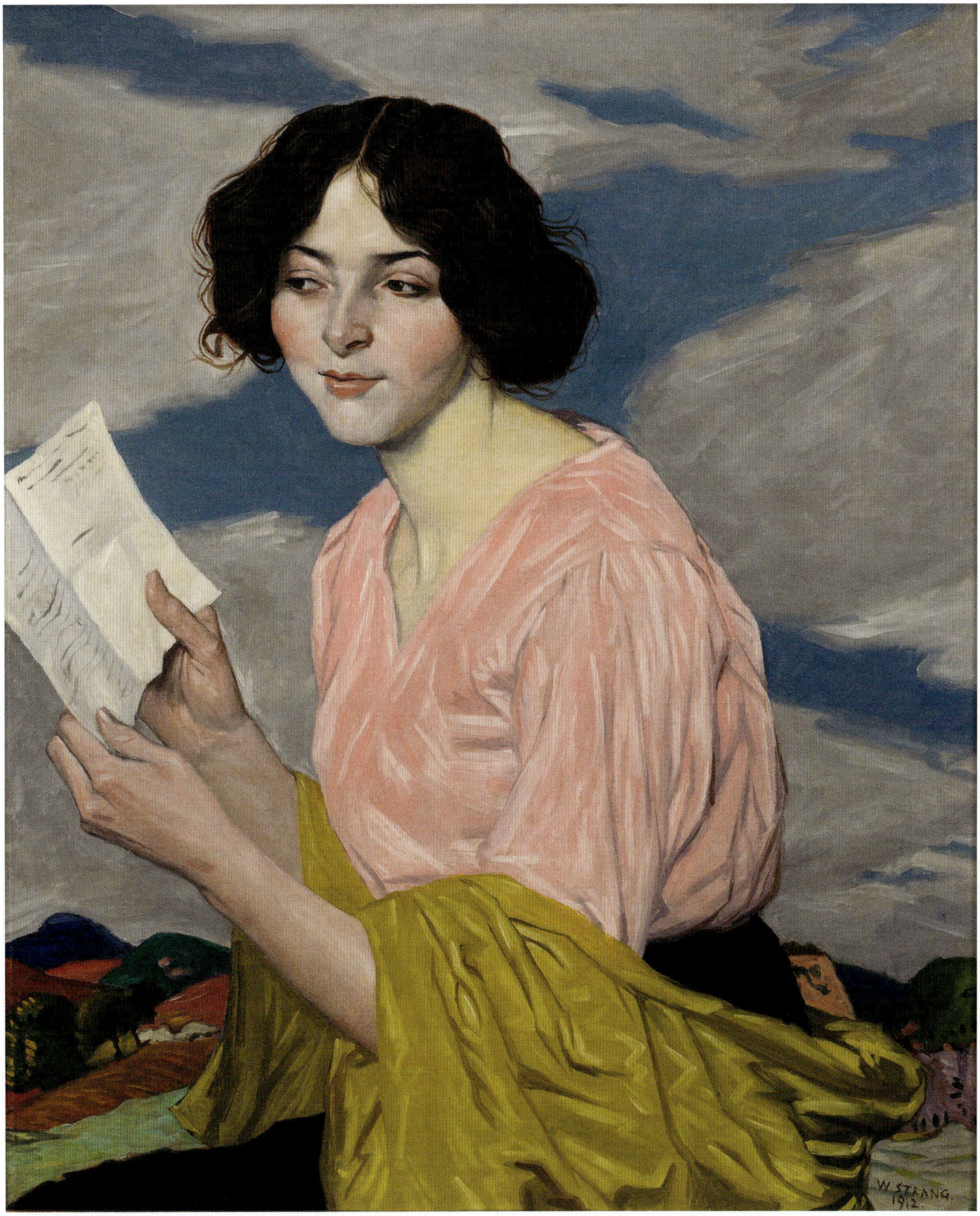


**85 William Strang** (1859-1921), *The Love Letter, (Portrait of Dora Labbette)*, 1912, signed and dated, oil on canvas, 30 x 25 in. (76 x 63.5 cm).

The model is Dora Labbette, an English soprano who was married briefly, in 1918, to David Strang, William Strang's son. After studying at the Guildhall School of Music, where she won many prizes, she went on to become a leading and much-loved British lyric, oratorio and operatic soprano, sometimes performing under the name Lisa Perli. A group portrait, *The Singer,* which features Dora, David Strang and William Strang himself, is known through an illustration from the *Illustrated London News,* but it is believed that this painting was destroyed by Strang when Dora and David separated. (**89**)

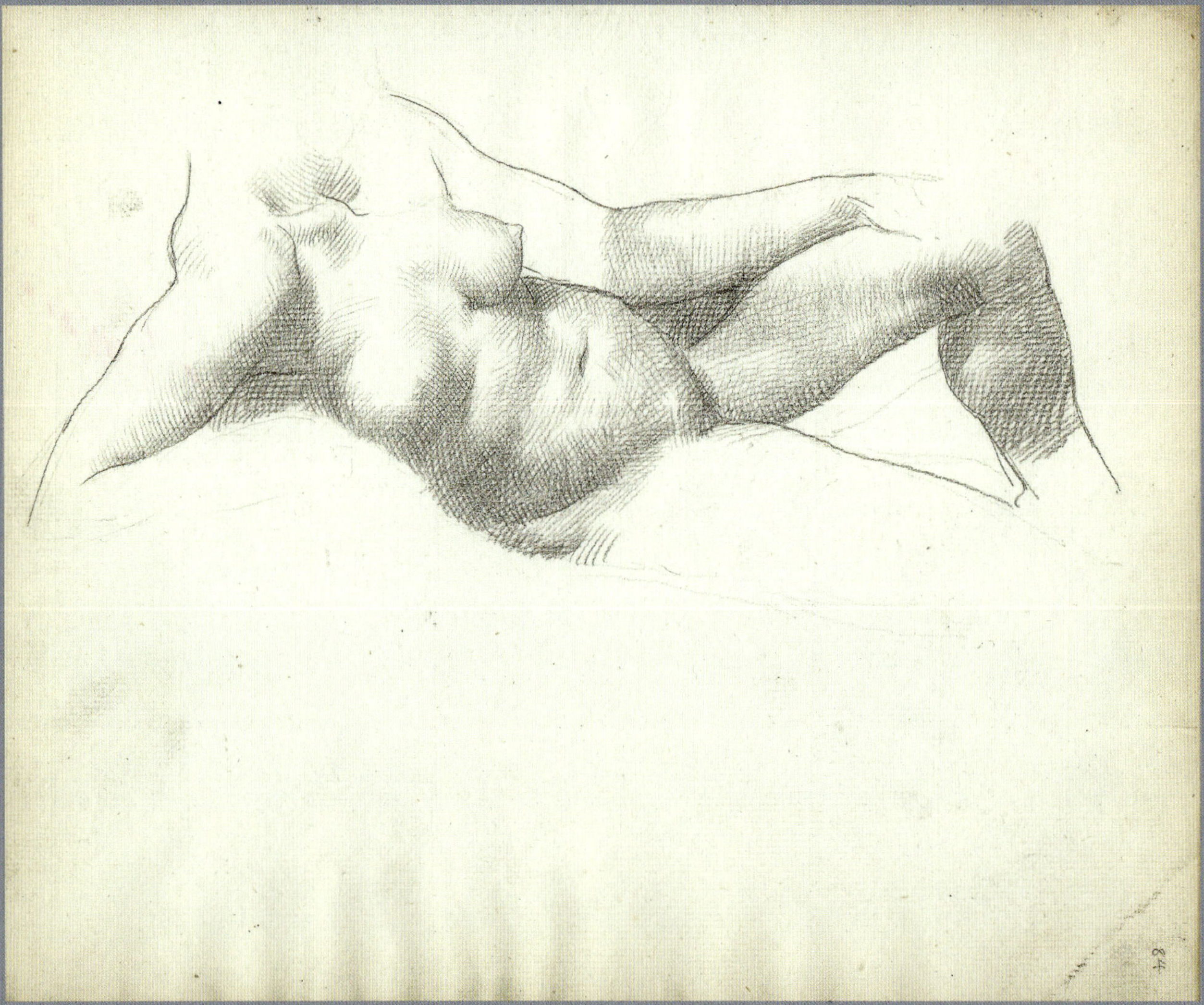

**86 William Strang** (1859-1921), *Reclining Nude*,
pencil with touches of silverpoint on paper, 7 ½ x 9 ¼ in. (19 x 23.5 cm).

William Strang received a rigorous training at the Slade School of Art (1875-1881) under Professor Alphonse Legros, a brilliant draughtsman and one of the chief exponents in the resurgence of metal point during the latter part of the nineteenth-century. Recognising Strang's own technical skill Legros appointed him assistant master in etching. Strang drew as he engraved using a distinctive technique where areas of tonality emerge through a system of parallel lines, hatching and cross-hatching.

**87 William Strang** (1859-1921), *Standing Nude, Rear View, Arms Raised*, signed with initials,
pencil on paper, 9 ¼ x 7 ½ in. (23.5 x 19 cm).

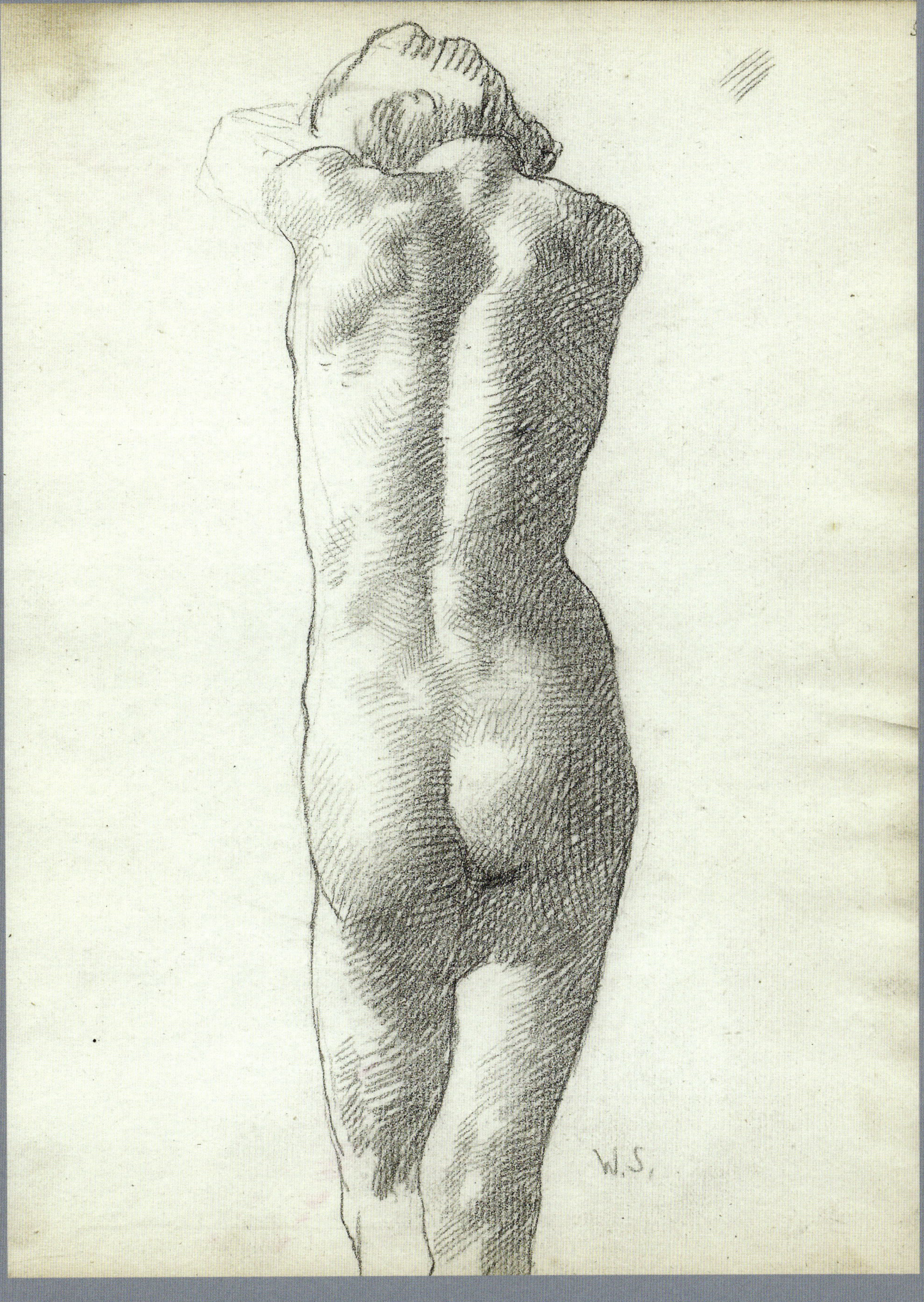
W.S.

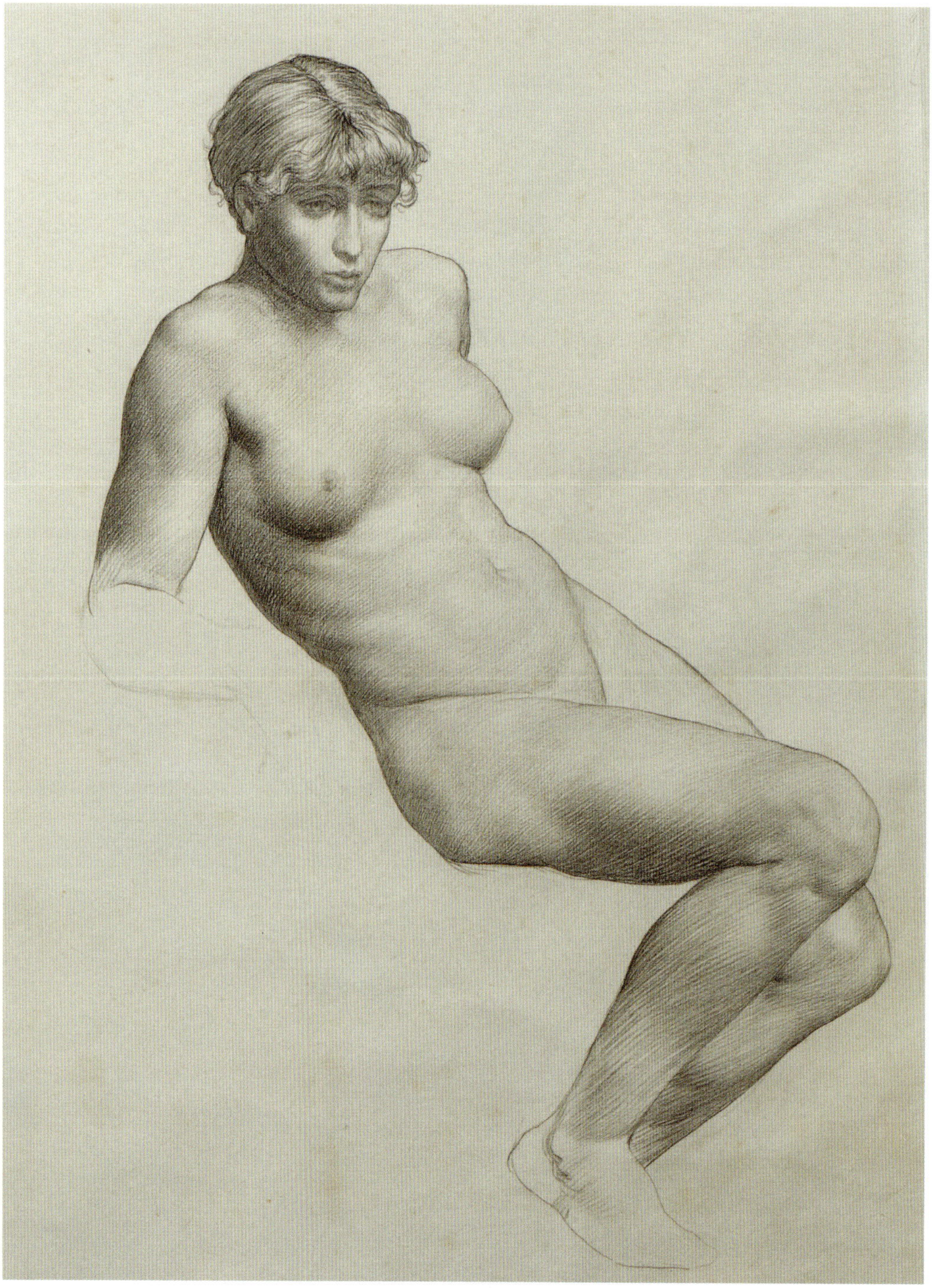

**88 William Strang** (1859-1921), *Seated Nude* (reclining, three quarter view), silverpoint on paper, 21 ¾ x 16 in. (55 x 41 cm).

Metalpoint is considered a challenging medium – unlike pen or chalk, which can produce strokes of varying thickness or darkness depending on how hard artists bear down on the instrument, silver leaves a nearly uniform line. The medium was perfectly suited to the subtlety and technical quality of Strang's draughtsmanship. C.R. Ashbee, who sat for Strang, recalled that: '. . . in each of his portraits there is some touch of his sitters' ugliness revealed in the beauty of the draughtsmanship . . .'

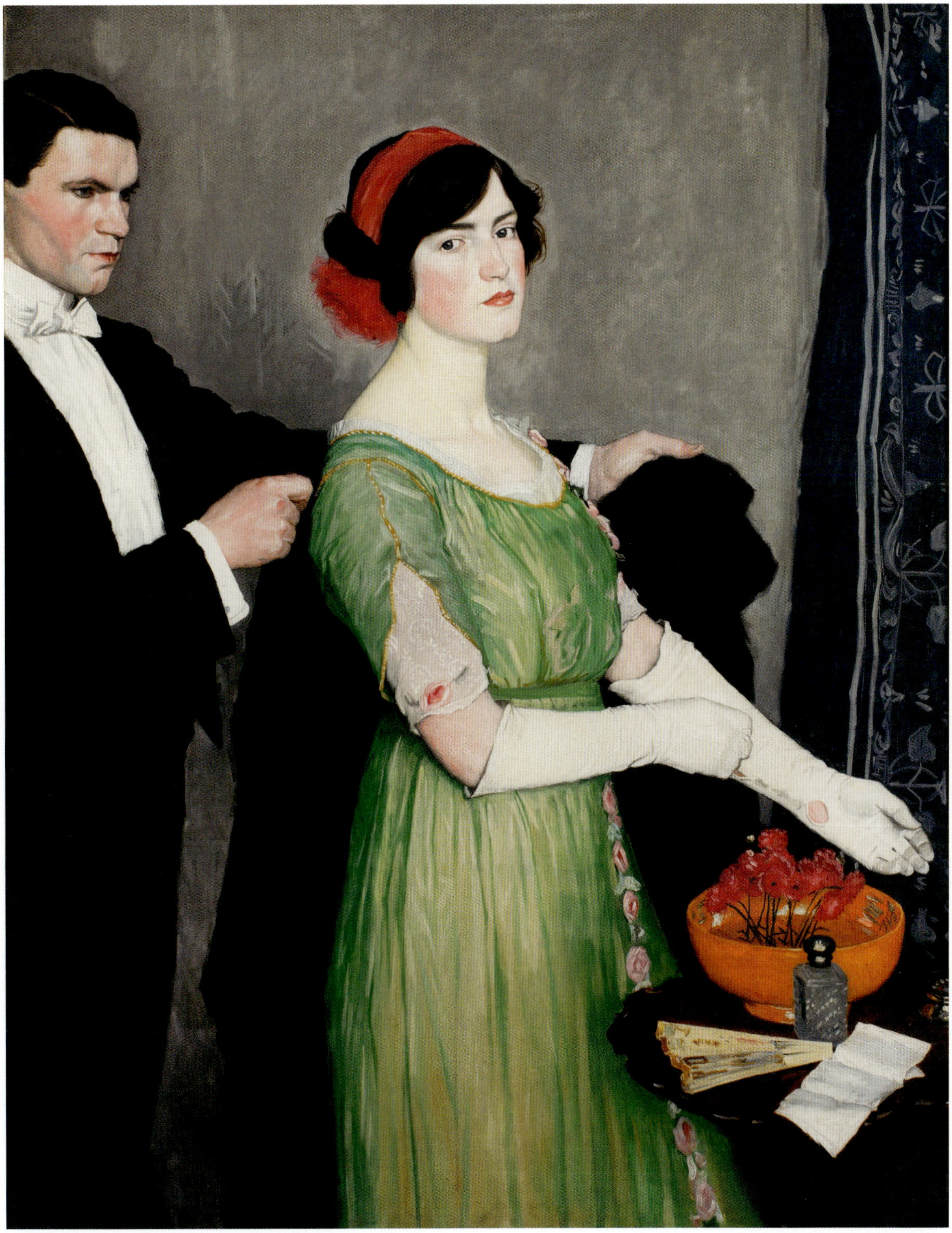

**89 William Strang** (1859-1921), *The Opera Cloak* (Portrait of Nancy Strang and David or Ian Strang), 1913, signed and dated, oil on canvas, 48 x 40 in. (122 x 102 cm).

Strang's only daughter Nancy held a particular place in her father's heart. C.R. Ashbee used to recount an anecdote that Strang once showed him a drawing remarking: 'I've tried all my life to do the pretty-pretty but it's no good . . . I can't'. He suddenly checked, looking at his little daughter Nancy and handed me a drawing of her, 'but what do you think of that?'

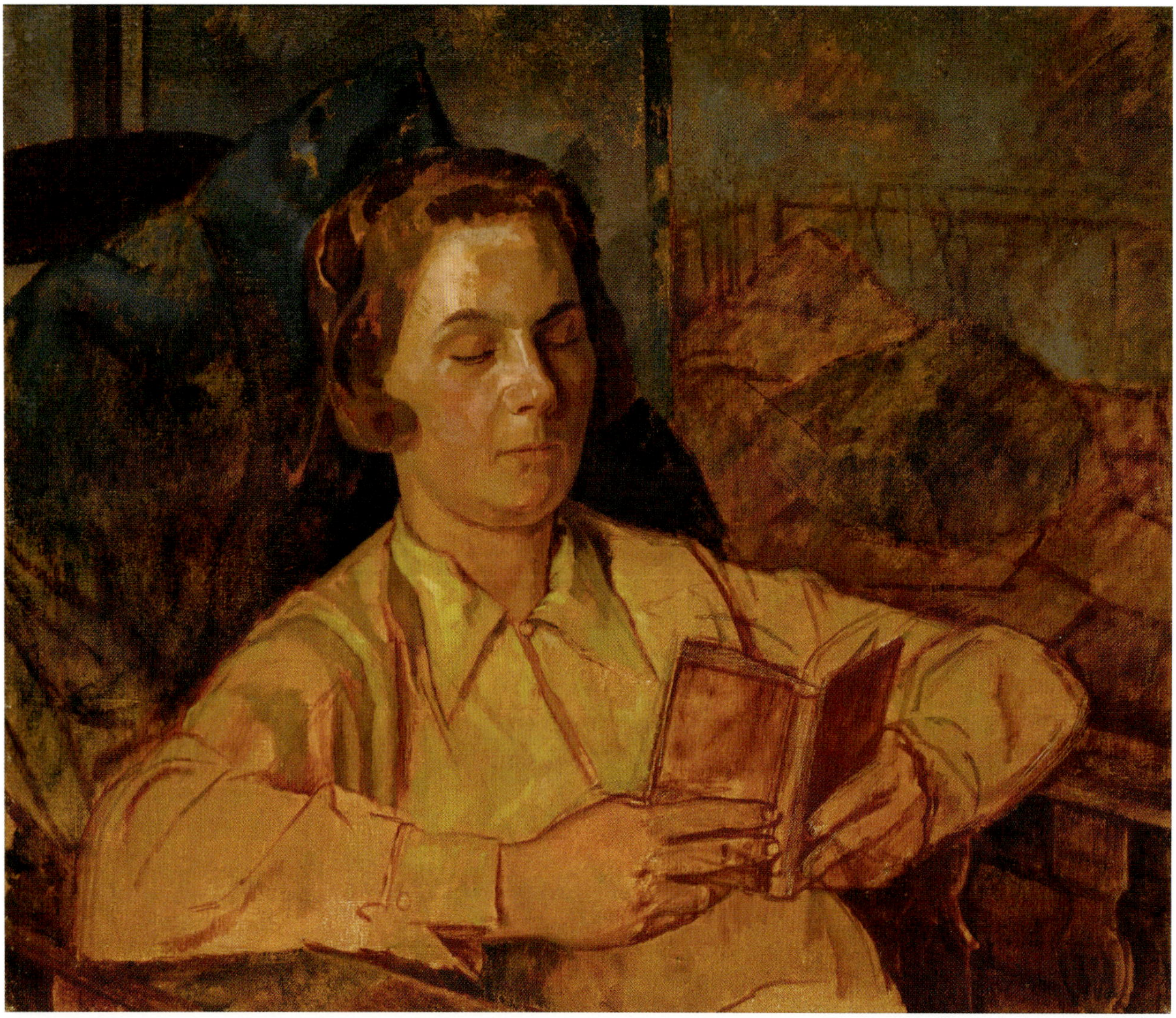

**90 Percy Horton** (1897-1970), *Joan Jenner-Rhoades Reading*, c.1925, signed with studio stamp on reverse (2/26), oil on canvas, 20 ¼ x 24 in. (51 x 61 cm).

Joan Jenner was a friend of Lydia, Percy Horton's wife. She married the painter Geoffrey Rhoades (**314**, **315**, **316**) in the mid-1930s having met him at a Royal College of Art ball. According to fellow artist Rodrigo Moynihan, 'Portraits, stripped of grandeur, familiar and unpretentious, are the subjects of Percy Horton's art and it would be vain to search for glamorous attitudes or passionate preferences. The passion is in the love of the task, the integrity and complexity of the drawing, in the affectionate interpretation of familiar scenes and people'.

**91 John Moody** (1906-1993), *Portrait of Anita Kowalska*, late 1920s, oil on canvas, 19 ½ x 15 ¾ in. (49.5 x 40 cm).

Anita Kowalska was a Polish model at the Royal Academy Schools in the late 1920s.

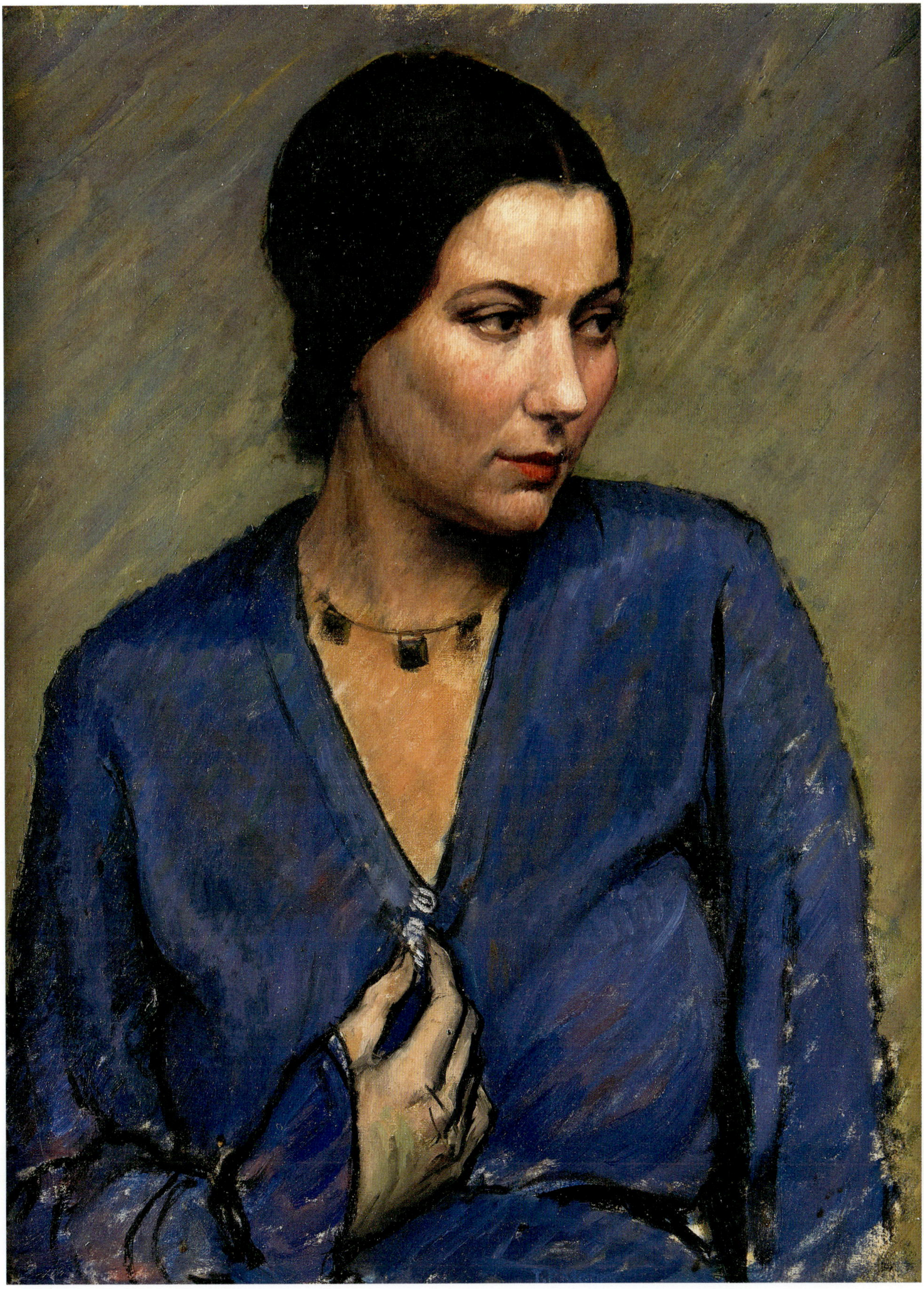

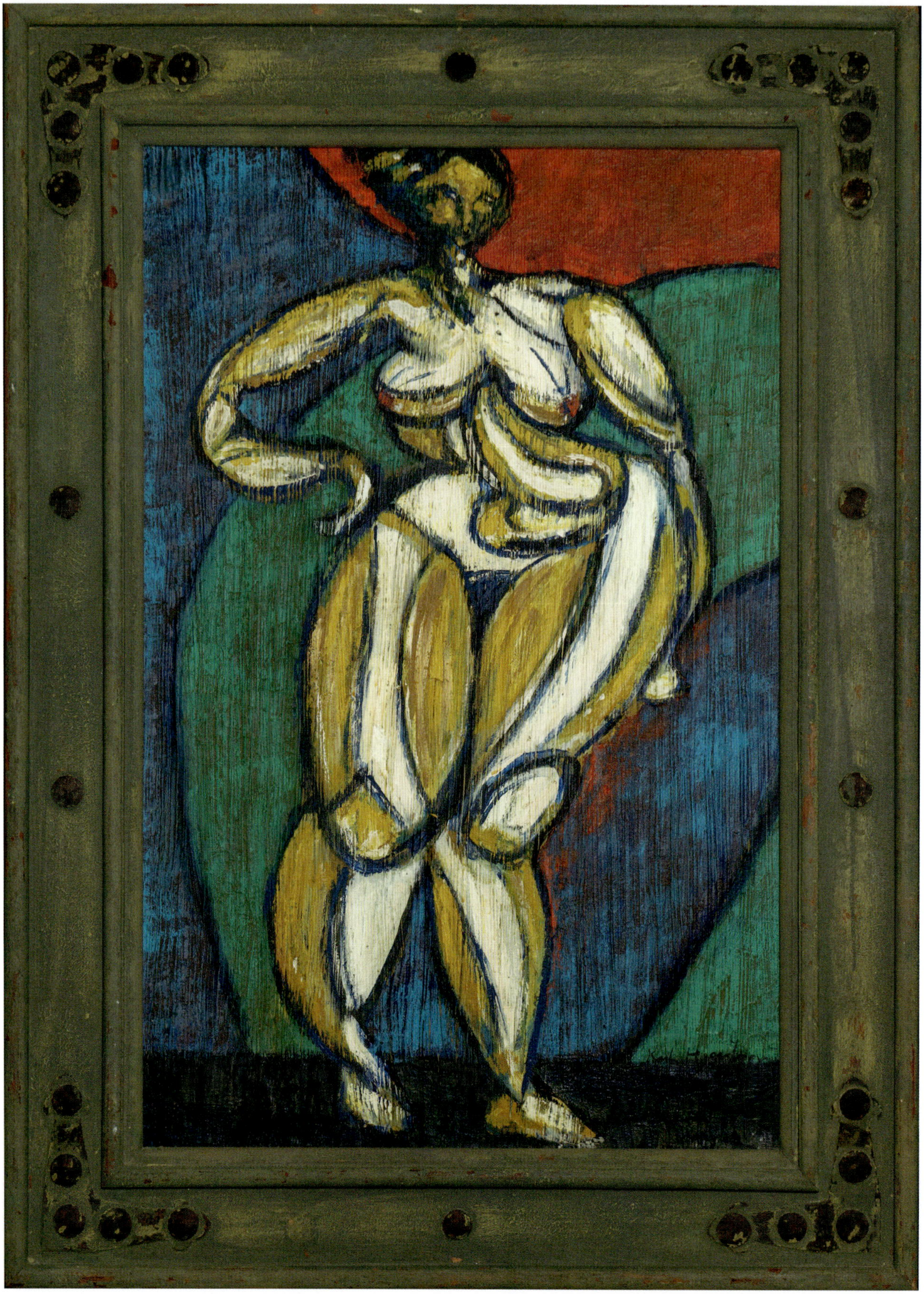

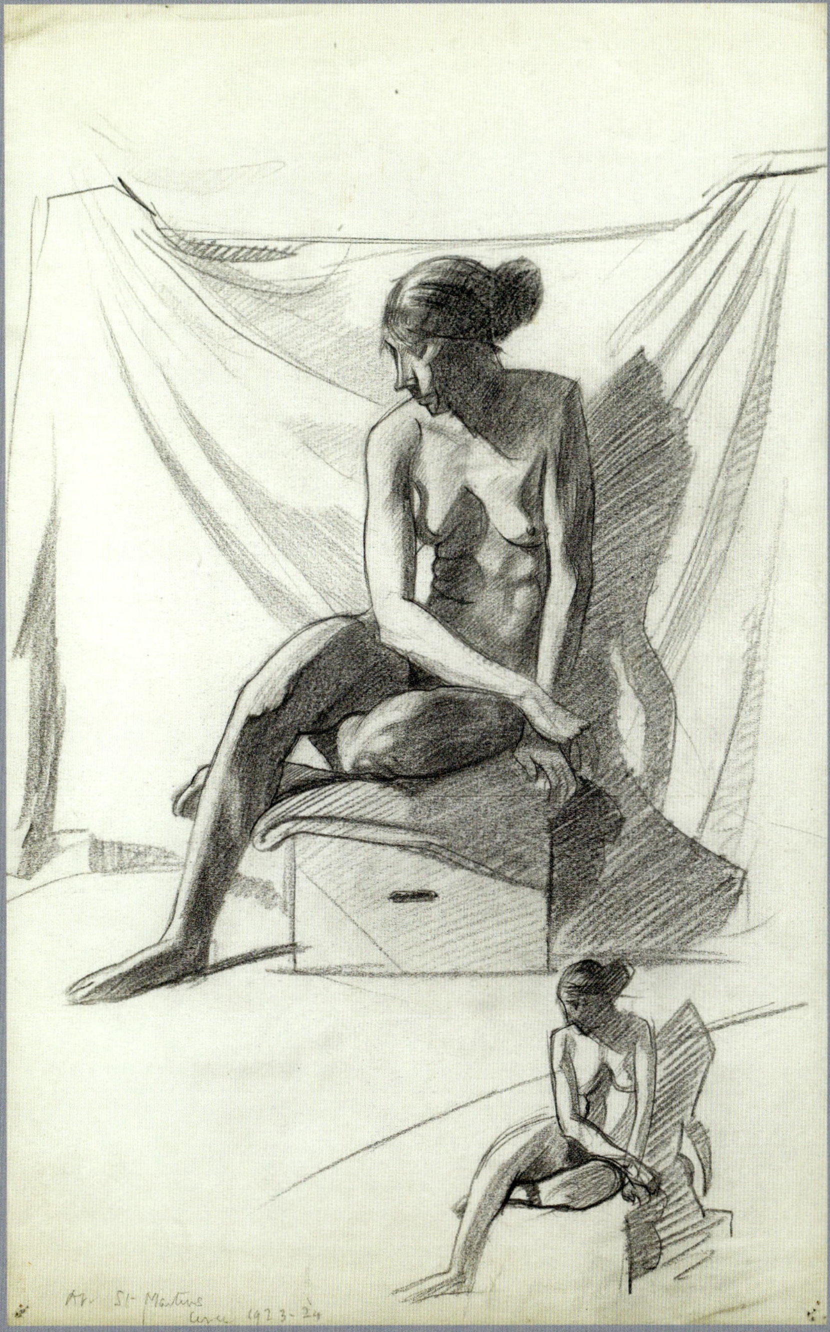


**93 Richard Carline** (1896-1980), *Life Study* (at St Martins), 1923-24, inscribed, pencil on paper, 18 x 12 in. (46 x 30.5 cm).

**92 Karl Hagedorn** (1889-1969), *Rhythmical Expression: Full-length Female Nude*, c. 1913, oil on canvas, 30 x 20 in. (76.2 x 50.8 cm). In a frame of the artist's own design.

Karl Hagedorn went to Paris in 1912 to complete his student training. He enrolled at the atelier of Maurice Denis, exhibited at the *Salon d'Automne*, and met with Henri Matisse. This experience proved formative and resulted in Hagedorn producing radically avant garde works, especially in terms of the status quo of British art of the time. (**321**, **322**, **323**)

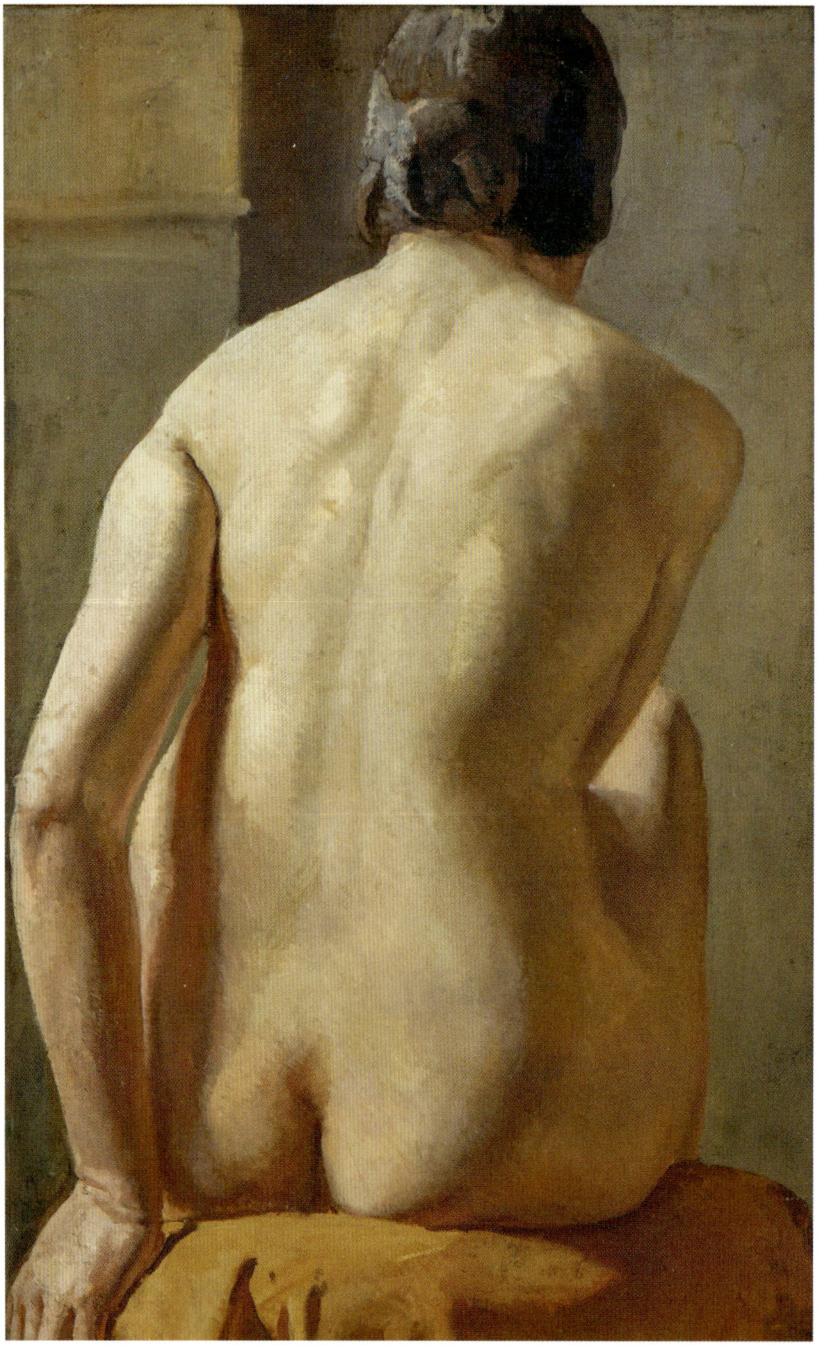

**94 Margaret Maitland Howard** (1898-1983), *Female Nude Seated, Rear View*, C.1920, oil on canvas 30 x 19 ¾ in. (76.5 x 50 cm).

**95 Margaret Maitland Howard** (1898-1983), *Female Nude, Seated, Three-Quarter Rear View*, c.1920, oil on canvas, 35 ¾ x 21 in. (91 x 51.5 cm).

Even after it became acceptable, early in the 20th century, for women to attend art school, drawing from a live model, rather than plaster casts, was often considered inappropriate. For at least the first half of the century it remained the case that women artists were discouraged from the nude as a genre.

The critic Alfred Lys Baldry observed in an article in *The Studio* (1925), that women painters had a 'plain matter of fact' approach to the painting of nudes suggesting that 'the frank fidelity of the woman artist', shared none of the characteristics of the 'idealized rendering of the female nude as seen by a male painter'.

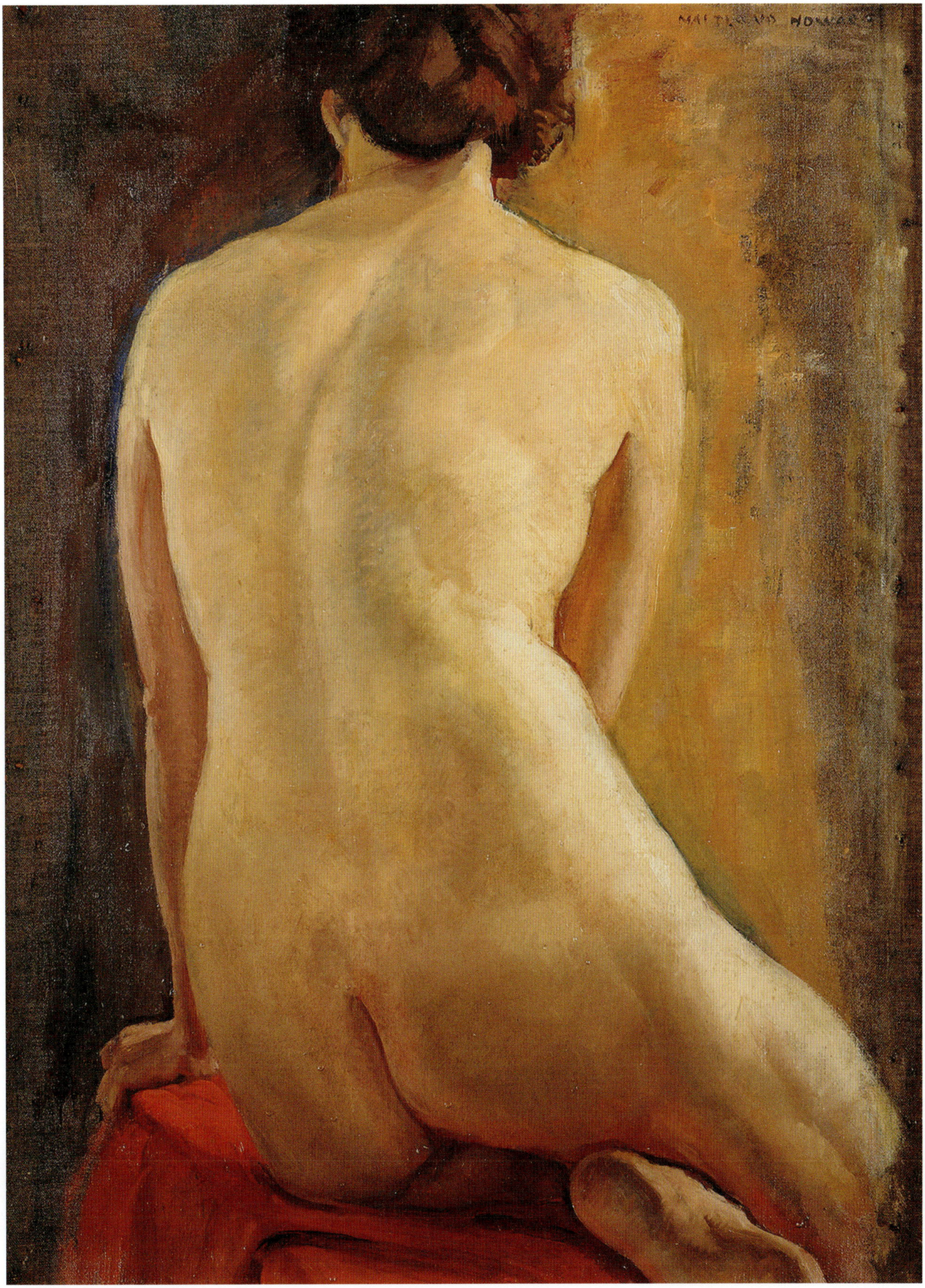

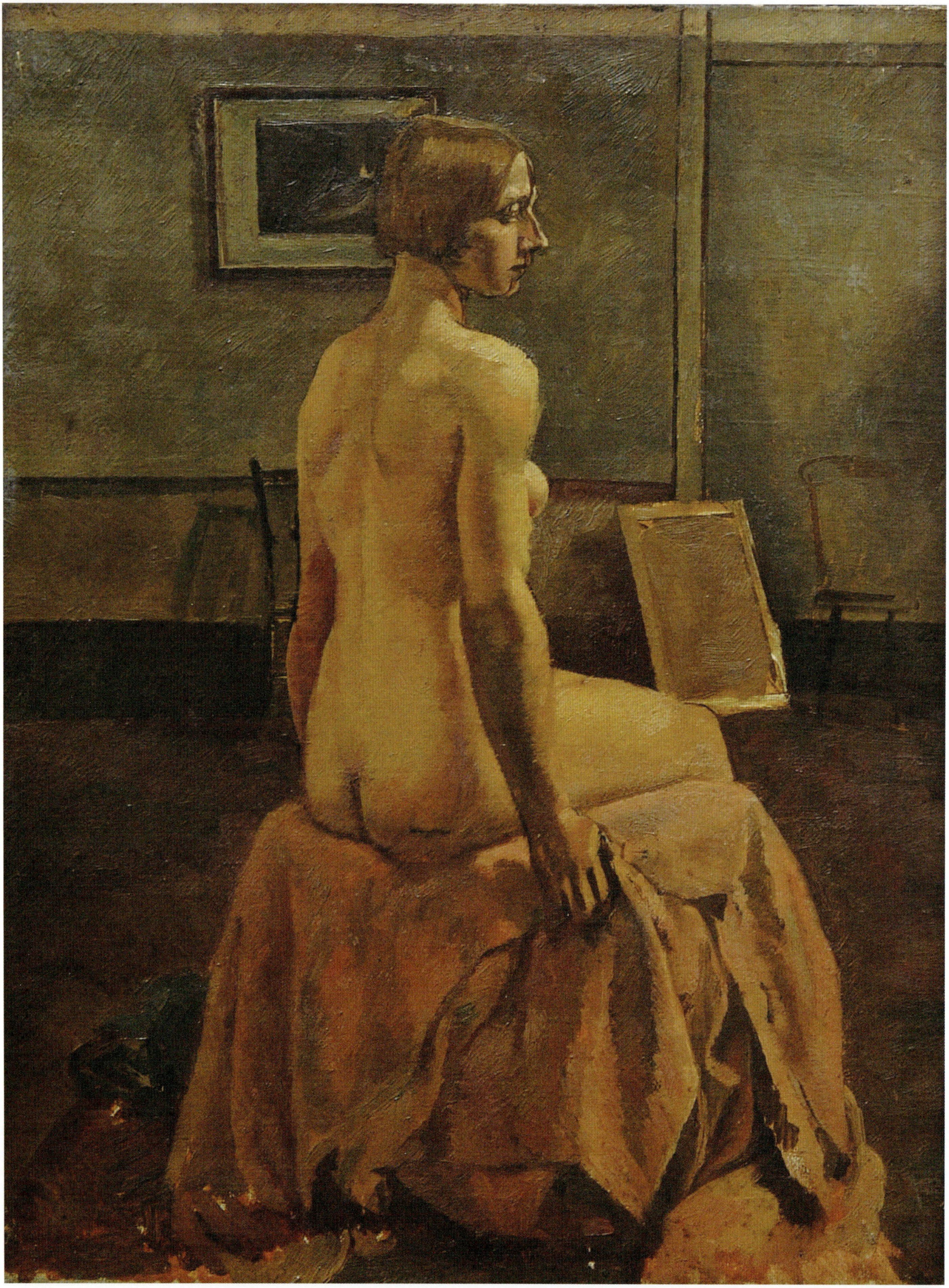

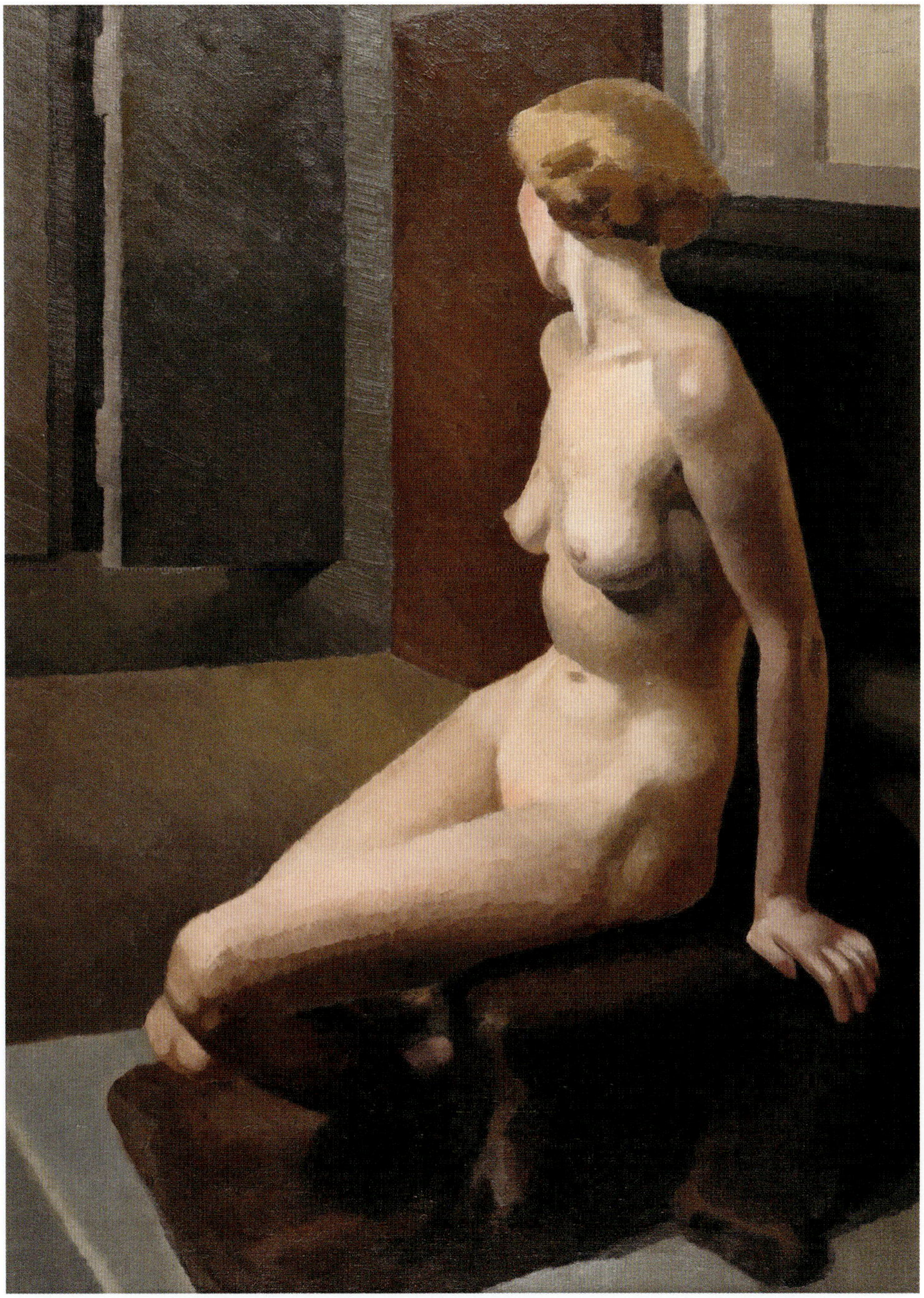

**97 Phoebe Willetts-Dickinson** (1917-1978), *A Seated Model in the Studio*, late 1930s, oil on canvas, 30 x 22 in. (76 x 56 cm).

Although by the interwar period it had become common for women attending art school to paint in the life class, some observers were still unenthusiastic. The idea that there was as 'something dangerously near to vulgarity' – as *The Times* critics had described Laura Knights' iconic *Self-portrait* (1913) – still lingered on.

**96 Percy Horton** (1897-1970), *A Seated Model in the Studio, Three Quarter Rear View*, c.1925, signed with studio stamp to canvas reverse (3/6), oil on canvas (D. Robertson and Co), 22 x 16 in. (56 x 40.5 cm).

During WWI Percy Horton became a conscientious objector and was sentenced to two years hard labour in Calton Prison, Edinburgh from 1916 to 1918. After the war he took up his studies again at the Central School of Art (1918-20) and then the Royal College of Art (1922-24). The culmination of a distinguished career was his appointment as Master of Drawing at the Ruskin School, 1949-64.

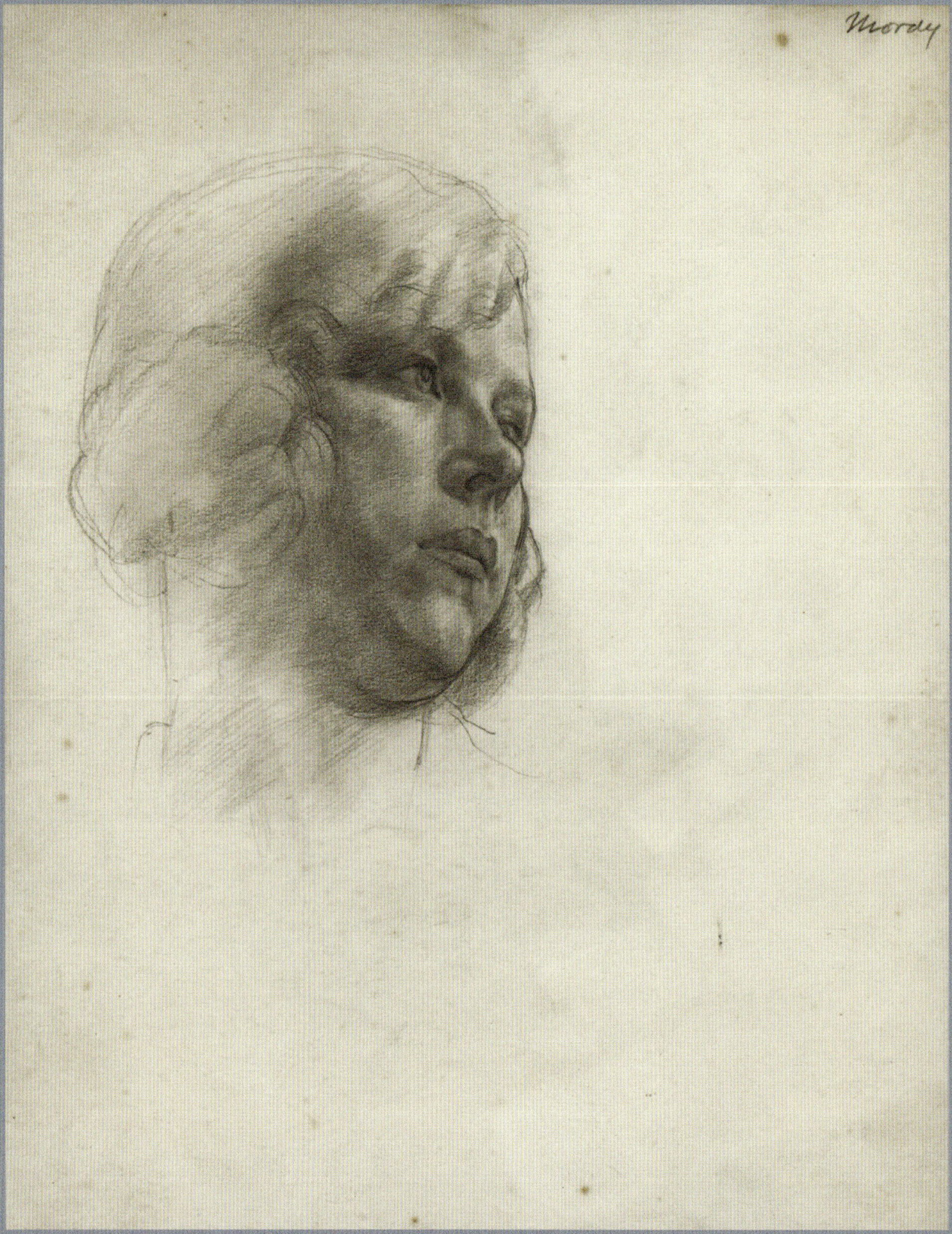


**98 Victor Hume Moody** (1896-1990), *Portrait of a Young Girl*, c.1920, signed, pencil on paper, 11 ¾ × 9 ½ in. (30 × 24 cm).

Moody's art school training lasted seven years, of which much was spent drawing from plaster casts and models. He struggled in the life drawing classes because of his short-sightedness, while his tutors enforced a recommended distance between students and models. As a result many of Moody's drawings were made at home and were based on studies of his family.

**99 David Foggie** (1878-1948), *Study of a Young Girl in a Green Dress with Yellow Floral Ornamentation*, c.1920, signed, oil on panel, 19 ¼ × 14 in. (49 × 36 cm).

The model in this study is the artist's future wife. A more formal portrait of her is in the collection of Dundee Art Gallery.

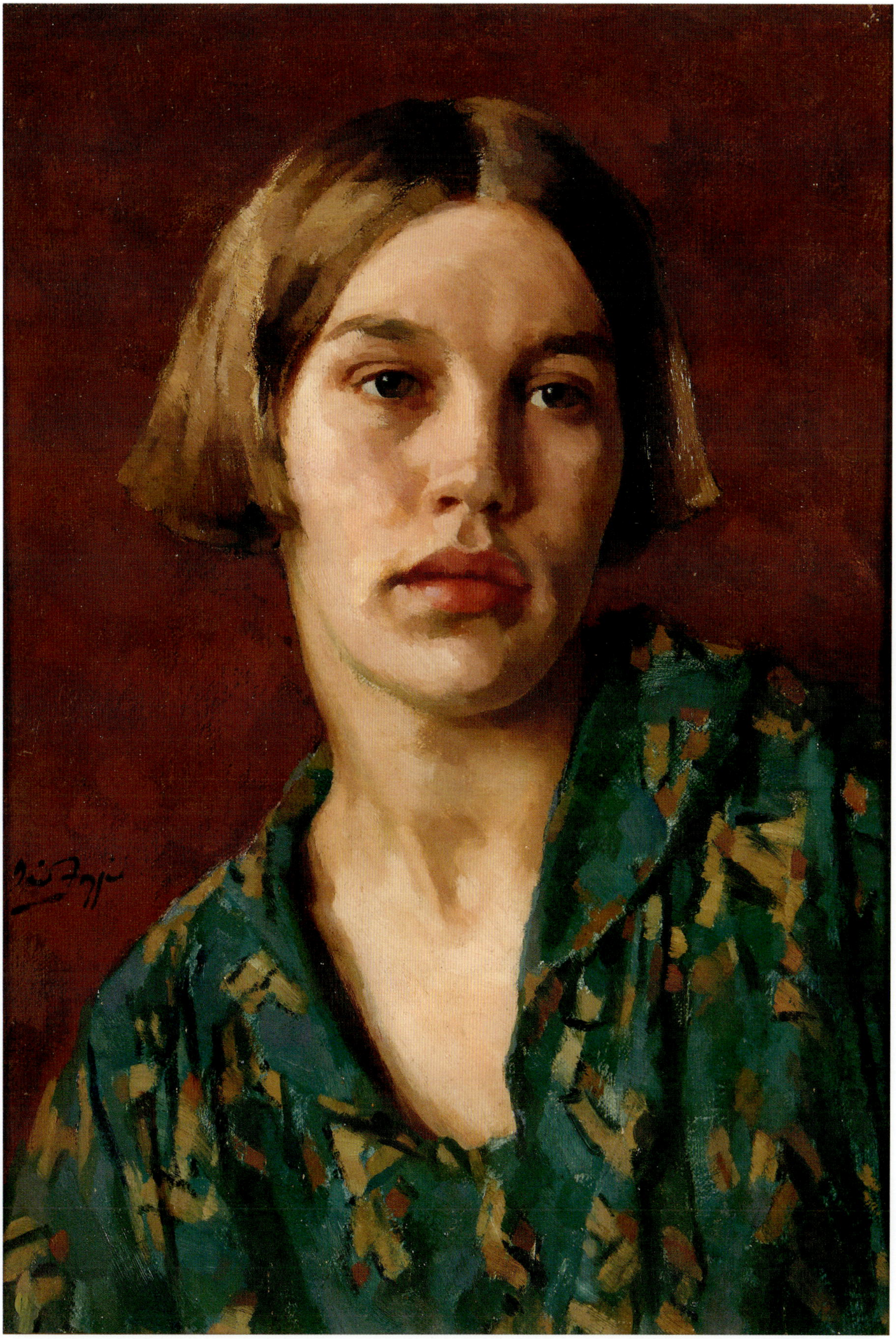

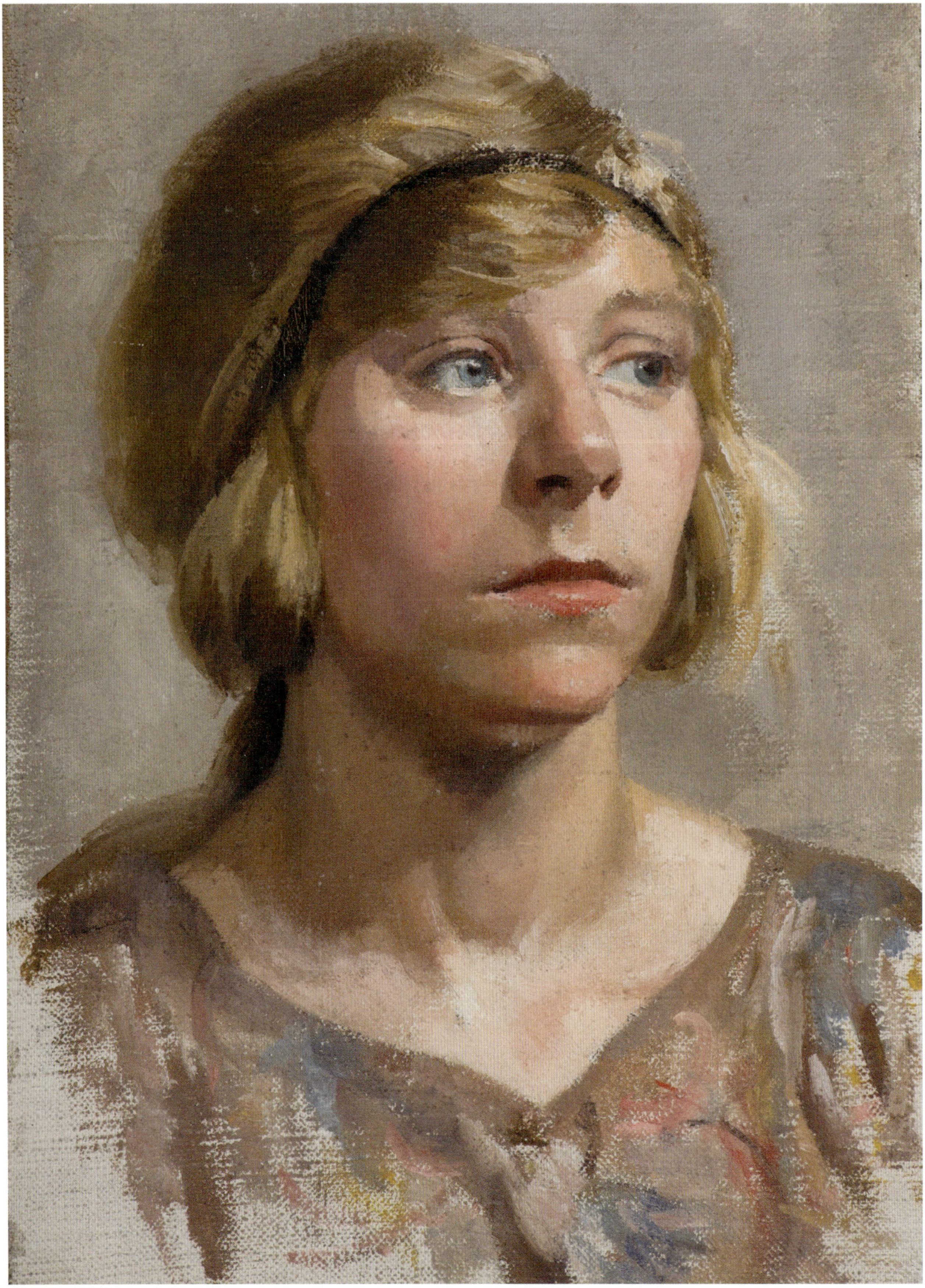

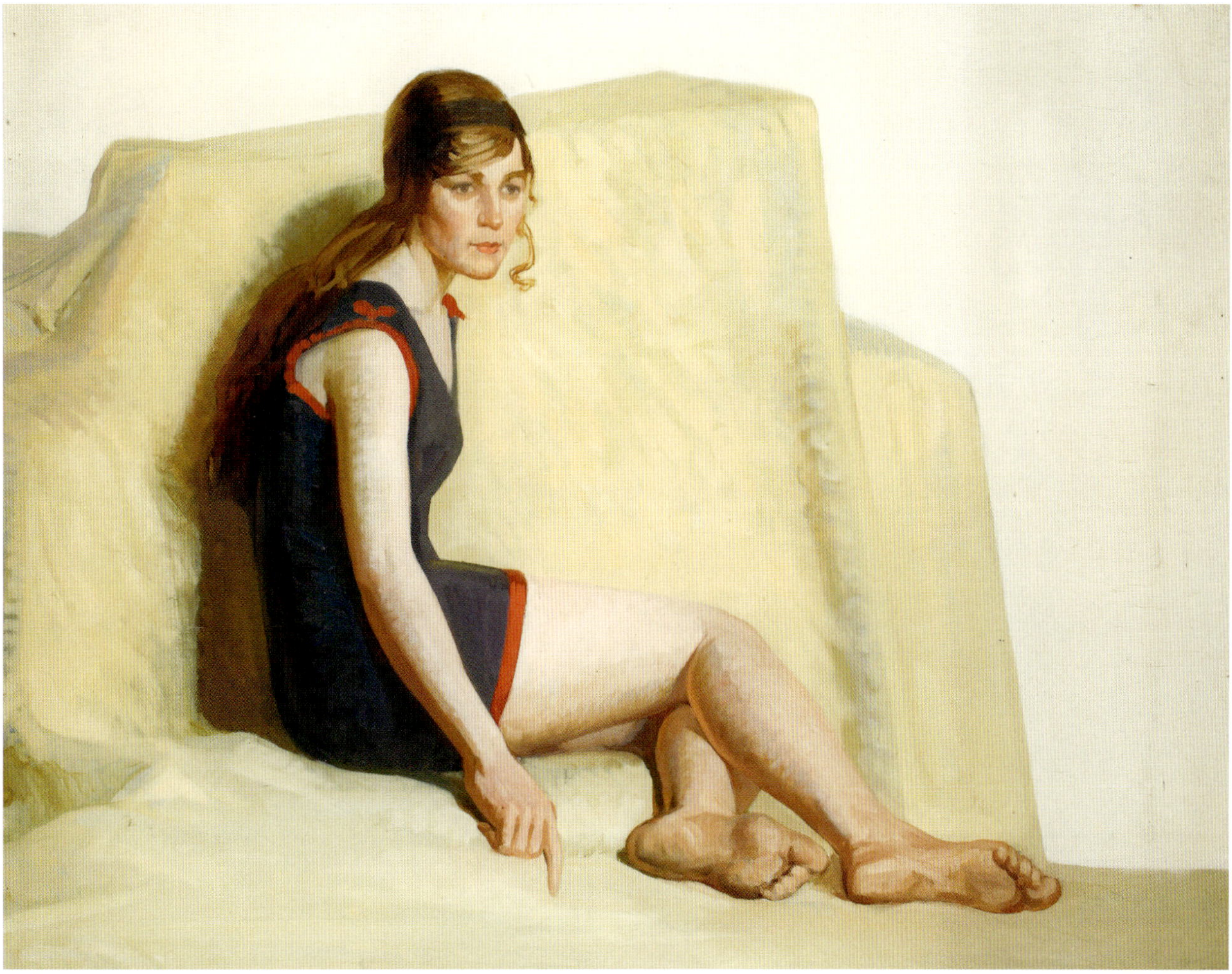

**101 Harold Dearden** (1888–1962), *Model in Bathing Suit, Posing in the Artist's Studio*, c.1922, signed on the reverse, oil on canvas, 32 × 42 in. (81.3 x 106.7 cm).

Painted in the artist's Oakley Street studio in Chelsea, this work depicts a model posed as if at the beach, with cliff-like forms simulated behind through the use of studio props.

**100 Phyllis Dodd** (1899-1995), *Portrait of a Young Woman* (possibly Muriel Minter), early 1920s, oil on canvas, 13 ¾ x 10 in. (35.3 x 25.4 cm).

Muriel Minter attended the Royal College of Art from 1921-23. Her peers included Ray Coxon and his future wife Edna Ginesi, Phyllis Dodd and her future husband Douglas Percy Bliss, and Gerald Cooper who Minter married in 1928. Portraits of many of theses students, Cooper and Minter amongst them, are included in Dodd's early Royal College of Art figure composition of a Baptismal group (**186, 187,188**).

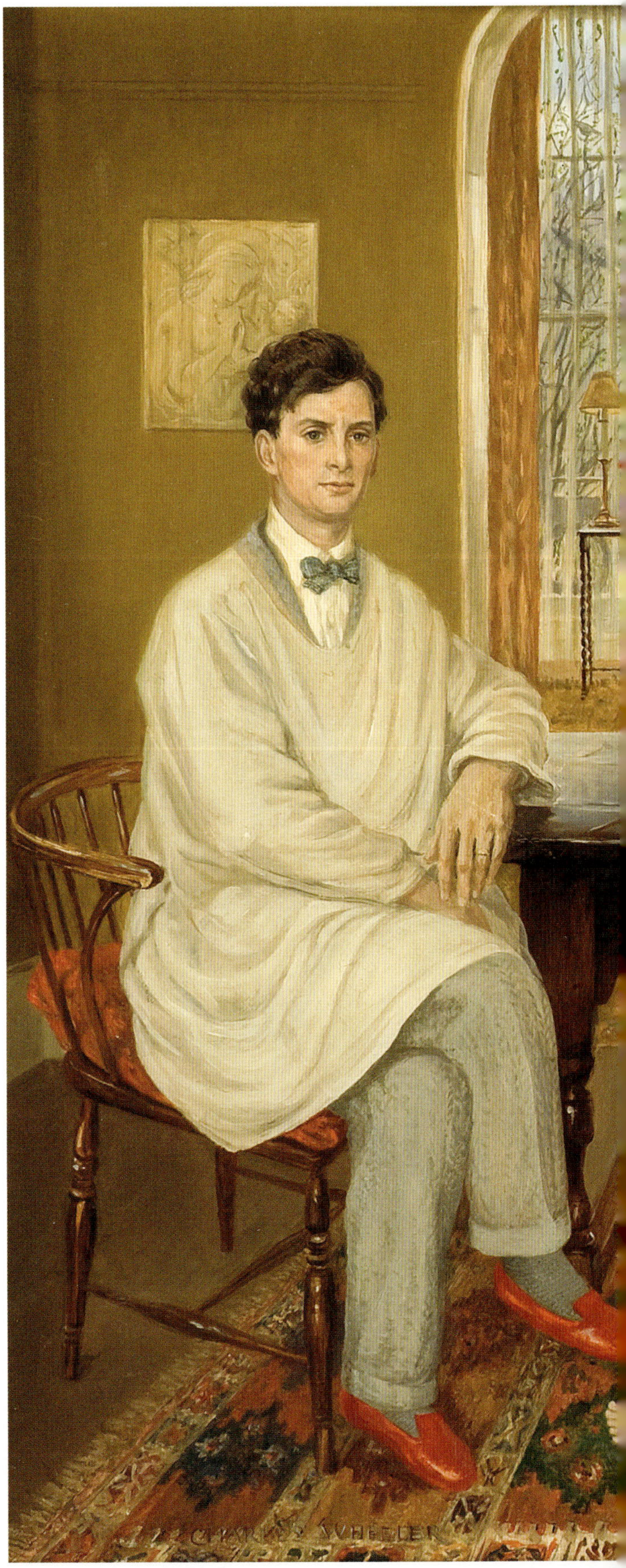

**102 Muriel Wheeler** (1888-1979), *Self and Family*, 1933, signed and dated, oil on panel, 21 ¾ x 28 in. (55.3 x 70.8 cm).

Although Muriel Wheeler produced predominantly sculpture after 1925, this accomplished family group dates to 1933. It includes portraits of her children Robin and Carol and her husband Charles (later Sir Charles, PRA) who is shown wearing an artist's smock. The setting is the dining-room of the Wheeler family home at 21 Tregunter Road, in South Kensington.

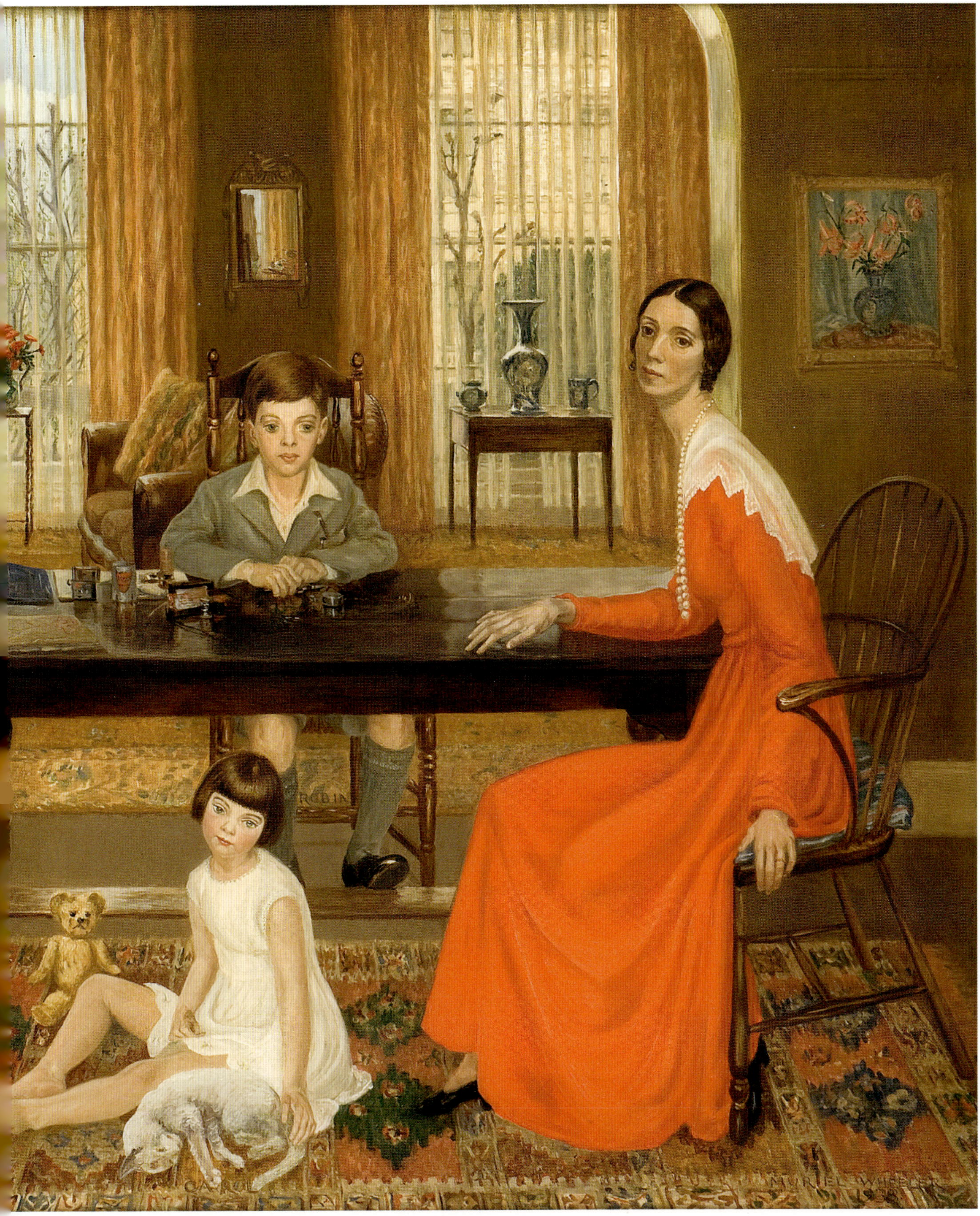
ROBIN
CAROL
MURIEL WHEELER

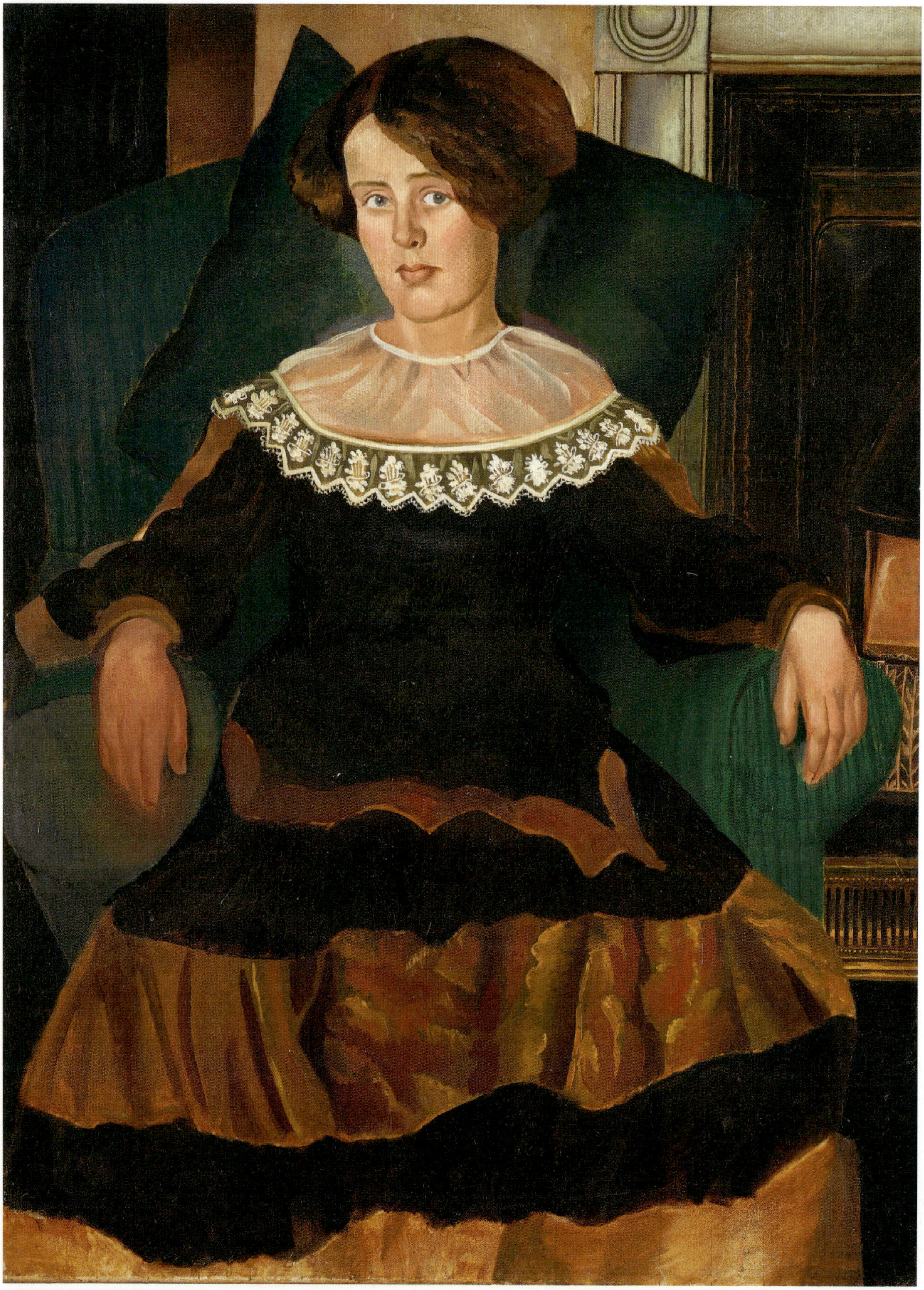

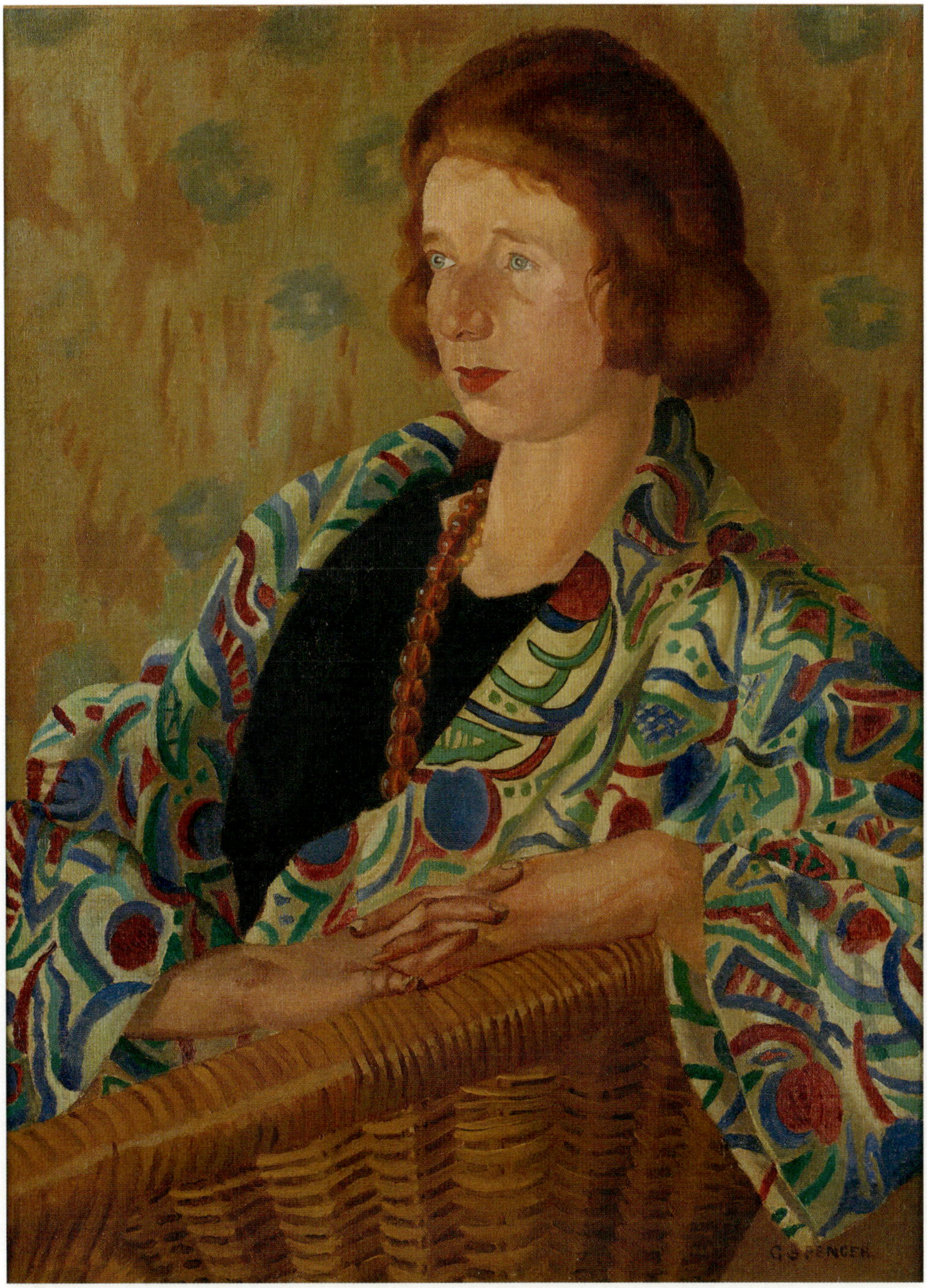


**104 Gilbert Spencer** (1892-1979), *Portrait of Joyce Peters*, signed, oil on canvas, 25 ½ x 17 ½ in. (65 x 45 cm).

Joyce Peters, an associate of the Bloomsbury Group, was a dancer. A life-long friend of Gilbert Spencer, she helped him secure a number of portrait commissions.

**103 Gilbert Spencer** (1892-1979), *Portrait of Doreen Harter*, mid 1920s, oil on canvas, 38 x 28 ½ in. (97 x 73 cm).

Doreen Harter was Sydney Carline's sister-in-law, and part of the artistic community in Hampstead of which Stanley and Gilbert Spencer were leading figures. Both Doreen and her sister Gwen were stage actresses.

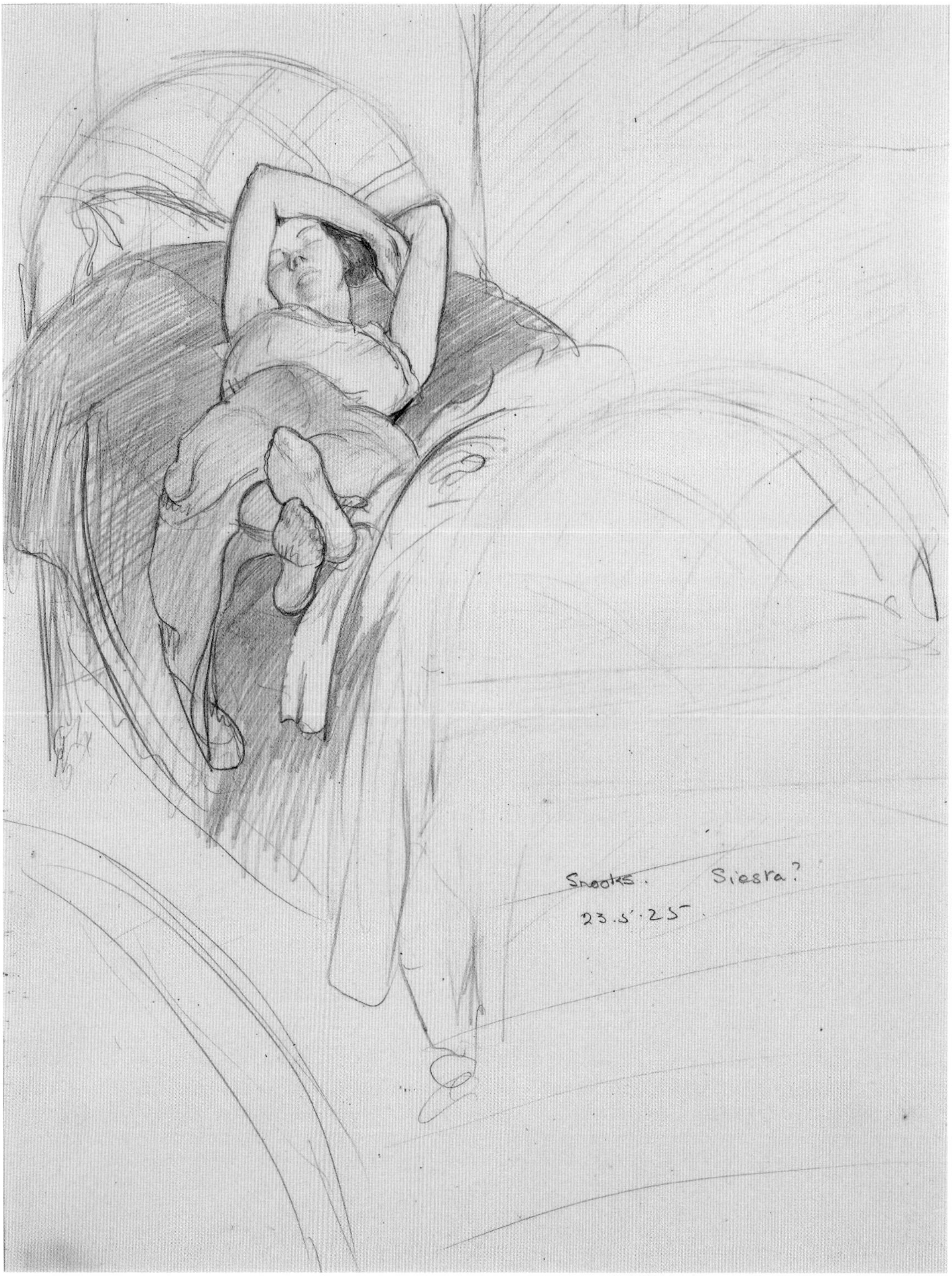


**105 Louise Larking** (fl 1920 to 1950), *Snooks, Siesta?*, 1925
pencil on paper, 10 ¼ x 7 ¼ in. (26 x 18.5 cm).

Figures reclining were a staple of art school training allowing students to hone their skills both in anatomy and perspective. Drawings made in the Life Room, often as timed exercises, formed a major part of all art school curricula. Thus Percy Horton's drawing, made towards the end of his time at Brighton School of Art, is inscribed '3 hours'. His training was cut short by WW1 when, as a conscientious objector, he was sentenced to two years of hard labour in Calton Prison, Edinburgh. Figures sleeping, in a domestic setting, afforded a similar opportunity to artists outside the life class. (**121**)

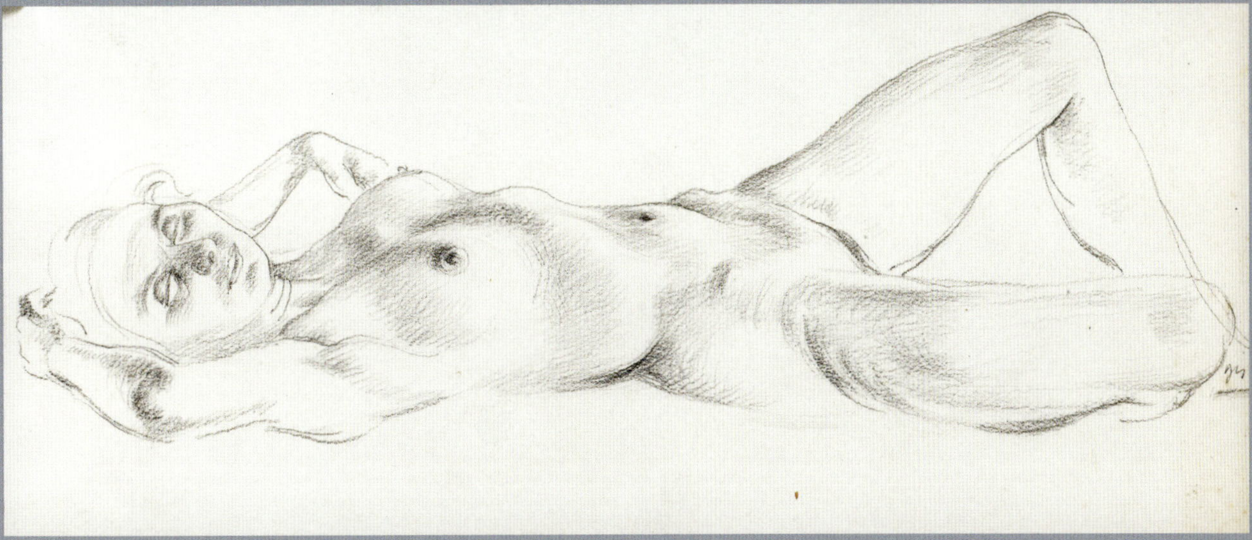

**106** **John Cecil Stephenson** (1889-1965), *Sleeping Female Nude*, c.1944, signed with initials, pencil on paper, 19 x 11 ½ in. (49 x 29 cm).

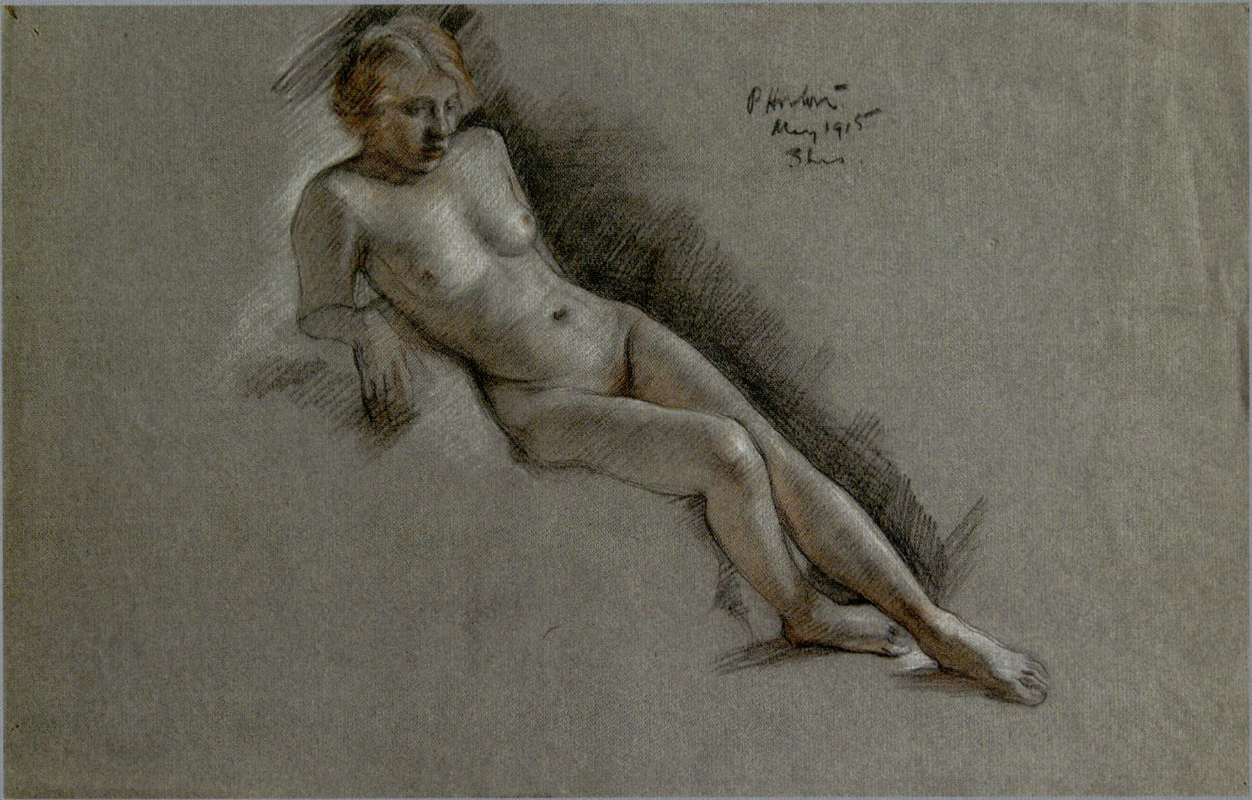

**107** **Percy Horton** (1897-1970), *Reclining Nude*, 1915, signed and dated, inscribed '3 hours', pastel and chalk on paper, 10 ¼ x 18 in. (26 x 45 cm).

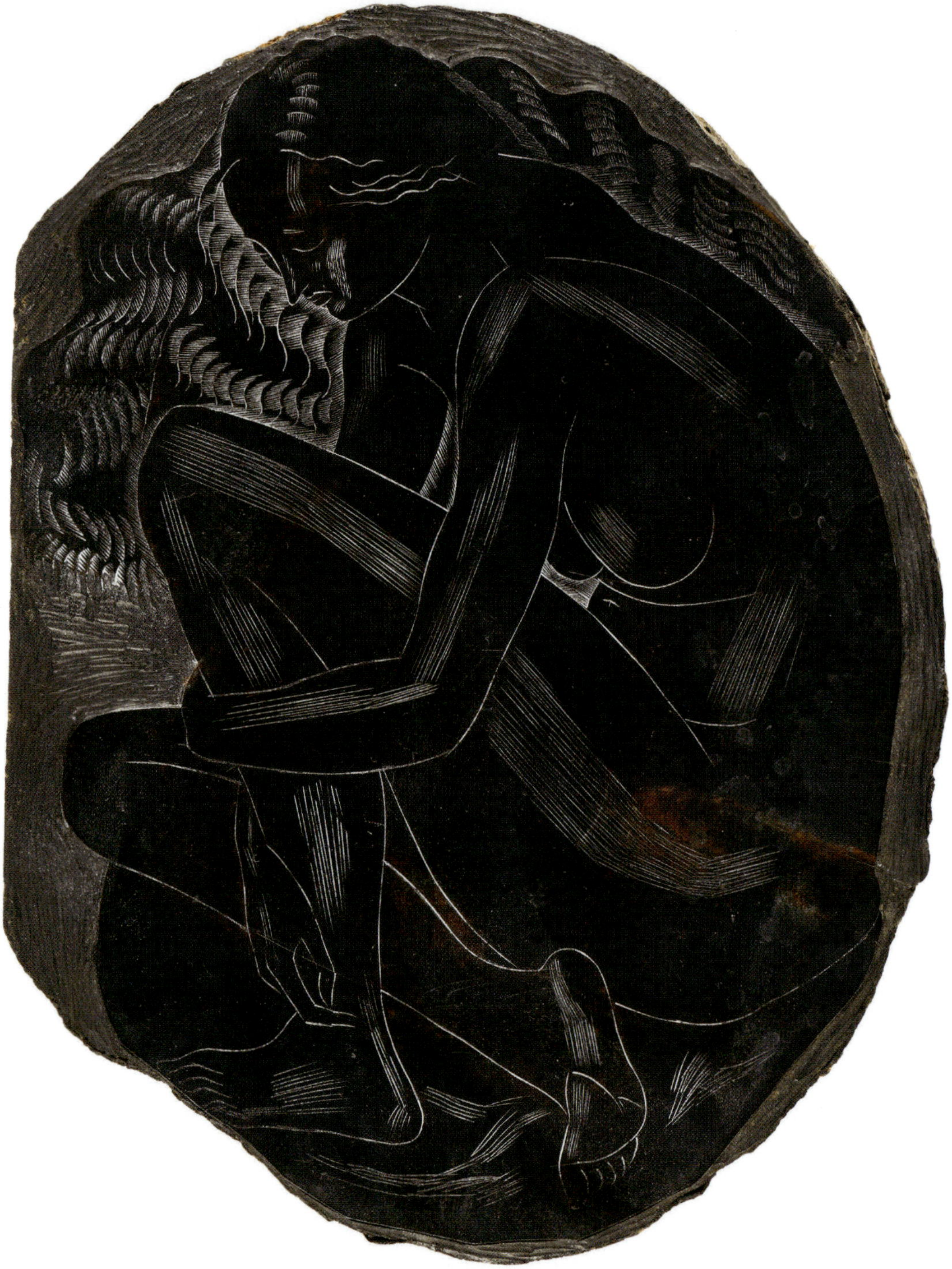

**108 Leon Underwood** (1890-1975), *Crouching Nude*, mid-1920s, original wood block 7 x 5 ¾ in. (17.8 x 14.8 cm).

Underwood began to produce wood engravings around 1924 at the same time as his early experiments with stone carving. At his Brook Green School Underwood offered an alternative art training to some of the most gifted artists of the inter-war generation, including Henry Moore, Eileen Agar, Blair Hughes-Stanton, and Gertrude Hermes. In 1925 Underwood and his pupils were to form the English Wood Engraving Society, reflecting the fact that their progressive imagery was at odds with the nostalgic work of many pastoral engravers of the same period. (**44**)

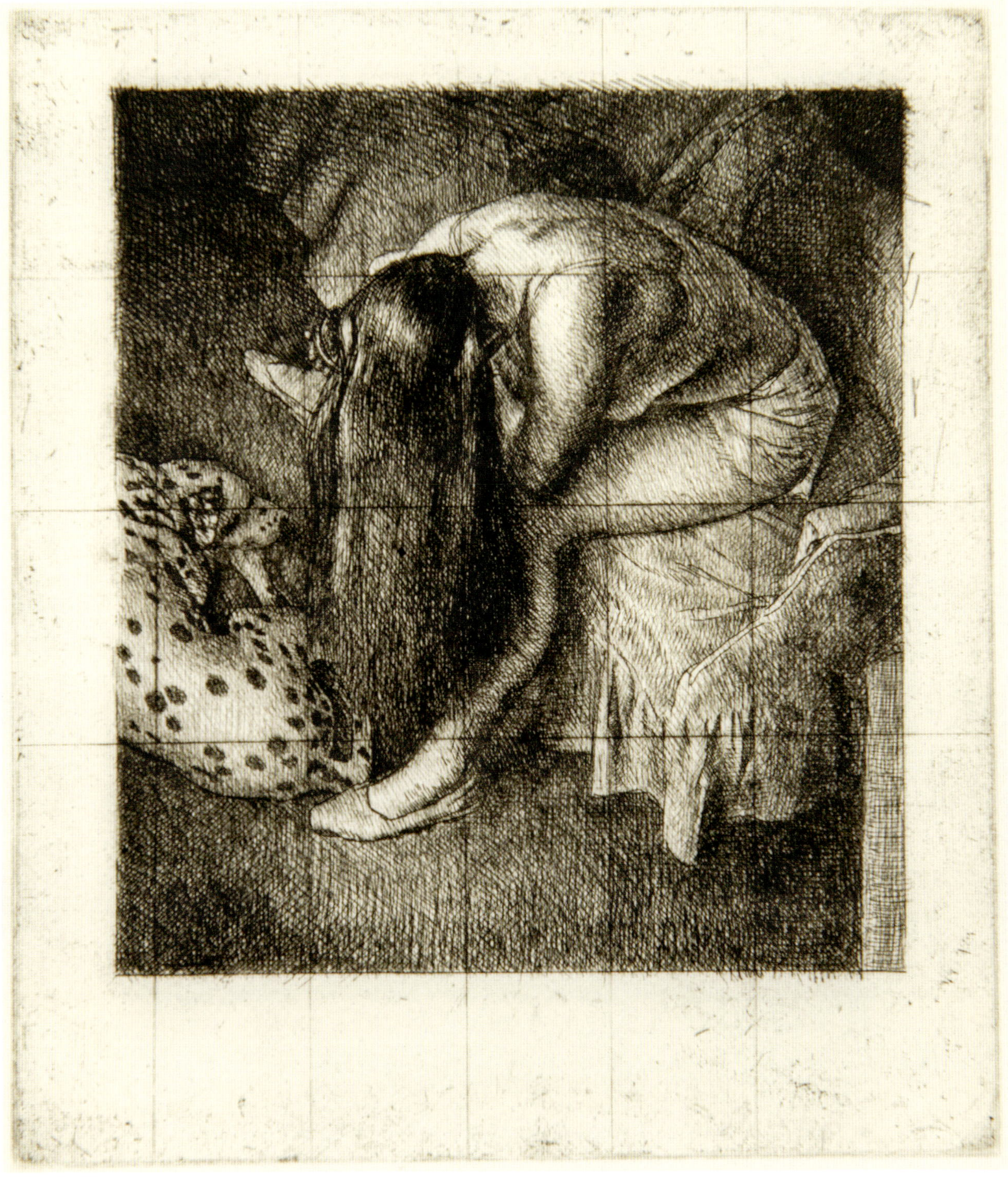

**109 Robert Austin** (1895-1973), *Girl Brushing Her Hair*, c. 1938,
etching on paper, (printed from the cancelled plate): 7 ½ x 6 ½ in. (19 x 16.5 cm), print: 11 x 9 ½ in. (28 x 24.5 cm).

Although Robert Austin's formidable reputation was secured by his line engravings of the mid to late 1920s, it was in the 1930s that he produced some of his most attractive engravings, often featuring single figures engaged in domestic activities: *Young Mother* (1935), *Girl on Stairs* (1937) and *Girl by a Gate* (1938). *Girl Brushing Her Hair*, which forms part of this series, has the added attraction of including the artist's Dalmatian, who was also the subject of a print titled 'Ling of Lingard' dating to 1936 (**141**, **142**).

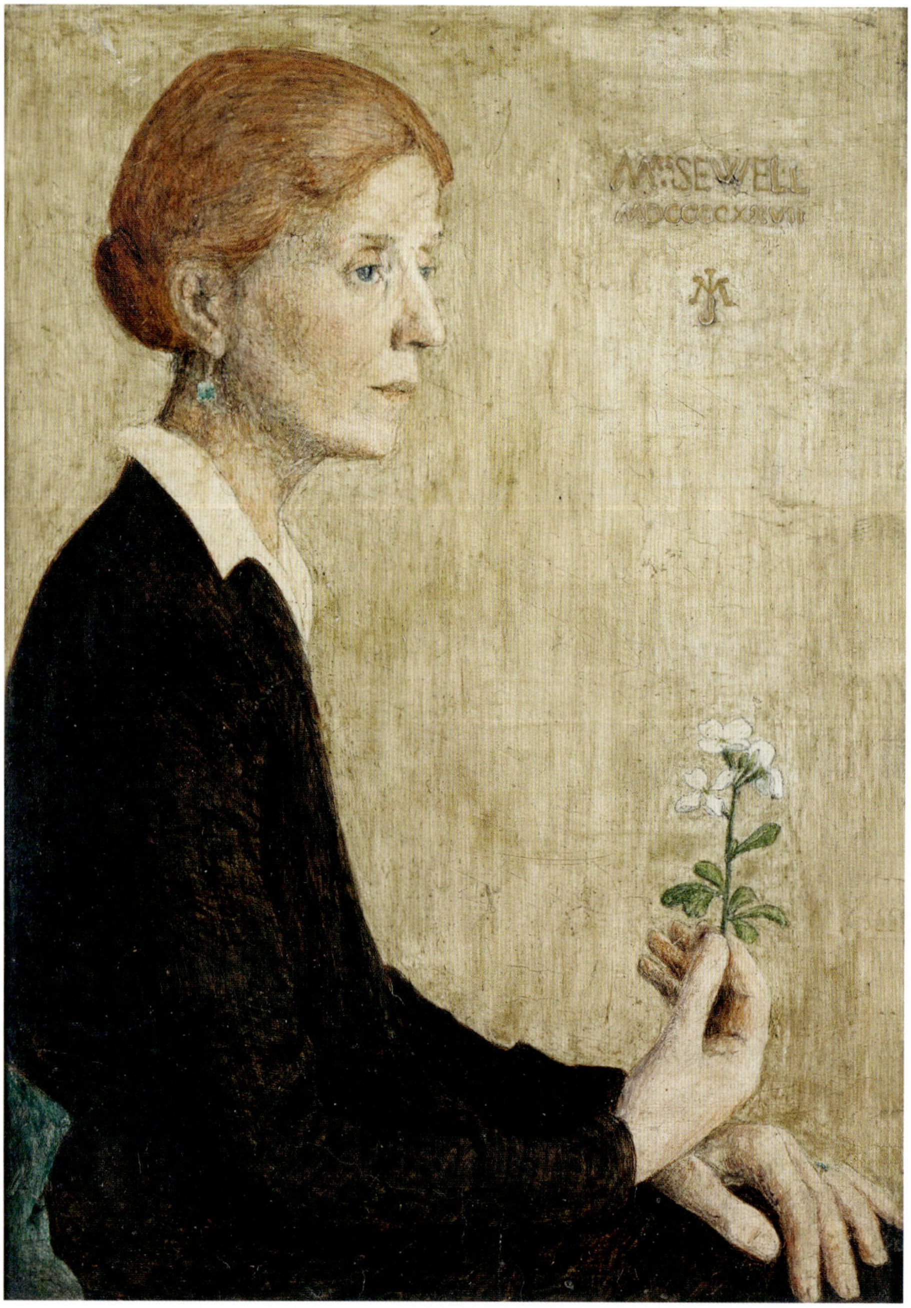


**110 John Moody** (1906-1993), *Margaret Sewell*, 1927,
egg tempera on board, 8 ¼ x 6 in. (20.9 x 15.2 cm).

Margaret Ley, a gifted miniaturist, and William Sewell, a talented artist and book illustrator, first met when students at Herkomer's Art School. In this poignant portrait of 1927, John Moody expresses the grief felt by Margaret on the tenth anniversary of her husband William's death – he died in 1917, aged 41 – at the battle of Arras.

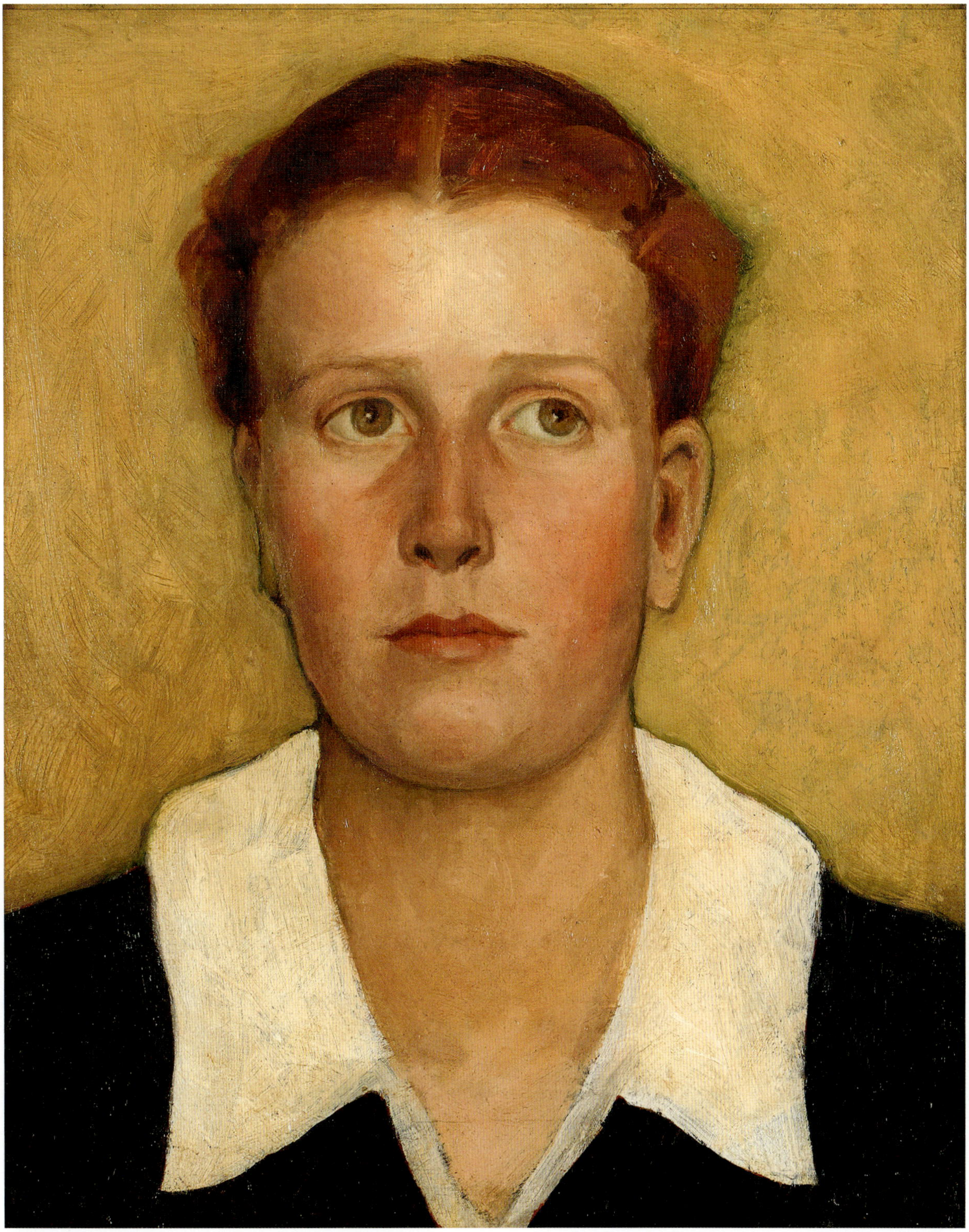

**111 John Moody** (1906-1993), *Portrait of Phillada Sewell*, mid 1920s, oil on canvas, 11 ½ x 9 ½ in. (29.5 x 24 cm).

John Moody and Phillada, the daughter of Margaret and William Sewell, were first cousins. Phillada was seven when her father died in 1917 at the battle of Arras. The bond she formed with her mother Margaret as a result was unbreakable. She trained first as a singer at the Webber Douglas School of Singing and Drama (John Moody and his future wife Nell Burra were also there) before moving into repertory theatre where she learned her trade as an actor. She appeared in numerous stage, television and big screen productions.

112

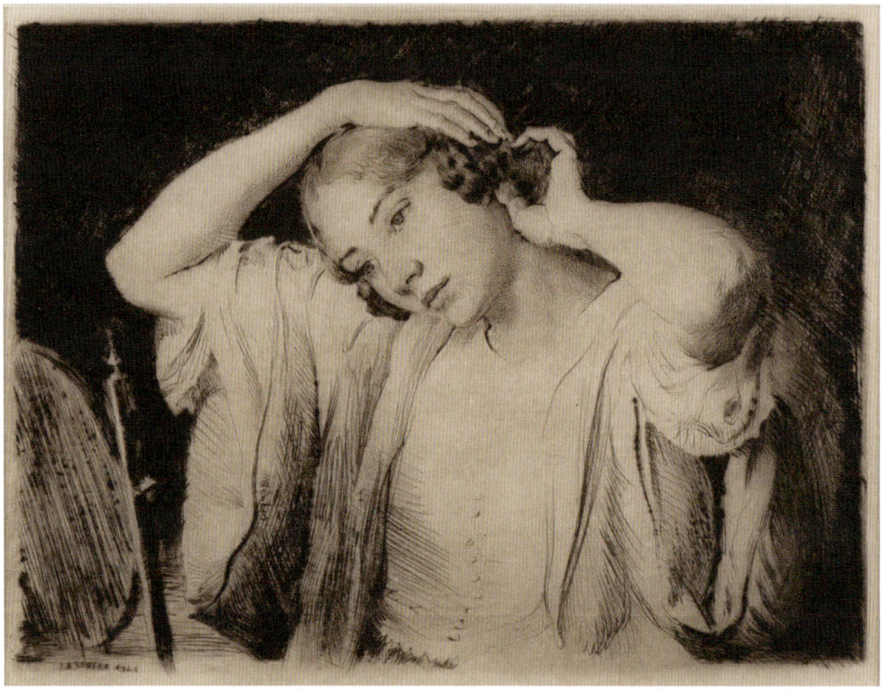

113

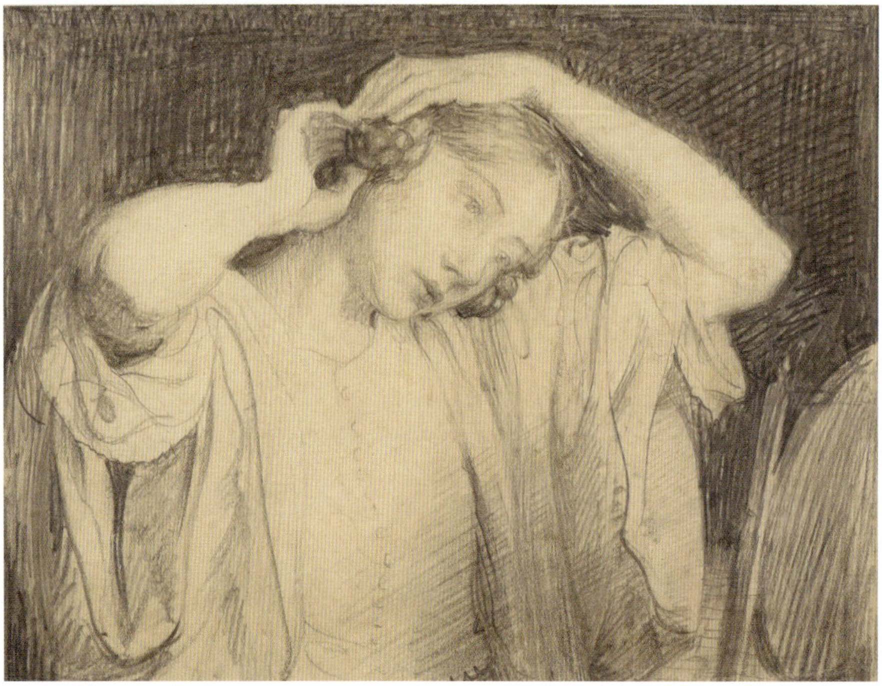

**John Bulloch Souter** (1890-1972),

**112** *The Artist's Wife, Dressing Her Hair*, 1925, signed and dated in the plate, etching on paper, 7 x 8 ¾ in. (17.8 x 22.3 cm).

**113** *The Artist's Wife, Dressing Her Hair*, 1925, pencil on paper, 7 x 8 ¾ in. (17.8 x 22.4 cm).

After serving in the Gordon Highlanders during WW1 Souter married and set up his studio in London, where he was able to find patrons for the portrait commissions that now formed the main part of his income. Christian, his wife, the subject of this sensitive drawing, also appears in the same pose (for which this is a study) in an etching. She is shown dressing her hair to cover her ears (*à la poissarde*).

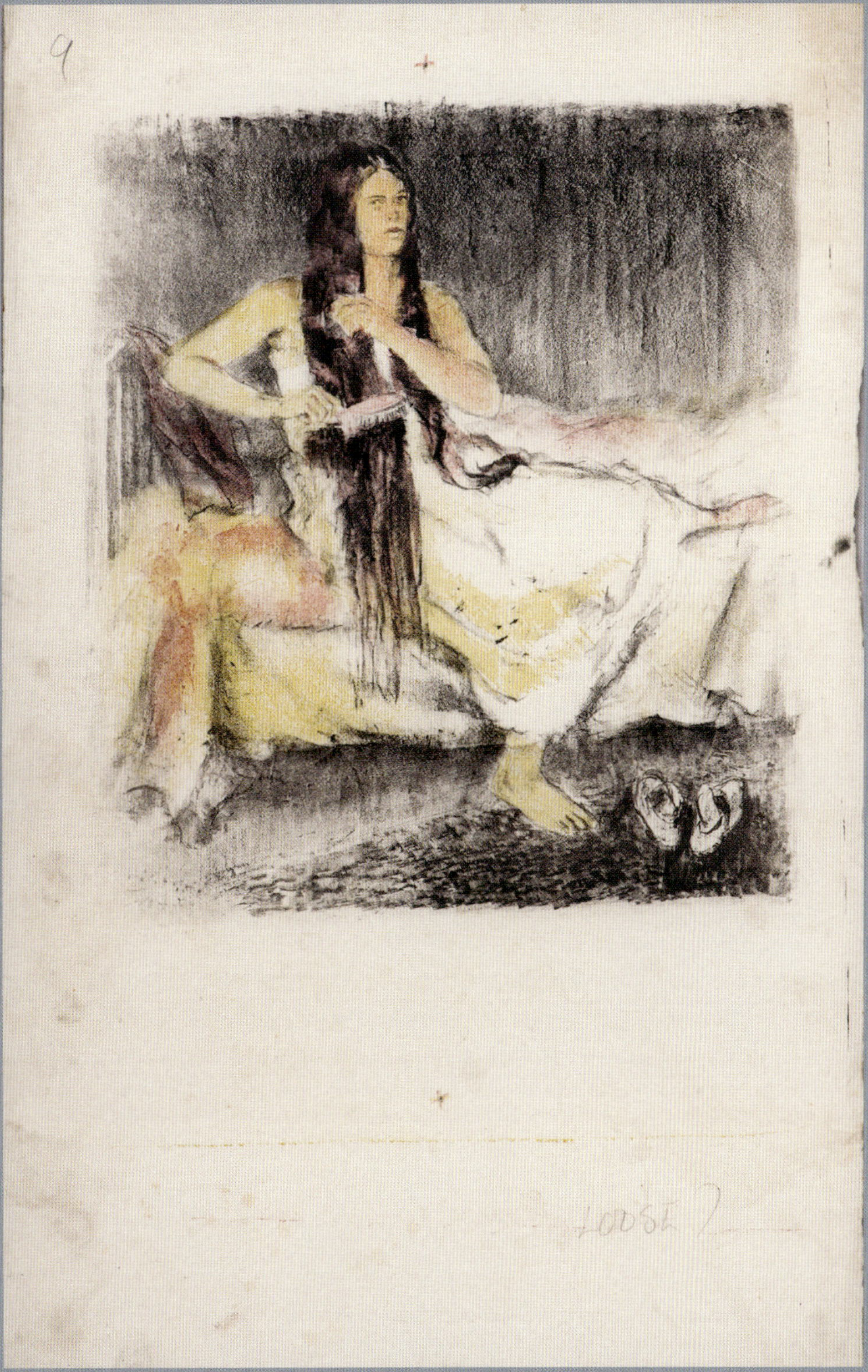

**114 James Fitton** (1899-1982), *Margaret Cook later Margaret (Peggy) Fitton*, 1925, lithograph, unique proof, image size 11 ½ x 10 ½ in. (29.2 x 26.7 cm).

Margaret Cook was a student at the Central School, where she met her future husband, James Fitton, a fellow-student three years her senior. He produced a related lithograph of Cook, in a studio setting rather than a bedroom, in the same year. In both pictures she is shown combing her long hair which she wore *à la poissarde*, wound into circular plaits over her ears.

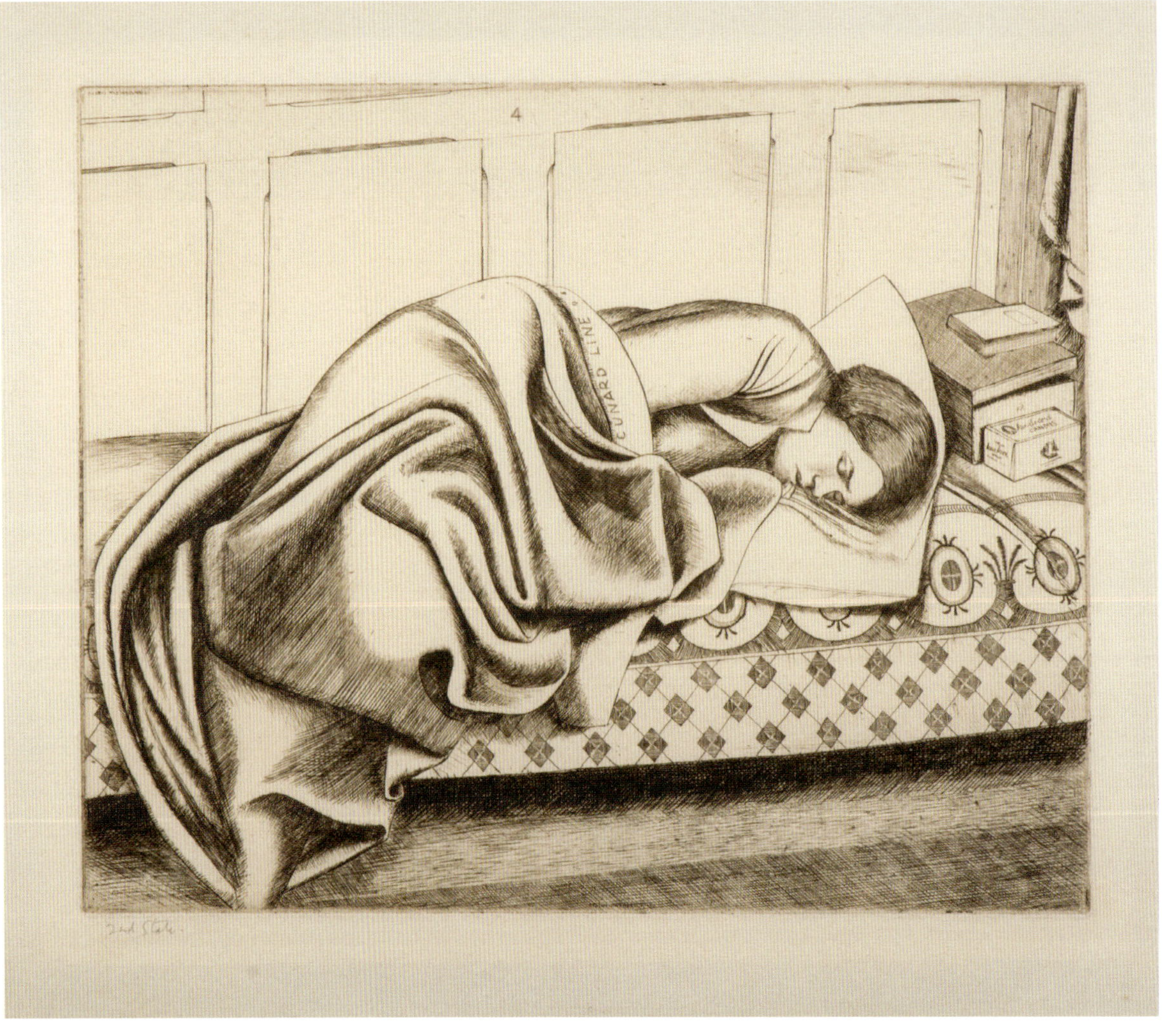


**115 Frederick Austin** (1902-1990), *Woman Sleeping (Cunard Line)*, 1932, etching, (2nd state) plate: 8 ¼ x 10 ¼ in. (21 x 26 cm) / paper: 11 ¾ x 12 ½ in. (30 x 34.5 cm).

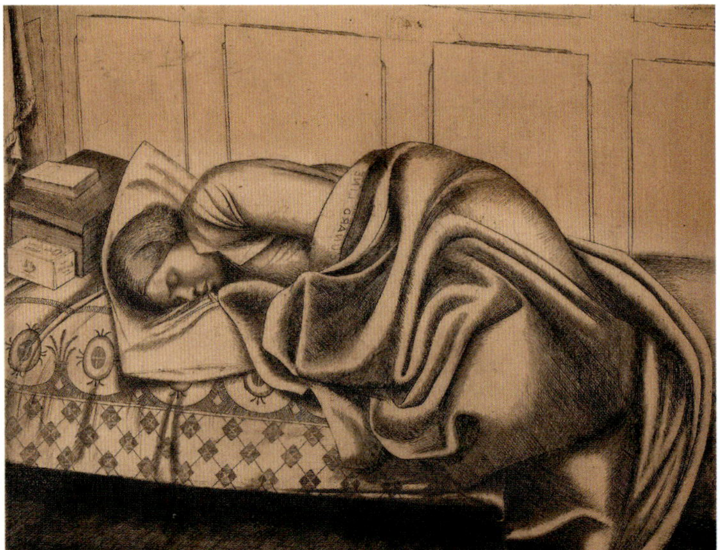

**116 Frederick Austin** (1902-1990), *Woman Sleeping (Cunard Line)*, 1932, original copper plate: 8 ¼ x 10 ¼ in. (21 x 26 cm).

This etching was created on the return from the Austin's honeymoon. The newly-wed Phyllis Austin (Keafsey), a Canadian opera singer, is shown sleeping in the cabin of the Cunard ship on which they sailed from Canada in 1932. A box of her favourite Laura Secord chocolates can be seen on the bedside table.

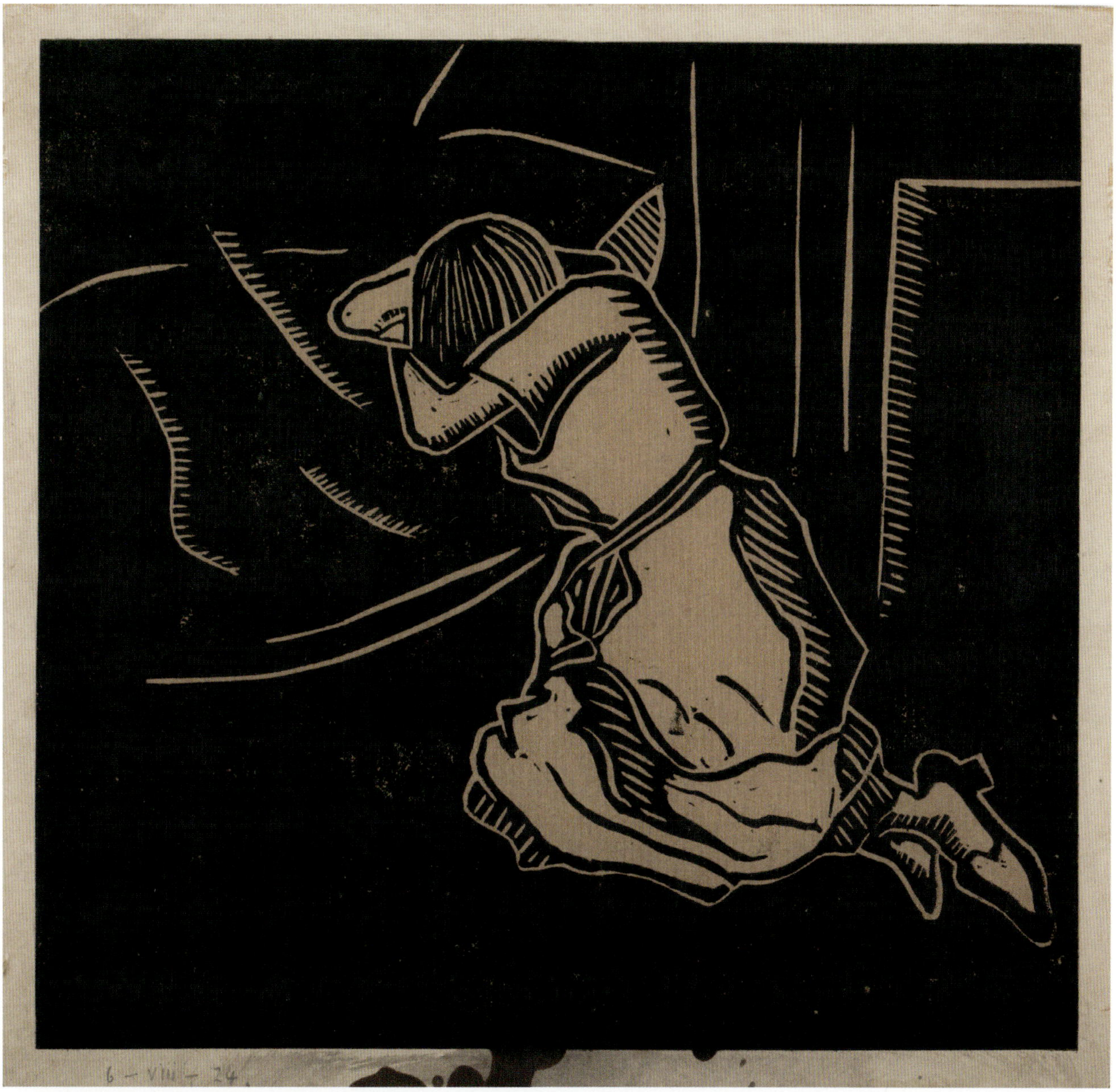

**117 Harry Epworth Allen** (1894-1958), *Study of the Artist's Future Wife Sleeping*, inscribed 6.viii. 24, pen and ink, 8 ¼ x 8 ¾ (21.2 x 22.2 cm).

In this early work by Allen, which dates to the period he was attending Sheffield Technical School of Art, the subject is portrayed in a reductive linear style that would later become the trademark of Allen's tempera paintings from the 1930s onwards. 'We are concerned primarily,' Allen wrote in 1942, 'with rhythm and design, and our colour must be employed for the purpose of reinforcing these fundamentals and strengthening form.'

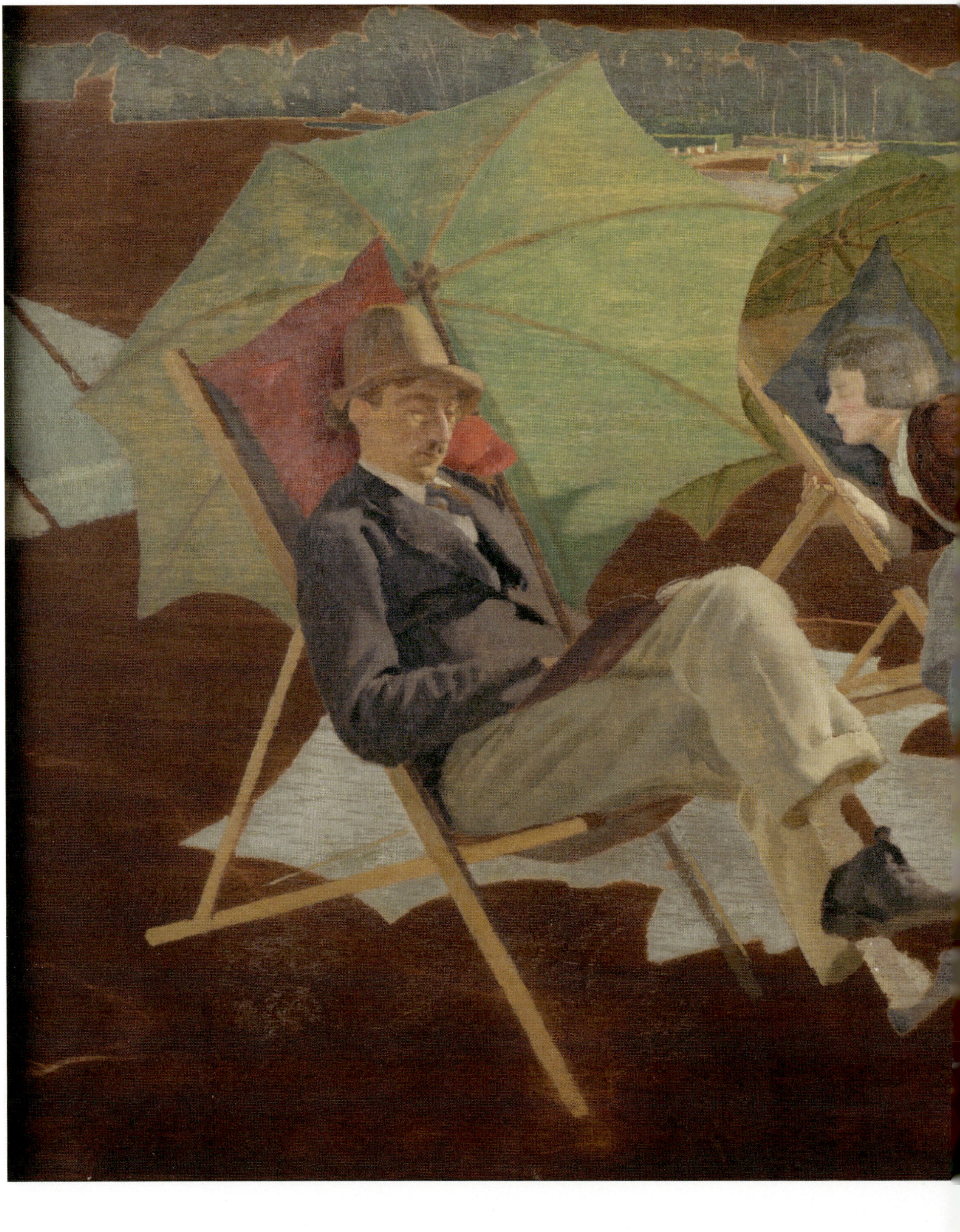

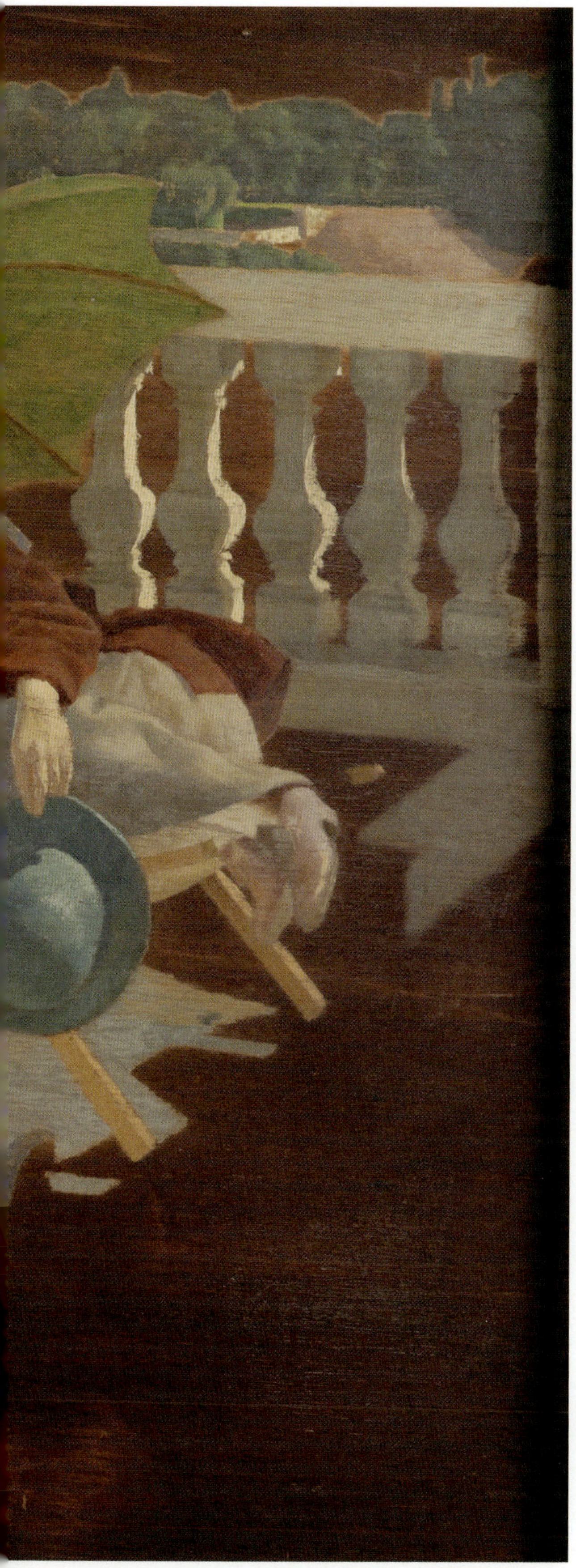

**118 Edward Irvine Halliday** (1902-1984),
*Roof-terrace of the British School at Rome*, 1926, signed and dated lower right, oil and tempera on panel, 14 ½ x 17 ½ in. (36.8 x 44.4 cm).

This evocative informal study shows Edward Halliday's fiancée, Dorothy Hatswell, and fellow-student Russell Meiggs (holder of the 1925 Pelham Studentship) relaxing in deck chairs on the roof terrace of the British School at Rome. A panoramic view of the Borghese Gardens can be seen behind.

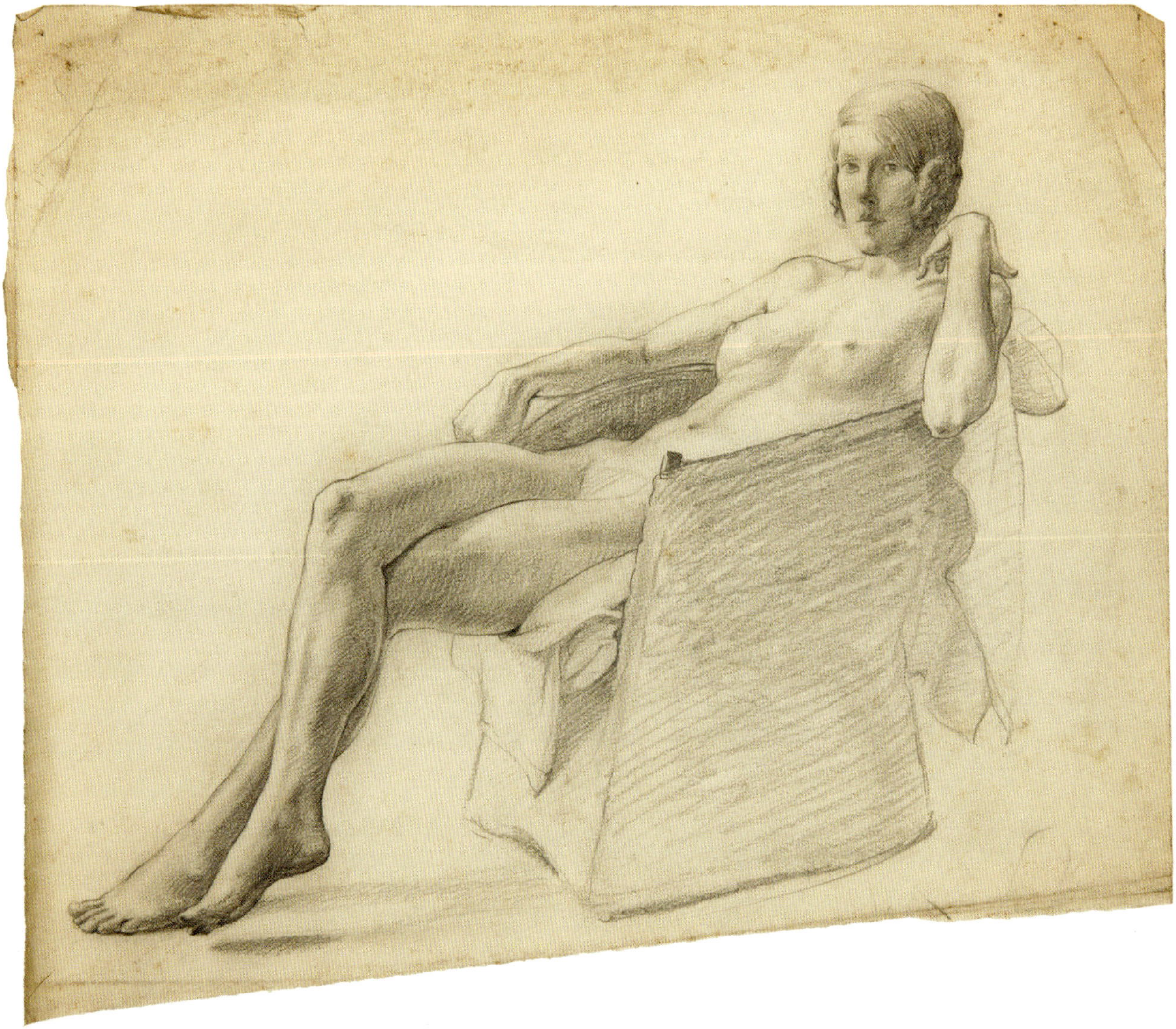

**119 Evelyn Dunbar** (1906-1960), *Seated Model with Hairstyle 'à la poissarde'*, early 1930s, pencil on paper, 12 ½ x 15 in. (32 x 38 cm).

As a student Evelyn Dunbar inevitably spent a lot of time in the life school at the Royal College of Art, but occasionally she did out-of-school life studies of fellow-students in non-approved postures, such as in this composition with its languidly posed model whose hair is dressed *à la poissarde*.

**120 Sir Gerald Festus Kelly** (1879-1972), *Portrait of Jane XIX*, inscribed 'XIX' on canvas edge, oil on canvas, 45 x 35 in. (114.3 x 88.9 cm).

Gerald Kelly first met Lilian Ryan in 1916, when she was working as an artist's model, and the two were married four years later. Affectionately nicknamed Jane, Kelly went on to depict her in over fifty oils, each numbered with a roman numeral, many of which were exhibited at the Royal Academy.

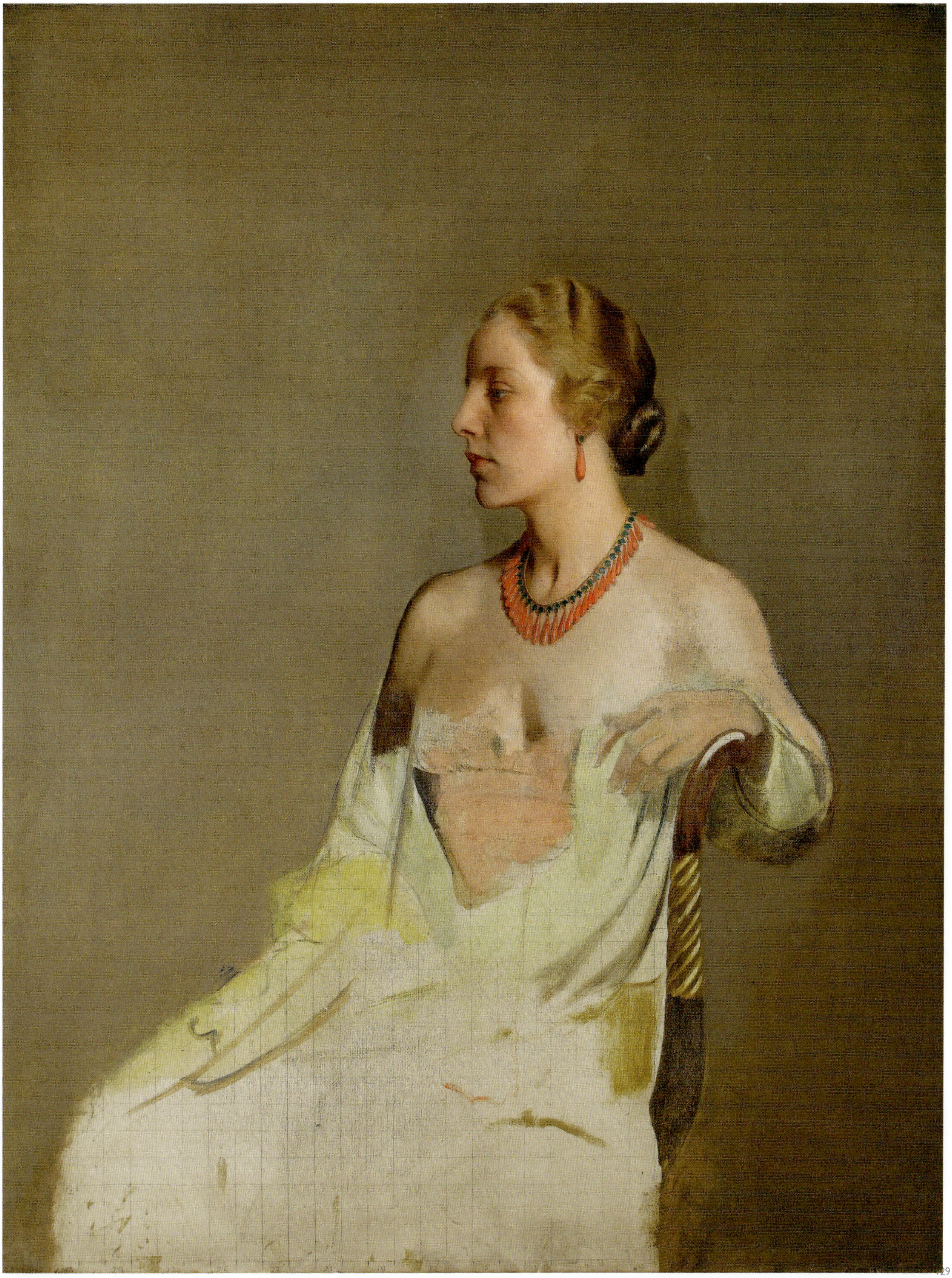

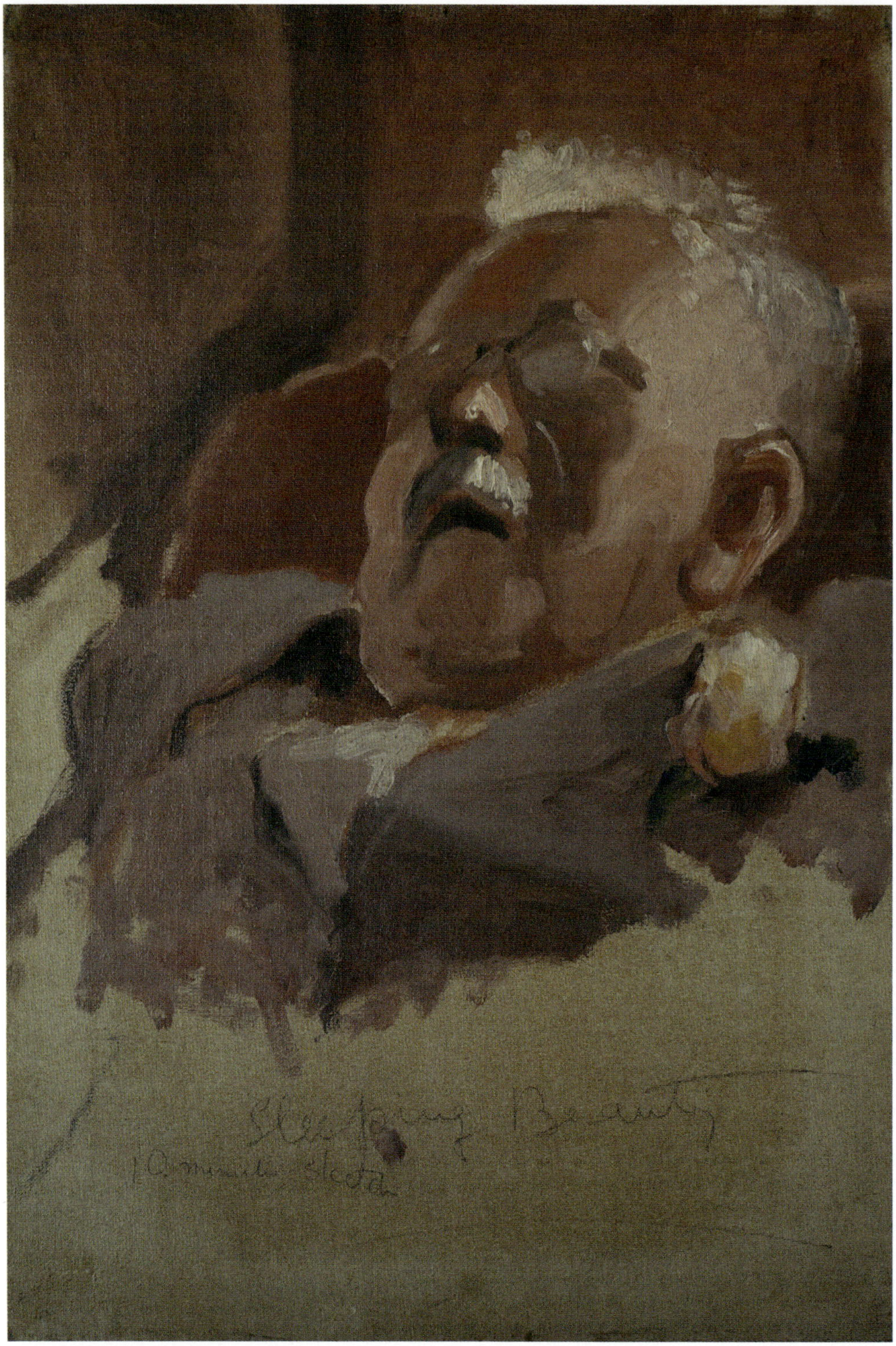


**121 Evelyn Dunbar** (1906-1960), *Sleeping Beauty, 10 minute sketch*, c.1928 (HMO 786),
inscribed in pencil with title,
oil on canvas, 19 x 13 in. (48 x 33 cm).

In this endearing portrait of her father, (in his mid 60s), Dunbar shows William having an after-lunch nap, during which he has slipped down inside his jacket. Always attentive to dressing well, as befitted a bespoke tailor, he wears a rose in his button-hole. The pencil inscription 'Sleeping Beauty 10 minute sketch', on the lower part of the canvas, appears to have been written by Florence, William's wife.

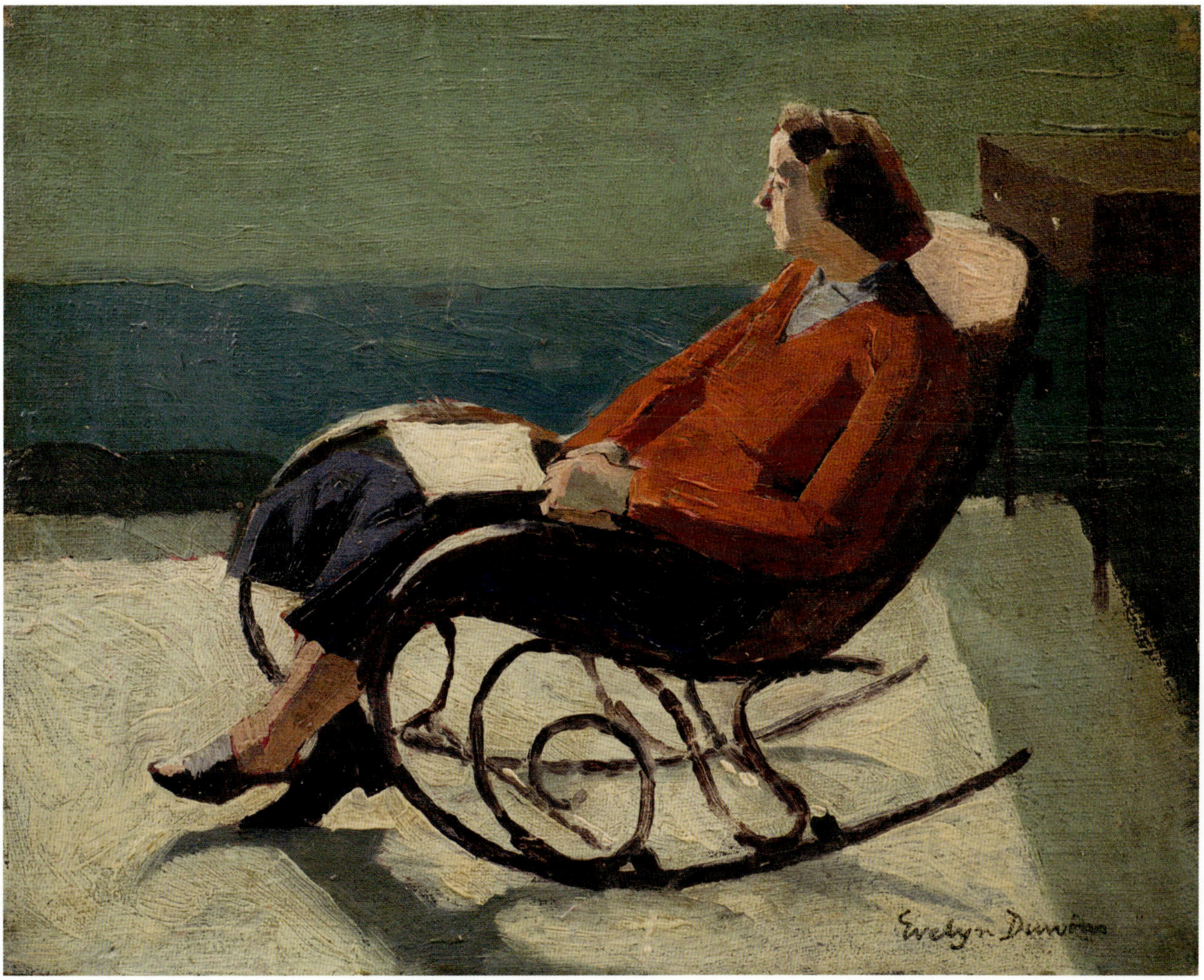


**122 Evelyn Dunbar** (1906-1960),
*Portrait of the artist's mother, Florence, on a bentwood rocking chair,* c.1930 [HMO 797], signed with studio stamp "Evelyn Dunbar", oil on canvas, 8 x 10 in. (20 x 25.4 cm).

Florence Dunbar, née Murgatroyd, was the daughter of a Bradford woolmaster. She met William Dunbar on one of his frequent visits to Bradford, where he would source textiles for his Reading bespoke tailoring and household linen business. They married in 1895. A tireless and green-fingered gardener, she also painted innumerable floral still lifes. Evelyn owed much to her unceasing encouragement. She died in 1944.

OVERLEAF:
**123 Evelyn Dunbar** (1906-1960), *Florence in the garden at The Cedars,* c.1938,
oil on canvas 12 x 18 in. (30.5 x 46 cm).

Florence, Evelyn's mother, was a gifted and devotedly hard-working gardener. She features frequently in Evelyn's studies of the family home, The Cedars, more often than not in the garden, and often wearing the same jacket. In this contemplative composition she waits patiently for Spring, filling in time knitting. Allegories of the relationship between mankind and the Creator were a consistent theme in Dunbar's work. (**373**)

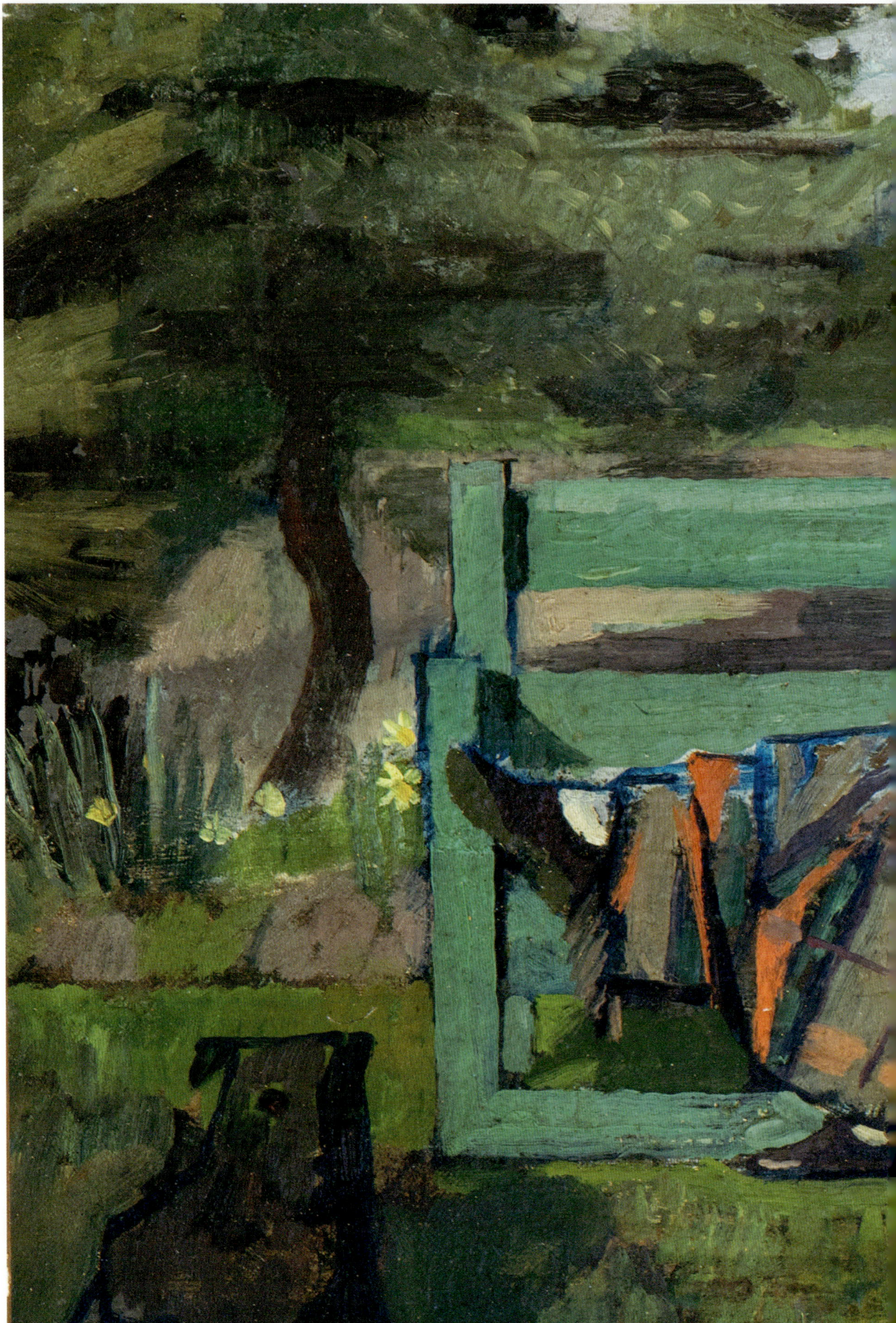

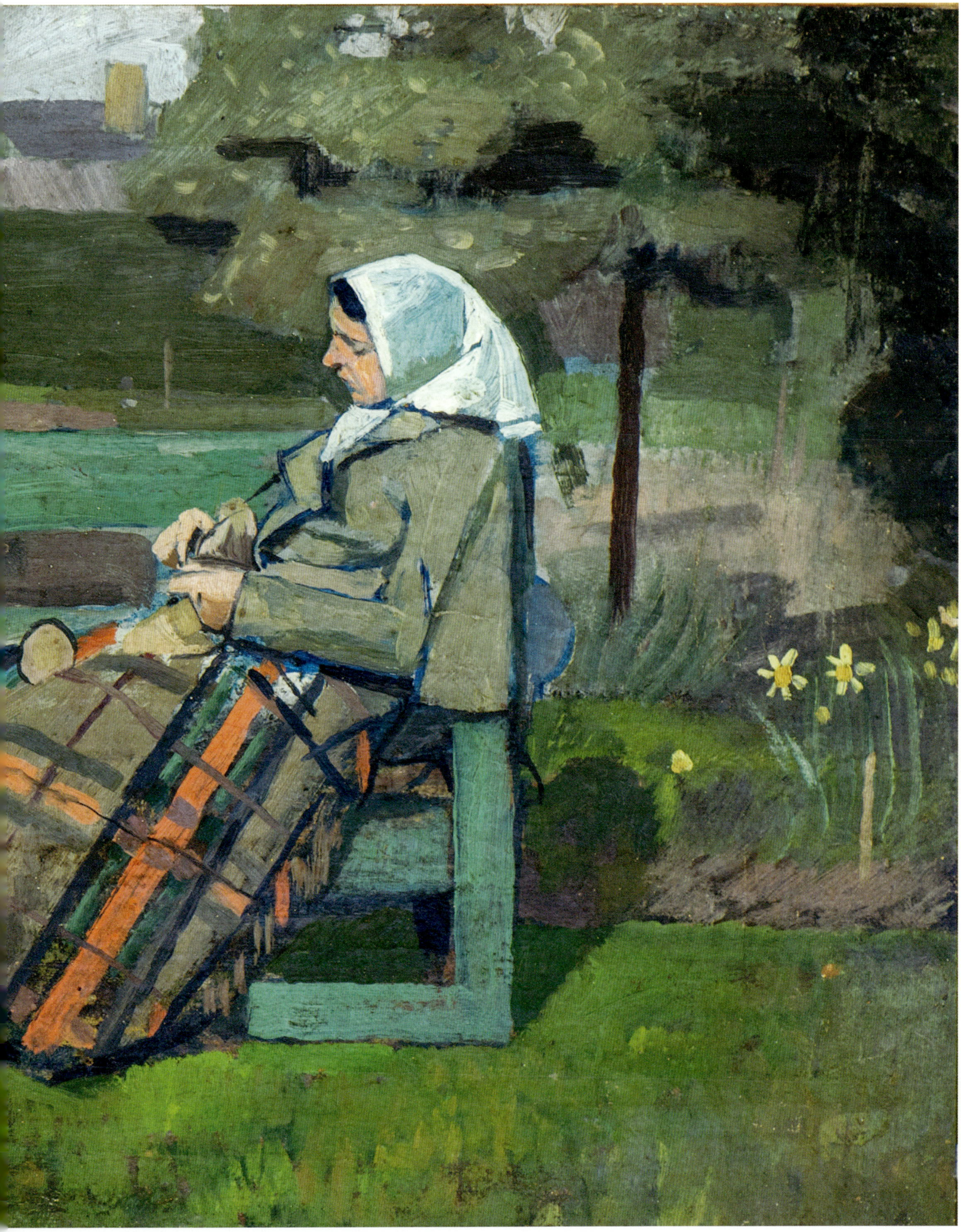

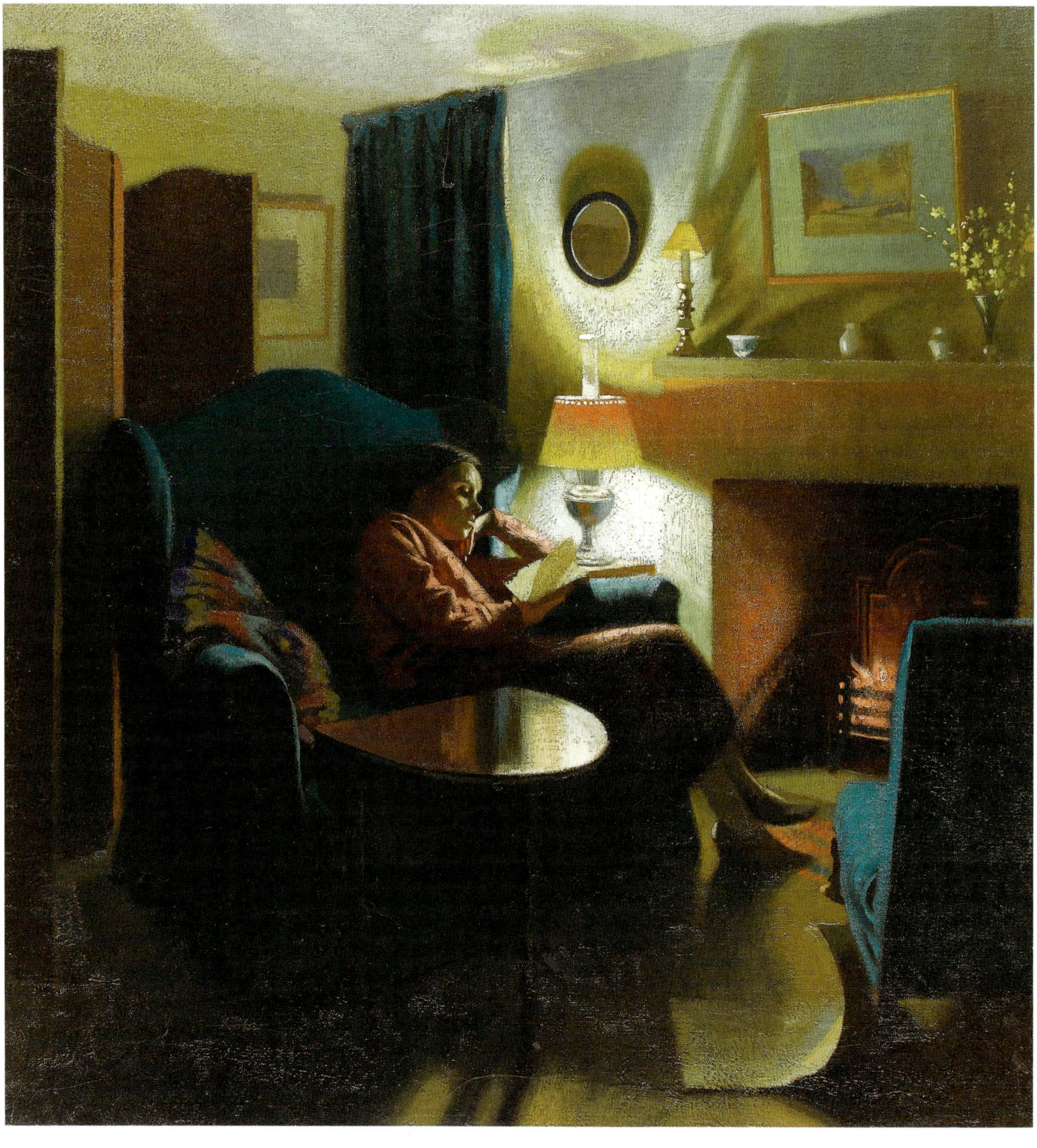

**124 Gerald Gardiner** (1902–1959), *The Artist's Wife, Evelyn, Seated Reading*, mid-1930s, inscribed on label on reverse: 'This picture is the property of Mrs Evelyn Gardiner', oil on canvas, 28 ¼ × 26 in. (71.5 × 66 cm). Collection: Cheltenham Art Gallery & Museum.

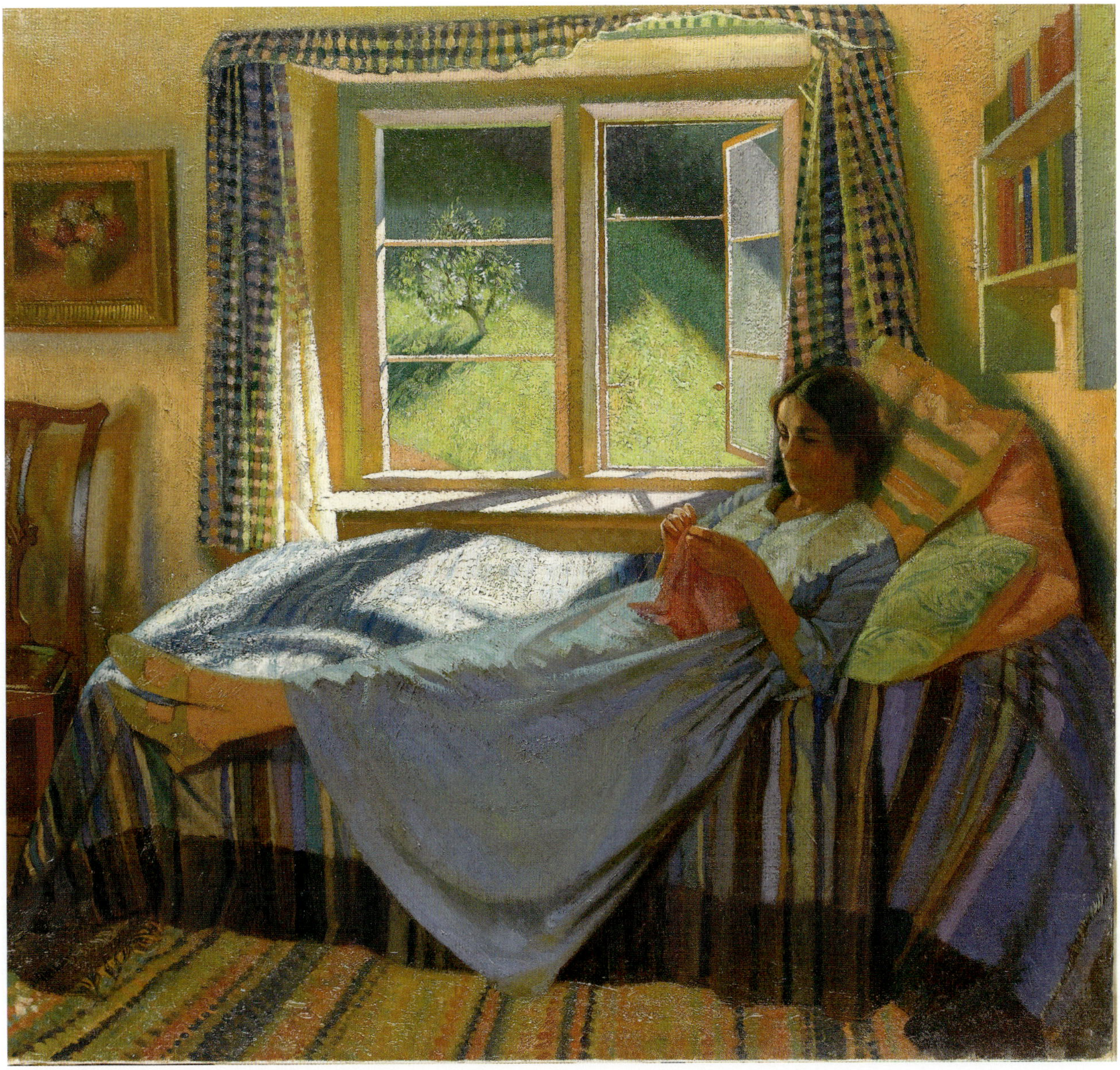

**125 Gerald Gardiner** (1902-1959), *The Artist's Wife, Evelyn, Knitting on a Daybed*, 1934,
inscribed on label on reverse: 'This picture is the property of Mrs Evelyn Gardiner'; dated on canvas return: '15th April '34',
oil on canvas, 28 x 30 ¼ in. (71 x 77 cm). Collection: Cheltenham Art Gallery & Museum.

These two paintings, which remained with the artist and his wife throughout their lives, are somewhere between genre paintings and portraits. The setting for both is the artist's home, Lower Nash End, Bisley in Gloucestershire, to which the Gardiners moved in 1934. While remaining a purely figurative painter, Gardiner delighted in applying thick impasto, often in pure colours, and had a remarkable ability to capture, through abstract patterns, both natural and artificial light, and the play of reflected light and shadows.

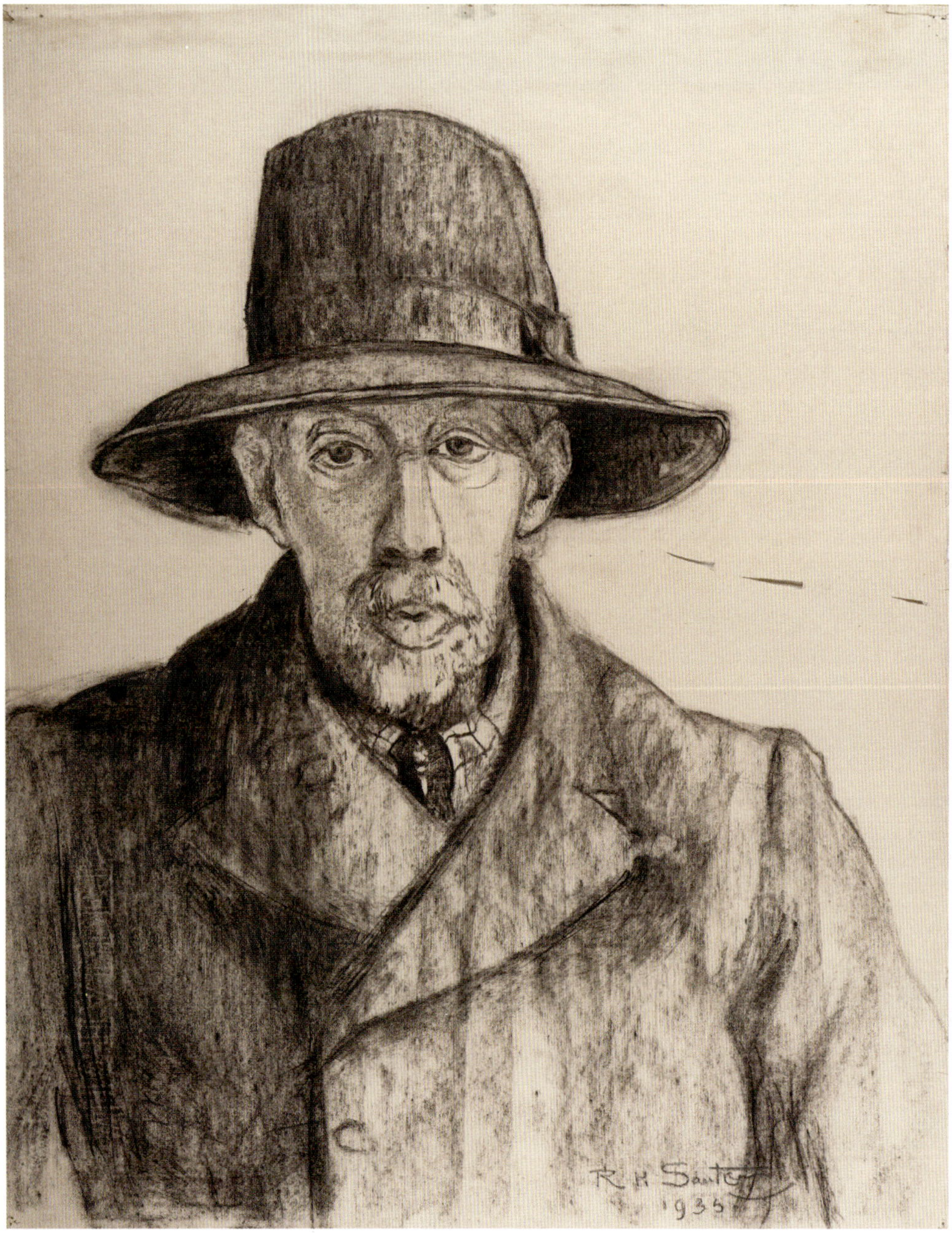

**126 Rudolf Sauter** (1895-1977),
*Portrait of Arthur William Symons* (British poet, critic and translator), 1935, signed and dated, charcoal on paper, 24 ¼ x 19 ¼ in.(62 x 49 cm).

Arthur William Symons (1865-1945) was a British poet, critic, translator and part of the vibrant literary community in the notorious Rhymers' Club, alongside poets like William Butler Yeats. Symons' career was cut short by a devastating mental breakdown in 1908. Little of his writing after that point has been published, save his volume *Confessions: A Study in Pathology* (1930).

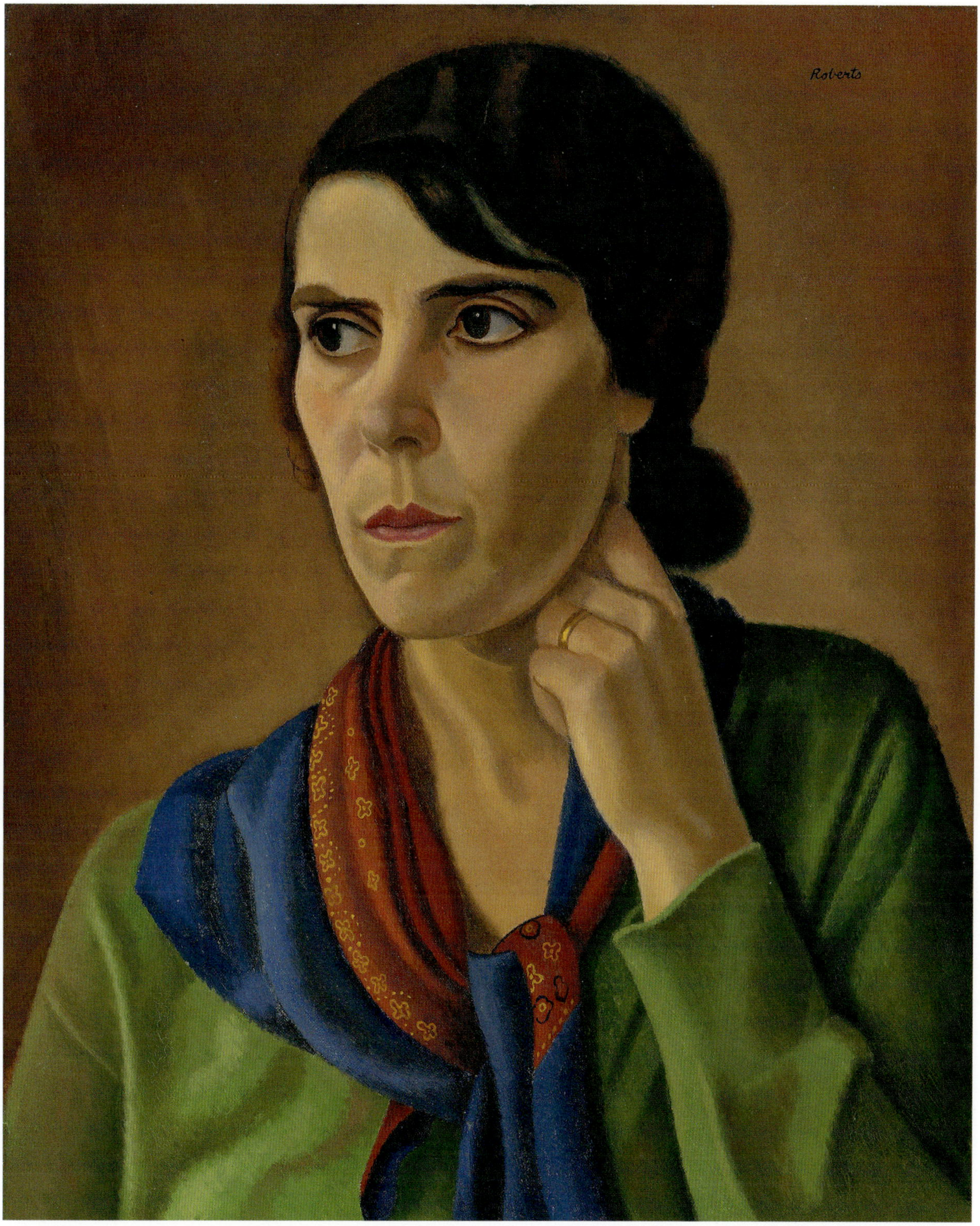


**127 William Roberts** (1895-1980), *Portrait of May Berry*, 1933, oil on canvas, 22 x 18 in. (55.6 x 45.5 cm).

May and her husband Joe Berry are recorded as having visited Mr and Mrs Roberts at Haverstock Hill, where they lived 1929-35. May is known to have owned at least one painting by Roberts, *The Park Bench*, which sold at Sotheby's in 1960. The extent of their friendship is unknown, but Roberts records that he went to see the Boat Race once from the windows of the Berrys' flat on Upper Mall, Chiswick.

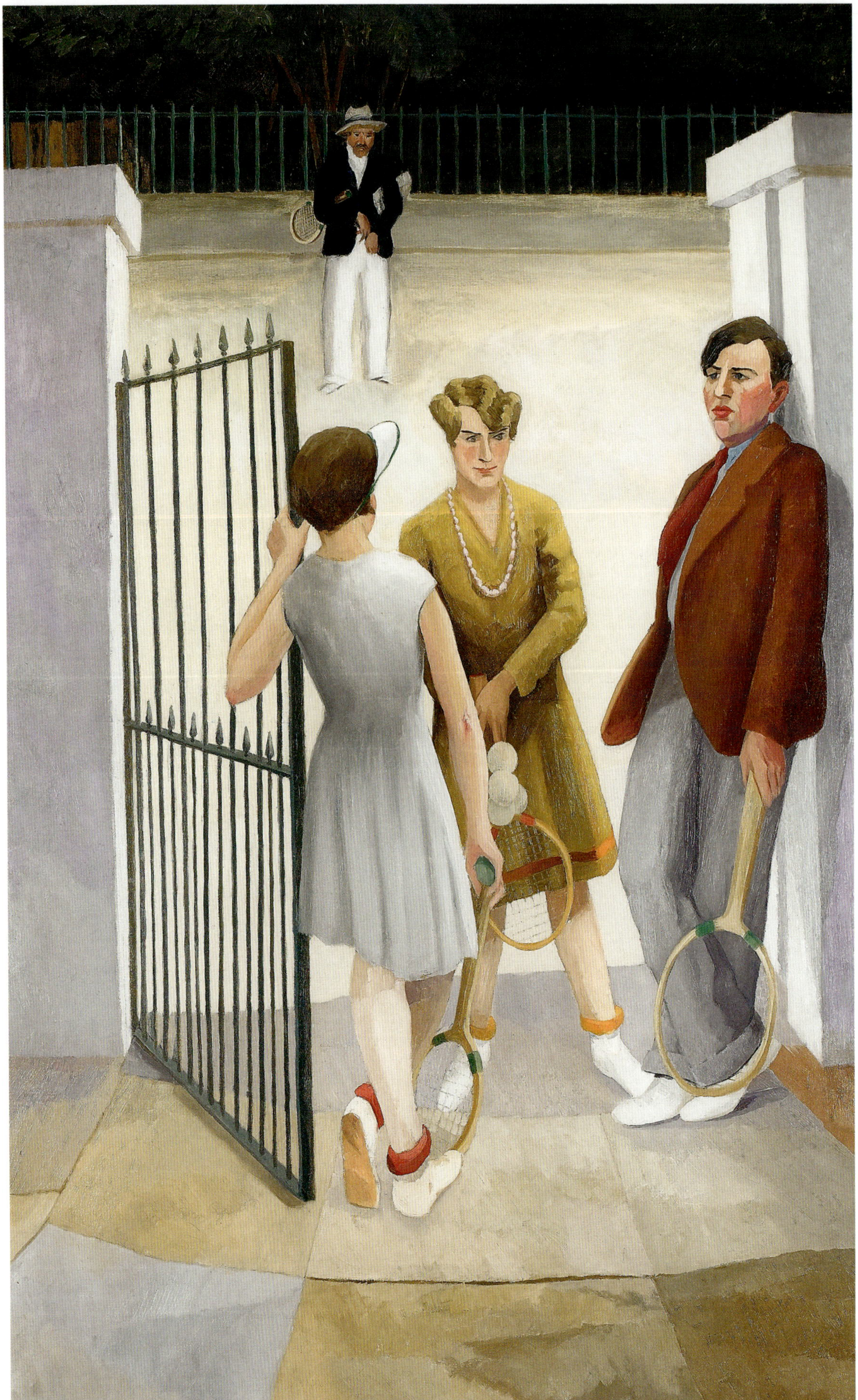

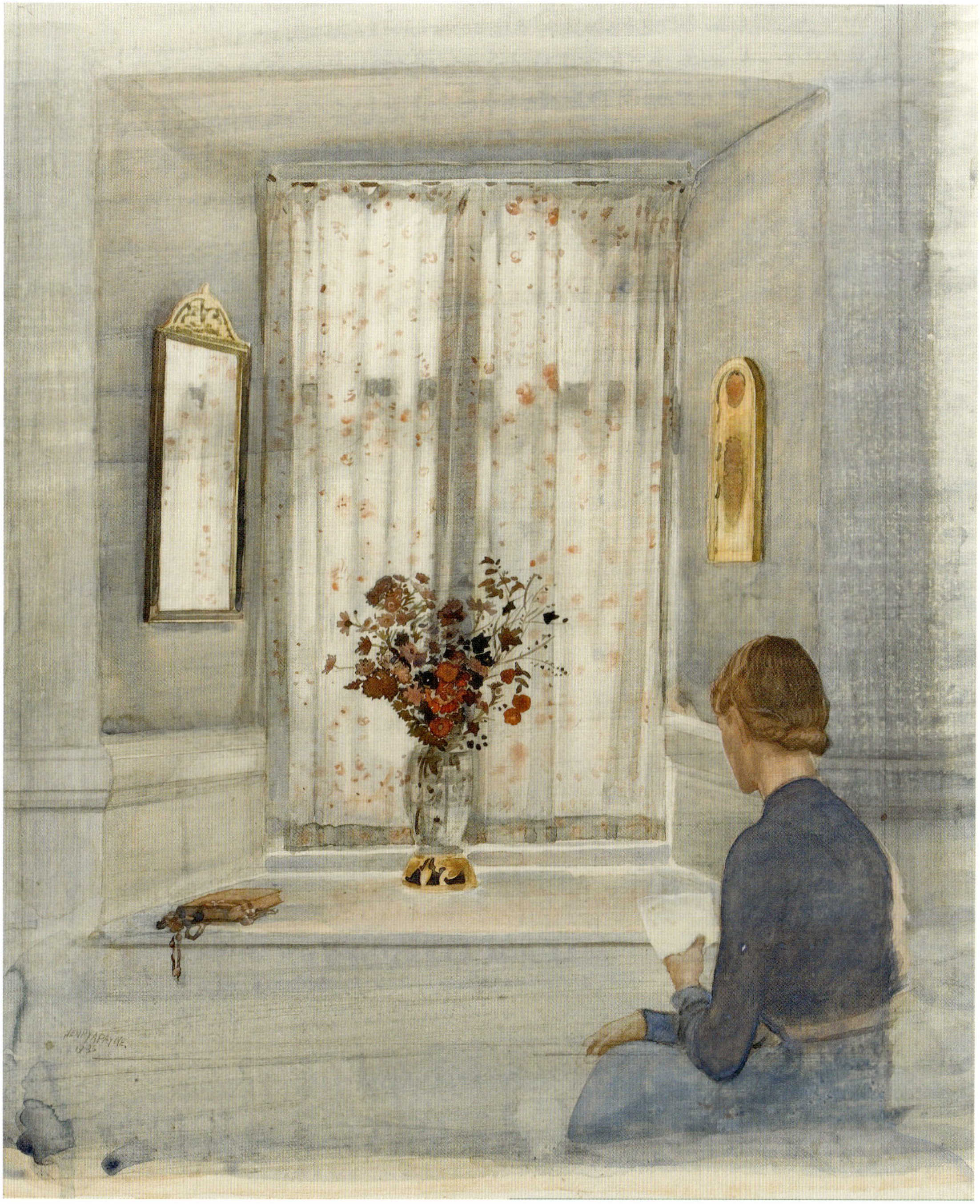

**129 Henry Payne** (1868-1940), *The Letter Reader,* 1935, signed and dated, titled on the reverse, pastel on buff paper, 17 ¼ x 13 ¼ in. (44 × 33 cm).

This possibly shows the artist's daughter at St Loe's House, the family home and studio in Amberley, Gloucestershire. The gilded tablet to the right is likely to be the work of Edith Payne, Henry's wife, who was a watercolourist and gilder.

**128 Richard Carline** (1896-1980), *Gilbert and Janet Pairing Up for Tennis,* early 1920s, inscribed on the reverse '63 U. Spencer', tempera, 61 ¾ x 37 ¾ in. (156.8 x 95.8 cm).

The painting depicts the artist Gilbert Spencer and the Carlines' maid, Janet Piggott. The setting is likely to be 47 Downshire Hill, Hampstead, home of the Carline family and in the 1920s a popular meeting place for many artists living in Hampstead. Gilbert's brother Stanley Spencer lived with the Carlines and in 1925 married Hilda Carline, to whose daughter this painting belonged. (**152**, **153**)

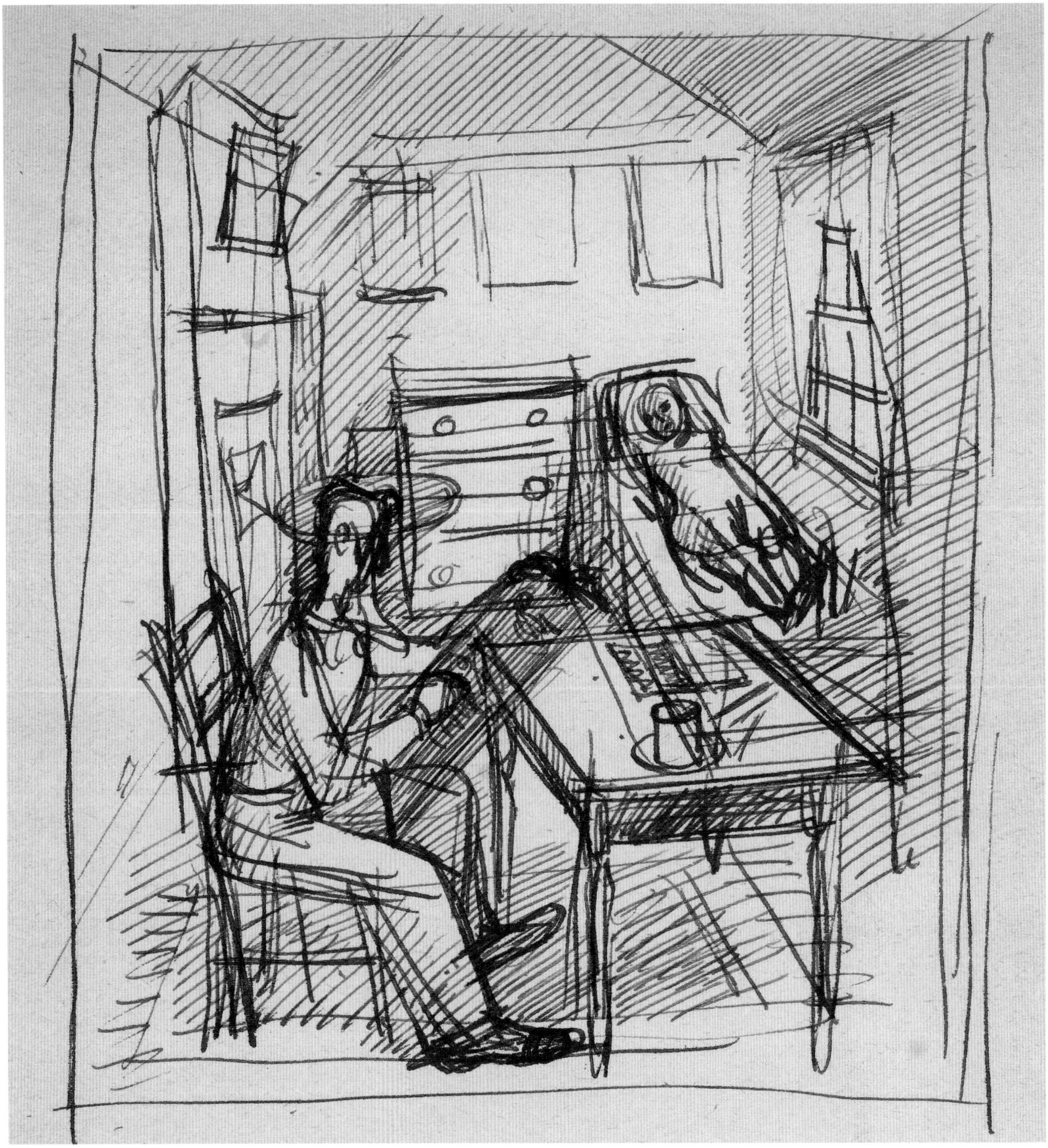

**130 Charles Mahoney** (1903-1968), *The Artist and His Model*, c.1935,
pen & ink on paper, 15 ½ x 11 in. (39.5 x 28 cm).

Though often described by his students as a serious and exigent teacher Mahoney had a quirky sense of humour. This pen & ink drawing caricatures poignantly the often cramped spaces in which Mahoney had to work.

**131 Eric Gill** (1882-1940), *Seated Female Nude* (from *Twenty-five Nudes*) (P951), c 1933,
signed with monogram, numbered '637' on reverse with T.N. Lawrence block maker stamp
engraved wood block, 9 x 5 1/2 in. (22.9 x 14.2 cm).

A similar version of this discarded block (P951) appeared in the 1938 book *Twenty-five Nudes*. The sitter has been identified as the illustrator and wood-engraver, Clare Leighton (1898-1989), who posed for Gill on 24 August 1933.

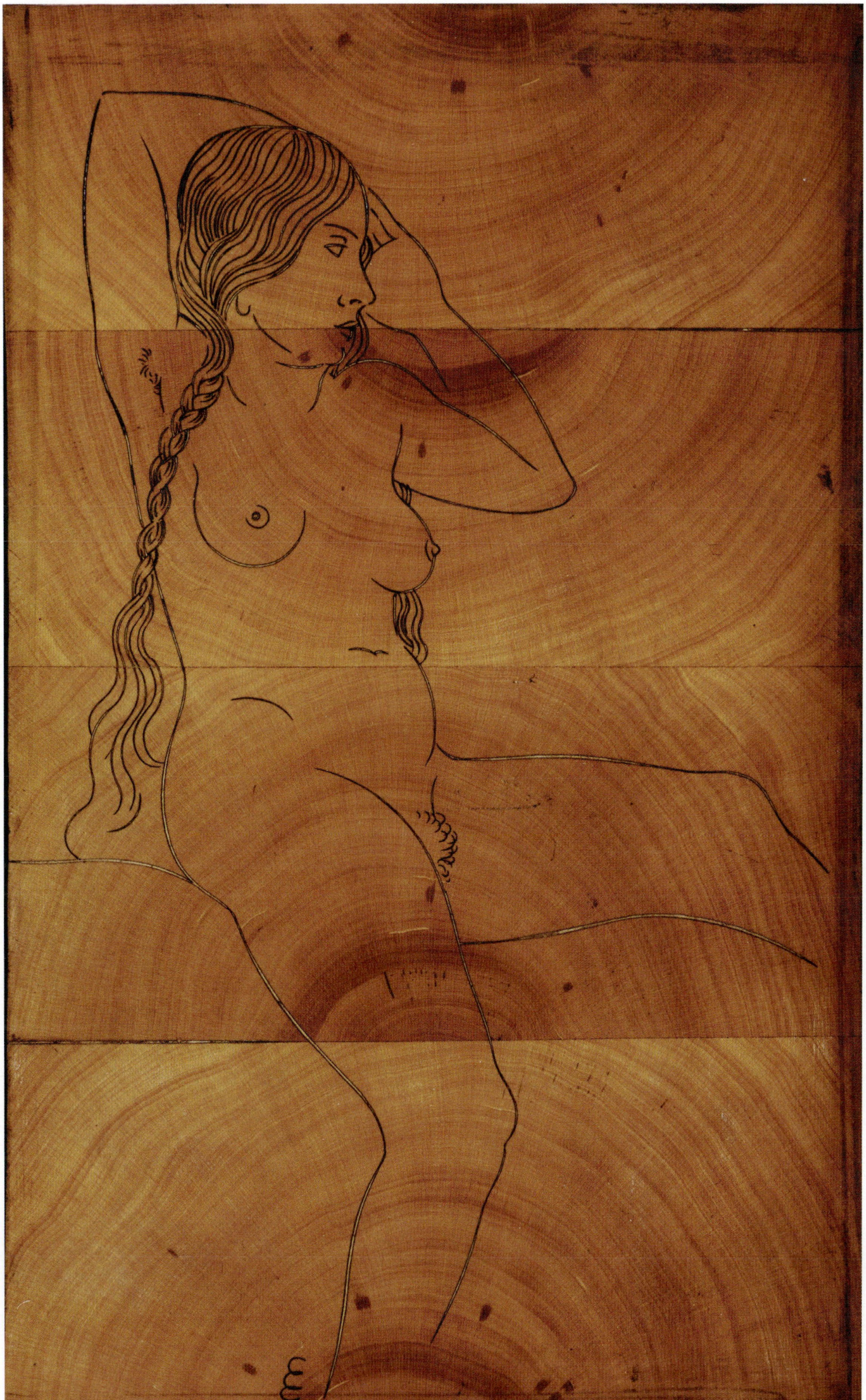

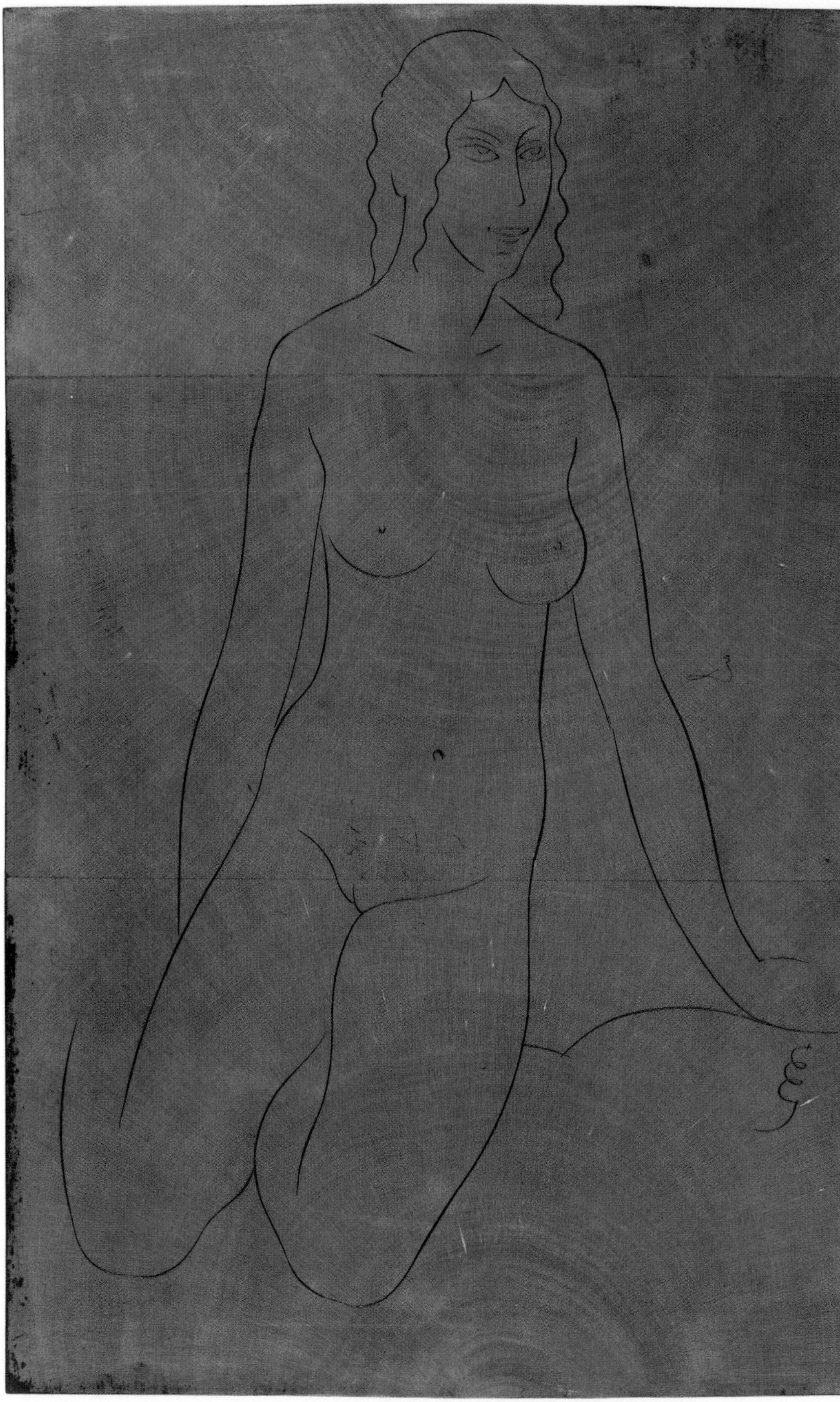

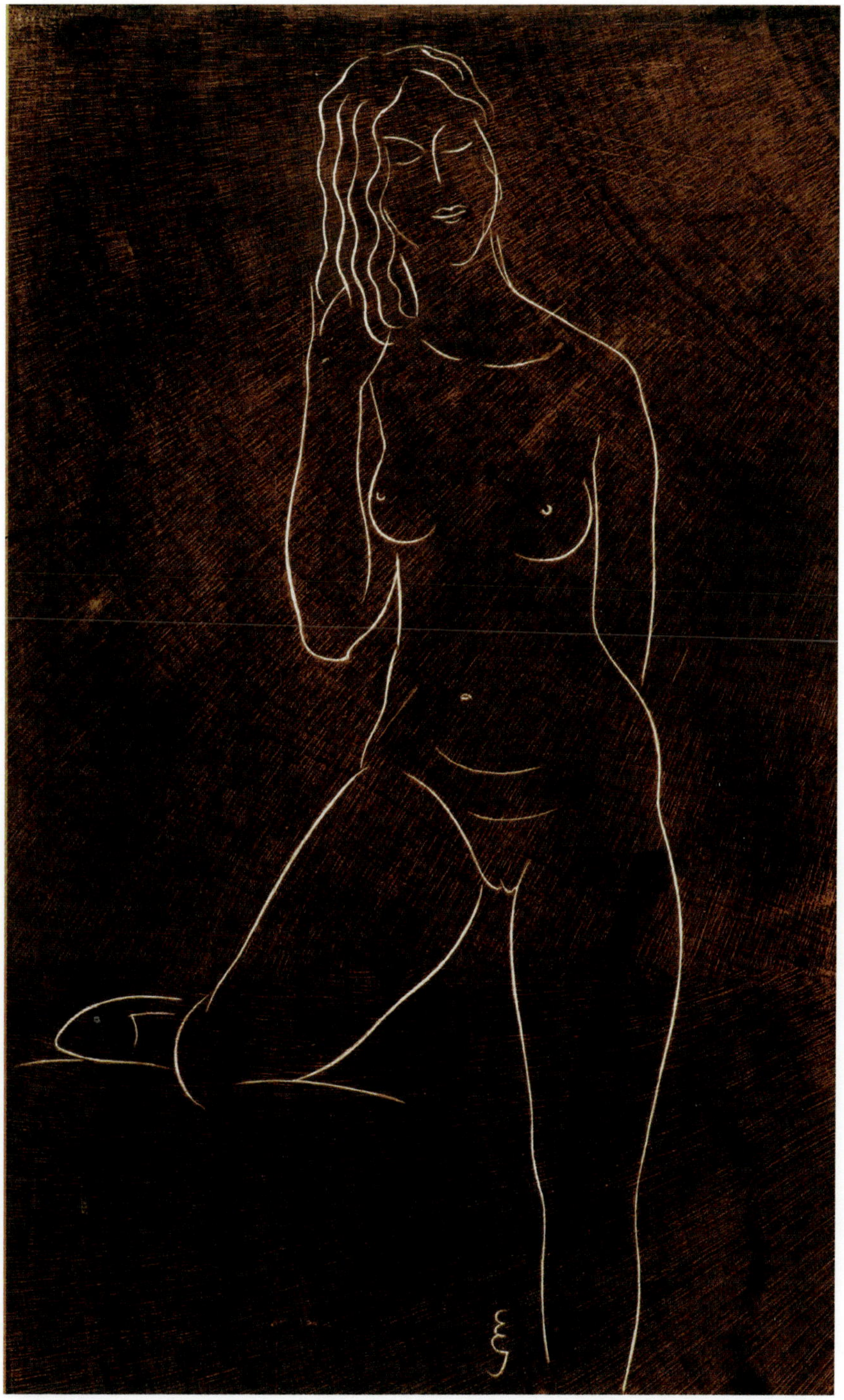

**133 Eric Gill** (1882-1940), *Female Nude* (from *Twenty-five Nudes*), c 1938, signed with monogram, numbered '633' on reverse with T.N. Lawrence block maker stamp, engraved wood block, 9 x 5 ½ in. (22.9 x 14.4 cm).

**132 Eric Gill** (1882-1940), *Standing Female Nude* (from *Twenty-five Nudes*), c 1938, signed with monogram, numbered '636' on reverse with T.N. Lawrence block maker stamp, engraved wood block, 9 x 5 ¾ in. (23.3 x 14.5 cm).

'For drawing, like any other art, is not merely a means to an end. Drawing is worth doing for its own sake; it is subordinate to no other end than the general end of life itself – man's final beatitude.' (Eric Gill) (**268**)

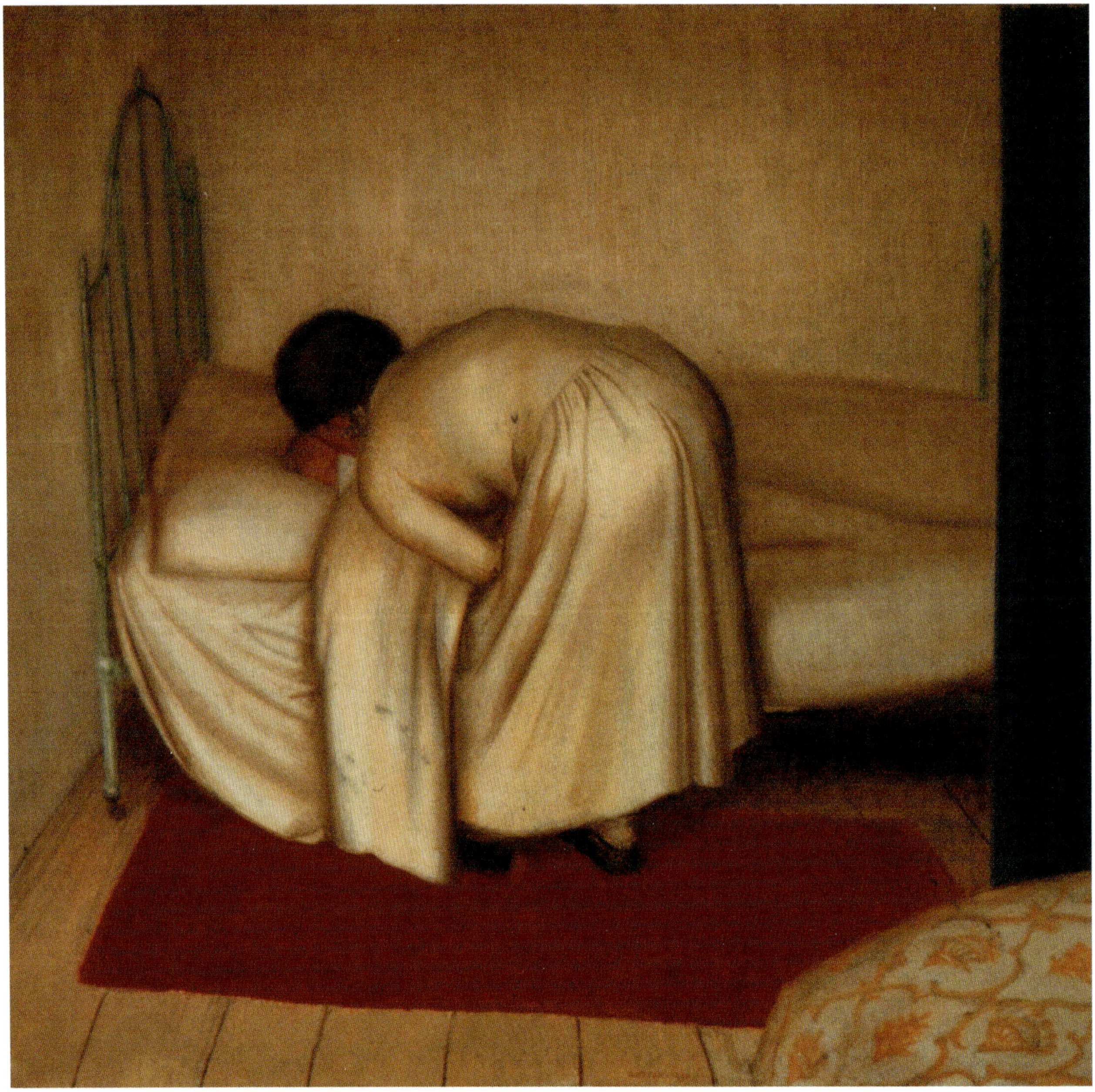

**134 Robert Austin** (1895-1973), *Child in Bed*, 1930, signed and dated, egg tempera, 10 ¼ × 11 in. (26.3 × 27.7 cm).

Figures resting or sleeping are amongst the subjects that Austin drew consistently. In the domestic family routine which formed the backdrop to his work, he found an endless source of inspiration. An etching and drypoint of the same subject was made by Austin the previous year (C.D. 89).

**Robert Austin** (1895-1973),

**135** *Child in Bed*, 1929, original copper plate (cancelled), 5 × 5 ½ in. (12.8 × 14 cm).

**136** *Child in Bed*, 1929, drypoint (printed from cancelled plate), 8 ¾ × 8 ¾ in. (22 × 22 cm).

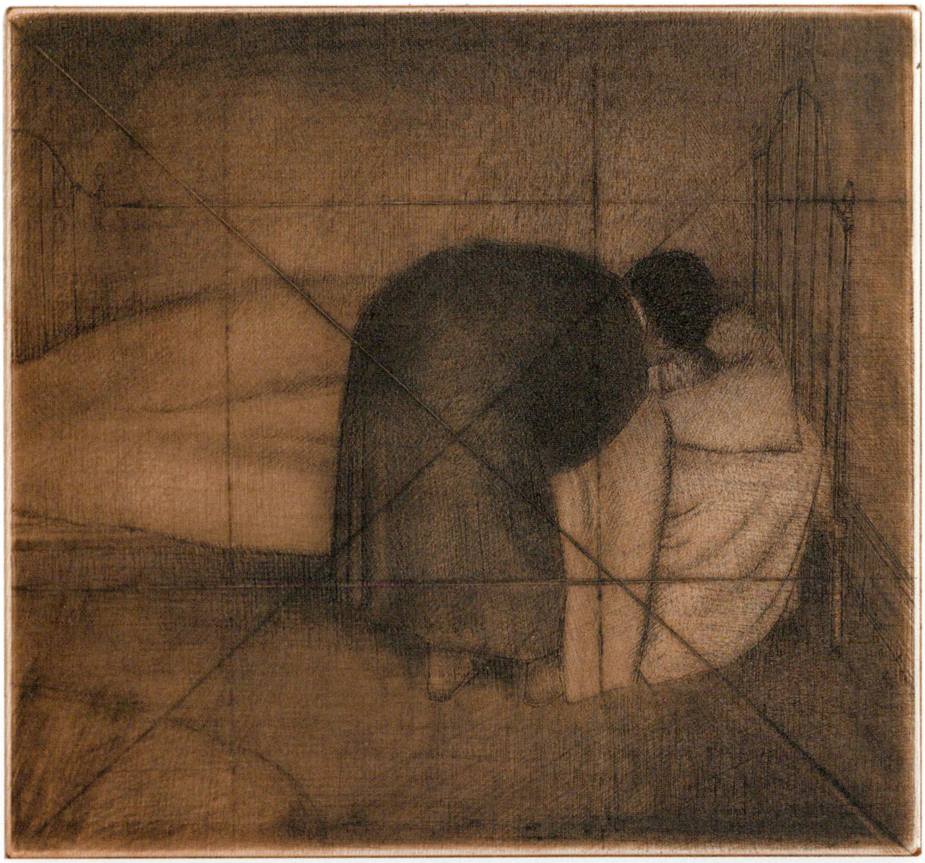

135

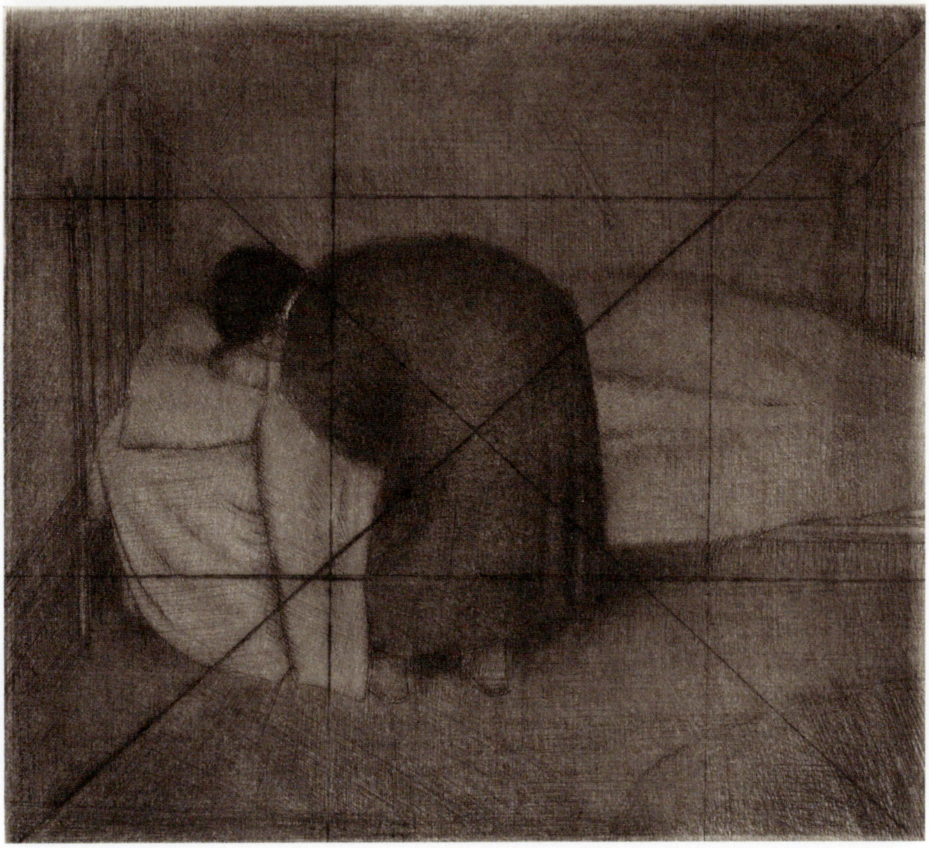

136

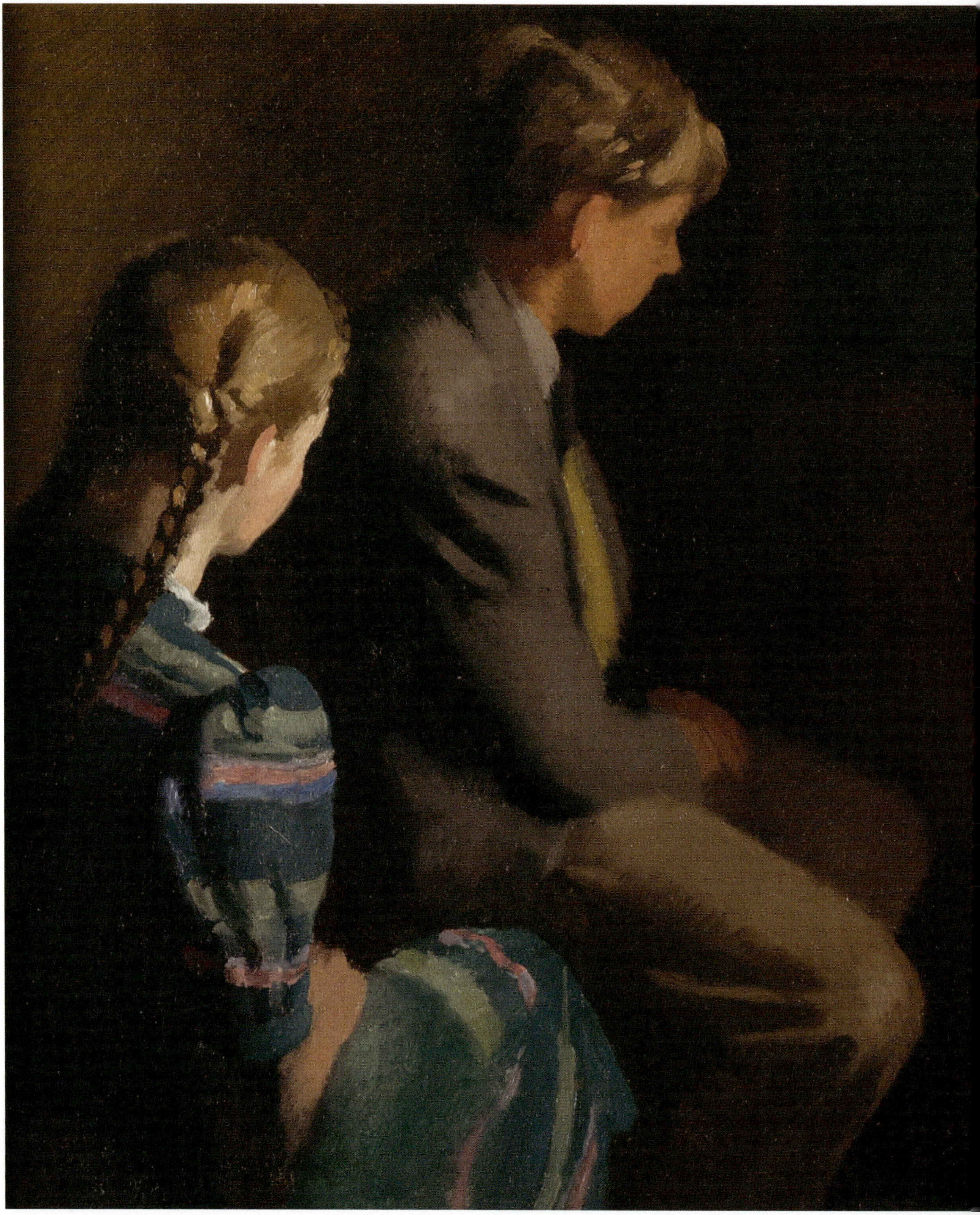

**137 Edward Irvine Halliday** (1902-1984), late 1940s, *Children's Hour,* titled on label on reverse, oil on canvas, 12 ½ x 17 in. (31.7 x 43.2 cm).

Halliday depicts his daughter (the painter Charlotte Halliday, b. 1935) and son watching television – a full two decades before television networks switched to colour in the mid-1960s. The first television children's programmes started in 1946, after the end of WWII, when there was a live Sunday afternoon transmission known as *Children's Hour.*

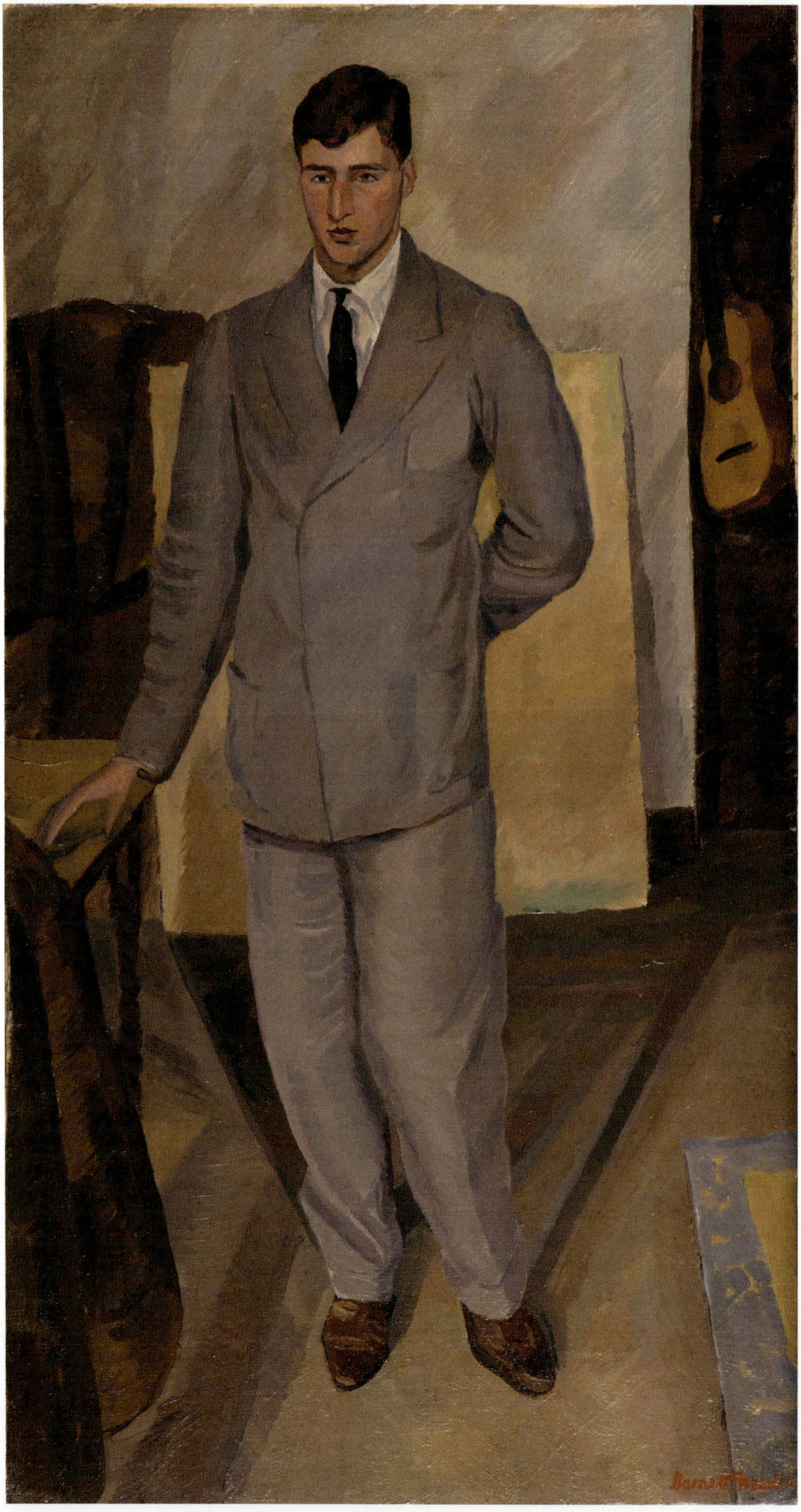

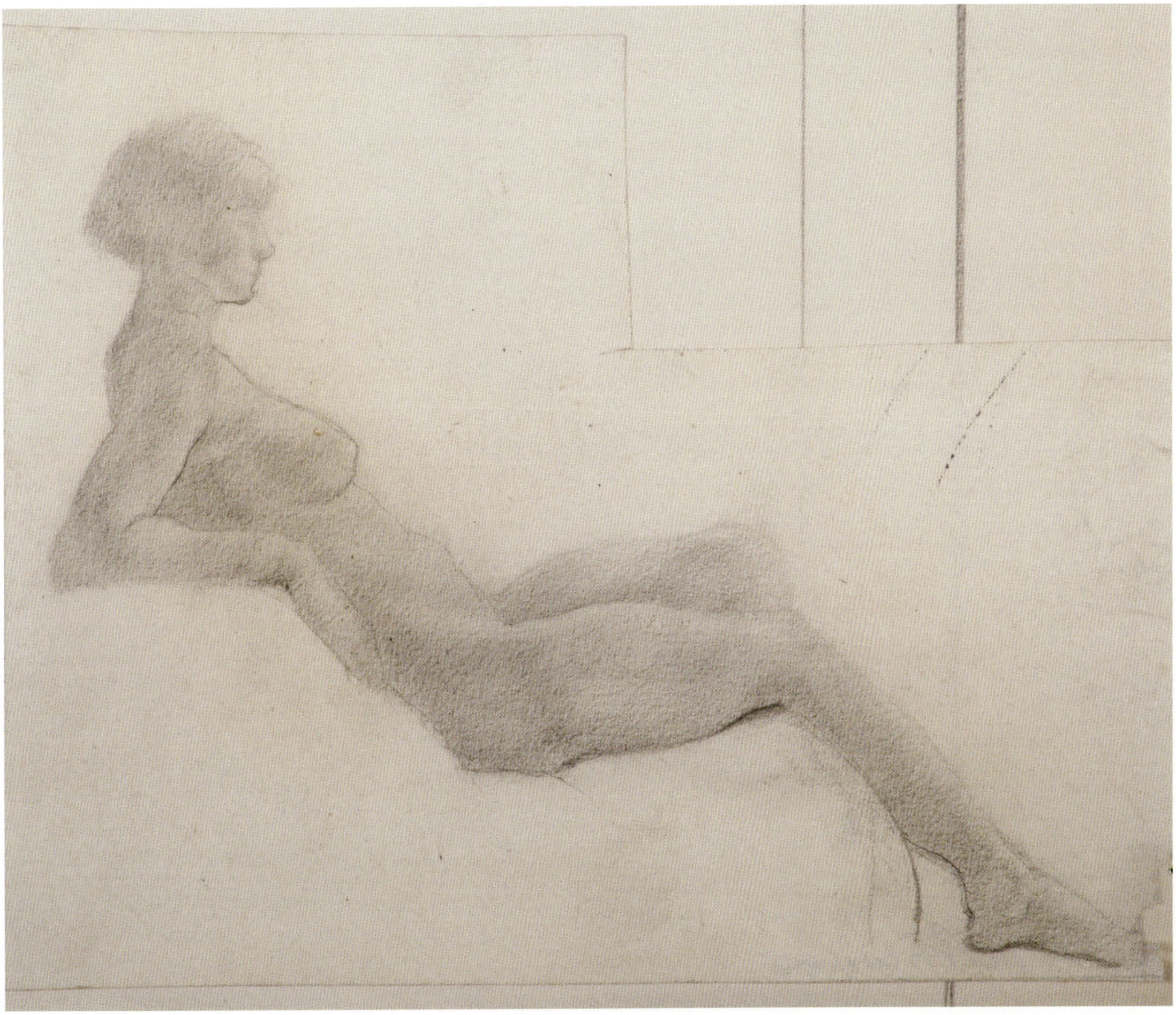

**139 Barnett Freedman** (1901-1958), *Nude*, mid-1920s,
pencil on paper, 6 ¼ x 7 ½ in. (15.8 x 19.1 cm).

As newly-weds Claudia and Barnett lived in two rooms near the Euston Road, one of which Freedman used as a studio as he sought to combine theatrical activities with oil painting, remarking later "I nearly starved". (**168**)

**138 Barnett Freedman** (1901-1958), Sketch for *Portrait of Young Man*, mid-1920s, signed, titled to reverse,
oil on board, 26 ¾ x 14 ½ in. (67.8 x 36.8 cm).

This full length figure study, set in the artist's studio, is likely to relate to Freedman's 1926 portrait painting *The Stanhope Street Group*. (**168**)

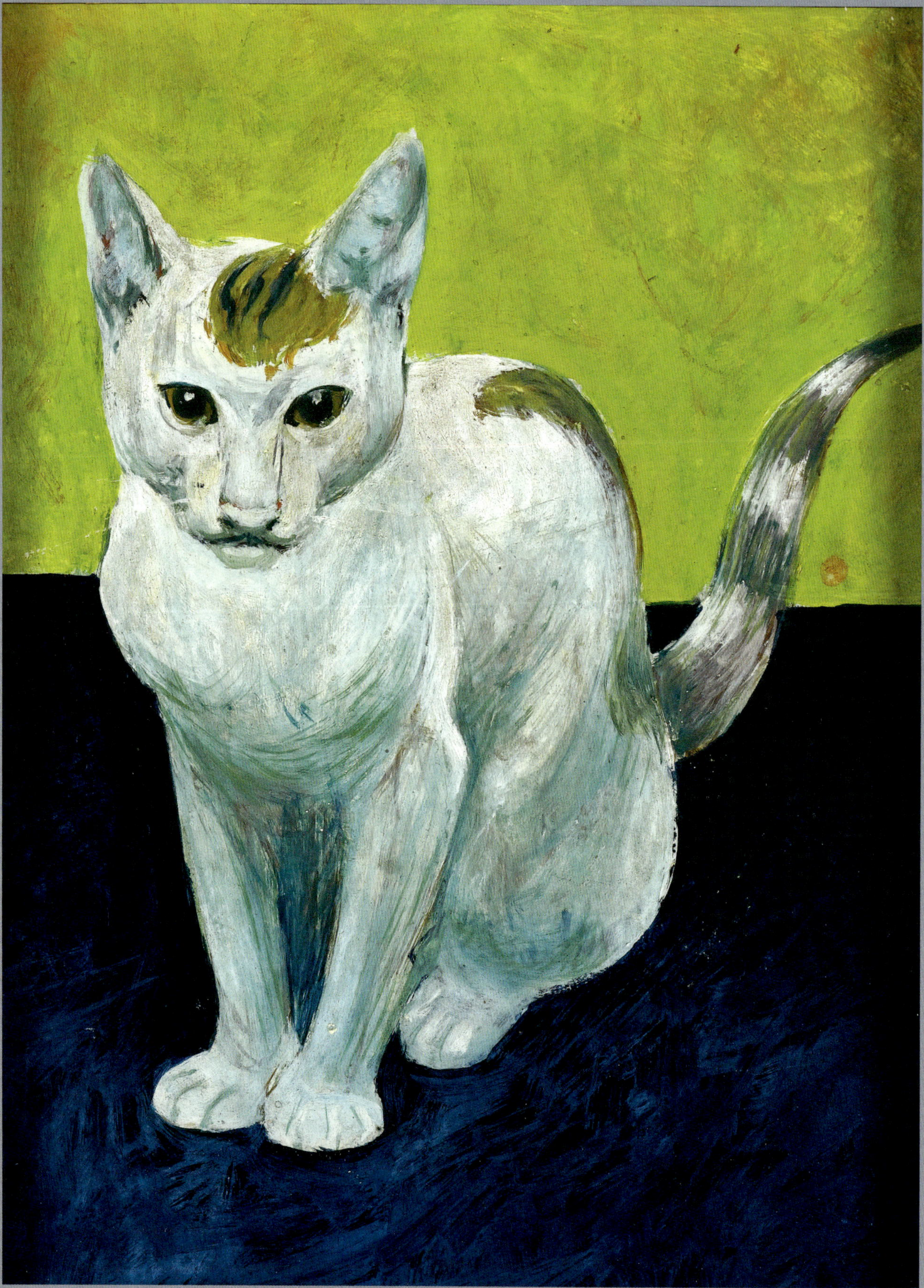

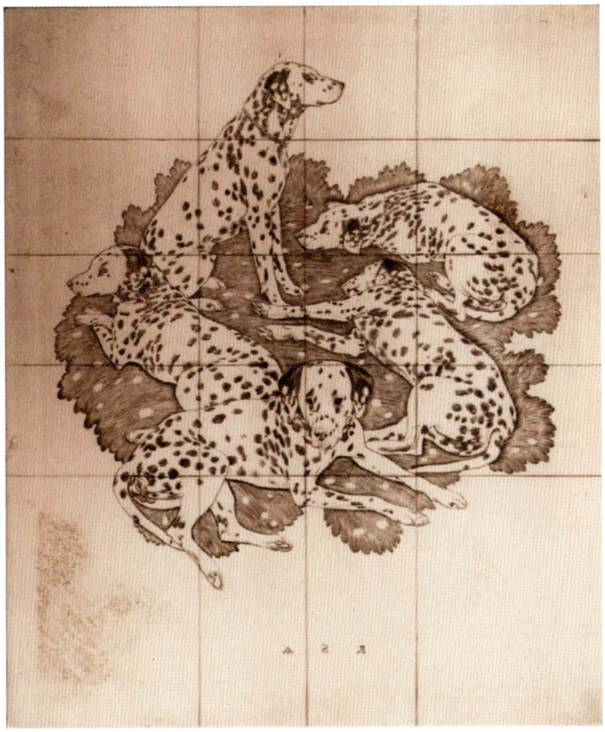

141

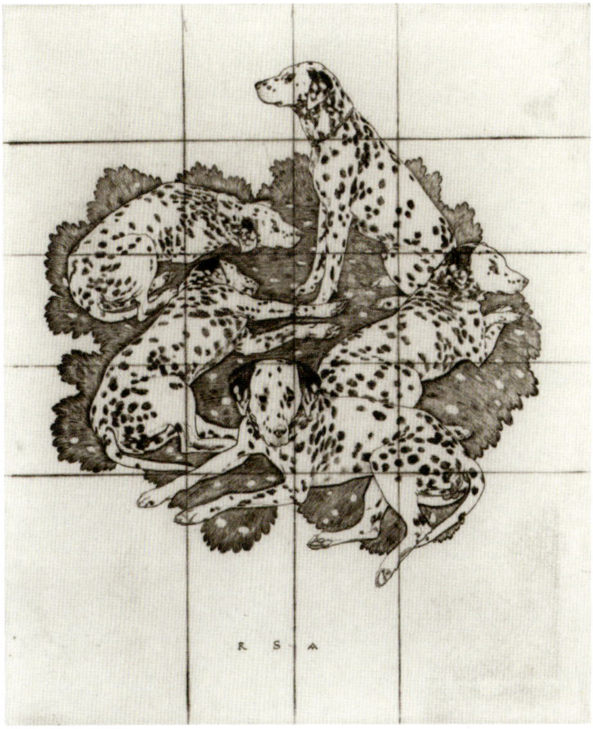


142

**Robert Austin** (1895-1973),

**141** *Ling of Lingard*, 1936, (CD 115), signed with initials in the plate, original copper plate (cancelled), 7 x 6 in. (17.5 x 15.2 cm).

**142** *Ling of Lingard*, 1936, (CD 115), engraving, printed from the cancelled plate, 9 x 8 in. (22.5 x 20 cm).

Ling was the name of the artist's Dalmatian, named after the family's home, Lingard House, in Chiswick. The engraving, produced in 1936, shows Ling in five different states of repose combined into a decorative cartouche. Austin included Ling in other compositions including *Girl Brushing Her Hair*. (**109**)

**140** **Fyffe Christie** (1918-1979), *The Artist's Cat, Carmen*, c.1955, oil on board, 10 ½ x 8 in. (27 x 20.2 cm).

After Fyffe and Eleanor (**229**, **230**) married in 1952 they rented a flat overlooking the Botanic Gardens in Glasgow, with one large living / dining room/ studio, and one small bedroom adjoining, sharing a tiny kitchen and bathroom with the other tenants and their white cat, called Carmen.

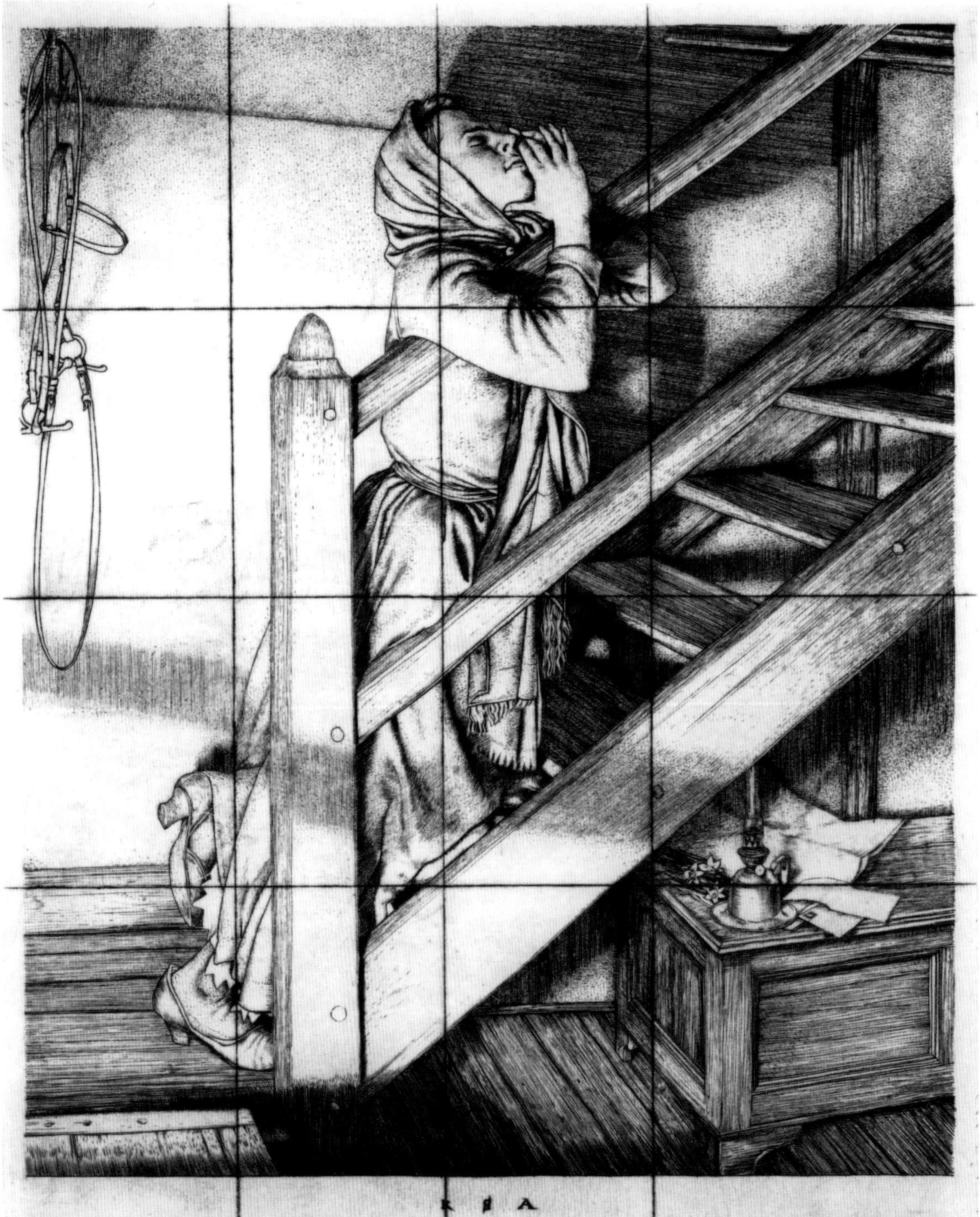

**143 Robert Austin** (1895-1973), *Evening*, 1939, signed in the plate,
engraving (printed from cancelled plate), 8 ¾ x 6 ¾ in. (22.5 x 17.2 cm).

*Evening*, a composition created in the first year of WW2, is one of Austin's most accomplished engravings. The figure praying was Austin's student and mistress Eleanor Hudson, a watercolourist, etcher and designer best known for her depictions of women at work during WW2. The setting of *Evening* is the former Primitive Methodist chapel at Burnham Overy Staithe, Norfolk, which Austin bought and converted in the mid-1930s for use when he was not working in London. He used the same setting for his self-portrait. (**257**)

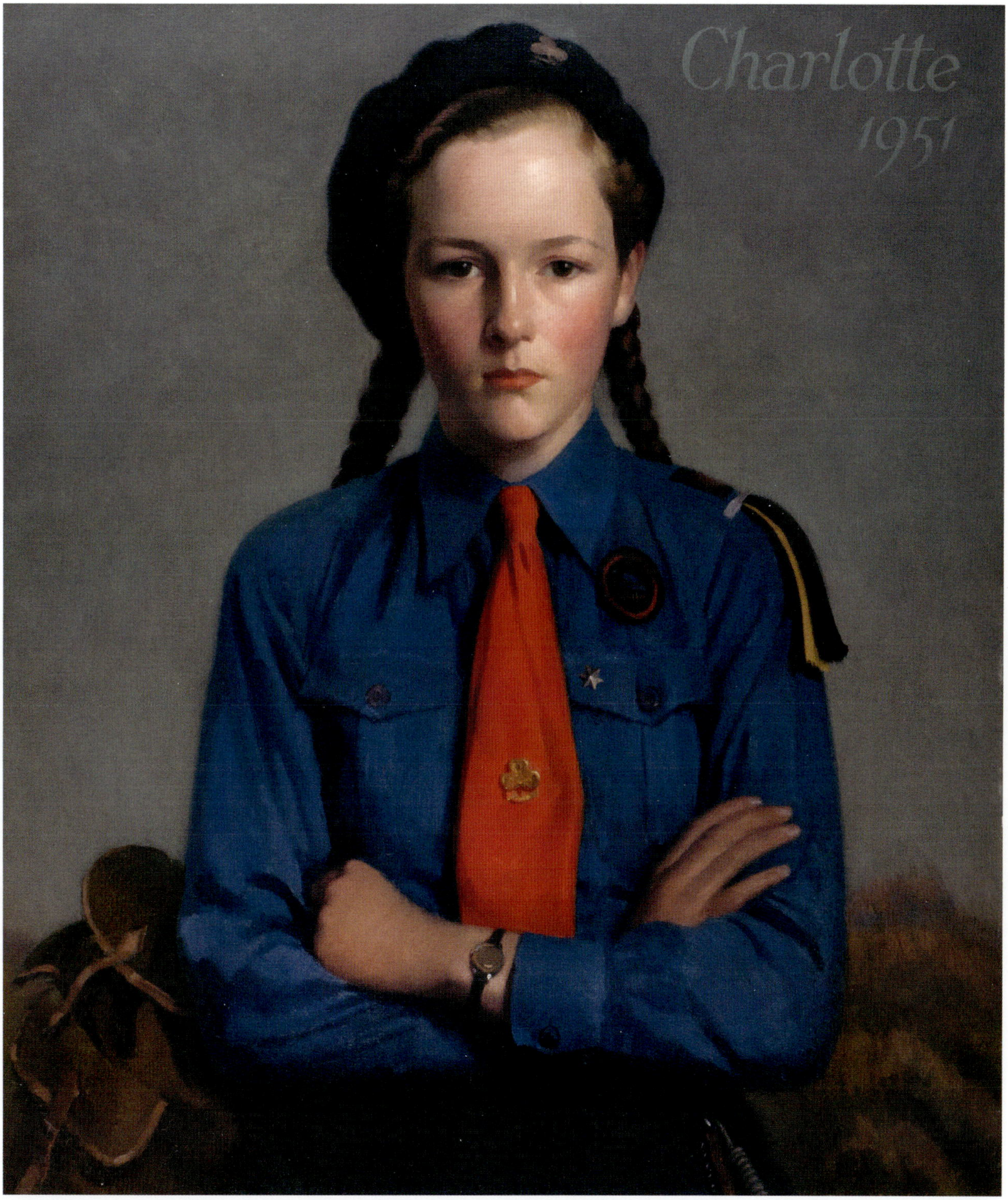


**144 Edward Irvine Halliday** (1902-1984), *Charlotte* (the artist's daughter), 1951, signed, titled and dated, oil on canvas, 30 x 25 in. (76.5 x 63.5 cm).

Charlotte, aged 16, is shown wearing the 'headquarters blue' tunic, traditional beret and red scarf of the Girl Guides. Two years after this portrait was painted she gained a place at The Royal Academy Schools to embark on her own career as a professional artist. (**301**)

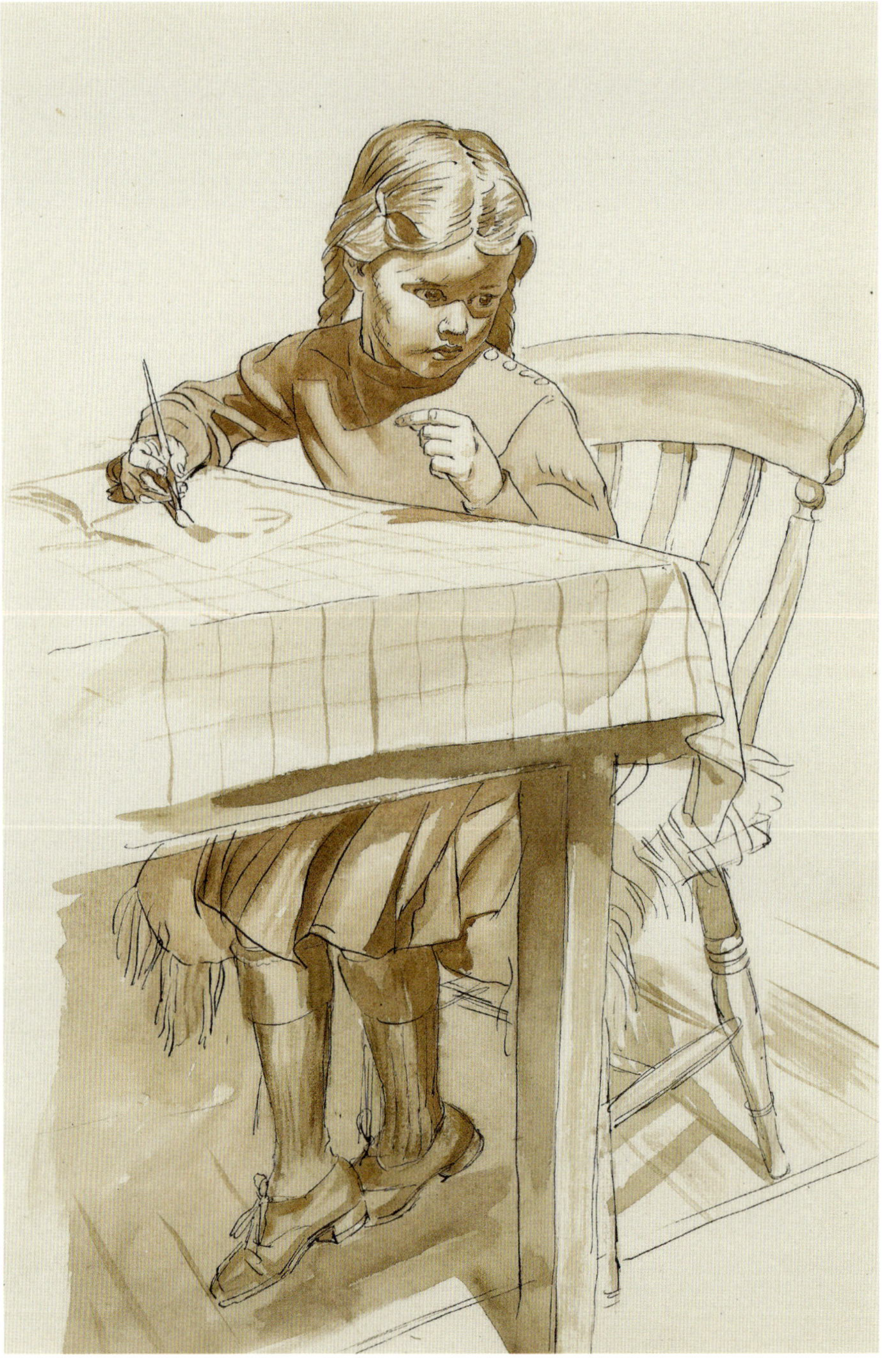

**145 Raymond Sheppard** (1913-1958), *Christine Sketching at Kitchen Table,* c.1952, pen & ink and watercolour on paper, 14 x 10 in. (36 x 25.5 cm).

**146 Raymond Sheppard** (1913-1958), *Michael with Toy Car*, c.1952, pen, ink and watercolour, 15 x 11 in. (38 x 28 cm).

Raymond Sheppard's children provided (mostly) willing models and a daily routine that offered him a rich variety of subject matter. 'I remember posing many, many times for my father. (**303**) Sometimes we were paid pocket money for sittings, especially when we didn't feel like sitting still! I think we wanted to help our dad and were, mainly, willing.' (Christine Sheppard)

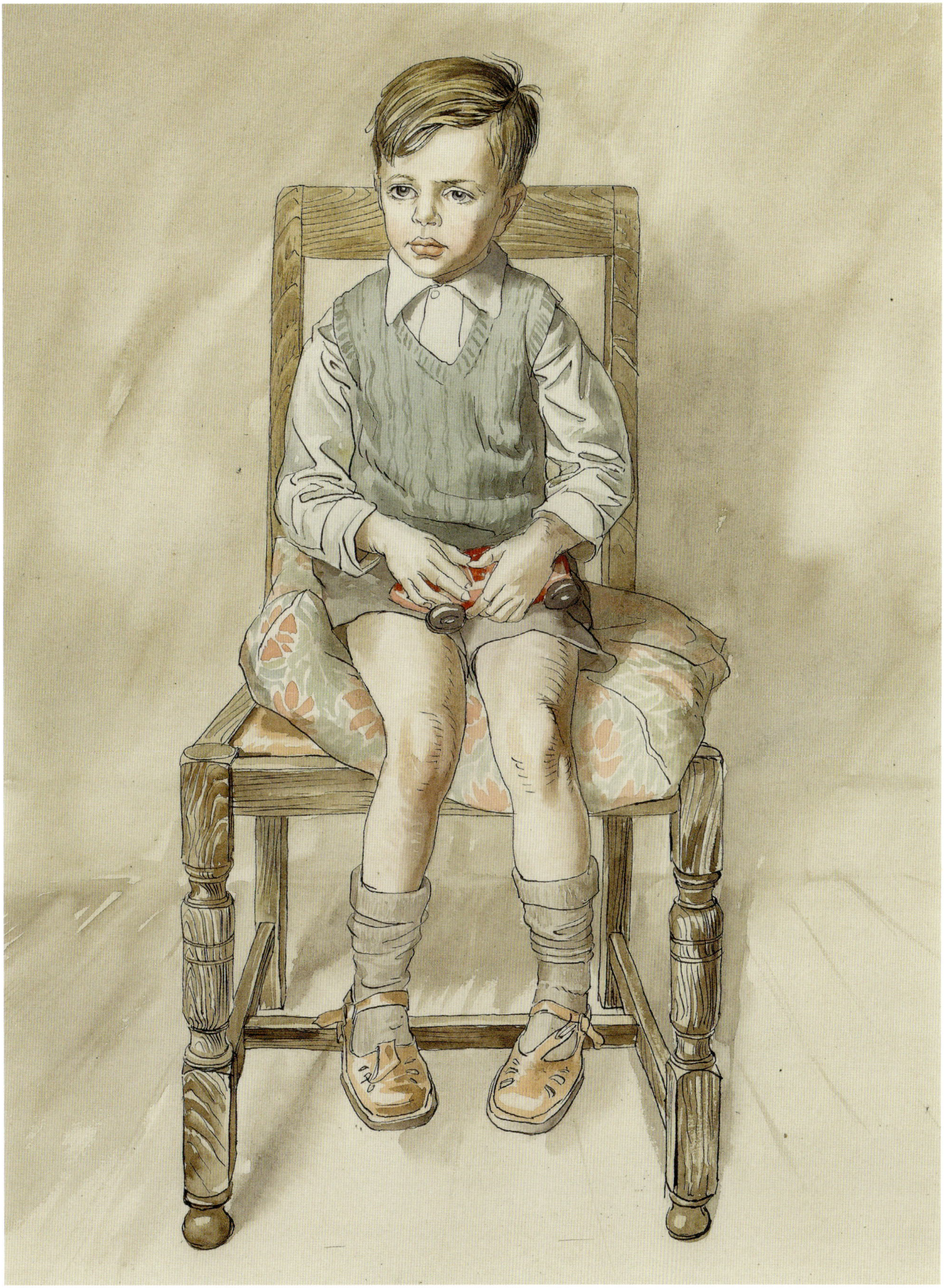

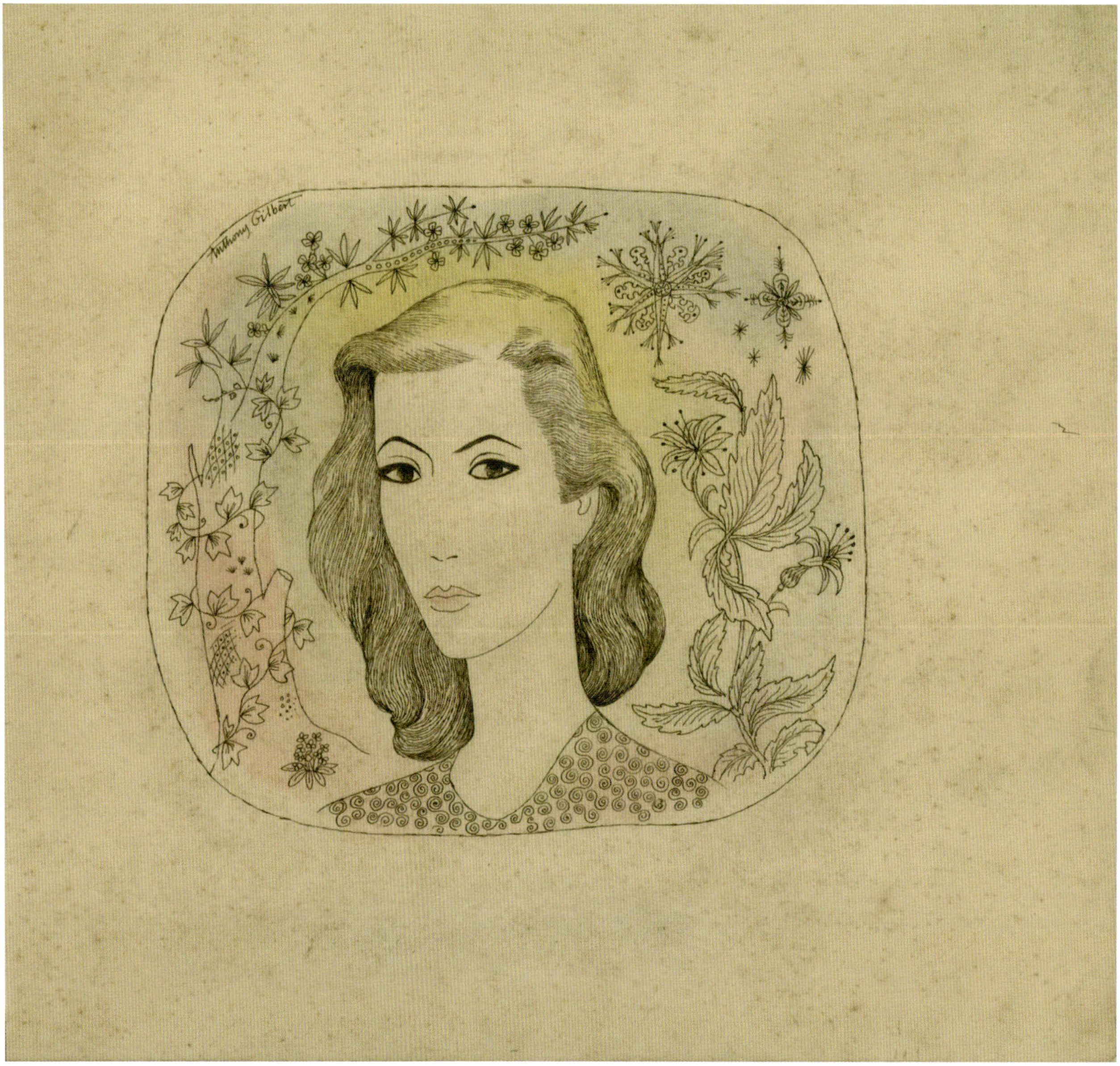


**147 Anthony Gilbert** (1916-1995), *Portrait of the Artist's Wife*, 1950's, signed, pen & ink and coloured pencil on paper, 10 ¼ x 12 ½ in. (25.9 x 31.7 cm).

*After Eight, Rose's Lime Cordial, Horlicks* – Anthony Gilbert designed artwork for these and many more iconic brands.

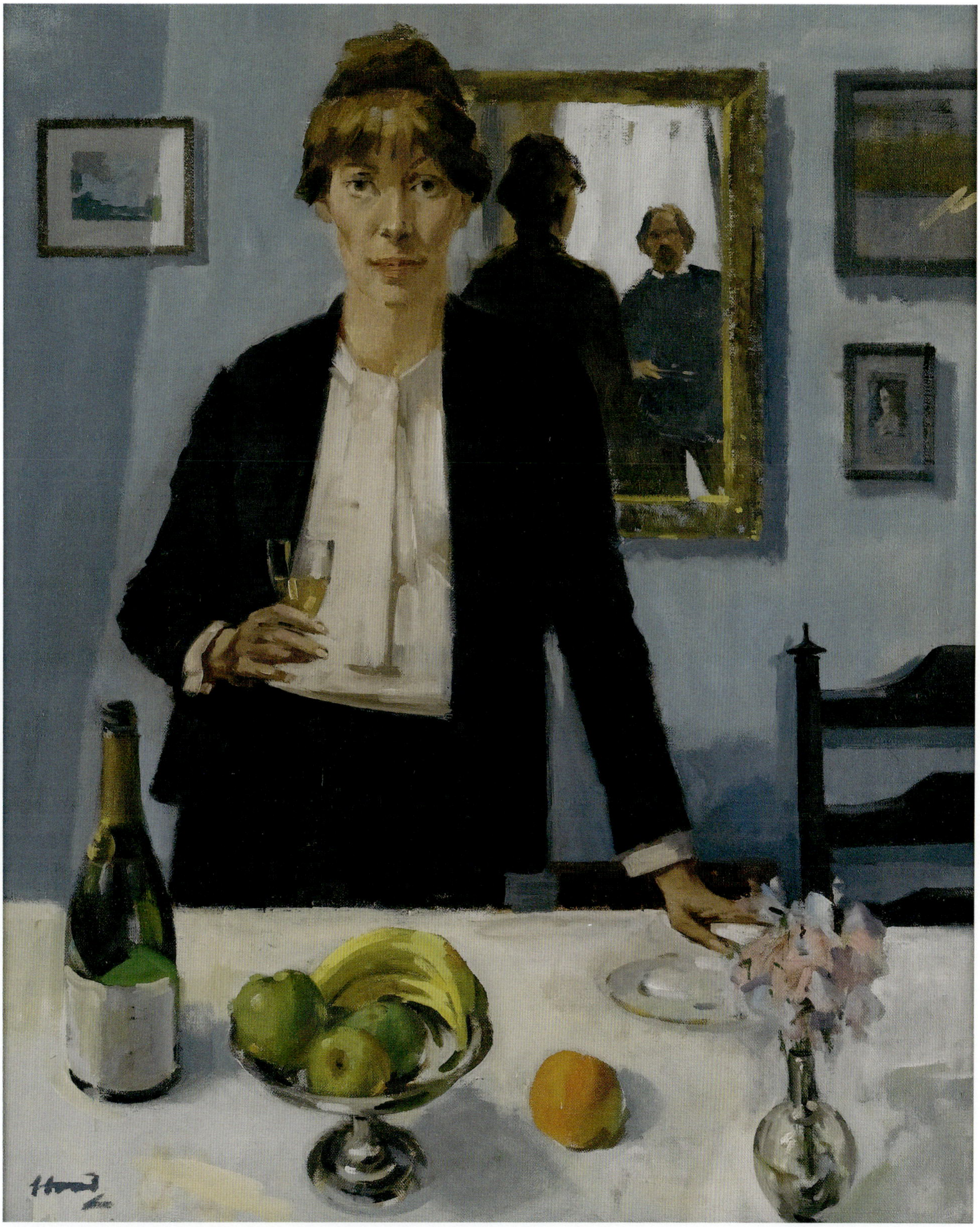

**148 Ernest Burnett Hood** (1932-1988), *Portrait of the Artist's Wife*, c.1970, oil on canvas, 34 ½ x 28 ¾ in. (88 x 73 cm).

Hood can be seen reflected in the mirror behind his wife and an outline of his reflection can also be discerned in the foreground champagne bottle. The composition makes reference to elements of Manet's celebrated *Bar au Folies Bergère*.

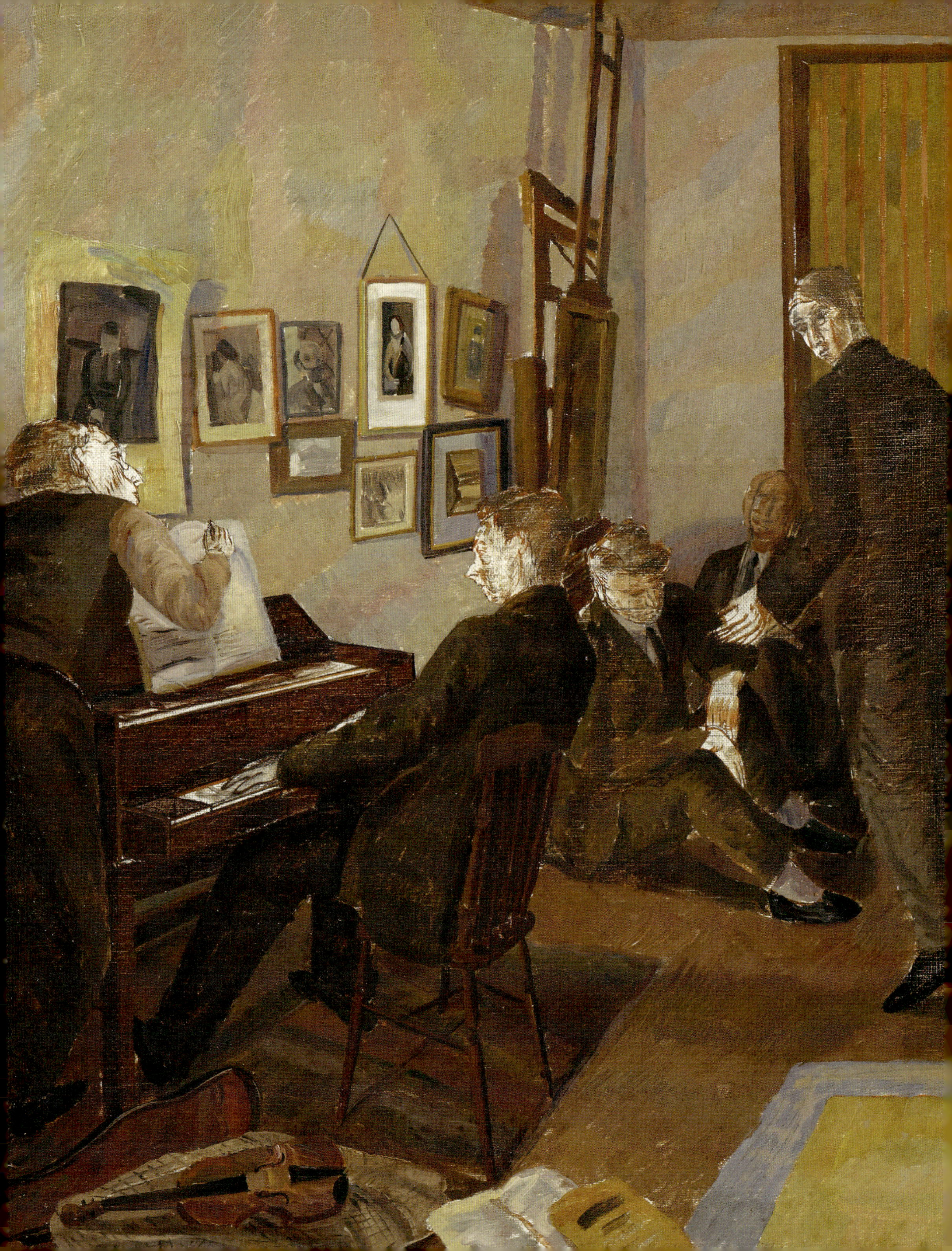

# ARTISTS BY ARTISTS

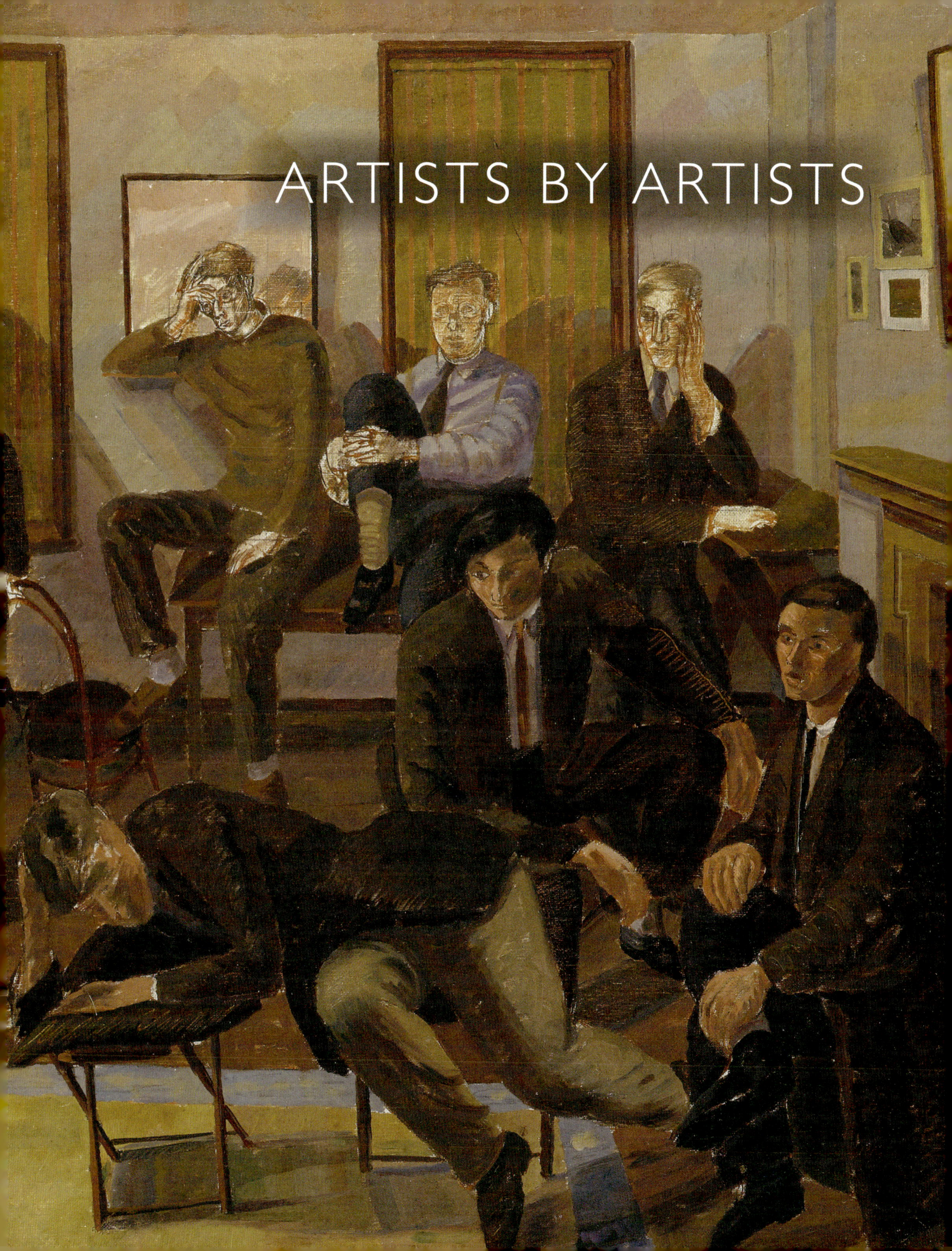

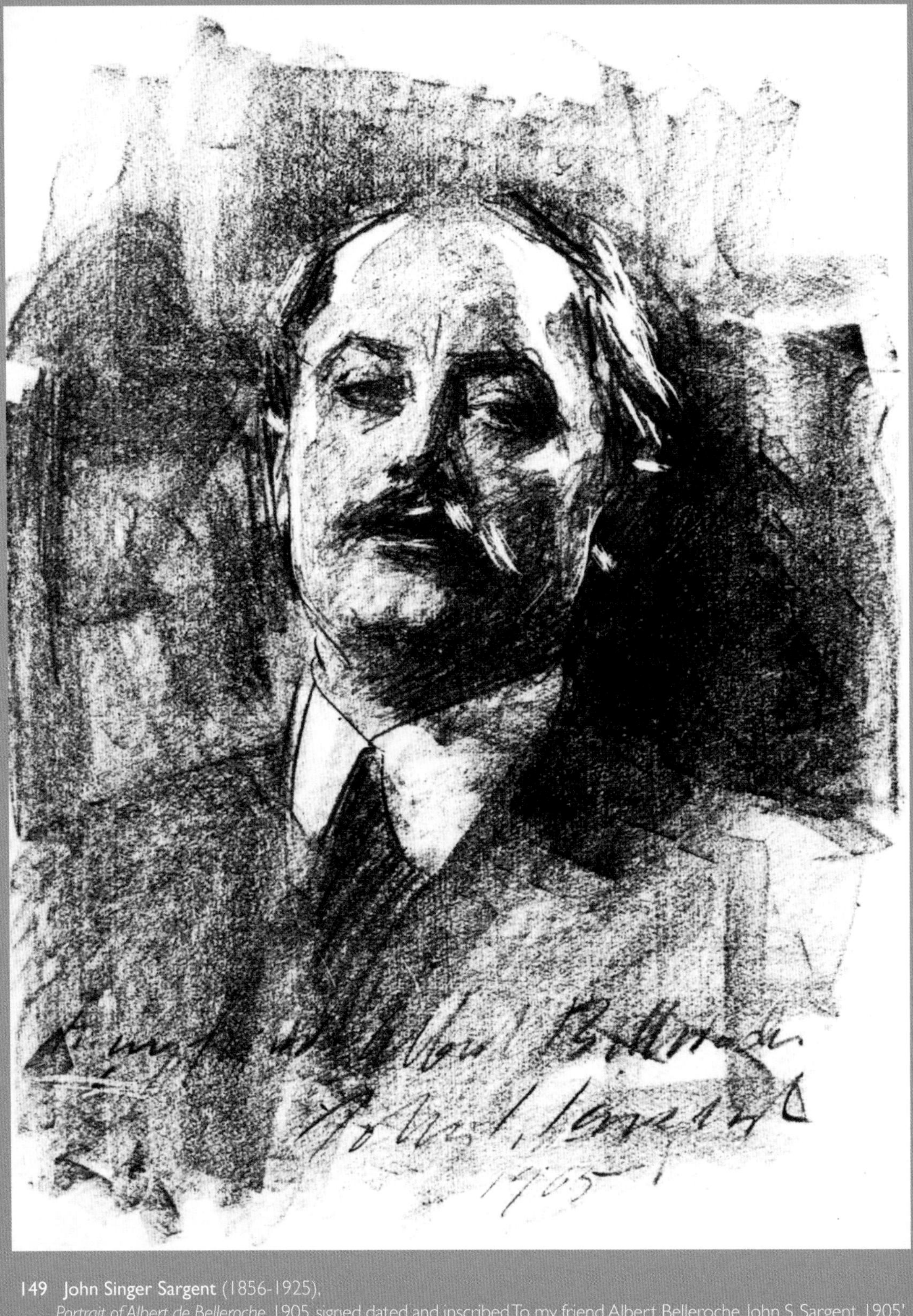

**149 John Singer Sargent** (1856-1925).
*Portrait of Albert de Belleroche*, 1905, signed dated and inscribed To my friend Albert Belleroche, John S. Sargent, 1905', lithograph on wove paper, 19 ¾ x 16 ¼ in. (50.5 x 41 cm).

John Singer Sargent and Albert de Belleroche met in 1882, when the latter was enrolled in the atelier of Carolus-Duran. A lifelong friendship resulted in them sharing studios in both London and Paris. Sargent made numerous portraits of Belleroche. The best known of these, painted in 1883, is now in the collection of the Metropolitan Museum of Art, New York.

# Artists by Artists

*'Every time I paint a portrait I lose a friend.'* John Singer Sargent

In spite of Sargent's quip, 'every time I paint a portrait I lose a friend', artists provided each other with the perfect subject. Unlike professional models, fellow artists usually did not have to be paid, and sittings might easily be reciprocal; Knights sat for Gill, Gill sat for Knights. Furthermore artists knew how to sit – and how to sit still – and how to pose: Belleroche, Dixon, Cundall, Brangwyn and Mahoney are amongst the many whose body language exudes confidence; others such as Whistler, Bone, Bliss and Hassall pose with a sense of swagger.

Most often artists portray each other at work – Cassatt, Adshead, Brangwyn, Cundall, Hassall, Brill, Bone and Goodwin – or at least in a studio setting, surrounded by the tools of the artist's trade and sometimes the fruits of his or her labour. There are however notable exceptions: Ososki, who won a medal for wrestling in the 1928 Olympics, is shown getting ready for a prize fight; Murray, an exceptionally talented violinist, is depicted pursuing his great love, other than print-making; and Freedman is shown directing a play. Amy Dyer is shown ironing, which poignantly brings to mind the disadvantages that women had in trying to balance running a household with a career.

Many of the portraits pay homage to other artists. Some may carry a dedication, as for instance 'To my friend Albert Belleroche, John S. Sargent, 1905'. Albert de Belleroche and Joseph Simpson both created images of Frank Brangwyn that were clearly intended to elevate him. Similarly Greaves painted Whistler in a formal and rather grandiose manner. Often there is a sense of benefit by association, a portrait being proof that its creator was moving in the right artistic circles, or, in the case of Rothenstein, nurturing the next generation. This was clearly the case when Hartrick painted Gauguin. Clearly less reverential was the inscription accompanying Douglas Percy Bliss' portrait of the same artist: 'It is impossible to love the man Gauguin. In his lifetime it is probable that he never loved anyone, man or woman. He simply used them. He was a ruthless egoist, harsh, sensual, arrogant. He was wretchedly unhappy for the most part even in this Polynesian Paradise. It takes more than a Sarong to make a Savage.'

Most portraits are attestations of friendship, especially amongst the student artist community. Carline drew Spencer, Dodd painted Ravilious, Garwood and Bawden; Townsend painted Mahoney, Mahoney painted Rhoades; Freedman painted an entire group of fellow students. The relationship between teachers and students is also a familiar theme, as in Dunstan's magnum opus or Rothenstein's remarkable double portrait of Finney and Houtheusen. Personalities like Hassall were painted numerous times. Winifred Knights, famed both for her beguiling looks and her striking talent, was the subject of portraits by more than ten artists, Gill, Monnington and Mason among them. Husbands, wives and lovers were frequent models; pictures by Rooke, Dring and Freedman commemorate engagements; Austin a honeymoon. Pieterson painted her husband Cundall; Rosalie Brill painted her husband, Reginald Brill. Monnington painted Knights and Bliss painted Dodd. Mary Adshead painted her husband Stephen Bone, and he in turn painted her numerous times.

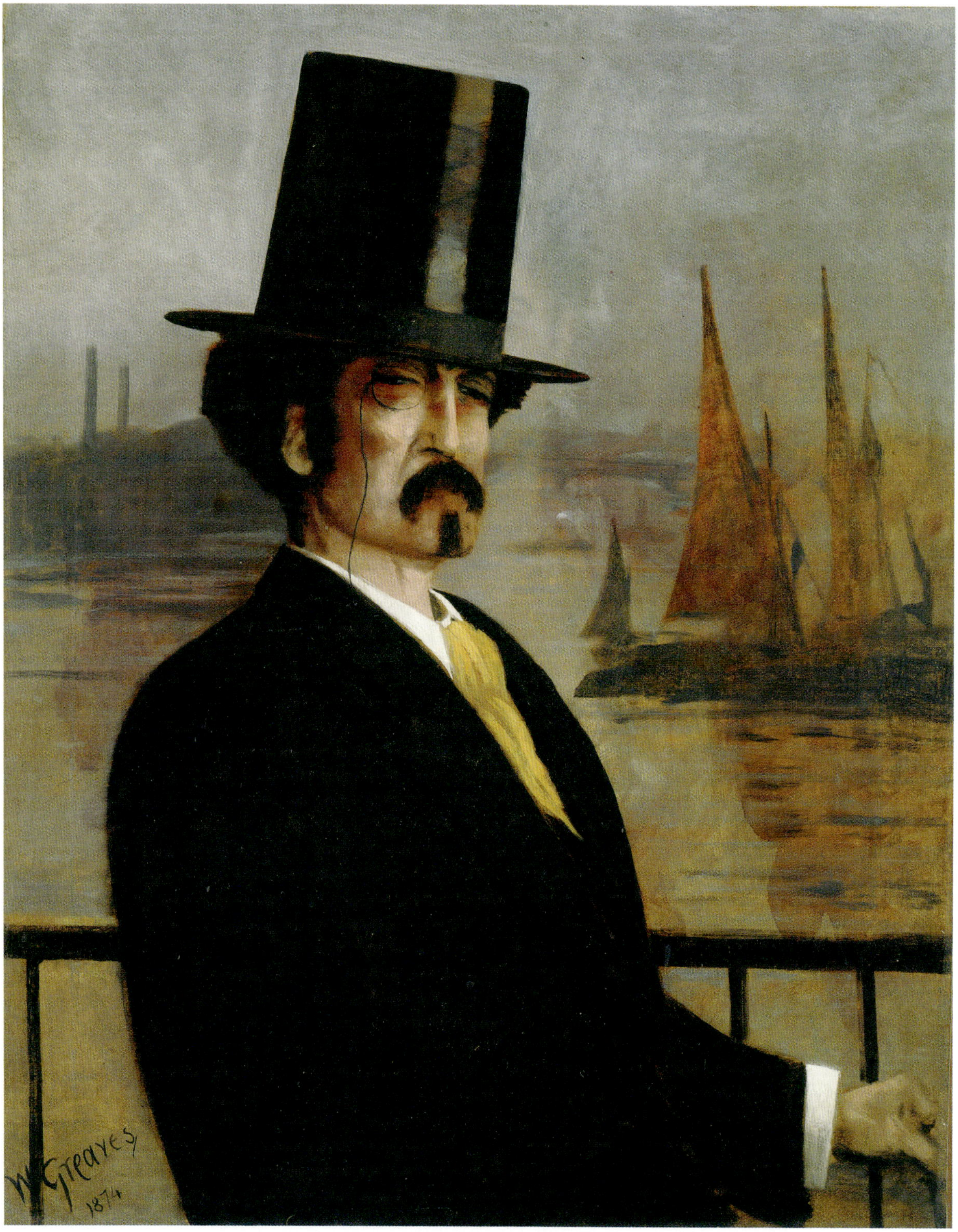


**150 Walter Greaves** (1846-1930), *Whistler on the Thames*, 1874, signed and dated, oil on canvas, 34 ¾ x 28 in. (88.3 x 71.5 cm). Collection: Ferens Art Gallery.

When Walter Greaves first met James Abbott McNeill Whistler in 1863, he was captivated and became Whistler's assistant and pupil. During the 1870s Greaves made a series of portraits of Whistler, with the Thames as a backdrop. Their friendship was jeopardised in the early 1880s when Joseph Pennell, Whistler's friend and biographer, damaged Greaves' reputation by suggesting that some of his canvases had in fact been painted by Whistler – a controversy that Greaves never recovered from.

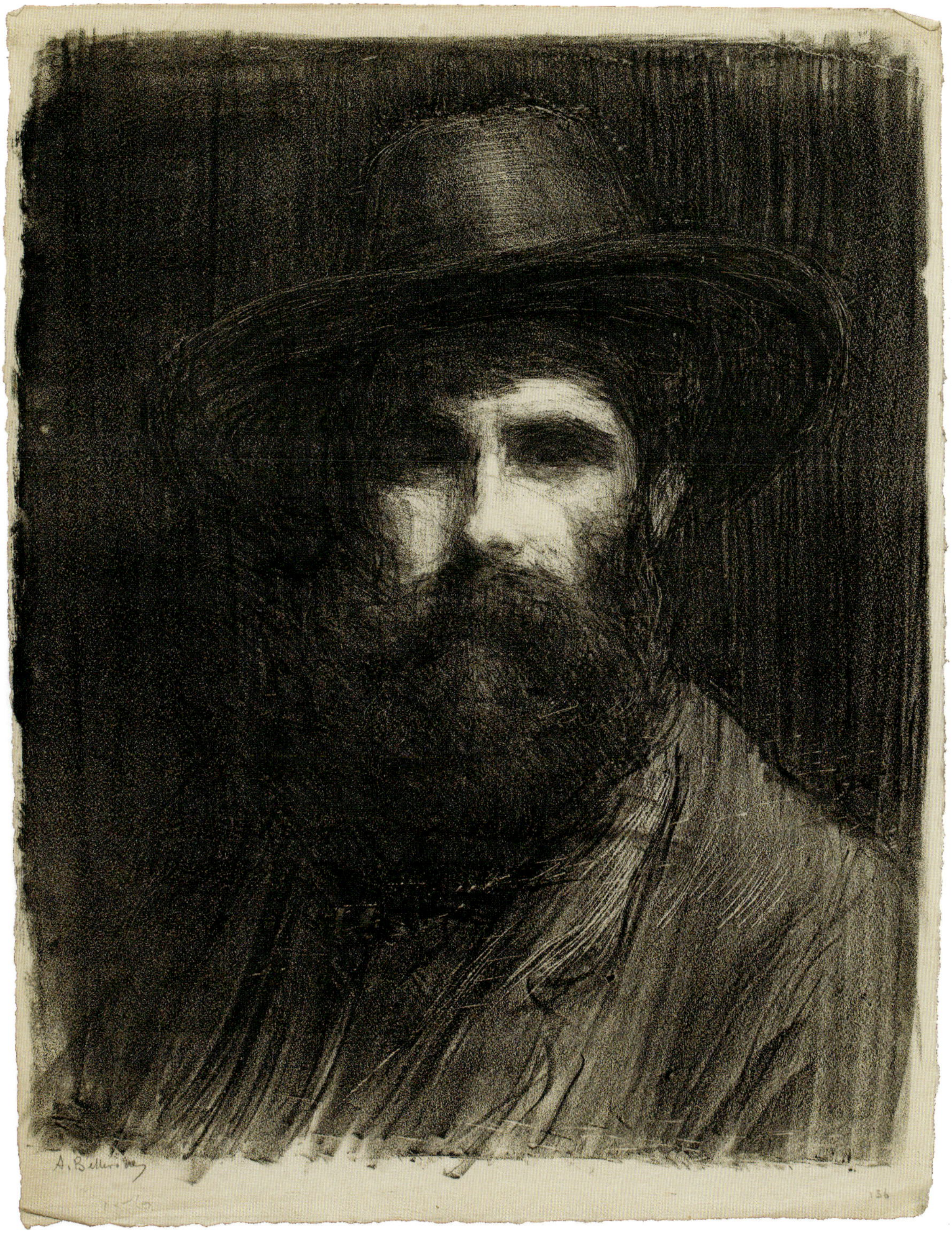

**151 Albert de Belleroche** (1864-1944), *Hermenegildo Anglada Camarasa* (1871-1959), signed, lithograph on paper, 23 ½ x 18 ½ in. (59.7 x 47 cm).

The painter Hermenegildo Anglada Camarasa (1871-1959) moved to Paris in 1894 to study at the Académie Julian. The nature of his friendship with Belleroche is undocumented, but evidence suggests that his style was influenced by that of Belleroche, (7 years his senior), as well as Degas and Toulouse-Lautrec. Later he graduated towards a brighter decorative palette, much influenced by the Vienna Secession.

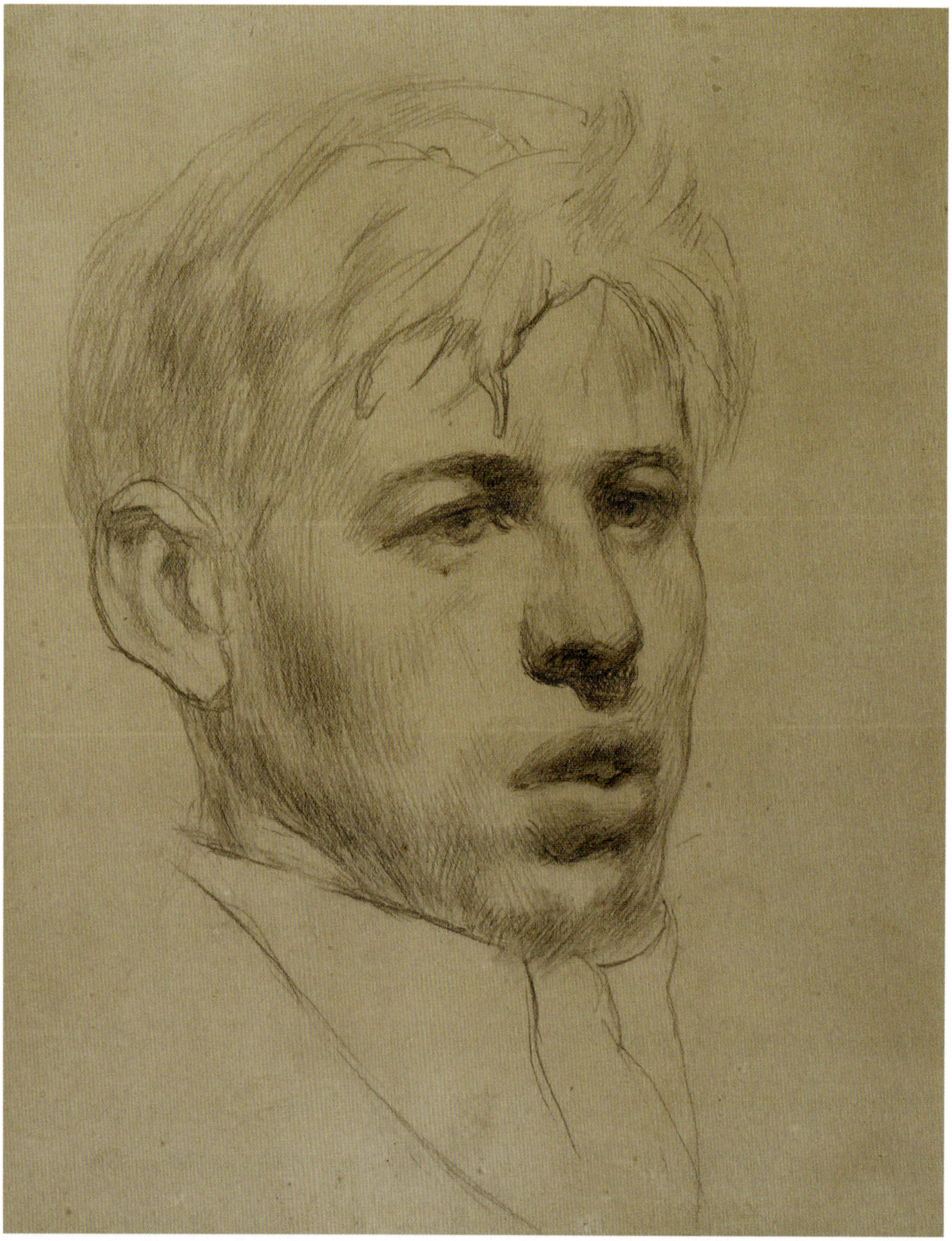

**152 Hilda Carline** (1889-1950), *Portrait of Gilbert Spencer*, c.1919, pencil on brown paper, 17 ¾ x 11 ¼ in. (45 x 30 cm).

Hilda Carline met Gilbert Spencer (**155**) while studying at the Slade School of Fine Art (1918-1922). Gilbert was the younger brother of Stanley, whom she went on to marry in 1925. These two portrait drawings, one executed in pencil, the other in red chalk, date to around 1919; in their vigour and directness they demonstrate the teachings of Professor Henry Tonks, who encouraged students to emulate the drawing methods of the Renaissance masters. (**325**)

**153 Hilda Carline** (1889-1950), *Portrait of Gilbert Spencer*, c.1919, inscribed 'Mr G Spencer', (**128**), red chalk on paper, 17 ¾ x 11 ¾ in. (45 x 30 cm).

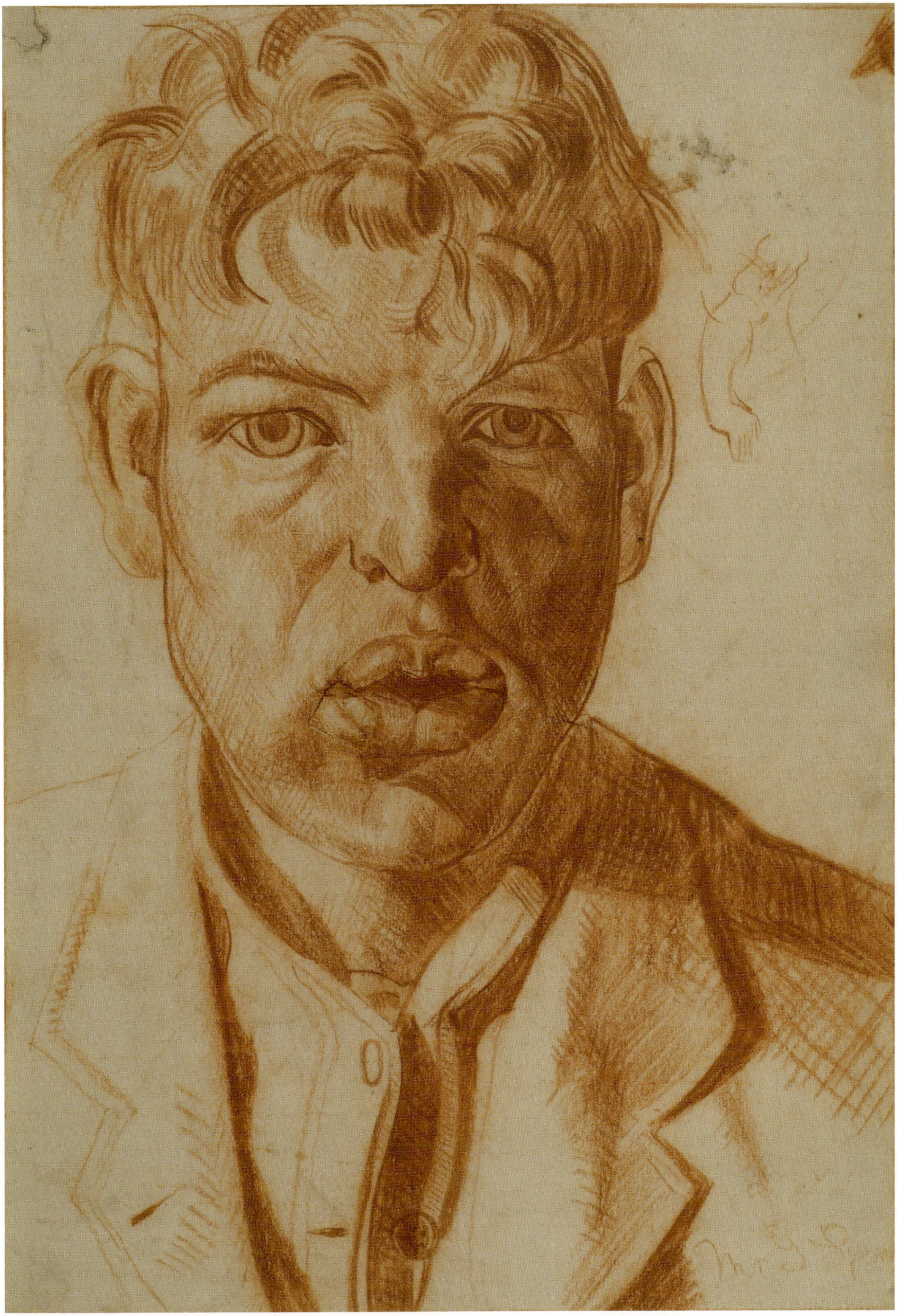

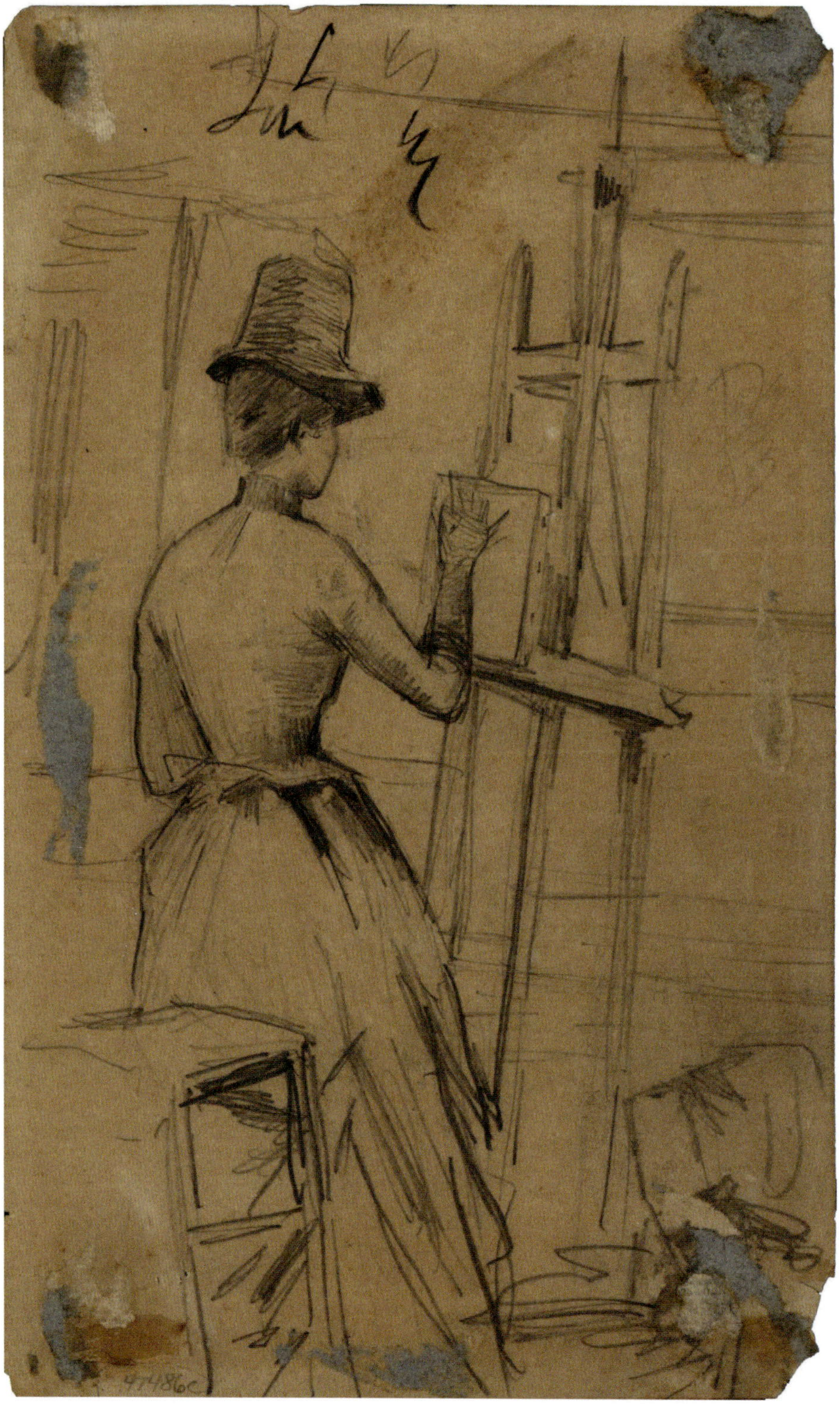

**154 Albert de Belleroche** (1864-1944), *Portrait of Mary Cassatt*, 1880s, pencil on paper, 7 ½ x 4 ¾ in. (19 x 12.2 cm).

Mary Stevenson Cassatt (1844-1926) was an American painter and printmaker born in Pennsylvania. She lived much of her life in France, where, like Belleroche, she befriended Edgar Degas and exhibited with the Impressionists. She was described by Gustave Geffroy as one of 'les trois grandes dames' of Impressionism alongside Marie Bracquemond and Berthe Morisot.

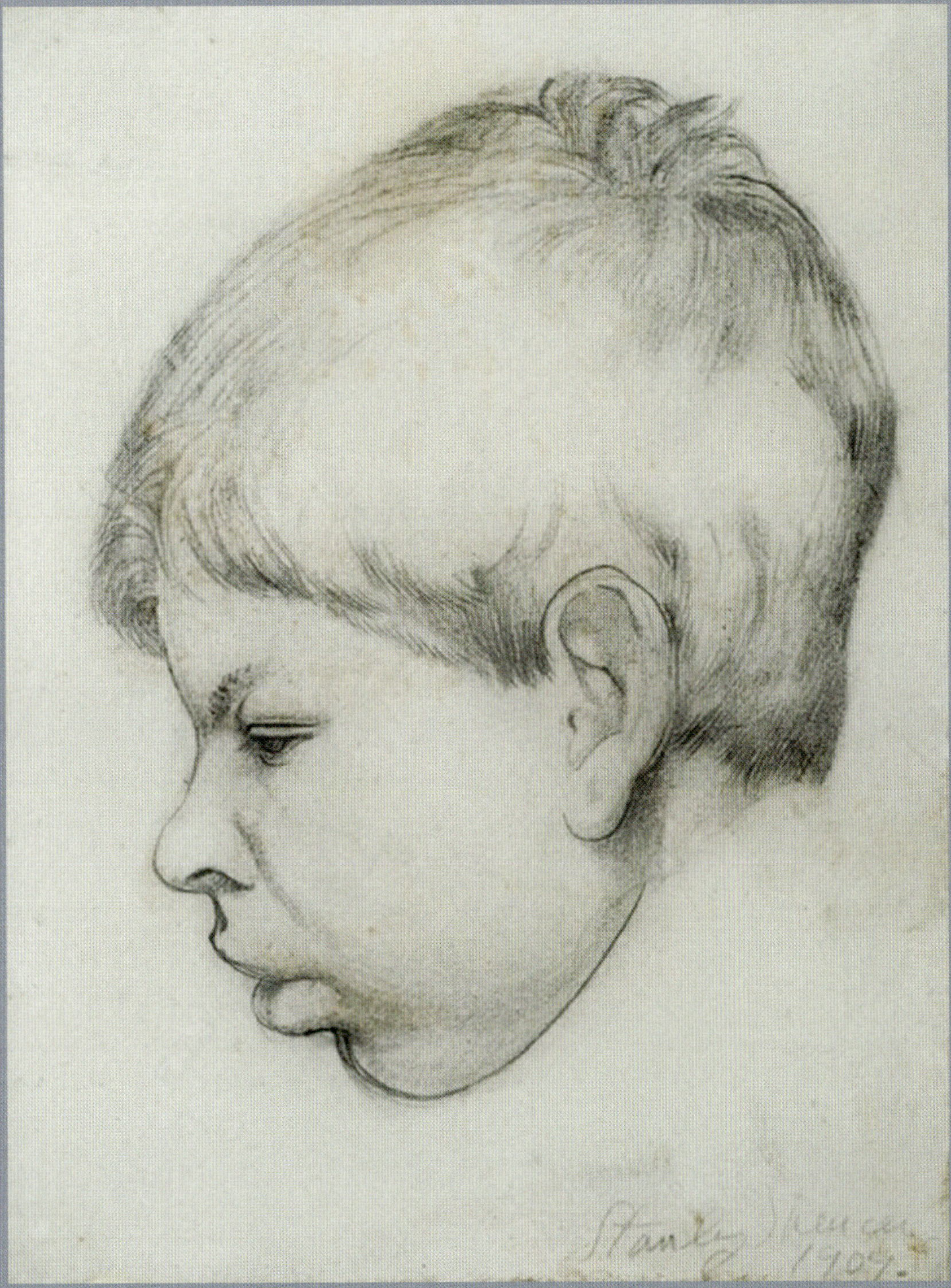

**155 Stanley Spencer** (1891-1959), *Portrait of Gilbert*, 1909, signed and date, pencil on paper, 8 1/2 x 6 in. (22 x 16 cm). On long-term loan to the Stanley Spencer Gallery, Cookham.

When Stanley Spencer made this affectionate profile portrait of his younger brother Gilbert (**325**) the two were already at art school – Stanley in his first year at the Slade, and Gilbert at The Ruskin School. Taught by the illustrious Henry Tonks, Stanley's contemporaries included Dora Carrington, Mark Gertler, Paul Nash, Edward Wadsworth, Isaac Rosenberg and David Bomberg.

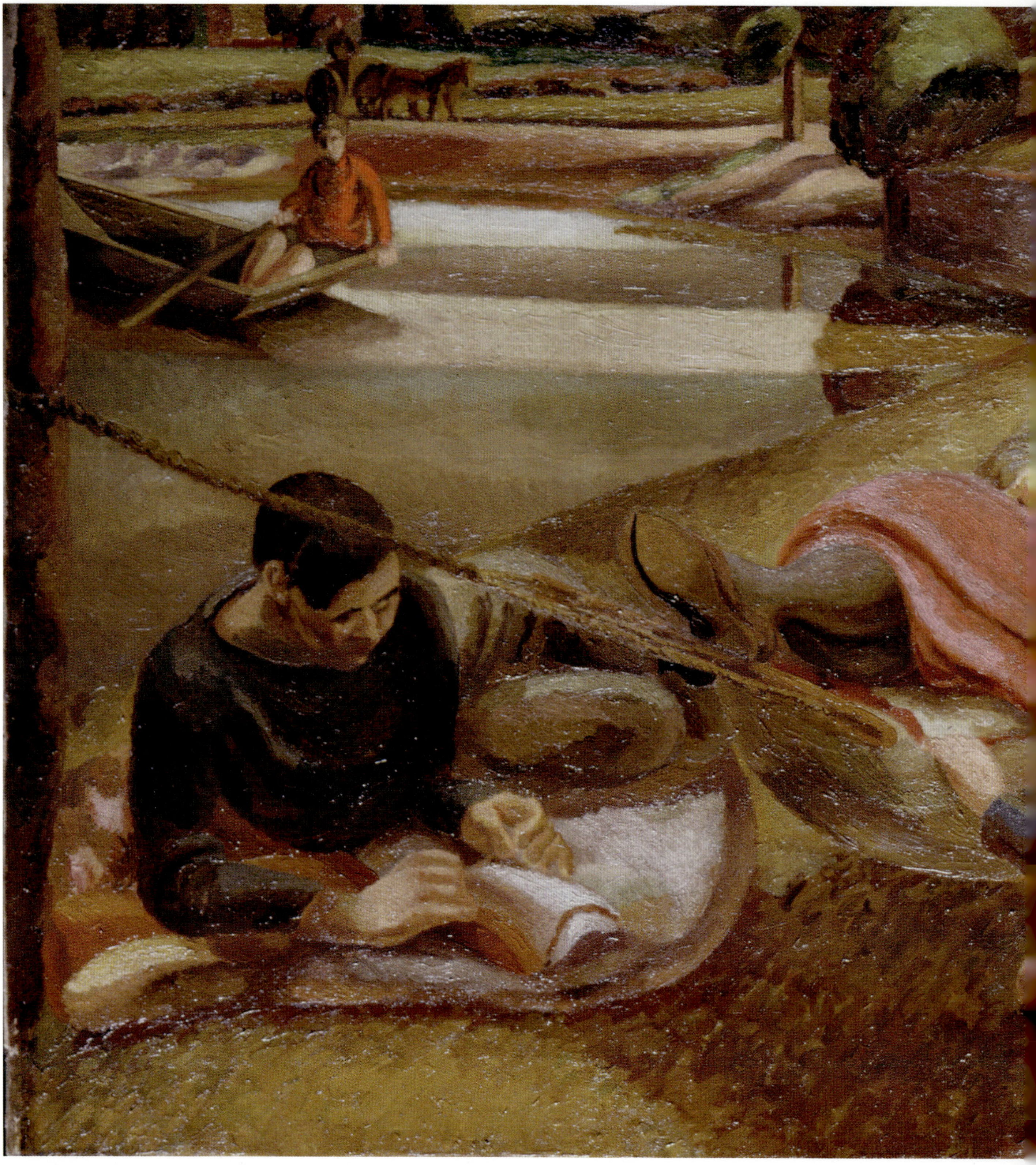

**156 Duncan Grant** (1885-1978), *The Hammock*, 1921-23, signed and dated,
oil on canvas, 32 x 57 ¾ in. (81.7 x 146.5 cm). Collection: Laing Art Gallery. 

The artist and designer Vanessa Bell is shown relaxing in a summertime scene. Her three children play around her in their garden at

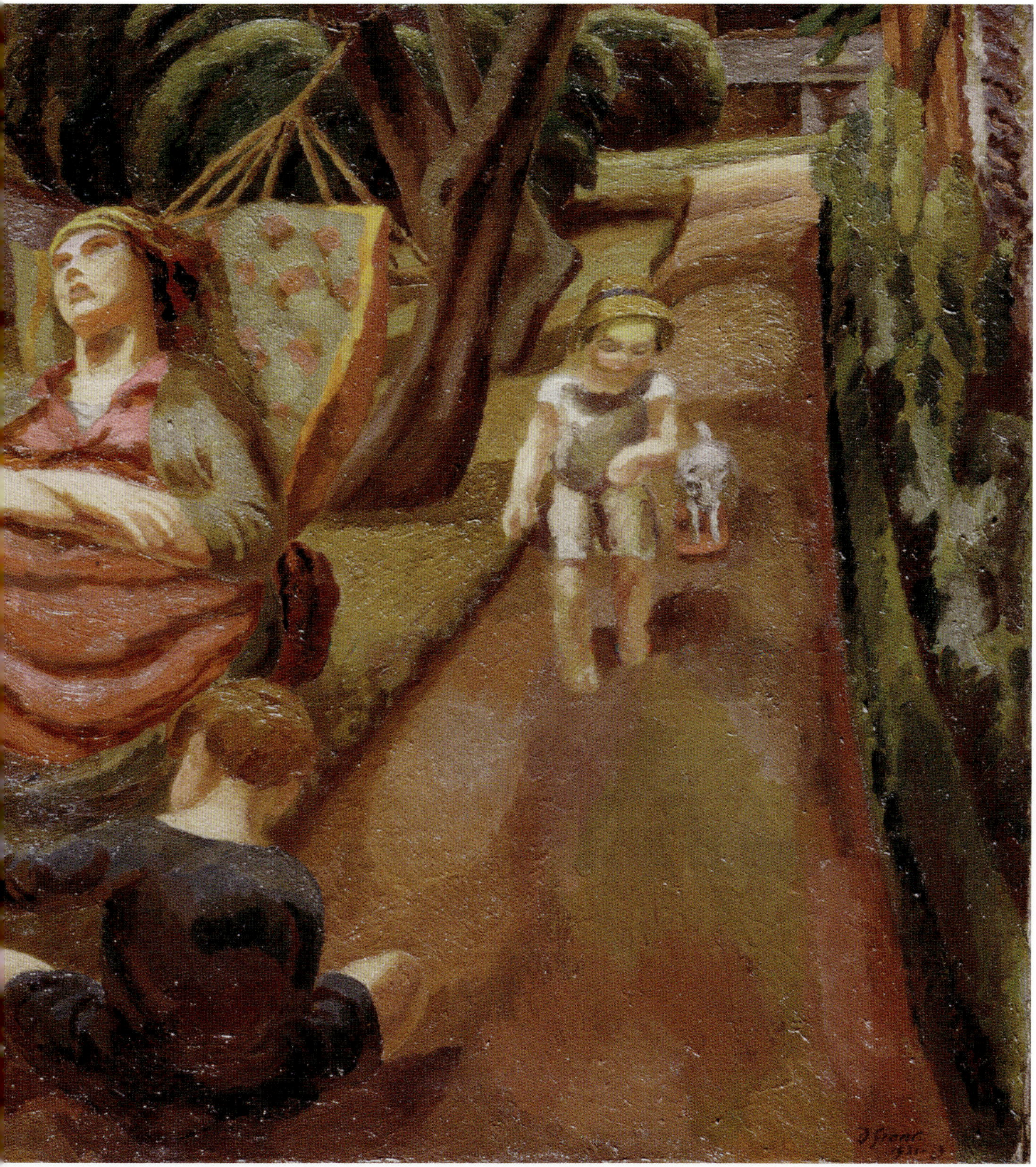

Charleston in Sussex. Angelica walks along the path, while Julian is in the punt on the left and Quentin rocks the hammock. Both Quentin and Angelica became artists, and Julian was a poet. In the painting, the young man reading a book is the boys' tutor, the sociologist W.J.H. (Sebastian) Sprott. Grant's pattern-like style of painting in this picture was influenced by French Post-Impressionist painters such as Cézanne. Both Vanessa Bell and Duncan Grant were members of the Bloomsbury Group of writers and artists.

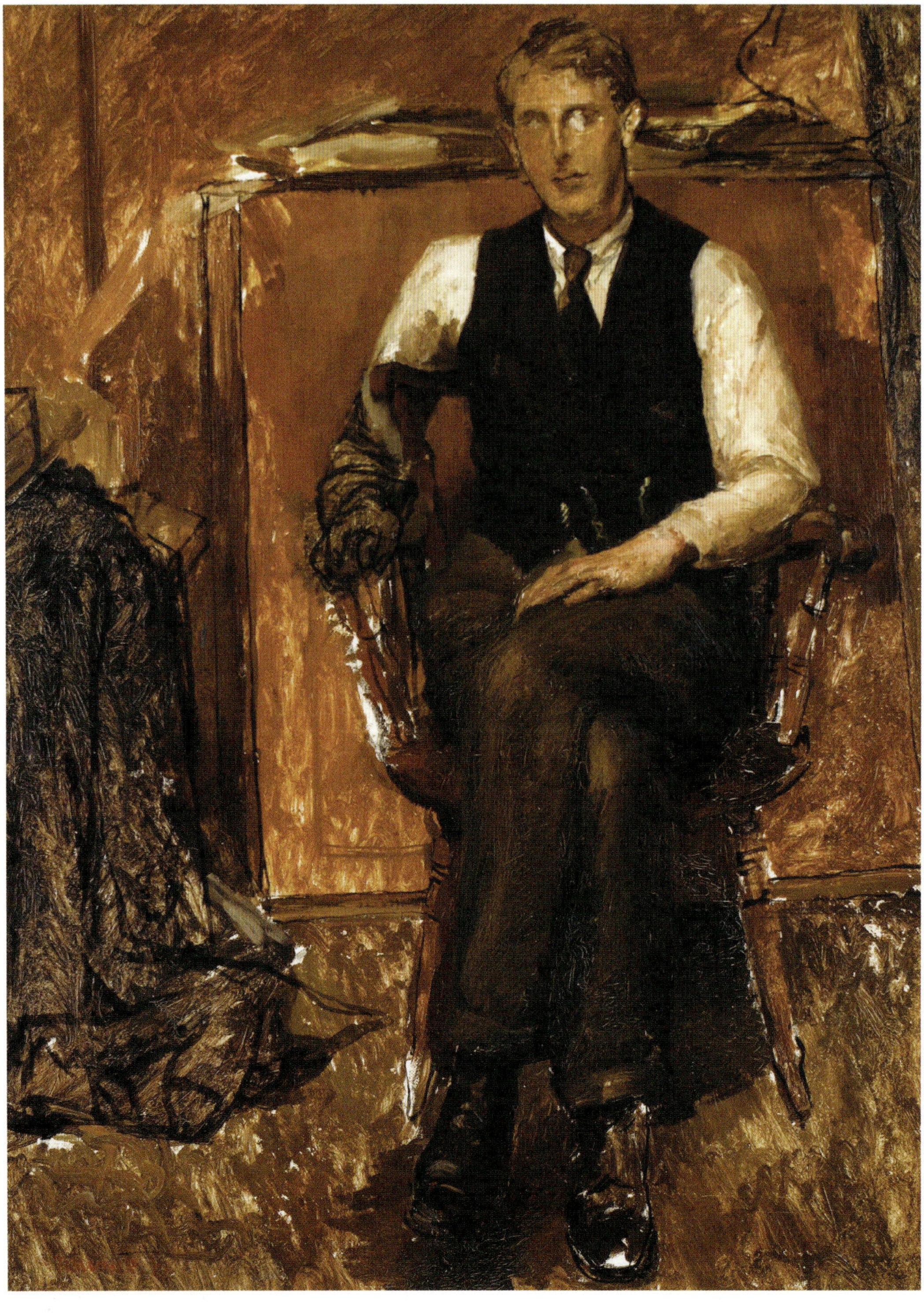

**157 Donald Chrisholm Towner** (1903-1985), *Portrait of Charles Mahoney*, 1926, signed and dated, oil on canvas , 24 x 18 in. (61 x 46 cm).

Mahoney and Towner were fellow students at the Royal College of Art. Mahoney was 23 years old when this portrait was painted. Perhaps deliberately, perhaps by chance, Mahoney's eye defect (Mahoney had lost the sight in one eye in a childhood accident) seems emphasised in this portrait sketch. Tirzah Garwood recounts several amusing anecdotes about Mahoney in *Long Live Great Bardfield* (Fleece Press, 2012; Persephone Books, 2015): 'Charlie had a glass eye but I thought that on the whole it improved his appearance, giving an interesting and piratical look to a face that as nature intended it, might have belonged to a Sunday School superintendent or a postman.'

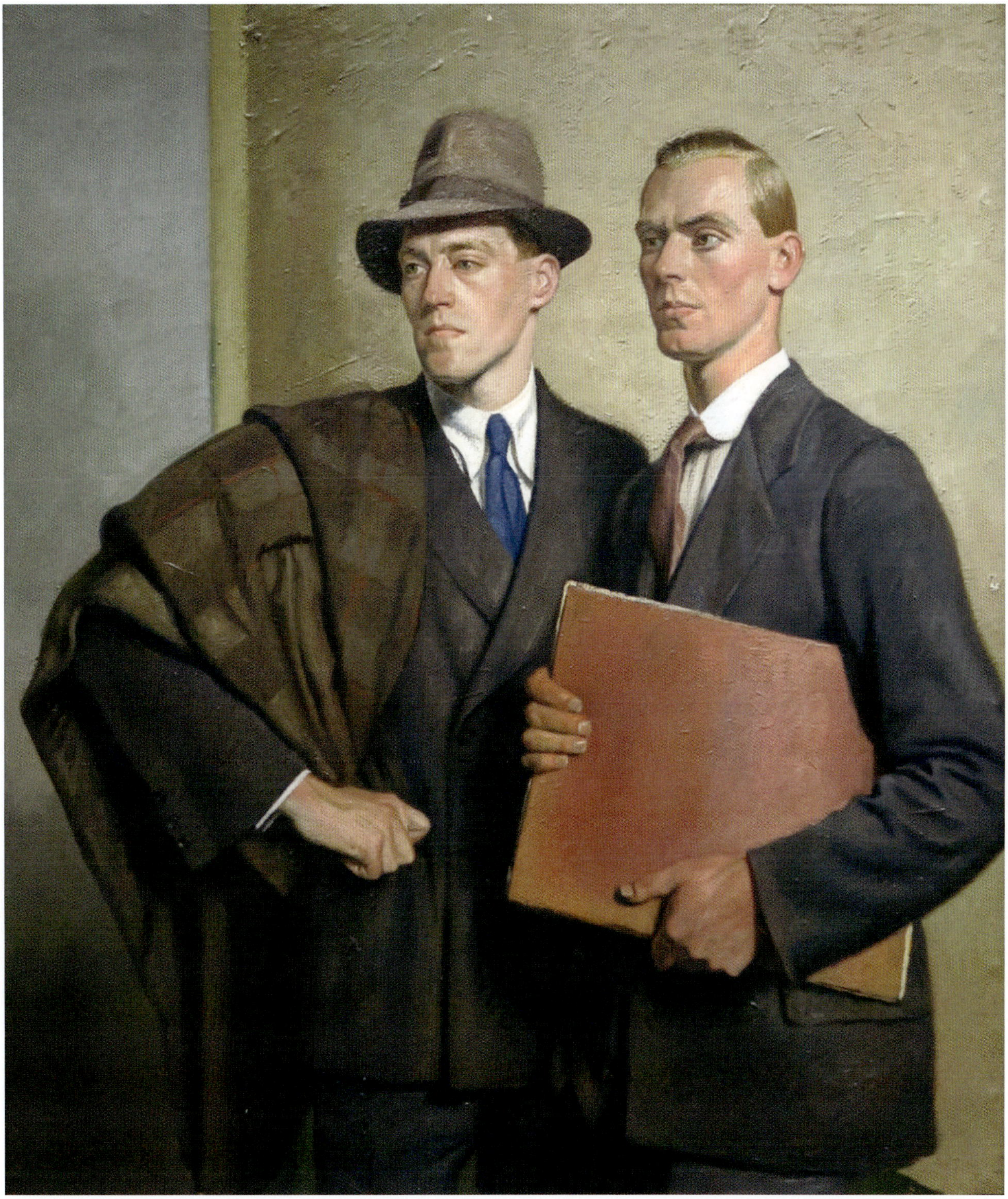

**158 William Rothenstein** (1872-1945), *Portrait of Albert Houthuesen and Hugh Finney as Students at the R.C.A*, c.1927, oil on canvas 35 ¾ x 31 in. (91 x 79 cm).

More than two hundred of Rothenstein's portraits can be found in the National Portrait Gallery collection. Rothenstein served as Principal at the Royal College of Art from 1920 to 1935. Albert Houthuesen and Hugh Arthur Finney overlapped as students at the R.C.A in 1927 (**310**, **311**, **324**), the year that Houthuesen completed his magnum opus *The Supper at Emmaus*. (**328**)

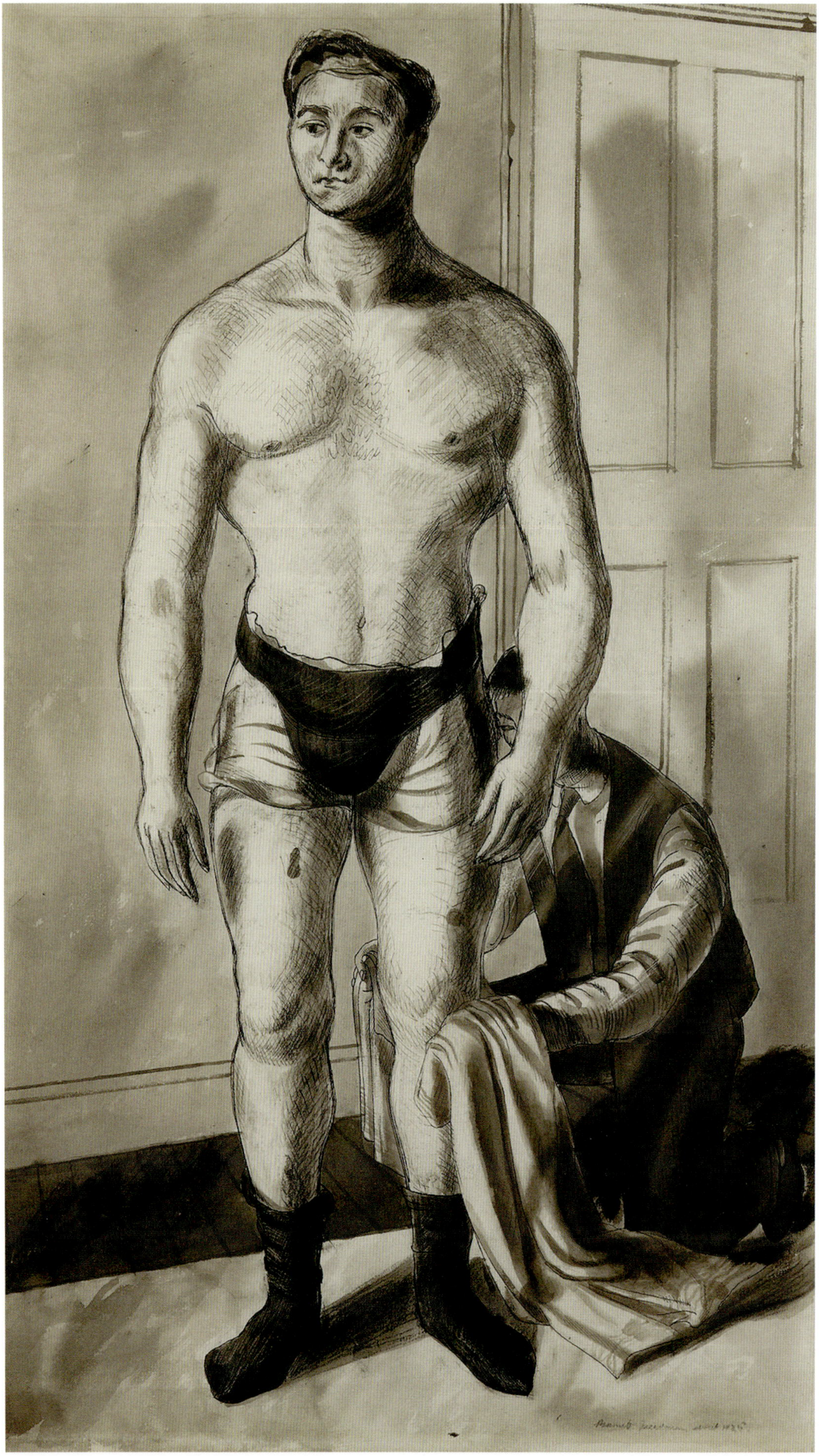

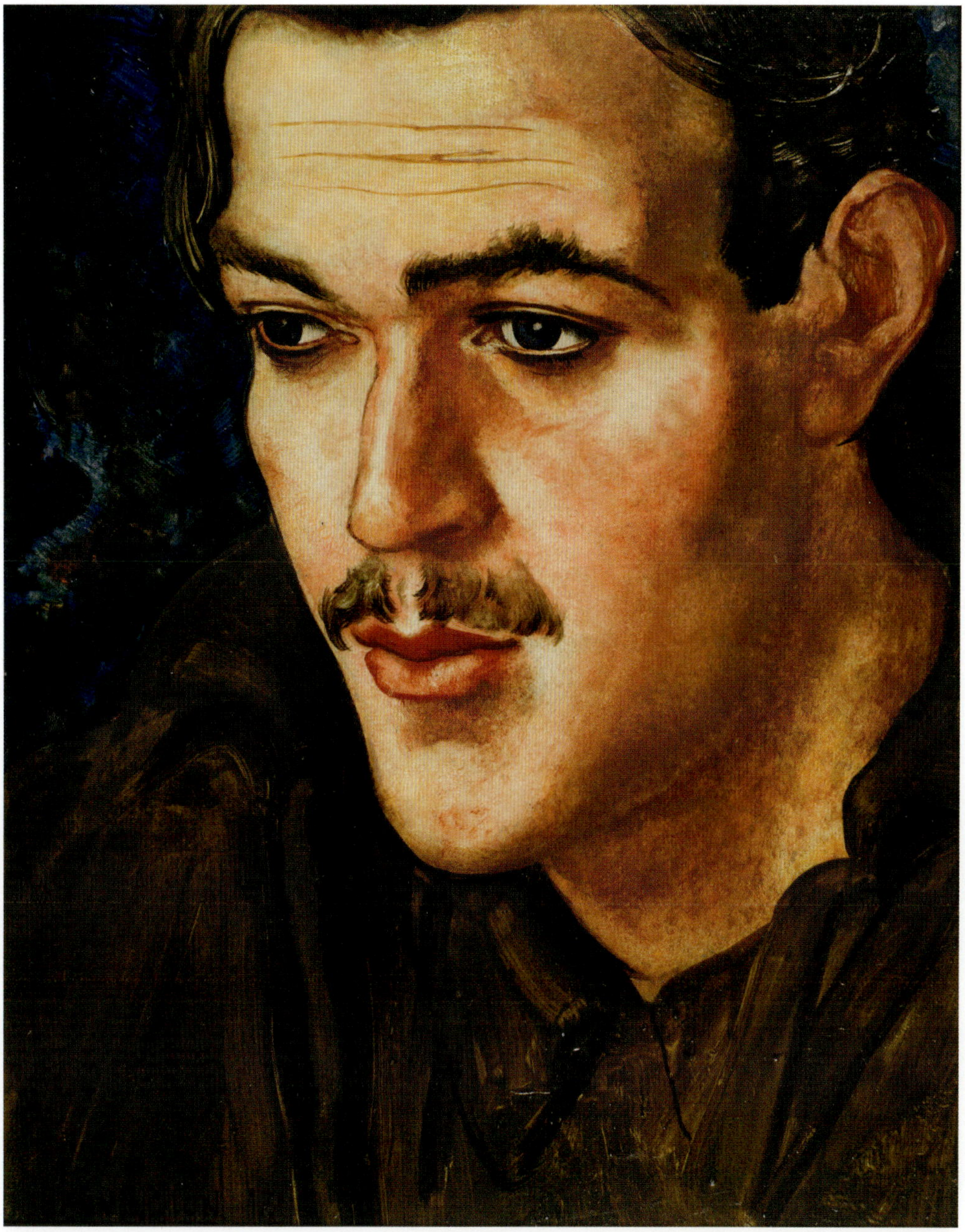

**160 Eric Kennington** (1888-1960), *Portrait of Cosmo Clark,* 1917, signed and dated, oil on panel, 12 x 9 ¾ in. (30.5 x 25 cm).

Cosmo Clark and Eric Kennington – childhood neighbours – were life-long friends. During WW1 both served with the Middlesex Regiment, to which Kennington was attached as an Official War Artist.

**159 Barnett Freedman** (1901-1958), *Portrait of Sam Rabin*, c. 1925, signed and dated, pen, brush and black ink on paper, 25 x 15in. (64.8 x 38.1cm).

Born Samuel Rabinovitch, 'Rabin' won a scholarship in 1914 to the Manchester Municipal School of Art, at 11 the youngest pupil ever to attend the college. In 1921 he gained a place at the Slade School of Fine Art. Rabin was physically strong and boxed and wrestled as an amateur to fund his career as an artist. He won a bronze medal in the middleweight division of the free-style wrestling at the 1928 Olympics in Amsterdam and turned professional in 1932. The figure kneeling behind, massaging Rabin's knee is the artist Gerald Ososki, who was a friend of both Freedman and Rabin. In 1949, Rabin began teaching drawing at Goldsmith's College of Art in New Cross, London. His students included Mary Quant, Bridget Riley and Tom Keating.

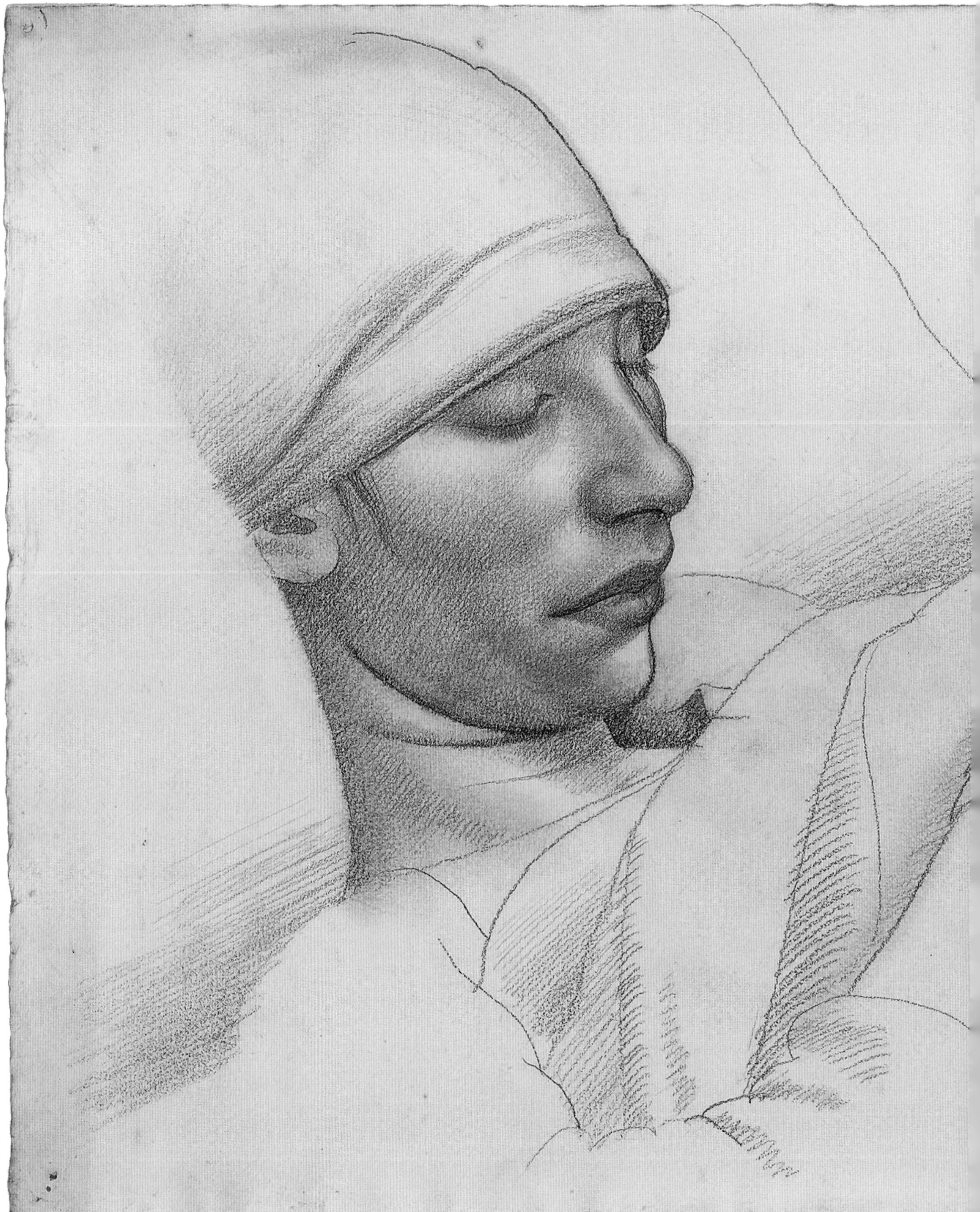

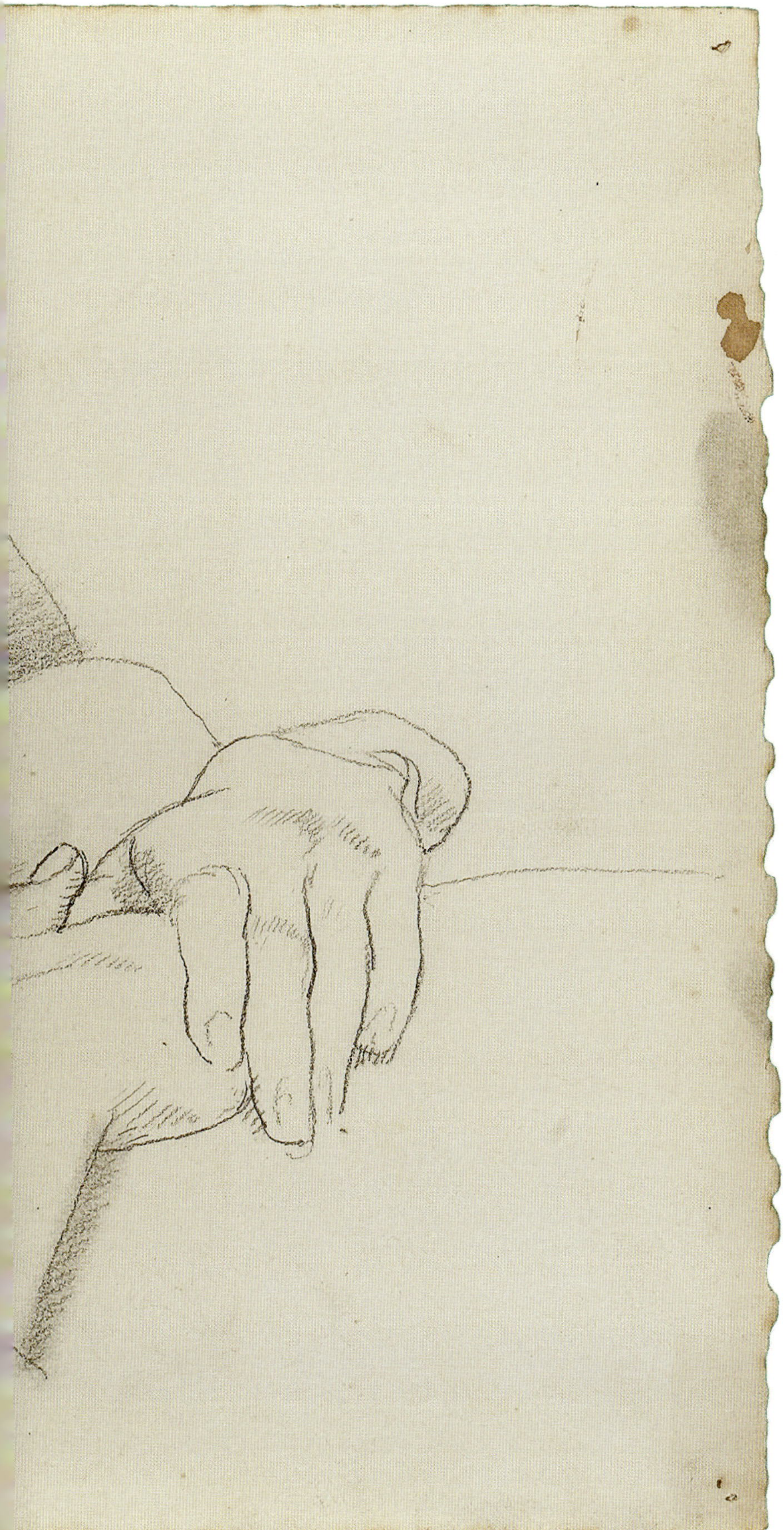

**161 Arnold Mason** (1885-1963),
*Portrait of Winifred Knights Sleeping*, c.1920,
pencil on paper, 11 x 15 ¼ in. (28 x 39 cm.).

In 1918, Arnold Mason enrolled at the Slade where he became a friend and later fiancé of Knights. (**164**) Although in 1924 Knights married fellow Rome Scholar Tom Monnington, the friendship with Mason endured and this pencil portrait was one which Knights retained throughout her life. In 1947 Mason exhibited a posthumous portrait at the Royal Academy, *The Late Winifred Knights*. A slightly earlier portrait of Knights by Mason is in the Queen's Collection (Royal Library Windsor, 23047).

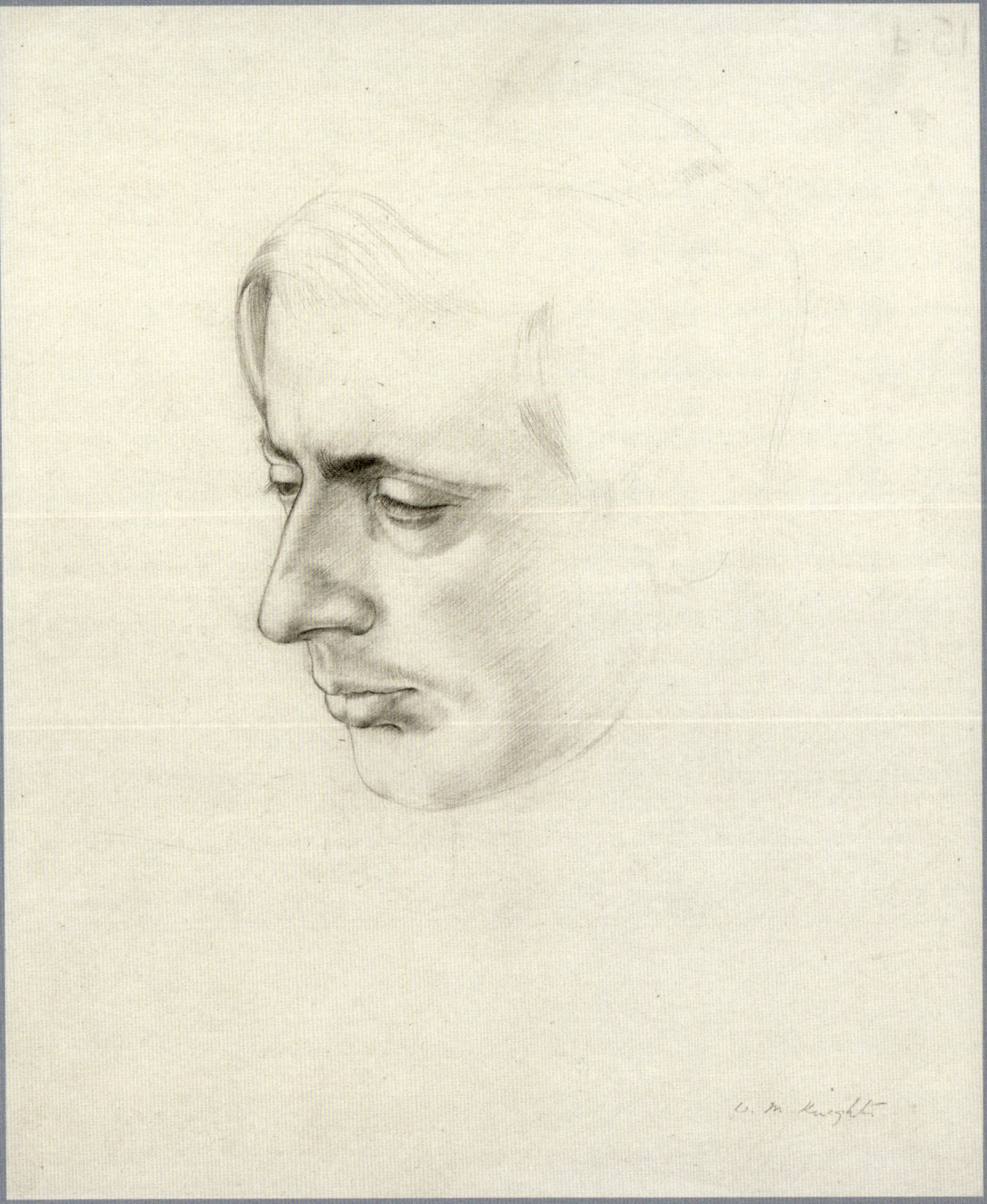

**162 Winifred Knights** (1899-1947), *Portrait of Colin Gill*, c.1921, signed, pencil on paper, 10 ¼ x 8 ¾ in. (26 x 22.2 cm).

Colin Gill was the first Rome Scholar in Decorative Painting. He completed his stay at the British School at Rome in 1921, shortly before Winifred Knights, the first woman to win the Scholarship, arrived at the end of 1920 as his successor. Each produced a pencil portrait of the other. Gill included Knights in a full-length portrait, holding a bird cage, in his British School at Rome masterpiece *Allegory* (**339**), completed in May 1921: 'I couldn't get [the newspaper] away from Gill; he had his nose glued to it for a whole morning, so I drew him – not at all a bad drawing' (Letter from Knights to her mother, 19th May 1920).

**163 Colin Gill** (1892-1940), *Portrait of Winifred Knights*, 1921, signed and inscribed 'Jane' on the original backboard, (**339**), pencil on paper, 17 ¼ x 12 ¾ in. (43.8 x 32.4 cm).

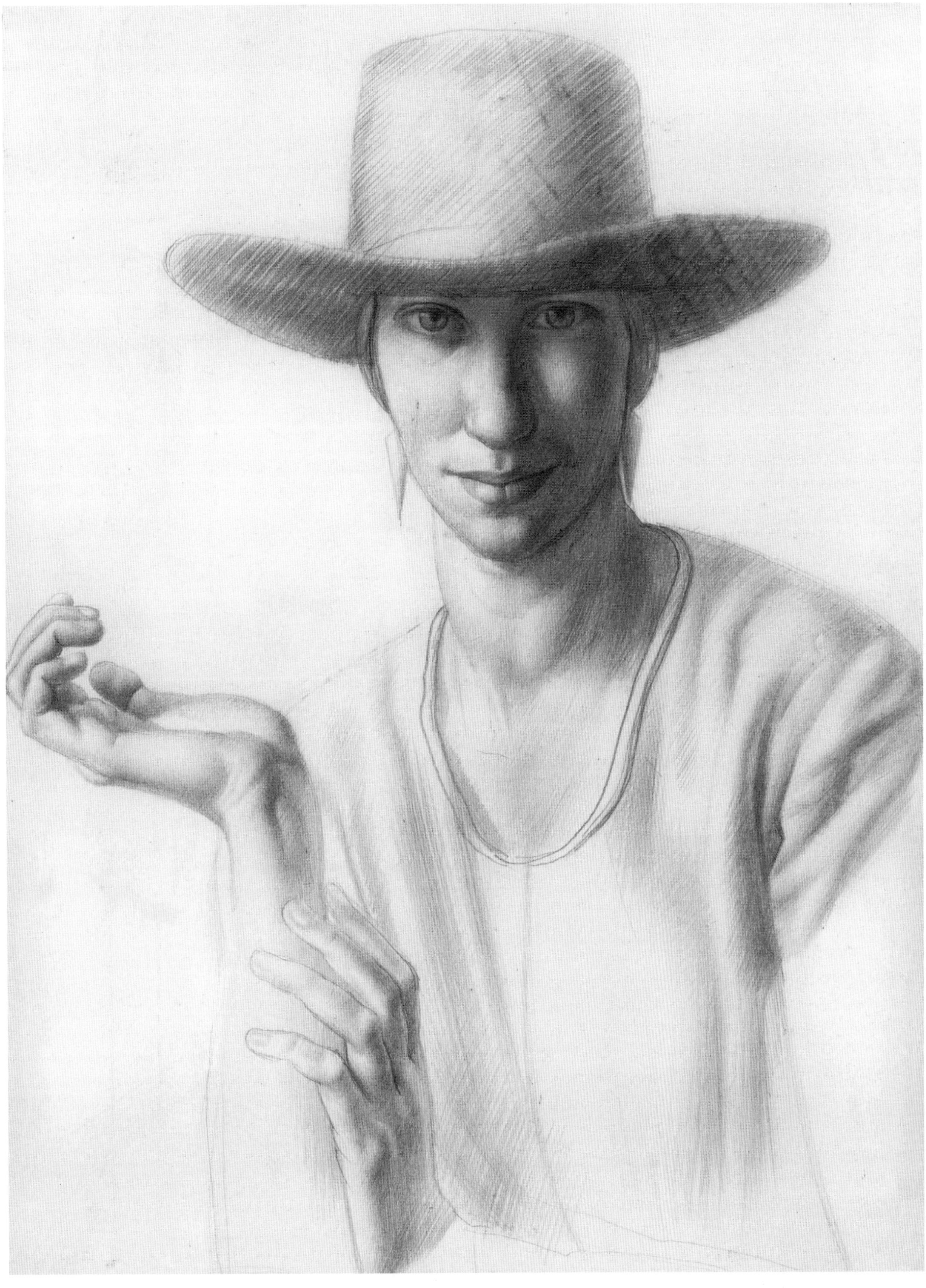

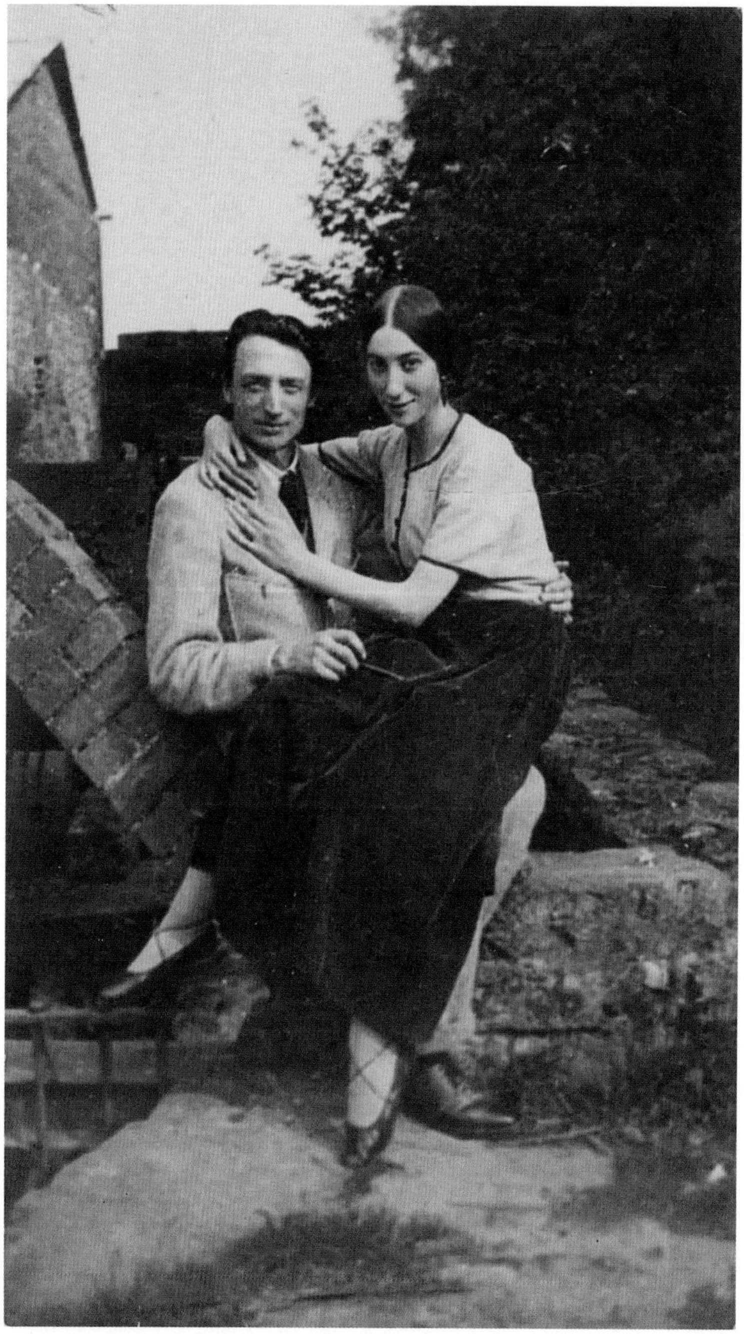

**164** **Winifred Knights** (1899-1947),
*Winifred Knights and Arnold Mason, Ludlow*, September 1920,
photograph, 10 x 5 ¾ in. (25.4 x 14.6 cm).

On the 21st of September 1920, while on holiday in Ludlow with her father, Arnold Mason and Mary Attenborough, Knights learnt that she had won the coveted British School at Rome Scholarship in Decorative Painting for 1920. (**161**)

**165** **Winifred Knights** (1899-1947), *Portrait Study of Colin Gill*, c.1921,
pencil on paper, 15 x 10 in. (38.2 x 25.3 cm).

In March 1921, Gill and Knights set off on a walking expedition in the countryside north west of Rome, and then travelled by bus to Viterbo, Orvieto, Assisi, Perugia and Florence. This portrait study likely dates from this expedition. (**261**)

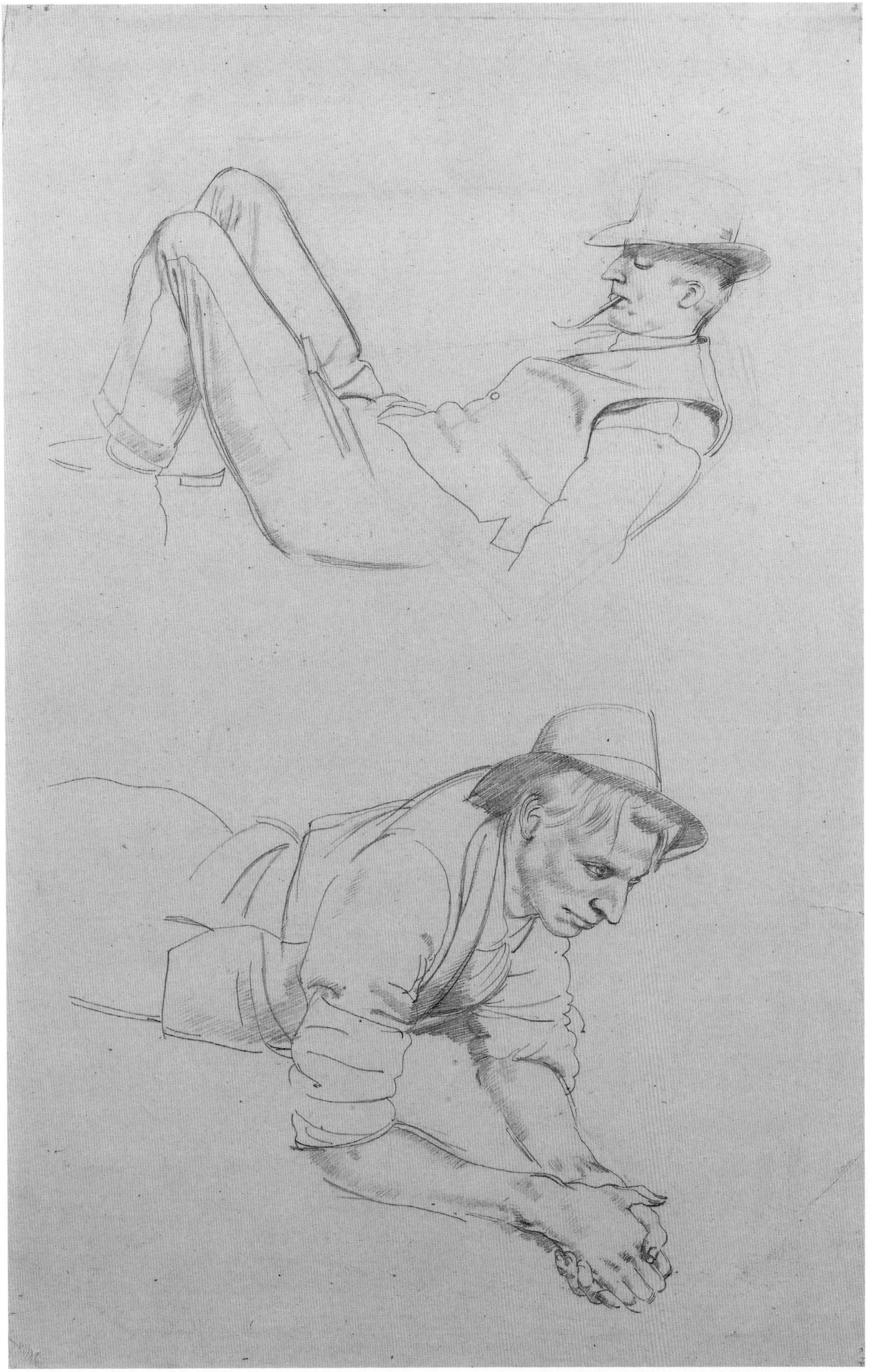

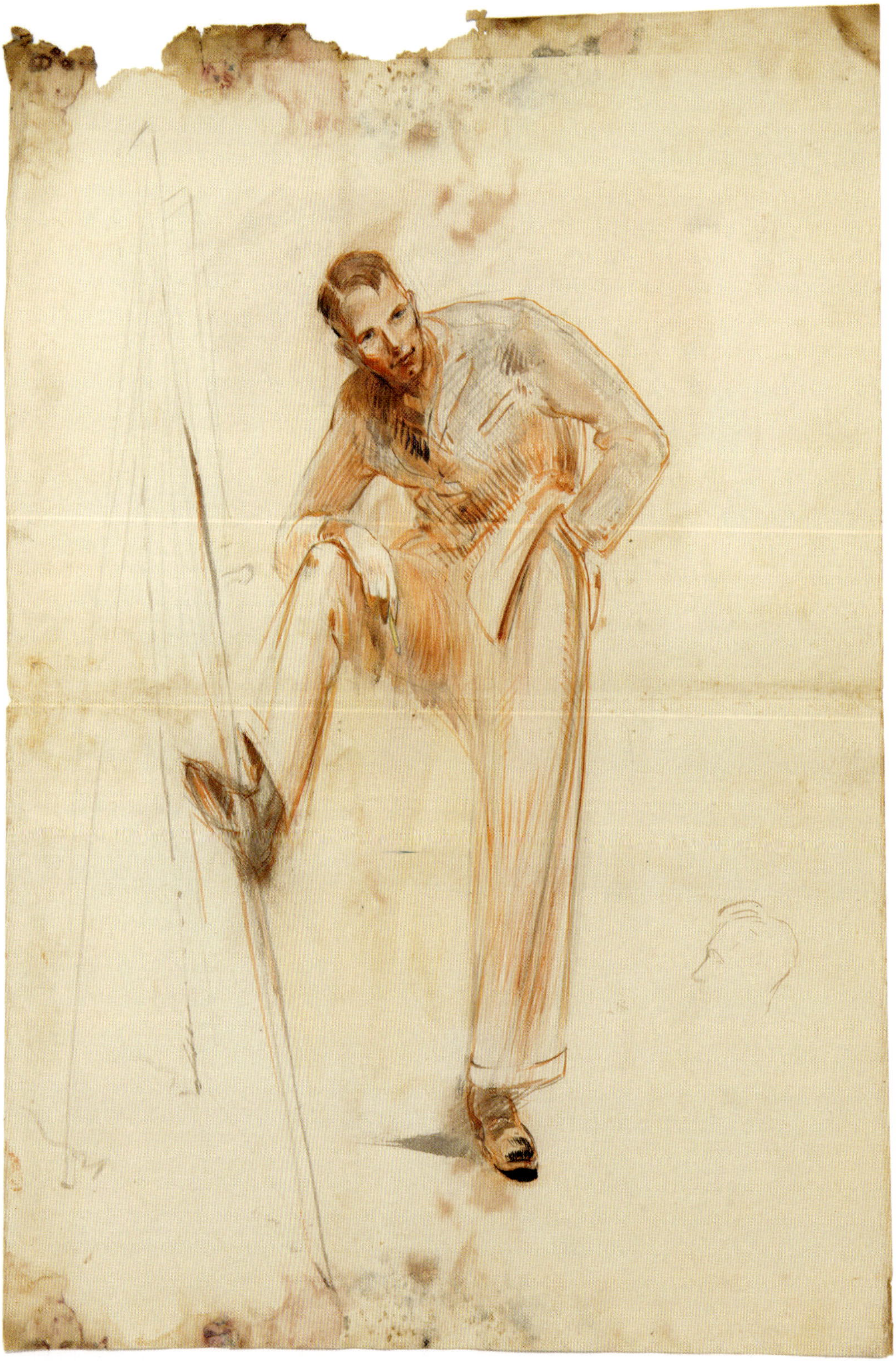

**166 Evelyn Dunbar** (1906-1960), *An Artist at His Easel* (probably Robert Lyon), late 1920s, pencil, watercolour and pen & ink on paper, 22 x 15 in. (55.5 x 38 cm).

The identity of this artist, with his foot resting nonchalantly on the easel, is thought to be Robert Lyon, who was a student at the Royal College of Art in the mid-1920s.

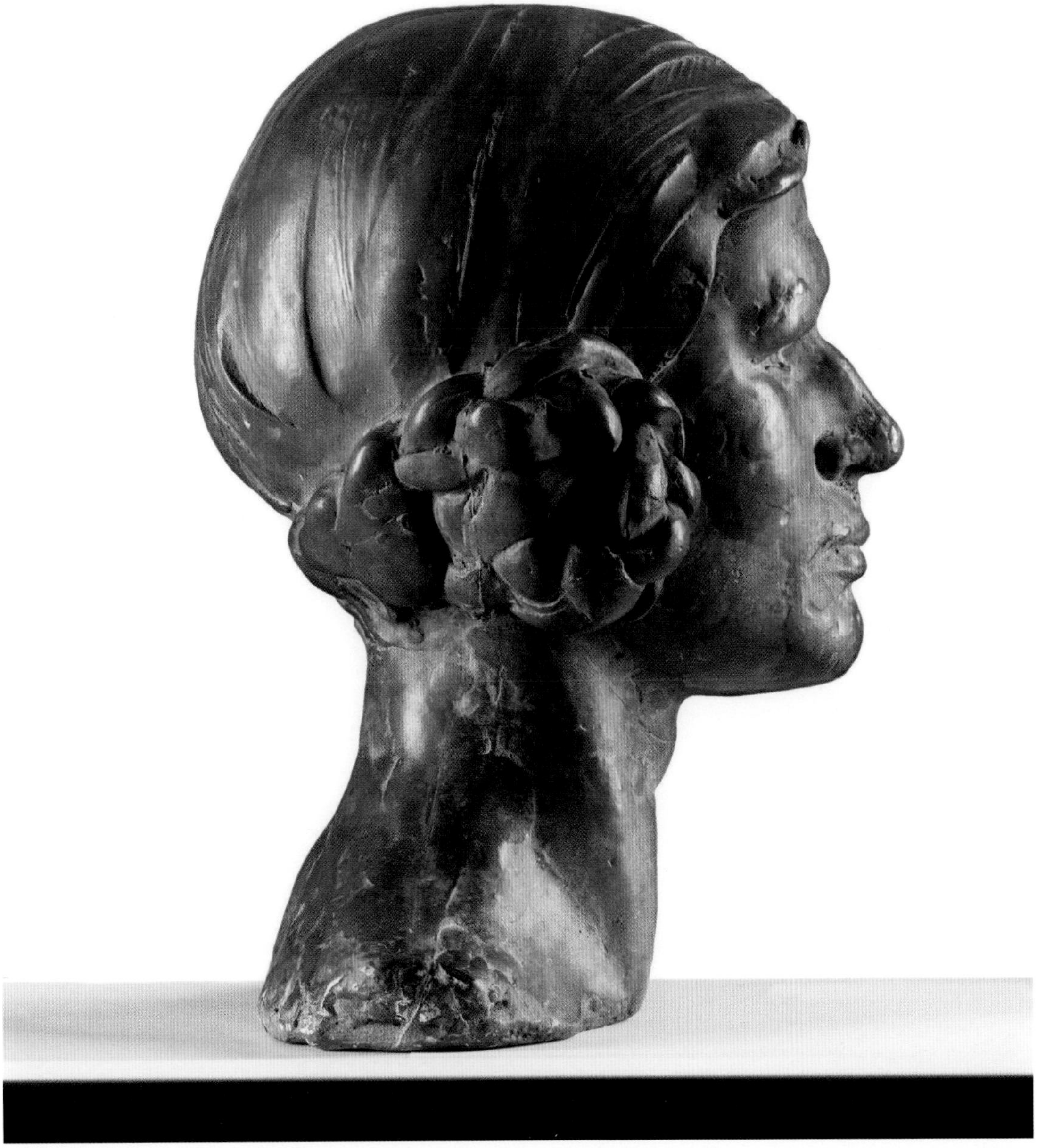

**167 Eric Kennington** (1888-1960), *Portrait Head of Jean Clark*, c.1924-5
plaster, with a green patina, height: 12 in. (32 cm) / base 9 x 4 in. (23.5 x 12 cm).

The painters Jean and Cosmo Clark were life-long friends of Eric Kennington. Cosmo and Eric were childhood neighbours and during the First World War both served with the Middlesex Regiment, to which Kennington was attached as an Official War Artist (**160**). Kennington, who lived on Chiswick Mall, near to the Clarks in St Peter's Square, was drawn to Jean Clarke as a sitter because he considered her forehead similar to that of T.E. Lawrence: 'Eric was planning a head of Lawrence of Arabia. Eric needed some "practice"' (Julia Rhys, the artist's daughter, letter to Paul Liss, 20 April 2004).

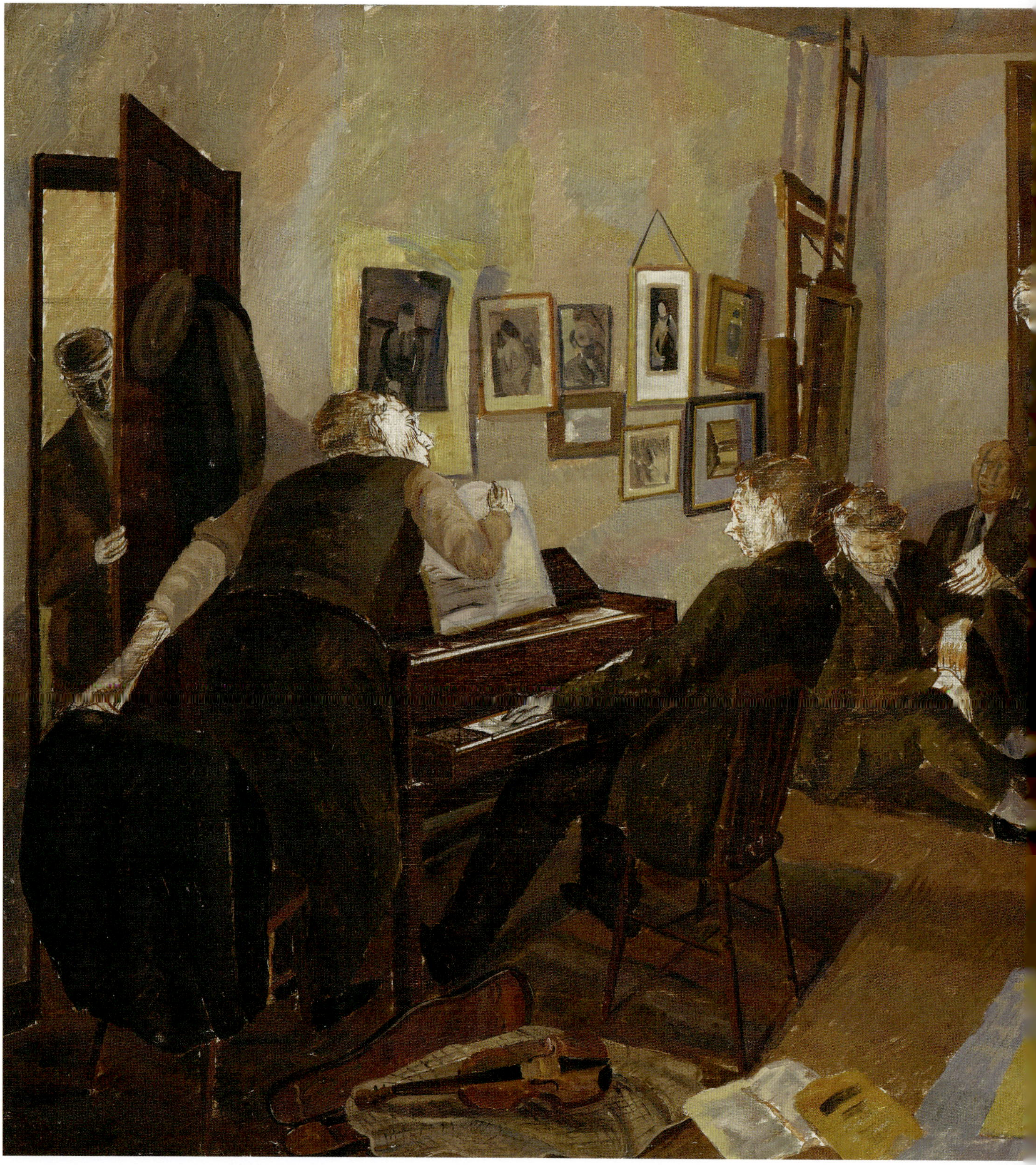

**168 Barnett Freedman** (1901-1958), *The Stanhope Street Group*, 1926, oil on canvas, 20 x 40 in. (50.8 x 101.8 cm).

The scene depicted probably records a rehearsal for a play directed by Freedman; he greatly admired the East End dramatist Israel Zangwill and was himself involved in productions at the Little, Fortune and Scala theatres. From various surviving studies several figures

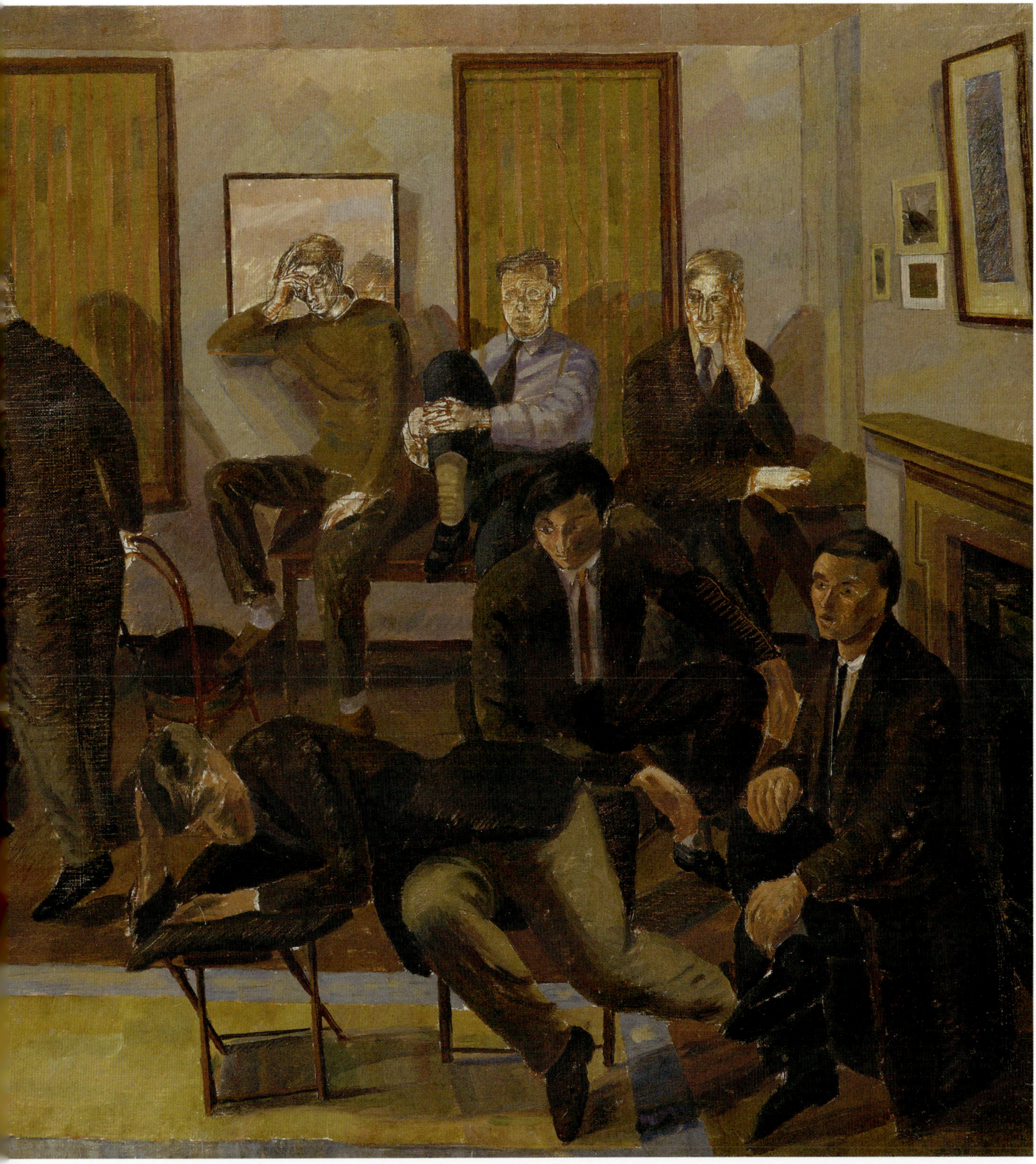

have been identified as Royal College of Art contemporaries. Roy Keevil is the figure coming through the door. Barnett Freedman has his back to the viewer with a violin at his feet, Frank Barber is at the piano. Francis Spear is most likely the figure seated at the foot of the easel; the older figure seated on the floor behind is likely to be William Rothenstein; Alan Sorrell is portrayed full length, looking back to the viewer, Charles Mahoney is seated on the table, probably with Percy Horton seated next to him, leg raised, and G.K. Branson. Gerald Ososki is seated on the stool, with Hugh Finney to his left. (**158**, **267**, **273**, **281**, **311**, **316**, **318**)

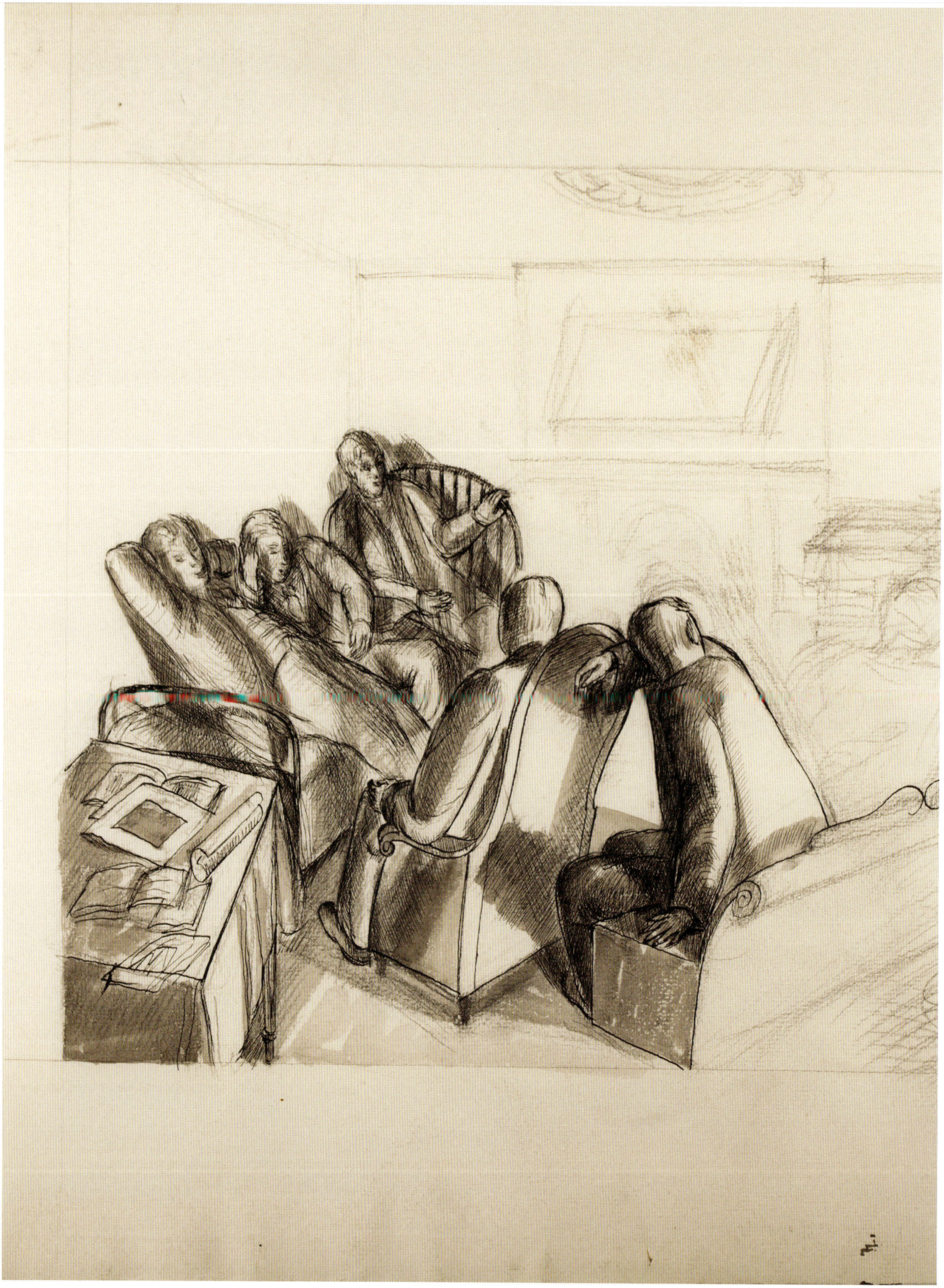

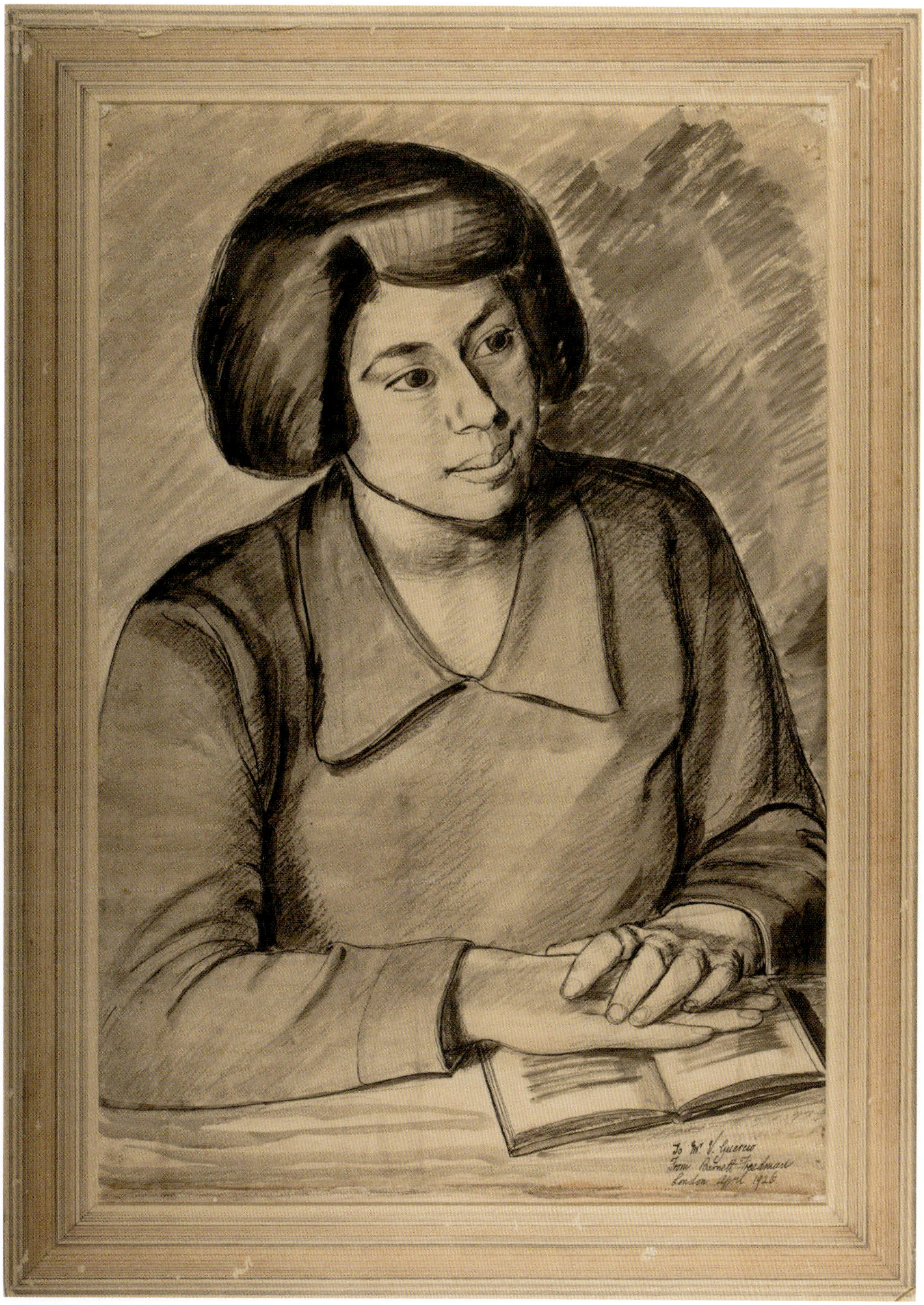


170

**Barnett Freedman** (1901-1958),

**169** Early Study for *The Stanhope Street Group*, (detail), c.1926, pencil, pen & ink and wash on paper, 15 x 22 ¼ in. (38.1 x 56.5 cm).

**170** *Portrait of Claudia Guercino, the Artist's Future Wife*, signed and dated April 1926, inscribed 'To Mr. V. Guercio, From Barnet Freedman, London, April 1926' pencil, pen & ink and wash on paper, 21 ½ x 14 ¾ in. (54.6 x 37.5 cm).

Freedman married fellow-student Claudia Guercio in 1926 in a match initially kept secret from her disapproving parents (**172**). They lived in Stanhope Street near the Euston Road, where they rented two rooms. One of these Freedman used as a studio, as he sought to combine theatrical activities with oil painting; neither proved satisfactorily remunerative and he later recalled 'I nearly starved'.

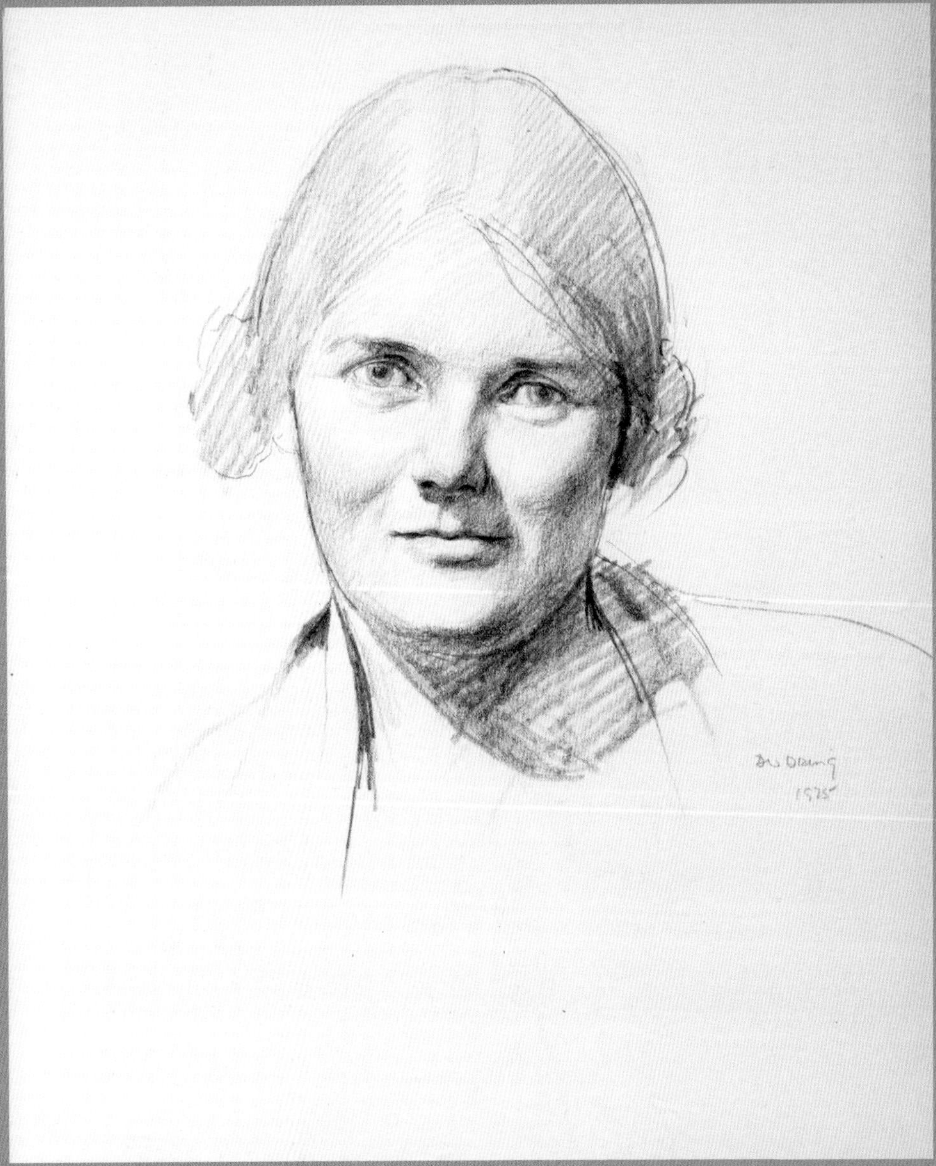

**171 William Dring** (1904-1990), *Portrait of the Artist Grace Elizabeth Rothwell, (Mrs Dring)*, 1925,
signed and dated, titled on label to reverse,
pencil on paper, 9 ½ x 7 ½ in. (24.1 x 19 cm).

The sitter is the artist Grace Elizabeth Rothwell, who later became the artist's wife. This portrait was made shortly after the two met at the Slade. They married on New Year's day in 1931. Under the name of Elizabeth Rothwell she exhibited at the New English Art Club and the Royal Academy of Arts during the late 1920s and early 30s, but after the birth of her children she largely gave up painting and reverted to textile design. 'Gray' Dring as she was known to family and friends has examples of her textile work in the collection of the Victoria & Albert Museum.

**172 Barnett Freedman** (1901-1958), *The Artist's Wife, Claudia* (née Guercio) *at Stanhope Street*, c.1926,
oil on canvas, 26 x 16 ¼ in. (66 x 41.3 cm).

Claudia Freedman's output was relatively small, but her talent, though never fully given the chance to flourish, was arguably a worthy match to that of Barnett Freedman. She studied at Liverpool School of Art and the Royal College of Art. Working initially under her maiden name, she took the name Claudia Freedman from 1930 when the two were declared as married, although they had secretly married when they first met at the Royal College of Art in 1924.

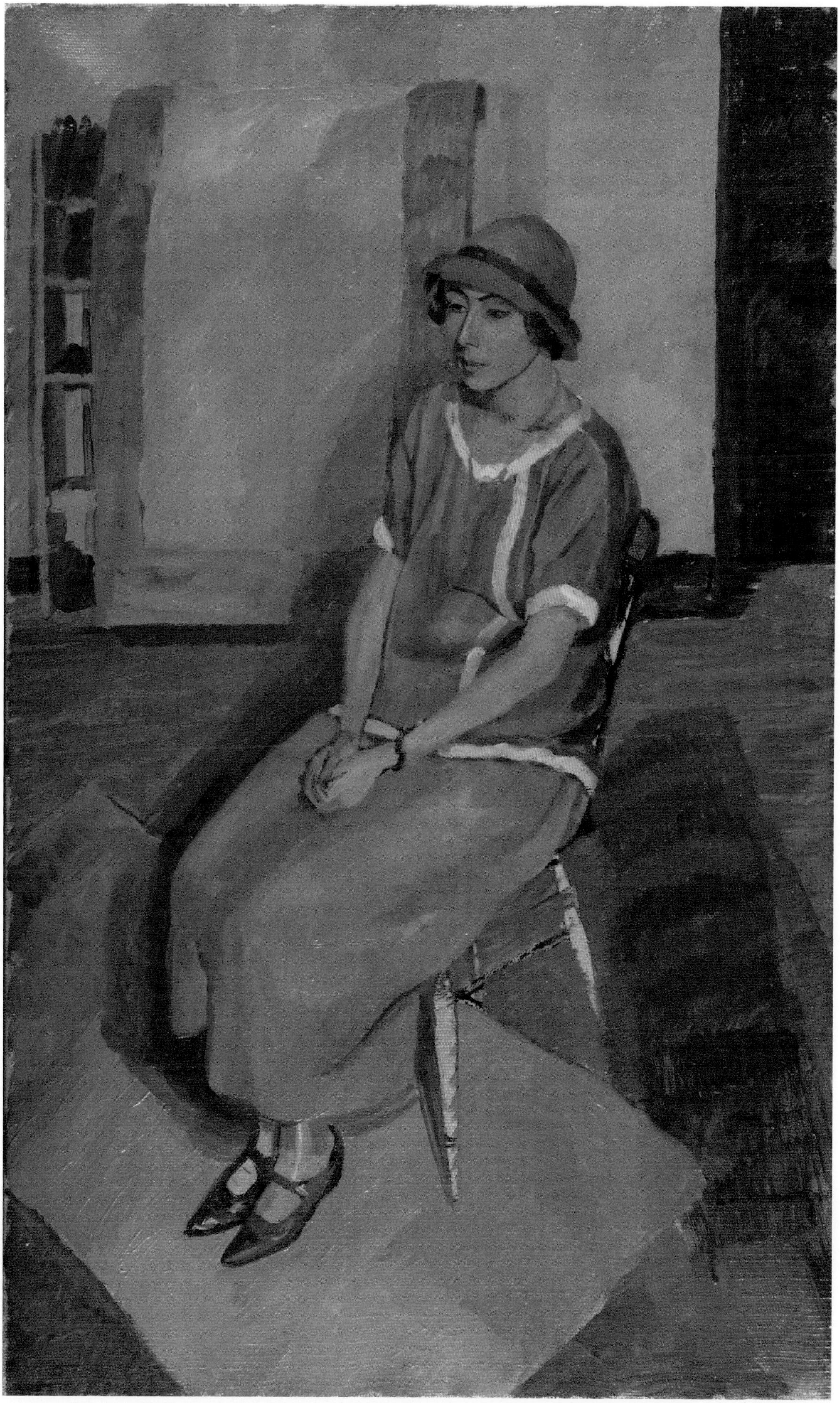

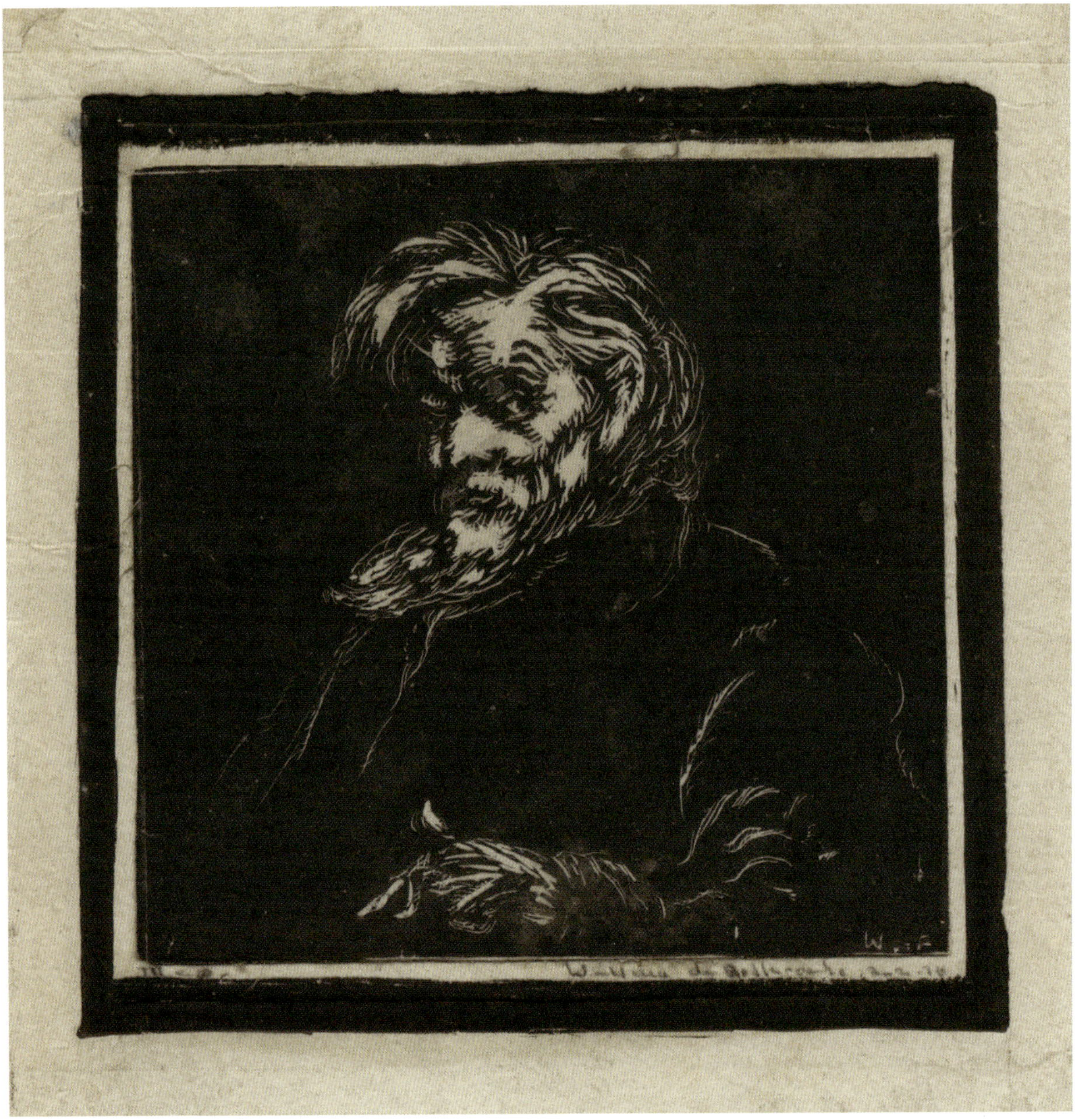

**173 William de Belleroche** (1912-1969), *Portrait of Frank Brangwyn*, 1936,
inscribed "WdeB" b.r. and "William de Belleroche 2-2-36" on the mount,
wood engraving on paper, 5 ¾ x 5 in. (14.7 x 12.6 cm).

William de Belleroche, the son of Brangwyn's contemporary and friend Count Albert de Belleroche, wrote two books on Brangwyn and sought to promote Brangwyn's work during his lifetime. This woodcut, produced when William de Belleroche was 24 and Brangwyn was 69 years old, was never published. This copy, which belonged to William de Belleroche all his life, is only one of a handful that are known. William de Belleroche's extensive collection of works by Brangwyn was sold at Christies in a single owner sale in 1961. (**299**)

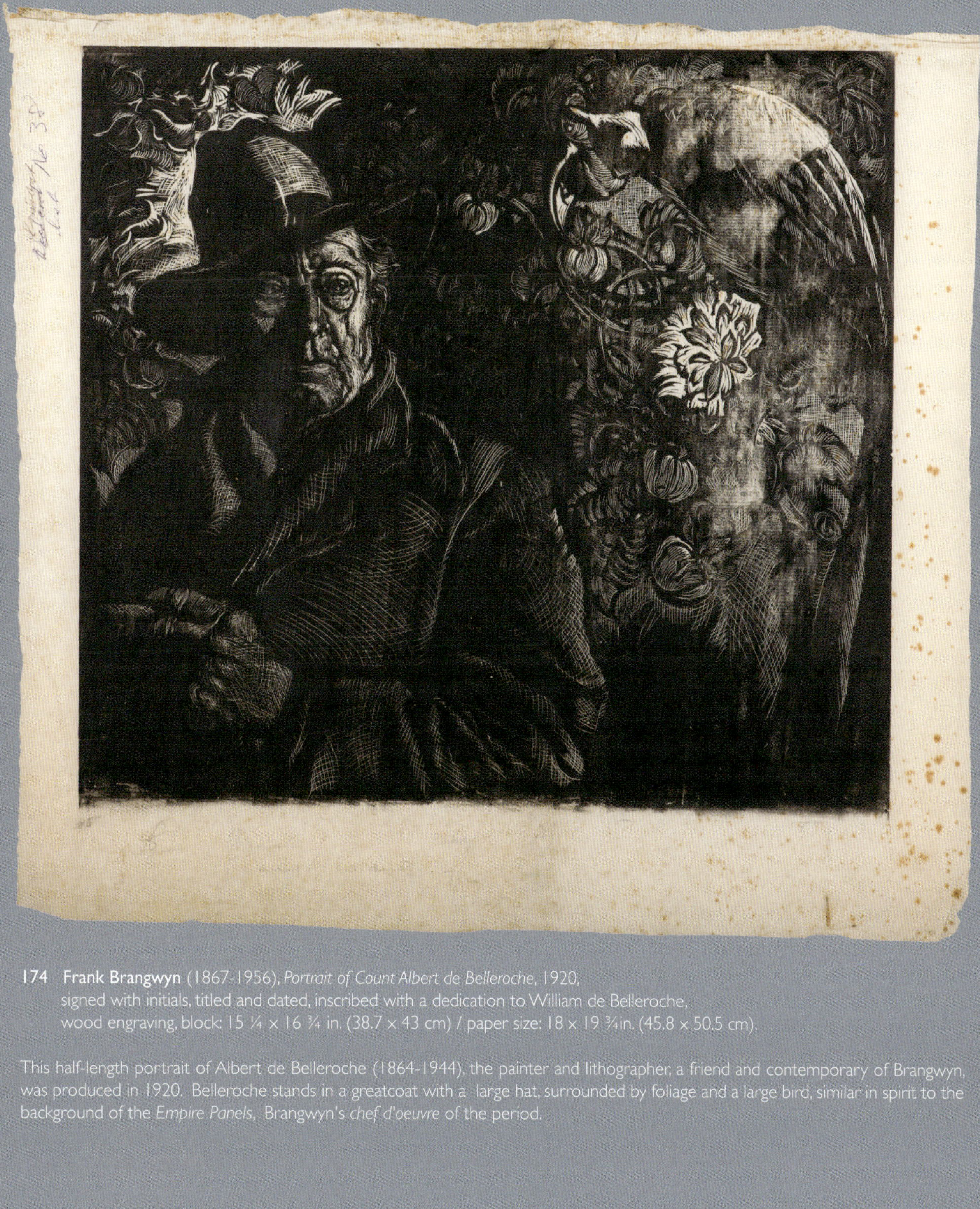

**174 Frank Brangwyn** (1867-1956), *Portrait of Count Albert de Belleroche*, 1920,
signed with initials, titled and dated, inscribed with a dedication to William de Belleroche,
wood engraving, block: 15 ¼ x 16 ¾ in. (38.7 x 43 cm) / paper size: 18 x 19 ¾in. (45.8 x 50.5 cm).

This half-length portrait of Albert de Belleroche (1864-1944), the painter and lithographer, a friend and contemporary of Brangwyn, was produced in 1920. Belleroche stands in a greatcoat with a large hat, surrounded by foliage and a large bird, similar in spirit to the background of the *Empire Panels*, Brangwyn's *chef d'oeuvre* of the period.

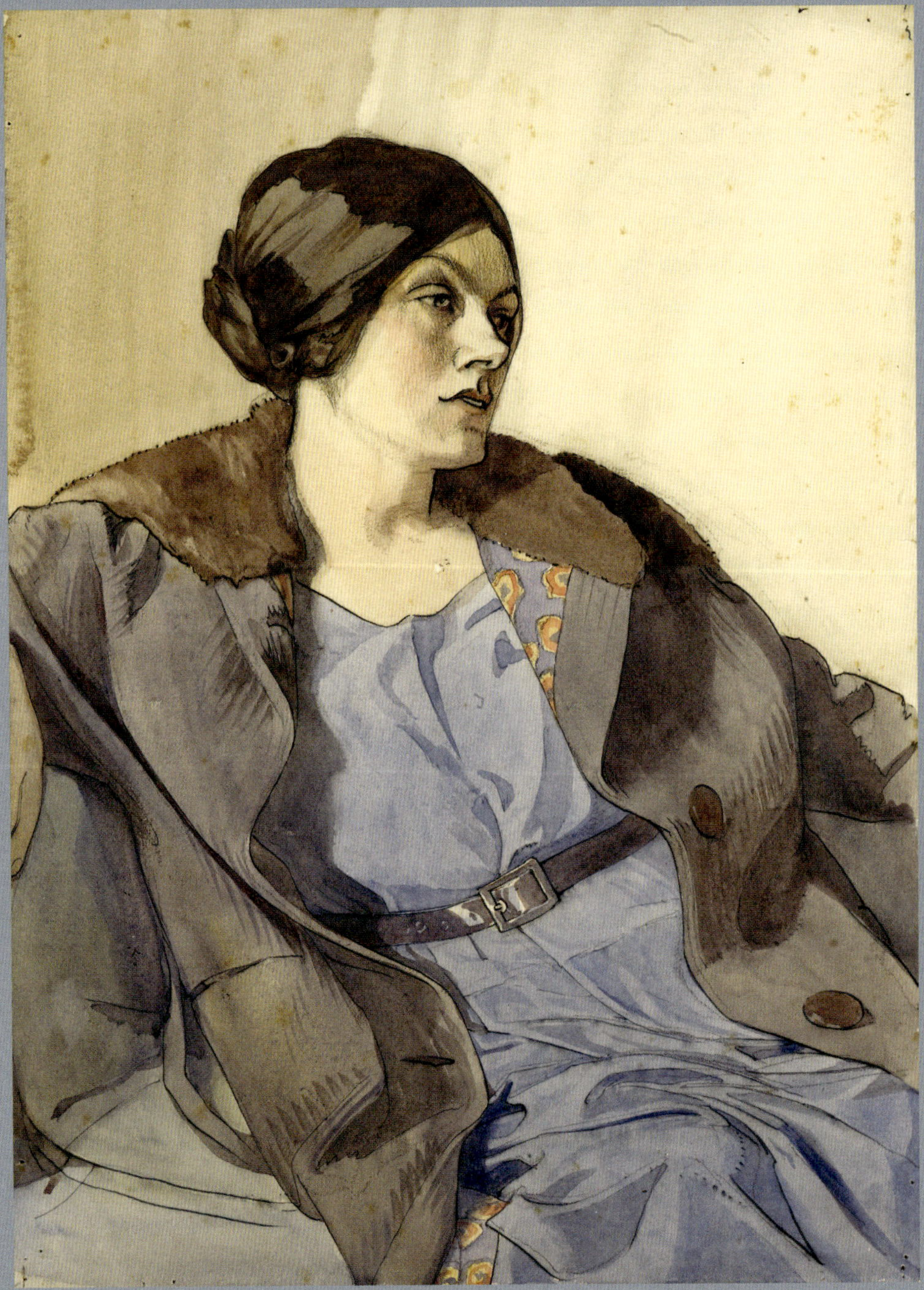

**175 Noel Rooke** (1881-1953), *Portrait of the Artist's Wife, Celia Fiennes*, late 1920s, watercolour over pencil on paper, 15 x 11 in. (38 x 28 cm).

This portrait probably dates to Fiennes' time at the Central School of Arts and Crafts, where she enrolled in 1924. Fiennes studied under Noel Rooke, whom she married in 1932. Together they made a major contribution to the revival of wood engraving in Britain in the twentieth century. (**265**)

**176 Joseph Simpson** (1879-1939), *Portrait of Frank Brangwyn at Work*, 1925, signed and dated, etching, paper: 14 x 10 in (35.5 cm x 25.3 cm) / plate: 11 ¾ x 8 ¼ in. (30 x 21 cm).

Joseph Simpson turned to etching, at the encouragement of Frank Brangwyn in 1909. In 1926 Simpson held his first print exhibition in Glasgow. Simpson shows Brangwyn at the height of his powers, one year after he was knighted, and at work on the *Empire Panels*. (**258**)

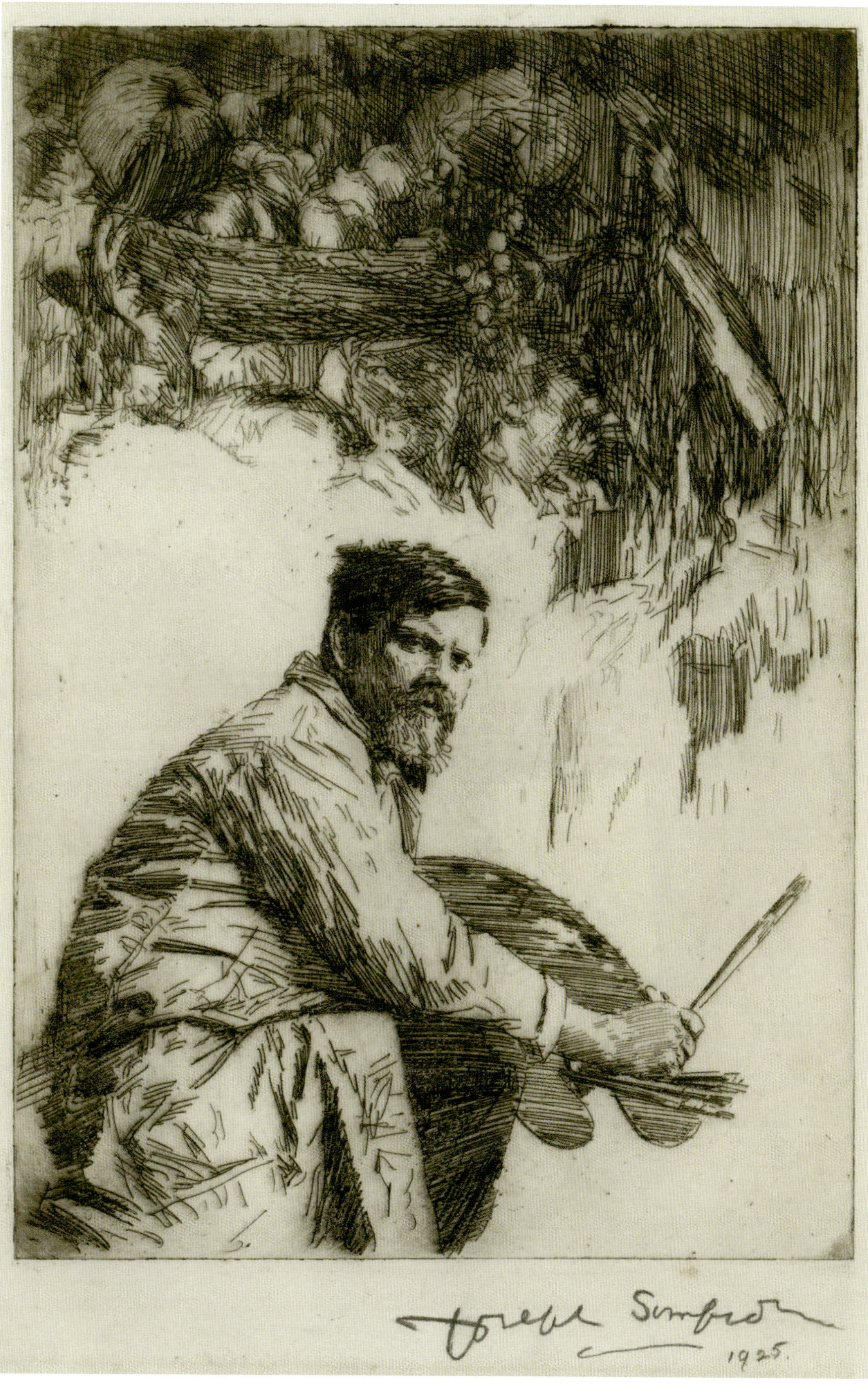
Joseph Simpson
1925.

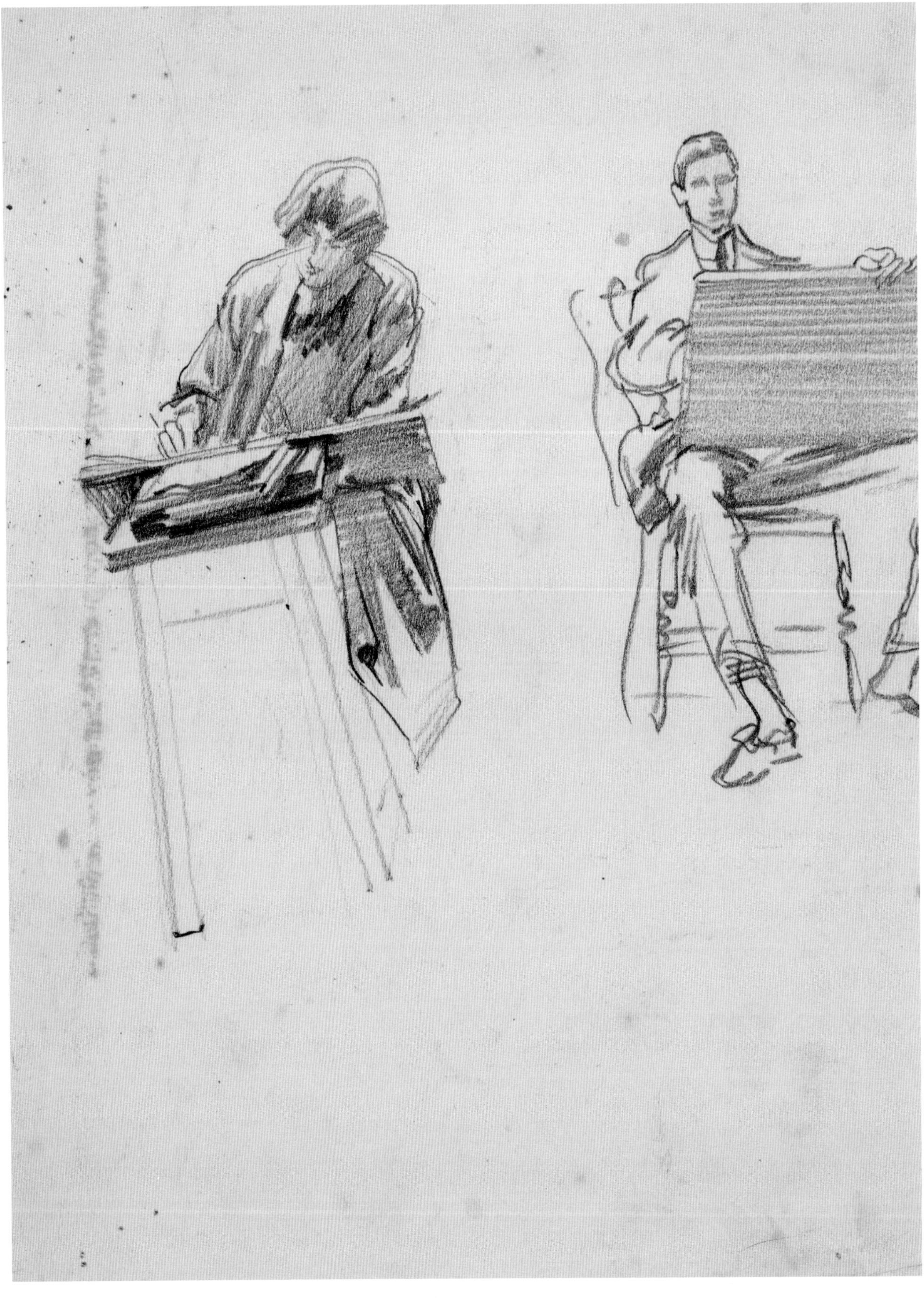

177

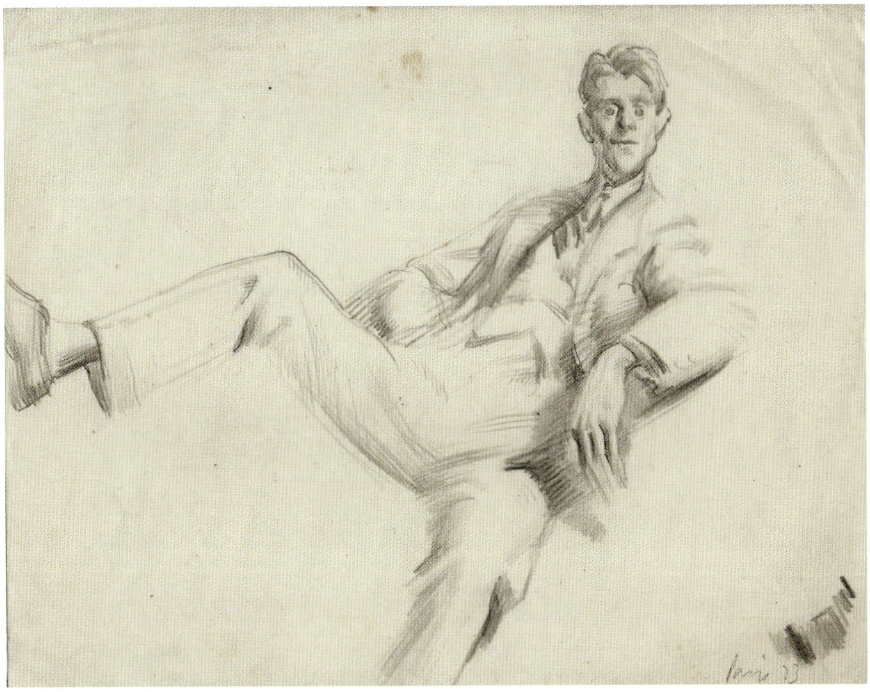

178

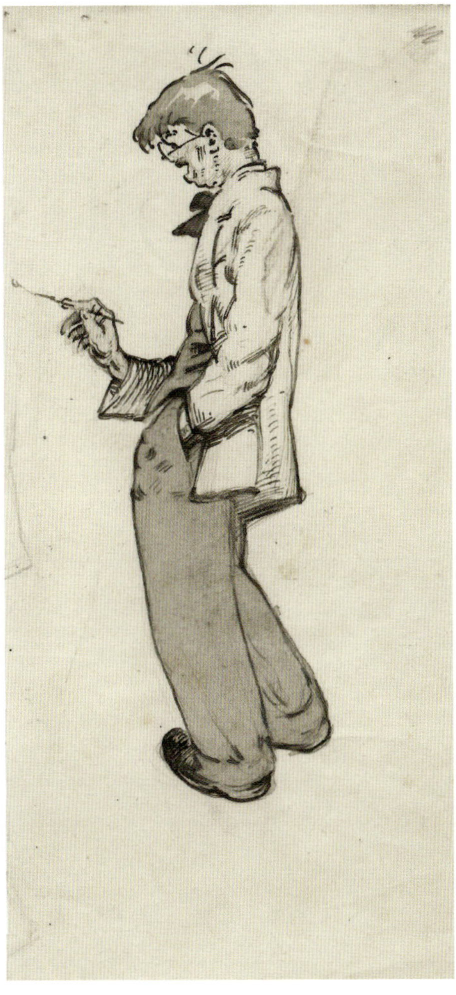

179

**Edward Irvine Halliday** (1902-1984),

**177** *Royal College Art Class*, c.1925,
signed with studio stamp, Inscribed 30 min
pencil on paper, 15 x 11 in. (38 x 28 cm).

**178** *Portrait of a Fellow Art Student*, inscribed and dated 'Paris 23',
pencil on paper, 8 ½ x 11 in. (21.6 x 28 cm).
Provenance: The Artist's Family; Private collection.

**179** *An Art Student Sketching*, early 1920s,
pencil, pen & ink, watercolour on paper, 11 ½ x 5 ¾ in. (29.2 x 14.6 cm).
Provenance: The Artist's Family; Private collection.

Timed sketches were a standard exercise for art students. (**107**, **121**) Edward Irvine Halliday first attended Liverpool College of Art. Halliday continued his studies and attended life drawing classes at Académie Colarossi (1922-1923), the Royal College of Art (1923-1925), and the British School at Rome (1925-1928). He was awarded the Prix de Rome for Decorative Painting in 1925. He established himself as a portrait artist with *Lord Darling* (1928).

During World War II, Halliday served in the Royal Air Force in Bomber Command. After the war in 1948, he received a painting commission for a portrait of Princess Elizabeth from the Drapers' Company of London. This was the start of many more royal portrait commissions. Other sitters for Halliday's portraits included Winston Churchill, Edmund Hillary, Lord Denning, Lord Widgery, Louis Gluckstein, Robert Stopford, Lord Hunt, Frank Whittle, Malcolm Sargent, Leon Goossens, Beryl Grey, Gladys Cooper, Wally Hammond, Brian Johnston and Ben Travers.

Halliday had two arts series radio programmes, *Artists at Work* (1932) and *Design in Modern Life* (1934). The success of these radio programmes led to further radio and television work. In the 1950s, Halliday was the voice behind the BBC Television Newsreel.

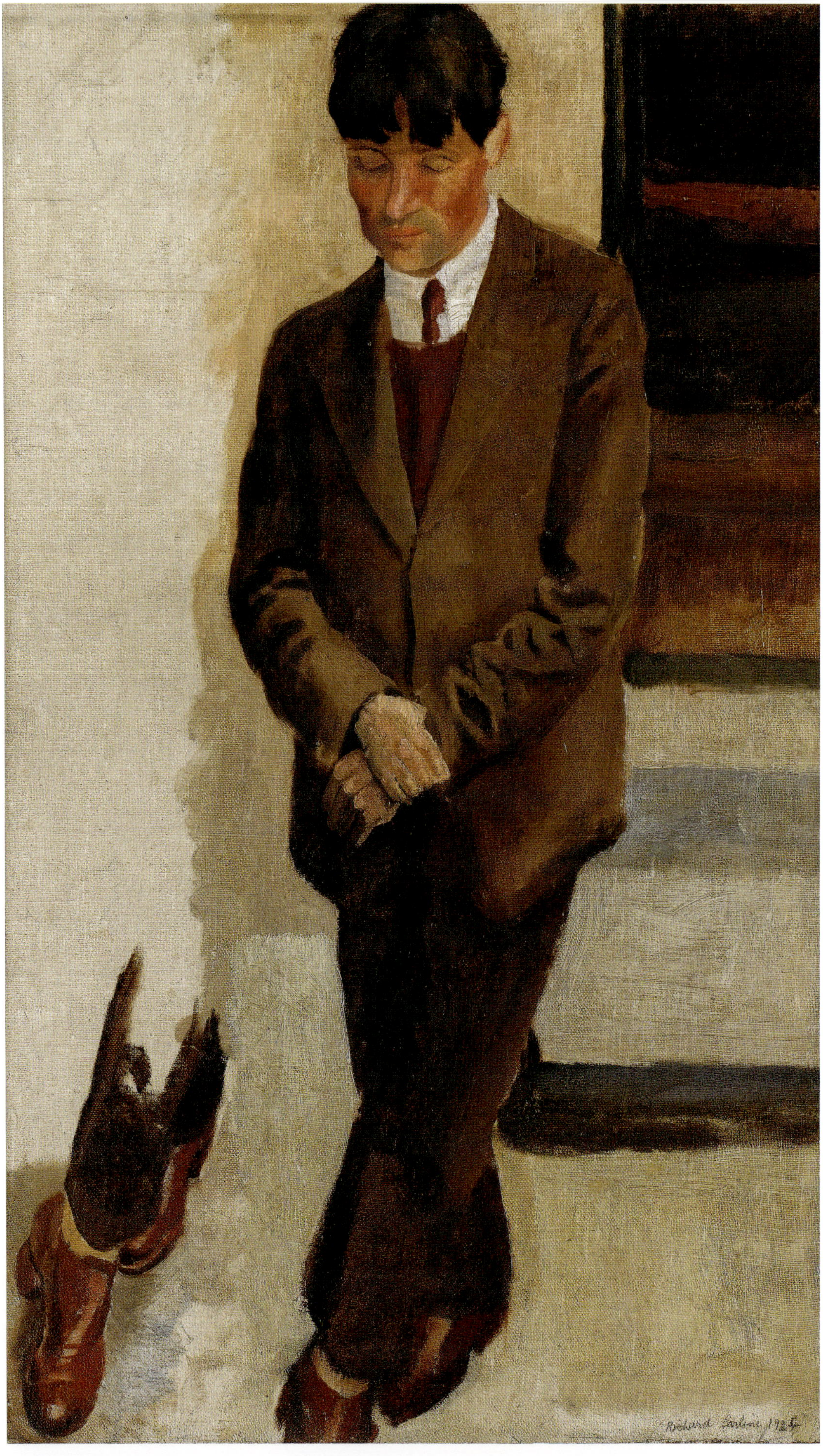
Richard Carline

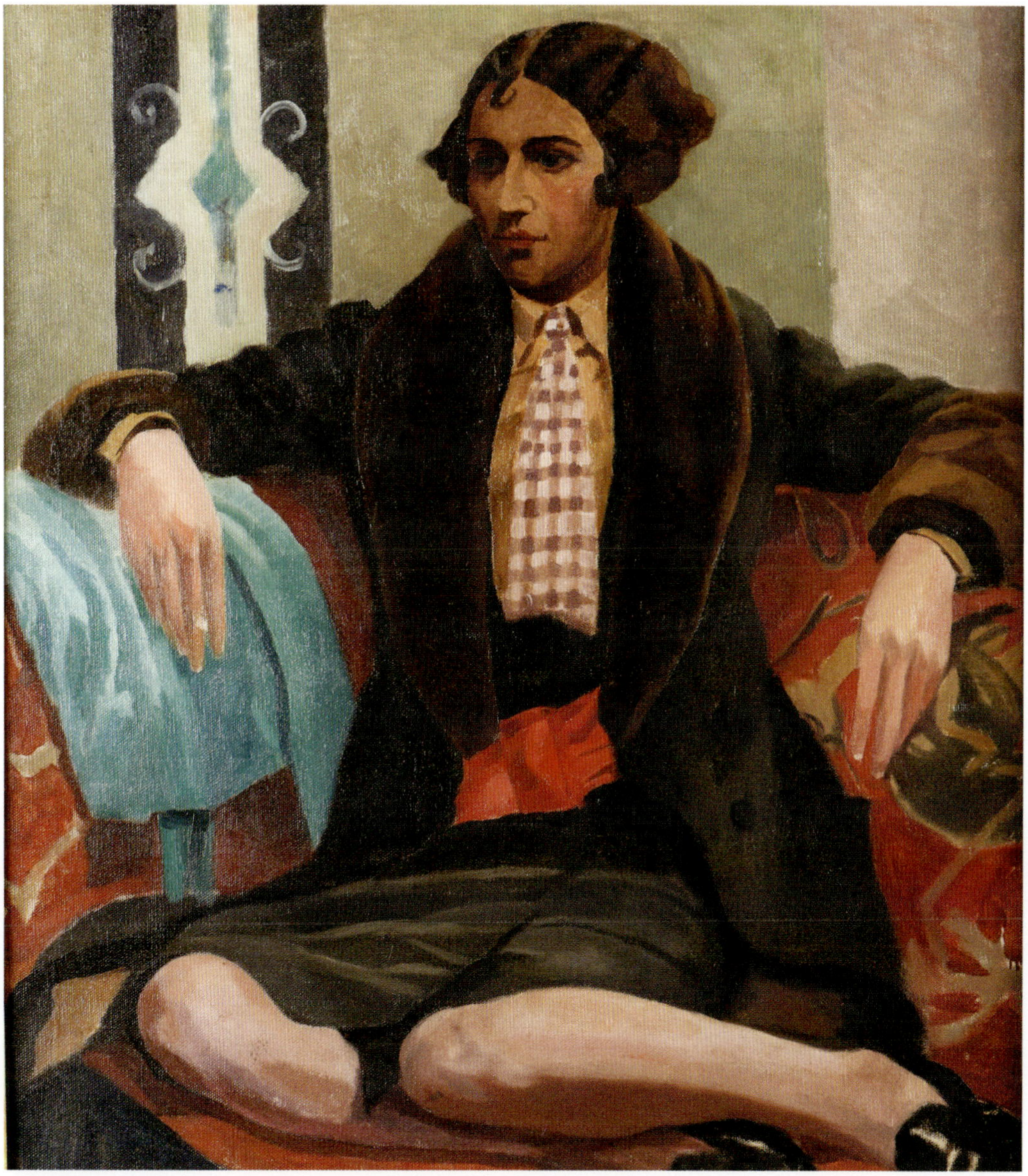

**181 Richard Carline** (1896-1980), *Portrait of Ivy Turner* (?),
oil on canvas, 31 x 28 in. (79 x 71cm).

The identity of this model remains uncertain – her physiognomy is close to that of Ivy Turner who attended the Slade in the early 20's and was part of the Hampstead group which included figures such as Stanley Spencer, Henry Lamb, as well as Hilda and Richard Carline. Elements such as her cropped hair, cigarette and caravat identify her as a progressive and independent woman, typical of the artistic and literary types that characterised the 'Roaring Twenties'.

**180 Richard Carline** (1896-1980), *Portrait of Stanley Spencer* (Study for 'Gathering on the Terrace at 47 Downshire Hill, Hampstead'), 1924-5,
signed, dated and inscribed on the reverse: 'Painted from life in the garden at 47 Downshire Hill, Hampstead, 1924'
canvas on board, 24 x 14 ½ in. (61 x 36.8 cm). Collection: Ferens Art Gallery.

'In 1921, I decided to attend the Slade under Henry Tonks. About this time, I painted a large family group seated round the dining table at 47 Downshire Hill, in Hampstead. Eddie Marsh bought it for the Contemporary Art Society but, alas, it was destroyed in the Tate Gallery flood. Three years later I painted a still larger family group on the terrace at Downshire Hill with Henry Lamb and Stanley Spencer, who was soon to marry my sister Hilda' (Richard Carline, introduction to his own exhibition catalogue, Anthony d'Offay Gallery, 1975). It is interesting to note that in both the (destroyed) Tate composition and the finished Ferens Art Gallery painting, for which this work is a study, Spencer is shown apart from the main group, leaning with arms folded and head bowed, deep in thought. (**223**)

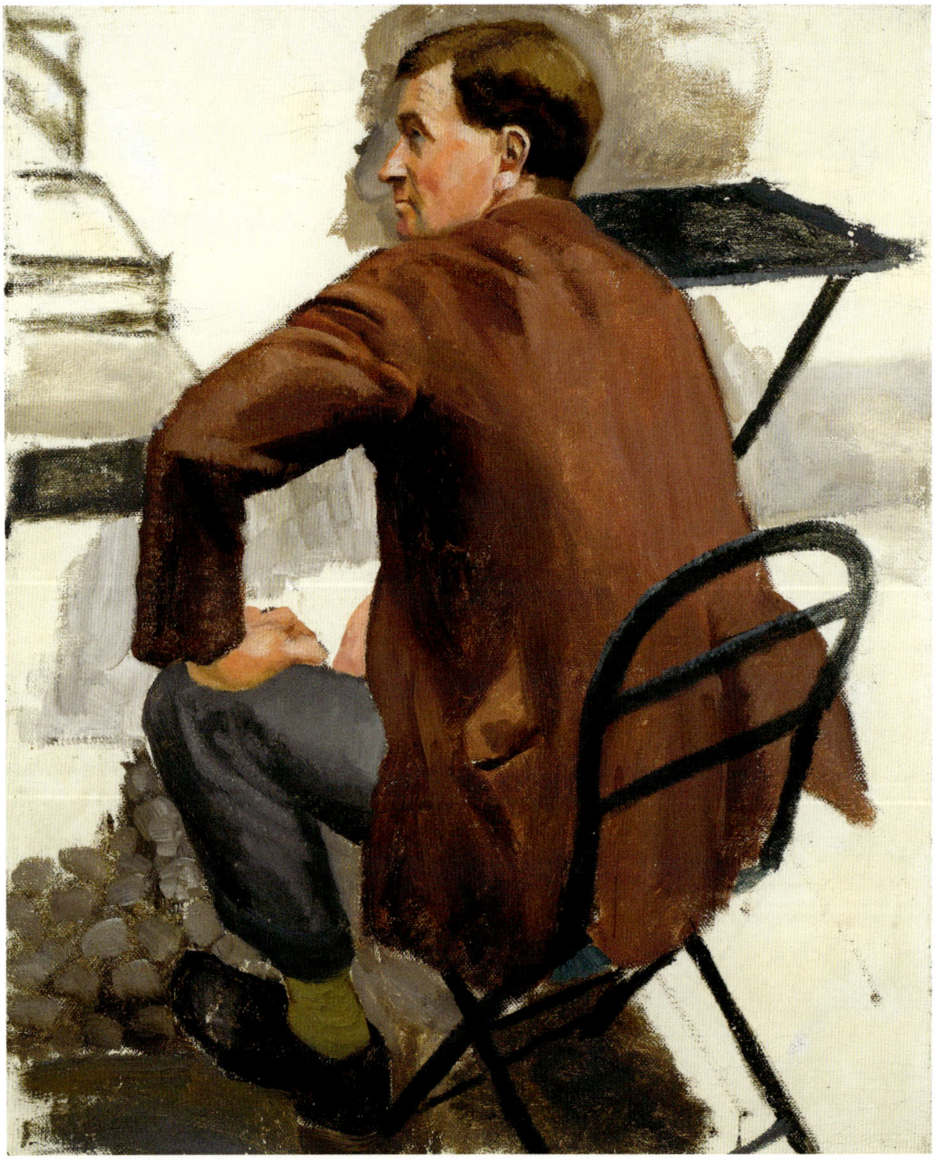

**182 Richard Carline** (1896-1980),
*Study of Richard Hartley for 'Gathering on the Terrace at 47 Downshire Hill, Hampstead'*, 1925
oil on canvas, 22 x 18 in. (56 x 46 cm).

Richard Hartley was a fellow student at the Slade School of Fine Art in the early 1920s and an acquaintance of both Richard and Hilda Carline. In his own words Carline '… sought to convey the conflicting personalities gathered at our house – Stanley peering up and down as he expounded his views on this or that, James Wood hesitating in the doorway whether to come or go, Hilda absorbed in her own thoughts, Hartley sitting at ease, Lamb courteously attentive to my mother, with Sydney always helpful….'

**183 Richard Carline** (1896-1980),
*Study of Annie and Sydney Carline for 'Gathering on the Terrace at 47 Downshire Hill, Hampstead'*, 1925,
oil on canvas 24 ½ x 18 in. (62 x 46 cm).

Sydney studied at the Slade school of Art, the son of the artists George Francis Carline and Annie Smith. His brother, Richard Carline and his sister Hilda were also artists, as was his sister-in-law, Nancy (née Higgins), and his brother-in-law, Stanley Spencer. Encouraged by the artists she had met through her children and husband, Annie Carline also took up painting, producing from 1927 landscapes and figures, usually in watercolour. The cubist painter André Lhote helped organise a solo exhibition of her work at the Galerie Pittoresque in Paris. Carline remained active as a painter until her death in 1945.

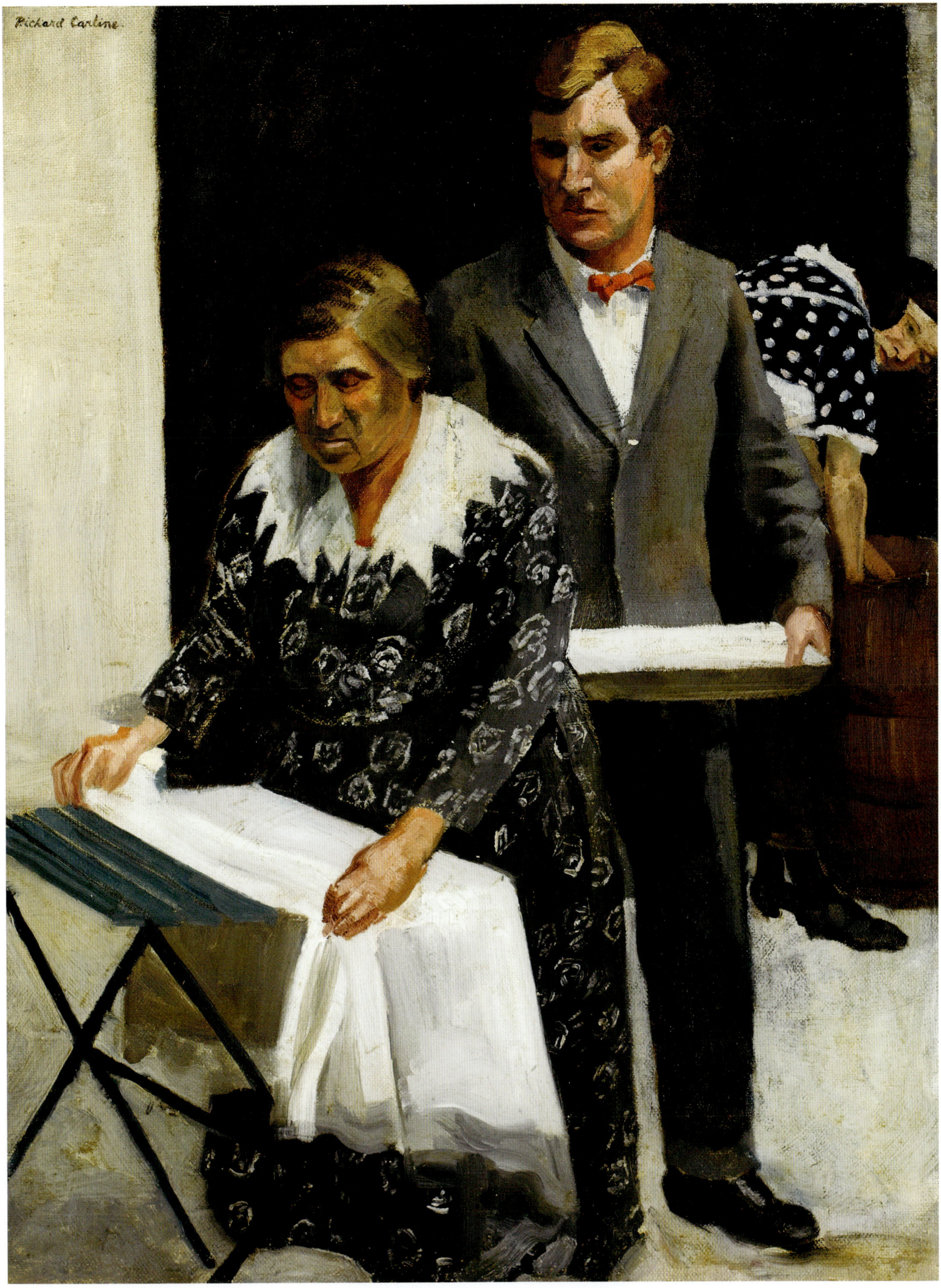
Richard Carline

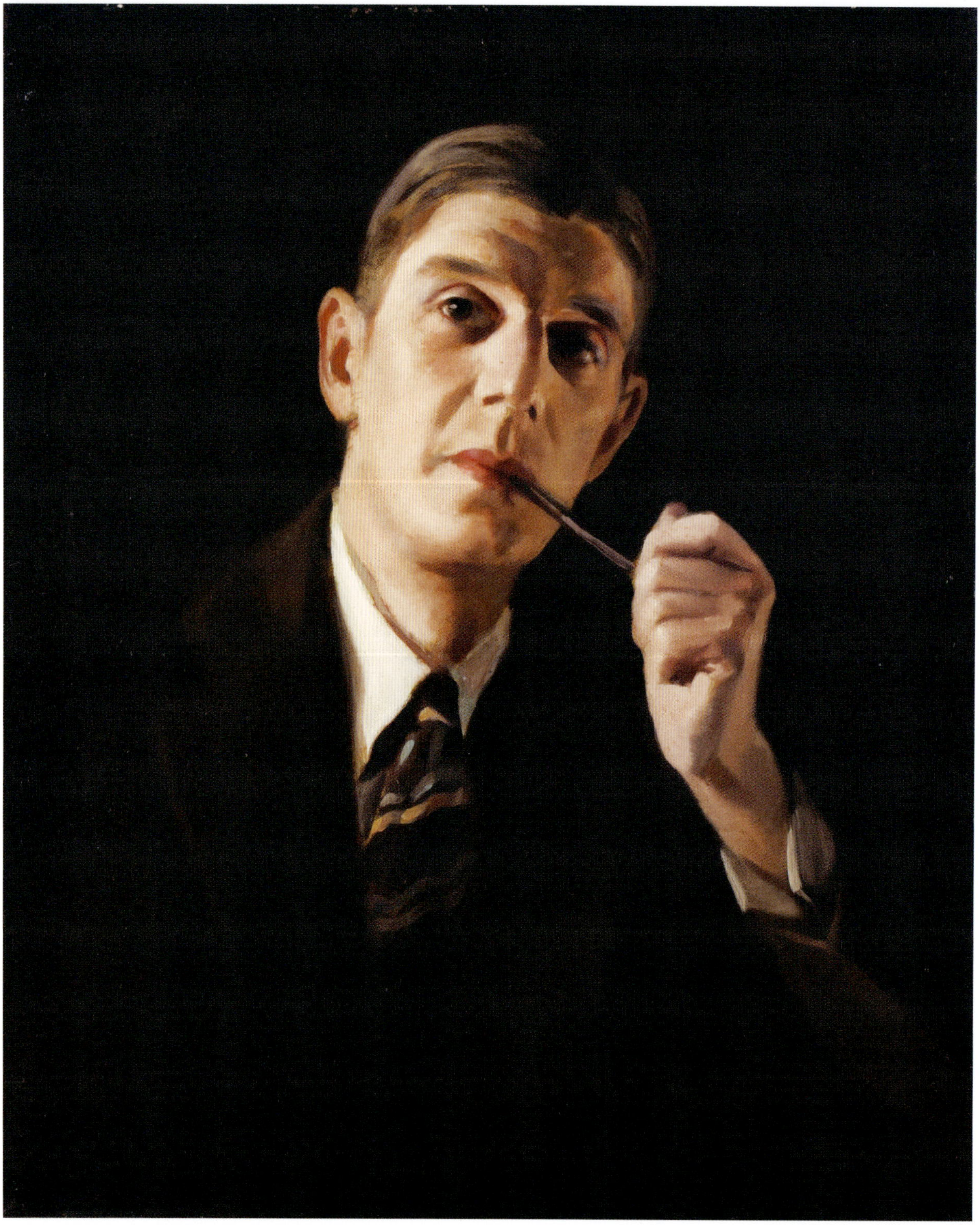

**184 Harry Dixon** (1888-1974), *Portrait of the Artist Harry Riley, Smoking a Pipe*, signed to reverse, oil on canvas, 23 ½ x 19 ¼ in. (59.7 x 49 cm).

Harry Dixon and Harry Riley met after WW1. Dixon's wife, Mabel Amelia Mann, a professional contralto, and Riley's wife, Mabel, were especially close and the two couples spent many sketching holidays together. Harry Riley first studied art at the Hammersmith School of Art and following active service in WWI he continued his studies at St. Martin's School of Art. He exhibited regularly at the Royal Academy, Royal Society of British Artists and the Royal Institute of Oil Painters, (**308**, **320**)

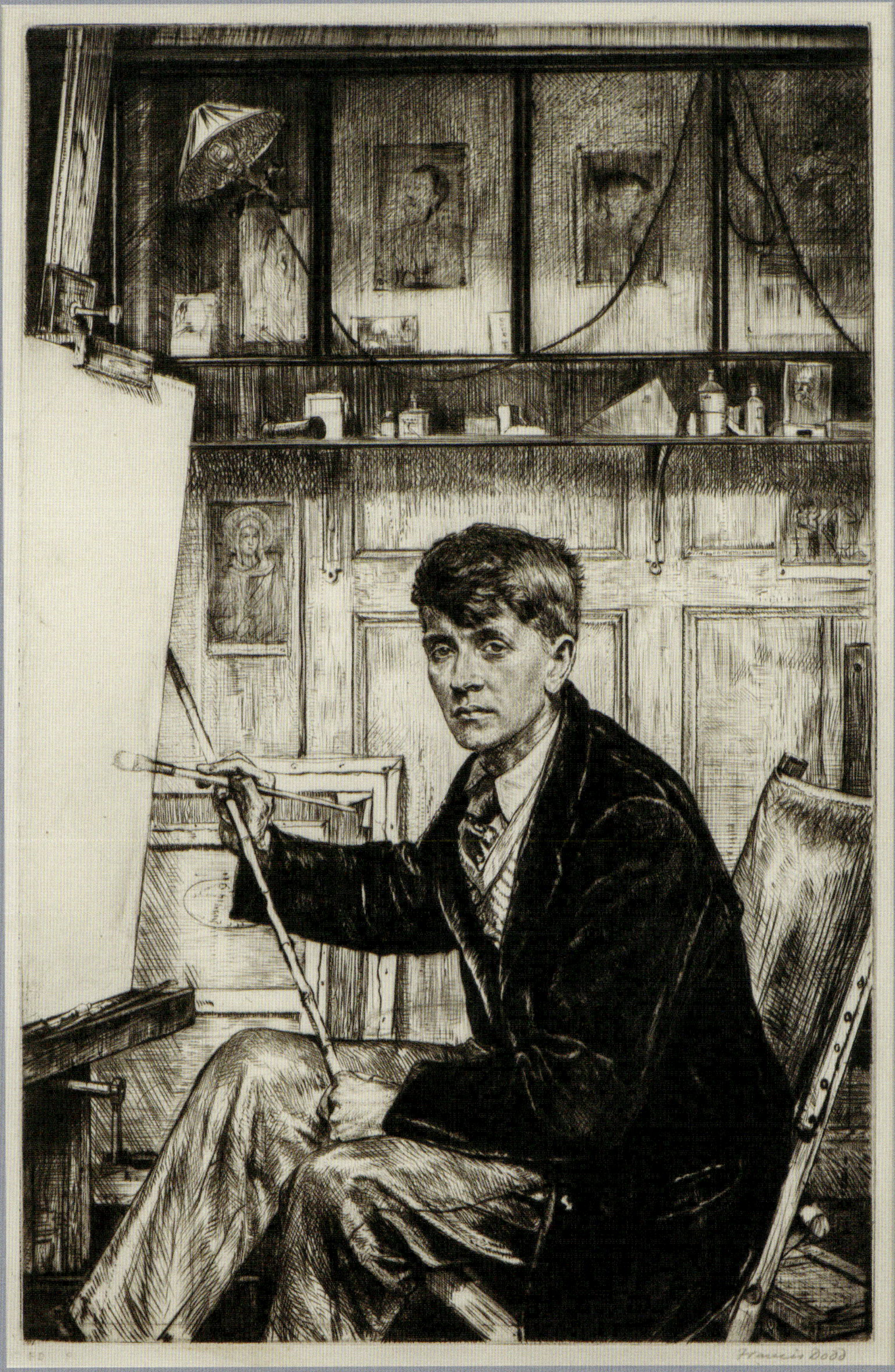

**185 Francis Dodd** (1874-1949), *Portrait of Charles Cundall*, c.1926, signed, inscribed with initials, dry point print: 18 x 11 ¾ in. (45.7 x 29.8 cm).

Francis Dodd belonged to the second generation of the Etching Revival movement, artists who sought to bring original prints back into fashion. Dodd often finished his prints by working directly on the plate after the model. A painter and lithographer, Charles Cundall (1890-1971) (**213**) had his first one-man show at Colnaghi the year after this impressive portrait was made

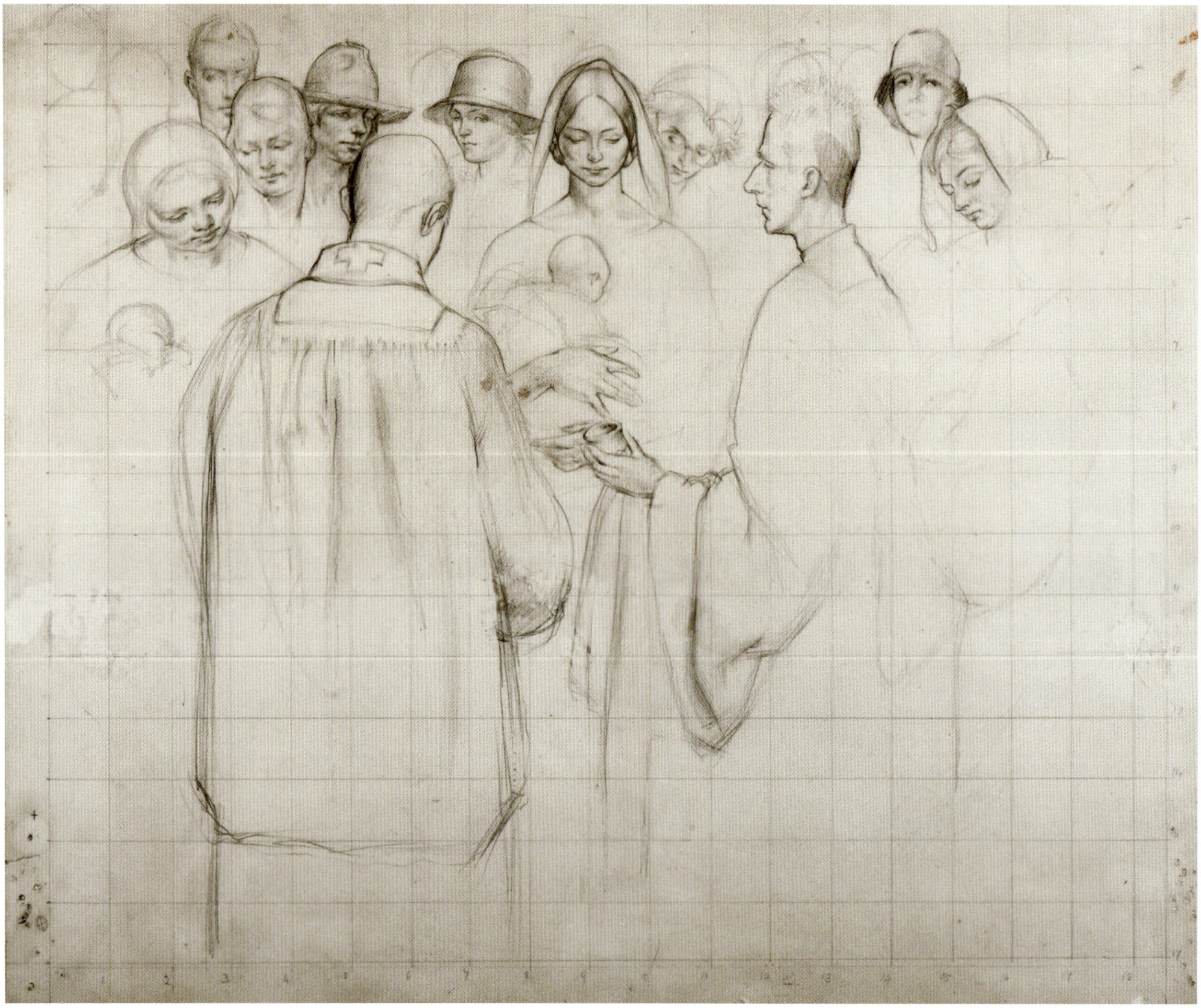

186

**Phyllis Dodd** (1899-1995),

**186** *Squared Study for Baptismal Scene*, c.1923
pencil on paper, squared, 12 ½ x 15 ¼ in. (31.8 x 38.6 cm).

**187** *Colour Study for Baptismal Scene*, 1923, inscribed with names on overlay,
pencil and watercolour on paper, 6 x 6 ¼ in. (15.2 x 15.9 cm).

**188** *Squared Colour Study for Baptismal Scene*, c.1923, inscribed with measurements,
pencil and watercolour on paper, squared, 6 ¼ x 6 ½ in. (15.8 x 16.8 cm),

Several informal but very good likenesses of fellow Royal College of Art students from the period demonstrate Phyllis Dodd's skill at portraiture. A series of sketches showing adults at a baptism includes recognisable portraits, aided by inscribed names on one of the colour sketches: Beryl Bowker, Edward Halliday, Kathleen Bridle (**192**), Dodd herself (**262**), Enid Marx, Gerald Cooper, Muriel Minter (**100**) and Marianne Thatcher.

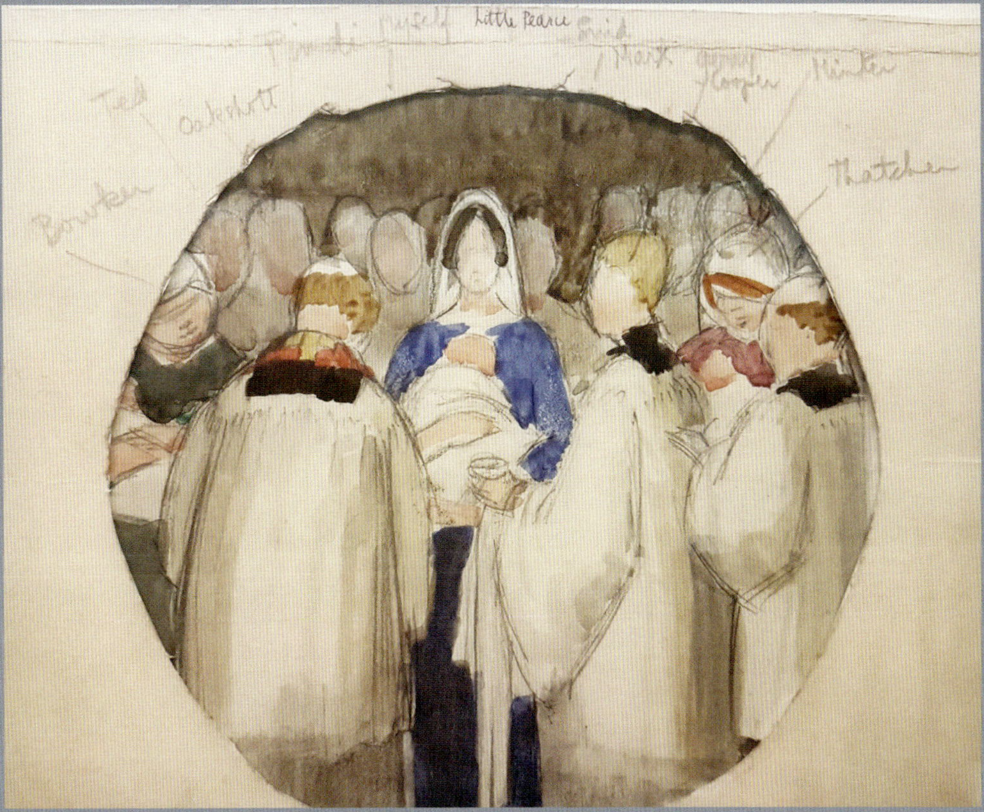
myself
Little Pearce
Mark
Cooper
Minter
Ted
Oakshott
Thatcher
Bowker

187

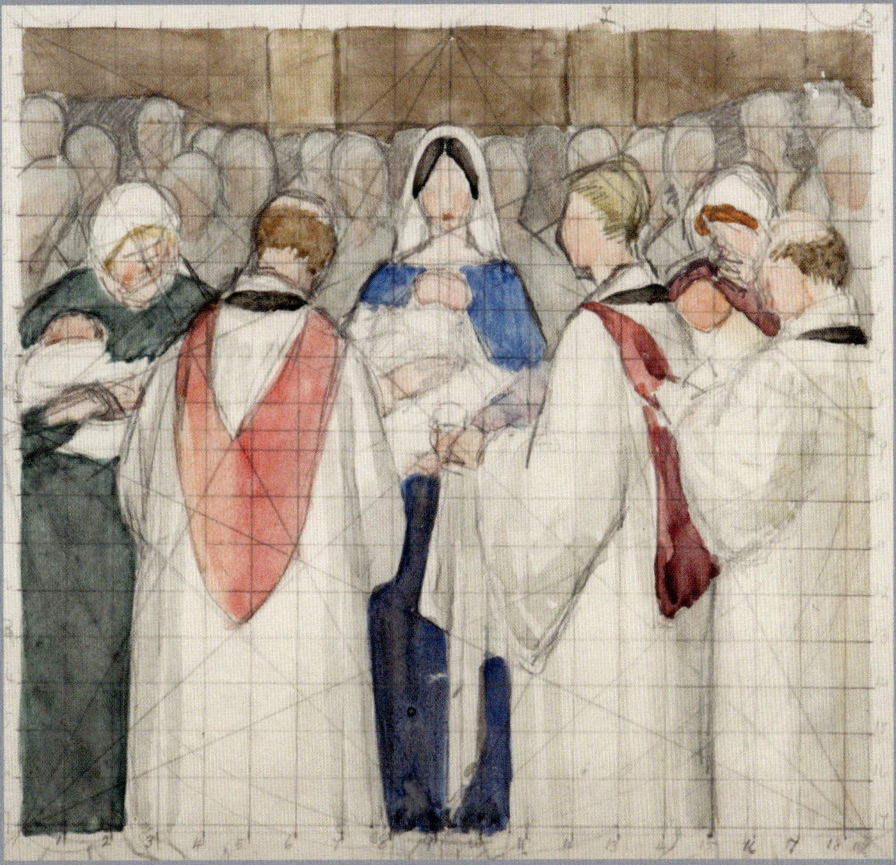

188

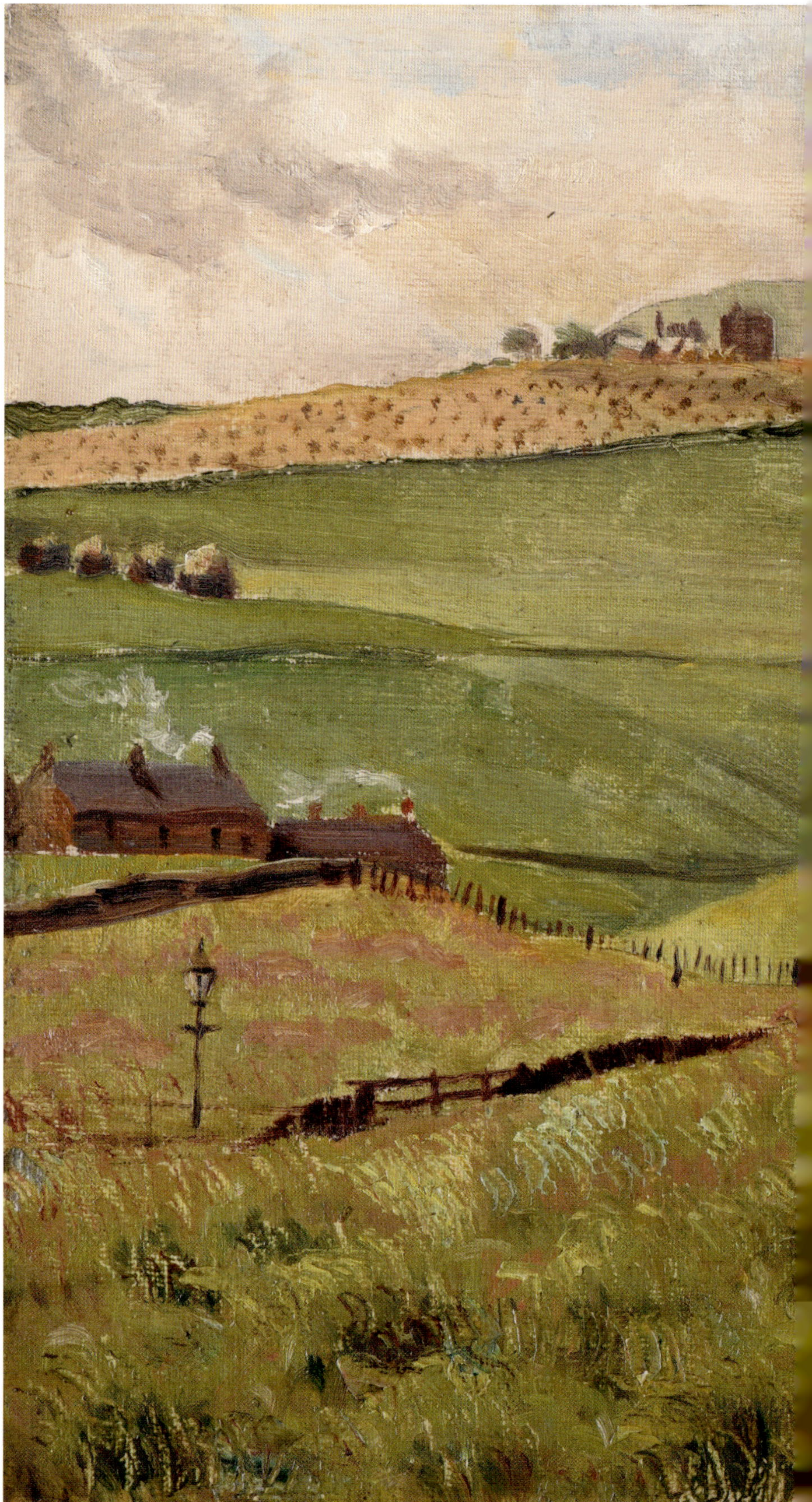

**189 Phyllis Dodd** (1899-1995),
*In the Pentlands*,
oil on George Rowney Birchmore Board,
10 x 14 in. (25.4 x 35.5 cm).

The reclining figure is Phyllis Dodd's husband, Douglas Percy Bliss (**190**, **263**). Admiring the composition, Bliss produced an almost identical version of this painting in 1955.

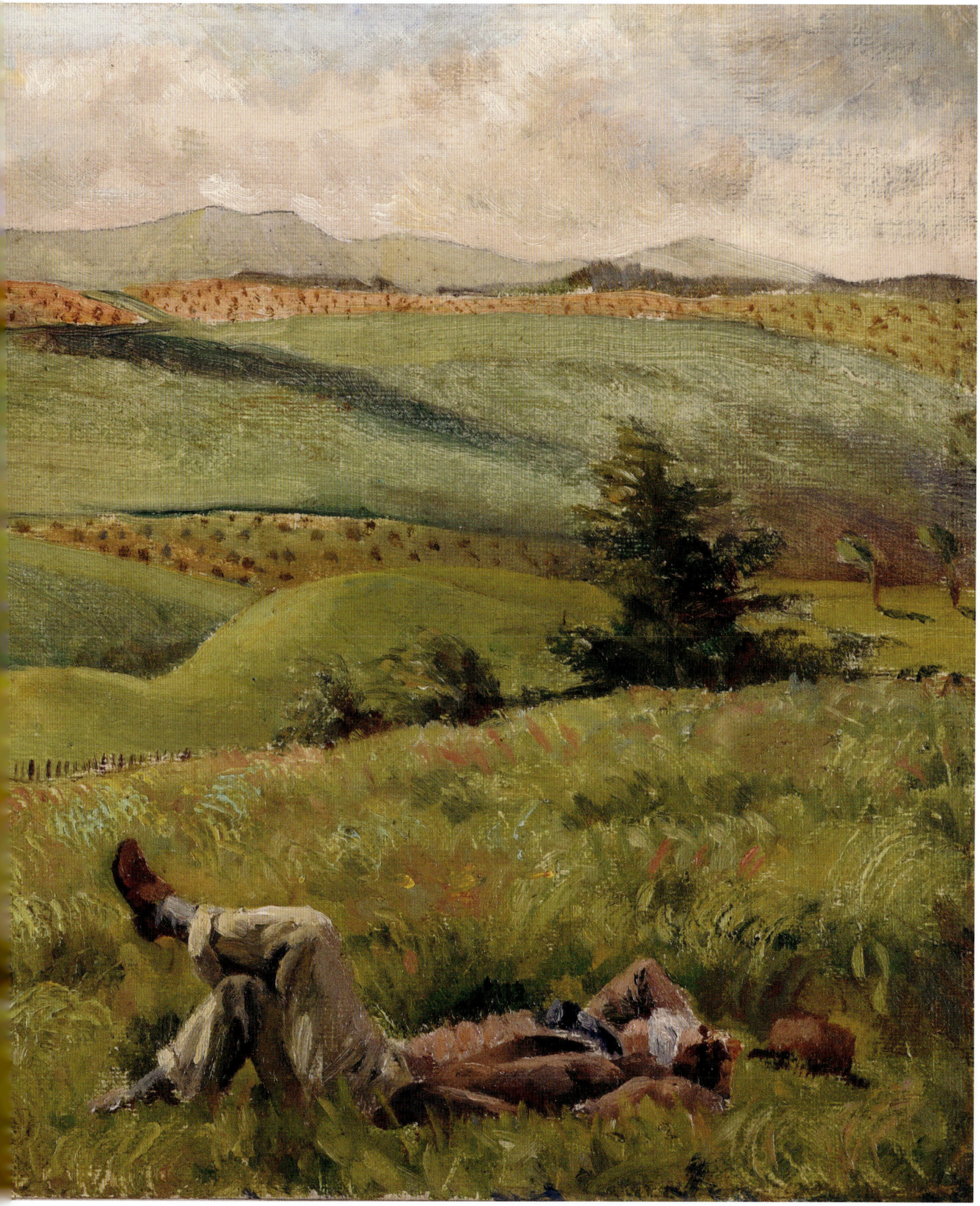

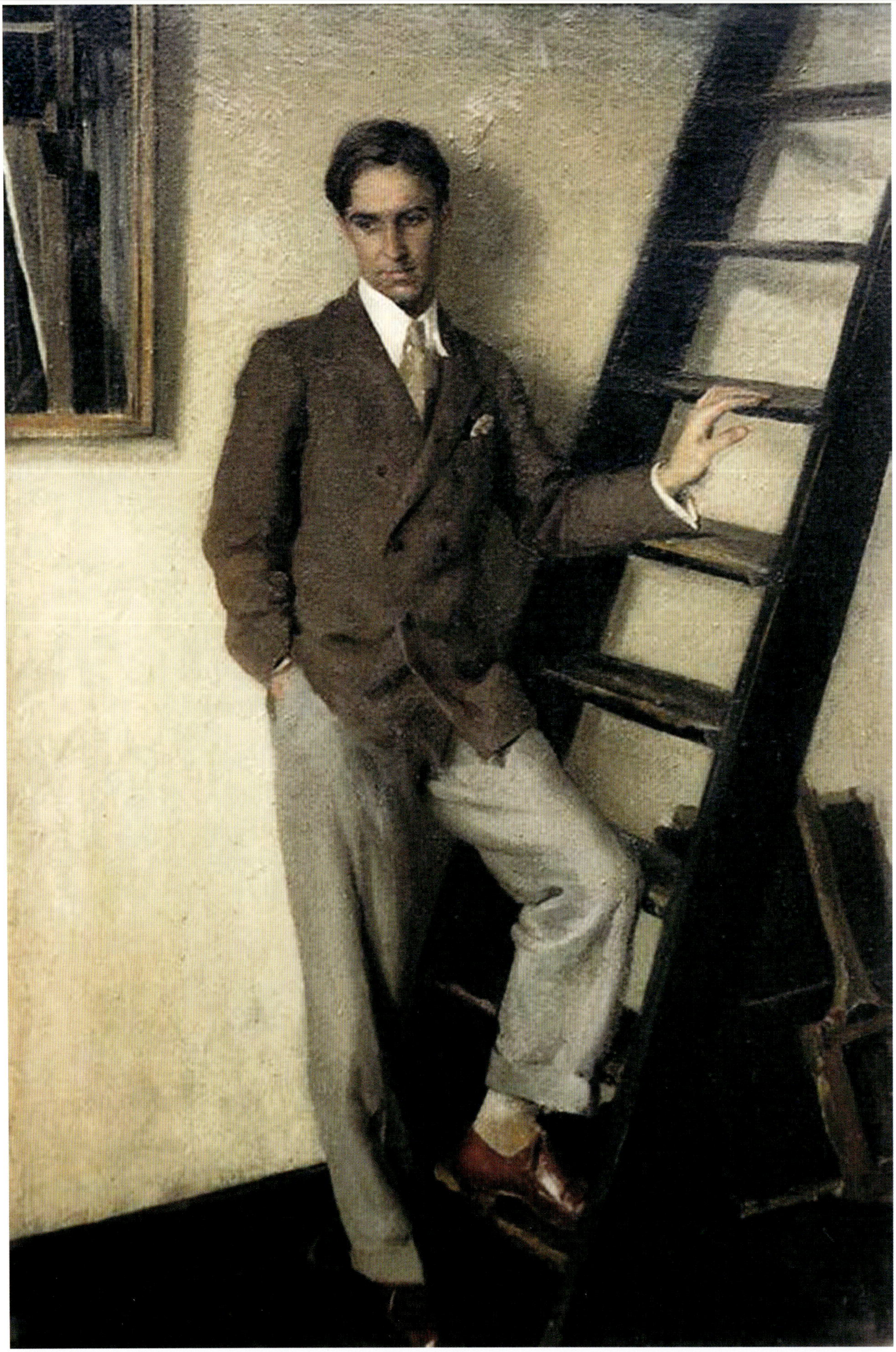

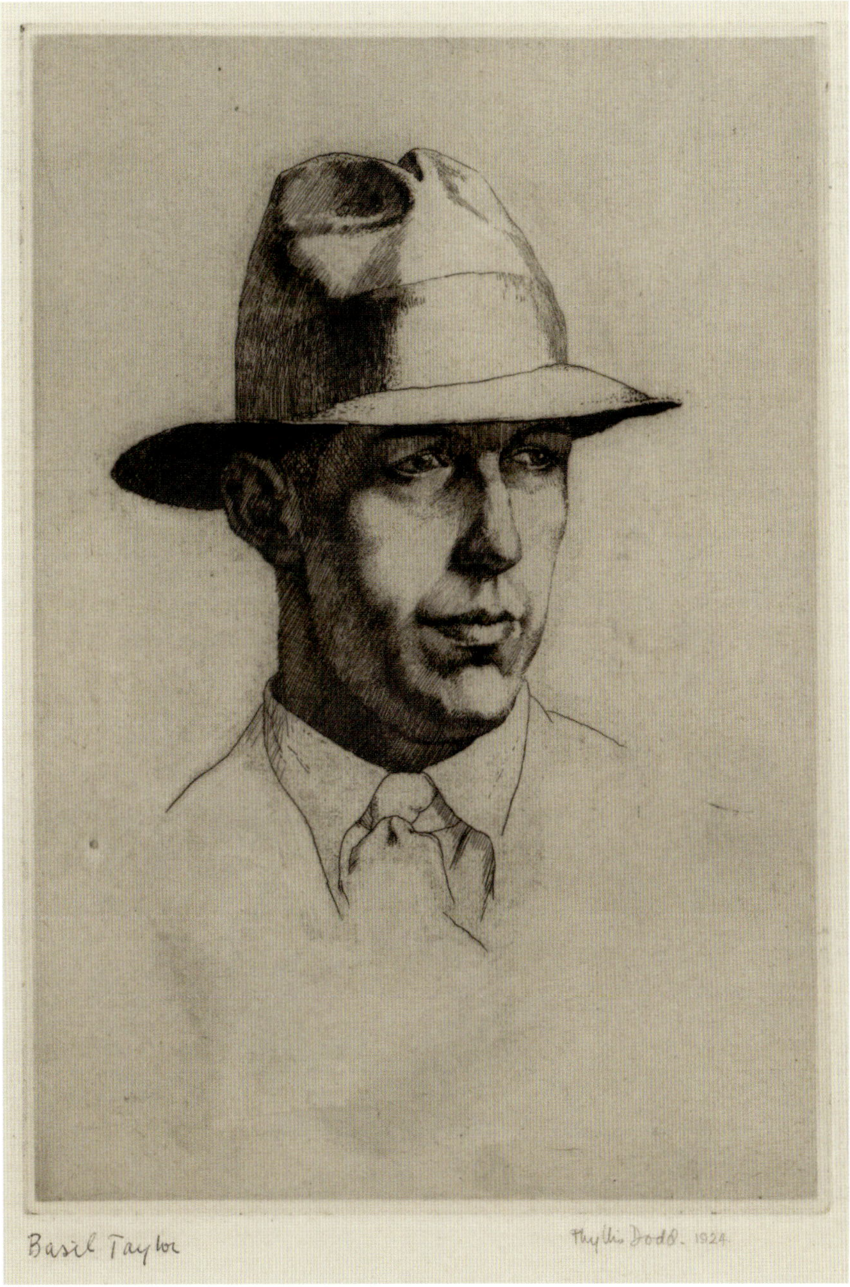


**191 Phyllis Dodd** (1899-1995), *Basil Taylor*, 1924, signed, dated and titled, etching, plate size: 7 ¾ x 5 ½ in. (20 x 14 cm) / paper size; 12 ½ x 9 in. (32 x 23 cm). Collection: National Gallery of Ireland.

Basil Taylor was a flamboyant critic and scholar. Described by Tirzah Garwood as 'a gypsy's warning of a young man', his suicide in 1935 shocked the Great Bardfield artistic community of which he was a part.

**190 Phyllis Dodd** (1899-1995), *Portrait of Douglas Percy Bliss,* 1926-27, oil on board, 30 x 20 in. (76 x 51 cm).

Phyllis Dodd studied at the Liverpool School of Art before moving to the Royal College of Art in London, where her future husband Douglas Percy Bliss was also enrolled. This portrait dates to the period during which Bliss' reputation as a wood engraver was on the rise. The couple married in 1928. In 1946 Bliss was appointed as Director of the Glasgow School of Art. (**263**)

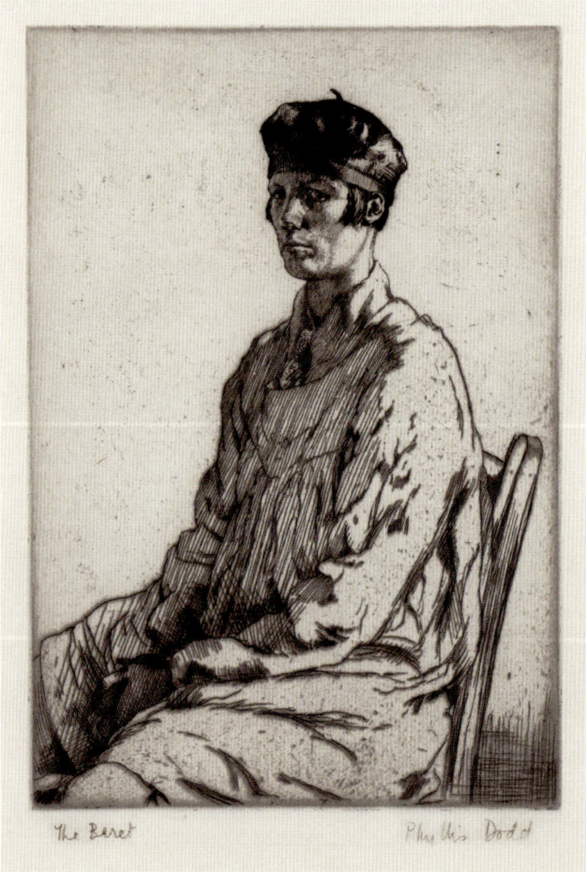


192

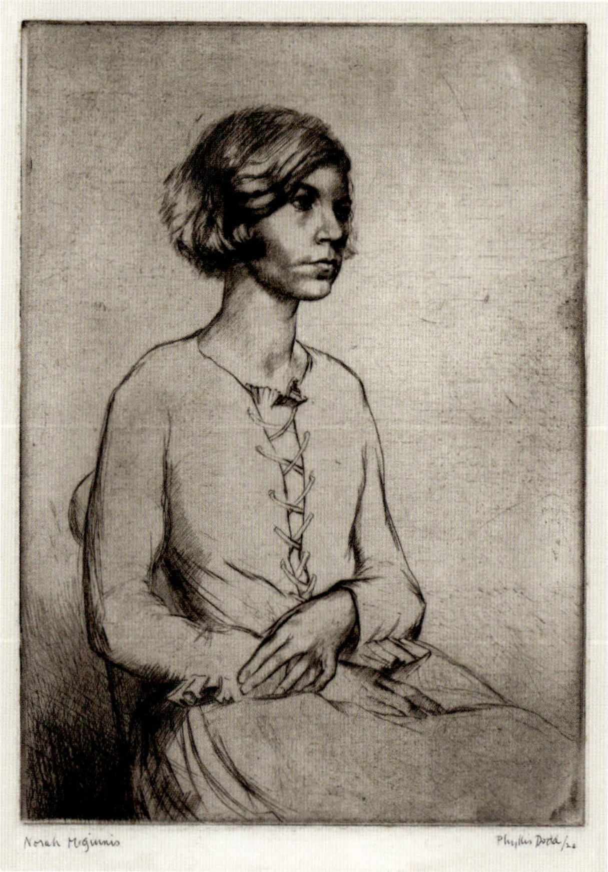


193

**Phyllis Dodd** (1899-1995),

**192** *The Beret* (portrait of Pindi), signed and titled,
drypoint print, plate size: 8 ½ x 6 in. (21.5 x 15 cm) / paper size: 15 x 10 ¾ in. (38.2 x 27.5 cm). Collection: National Gallery of Ireland.

**193** *Norah McGuinness*, 1926, signed, titled and dated,
drypoint print, plate size: 10 ½ x 8 in. (27 x 20 cm) / paper size; 15 x 10 ¾ in. (38 x 27.5 cm). Collection: National Gallery of Ireland.

Pindi was the pet name for Dodd's fellow student and friend, Kathleen Bridle (1897-1989). Kathleen Bridle won a scholarship from the Dublin Metropolitan School of Art to the Royal College of Art in 1920. Phyllis Dodd, Kathleen Bridle and Norah McGuiness shared student accommodation in London. Phyllis Dodd won the George Clausen Prize at the RCA for her 1924 portrait of Norah McGuiness.

After studying at the Dublin Metropolitan School of Art, Norah McGuiness attended the Chelsea Polytechnic. She married Geoffrey Phibbs, but they divorced in 1930 after he had left her more than once, notably for the poet Laura Riding, a mistress of Robert Graves.

**194** **Phyllis Dodd** (1899-1995), *Geoffrey Phibbs*, c.1927, signed,
pencil on paper, 15 x 11 in. (38 x 28 cm). Collection: The National Gallery of Ireland.

Jeoffrey 'Geoffrey' Basil Phibbs was an English-born Irish poet; he took his mother's maiden name and from about 1930 called himself Geoffrey Taylor.

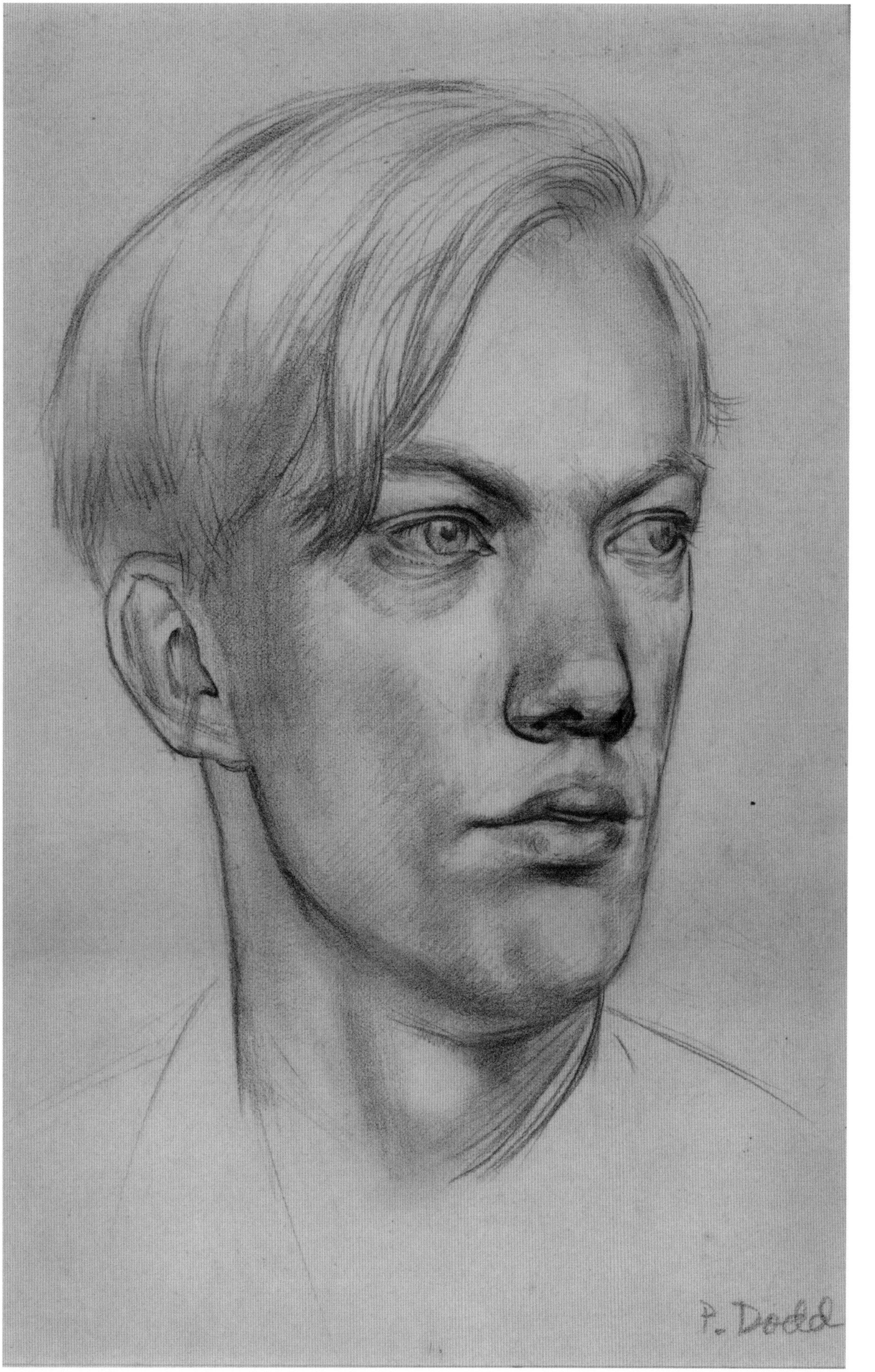
P. Dodd

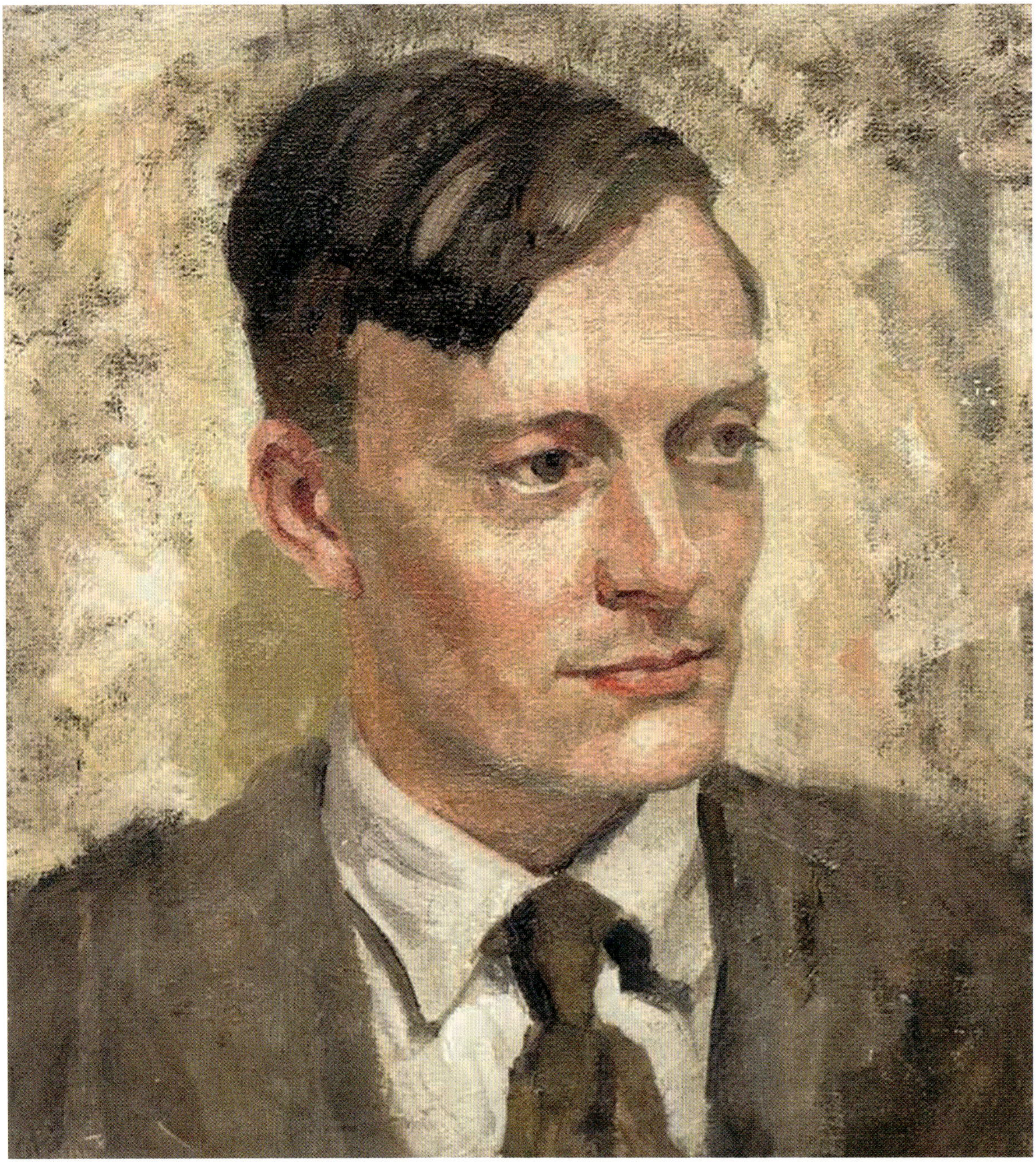

**195 Phyllis Dodd** (1899-1995), *Portrait of Eric Ravilious*, 1929,
oil on canvas, 13 ¾ x 11 ½ in. (35 x 29 cm).

Douglas Bliss found Eric Ravilious 'gay, elegant, sensitive, he could dance and he could whistle; Bawden and I liked him immensely'. Bliss was in the School of Painting at the Royal College of Art, while his two friends were in the School of Design. They gave each other nicknames: Bawden was 'The Pale Spirit', Bliss was 'Mahatma' and Ravilious 'The Boy'. (**199**)

In July 1930 Ravilious married Tirzah Garwood, the most outstanding of his wood engraving students at the Eastbourne School of Art: Bawden was the best man and the Blisses, Rothenstein, Freedman, Edna and Raymond Coxon were there in support. Tirzah had been a member of the group for some time, and the year before the wedding Phyllis had painted a head and shoulders portrait of her in a green cloche hat, executed in one sitting on a hot Sunday afternoon in the Lambeth flat.

**196 Phyllis Dodd** (1899-1995), *Portrait of Tirzah Garwood,* 1929, (**200**, **201**),
oil on board, 23 ½ x 19 ½ in. (60 x 50 cm).

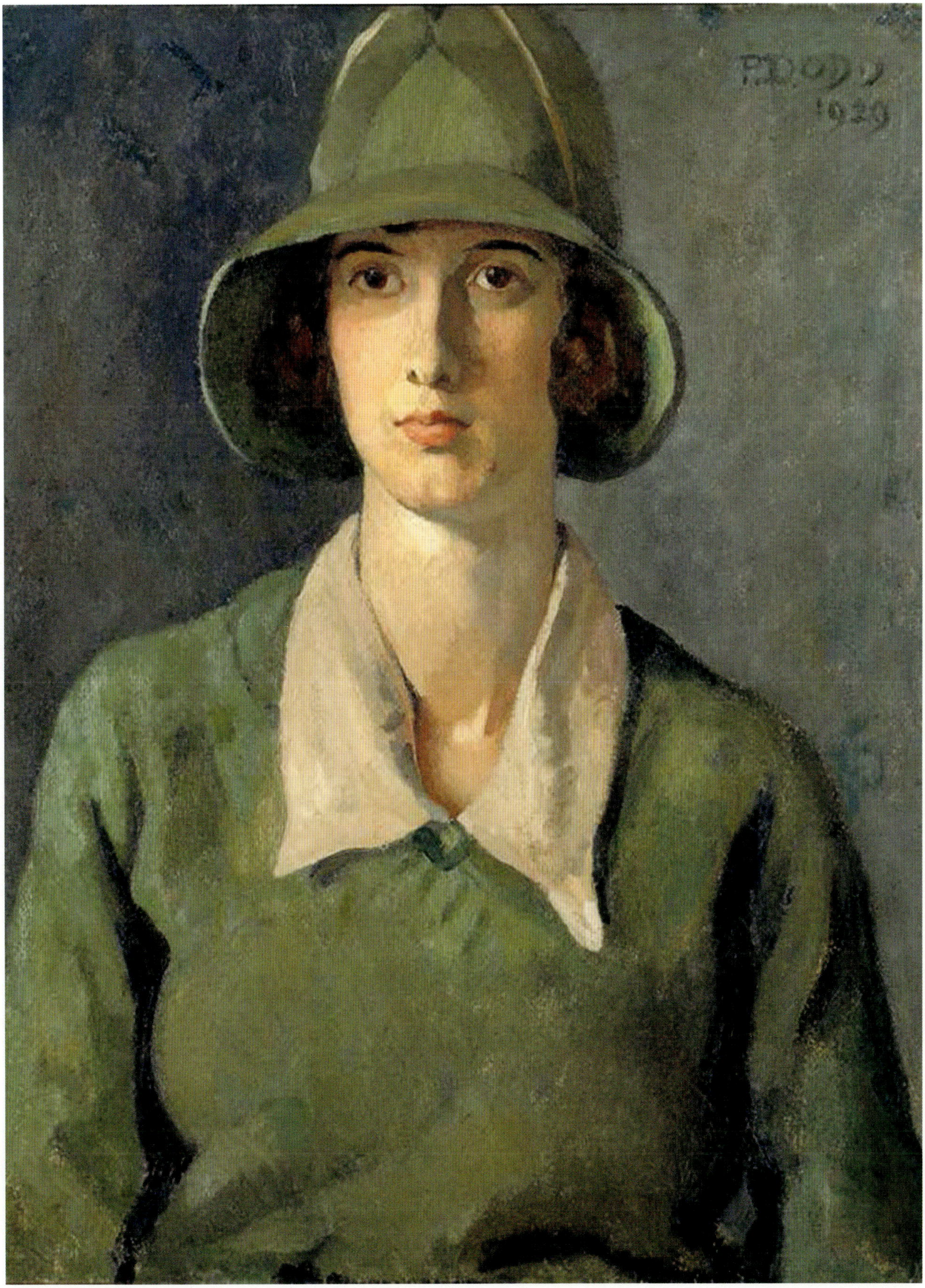
P.DODD
1929

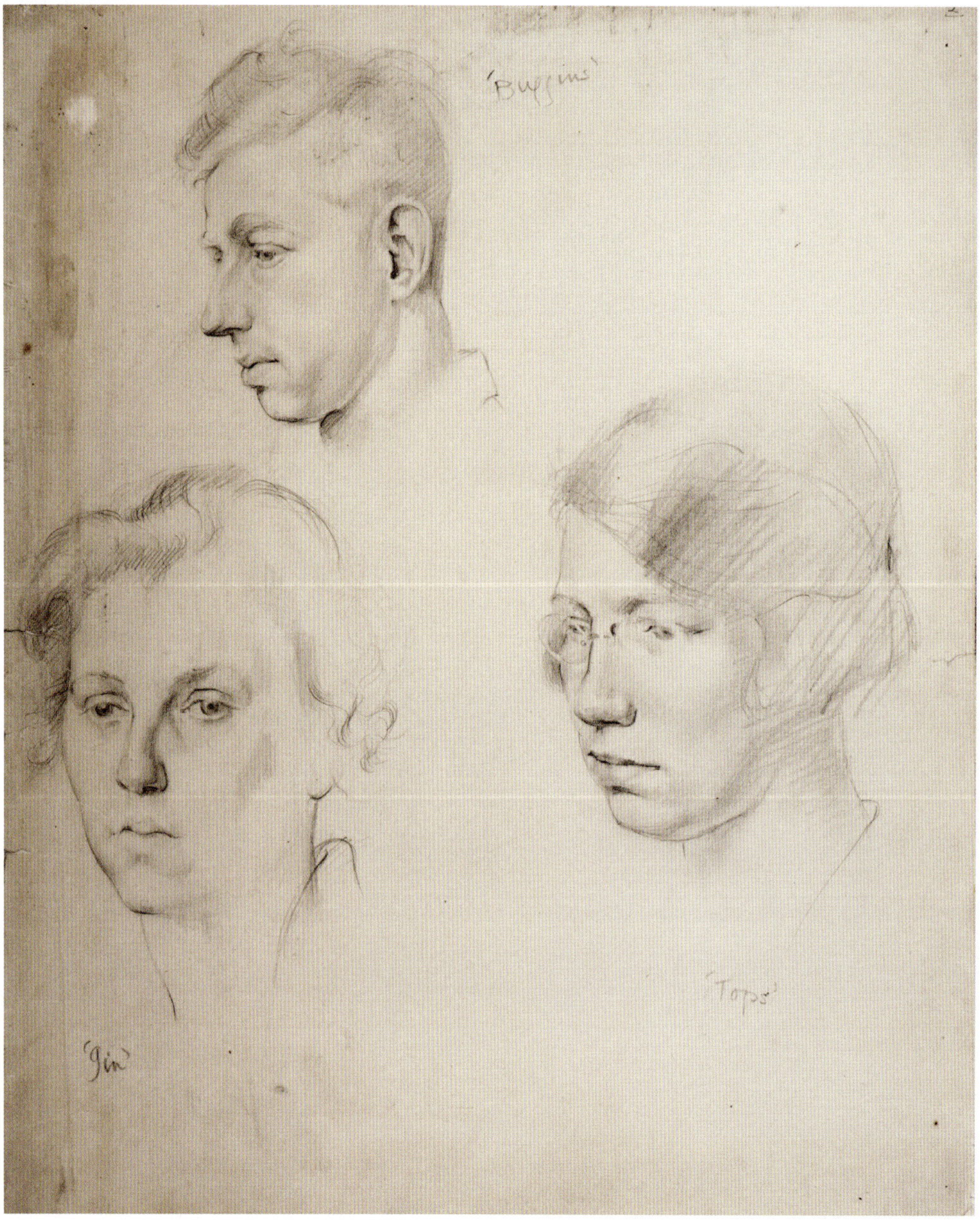


**197 Phyllis Dodd** (1899-1995), *'Buggins','Gin' and 'Tops',* pencil on paper, 15 x 12 ½ in. (38.5 x 31.5 cm).

'Gin' was the nickname given to Edna Ginesi, who studied at Leeds College of Art in 1920-21. At Leeds she met the artist Raymond Coxon (1896-1997), whom she married in 1926. Both Coxon and Ginesi attended the Royal College of Art from 1921 to 1925 where, together with Henry Moore, Barbara Hepworth and Vivian Pitchforth, they formed what was known as 'the Leeds table'. The painter and printmaker Horace Brooks, otherwise known as 'Buggins', who also had studied at Leeds, was another member of this group.

**198 Phyllis Dodd** (1899-1995), *Edward Bawden when a Student at the Royal College of Art,* 1929, oil on canvas, 28 x 18 ¾ in. (71 x 47.5 cm).

Malcolm Yorke has observed that, 'Bawden lived to work: he neither smoked nor drank, nor had any serious interest in sports, theatre, film, politics or dancing. He was wary of women ('the great untouchables') and cripplingly shy, although this did not prevent him having a scathing sense of humour. Douglas Percy Bliss found him abrasive, tactless, self-absorbed and a social liability. He discussed with Ravilious whether to drop him, but they concluded that Bawden was unique and that they were lucky to have him.' The portrait was painted in Cecilia Dunbar-Kilburn's studio at 37 Redcliffe Road, Kensington.

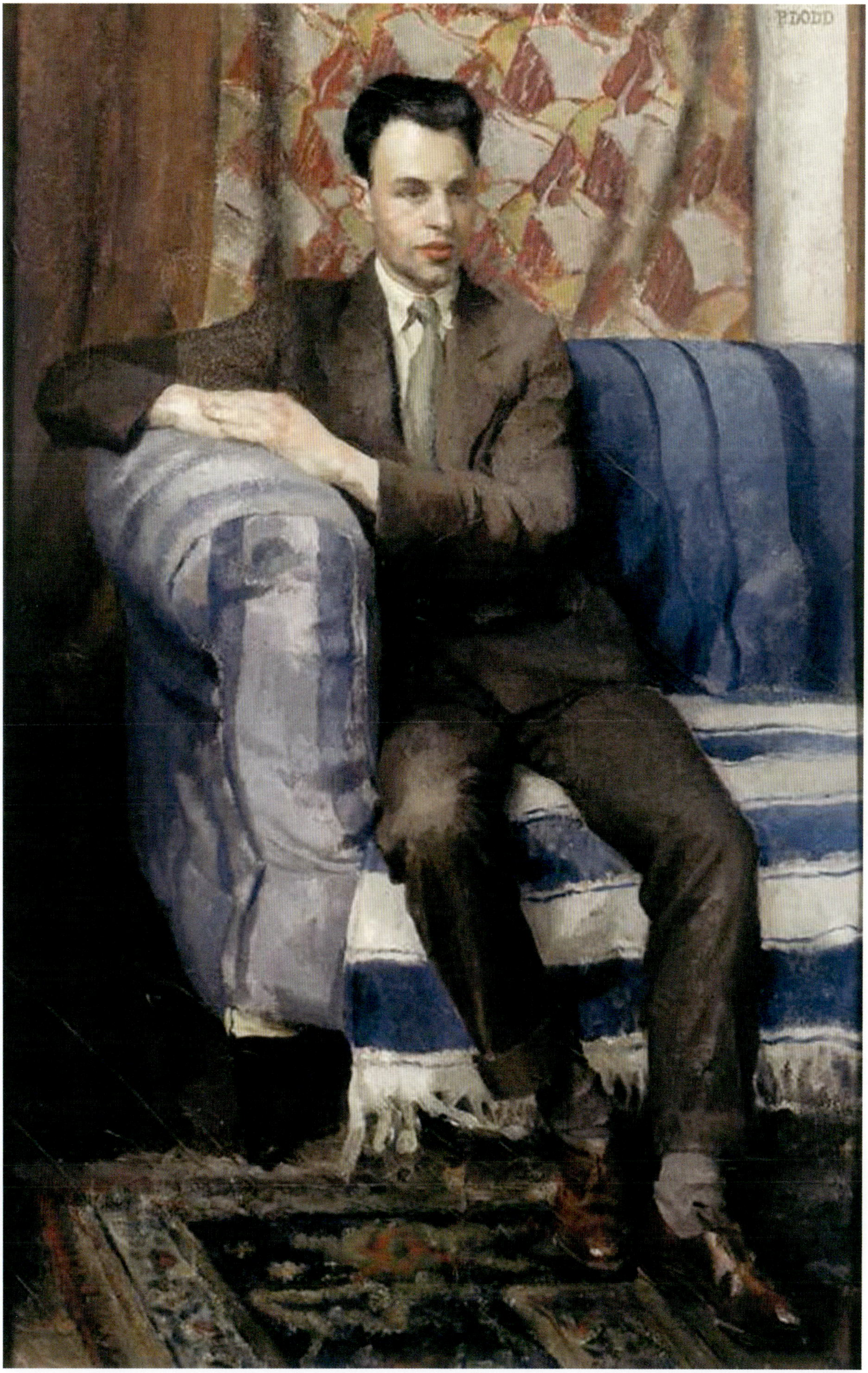
P DODD

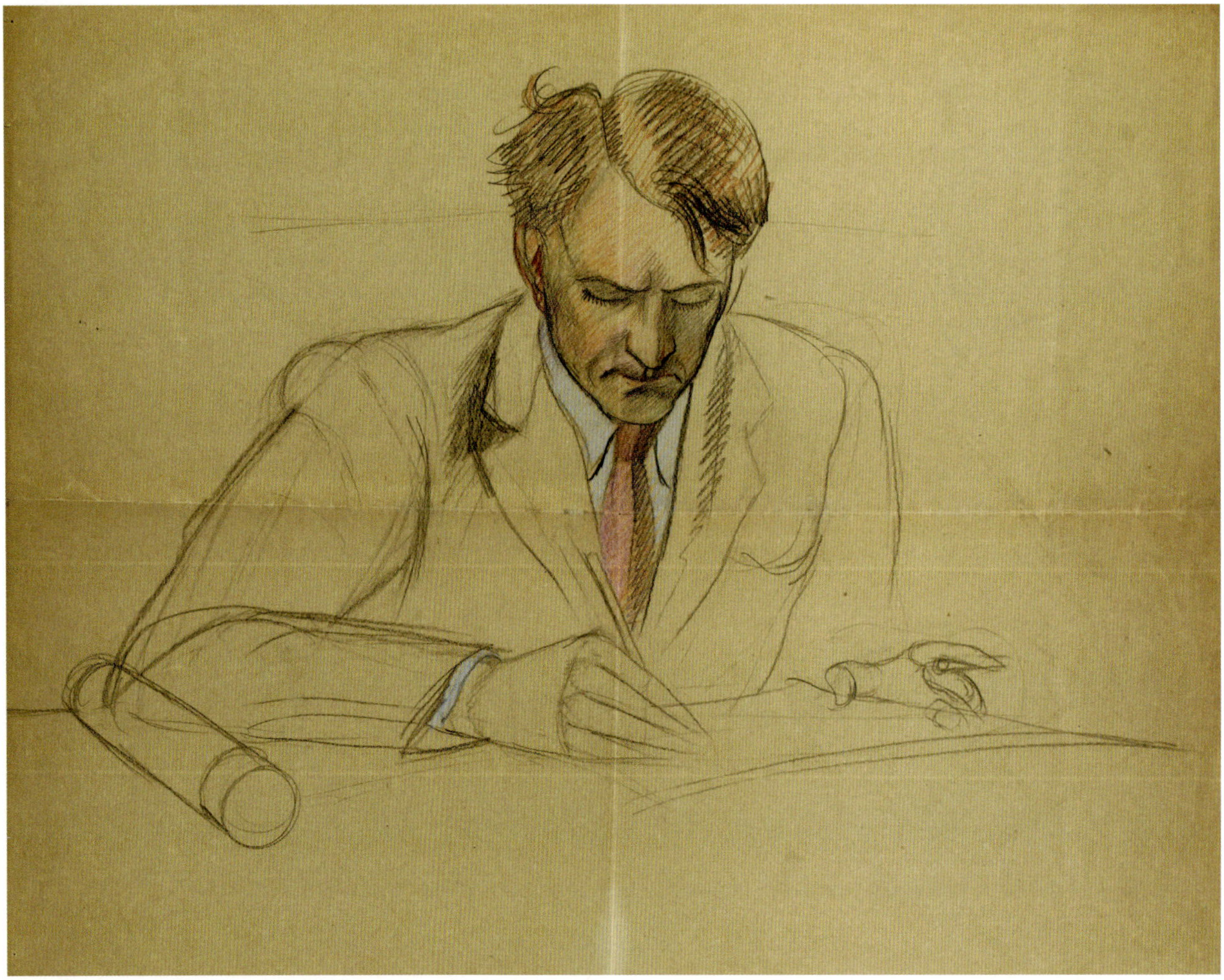

**199 Peggy Angus** (1904-1993), *Portrait of Eric Ravilious*,
pencil and colour on paper, 12 ¼ x 18 in. (31 x 46 cm). Collection: Towner Art Gallery, Eastbourne.

Peggy Angus first met Eric Ravilious in the early 1920s when both were students at The Royal College of Art. Other students included Henry Moore and Barbara Hepworth, Edward Bawden, Barnett Freedman and Enid Marx. From 1933 onwards Angus rented a shepherd's cottage, Furlongs, near Beddingham at the foot of the South Downs, and made that a home to which a circle of artists of gathered. Ravilious considered that his time at Furlongs: '...altered my whole outlook and way of painting, I think because the colour of the landscape was so lovely and the design so beautifully obvious ... that I simply had to abandon my tinted drawings.' (**195**)

**Eric Ravilious** (1903-1942),

**200** *Tirzah on a Cockerel*, 1931,
original boxwood block, 8 x 9 ½ in. (20.5 x 24.2 cm).

**201** *Tirzah on a Cockerel*, 1931,
wood engraving, image size: 8 x 9 ½ in. (20.5 x 24.2 cm).

Used on the cover of the Golden Cockerel Press Autumn List, 1931, this flamboyant lady is based on Ravilious' wife Tirzah. Robert Gibbings had asked Ravilious if he could engrave a device 'for a fiver and the block which I can send you'. He outlined a design based on a merry-go-round cockerel, suggesting a 'robust animal with a naughty twinkle in its eye and a comb suggesting a drunken coronet'. Its rider should be a 'luscious lady'. The block bears a vague outline nude drawn on the underside. On 11 September 1931 Gibbings wrote to Ravilious explaining that he had done this 'for the benefit of Pathé who were down here yesterday filming us at work for their Pictorial'. When he had finished the engraving, Ravilious wrote 'it was fun to do', hoping that Gibbings would not mind that he had deviated slightly from the suggested design. Very few of Ravilious' blocks survive, and this one was never printed by the artist.

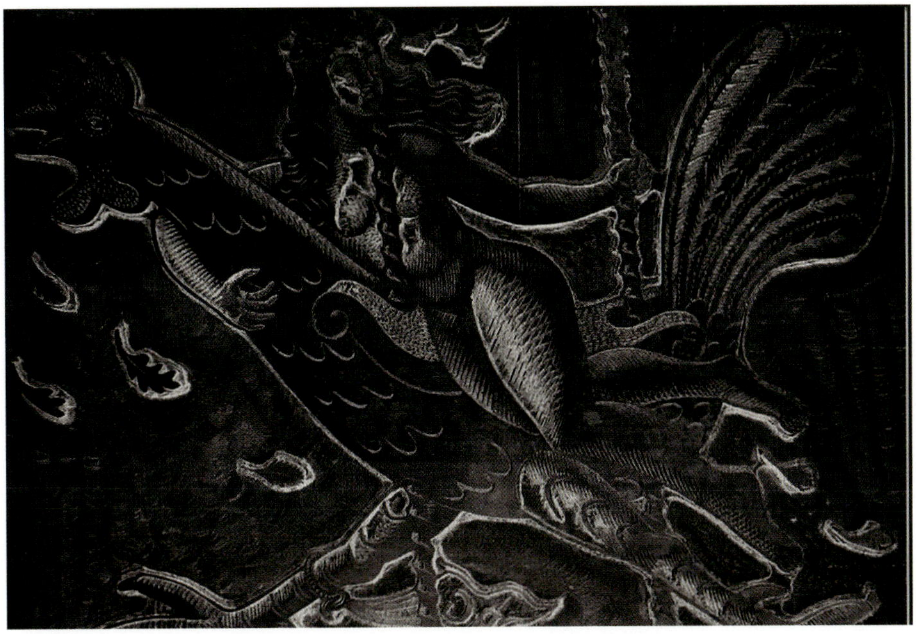

200

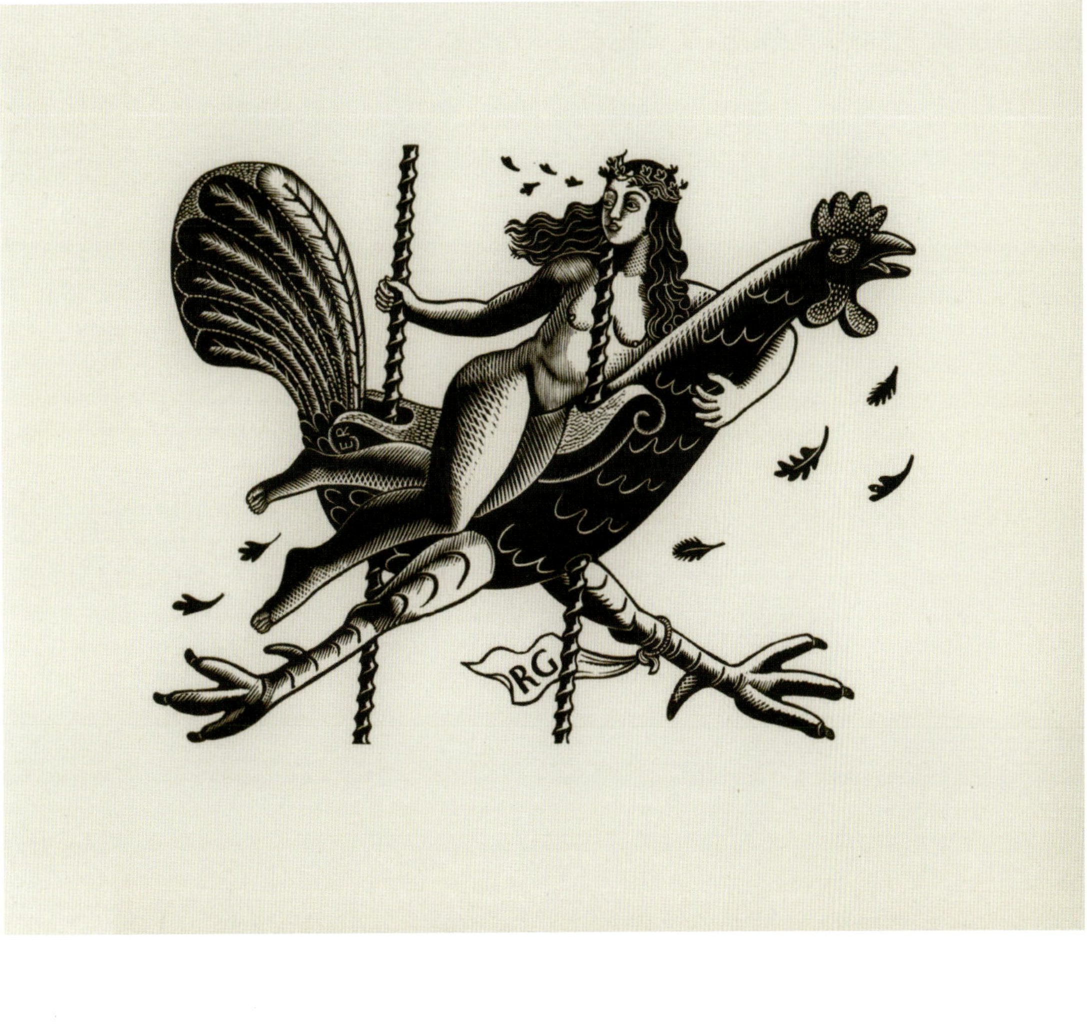


201

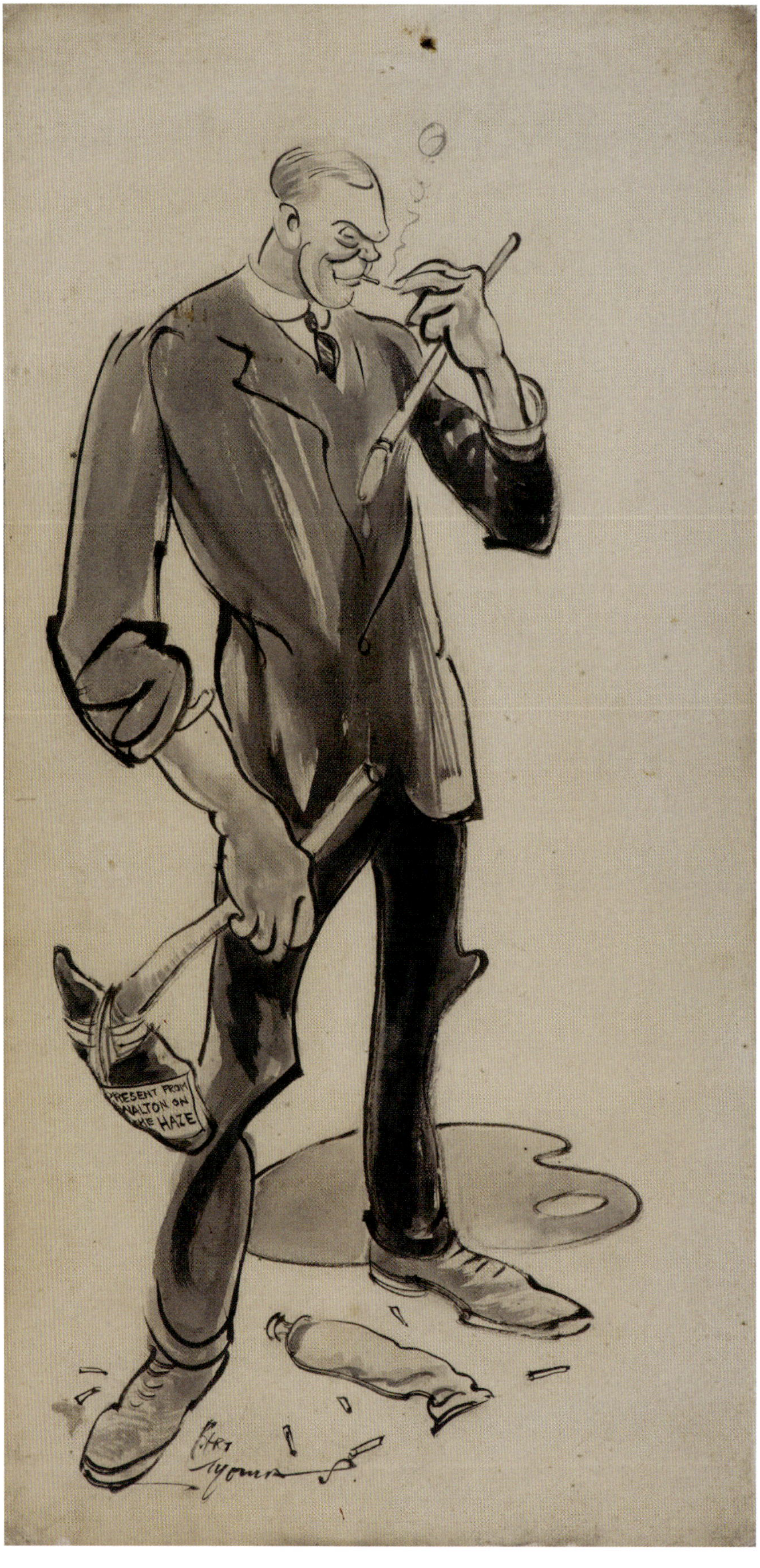

**202 John Hassall** (1868-1948),
*Portrait of Bert Thomas*,
signed and inscribed,
Bert, yours J.
'Present from Walton on the Haze'
pen & ink on board,
16 ¾ x 8 ½ in. (42.6 x 21.5 cm).

Having studied in Antwerp and Paris, during which time he was influenced by the famous poster artist Alphonse Mucha, John Hassall became one of Britain's most successful graphic artists of the late 19th century. His work was characterised by the use of flat colours enclosed by thick black lines, a style widely recognised when, from 1895 he began work as an advertising artist for David Allen & Sons. Over his fifty-year career he produced many iconic posters, including 'Skegness is so Bracing' (1908). Between 1896 and 1899 alone, he produced. over 600 theatre poster designs for the firm.

In 1900, Hassall opened his own New Art School and School of Poster Design in Kensington. The Hassall brand was thus passed on to a new generation: Annie Fish, Bert Thomas (**209**), Bruce Bairnsfather, H. M. Bateman and Harry Rountree (**207**) were among his students. He also belonged to several clubs, including the Langham, the Savage and the London Sketch Club, of which he was a President from 1903-1904. Dudley Hardy (**242**) and Cecil Aldin were his life-long friends. Hassall was, not surprisingly, the subject of numerous portraits by his students and admirers. (**280**)

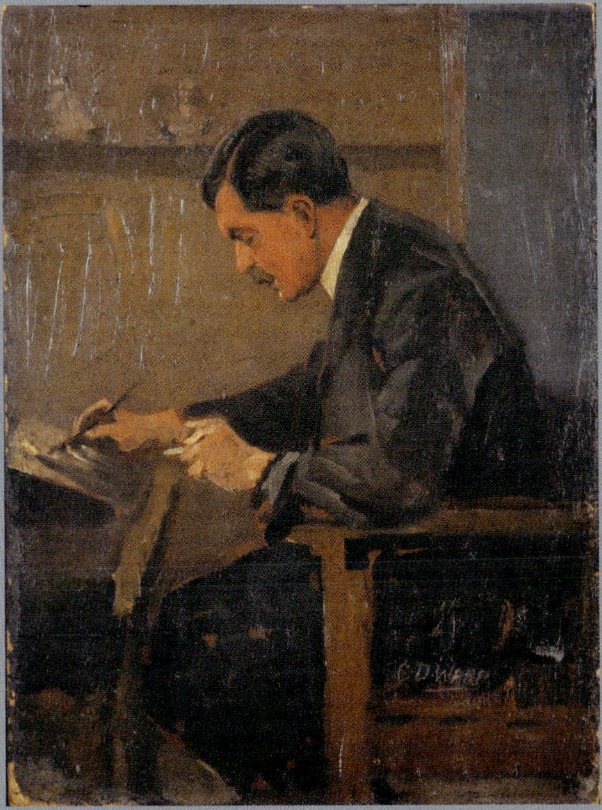

203

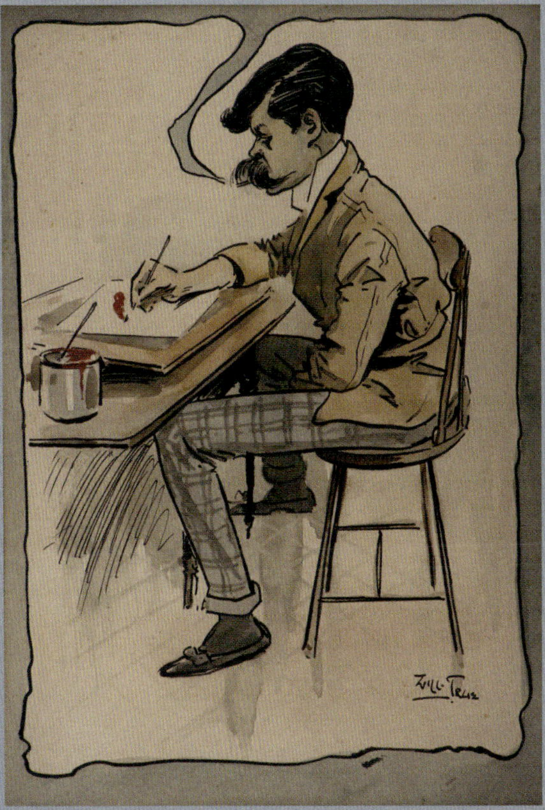


204

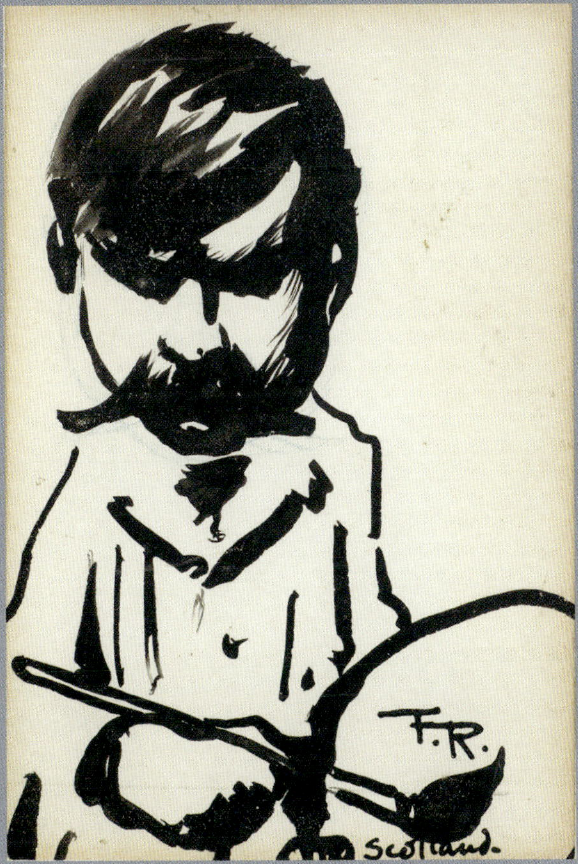


205

**203 Charles Daniel Ward** (1872-1935),
*John Hassall at Work*,
oil on board, 12 x 9 in. (30.5 x 22.9 cm).

**204 Will True**,
*Portrait of John Hassall, Seated at Table, Painting*,
signed, inscribed to reverse 'published in Savage Club',
pen, Ink and gouache on paper,
11 ½ x 8 in. (29.2 x 20.3 cm).

**205 Frank Reynolds** (1876-1953),
*Portrait of John Hassall Painting*,
signed with initials, inscribed 'Scotland',
black ink on paper,
4 x 3 in. (10.4 x 7.7 cm).

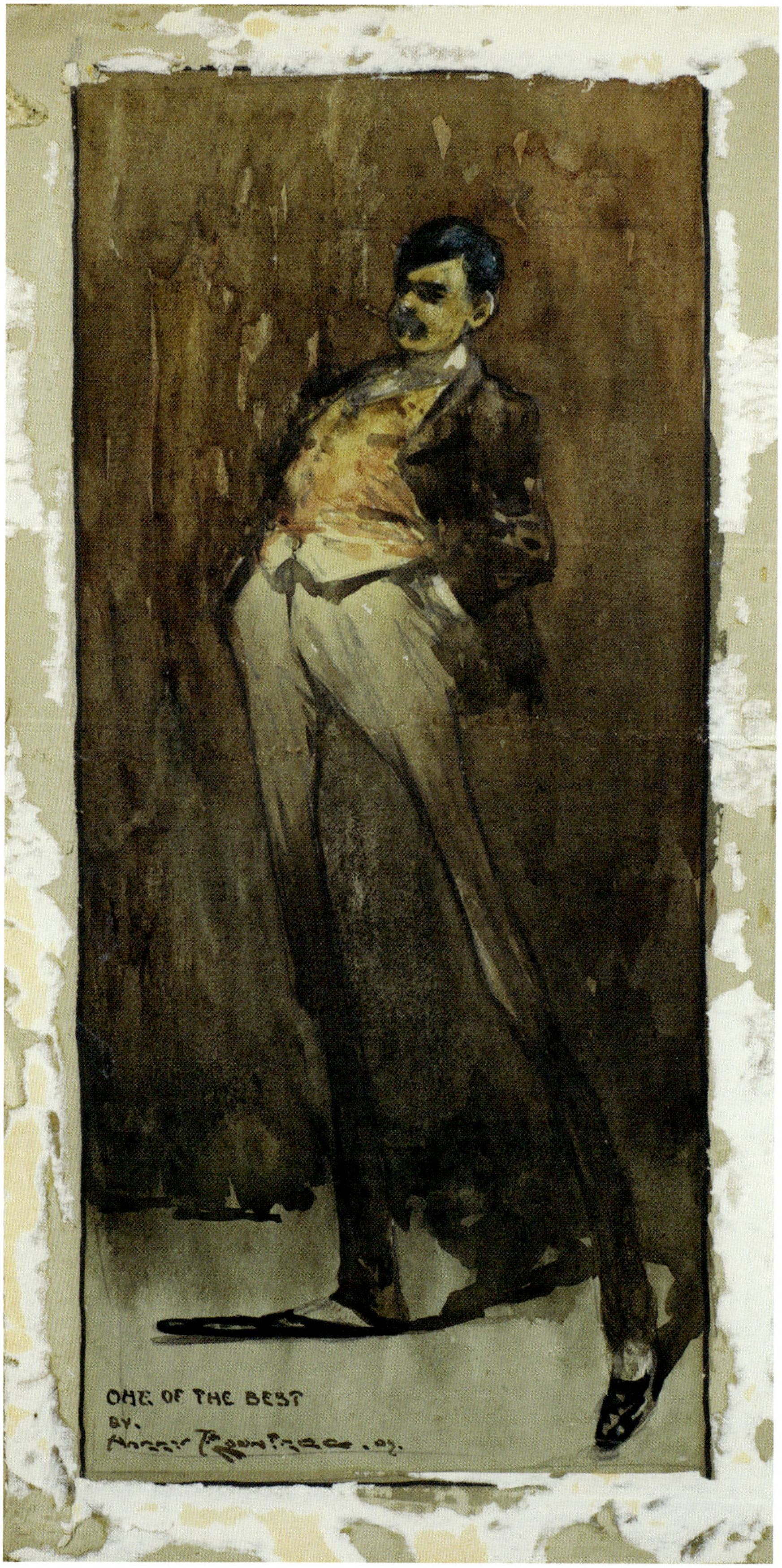


**206** **Harry Rountree** (1878-1950),
*'One of the Best' Portrait of John Hassall*,
signed, inscribed with title,
gouache on card,
9 x 4 ¼ in. (22.9 x 10.8 cm).

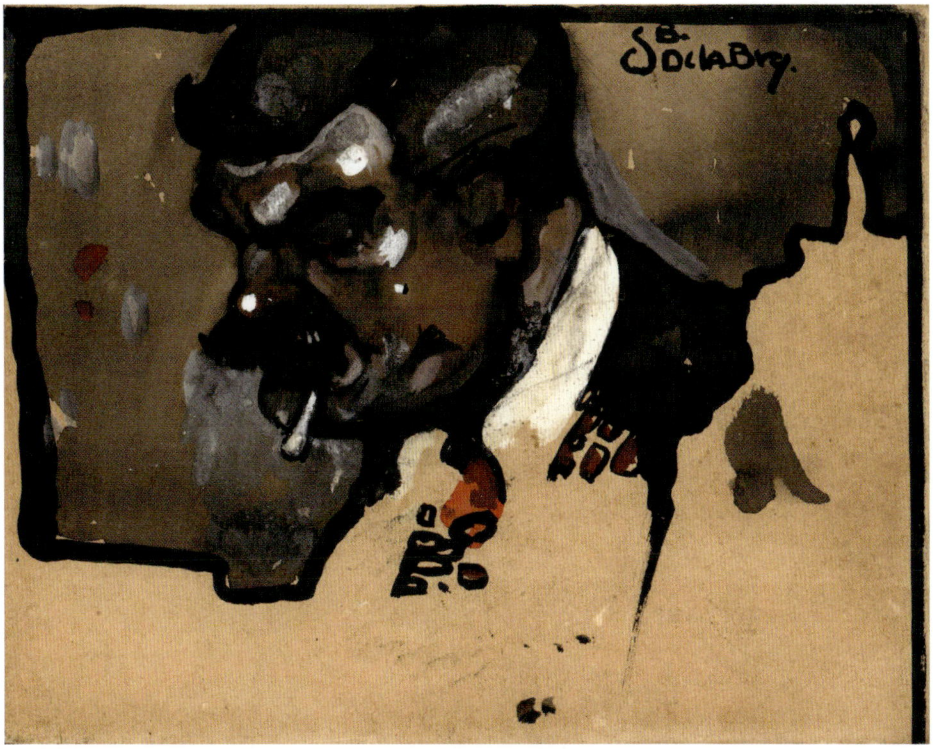

**207** **Stephen Baghot de la Bere** (1877-1927), *Portrait of John Hassall Smoking*, gouache on card, 5 ¾ x 7 ½ in. (14.7 x 19 cm).

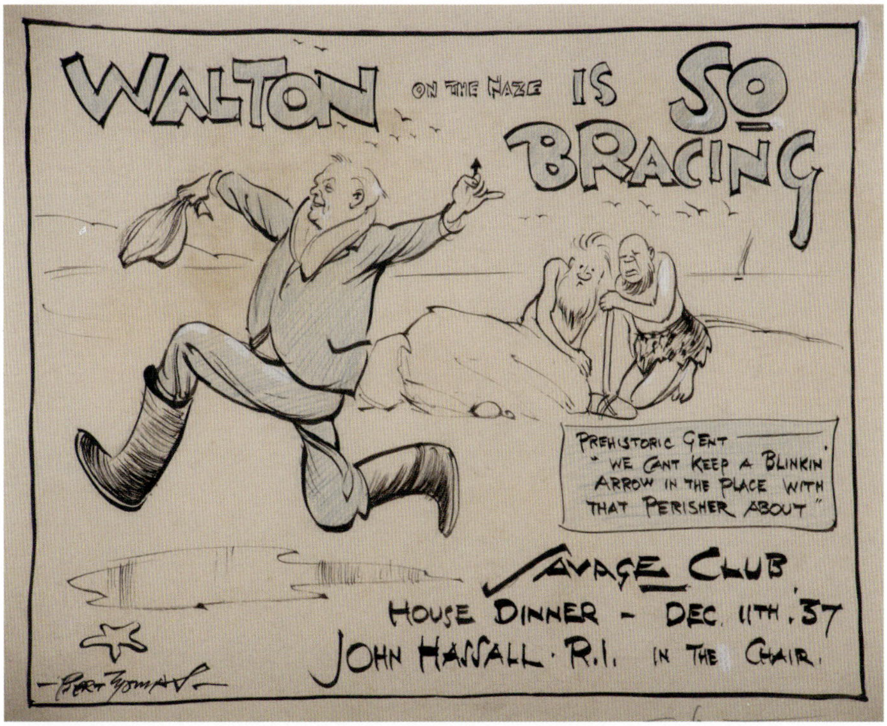


**208** **Bert Thomas** (1883-1966), *Walton on the Naze is So Bracing, Savage Club House Dinner*, 1937, signed and inscribed, pen & ink and crayon with highlights in white on Reeves commercial art board, 10 ½ x 15 in. (26.8 x 38.2 cm).

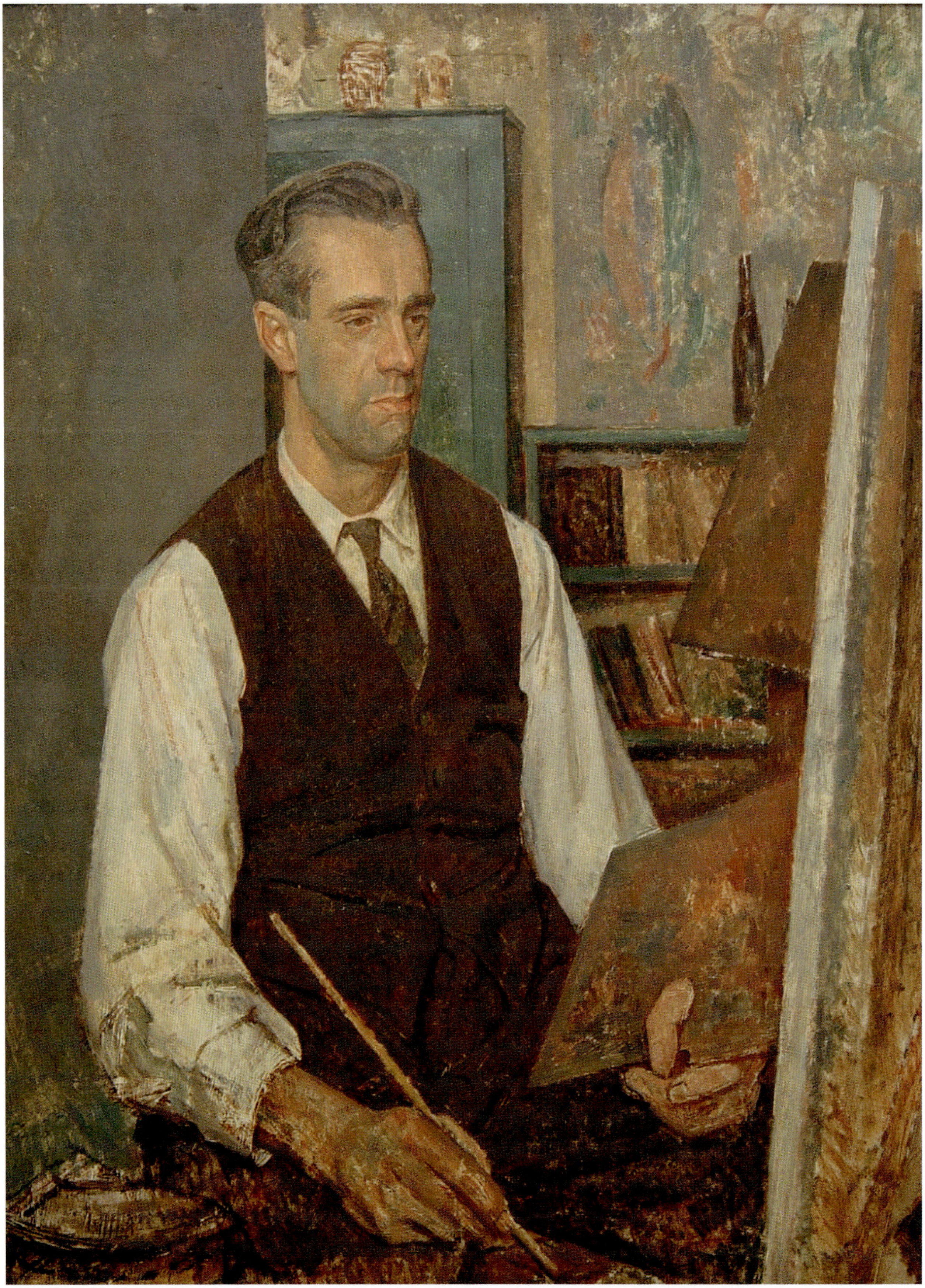

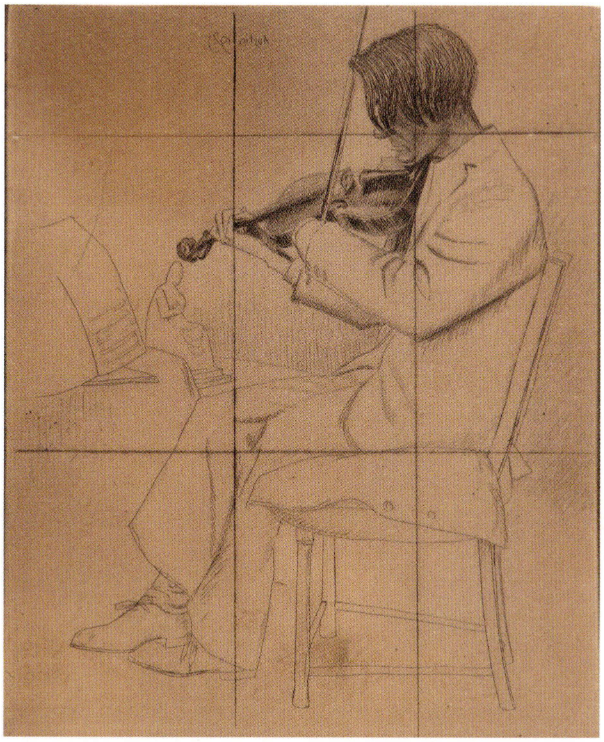

210

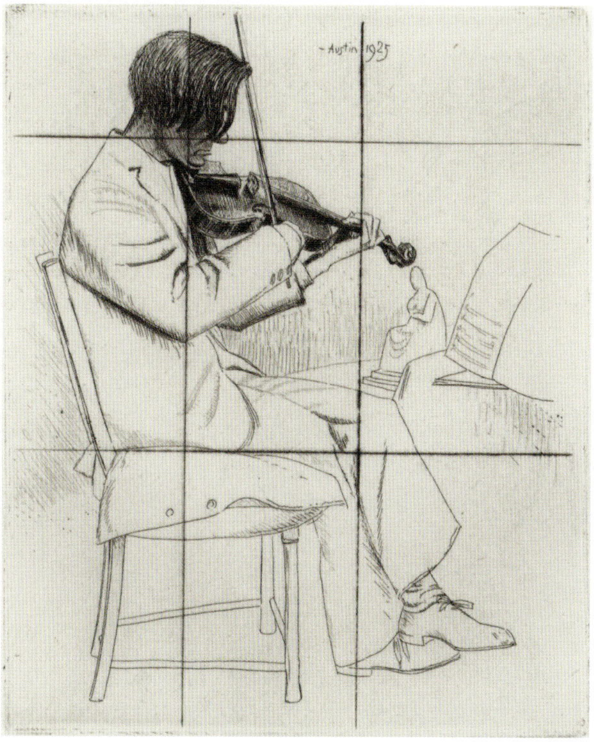

211

**Robert Austin** (1895-1973), *Portrait of Charles Murray*, 1925 (CD 55),

**210** original copper plate (cancelled), signed in the plate, 5 ¼ x 4 ½ in. (13.5 x 11.2 cm),

**211** etching (printed from the cancelled plate), 9 x 7 ¼ in. (23 x 18.7 cm).

Robert Sargent Austin (**256**) and Charles Murray were Rome Scholars in Engraving respectively for 1922 and 1923. Their time at The British School at Rome overlapped by two years. This portrait of Murray, who was a gifted violinist, is numbered '55' in Campbell Dodgson's *A Catalogue of Etchings and Engravings by Robert Austin RE 1913-1929*.

**209 Percy Horton** (1897-1970), *Portrait of an Artist*, c.1925,
signed with studio stamp to reverse, reference number 2/8,
oil on panel, 24 x 18 in. (61 x 46 cm).

The paintings in the background suggest a link with an artist of the Bloomsbury Group. The sitter bears a resemblance to Cecil Stephenson and Stanley Badmin; the latter was a fellow-student of Horton at the Royal College of Art. However, apart from his Royal College of Art acquaintances, the sitter might well be an artist from Ruskin College or The Artists' International Association.

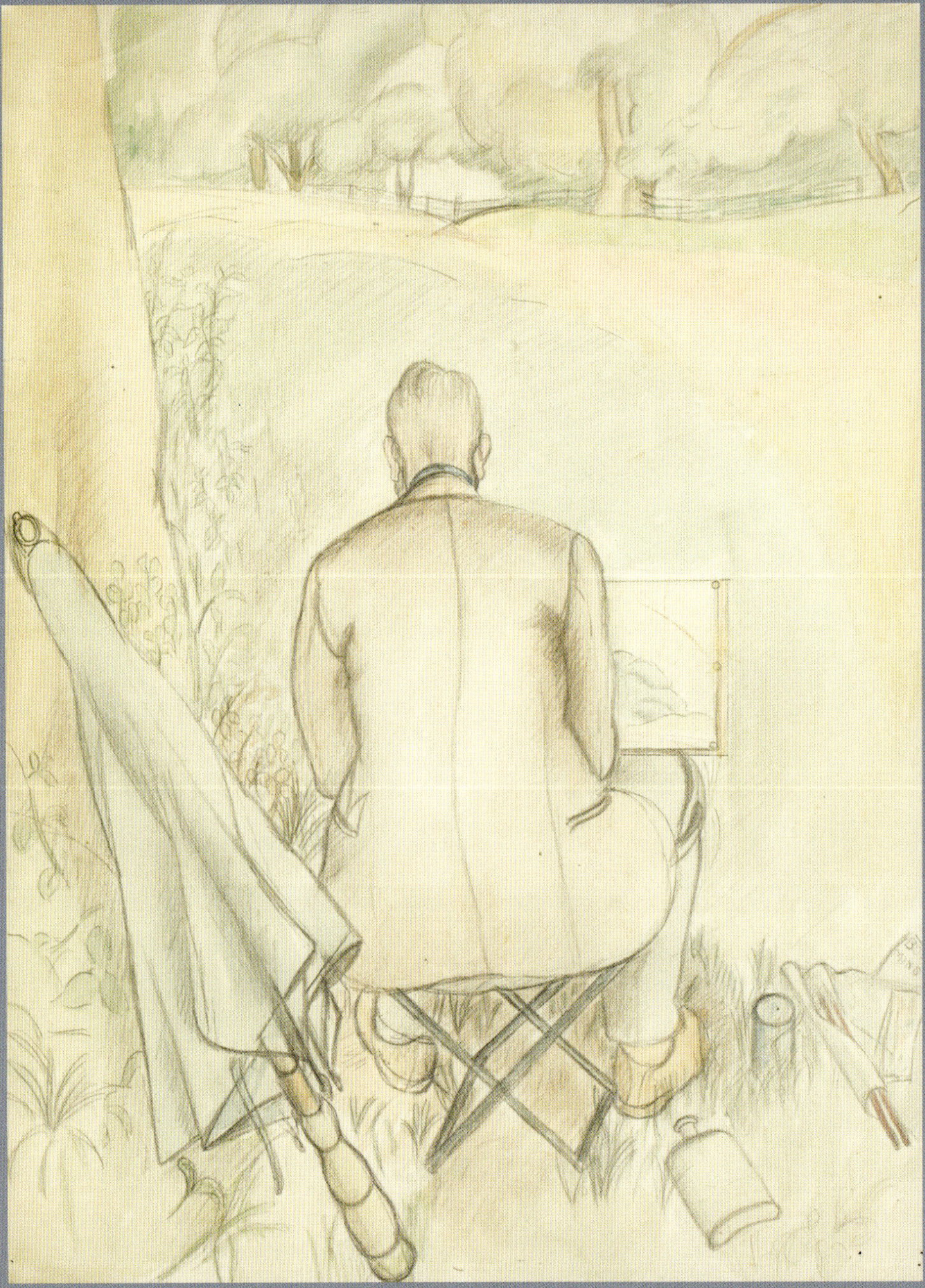

**212 Rosalie Brill** (1903-1992), *Portrait of the Artist's Husband, Reginald Brill, Sketching*, c. 1930, watercolour and pencil on paper, 15 x 11 in. (38 x 28 cm).

Rosalie Clarke (**264**) married Reginald Brill in 1925. She served as her husband's model throughout the early years of their marriage. In 1927 she accompanied him during his two-year scholarship in Decorative Painting at the British School at Rome. Rosalie was an accomplished artist herself, with a particular propensity for flower subjects. She exhibited occasionally at the Royal Academy.

**213 Jacqueline Pietersen** (1899-1984), *Charles Cundall at Work*, signed, oil on board, 13 ½ x 10 in. (34.2 x 25.5 cm).

Jacqueline Pietersen (1899-1984) studied at the Royal College of Art, where she met her future husband Charles Cundall (**185**). They were married in 1923 and lived in Paris. She exhibited regularly at the Royal Academy and the New English Art Club.

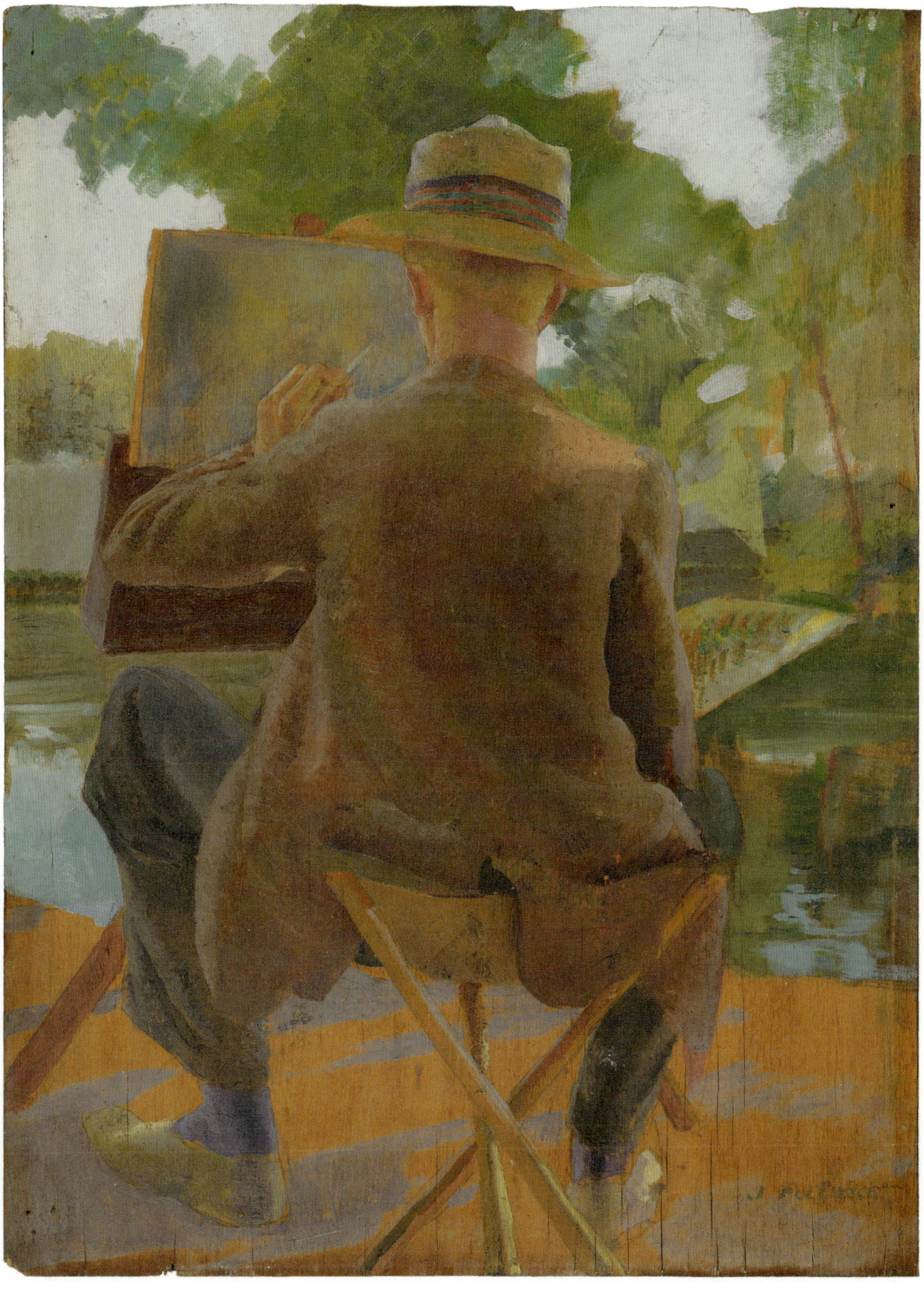

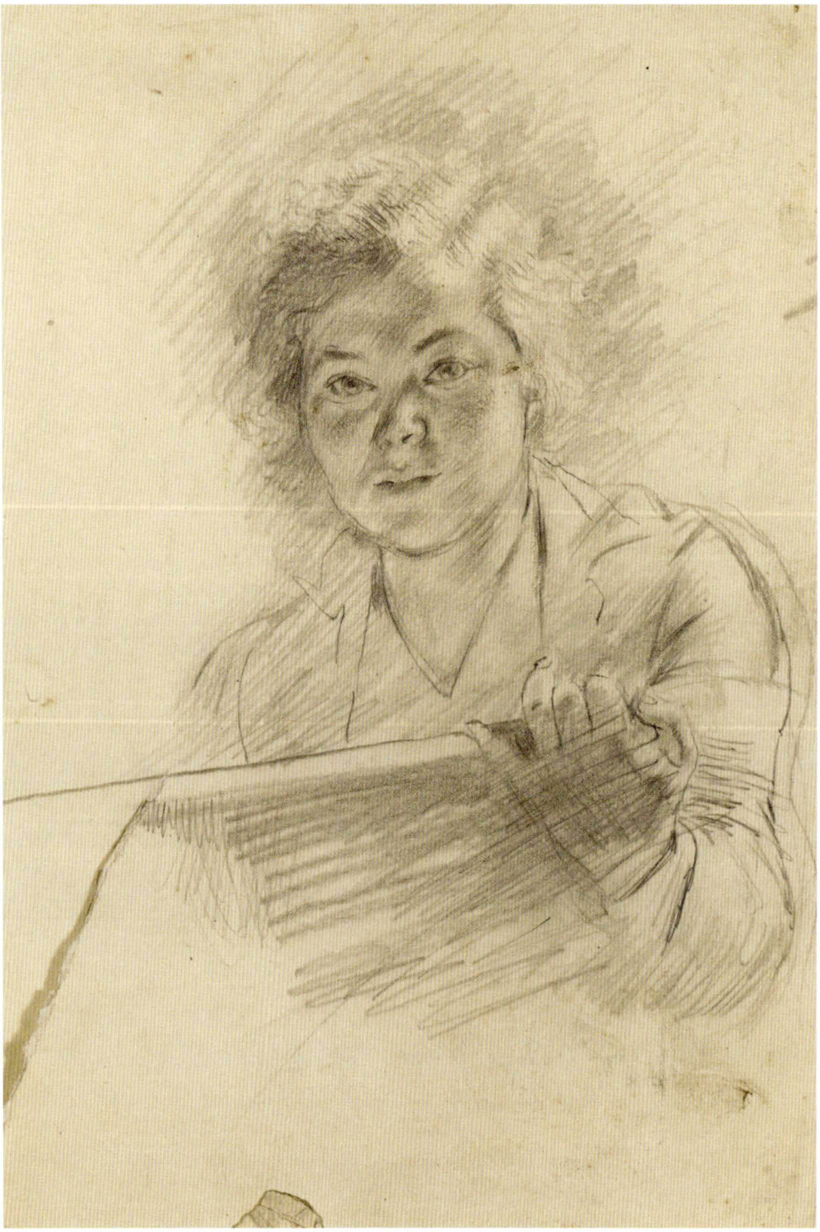

**214 Evelyn Dunbar** (1906-1960), *Portrait of the artist Margaret Goodwin*, c.1930, pencil on paper, 11 x 9 in. (28 x 23 cm).

Margaret Goodwin, a friend and contemporary of Evelyn Dunbar at the Royal College of Art, attended the school from 1929 to 1933. The two remained life-long friends. A high point of their friendship was a sketching and – for Dunbar – rock-climbing holiday in the Lake District with Roger Folley, Dunbar's future husband, in April 1941. (**292**, **293**, **294**, **295**)

**215 Thomas Monnington** (1902-1976), *Portrait of Winifred Knights*, c.1931, tempera on canvas, 14 x 11 in. (36 x 28 cm).

Thomas Monnington and Winifred Knights married in Rome in April 1924. This profile portrait dates to the early 1930's when Knights and Monnington were living in Crawley Down, West Sussex. At this time Monnington was working on his *Supper at Emmaus* altarpiece, with which this painting has stylistic affinities.

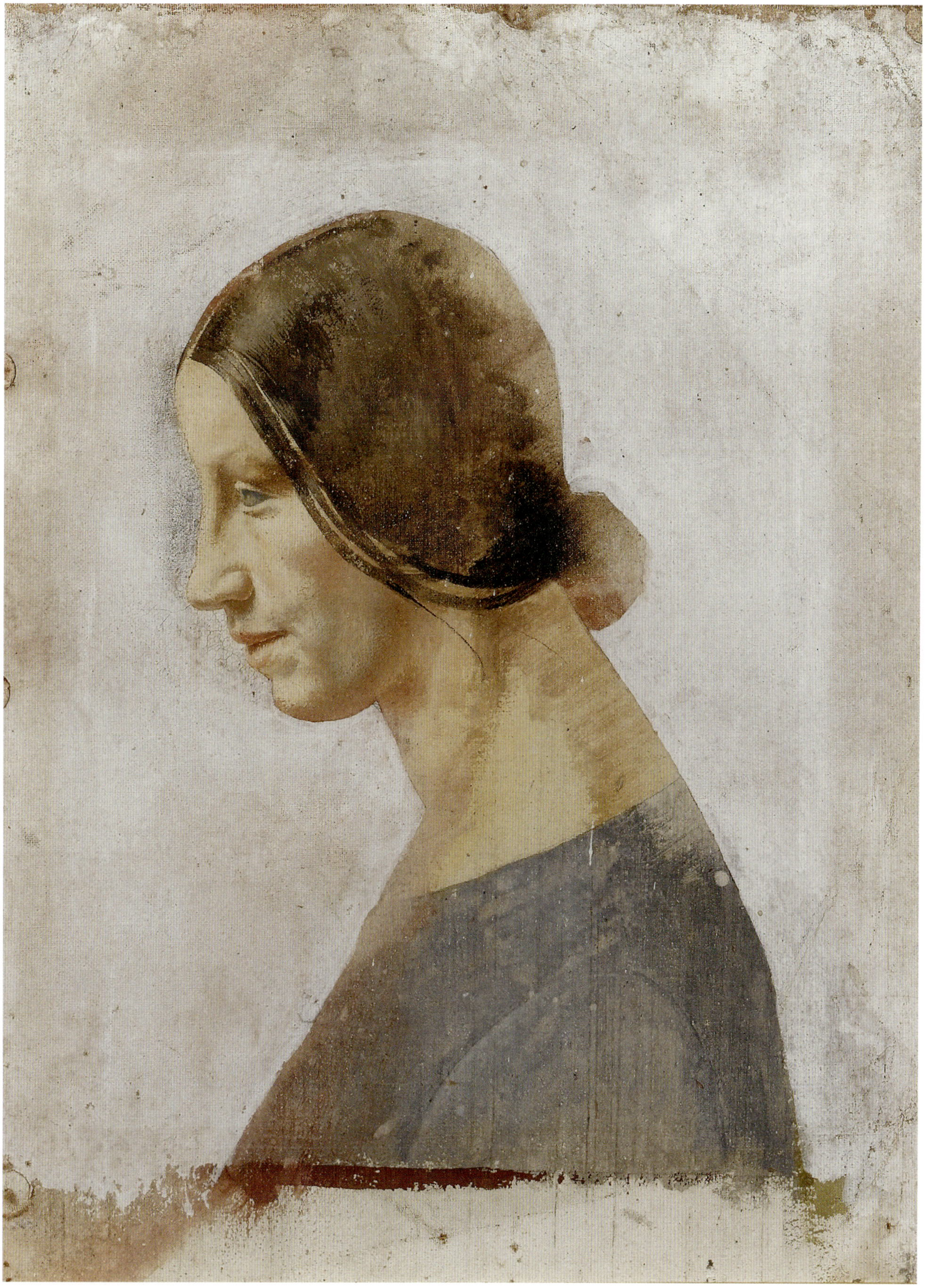

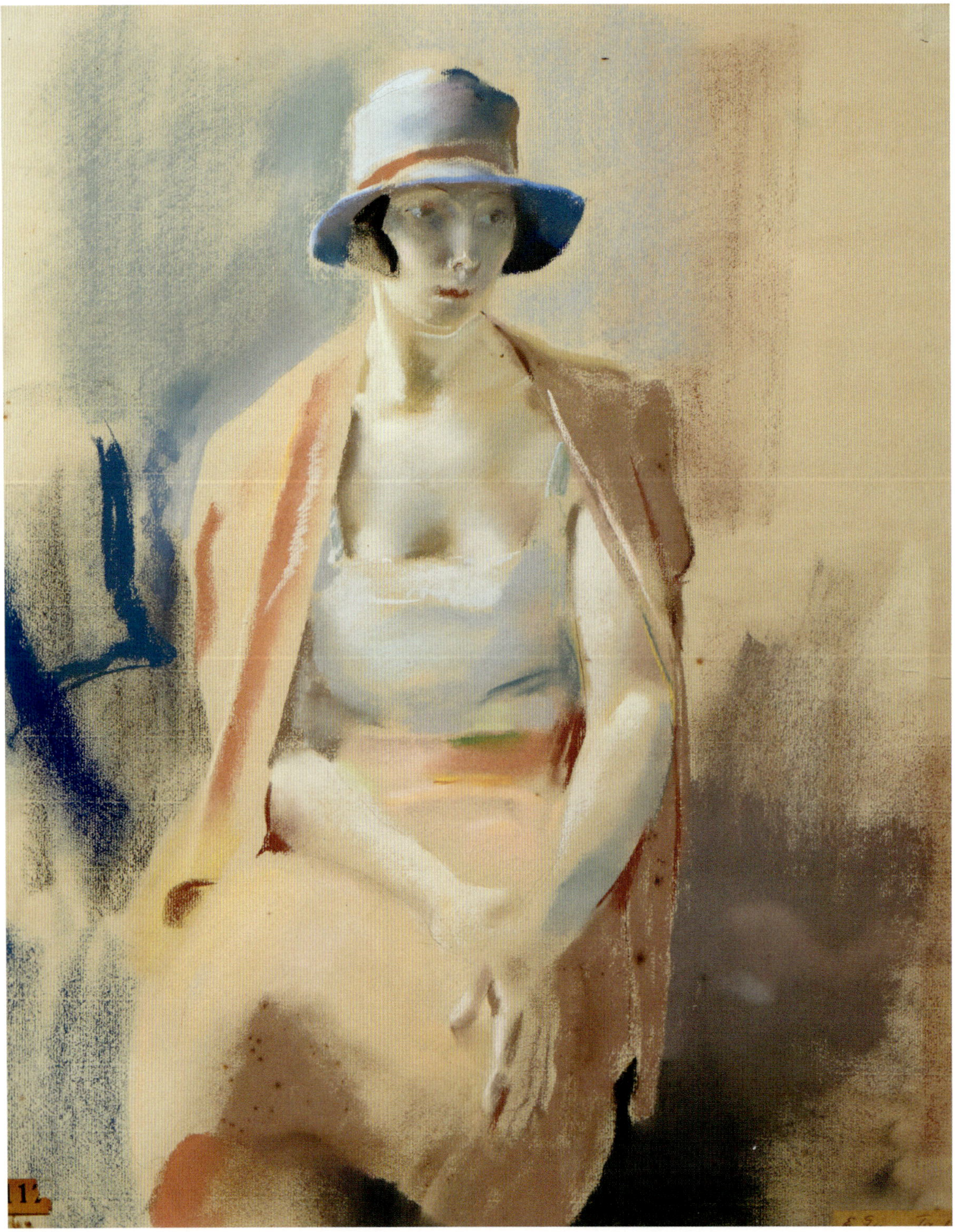

**216 Edith Granger-Taylor** (1887-1958), *Olive in a Blue Hat*, signed, pastel on paper,, 20 x 16 ½ in. (51 x 42 cm).

This composition shows Edith Granger-Taylor's sister-in-law, and frequent model, the artist Olive Deakes. In 1958 a joint retrospective of the two artists was planned at Walker's Gallery in New Bond Street. That summer Granger-Taylor died in a car accident. The exhibition went ahead, but attracted little critical notice. Reporting on her 1932 exhibition at the Beaux Arts Gallery, the art critic from *The Scotsman* wrote that Granger-Taylor uses pastel with 'extraordinary facility and intelligence, and designs with grace. She has a style personal and fluent [...], full of pleasant flourishes and tricks of technique'.

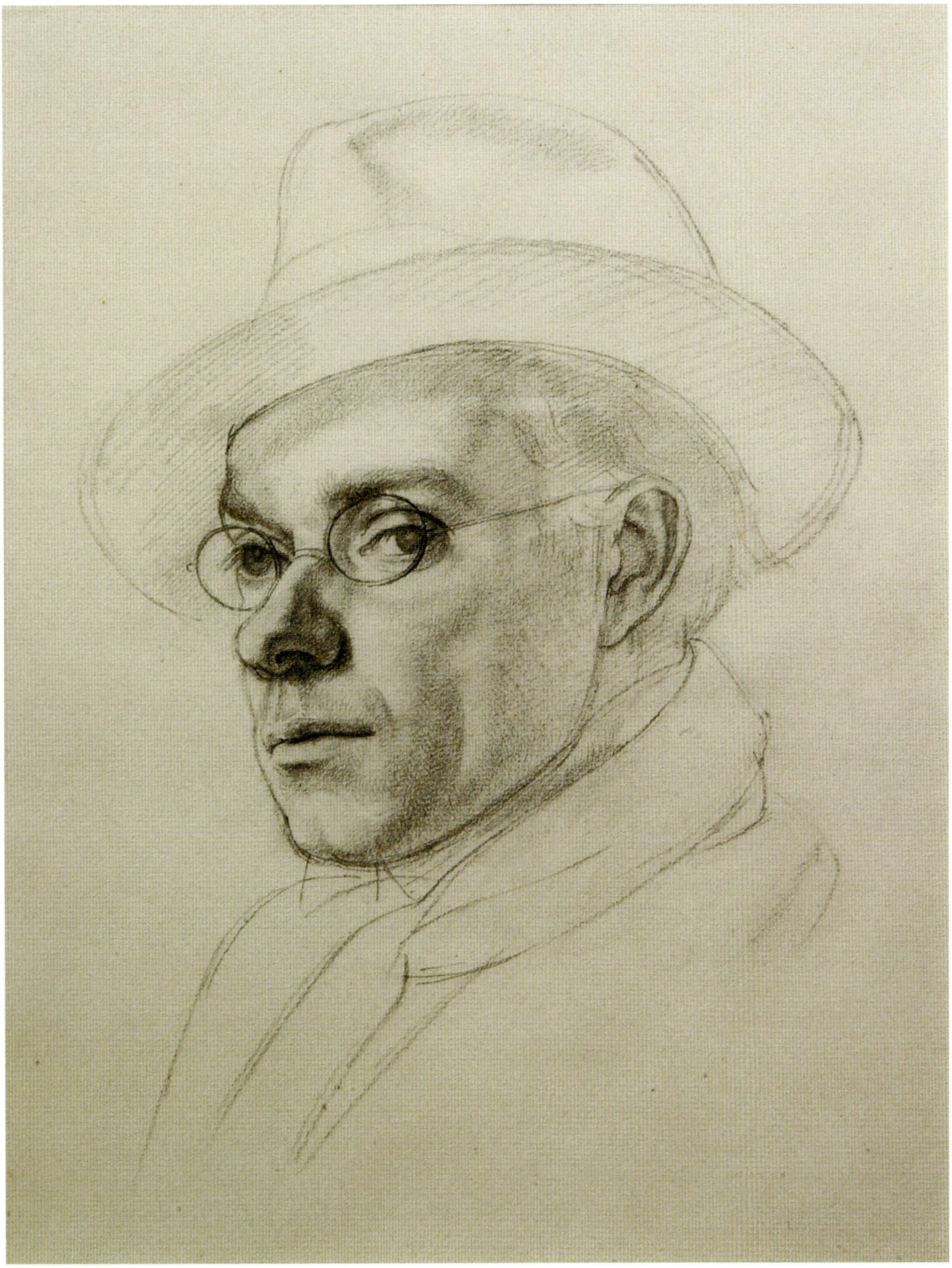

**217 Percy Horton** (1897-1970), *Portrait of the Artist's Brother, Ron*, mid-1920s, pencil on paper, 15 ¼ x 10 ¼ in. (39 x 26).

Ronald Horton was the younger brother of Percy Horton (**281**, **282**). A painter, printmaker, teacher and bibliophile with strong left-wing convictions, he was born and bred in Brighton where he attended Brighton School of Art, studying under Louis Ginnett, 1919-23. In 1924 he moved to London to work for the sculptor William Aumonier and later assisted Rex Whistler with murals and stage designs, 1930-36. From 1920 until his death Horton was a member of the Communist Party. His first wife was the artist Sofy Asscher.

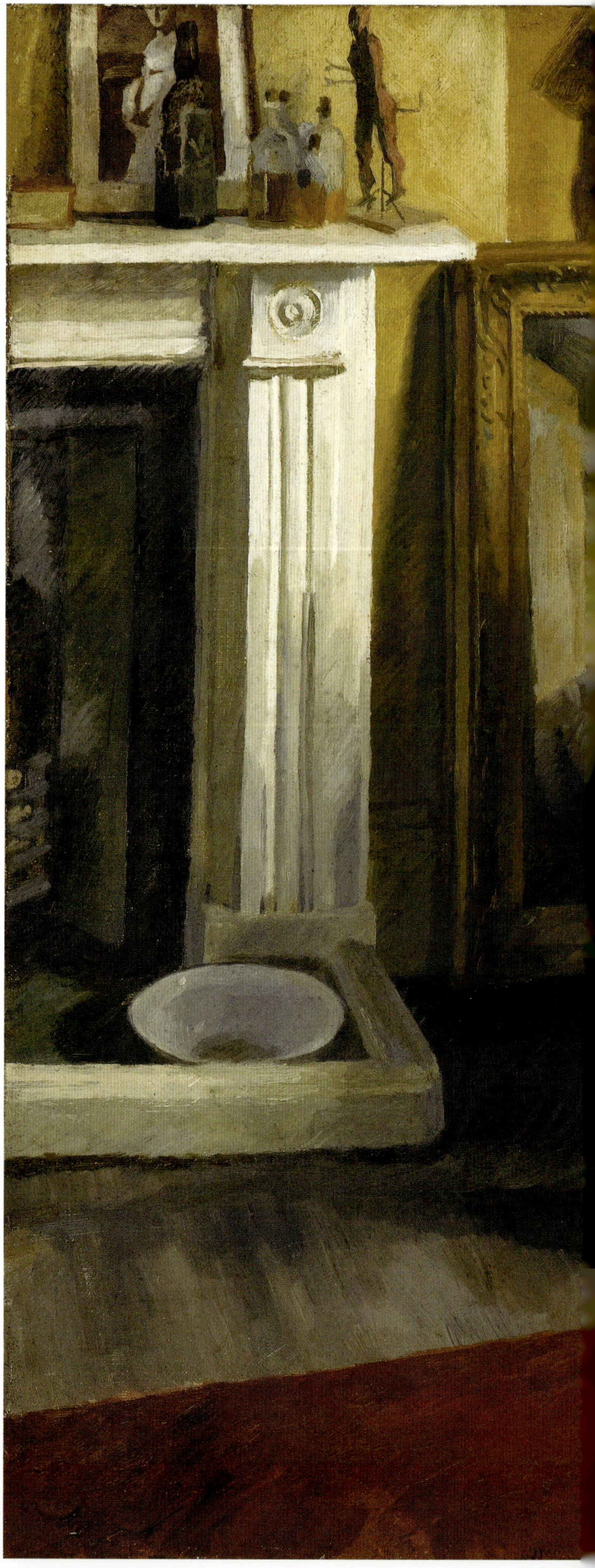

**218 Charles Mahoney** (1903-1968), *Portrait of Geoffrey Rhoades*, 1930, titled on a label to the reverse, oil on canvas, 20 x 24 in. (51 x 61 cm).

Mahoney and Rhoades (**314**, **315**, **316**) first met as students in 1924, Mahoney at the Royal College of Art and Rhoades at the Slade School of Fine Art. In 1930, the date of this painting, Mahoney was lodging at 1 Kensington Crescent in London; Geoffrey Rhoades lived at number 14. Set in Mahoney's sitting room, which also served as a studio, a (lost) composition of *The Prodigal Son* can be seen in the background, along with a stack of unpainted canvases.

In August 1930 Rhoades, Mahoney and Percy Horton had a two-week holiday in Marden, Kent. The former two would spend much of the winter helping Edward Bawden decorate Brick House in Great Bardfield, as part of Bawden's newly conceived idea to start an artists' colony there.

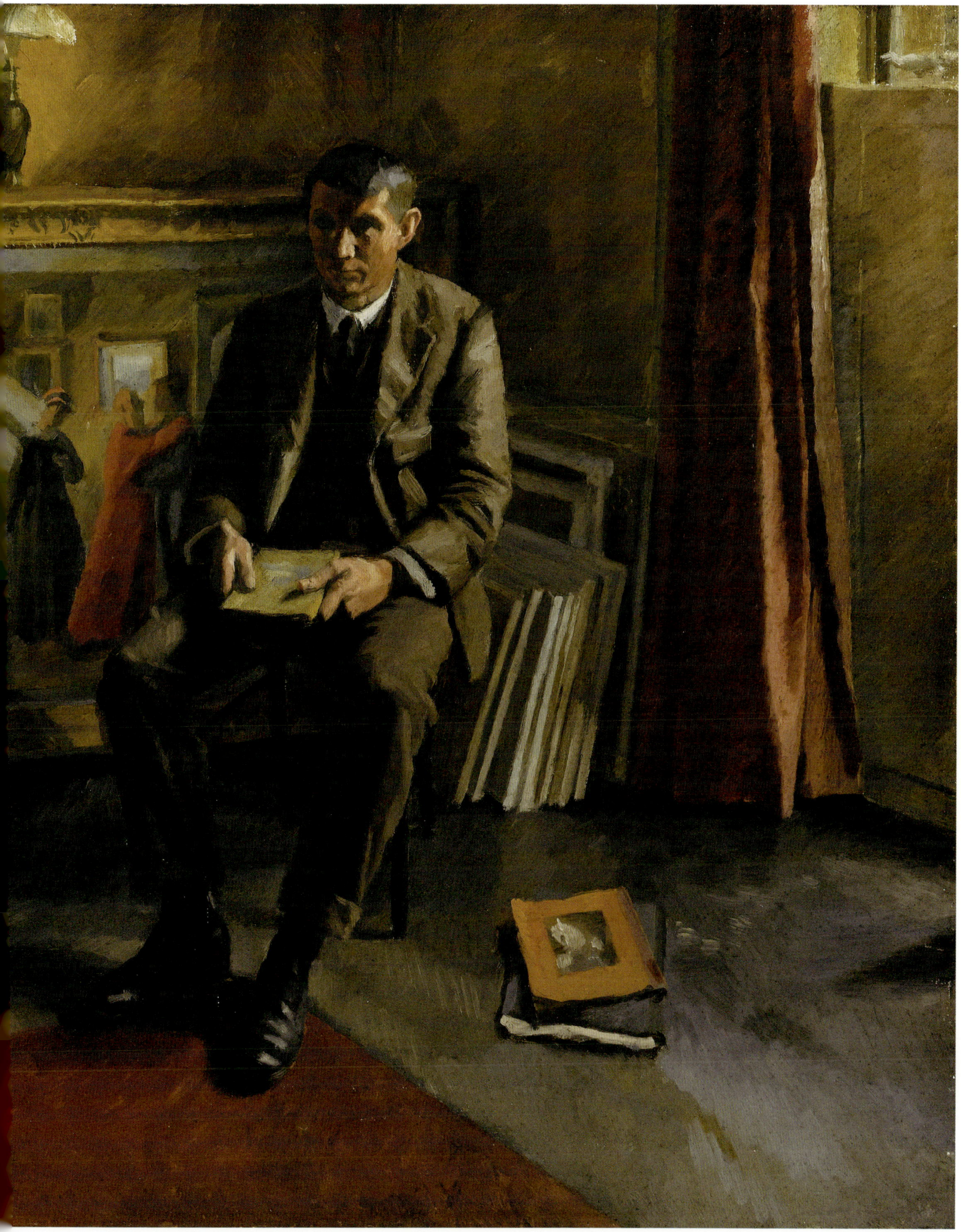

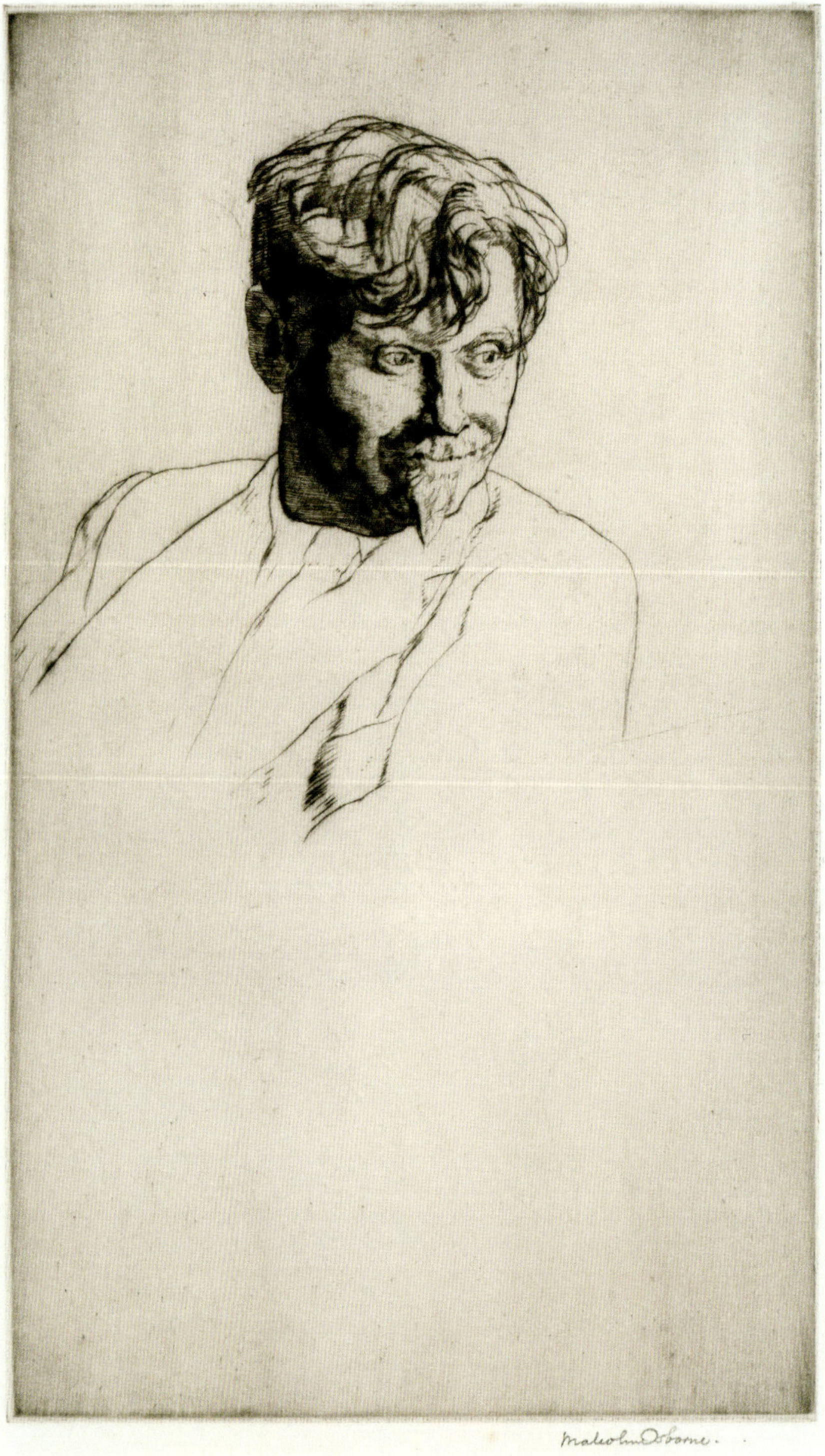

**219 Malcolm Osborne** (1880-1963), *Portrait of Job Nixon*, c.1930
etching, 13 x 8 in. (33 x 20.3 cm).

Nixon is best known for his etchings, drypoints and line engravings, which he started producing from 1913. In 1923 he won the first competition for the newly endowed British School at Rome Scholarship in Engraving. Here he met fellow Rome Scholar Winifred Knights, to whom he later gave this portrait. After returning to England he was appointed as assistant to Malcolm Osborne in the Engraving School at the Royal College of Art.

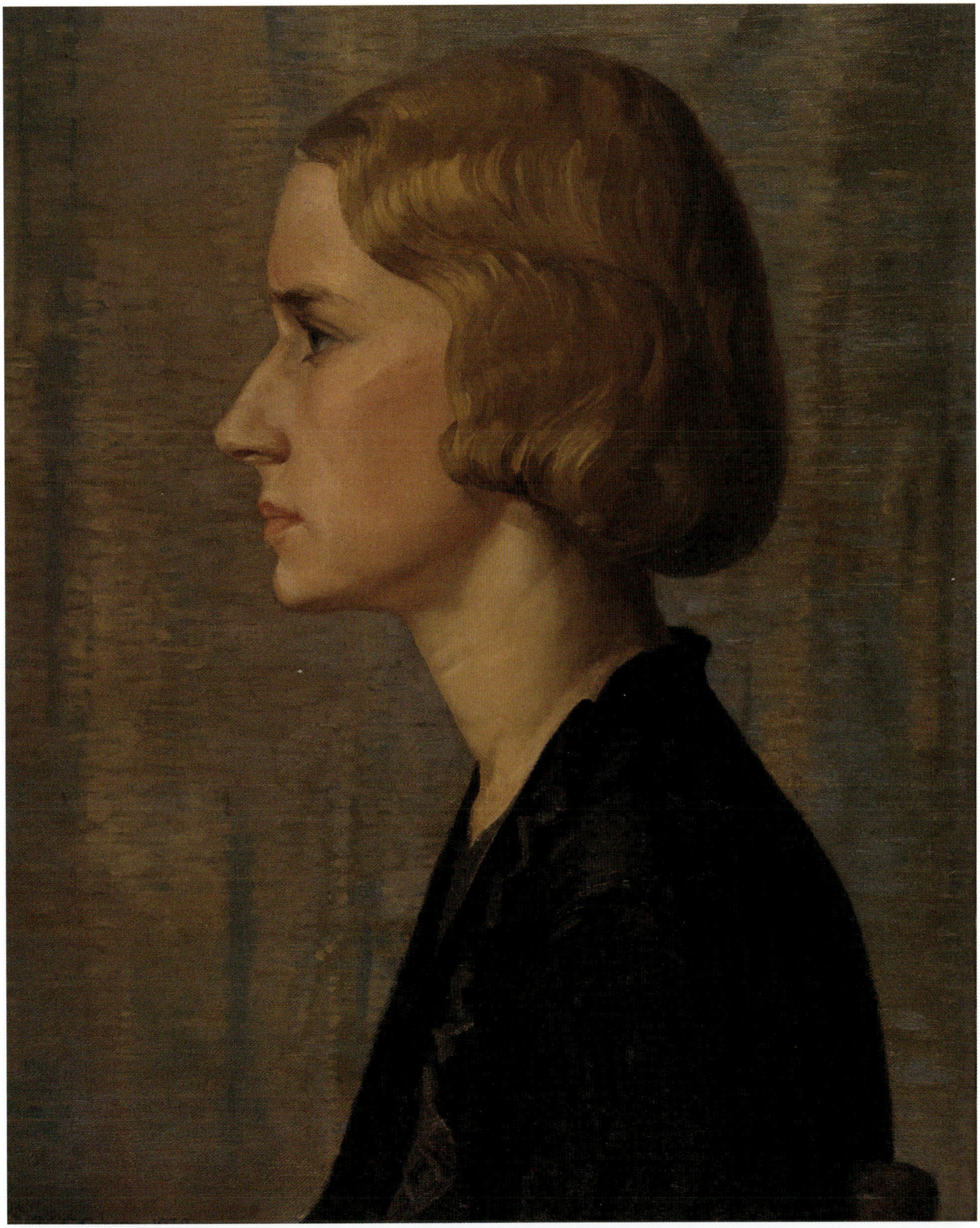

**220 Mary Gwenillan Gibson** (1888-1966), *Portrait of Gwynneth Cobden Holt, Wife of T. Huxley Jones*, 1932, signed, dated and titled on label to reverse, oil on canvas, 20 x 16 in. (50.8 x 40.6 cm).

Gwynneth Cobden Holt, married to her fellow-sculptor T. B. Huxley Jones, worked in a variety of media including ivory. Holt served as the model for a related painting by Gibson, of the Virgin, which is in the collection of Wolverhampton Art Gallery.

**Douglas Percy Bliss** (1900-1984),
*Masters in the Making,*

From the late 1920s onwards Bliss produced two series entitled 'Masters in the Making', satirical sketches of Old Masters and 19th century painters in their studios. This combined Bliss's erudition, irreverence, and skill as a caricaturist. The works were exhibited in London exhibitions in 1934 and 1937. Bliss annotated his drawing of Gauguin: 'Here is Gauguin at work in a native hut with a native audience. This terrific, half-demented being carried his torment with him wherever he went. It is impossible to love the man Gauguin. In his lifetime it is probable that he never loved anyone, man or woman. He simply used them. He was a ruthless egoist, harsh, sensual, arrogant. He was wretchedly unhappy for the most part even in this Polynesian Paradise. It takes more than a Sarong to make a Savage. Gauguin 'went Native', as they say; but it takes more than the presence of 'yaller girls' or the absence of white men, to decivilise a man nobly, to make a simple and dignified Primitive out of a European neurotic.'

Ravilious, after seeing the exhibition in 1934, wrote to Bliss: 'What an awfully good and lively show that was. Cezanne (sold I noticed) and Van Gogh were damn good drawings – the landscape in the latter was boiling point. I loved it. Holman Hunt, Toulouse Lautrec and Turner were the others I enjoyed most, the Turner I would have taken home if I could rub two halfpennies together.... Congratulations on the show....You should do well with these drawings. They are the goods. (Letter from Ravilious to Bliss, 10 November 1934.) (**263**)

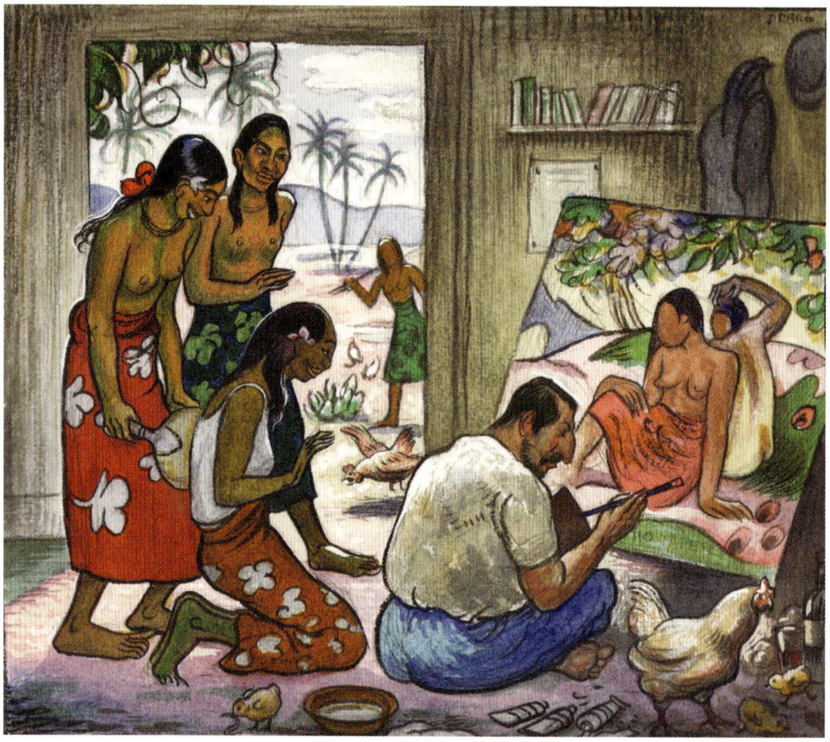

**221** *Paul Gauguin in His Polynesian Paradise*, early 1930s,
pencil, watercolour, gouache and pen & ink on paper, 12 ½ x 15 in. (31.8 x 38.2 cm).

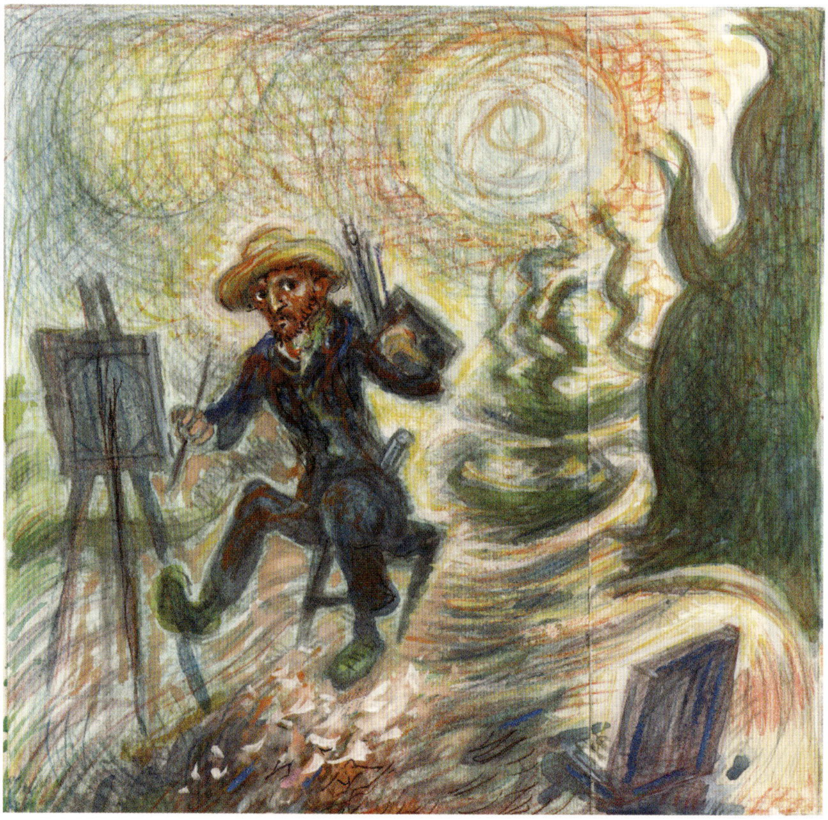

**222** *"The Sun, the Sun"!! – Vincent Van Gogh at Arles*, early 1930s,
pencil, watercolour, gouache and pen & ink on paper, 9 ¾ x 9 ¼ in. (25 x 23.2 cm).

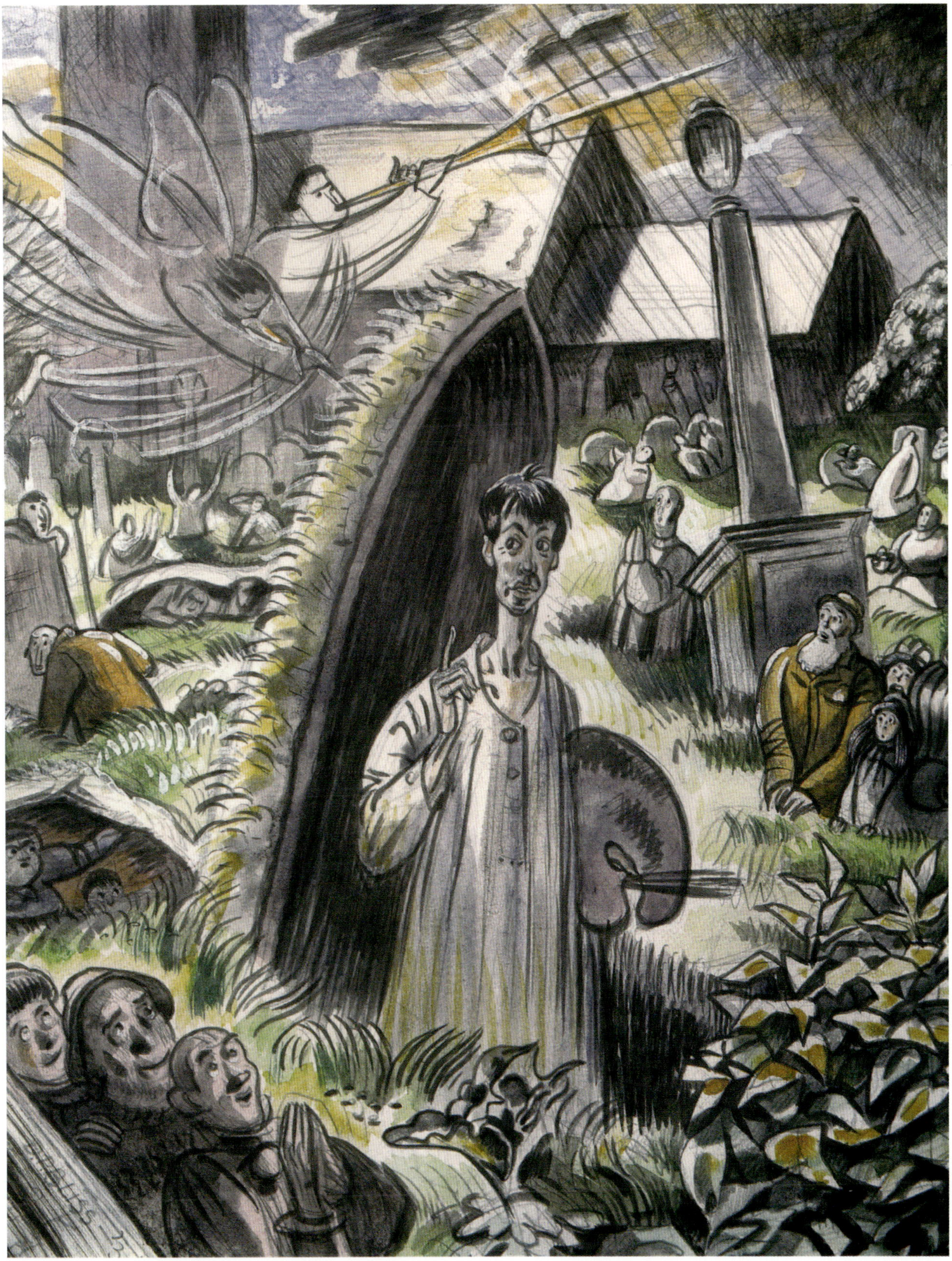

**223** *The Resurrection of Stanley Spencer*, early 1930s, (**180**)
pencil watercolour and pen & ink on paper.

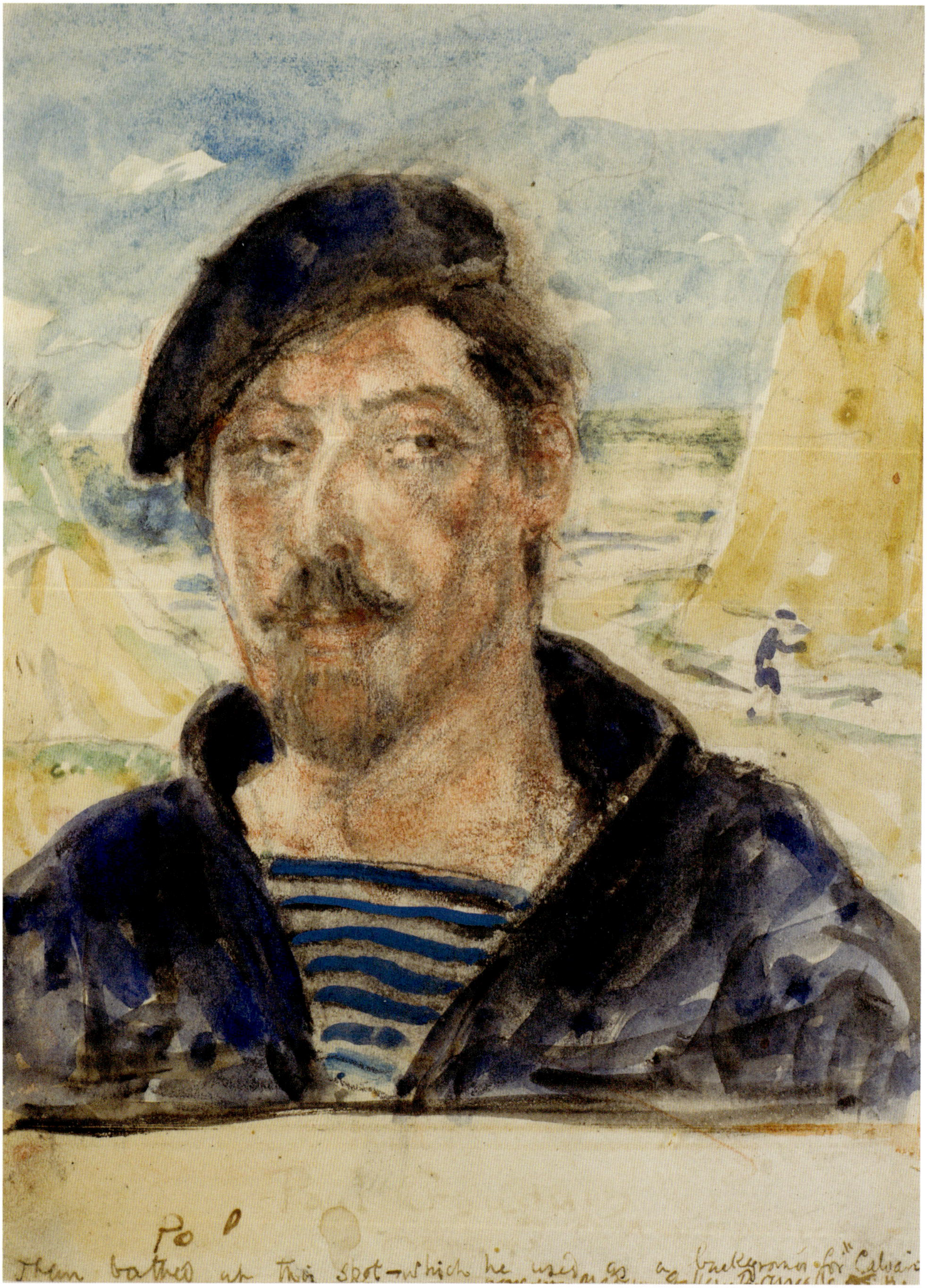
Pol
Them bathed at this spot—which he used as a background for "Calvai

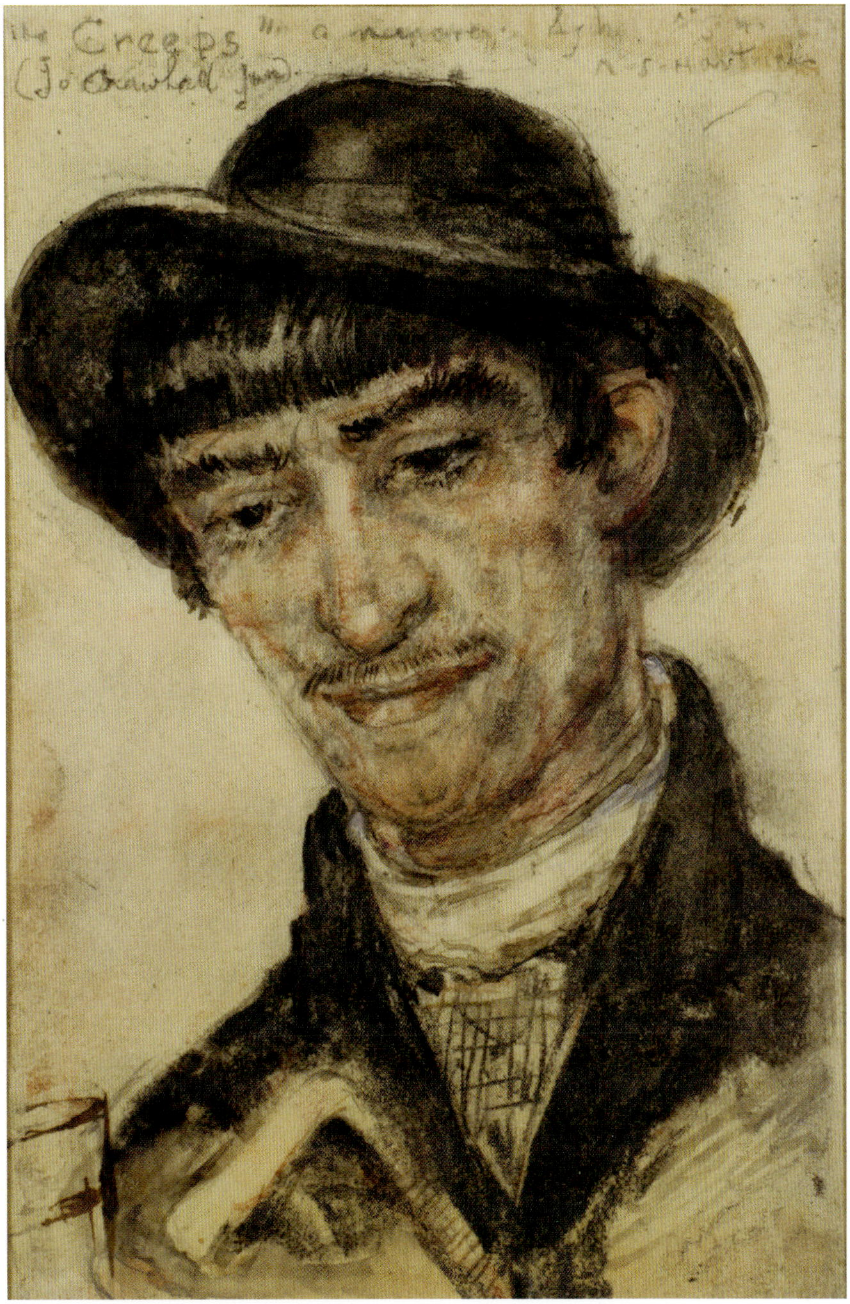

**225 Archibald Standish Hartrick** (1864-1950), *The Creeps* (Portrait of Joseph Crawhall), c.1939, signed, titled and inscribed in pencil, red and black chalks, pen &ink, and watercolour on paper, 6 ¾ x 4 ½ in. (17 x 11 cm).

**224 Archibald Standish Hartrick** (1864-1950), *Paul Gauguin at Poulhan*, c. 1939, titled and inscribed in pen, red and black chalks and watercolour on paper, 7 x 5 in. (18 x 13 cm). Collection: The Courtauld Institute of Art.

The Scottish painter Archibald Standish Hartrick (1864-1950) spent some months in 1886 working in Pont-Aven, an artists' colony in Brittany. He later published a lively account of his meetings there, particularly with the artist Paul Gauguin. Both Hartrick and Gauguin lodged at the Pension Gloanec, a favourite haunt of visiting artists, in the central square of the village. Hartrick recalled his initial impression of Gauguin: 'Tall, dark, rather handsome, with a fine powerful figure, and about forty years of age, wearing a blue jersey, and a beret on the side of his head, is how I saw him first.' This is the guise in which Hartrick paints Gauguin in this portrait; an image he later reproduced in his memoir 'A Painter's Pilgrimage through Fifty Years', 1939.

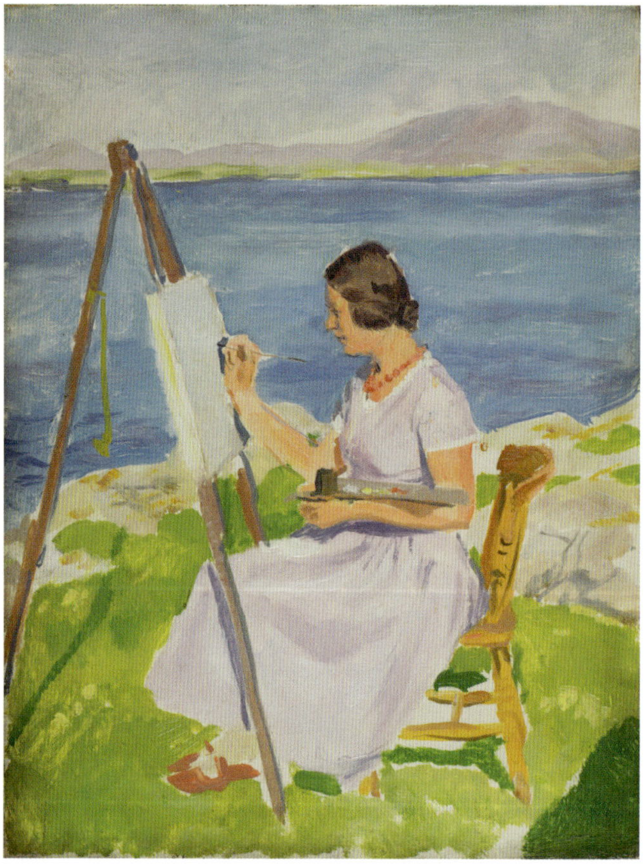

**226 Stephen Bone** (1904-1958),
*Mary Adshead at Work*, 1930s, signed,
oil on panel, 16 x 13 in. (40.6 x 33 cm).

Bone's rapidly painted 'en plein air' sketches were the subject of popular one-man shows at Lefevre, Redfern, The Leiceister Galleries and The Fine Art Society. He painted his wife Mary at work on several occasions.

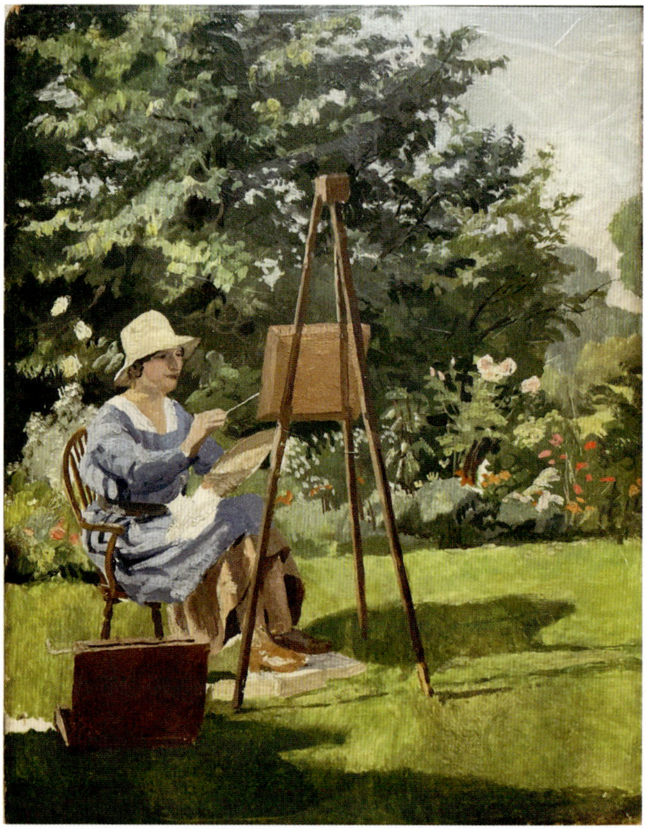

**227 Stephen Bone** (1904-1958),
*Portrait of Mary Adshead*, 1940s,
(probably at work in the artist's garden at Haverstock Hill, London), (**47**),
oil on board, 16 x 13 in. (40.6 x 33 cm).

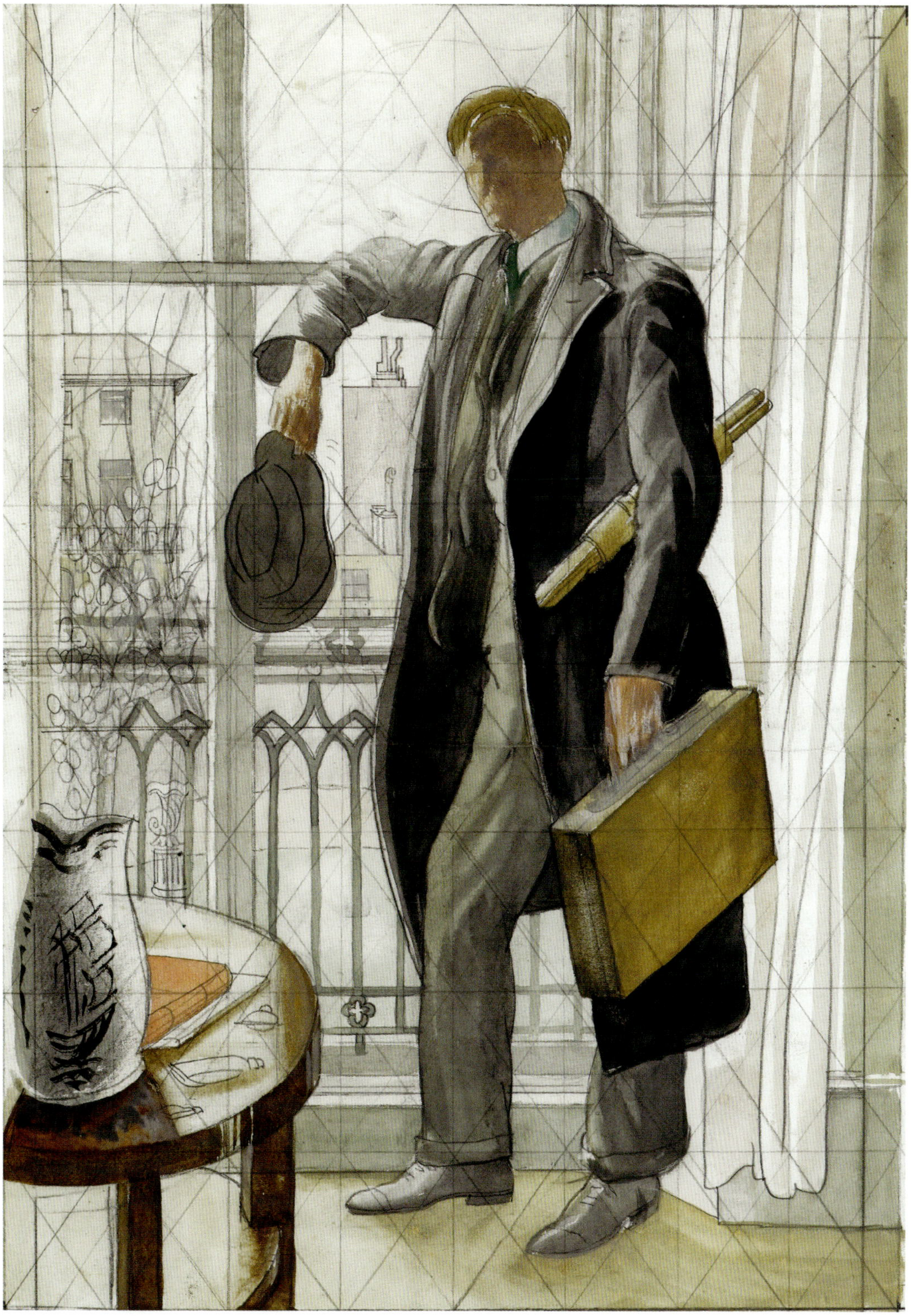

**228 Mary Adshead** (1904-1995), *Portrait of Stephen Bone*, lat 1930s, watercolour on paper, squared in pencil, 18 x 12 in. (46 x 30.5 cm).

In his early days Bone, a very tall man, strode huge distances to reach his painting locations.. He carried his wooden paint-box fitted out with paints, brushes and a rack of 3 or 4 primed panels everywhere. His equipment also included a three-legged folding wooden stool with a leather seat, a broad brimmed felt hat and, in winter, fingerless woollen mittens. The setting for this portrait is 43 Haverstock Hill, to where Bone and Adshead moved in 1938. (**47**)

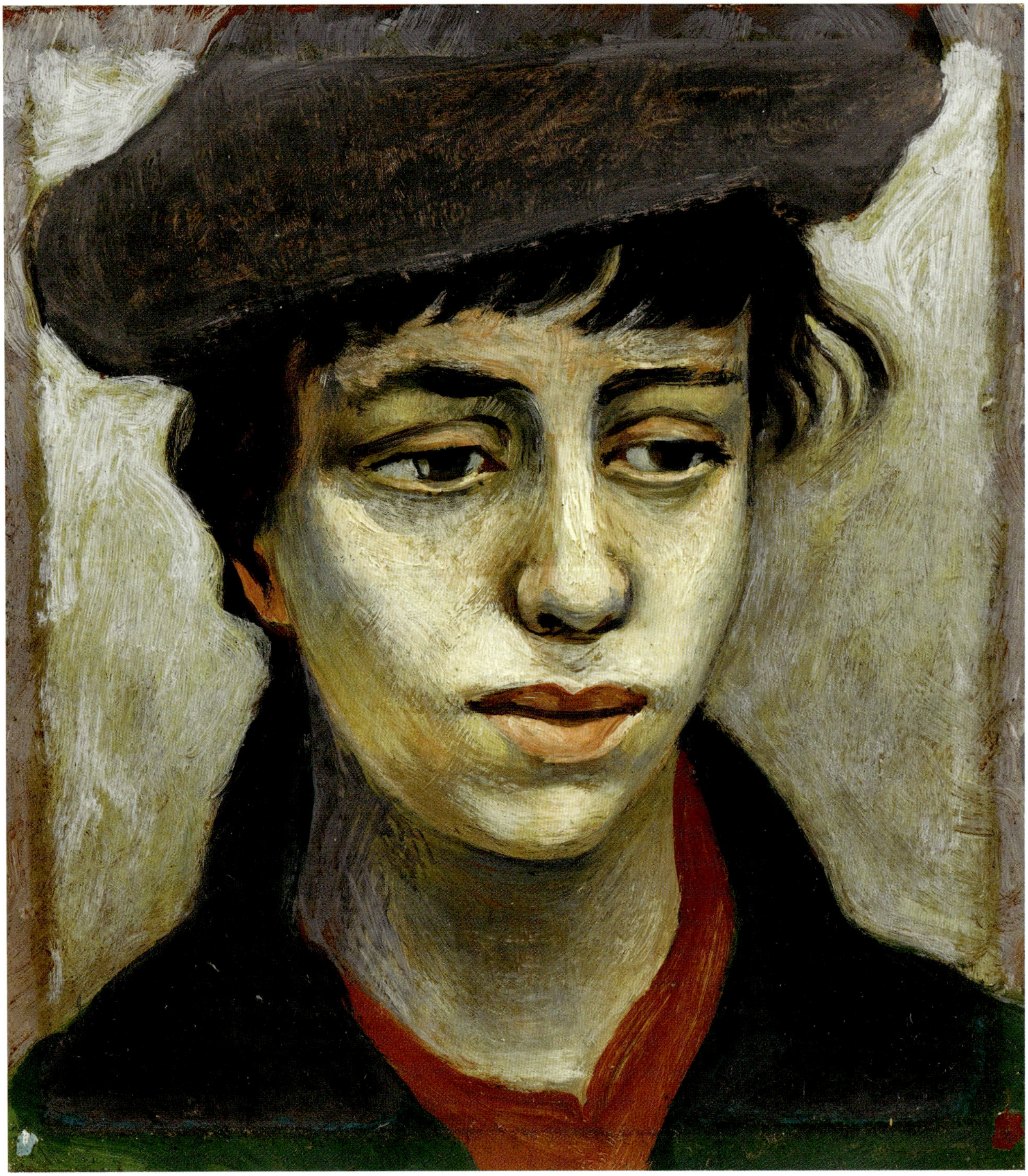

**229 Fyffe Christie** (1918-1979), *Portrait of the Artist's Wife Eleanor*, oil on panel, 6 ¼ x 5 ¾ in. (16 x 14.5 cm).

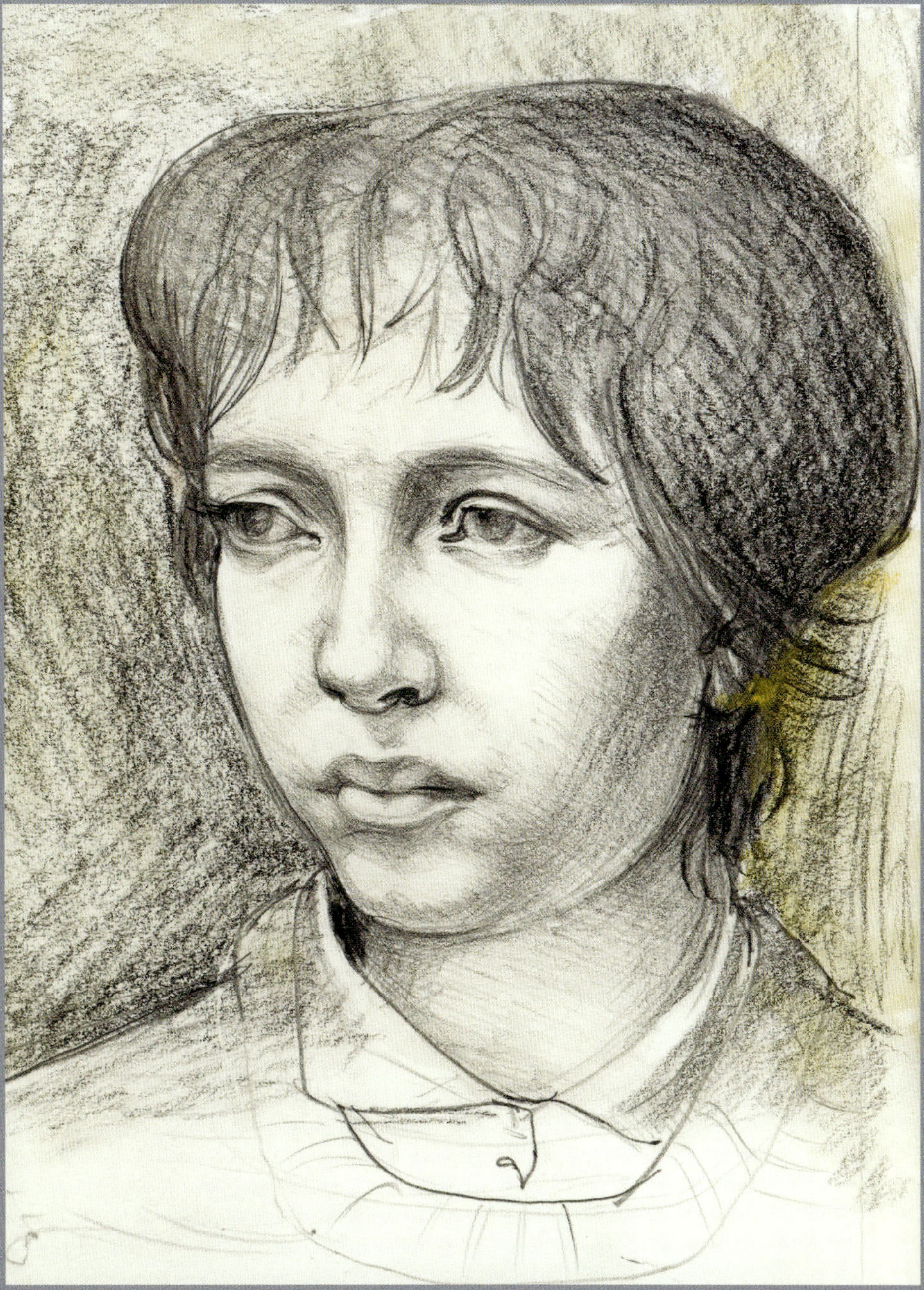

**230 Fyffe Christie** (1918-1979), *Portrait of Eleanor, the Artist's Wife*, mid 1950s, pencil and graphite with highlights in yellow, 8 in x 6 in. (20.3 x 15 cm).

Fyffe Christie met his future wife Eleanor, a sculptor, in 1950 when teaching evening classes at the Glasgow School of Art. They moved to London in 1957 where he again taught, while completing murals and much other work. Christie and his wife held a show at Woodlands Gallery in 1979, shortly before he died. Fyffe Christie also portrayed the couple's cat. (**140**)

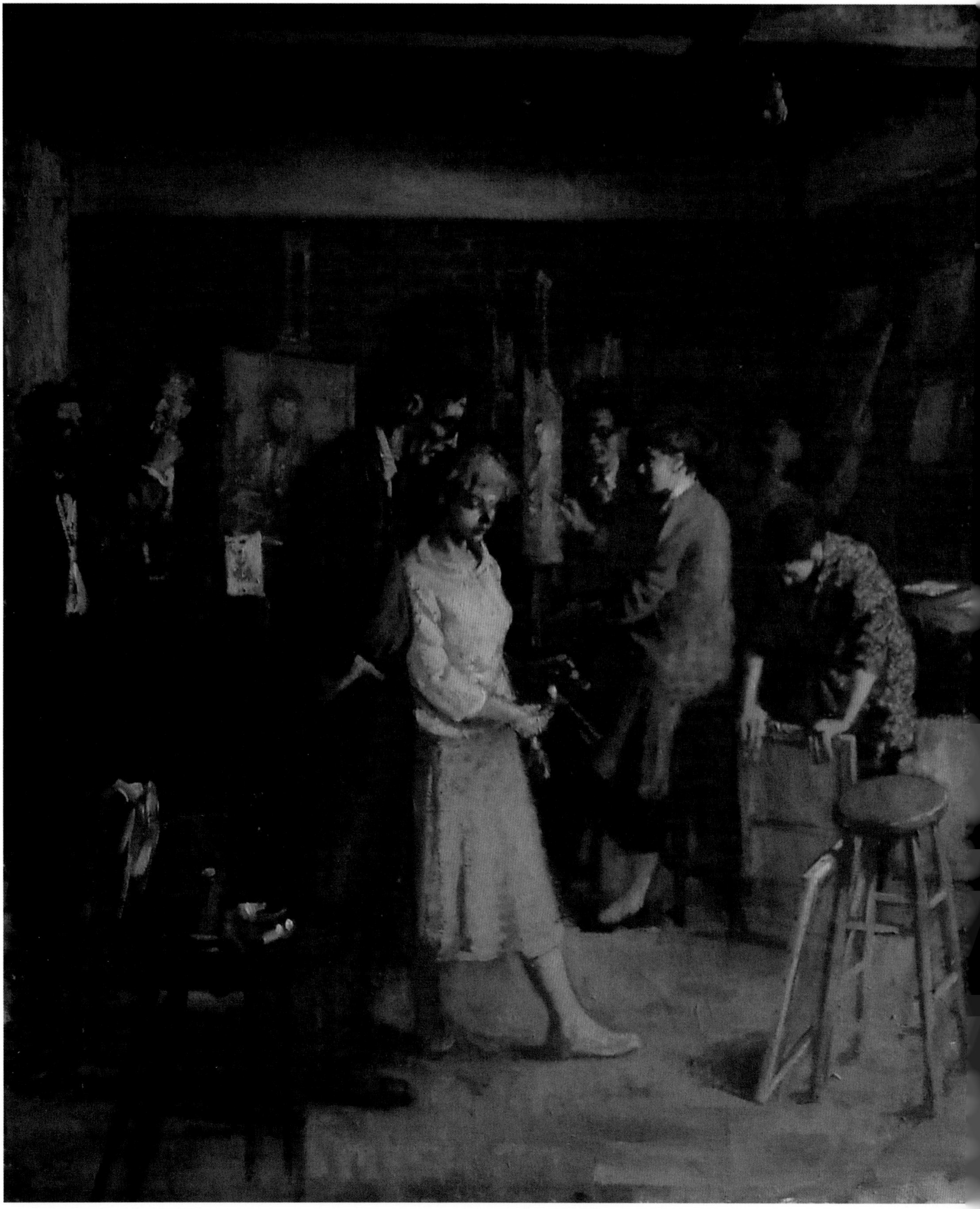

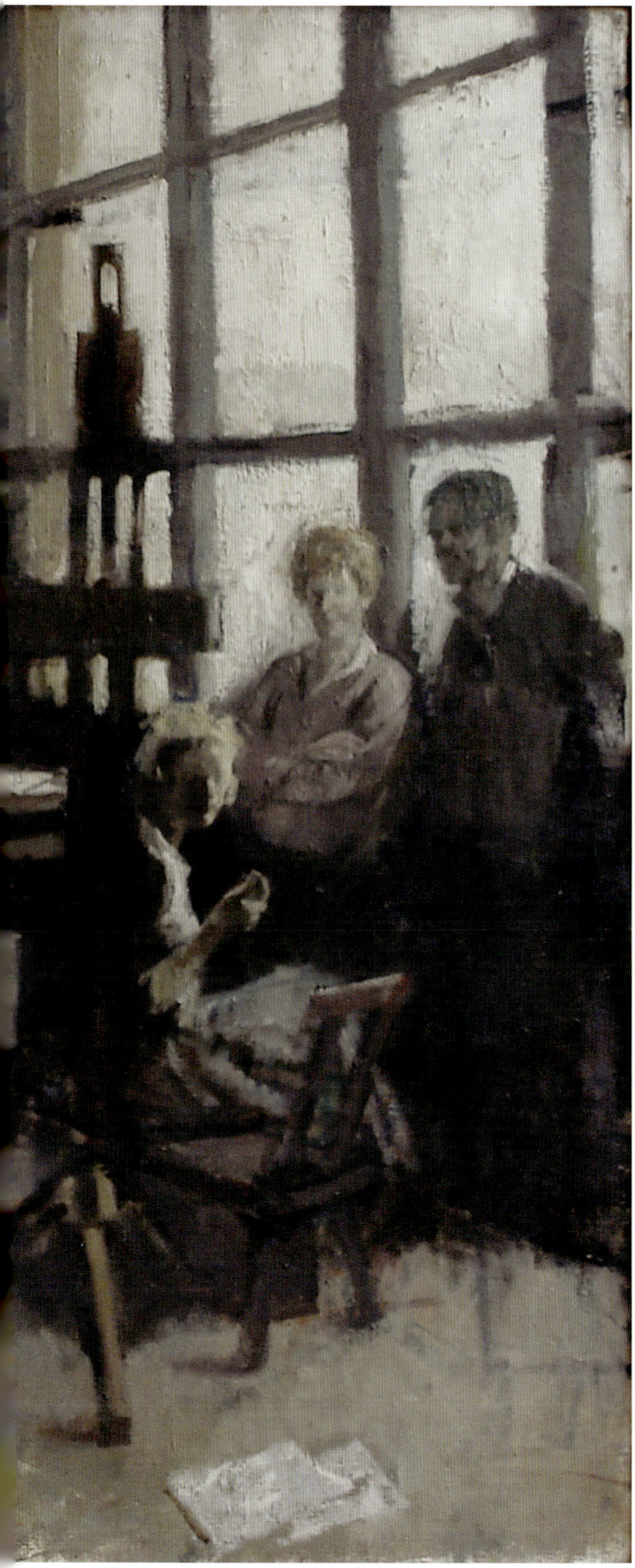

**231** **Bernard Dunstan** (1920-2017), *Interior: The Byam Shaw School*, 1960s, oil on canvas, 40 x 50 ¼ in. (102 x 128 cm).

Charles Mahoney (**318**) is the main figure in this interior scene; Rodney Burn and Elizabeth Riches can also be identified, the latter (to whom this interior scene belonged) holding up a painting in the background.

Bernard Dunstan was a student at The Byam Shaw School of Art in 1939 and taught there from 1953 to 1974. 'I first met Charles Mahoney when I was teaching at the Byam Shaw art school in the sixties. He came to join the staff at the suggestion, I think, of Peter Greenham. The Byam Shaw had been run for many years by F.E. Jackson, a great teacher of classical draughtsmanship, who inspired a remarkable degree of loyalty and respect among his students. After his death the school continued along his lines, though without his driving force; and as soon as Charles arrived it was clear to all, students and staff alike, that he had the same sort of strength as a teacher.'

The Byam Shaw School of Art was absorbed by Central Saint Martin's College of Arts and Design in 2010. In addition to Dunstan, the school's former students include Winifred Nicholson, Yinka Shonibare, and Mona Hatoum.

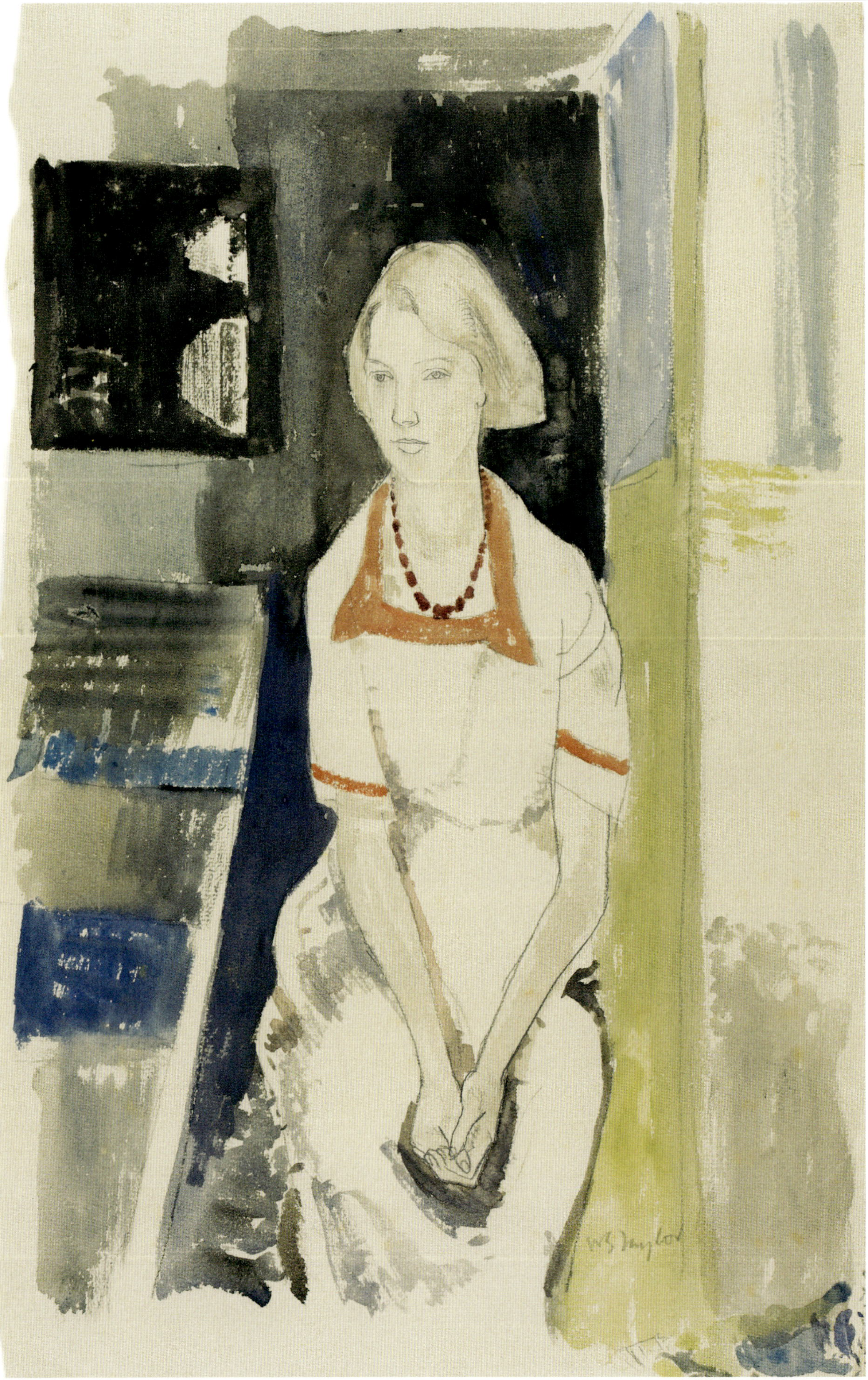

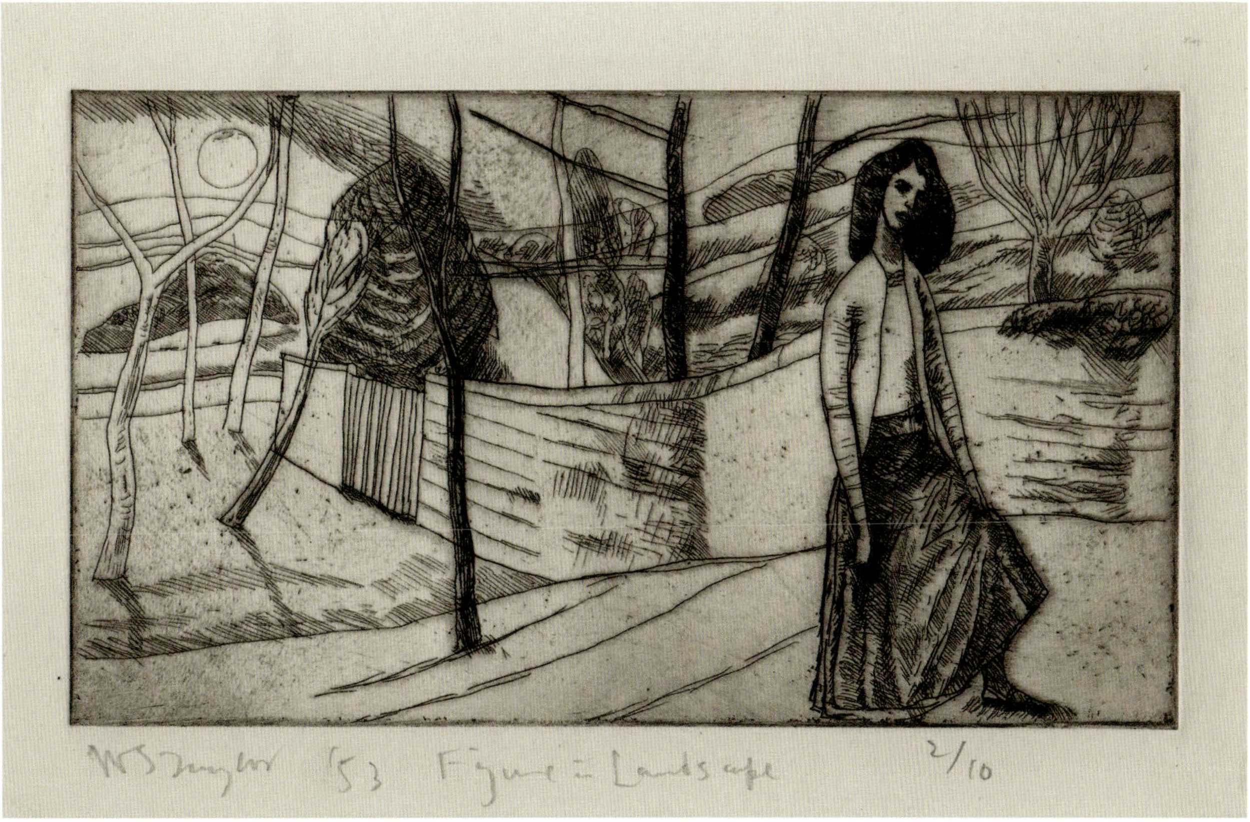


**233 William S Taylor** (1920-2010), *Figure in Landscape*, 1953, signed, dated, numbered 2/10 and inscribed with title, etching on paper, 6 x 10 in. (15.2 x 25.4 cm).
The model for this etching is the artist's wife Audrey Wallis (1919-1997), sculptor and painter.

Taylor's pictures combine figure and landscape with strong Neo-Romantic overtones, and are saturated with lyricism and a sense of longing. (**380**, **381**, **382**, **383**) His compositions are frequently set in the artist's Devonshire garden and almost always include portraits of his wife, Audrey Wallis (1919-1997) who, in addition to being his muse and model, was a sculptor and painter. She taught at Sheffield College of Art from 1948 to 1980.

**232 William S Taylor** (1920-2010), *Audrey Seated with Coral Necklace*, signed, mid-1950s, pencil and watercolour on paper, 19 x 12 ¼ in. (48.3 x 31.2 cm).

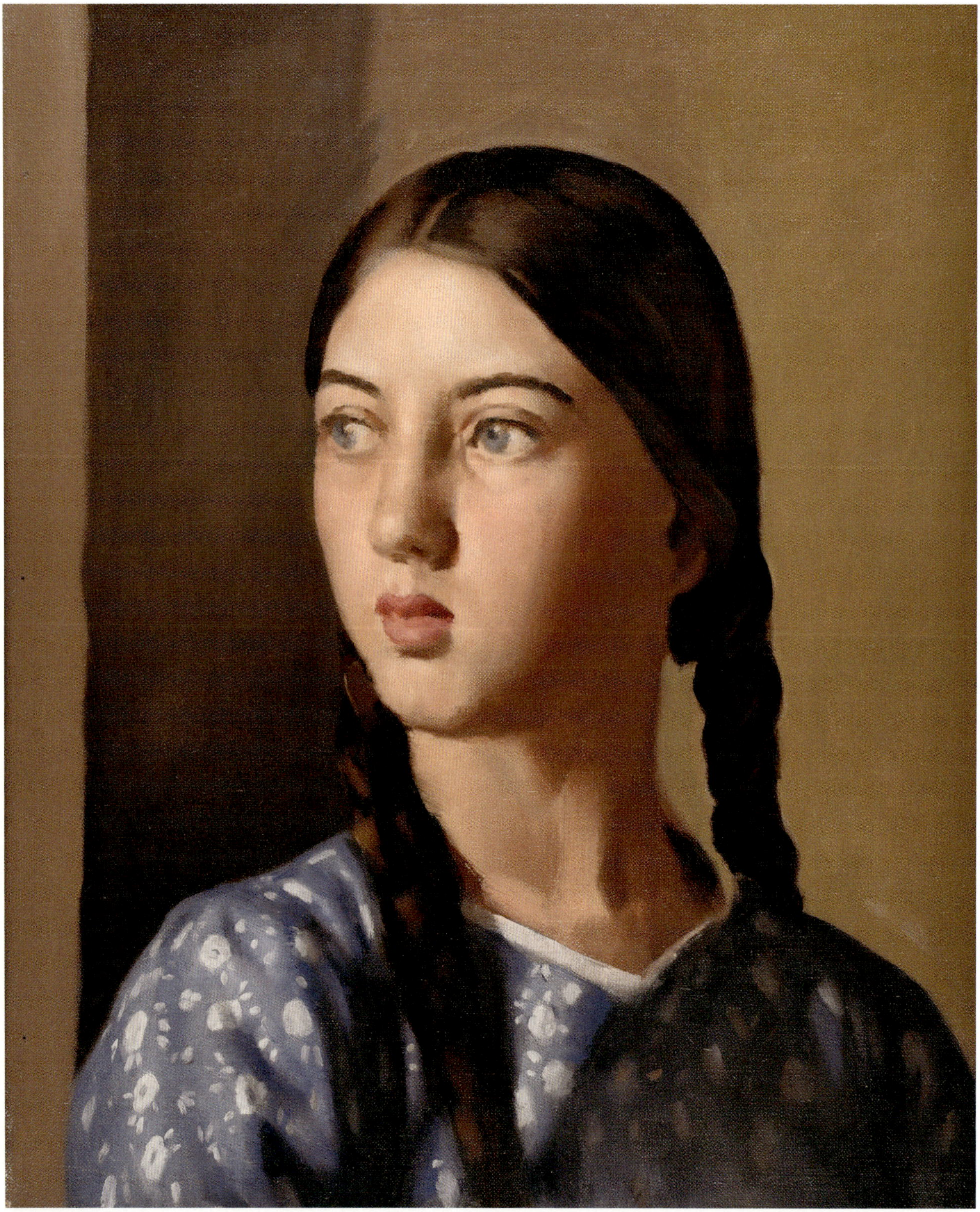

**234 Victor Hume Moody** (1896-1990), *Portrait of the Artist's Daughter, Catherine Moody*, late 1930s, oil on canvas, 18 x 15 in. (46 x 38 cm).

Catherine Olive Moody was the daughter of the artist Victor Hume Moody. (**270, 271, 272**) She studied under him at Malvern School of Art, at the Royal College of Art with Gilbert Spencer and at Birmingham College of Art under Bernard Fleetwood-Walker. She taught at Manchester College of Art, then was head of Malvern School of Art, 1962-80. (**45, 48**)

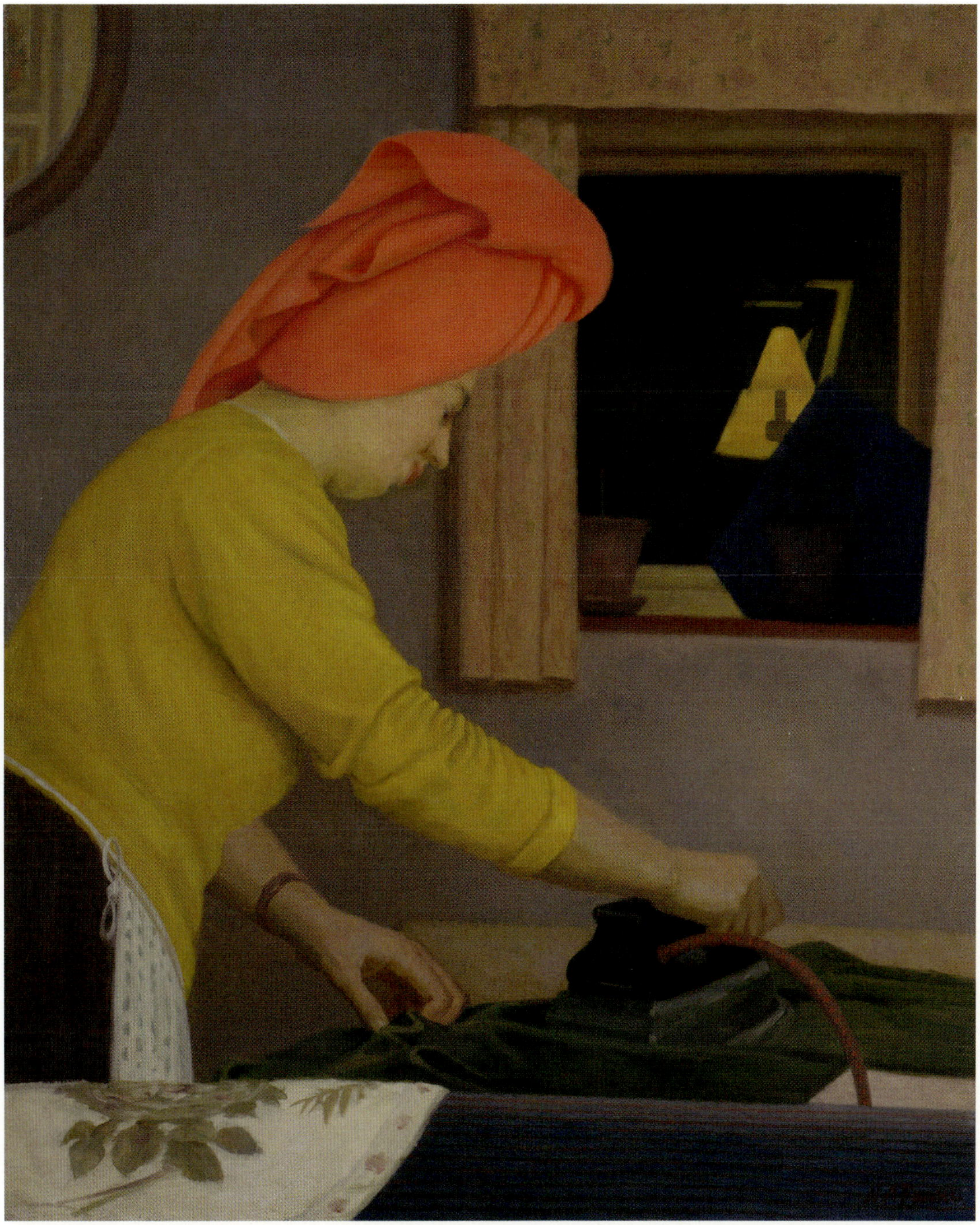

**235 Hubert Arthur Finney** (1905-1991), *Amy Ironing*, c.1953, signed, inscribed on stretcher 'Woman Ironing after washing her hair, no 33', oil on canvas, 30 x 25 in. (76 x 63.5 cm).

This composition shows Finney's second wife, Amy Finney (Dyer), ironing at home in Wokingham. Finney met Dyer whilst convalescing in 1945. He described her as 'a lovely intelligent woman with gifts in the visual arts as a designer'. She had attended design and drawing classes at Reading University, and knew Professor Betts, who was head of the Fine Art Department. Through this conection Dyer was able to secure Finney a part-time teaching post. In due course he became head of Life Drawing, a position which he held until his retirement in 1970. (**310**, **311**, **324**)

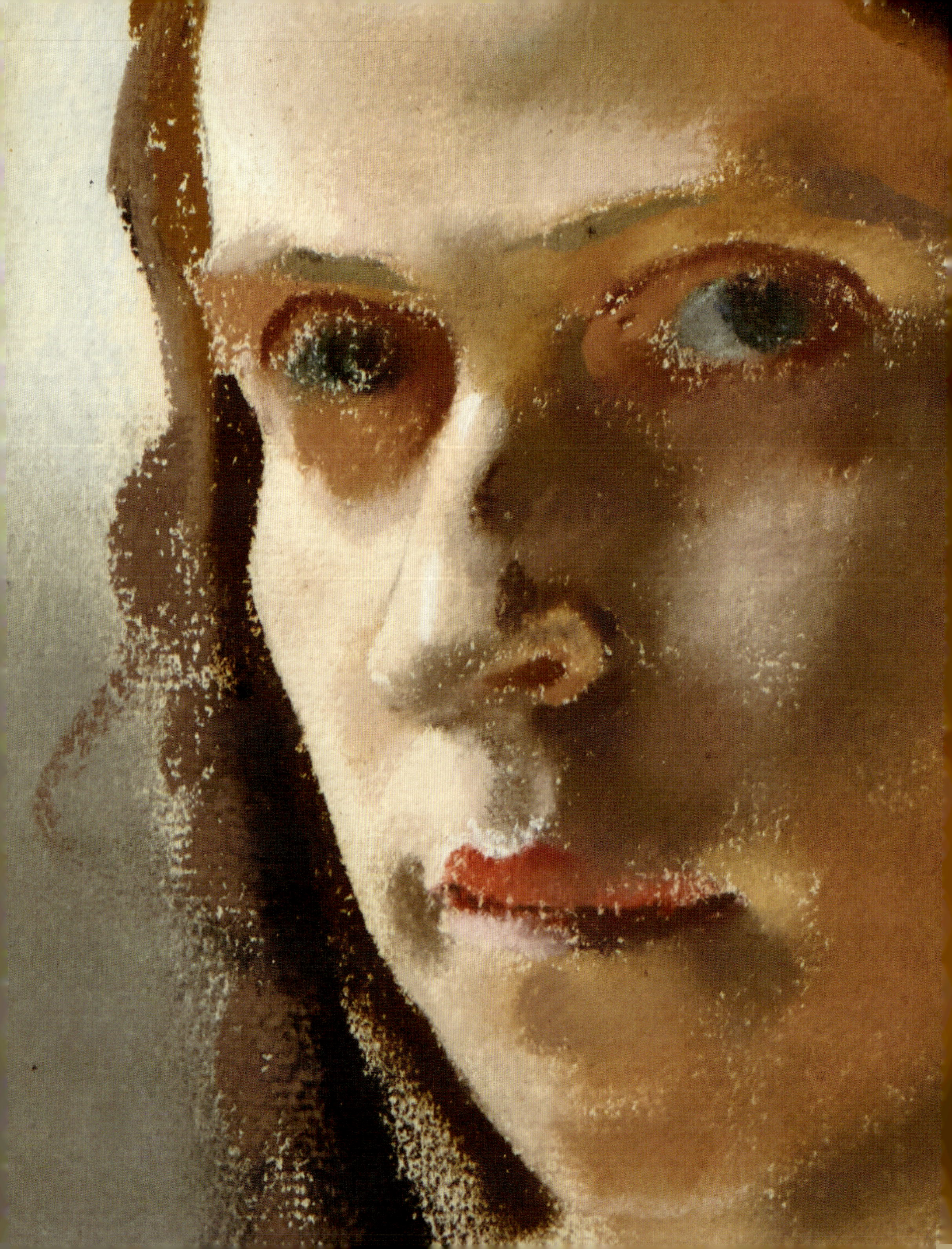

# SELF-PORTRAITS

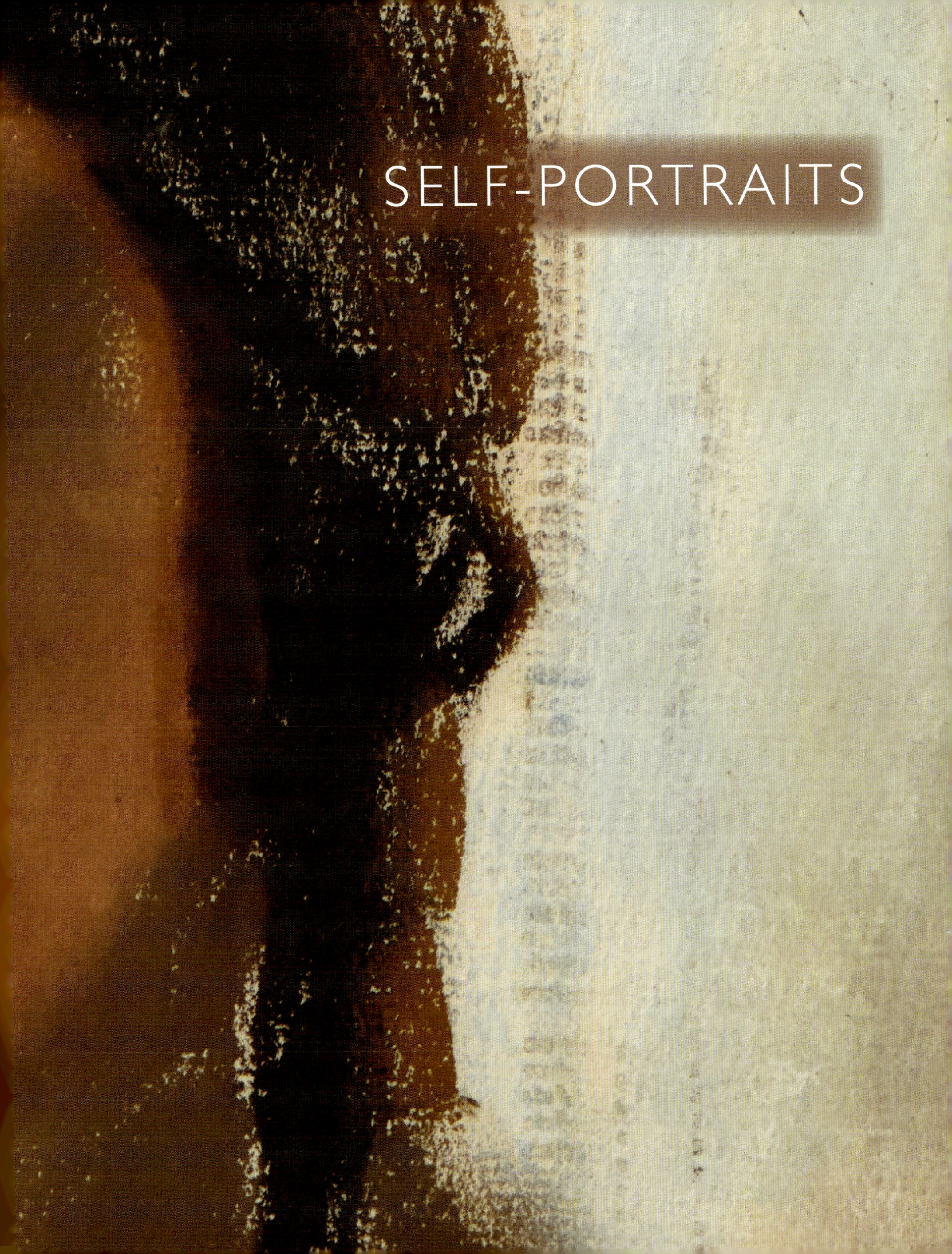

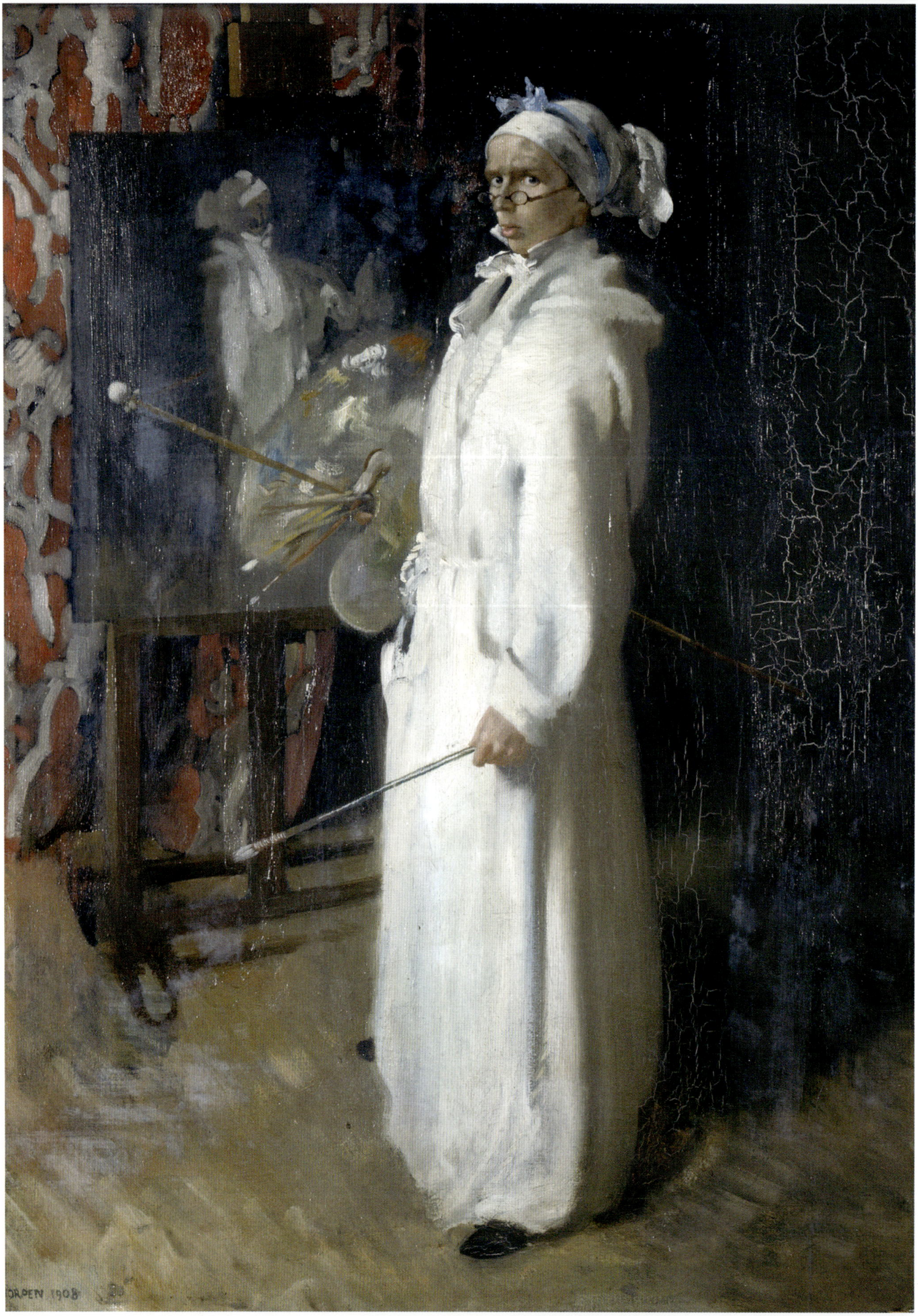
ORPEN 1908

# Self-portraits

*'I suspect the existence of most self-portraits is due to the absence of another model, whether by cancellation or in the case of dedicated portrait painters, a temporary drying up of commissions.'* Tom Phillips, R.A

Although self-portraiture can be traced back to Greek art, it was not until the Renaissance that it became a genre of its own, nurtured by treatises such as Vasari's *The Lives of the Most Excellent Painters* (1550) and the subsequent creation of a cult of celebrity. From this came the tradition, most commonly associated with Dürer and Rembrandt, that artists were melancholic geniuses battling with the meaning of their existence, usually through a deeply introspective gaze. Such is the mood of James Gunn's grand scale self-portrait in which the artist asserts his status as a serious painter in a serious tradition. On a more intimate scale, but with a similar mood of stygian gloom, there are the searingly honest self-portraits of Victor Moody. While such brutal honesty plays a part in self-portraiture, the quality usually most in evidence is vanity. As W. H. Auden explained: 'An honest self-portrait is extremely rare because a man who has reached the degree of self-consciousness presupposed by the desire to paint his own portrait has almost always also developed an ego-consciousness which paints himself painting himself, and introduces artificial highlights and dramatic shadows.' Such is the case with the self-portraits by Sheppard, Wood, Gill, Withey, Sorrell, Austin and Ray-Jones, all of whom show themselves as irresistibly youthful. Self-portraits by these artists in old age are much rarer. Edgar Holloway was an exception. His first self-portrait was a drypoint made in 1931, aged 16; *The Fedora*, his 33rd self-portrait, was etched in 2002, when he was 88 years old. Holloway made more etched self-portraits than any other British printmaker.

Self-portraiture sometimes had its origins in the most banal of reasons: the lack of an alternative model. Many artists have pointed this out, among them Tom Phillips and indeed Francis Bacon, who said "I loathe my own face, and I've done self-portraits because I've had nobody else to do." Most artists show themselves at work or in their studios with the tools of their trade to the fore. But notably some artists broke ranks, and to good effect: what could be more poignant and ultimately harrowing than Harry Riley's self-portrait *Me* (1940-42), where his face is obscured by a gas mask? Or more striking than Percy Shakespeare in his underwear doing his daily dozen? Karl Hagedorn shows himself rowing, Rudolf Sauter in his army kit, Hugh Arthur Finney convalescing, Evelyn Dunbar naked, John Hassall wearing an Indian headdress, Winifred Knights in the guise of Miss Muffet and, memorably, Joseph Southall with his wife standing on the beach in Southwold.

Self-portraits by women are especially interesting given that the emerging voice of these artists was one of the transformative aspects of 20th century art. This section includes self-portraits by 13 women: Knights, Gibbs, Ginger, Spencer, Granger-Taylor, Kuhlenthal, Dodd, Fiennes, Brill, Weber, Dunbar, Mort and Dobrée – strikingly honest images imbued with a strong sense of individuality, self-knowledge, self-awareness and self-determination.

**236 William Orpen** (1878-1931), *Self-portrait as Chardin*, 1908, signed and dated, oil on canvas, 36 ½ x 28 ¼ in. (92.8 x 72.1cm). Collection: Laing Art Gallery.

William Orpen was one of the most successful portrait painters of the early 20th century. Orpen greatly admired the careful control of light and shadow in the work of the 18th-century French artist Jean-Baptiste-Siméon Chardin. This self-portrait is in homage to Chardin, who had painted himself with a similar white head covering. However, Orpen has used his own looser style of brushwork.

**William Strang** (1859-1921),

**237** *Self-portrait,* 1895,
signed and dated in the plate,
etching, with fold marks,
9 ¾ x 7¾ in. (24.8 x 19.6 cm).

**238** *Self-portrait, 78-6,*
inscribed 78-6,
pencil on paper, 9 ¼ x 7 ½ in. (23.5 x 19 cm).

**239** *Self-portrait, 154,*
signed with initials, numbered 154
pencil on paper, 9 ¼x 7 ½ in. (23.5 x 19 cm).

This self-portrait by Strang is the original drawing for his etching of 1890 (hence the same composition in reverse). The artist, aged 41, was in mid-career and already renowned as an etcher by this point. The technique and composition owes much to Alphonse Legros (1837-1911), who had taught Strang earlier at the Slade. Strang subsequently became the assistant master in Legros' etching class.

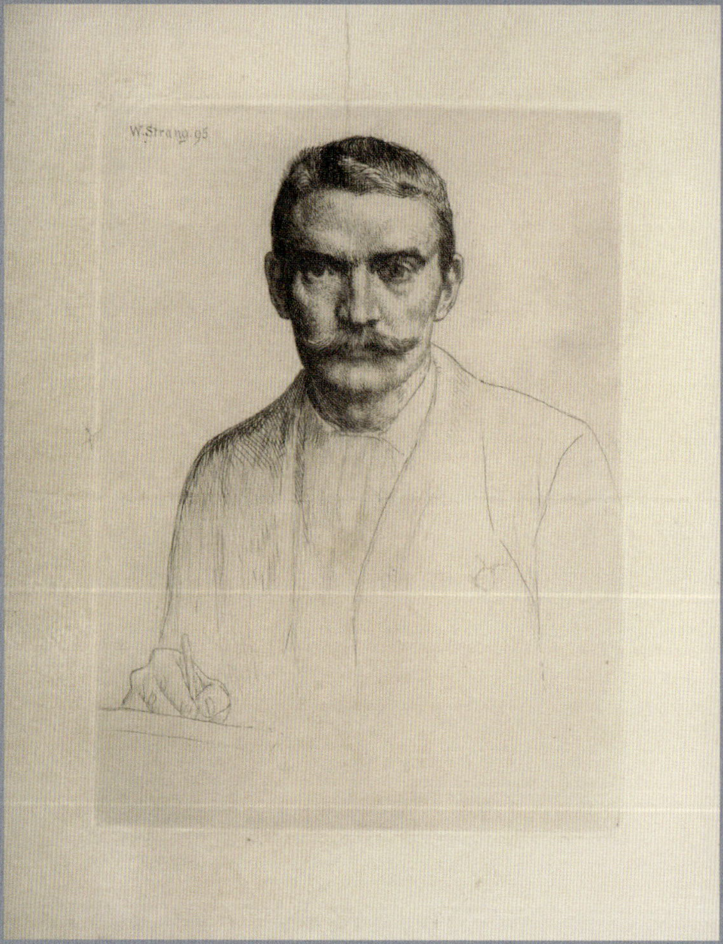


237

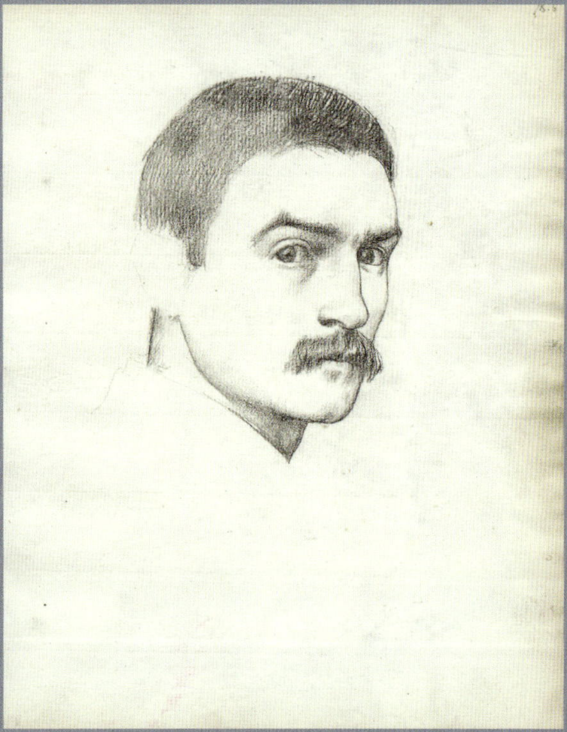

238

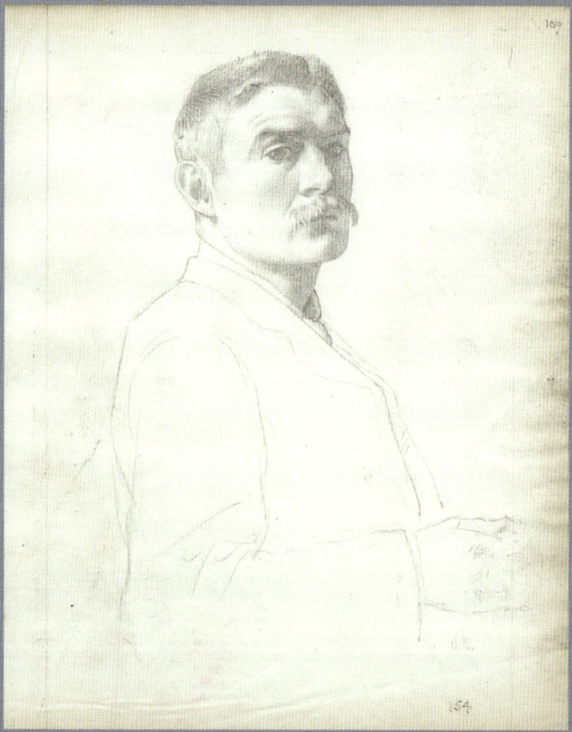

239

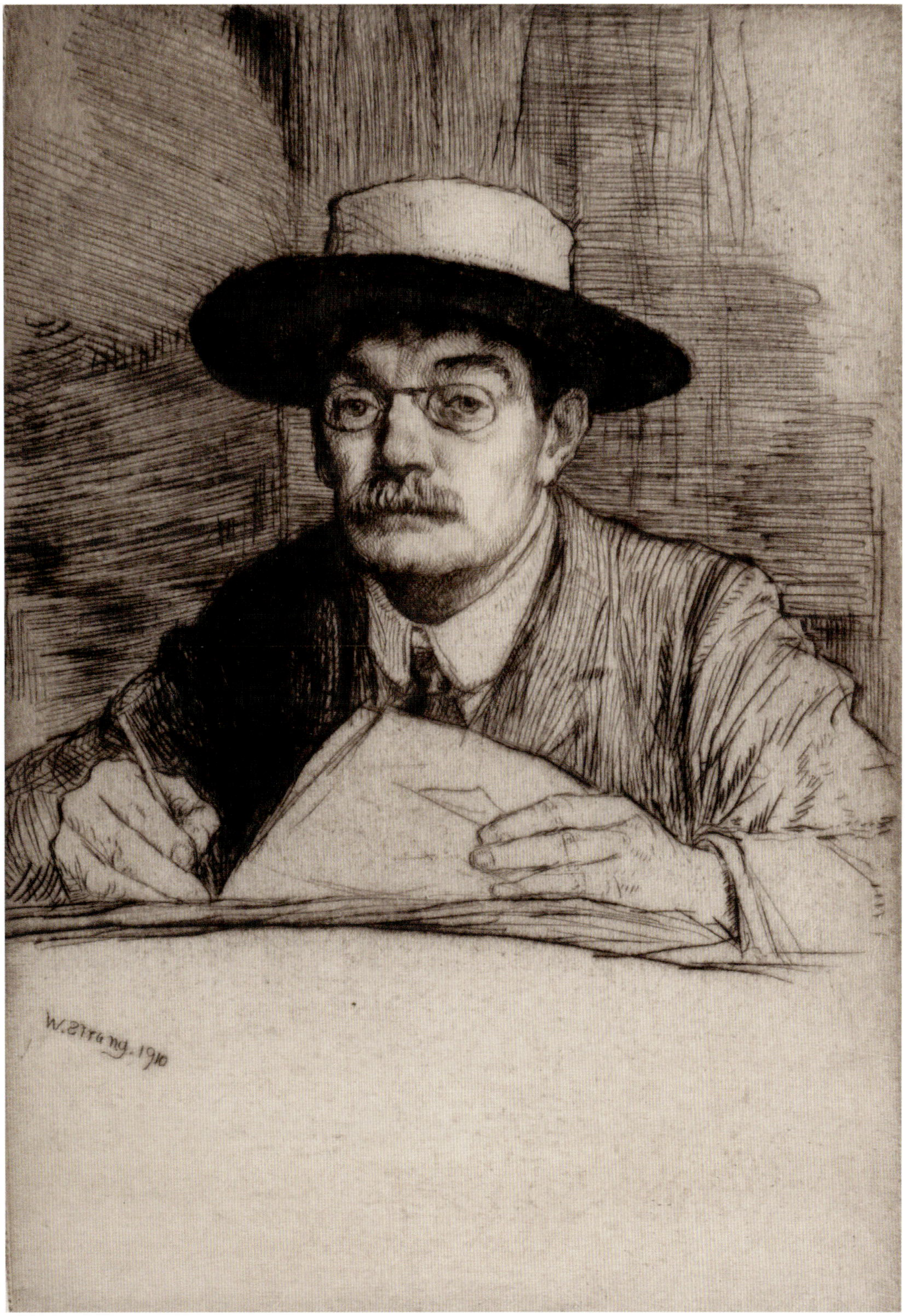


**240 William Strang** (1859-1921), *Self-portrait*, signed in reverse and dated 1910, inscribed "to Harry Paul from W Strang", etching, plate size: 8 x 5 ½ in. (20.3 x 14 cm).

In his younger years Strang was a noted serial self-portraitist. The etchings have a wide variety of poses and settings, or are distinguished by the wearing of hats. Joseph Pennell, himself a keen print-maker, commented: 'They are mainly portraits, simple and dignified, with a touch of severity that has its charm.'

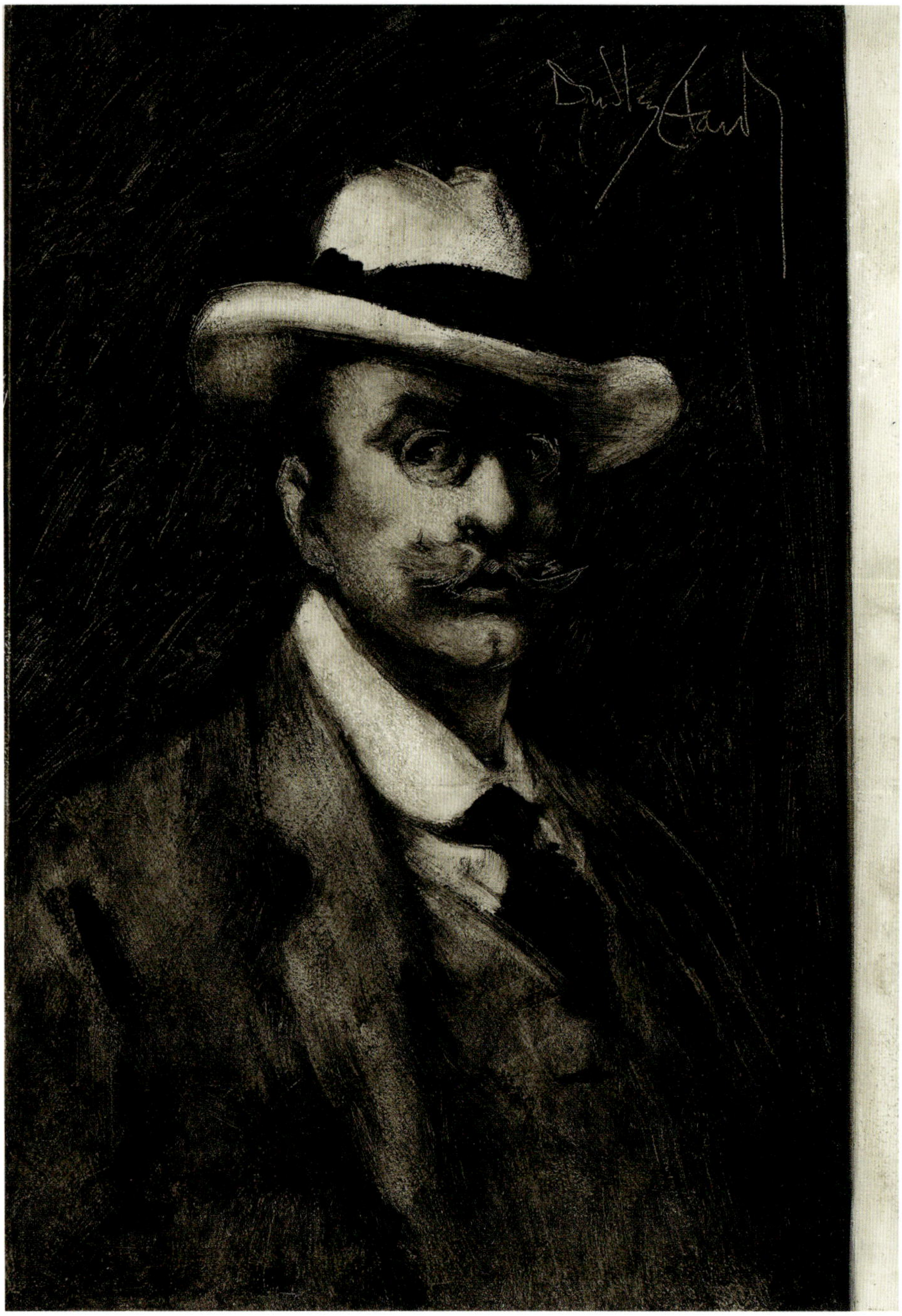

**241 Dudley Hardy** (1867-1922), *Self-portrait*, 1896, signed, inscribed on the reverse, oil on panel, 12 x 8 ½ in. (31 x 22 cm).

This self-portrait, showing the artist in his late 20s, was reproduced in the *Magazine of Art* in 1896. A prolific graphic artist and painter in oils, Hardy had, three years earlier, already produced the poster design, *A Gaiety Girl*, for which he is best known.

**242 George William Filliter** (1879-1960), *Self-portrait – Georgius Gulielmus Filliter / Princeps Ballagorriae*, c.1905, signed & inscribed 'Georgius Gulielmus Filliter / Princeps Ballagorriae', watercolour with pencil on paper, 10 ½ x 8 in. (27 x 20.5 cm).

Filliter studied architecture at Oxford University and worked in Manchester and the Isle of Man. The legend Princeps Ballagorriae ('Prince of Ballagorry') may be a witty reference to Ballagarey on the Isle of Man where Filliter is known to have undertaken a commission.

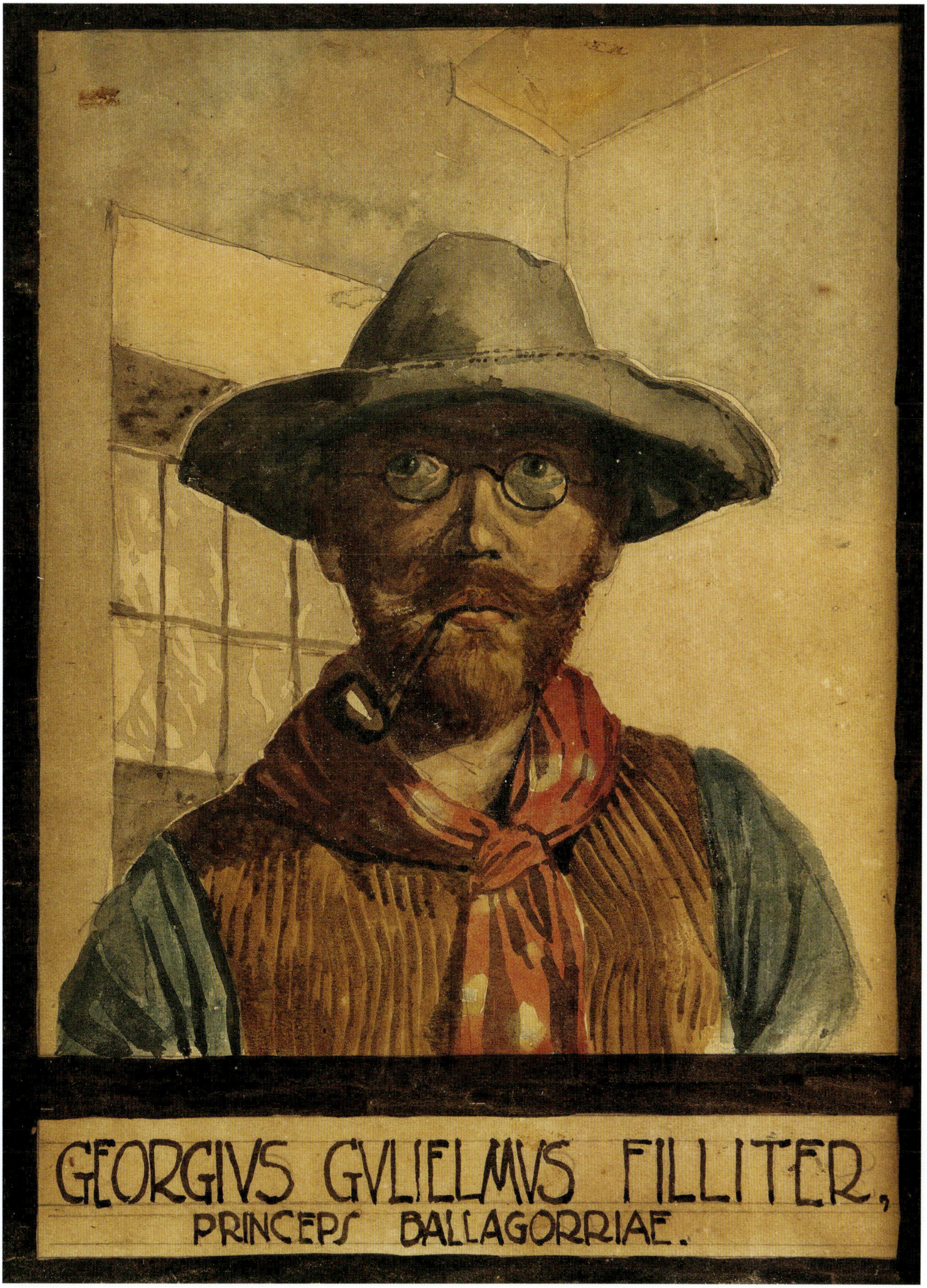
GEORGIVS GVLIELMVS FILLITER,
PRINCEPS BALLAGORRIAE.

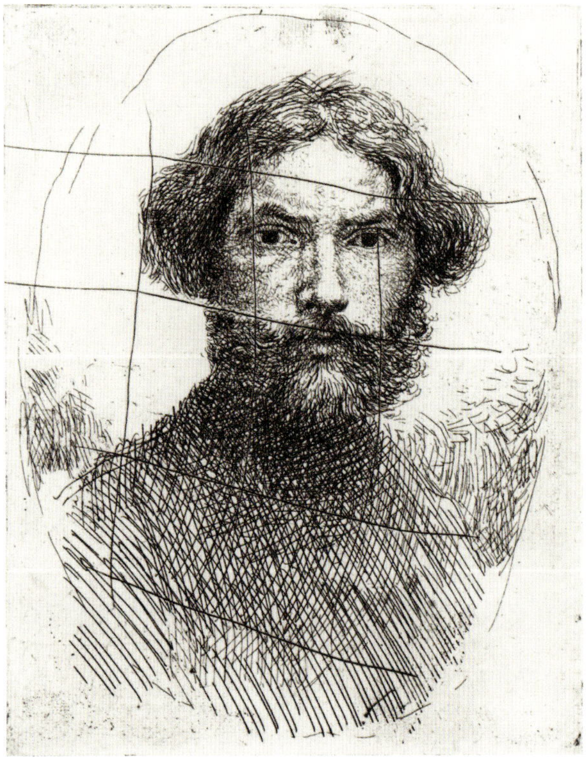

243

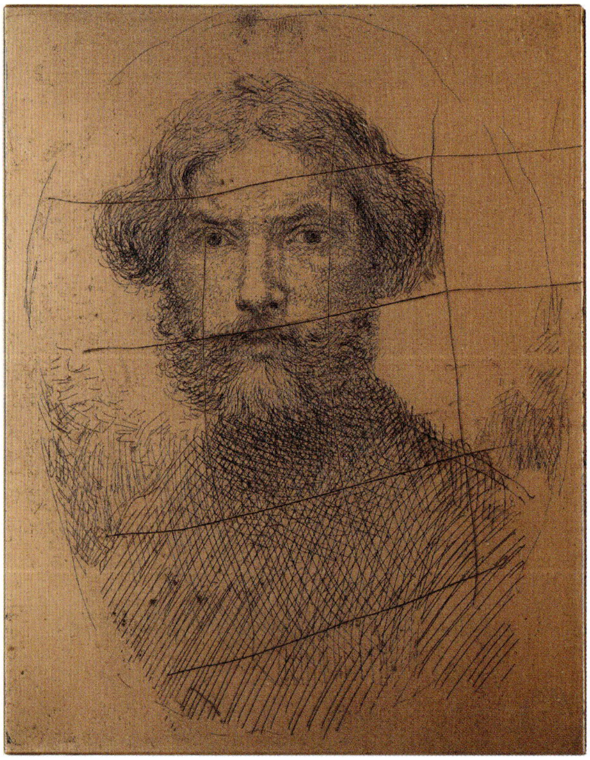

244

**Augustus John** (1878-1961), *Self-portrait*, 1906,

**243** etching, printed posthumously from cancelled plate, 8 ½ x 7 in. (21.5 x 18 cm).

**244** original cancelled copper plate 5 x 4 in. (12.5 x 10 cm).

John made 140 etchings, the majority between 1901 and 1906, culminating in an exhibition organised by Charles Knewstubb at the Chenil Gallery, London, in 1906.

Thought to have been produced during Augustus John's stay in Liverpool, where he taught at the University from 1901 to 1902, this etching was not published in a formal edition until issued by the Chenil Gallery in 1906 (in an edition of 25). The plate was then scored with cancellation lines by John. It was one of a series of self-portraits, all of which are deeply introspective and highly personal, the best known of which *Tête Farouche* is of a similar format though produced a few years earlier.

**245 Joseph Southall** (1861-1944), *The Agate (Portrait of the Artist and his Wife)*, 1911, signed with initials and dated, tempera on linen, 38 ¾ x 19 ¼ in. (98.4 x 48.8 cm). Collection: National Portrait Gallery.

This striking self-portrait shows the artist and craftsman Joseph Southall with his wife, Anna Elizabeth (known as Bessie) (**78**). They are standing together on a beach, most likely to be at Southwold, Suffolk, where they spent their honeymoon in 1903 and later enjoyed holidays together. Bessie is shown handing her husband an agate, a gemstone which can be found on the seashore in this area, and traditionally is associated with the strengthening of relationships. It was also the stone Bessie used to burnish the gilded frames that she made for her Joseph Southall's pictures.

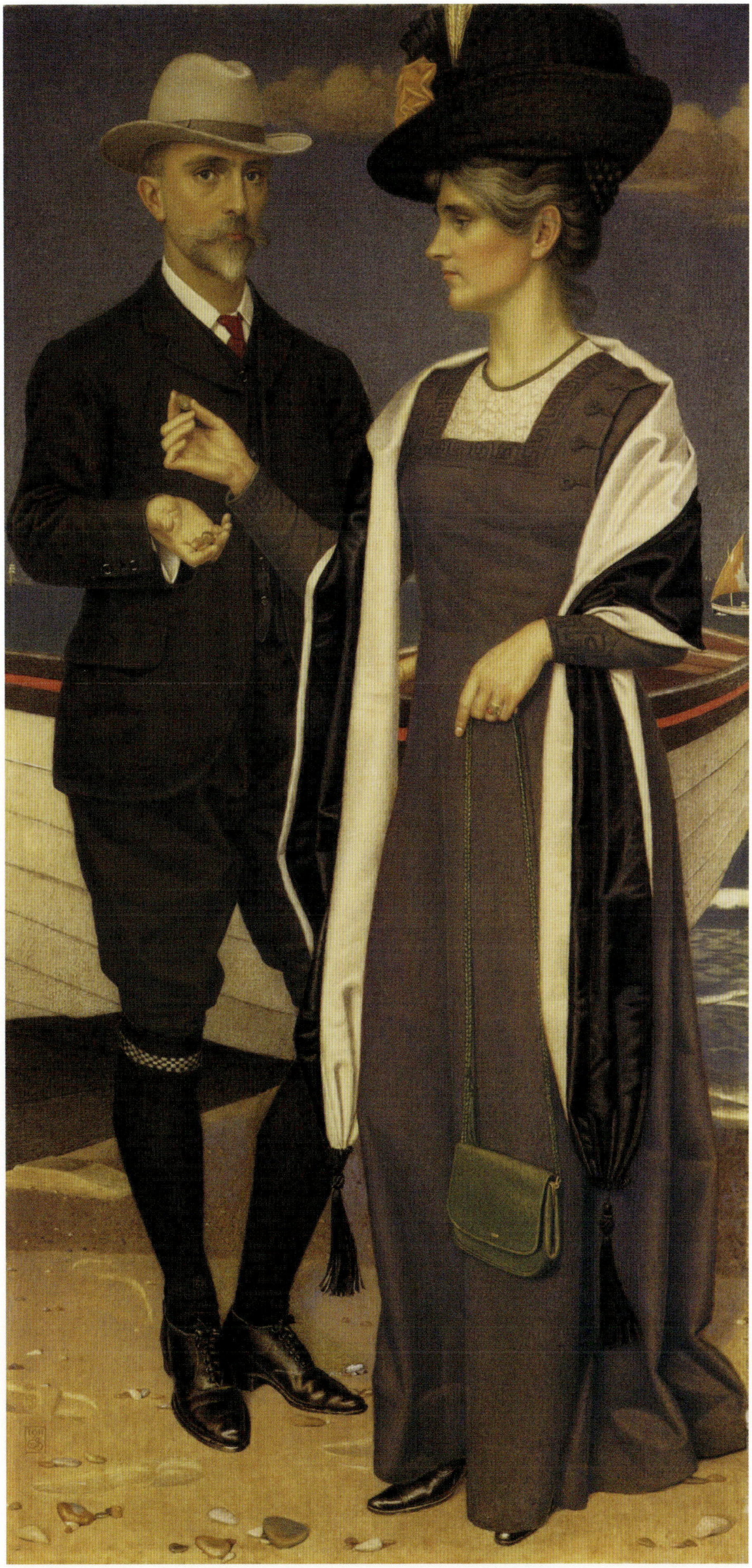

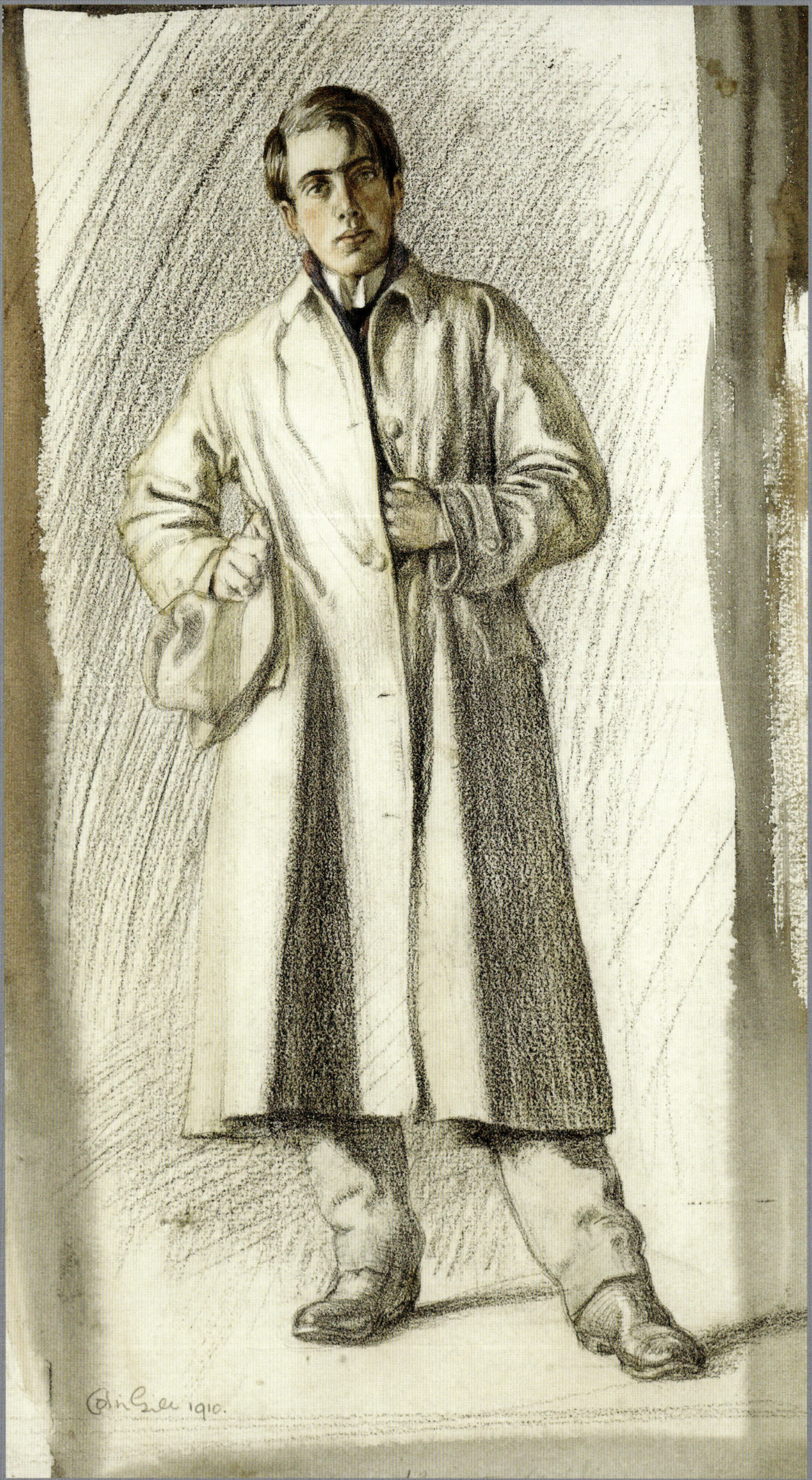
Colin Gill 1910.

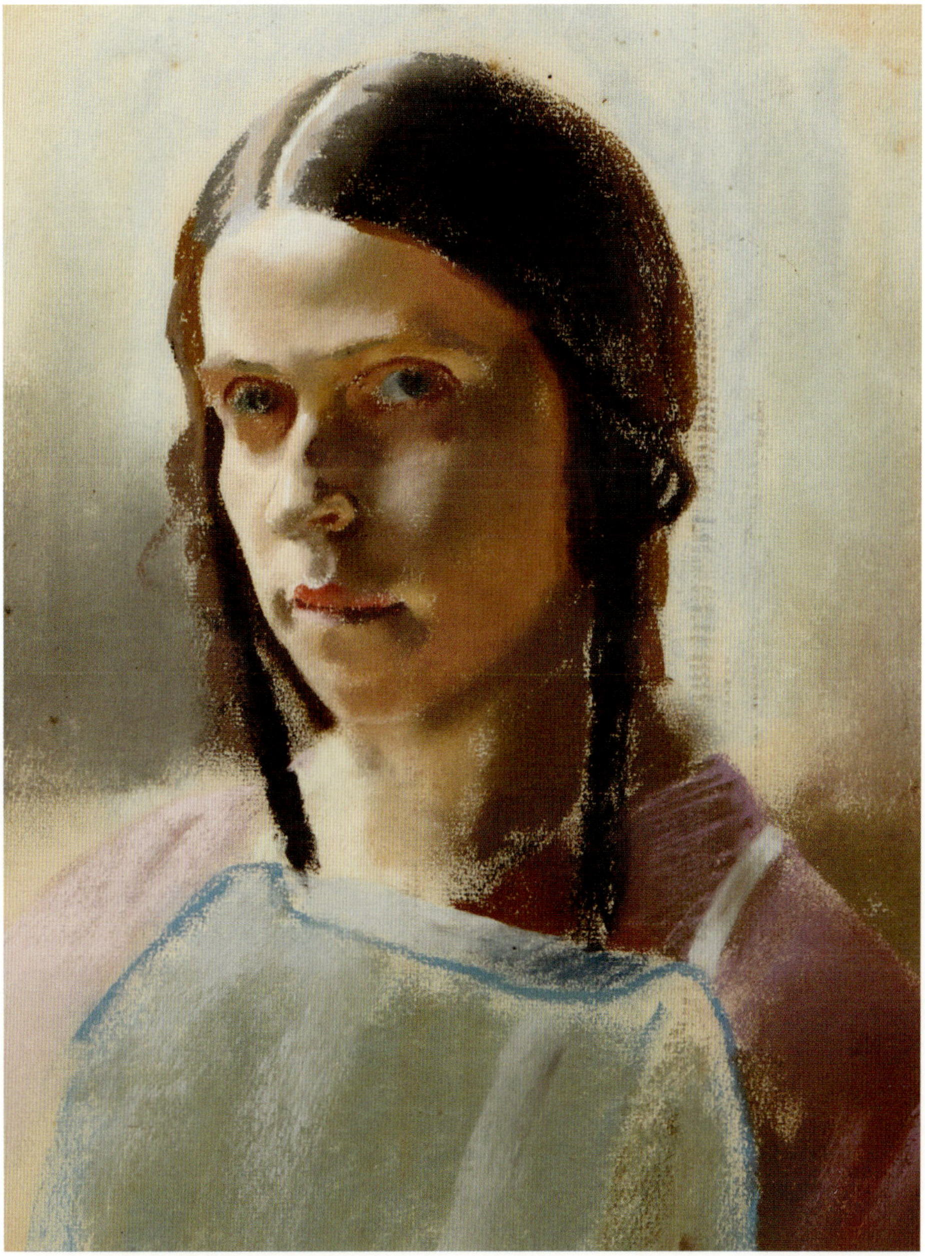

**247 Edith Granger-Taylor** (1887-1958), *Self-portrait*, c.1920
pastel on paper, 13 ¼ x 10 ¼ in. (34 x 26 cm).

Having learnt pastel from Henry Tonks whilst attending the Slade in 1919, Edith Granger-Taylor worked almost exclusively in this medium, or crayon, for the rest of her life.

**246 Colin Gill** (1892-1940), *Self-portrait with Coat and Hat*, 1910, signed and dated,
pencil, coloured crayon and watercolour on paper, 14 x 8 ¼ in.(35.6 x 21 cm).

Colin Gill attended the Slade in its heyday, the years leading up to WWI. While never formally associated with the self-styled Slade 'Neo-Primitives', Gill shared a close friendship with Mark Gertler and William Roberts. In 1913 Gill became the first recipient of the Rome Scholarship in Decorative Painting to the British School at Rome. (**162**, **251**, **339**)

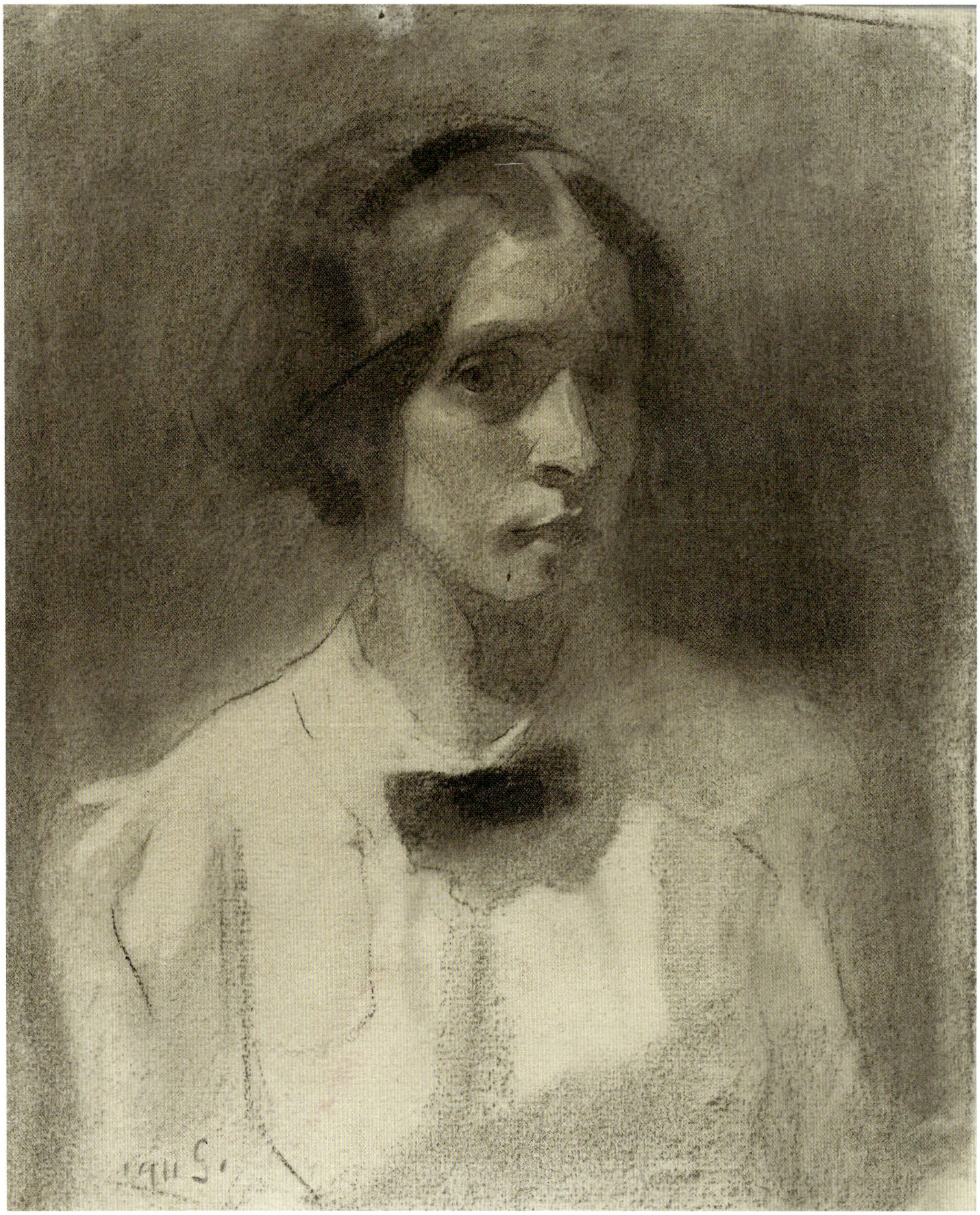


**248 Edith Granger-Taylor** (1887-1958), *Self-portrait*, 1911, signed with initial, dated, pencil and black chalk on paper, 9 ½ x 8 in. (24.2 x 20.3 cm).

Reporting on her 1932 exhibition at the Beaux Arts Gallery, London, the art critic from *The Scotsman* wrote that Granger-Taylor used pastel with 'extraordinary facility and intelligence, and designs with grace. She has a style personal and fluent [...], full of pleasant flourishes and tricks of technique'. The writer goes on to praise the tone and shape of Granger-Taylor's near-abstract style, saying that the 'peculiar sweetness (of pastel) proves fatal to all but draughtsmen with a strong and healthy colour sense'.

In spite of such critical reception, her increasing frustration as a female artist working in the inter-war years caused Granger-Taylor to retreat from the art world, and after the 1930s her work would not be exhibited again in her lifetime. Her remarkable abstract compositions date to the 1930s.

**249 Edith Granger-Taylor** (1887-1958), *Self-portrait*, c. 1920, pastel on paper, 9 ½ x 7 ¾ in. (24 x 20 cm).

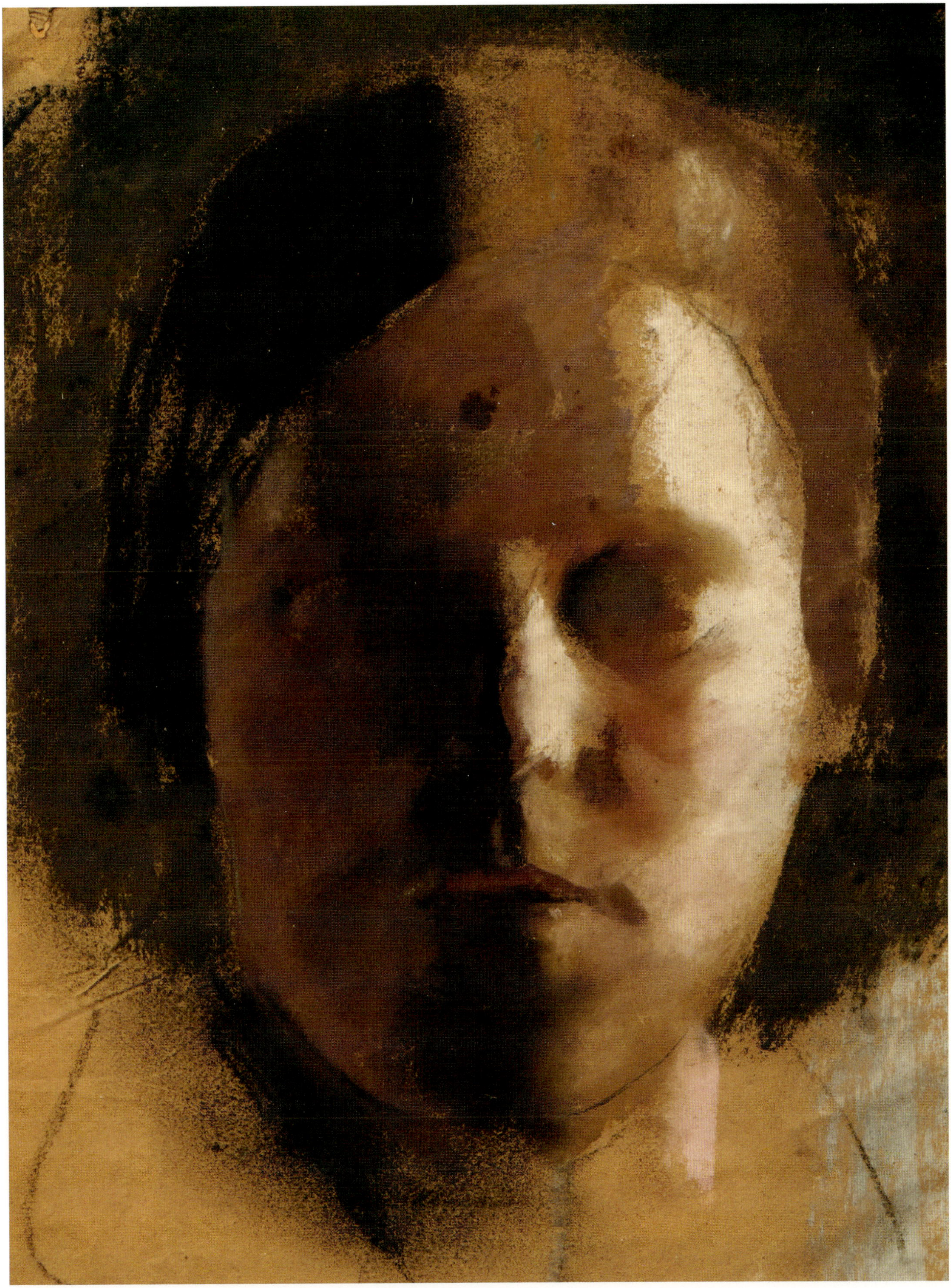

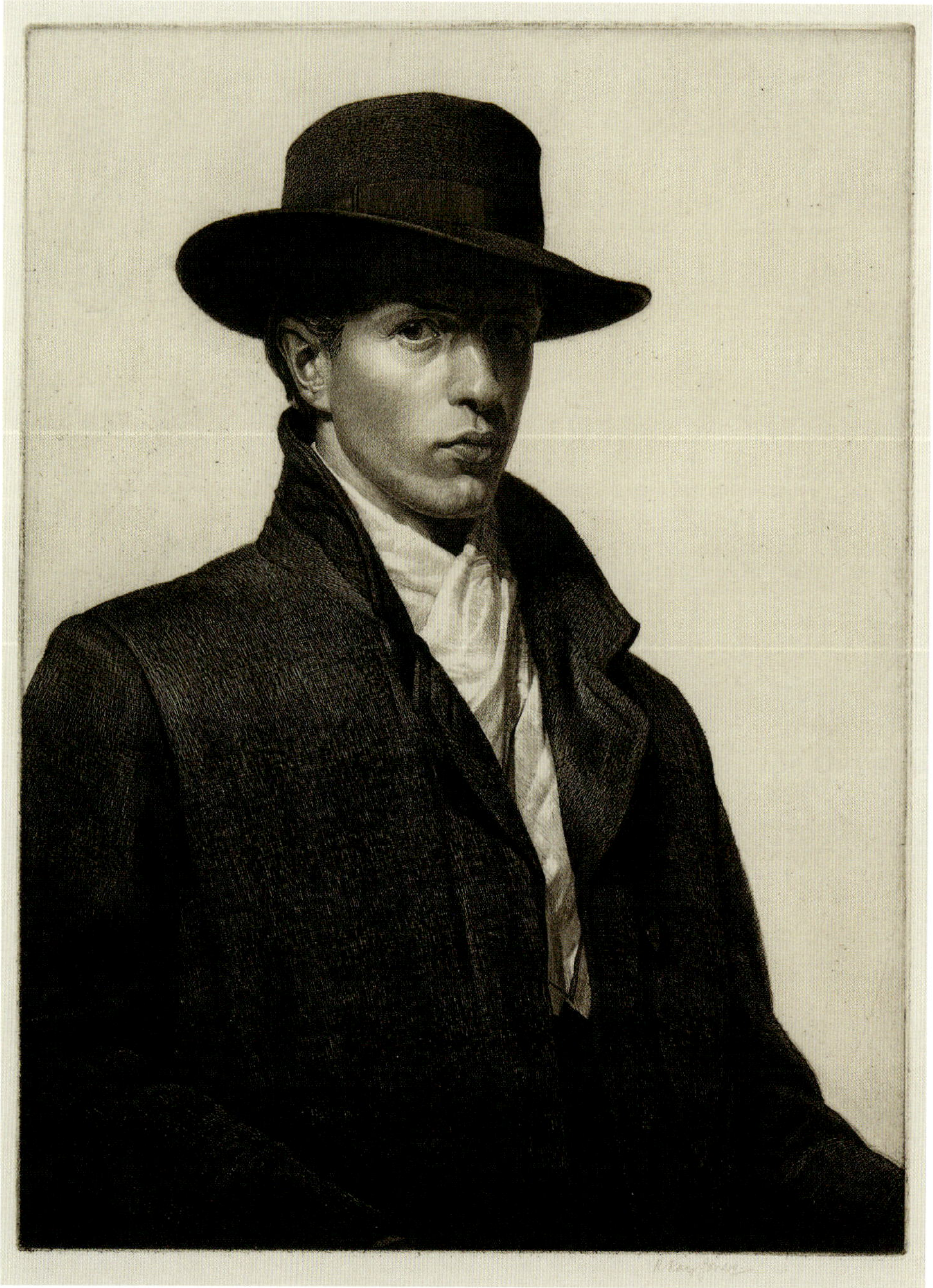

**250** **Raymond Ray-Jones** (1886-1942), *Self-portrait Wearing a Hat*, c.1915, signed in pencil, etching on laid paper, watermarked F.J. Head & Co., 13 x 9.7 in. (33 x 24.7 cm).

Considered to be the artist's greatest print, this self-portrait was exhibited at the Seventh Exhibition of Modern Masters of Etching at the Leicester Galleries in 1922, at which all impressions were sold out on the first day. The work was described as 'one of the finest etched portraits of contemporary times'. Ray-Jones also produced an etching of his wife. (**84**)

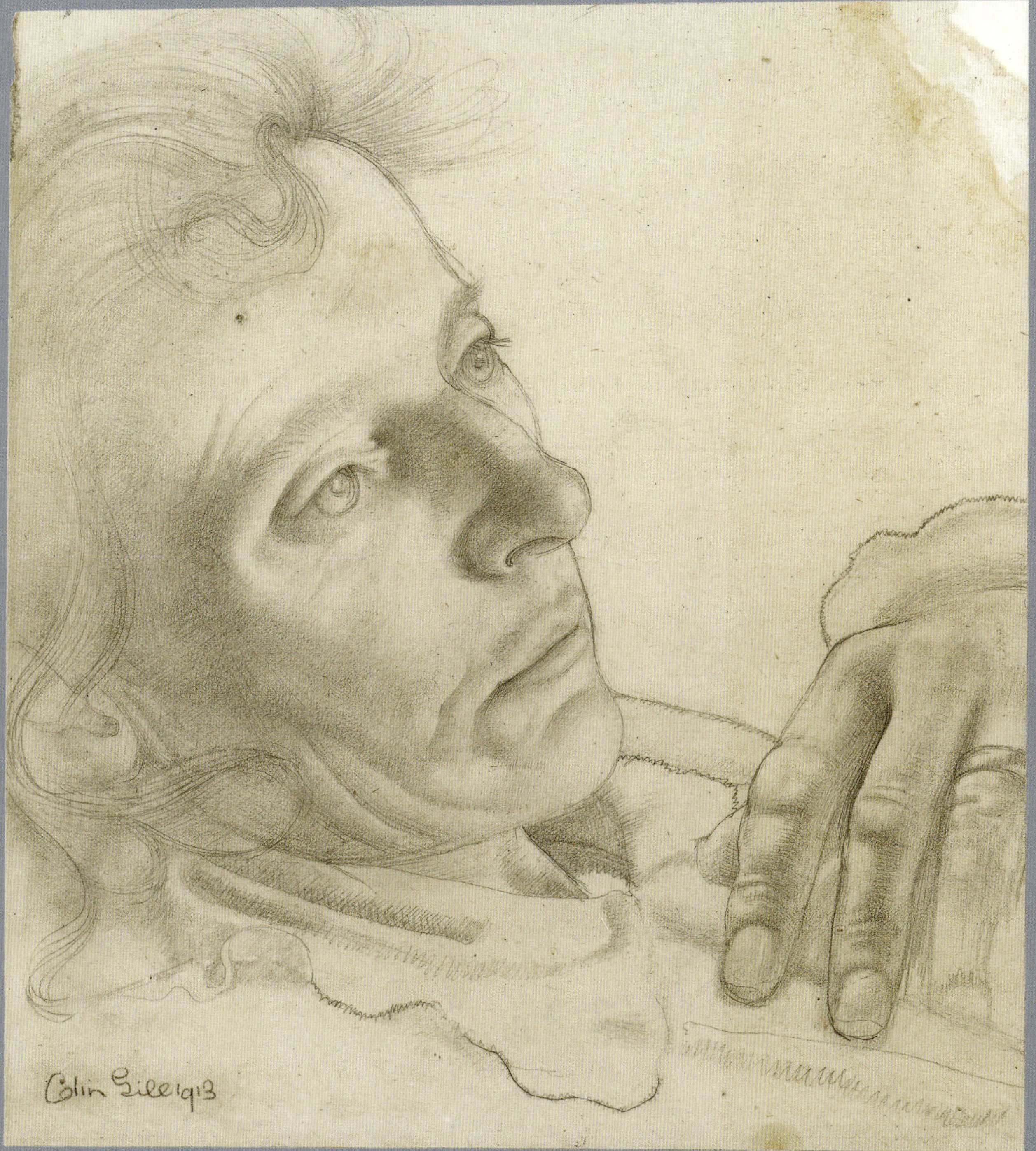

**251 Colin Gill** (1892-1940), *Self-portrait* (?), 1913, signed and dated,
pencil with white chalk highlights on paper. 8 ¾ x 9 ½in. ( 22.5 x 24.5 cm).

This drawing, which is likely to be a self-portrait, dates to 1913, the year in which Gill won the first scholarship in Painting to the British School at Rome. (**162**)

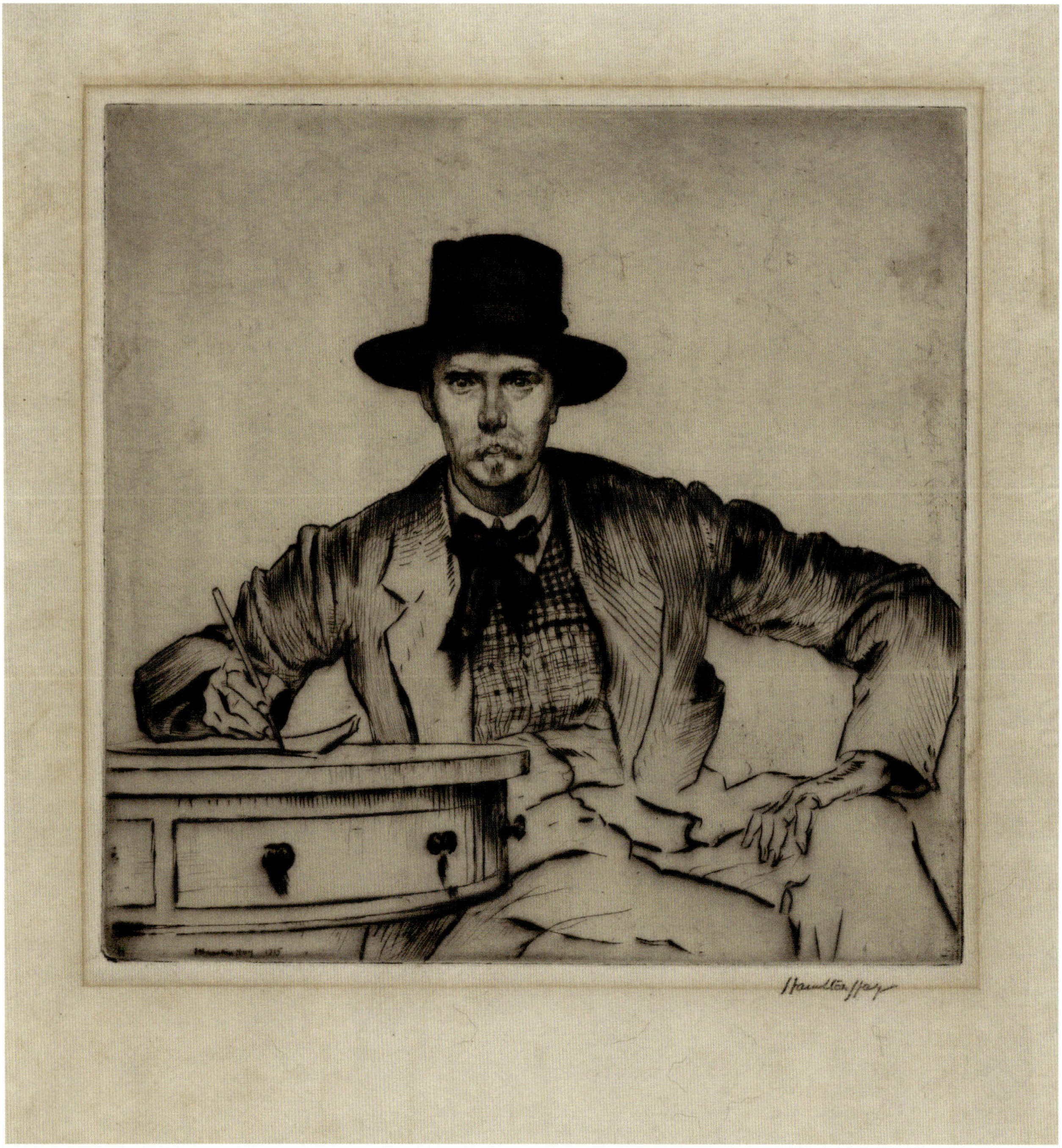

**252 James Hamilton Hay** (1874-1916), *Self-portrait*, 1915, signed and dated, titled and inscribed 'Specimen Copy' to reverse, drypoint print, 9 x 9 in. (22.8 x 22.8 cm).

James Hamilton Hay took up drypoint etching in 1913, inspired by Francis Dodd, who had produced a portrait of him the previous year. In the following three years, prior to his death in 1916, Hay produced 53 works in this medium.

**253 Christine Kuhlenthal** (1895-1976), *Self-portrait*, c.1915 pencil and watercolour on paper, 12 x 9 in. (30.5 x 22.8 cm).

Christine Kuhlenthal studied at the Slade School of Fine Art, but poor eyesight eventually prevented her from becoming a professional artist. In May 1918 she married John Nash.

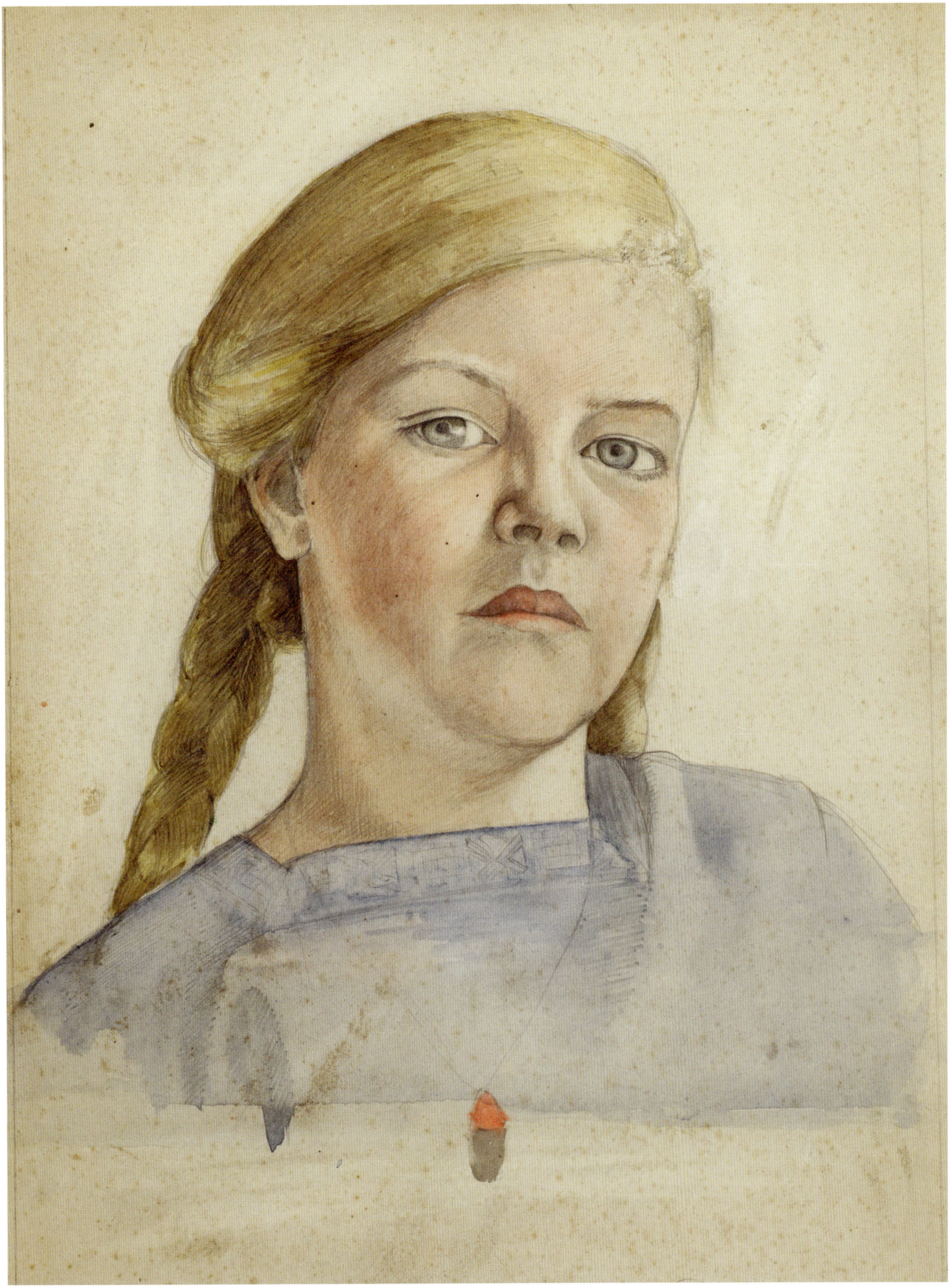

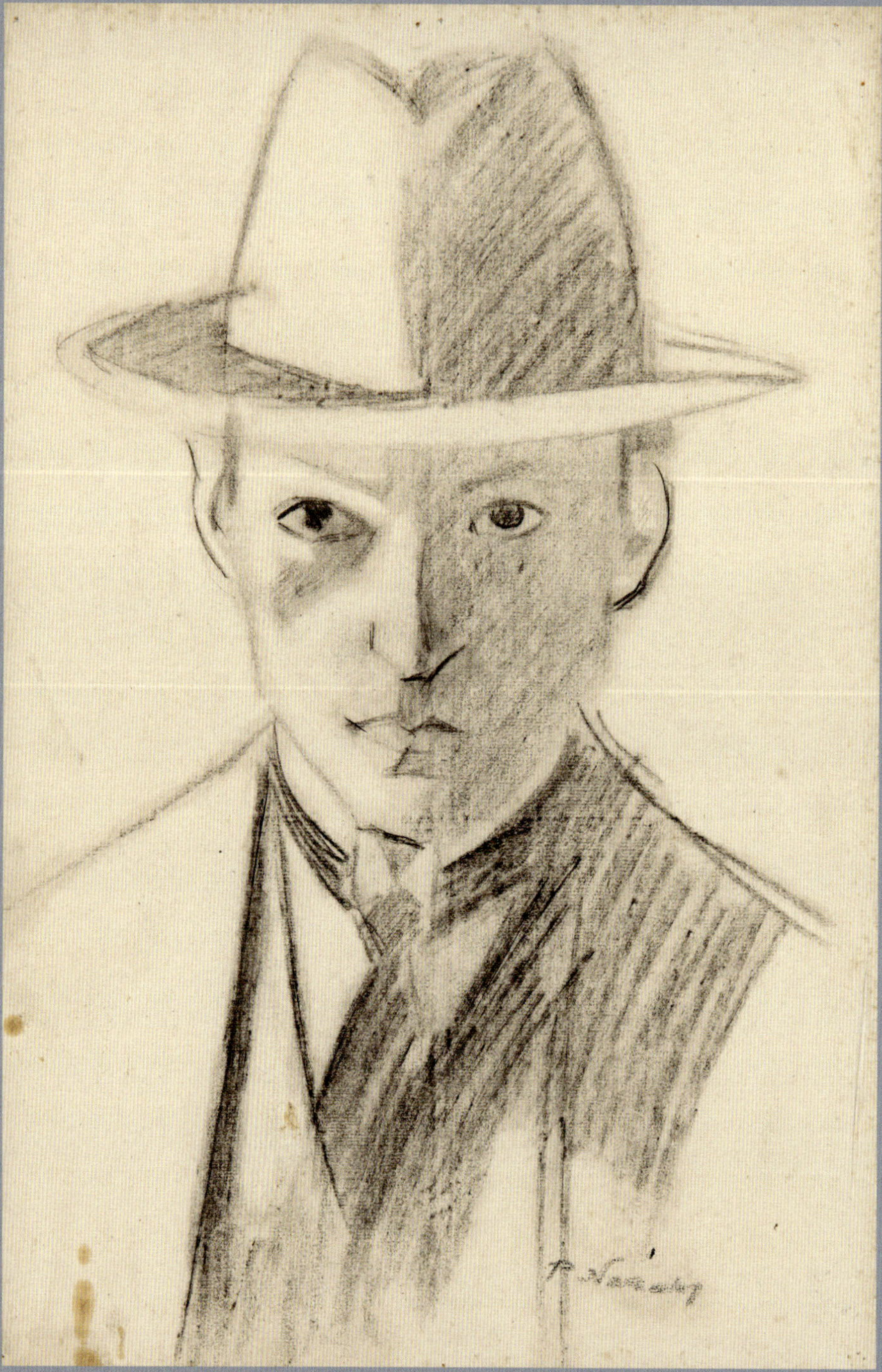

**254 Philip Naviasky** (1894-1983), *Self-portrait*, c.1920, signed, charcoal on paper, 18 ½ x 12 ¼ in. (47 x 31 cm).

This confident self-portrait shows Philip Naviasky on completion of his training at Leeds School of Art, which he attended from 1910-12. Thereafter he studied at the Royal Academy Schools (1912-14) and, on a scholarship, at the Royal College of Art (1914-16).

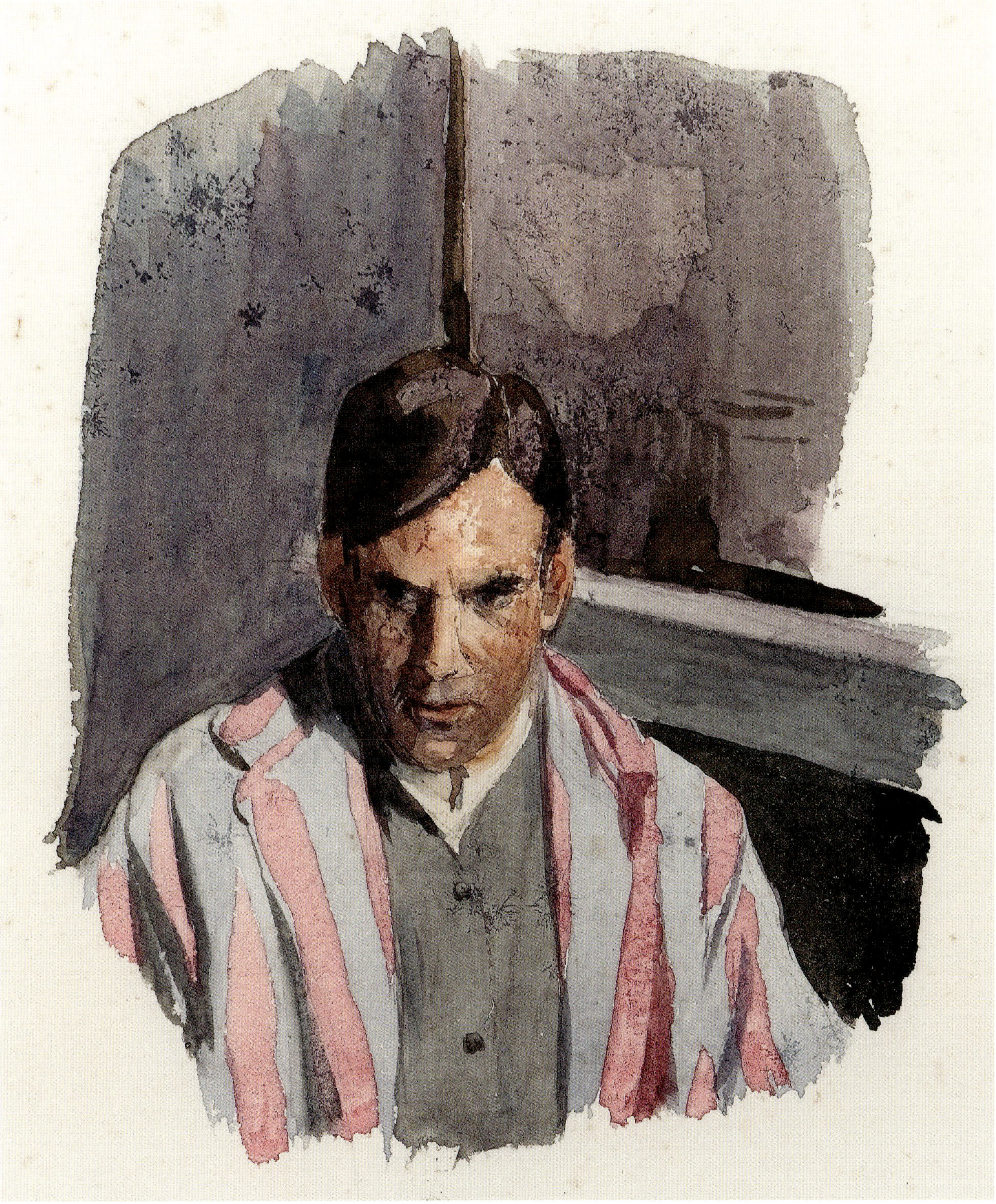

**255 James Wood** (1889-1975), *Self-portrait*, c.1918, watercolour on paper, 7 ½ x 6 ½ in. (19.5 x 16 cm).

This early self-portrait, with Wood wearing a dressing gown, dates from WW1. Wood read history at Cambridge and studied art in Paris and Munich. After service in the Royal Flying Corps in WW1, he worked on aircraft camouflage, partly in association with his life-long friend Richard Carline. (**278**)

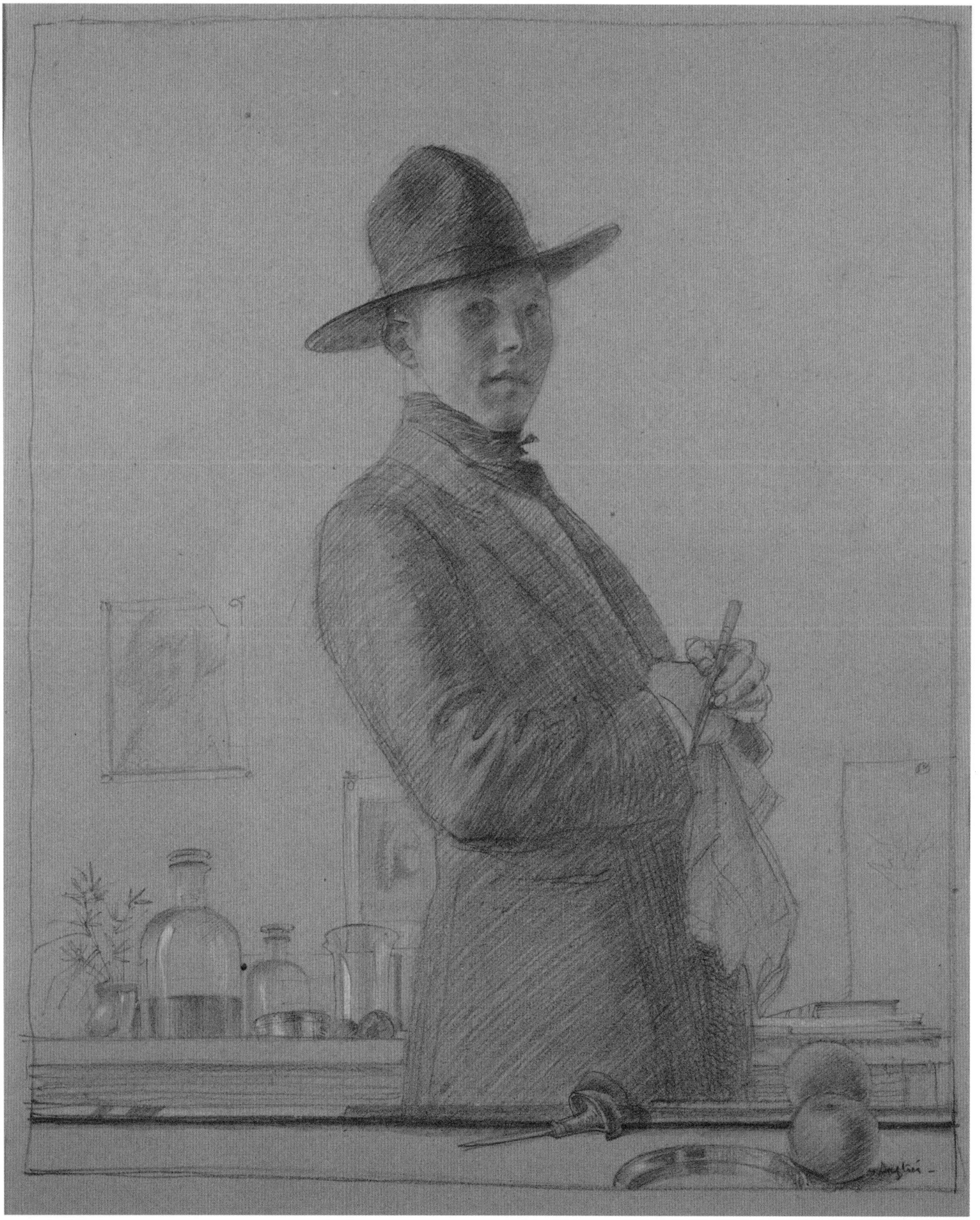

**256 Robert Austin** (1895-1973), *Self-portrait in Roman Hat*, mid-1920s, inscribed under mount, pencil and watercolour on paper, 10 x 8 in. (25.4 x 20.3 cm).

This self-portrait was given by Austin to Eleanor Hudson, his student and mistress. She was a watercolourist, etcher and designer best known for her depictions of women at work in WW2. Hudson was the model for Austin's engraving *Evening* (**145**).

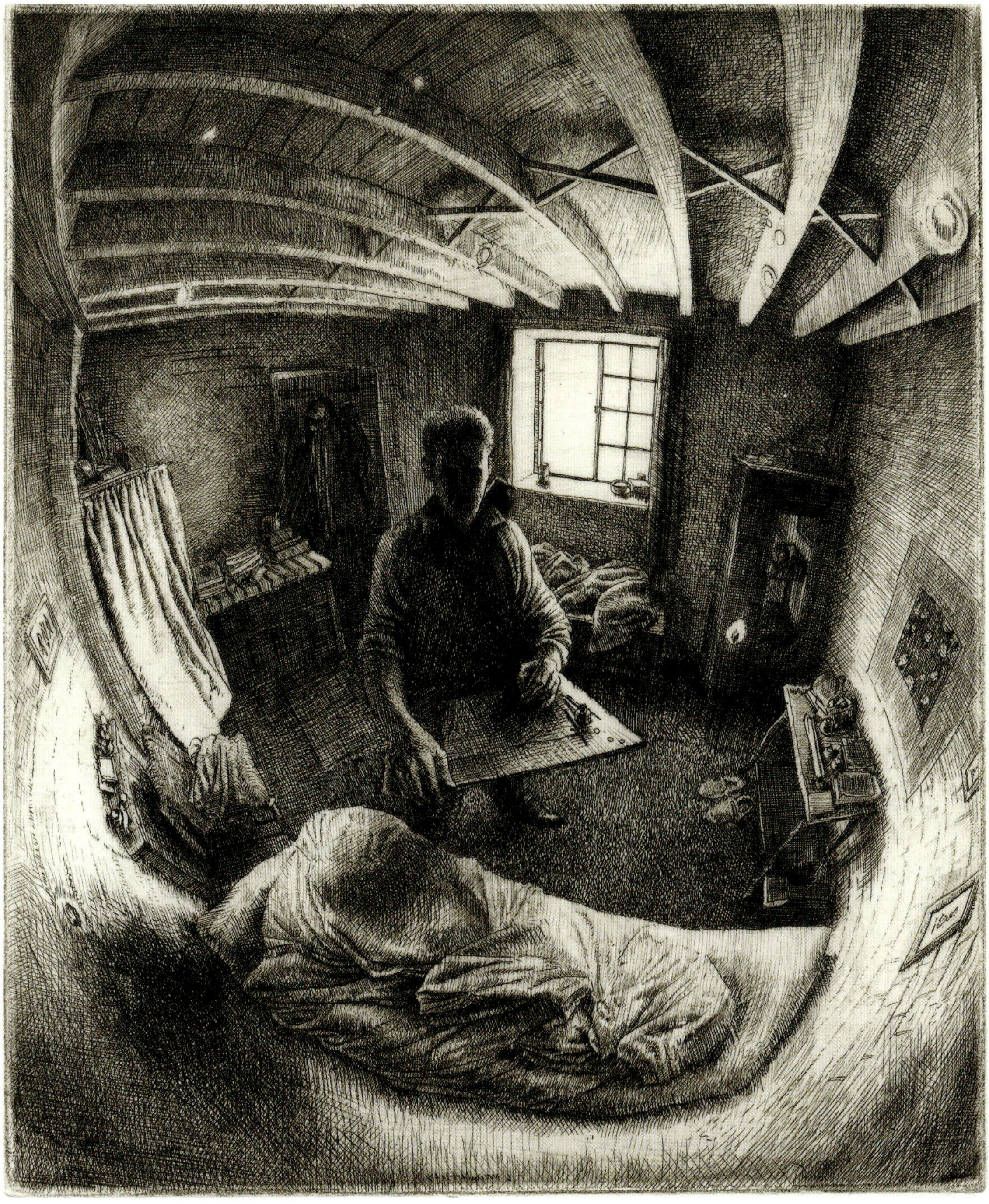

**257 Robert Austin** (1895-1973), *Self-portrait and Jackdaw,* 1949, signed in pencil, etching on paper, 8 x 6 ¾ in. (20.3 x 17.3 cm).

During WW2 Robert Austin worked for the War Artists' Advisory Committee. This enigmatic fish-eye lens self-portrait, dated 1944, shows Austin working in the attic studio of the disused Norfolk chapel he bought in 1936. (**143**) Despite the title no jackdaw is in evidence, except perhaps symbolically, as an inveterate gatherer of bits and pieces to furnish its nest.

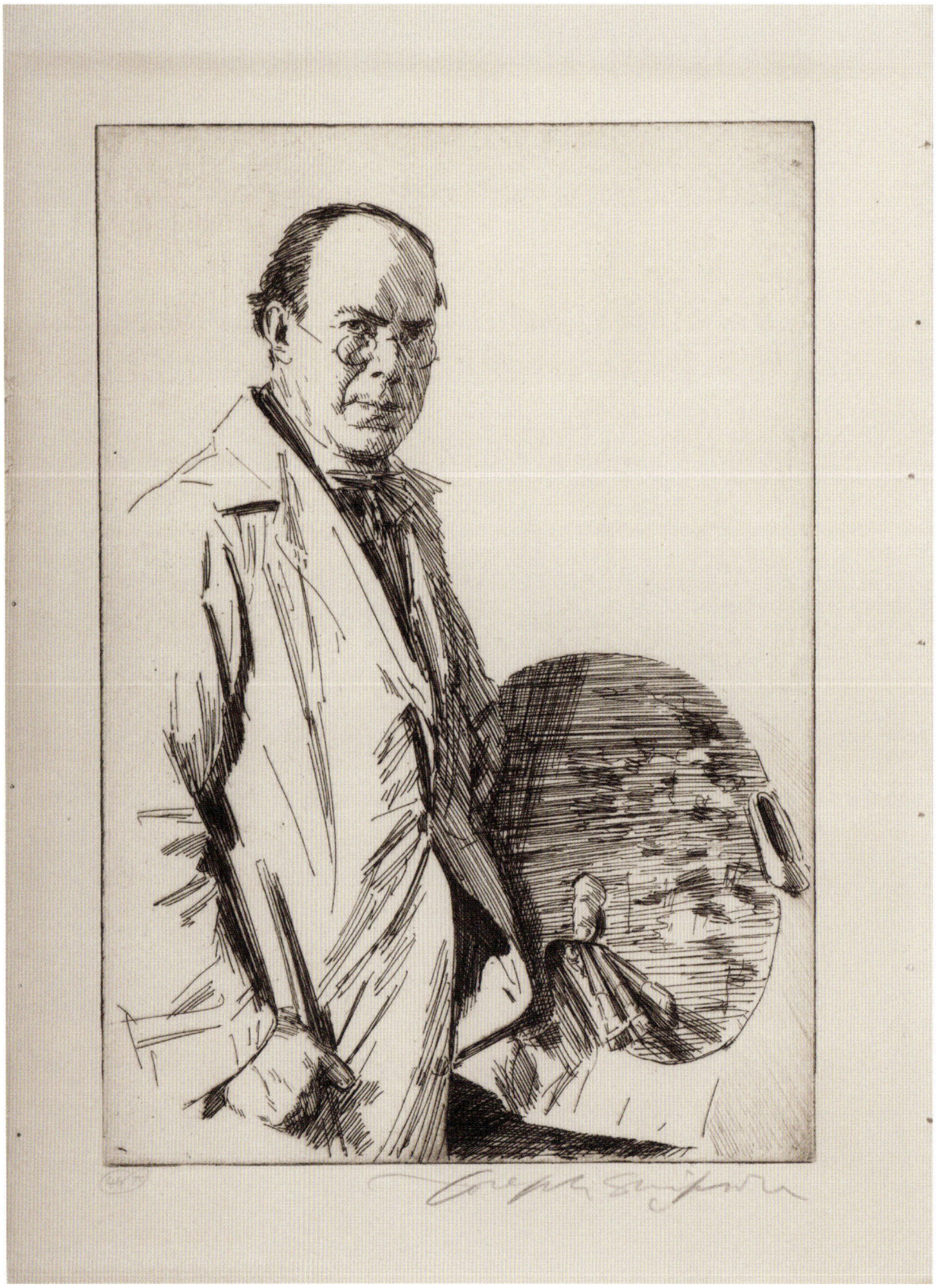

**258 Joseph Simpson** (1879-1939), *Self-portrait, The Artist Standing*, 1925, signed in pencil, titled and dated to reverse, etching (produced in an edition of 75), 14 ¾ x 11 ¼ in. (37.5 x 28.6 cm).

Dated 1925, when the artist was 46 years old, this self-portrait was produced one year before Joseph Simpson held his first exhibition of etchings. His career as an etcher had begun in 1909 at the suggestion of Frank Brangwyn. (**176**)

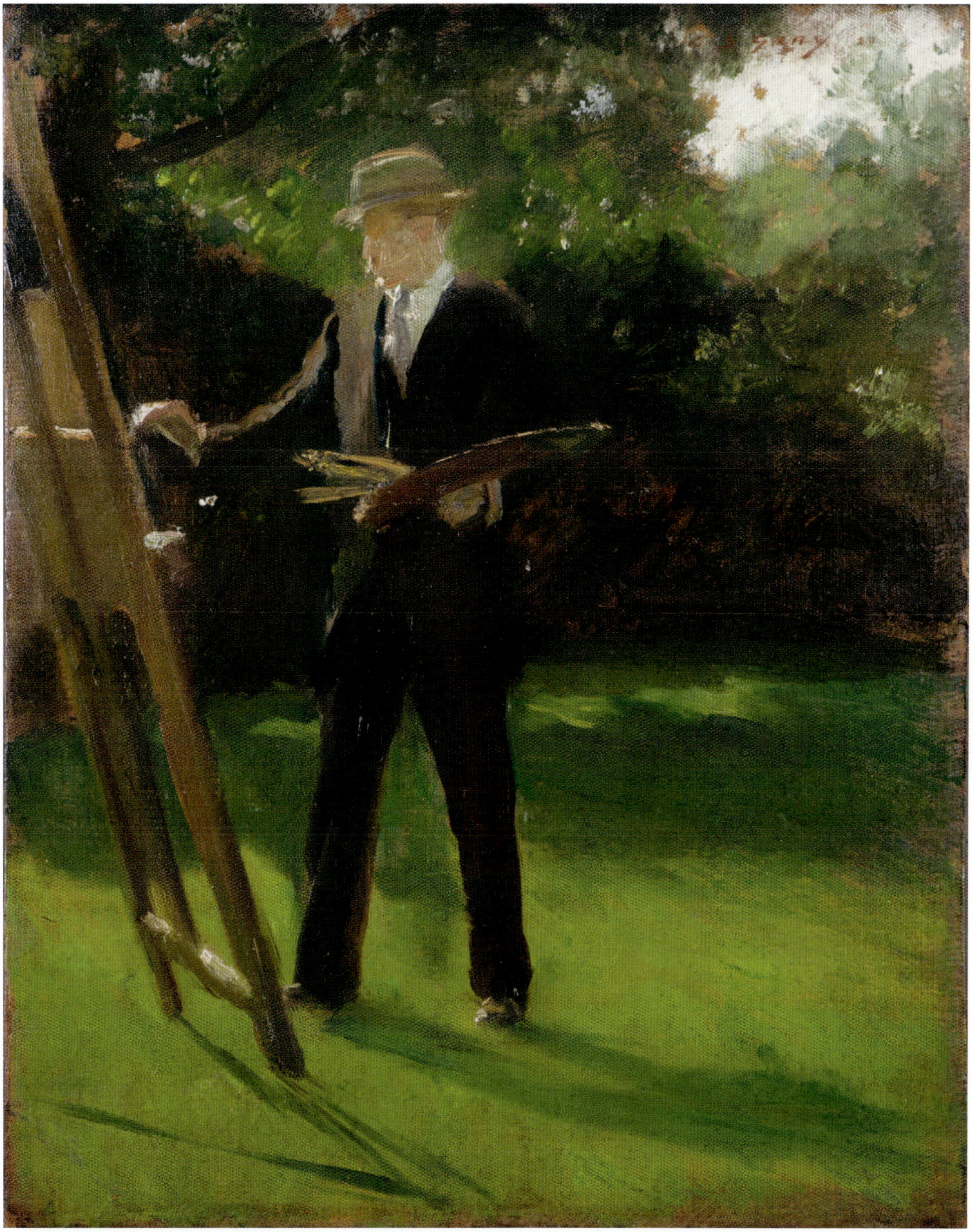

**259 Douglas Stannus Gray** (1890-1959), *Self-portrait Painting at an Easel Outdoors*, 1920, signed and dated, oil on canvas board, 18 x 14 ½ in. (45.7 x 36.9 cm).

Douglas Stannus Gray lived for most of his life in Clapham, where his garden at 102 King's Avenue was used as the setting for many of his portraits. The influence of John Singer Sargent, under whom he trained at the Royal Academy, is evident in the loose, wet-on-wet handling of paint which gives this panel its sense of spontaneity.

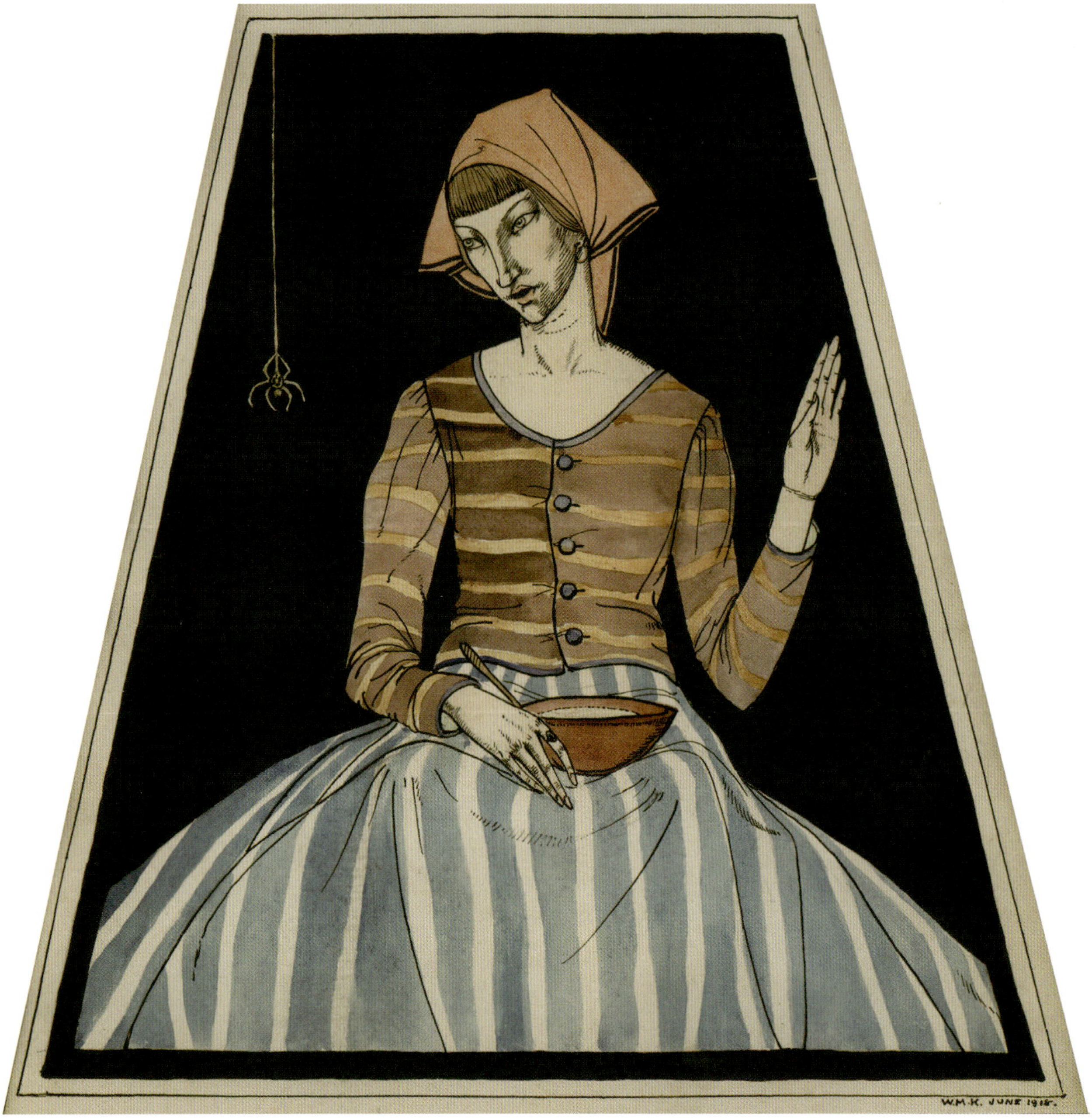

**260 Winifred Knights** (1899-1947), *Self-portrait as Little Miss Muffet*, signed and dated June 1918, ink and watercolour on paper, 10 ½ x 10 ½ in. (27 x 27 cm).

Winifred Knights frequently included herself as the main protagonist in her pictures. (**340**) This drawing reveals a strong sense of design which marks a clear departure from Knight's earlier Art-Nouveau-inspired compositions. The treatment of face and hands – elongated and symmetrical, with strong outline and an emphasis on the underlying anatomical geometry – would now become a defining characteristic of her figurative work.

**261 Winifred Knights** (1899-1947), *Self-portrait*, 1920, pencil on paper, 7 x 6 in. (18 x 15 cm).

This self-portrait dates to 1920 when Winifred Knights became the first woman to win a scholarship to The British School at Rome. She gave this drawing to her friend Marjory Allen, after she had accompanied Knights and Gill on an expedition to Viterbo, Orvieto, Assisi, Perugia and Florence. (**165**) Knights had striking features and portraits of her were made by Colin Gill, Arnold Mason and Tom Monnington, amongst many others, and portrait busts by sculptors David Evans, Professor Alfred Gerard, and Alfred Hardiman.

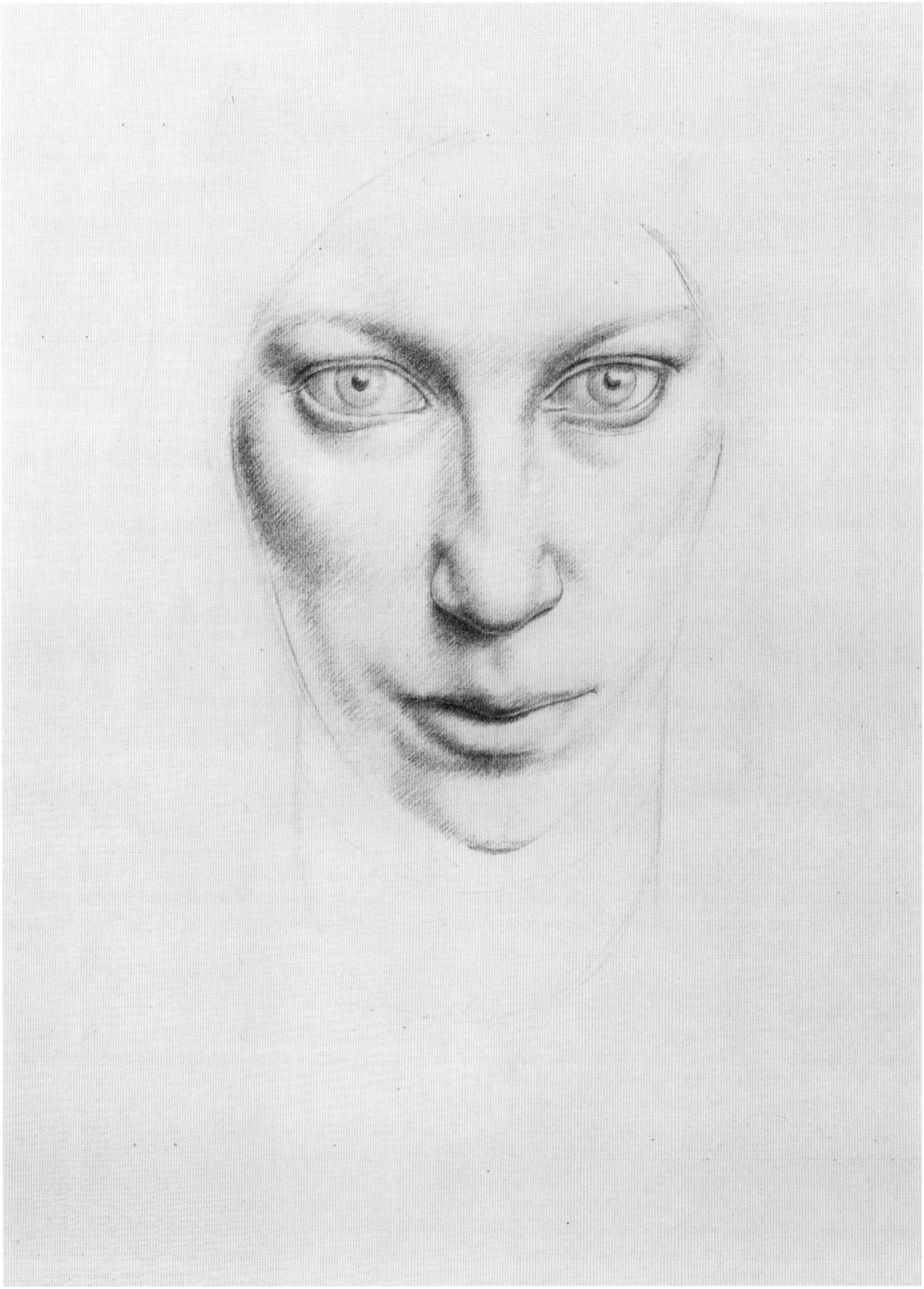

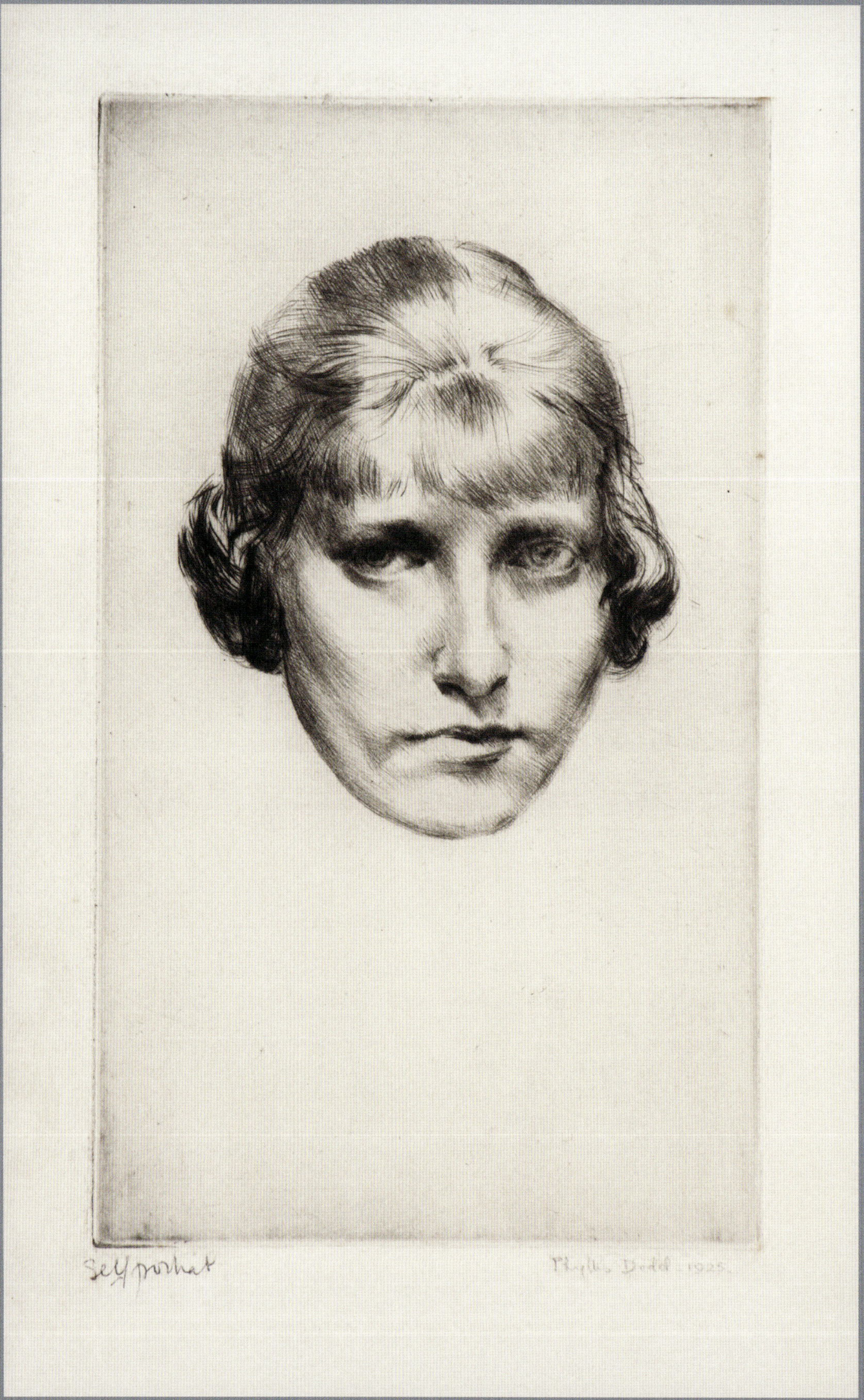
Self portrait
Phyllis Dodd 1925

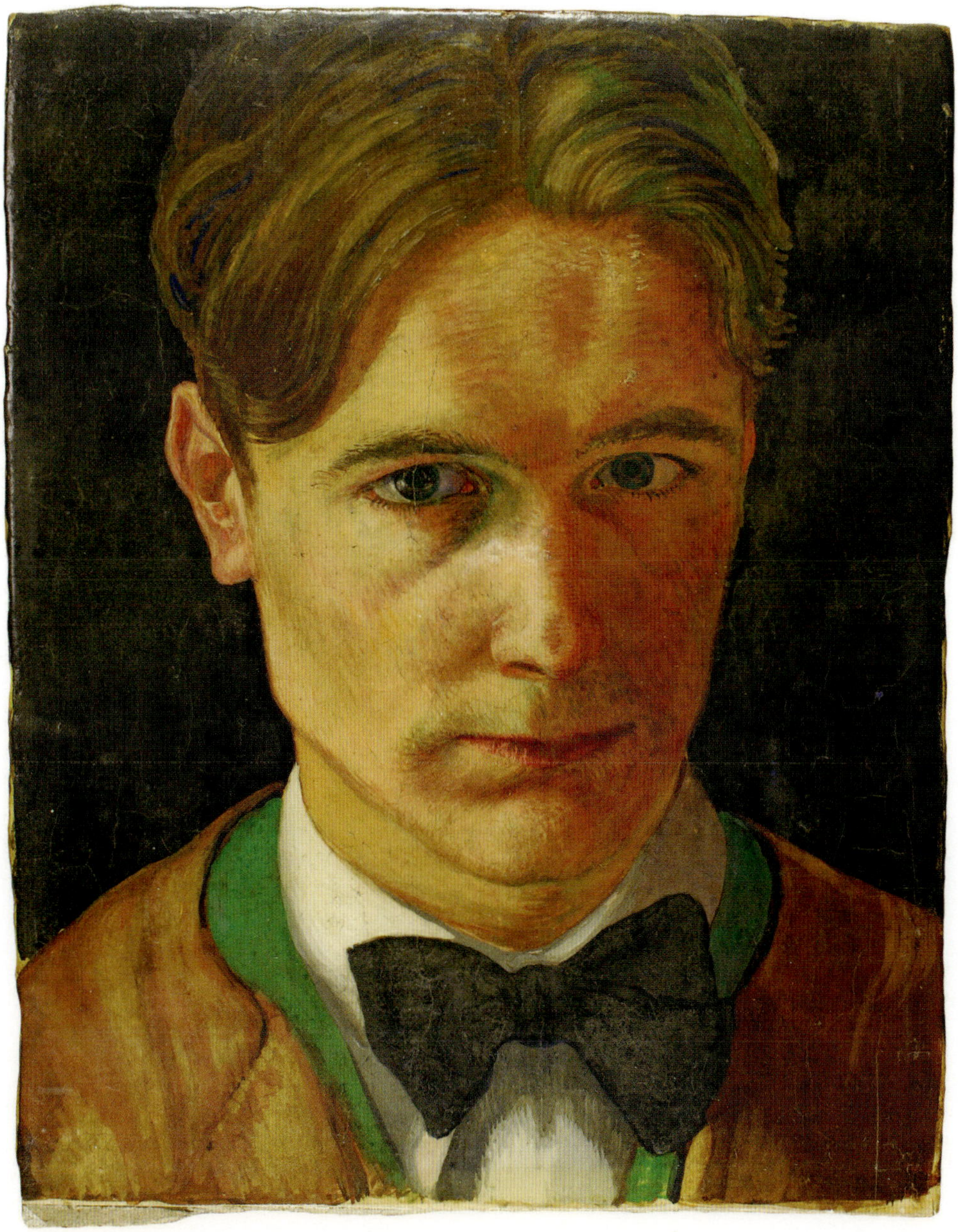

**263 Douglas Percy Bliss** (1900-1984), *Self-portrait*, 1923, tempera on stone tile, 10 x 8 in. (25.5 x 20.3 cm).

In 1923 Douglas Percy Bliss was midway through his painting diploma at The Royal College of Art. In December of that year he was elected editor of the student magazine, with Miss P. Dodd as secretary. Bliss and Dodd married in 1928. (**189**, **190**) This self-portrait was done in the class of Professor Tristram.

**262 Phyllis Dodd** (1899-1995), *Self-portrait*, 1925, signed and dated in pencil, inscribed 'self portrait', drypoint on paper, 9 x 8 ¾ in. (23 x 21.5 cm). Collection: The National Gallery of Ireland.

Phyllis Dodd received a Royal Exhibition Scholarship to attend the Royal College of Art (RCA) for four years, from 1921-25, alongside Henry Moore (1898-1986), Raymond Coxon (1896-1997) and Edna Ginesi (1902-2000). In 1924, having achieved her Painting Diploma in two years (rather than the usual three), she embarked on a scholarship course in etching and aquatint under Frank Short. Her confident self-portrait, dating to 1925, shows how well she mastered etching. Unfortunately, she produced no more prints after leaving college despite Short's advice that she should concentrate on etching portraits because she was so fluently skilled in these. It was good advice at the time, but after the Wall Street crash, interest in this medium collapsed and never really recovered.

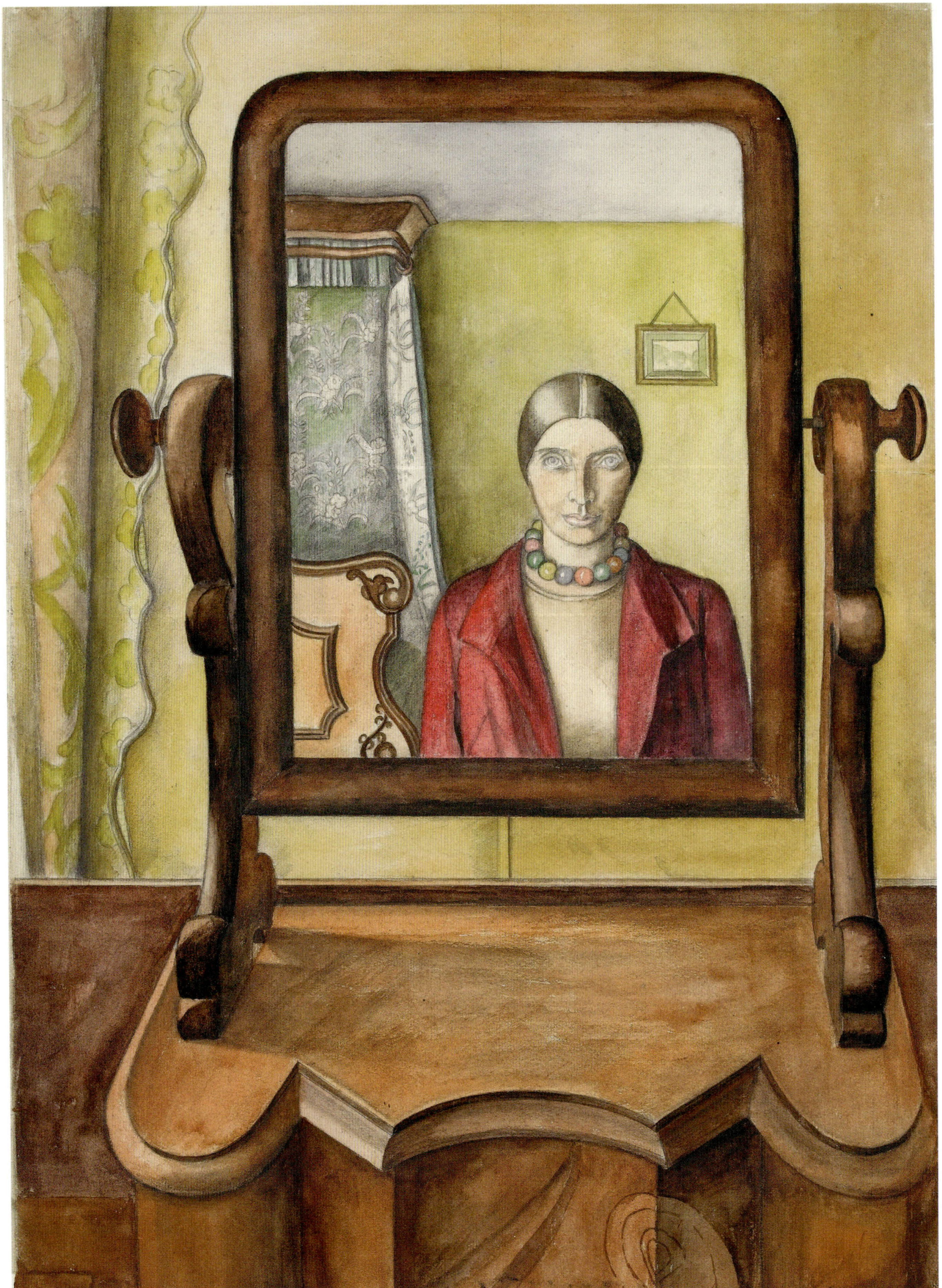

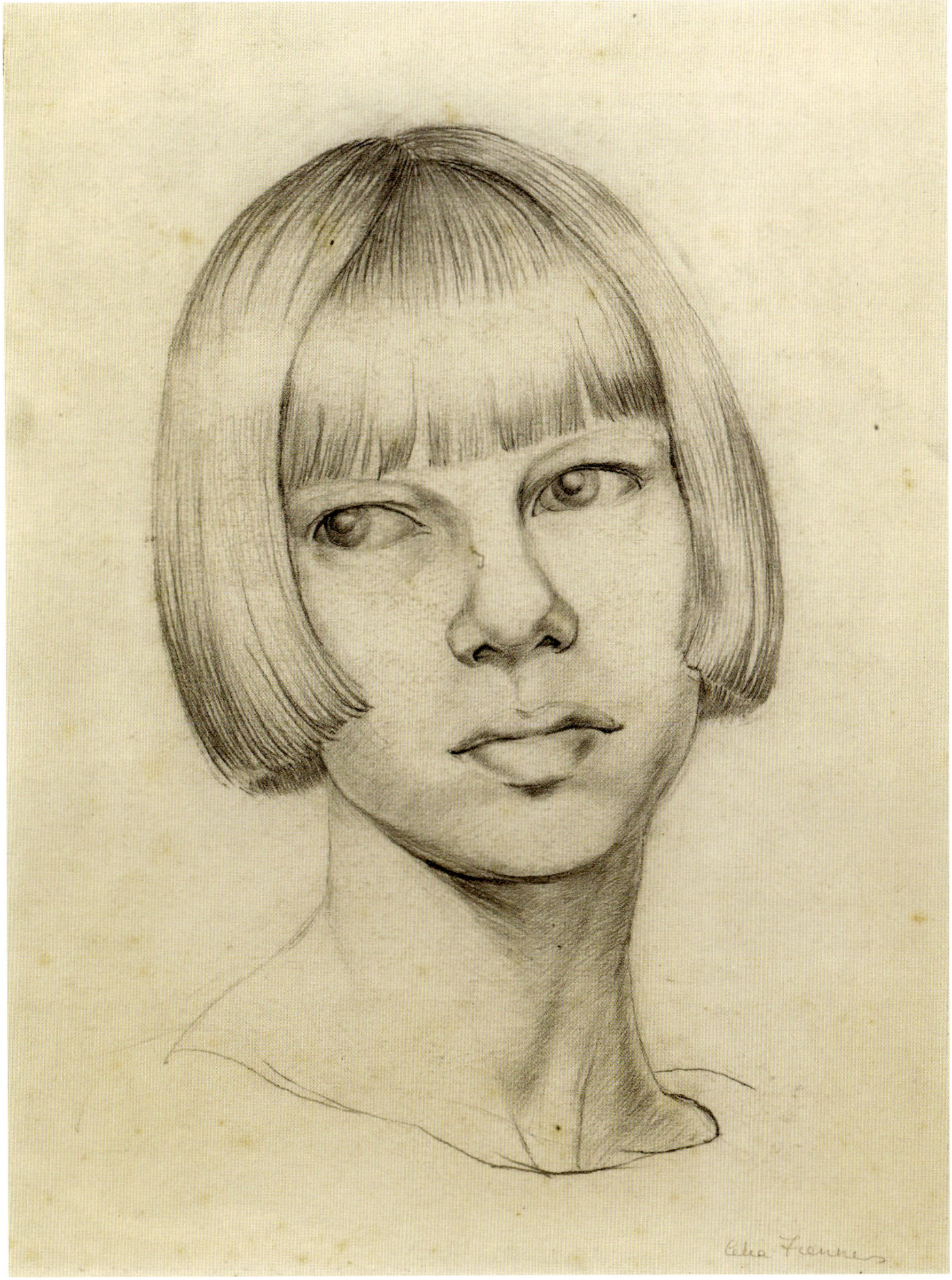


**265 Celia Fiennes** (1902-1998), *Self-portrait*, c.1925, signed,
pencil on paper, 10 x 8 ½ in. (25.5 x 20.4 cm).

This striking self-portrait by Celia Fiennes dates to her time at the Central School of Arts and Crafts, where she enrolled in 1924. Fiennes studied under Noel Rooke, whom she married in 1932. (**175**) Together they made a major contribution to the revival of wood engraving in Britain in the twentieth century.

**264 Rosalie Brill** (1903-1992), *Self-portrait*, late 1920s,
watercolour, on paper, 21 ¾ x 16 (55 x 40.5 cm).

Rosalie Brill, who had married the artist Reginald Brill (**212**) in 1925, accompanied him to Italy during his two year scholarship at The British School at Rome. A painting by Reginald Brill, *Young Woman in Rome*, 1930, shows the artist's wife wearing the same distinctive large beaded necklace.

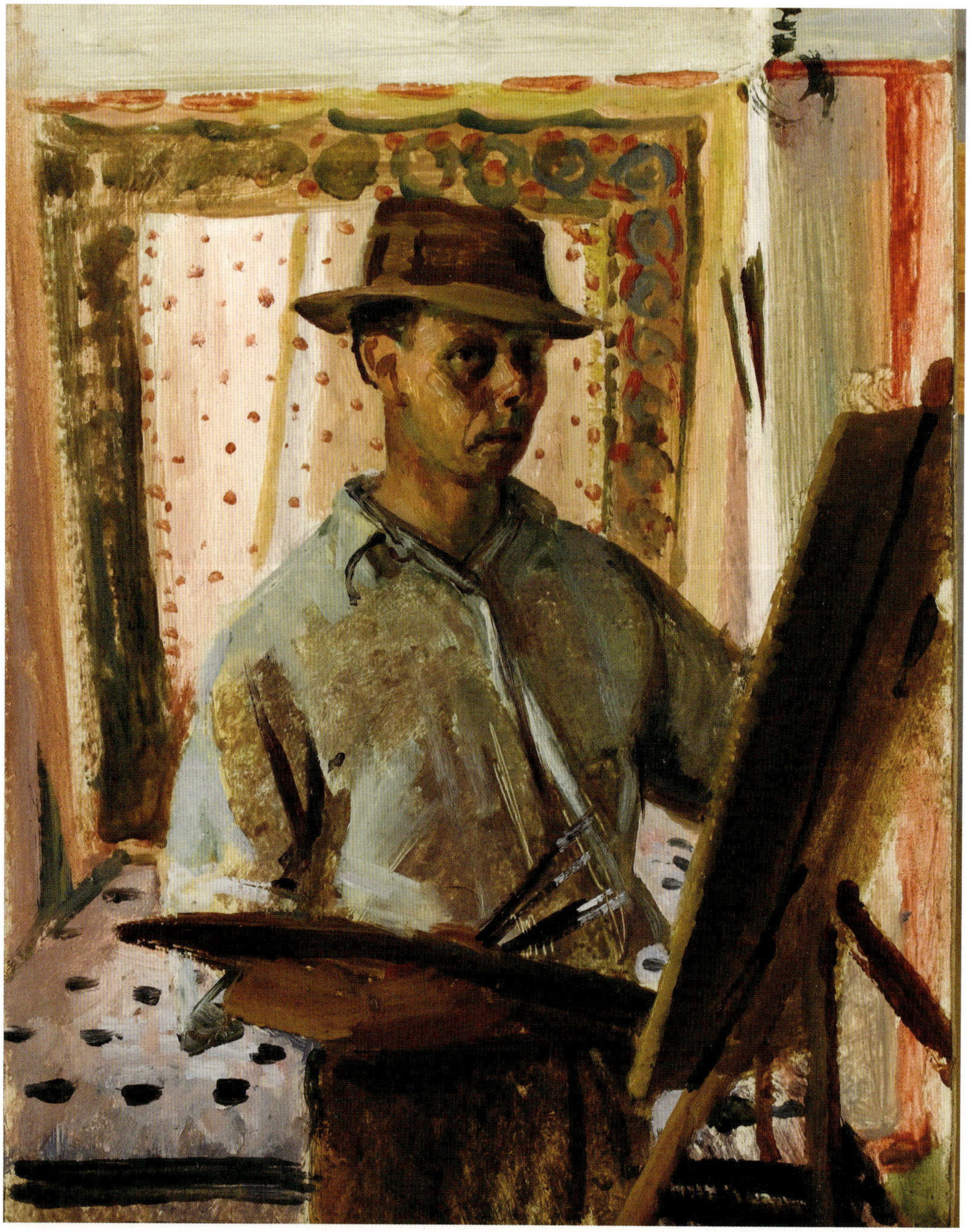

**266 Alan Sorrell** (1904-1974), *Self-portrait* (painted in 'the Vestry' at Thors Mead), c.1948, oil on board, 15 x 11 ¾ in. (38 x 30 cm).

In its bright palette this self-portrait, dating to Sorrell's second marriage, strikes an unusually optimistic note. Setting up his new home in a disused chapel at Daws Heath, Essex, Sorrell created an ideal studio, relishing the north-south orientation of the large hall, with its small Vestry attached at the far end.

**267 Alan Sorrell** (1904-1974), *Self-portrait*, 1928, signed and dated '1928 Nov.', pencil, ink and white gouache on paper, 21 ¾ x 14 ½ in. (55.2 x 37 cm).

Sorrell undertook this self-portrait one month after he had arrived in Rome on his two-year scholarship. He portrays himself in his studio at the British School at Rome; the intensely observed and sharply delineated drawing demonstrates his appreciation of Renaissance masters such as Masaccio and Piero della Francesca. Sorrell's presentation is introspective and melancholic, reflecting the tone of the diaries he wrote during these early days in Rome. (**360**)

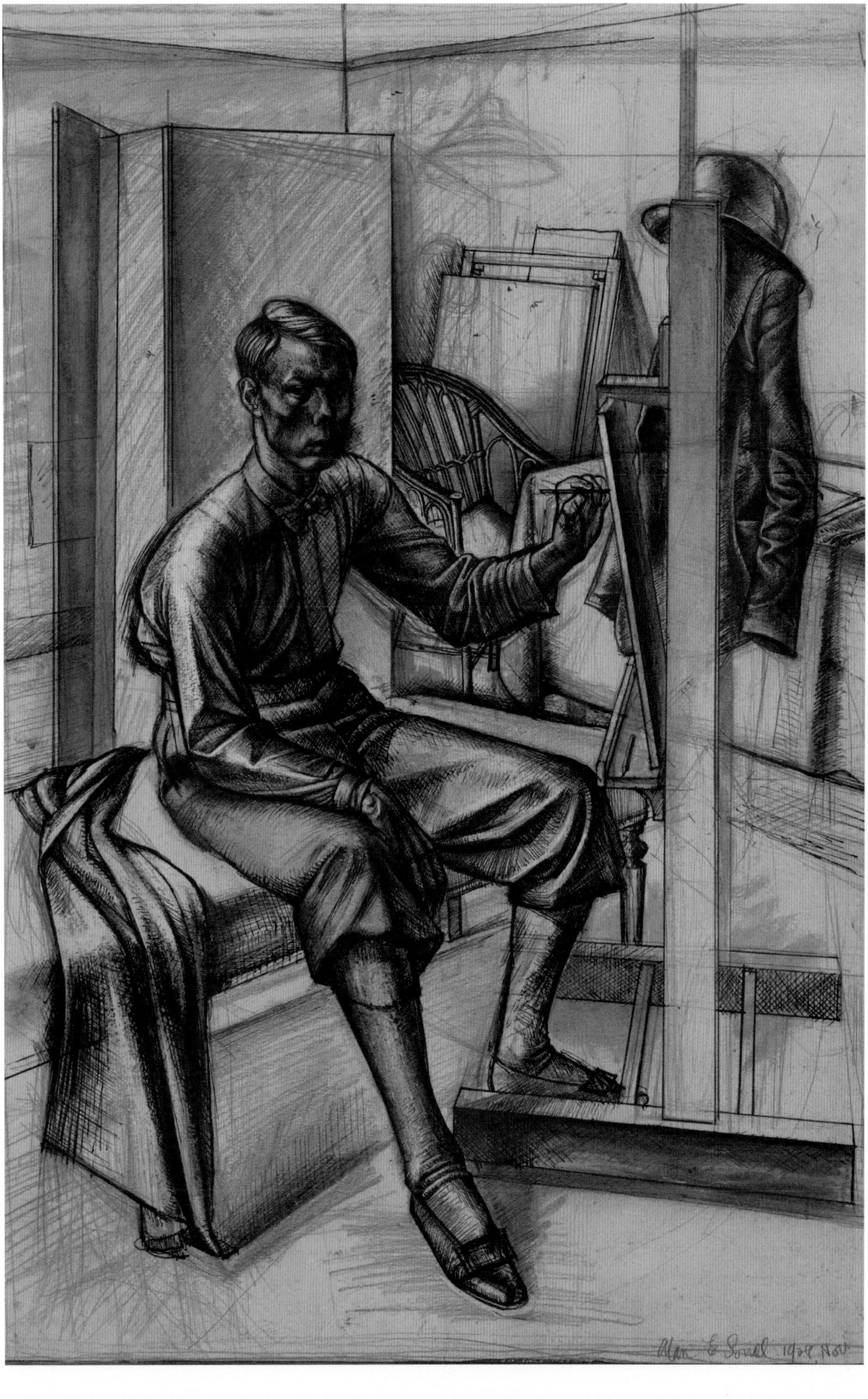

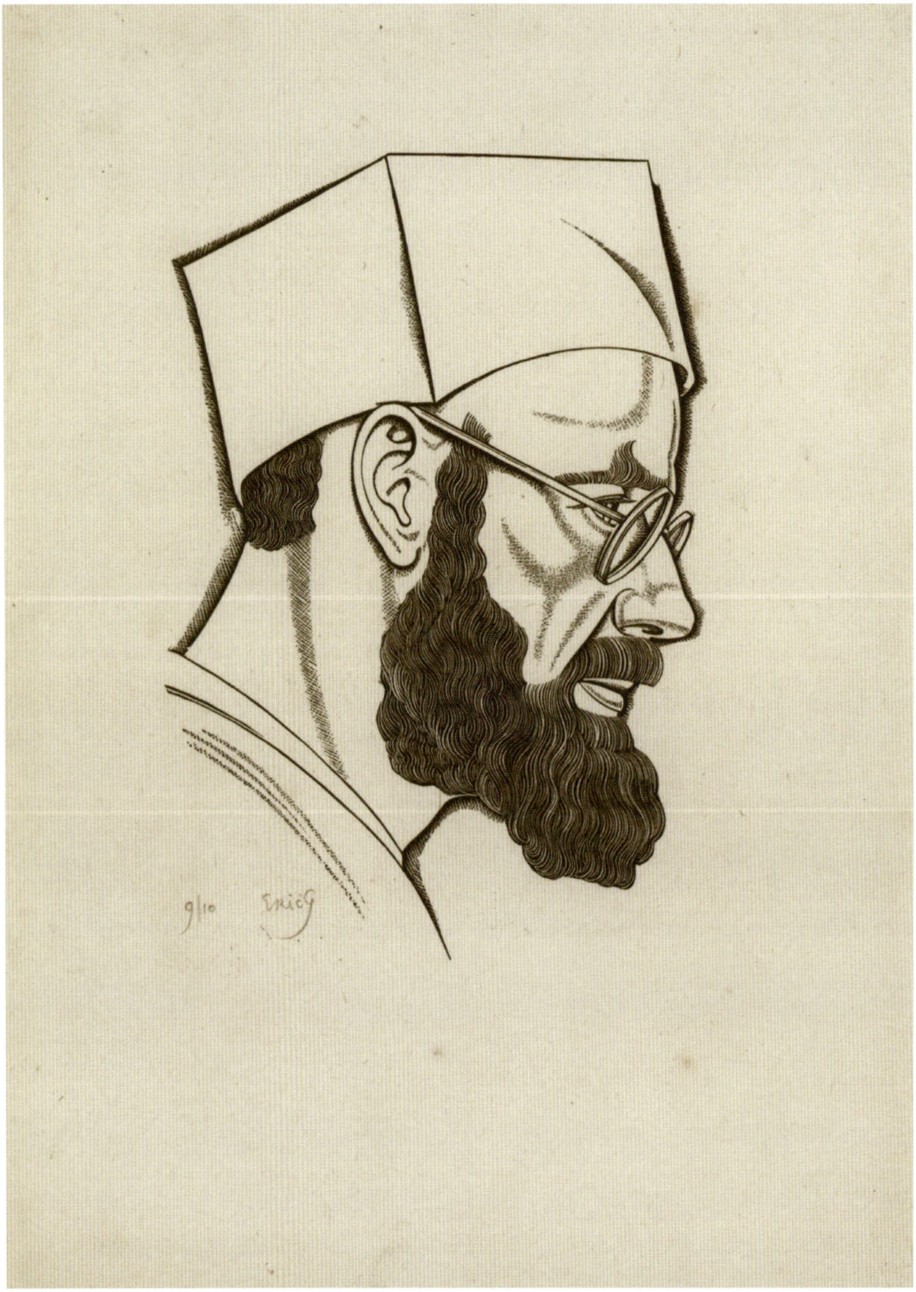

**268 Eric Gill** (1882-1940), *Self-portrait* (Physick 497), 1927, signed and numbered 9/10, wood engraving 11 ½ x 8 ¼ in. (29.2 x 20.9 cm).

This wood engraving, based on a drawing of the same date, was used as a frontispiece to *Engravings by Eric Gill*, printed by the Fanfare Press, London in 1929. Gill is wearing a version of the paper hat traditionally worn by stone masons. Produced in 1927 and limited to ten impressions, one from the same edition is in the collection of Tate Britain. An edition of 400 (unsigned) prints were also issued. (**131**, **132**, **133**)

**269 Hamish C. Paterson** (1890-1955), *Self portrait, Night*, 1910s, charcoal with highlights in white on brown paper, 9 x 7 in. (22.7 x 17.8 cm).

Many artists, especially within the Northern European tradition – most famously Rembrandt, Reynolds and Joseph Wright of Derby – experimented with painting in artificial light, relishing the challenge of capturing different light effects, such as those created by candlelight.

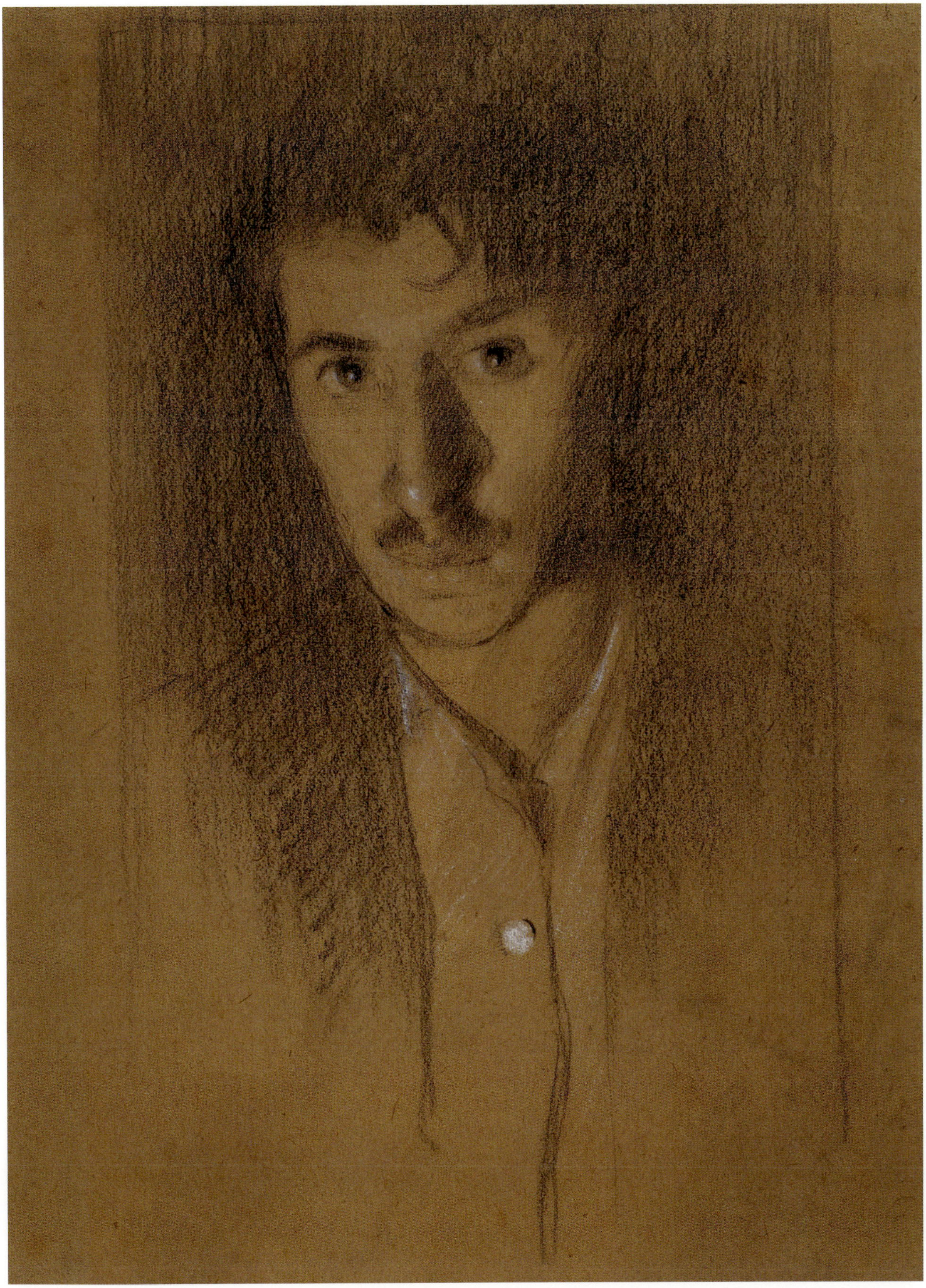

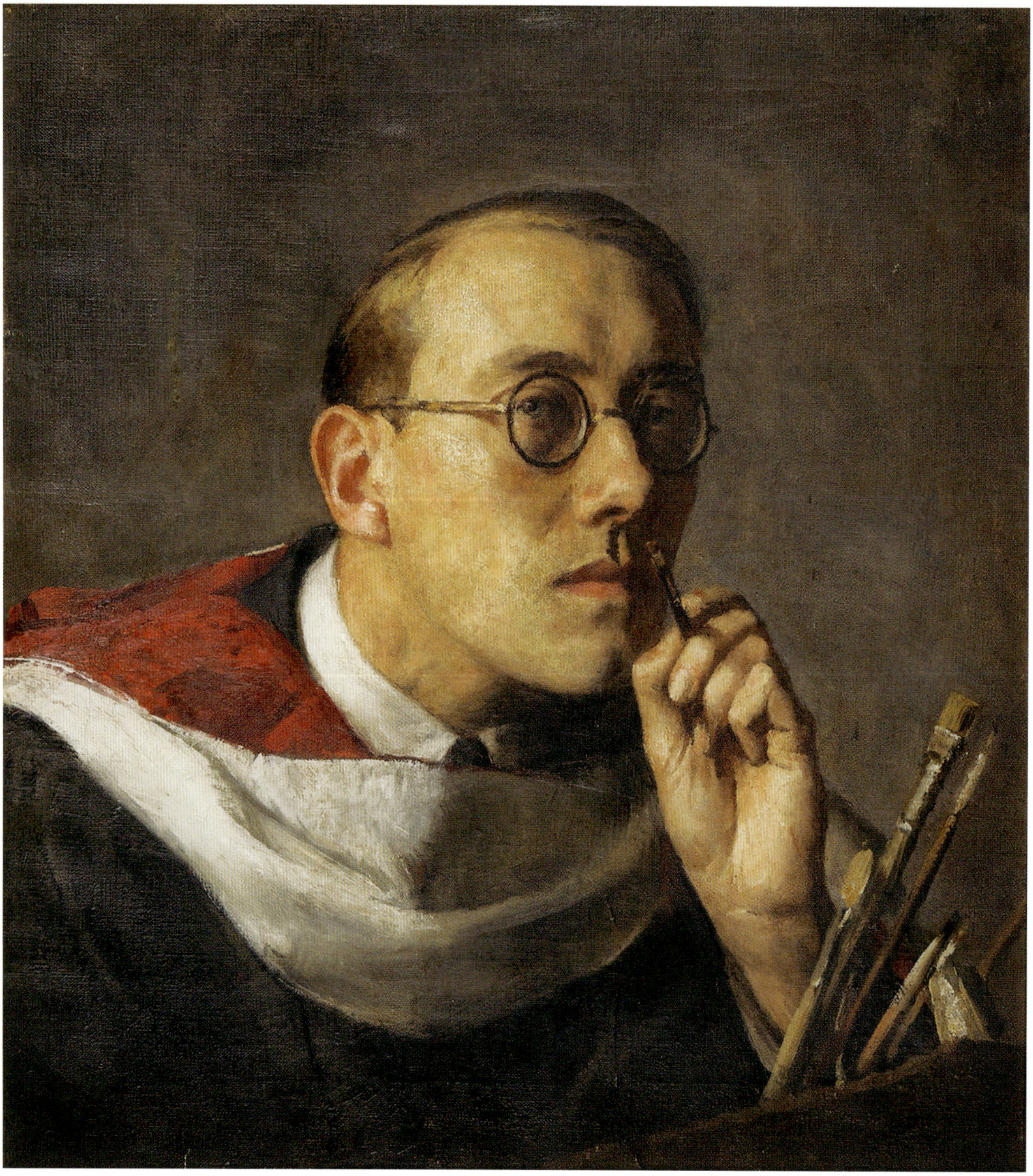

270

**Victor Hume Moody** (1896-1990),

**270** *Self-portrait, 1929*, oil on canvas, 20 1/8 x 18 1/8 in. (51.3 x 46.2 cm).
Diploma portrait painted at the end of his studies at the Royal College of Art.

**271** *Self-portrait*, mid-1930s, oil on canvas, 20 x 18 in. (50.8 x 45.7 cm).

**272** *Self-portrait*, c.1930, oil on canvas, 17 x 16 in. (43.2 x 40.6 cm).

'Self-portrait, 1929' was Victor Moody's diploma portrait, painted at the end of his studies at the Royal College of Art. In addition to his brutally honest self-portraiture, Moody also painted George Bernard Shaw, J.B.Priestley and Ernest Thesiger.

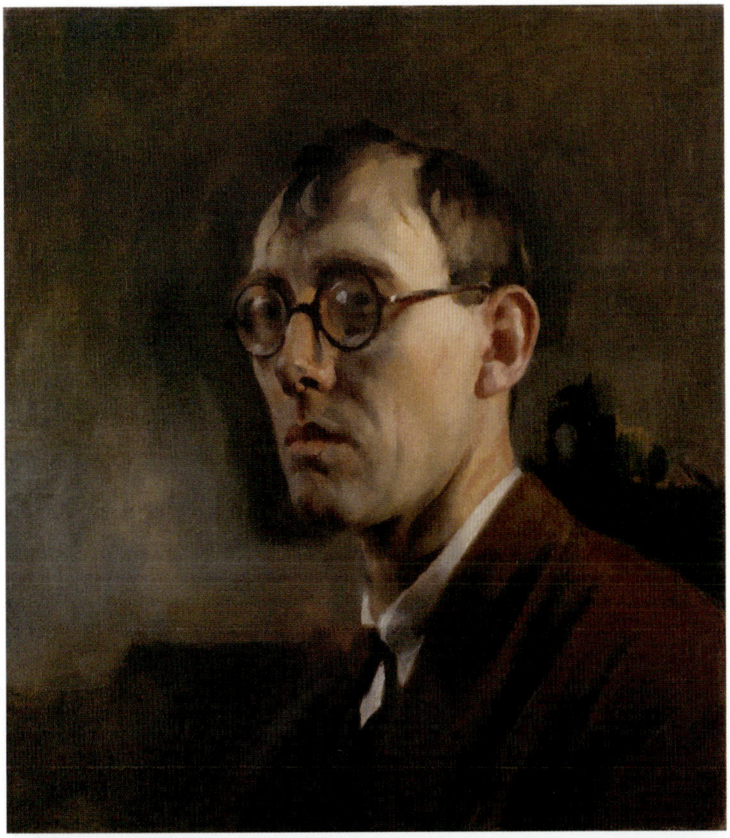

271

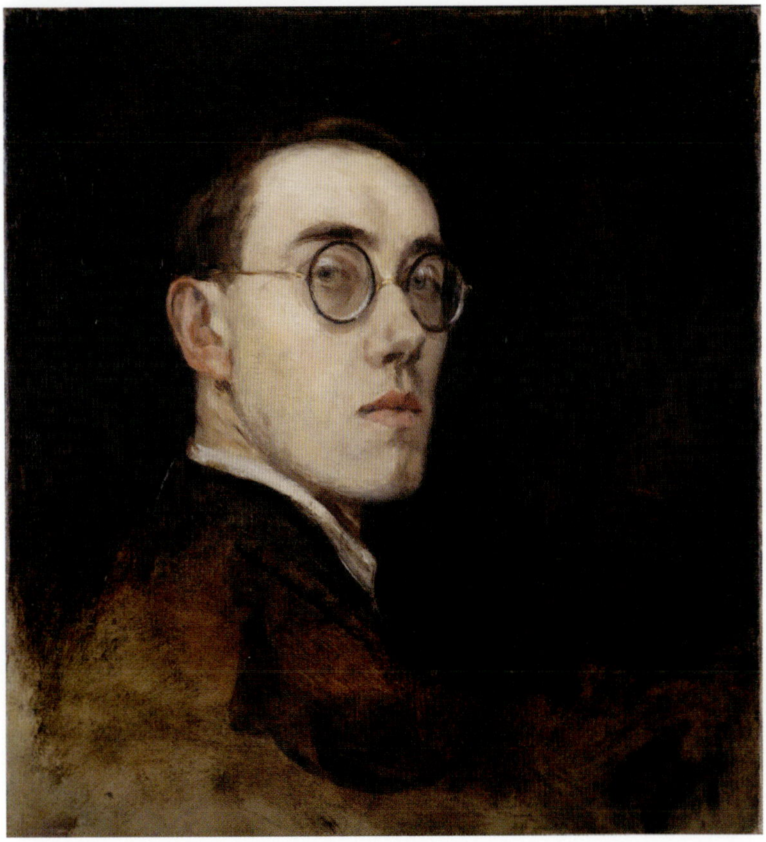

272

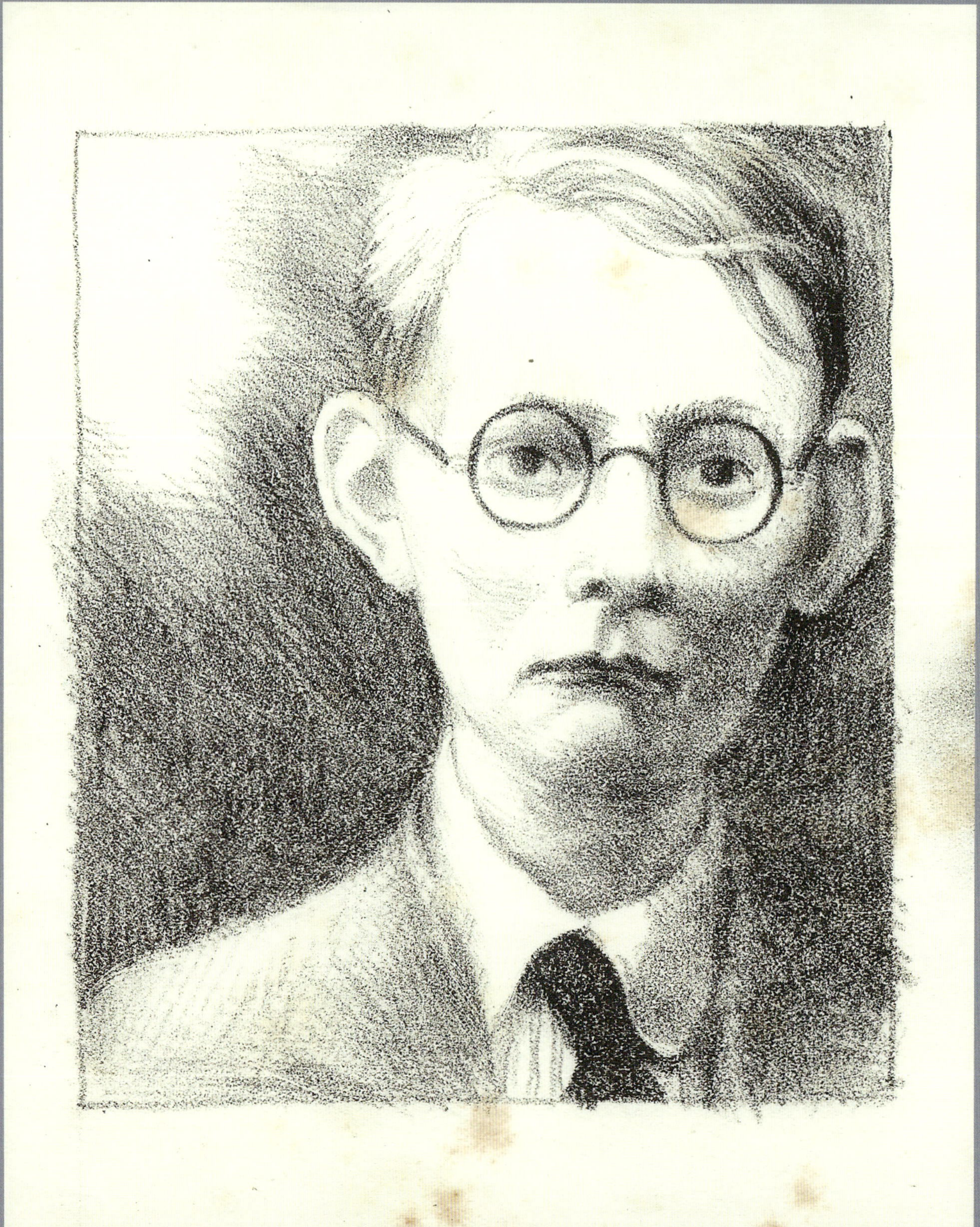

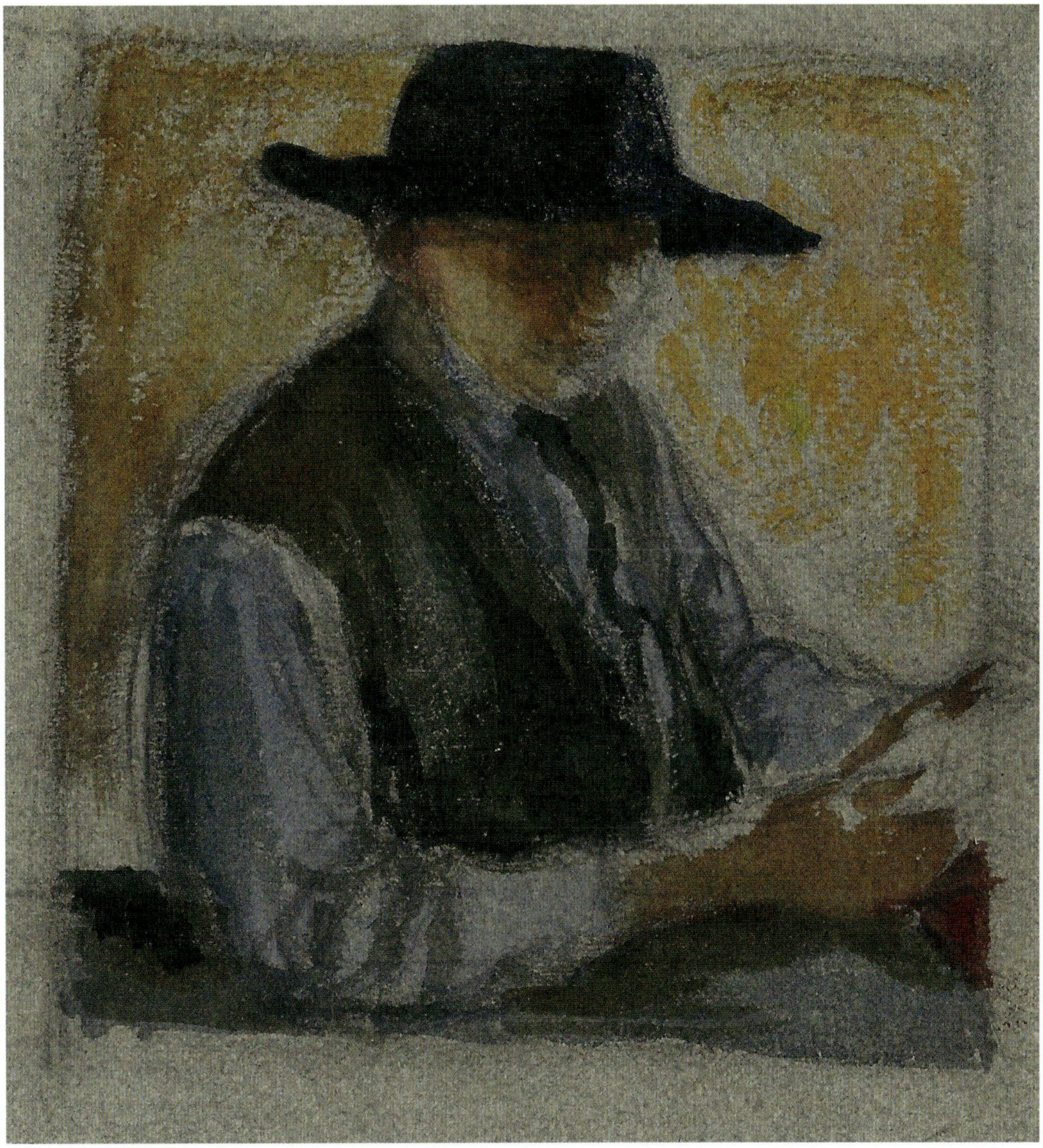

**274 Francis Spear** (1902-1979), *Self-portrait in a Large Brimmed Black Hat*, c.1930, watercolour on grey paper, 4 ¼ x 4 in. (10.8 x 10.2 cm).

**273 Francis Spear** (1902-1979), *Self-portrait with Round Spectacles*, mid-1920s, lithograph, unique proof, 7 ½ x 5 ¾ in. (19 x 14.1 cm).

In the mid-1920s Francis Spear was a member of a group of artists who owned their own lithographic press. They used to meet regularly in Howland St, Fitzrovia, near the Central School. Spear started teaching lithography at the Royal College of Art in 1929.

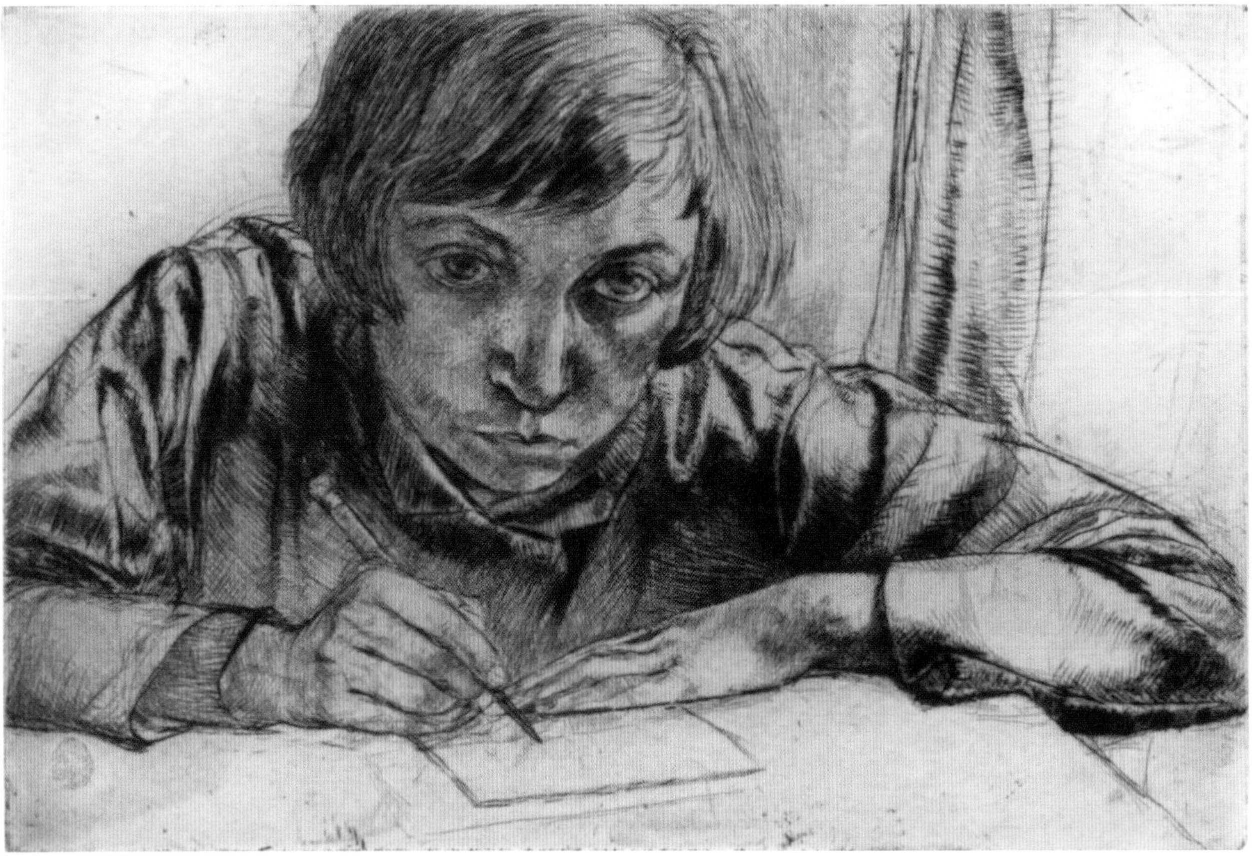

**275 Evelyn Gibbs** (1905-1991), *Self-portrait,* 1927, numbered in pencil, blind stamp lower right, dry point, 3 ¾ x 5 in. (8.6 x 12.7 cm); edition of 60 printed posthumously by the executor of the artist's estate.

Evelyn Gibbs' *Self-portrait*, made whilst at the Royal College of Art in 1927, a year before she applied for and won the coveted Rome Scholarship in Engraving, has much in common with, and might have been inspired by, Henry Fuseli's *Self-portrait* of 1770. Gibbs shows herself in the process of producing a drypoint, the blank copper etching plate on which she is working soon to become the self-portrait we are looking at. Gibbs appears as one of the models in Alan Sorrell's 1928 composition *People Seeking After Wisdom*. (**351**)

**276 Stanley Lewis** (1905-2009), *Self-portrait*, c.1930, black chalk with white highlights on buff paper, 6 x 6 ¾ in. (15.5 x 17.2 cm).

Stanley Lewis never travelled anywhere without his sketchbook to hand: 'I want to paint life; life everywhere, rather than death – an artist must have a theme; a trick I've enjoyed every minute of it with a pencil in my hand or a brush. Look at Dürer – he never left the house without a sketchbook, recording a broken wall, a tree, a figure walking….' (**359**)

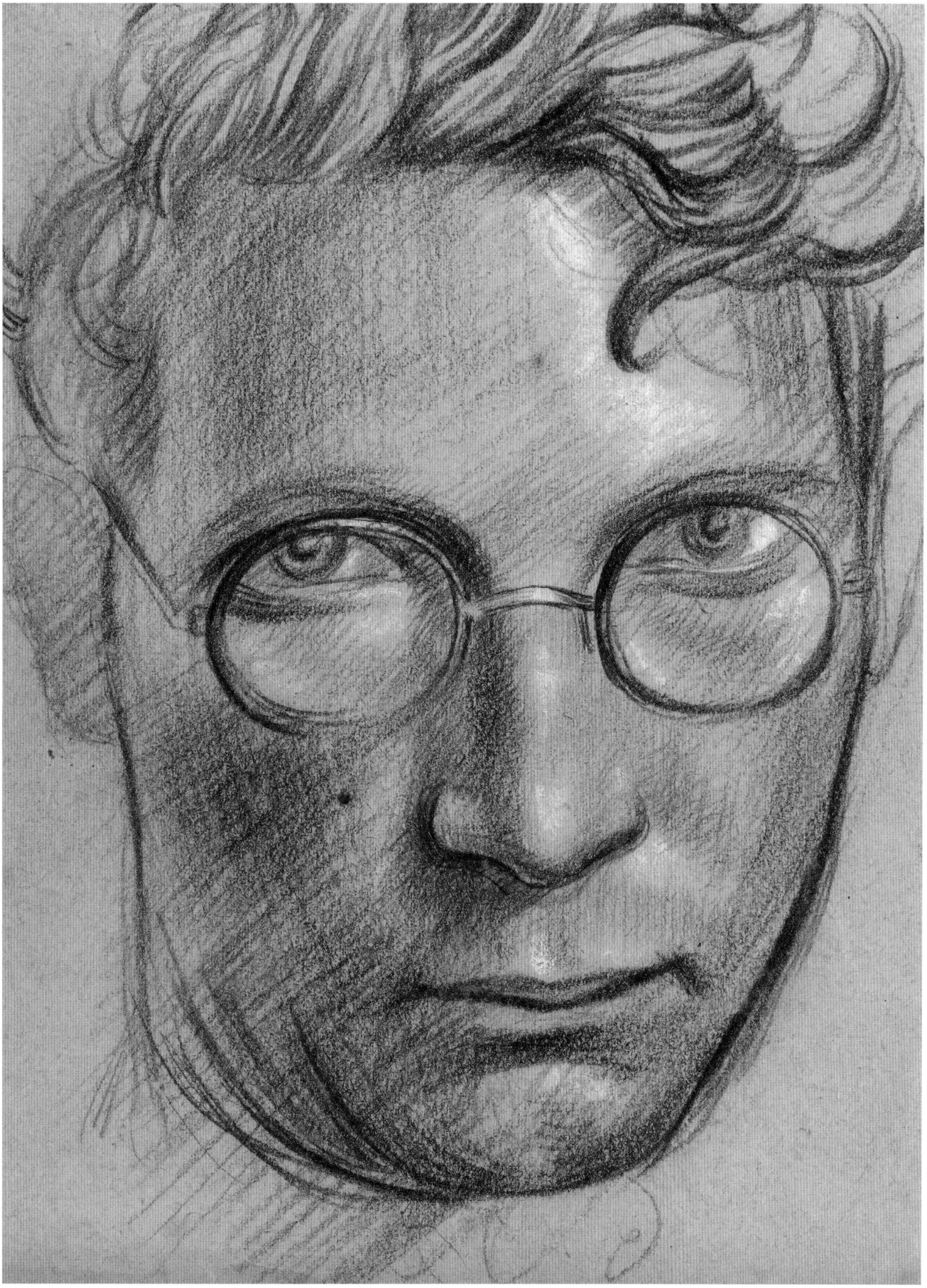

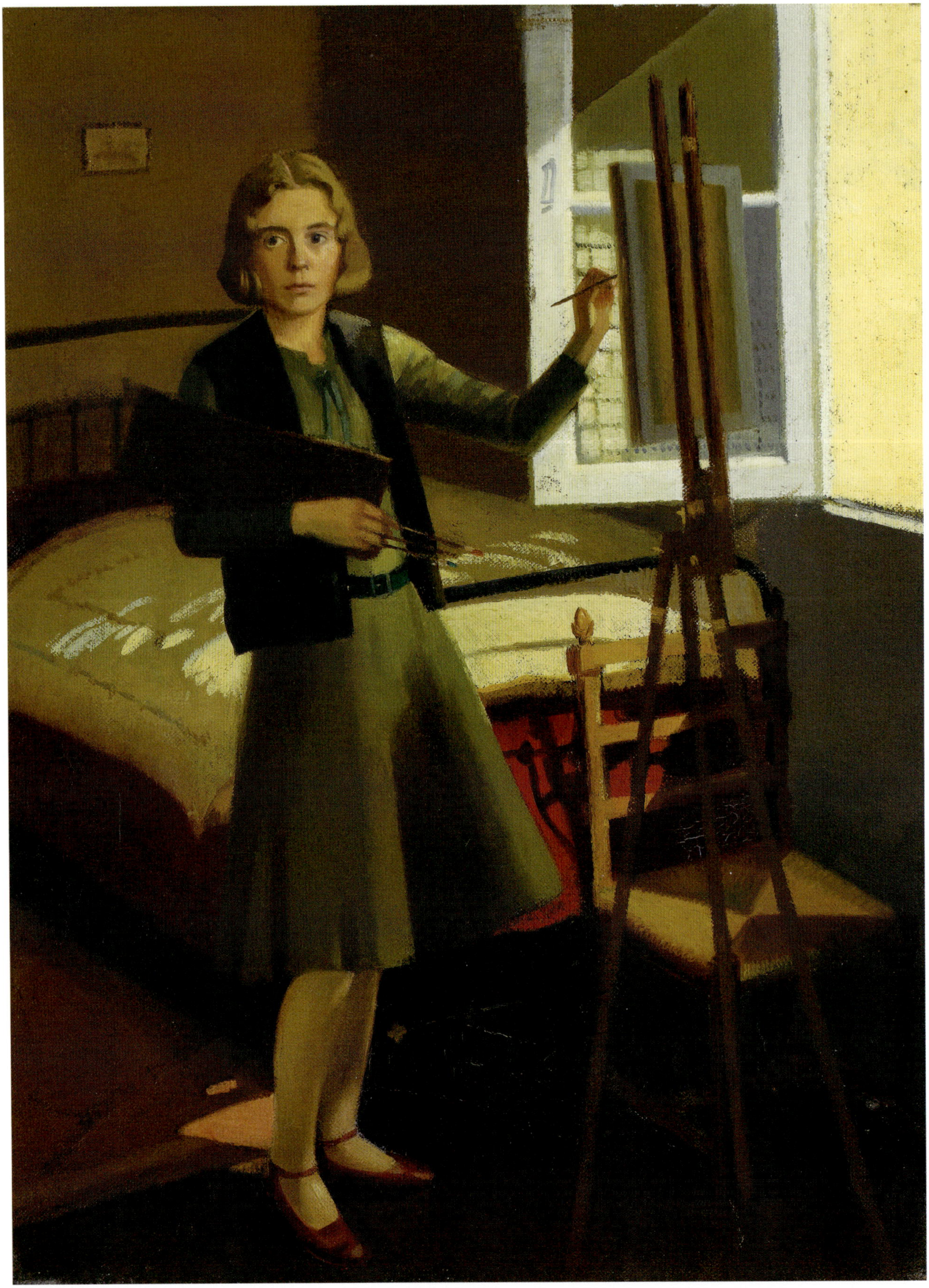

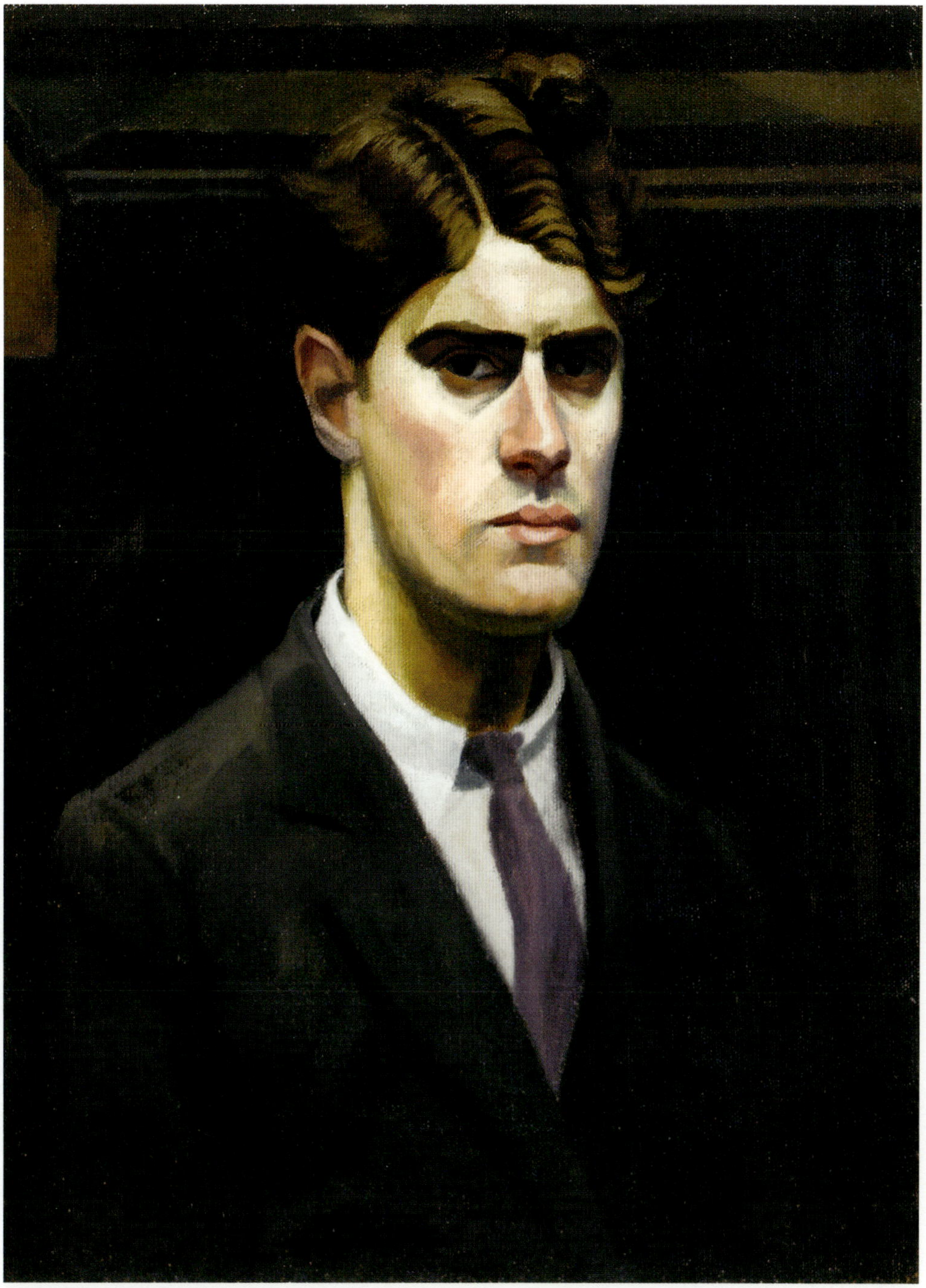

**278 Richard Carline** (1896-1980), *Self-portrait*, 1923, signed and dated, oil on canvas, 24 x 17 in. (61 x 43 cm).

This self-portrait shows Richard Carline aged 27. In the same year Stanley Spencer painted Carline's portrait and two years later, in 1925, Spencer married Carline's sister Hilda. An earlier self-portrait aged 22 (*Self-portrait in Uniform*) is in the collection of The Imperial War Museum.

**277 Audrey Weber** (1898-1981), *The Artist Painting in her Studio* (possibly a self-portrait), mid-1920s, oil on canvas, 15 ¾ x 11 ½ in. (40 x 29.5 cm).

The setting appears to be a French interior. Weber was painting possibly while travelling in the south of France, her bedroom turned into an impromptu studio.

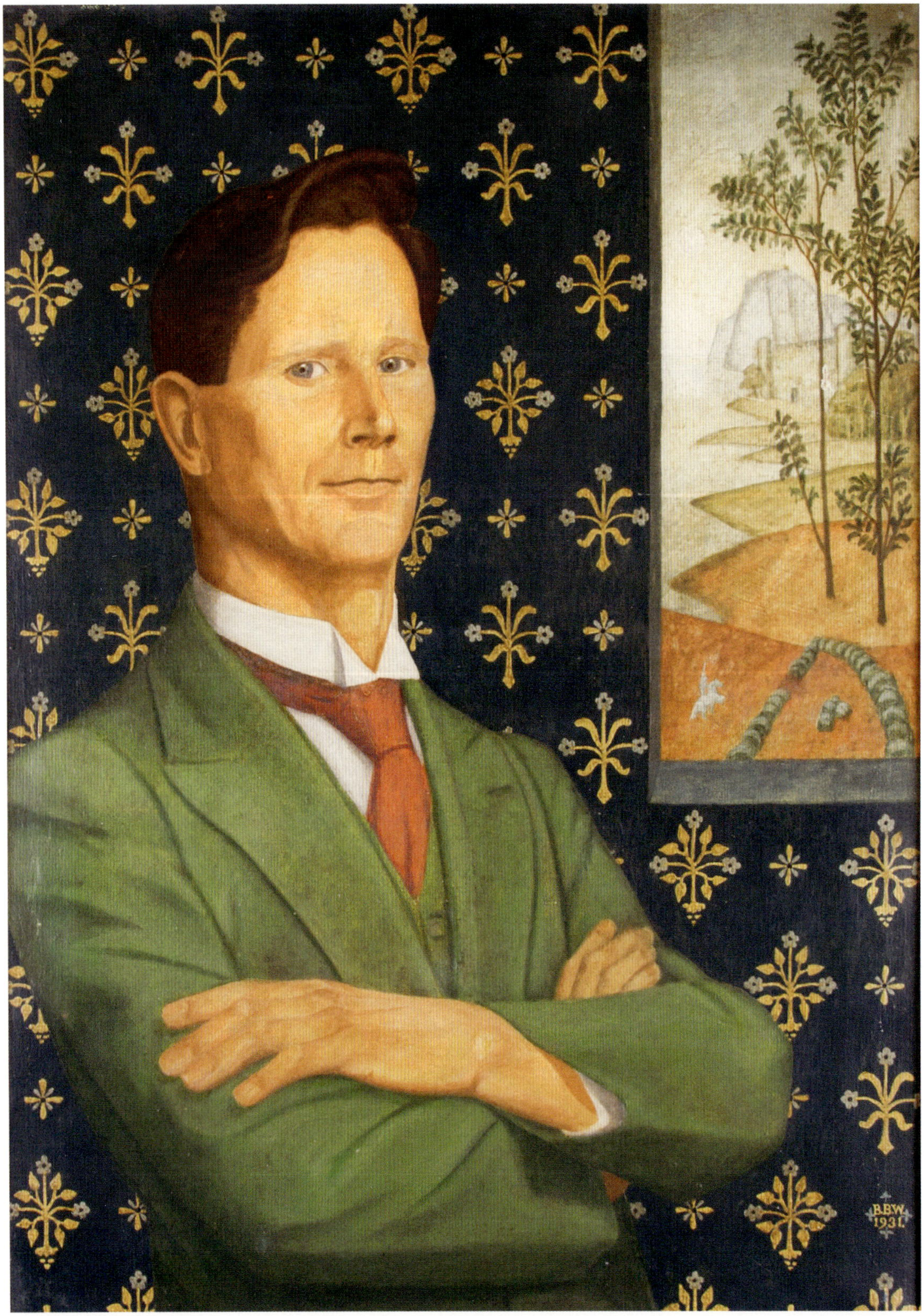


**279 Bernard Blane Withey** (1895-1976), *Self-portrait*, 1931, signed with initials and dated, oil on canvas, 29 ¾ x 21 ¾ in. (75.5 x 55 cm).

In this self- portrait the artist wears an artfully-contrived version of fashionable dress which is conventional, even conservative in style, but that employs unusual, eye-catching colours, suggesting that he is a man of aesthetic inclinations and singular taste.

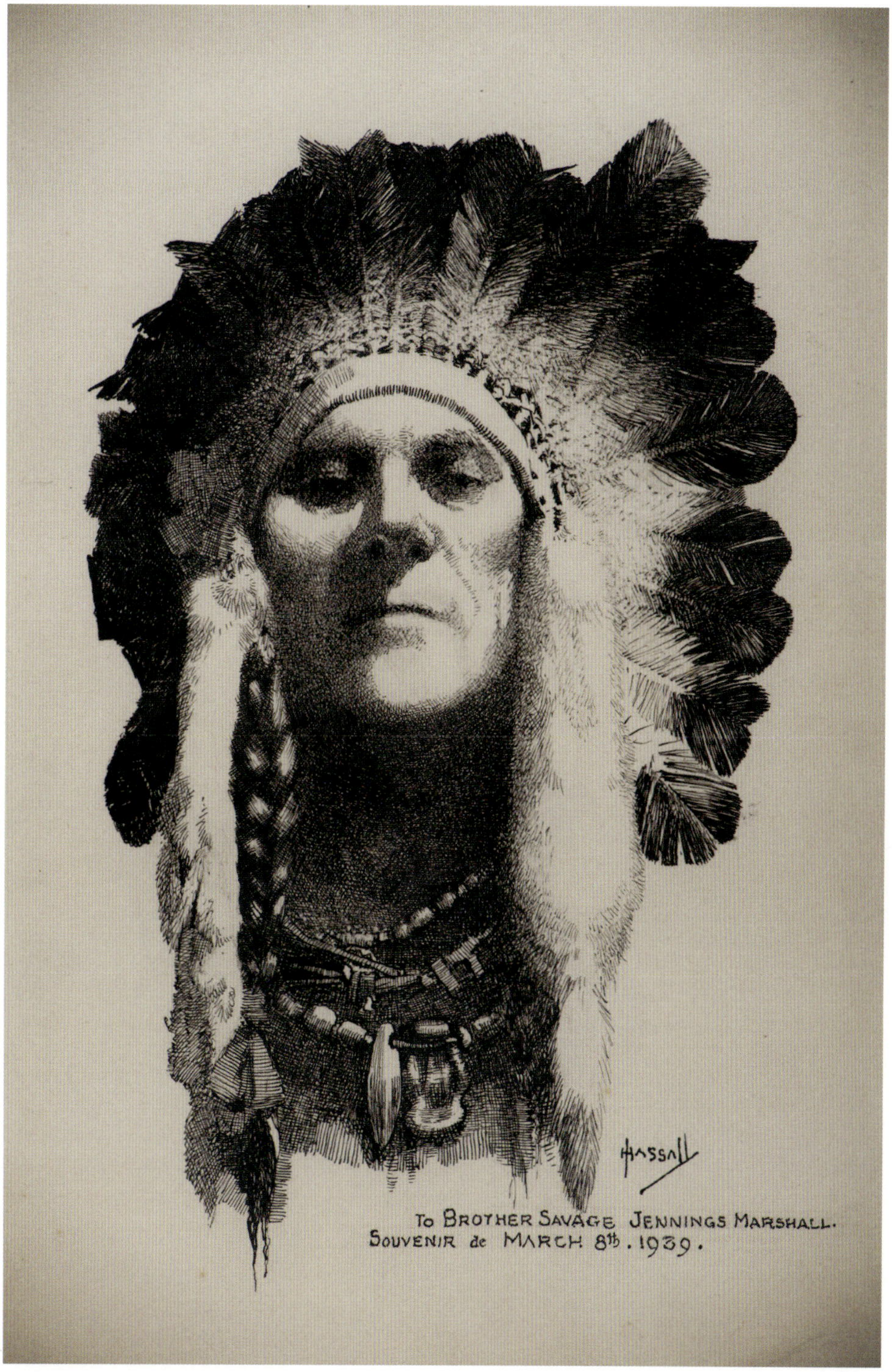


**280** **John Hassall** (1868-1948), *Self-portrait with Indian Headdress*, 8 March 1939,
signed, inscribed 'To Brother Savage Jennings Marshall. Souvenir de March 8th. 1939.
pen and ink on Whatman Drawing board, 15 x 10 ½ in. (38.2 x 26.2 cm).

A keen member of London gentlemen's clubs, John Hassall wore an Indian head-dress for Savage Club events and at the Sketch Club Ball. This self-portrait drawing was part of a tribute given by members of The Savage Club to the baritone Georges Baker (1885-1976), who was the honorary secretary and trustee of the club. (**202**, **203**, **204**, **205**, **206**, **207**, **208**)

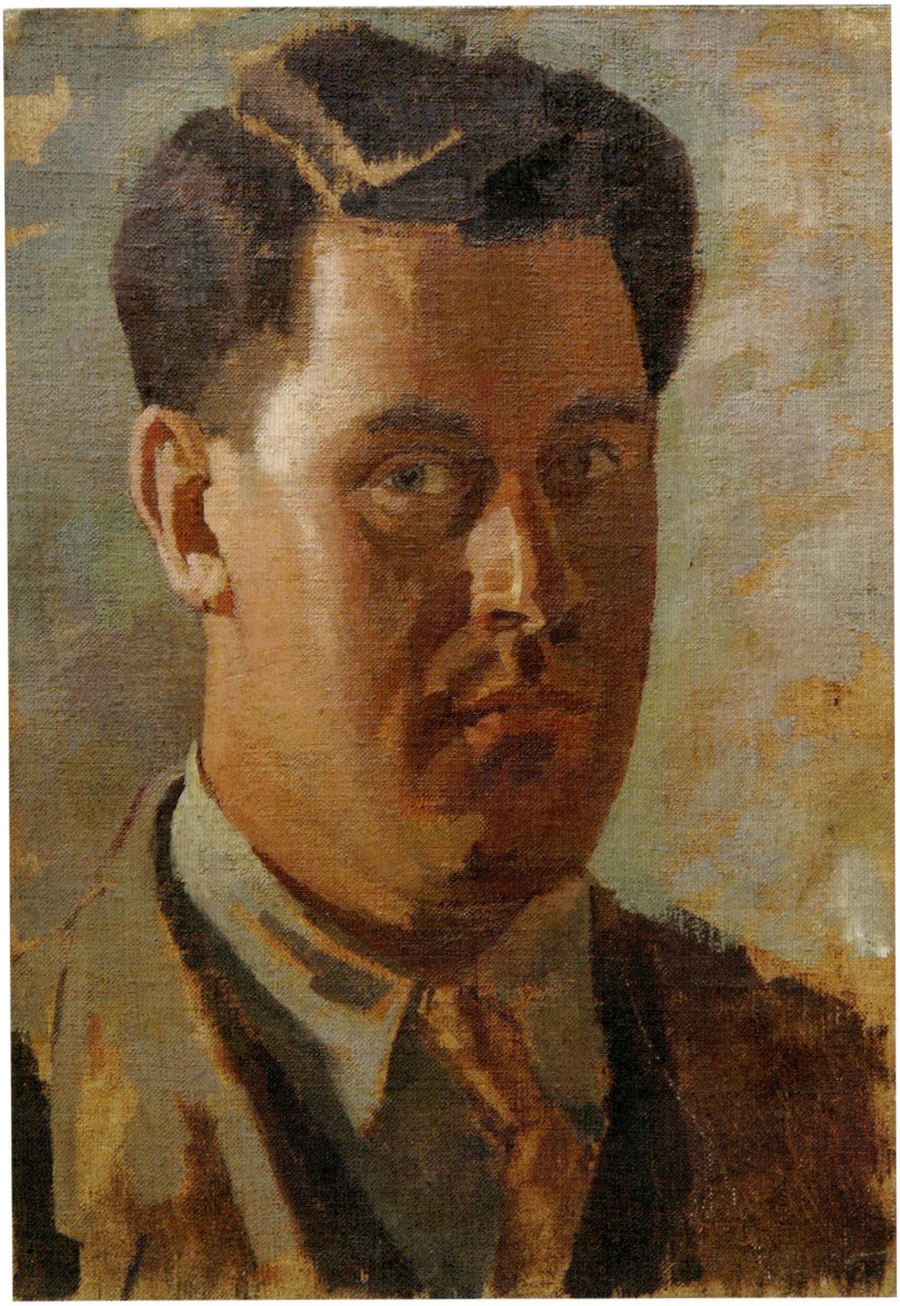

**281** **Percy Horton** (1897-1970), *Self-portrait*, c.1925, signed with studio stamp to canvas reverse (4/6), oil on Reeves Artists Canvas Board, 14 x 10 in. (35.5 x 25 cm).

This portrait dates to Percy Horton's final training at the Royal College of Art, where he was awarded a solo Royal Exhibition and ARCA Diploma with Distinction in Painting, together with the RCA Drawing Prize for 1924. His contemporaries at the College included Henry Moore, Edward Bawden, Eric Ravilious and Barnett Freedman. (**168**)

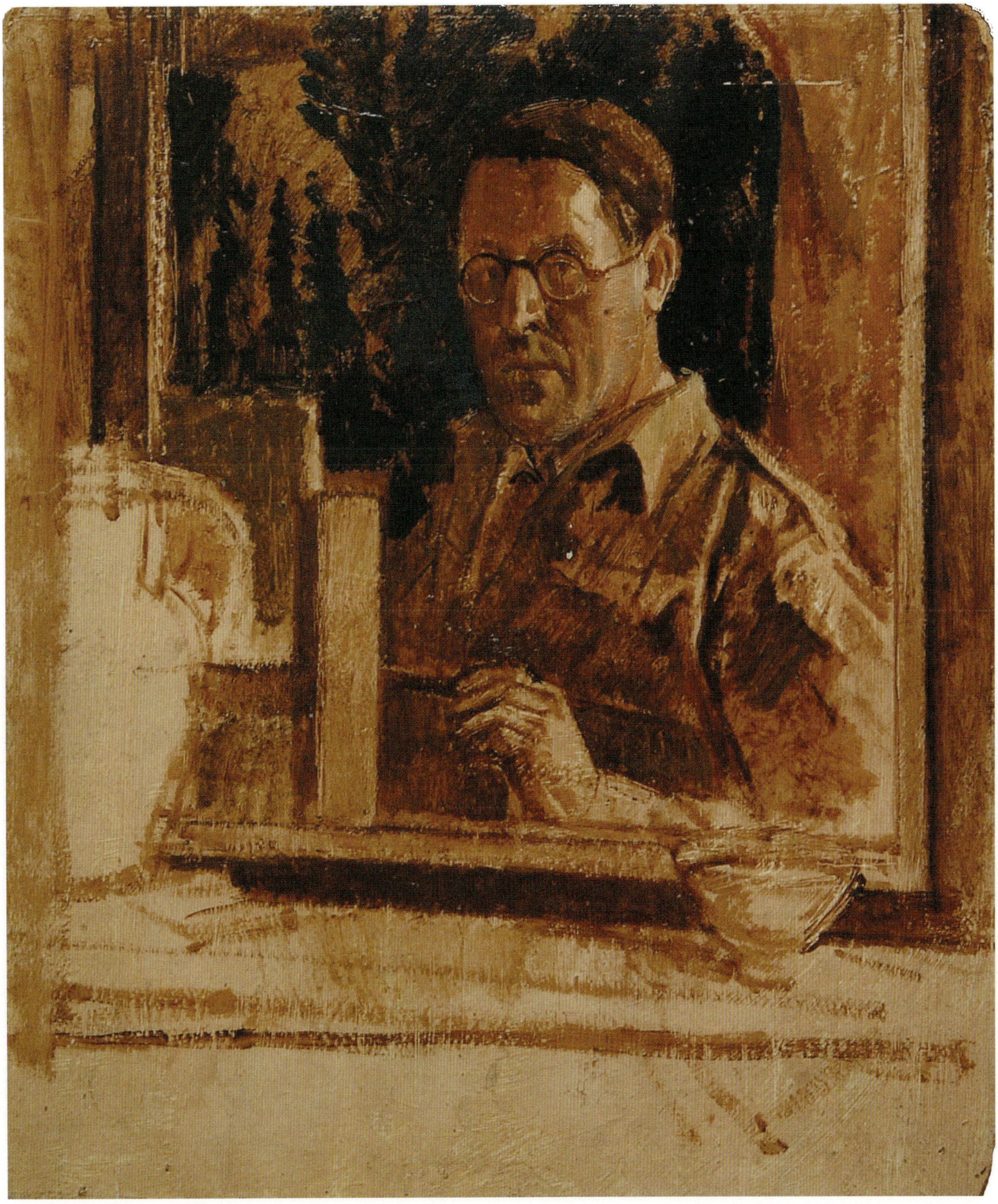

**282** **Percy Horton** (1897-1970), *Self-portrait at Easel*, c.1940, signed with studio stamp on reverse (4/7), oil on board, 15 x 12 ½ in. (38 x 32 cm).

In 1930 Horton was invited by Sir William Rothenstein to join the staff at the Royal College of Art. He remained there for 19 years, instructing in the Painting School. This portrait dates to 1940, when the RCA was evacuated to Ambleside. During this period Horton received a number of short-term commissions from the War Artists' Advisory Committee to paint portraits of Civil Defence staff and civilian factory workers.

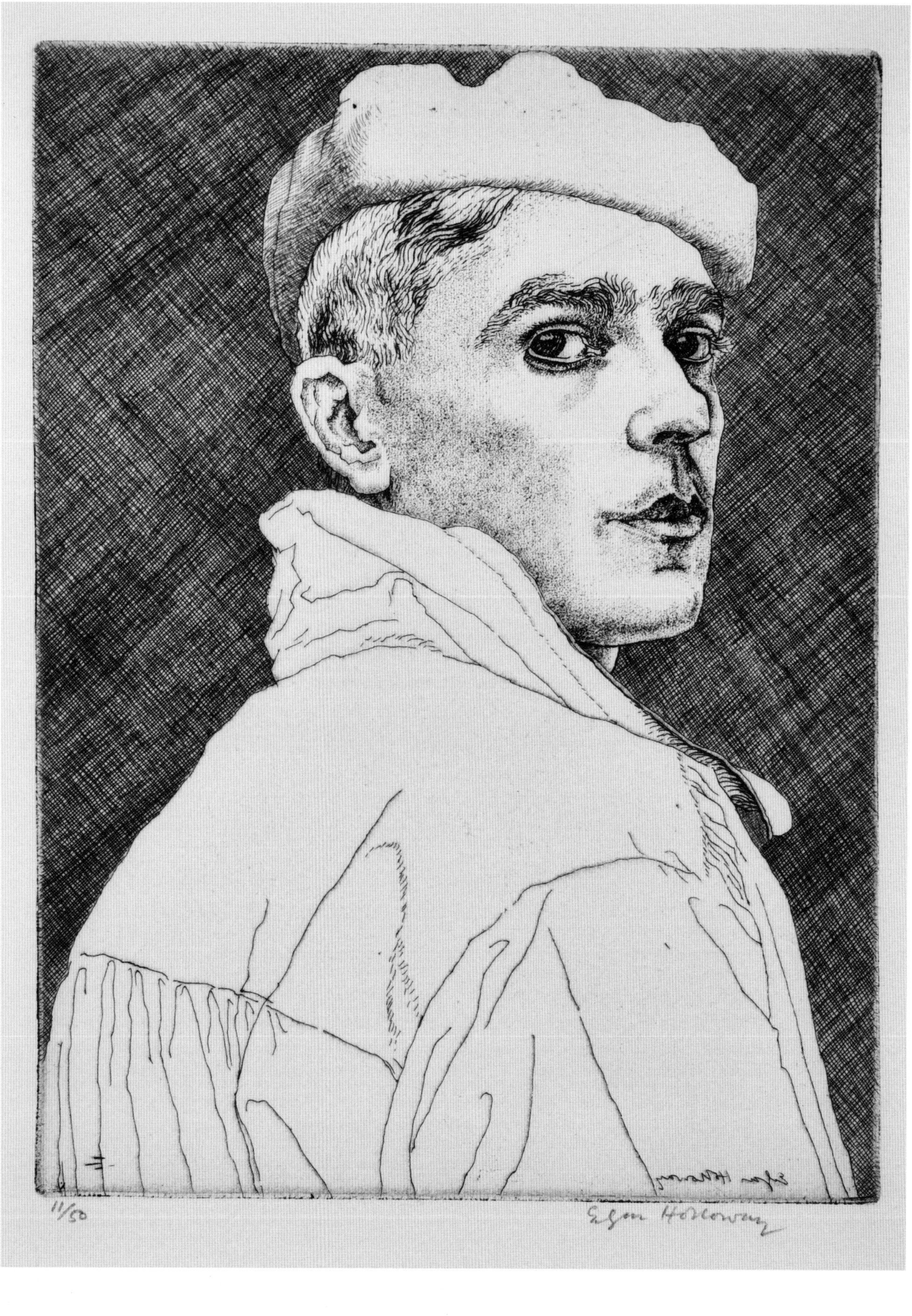


283

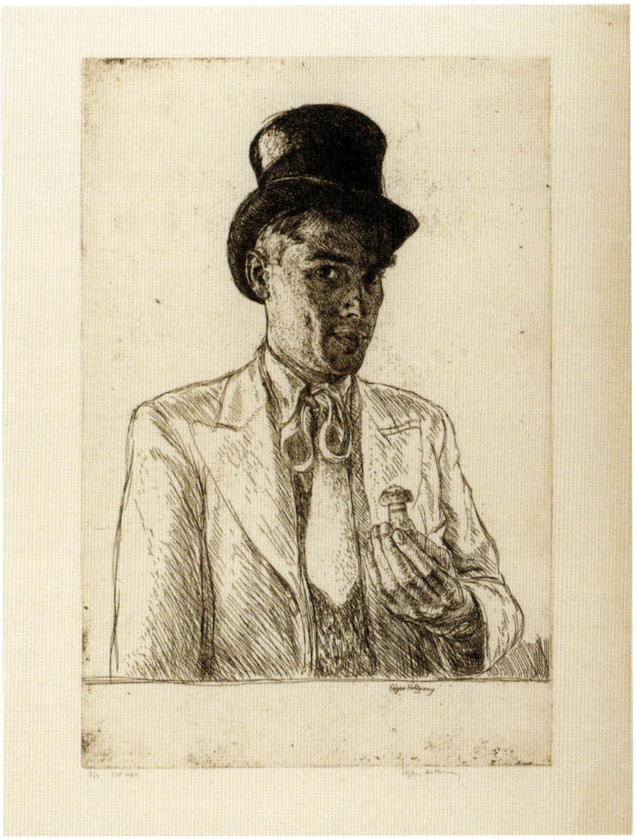

284

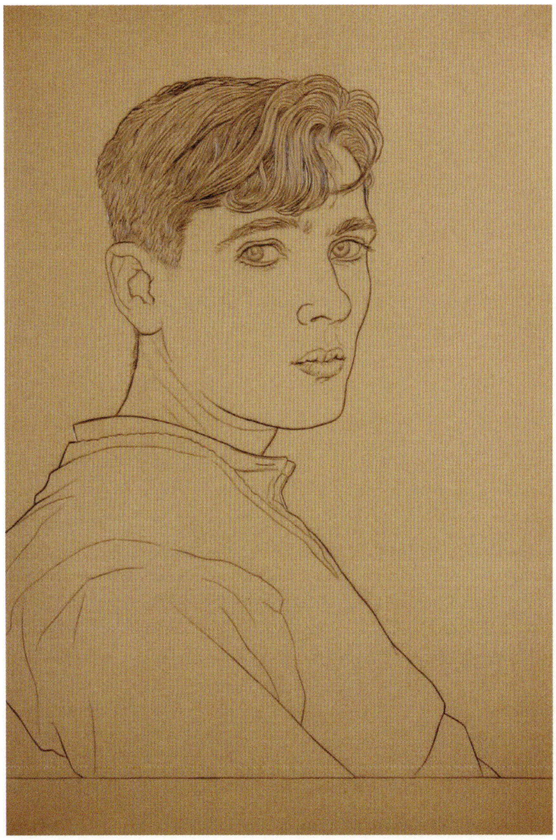

285

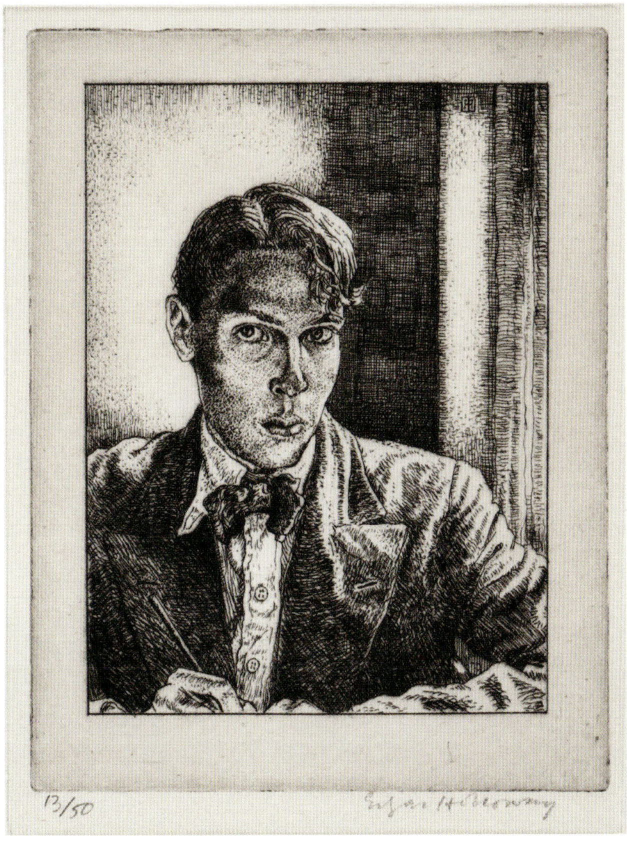


286

**Edgar Holloway** (1914-2008),

**283** *Self-portrait No. 25, Goodbye to All That!*, 1947,
signed in plate, signed in pencil, numbered 11/50
etching, 7 ¾ x 5 ¾ in. (20 x 15 cm).

**284** *Top Hat*, 1937,
signed in pencil and signed in plate, titled and numbered,
etching, plate size 11 ½ x 8 in. (29.5 x 20.3 cm),
paper size 14 x 10 ¾ in. (35.5 x 27.3 cm).

**285** *Self-portrait No. 17, Artist as a Young Man*, 1932,
original copper plate,
9 ½ x 6 ½ in. (24.3 x 16.2 cm)

**286** *Self-portrait No. 20* (Meyrick Cat. No. 251), 1932,
signed and numbered 13/50,
etching, 5 x 3 ½ in. (12.7 x 8.9 cm)

Edgar Holloway made more etched self-portraits than any other British printmaker. His first was a drypoint of 1931, aged 16; *The Fedora,* his 33rd, was etched in 2002, at the age of 88. Holloway was influenced by Rembrandt's use of light and dark and by contemporary etchers including Augustus John, Ernest Lumsden and Joseph Webb.

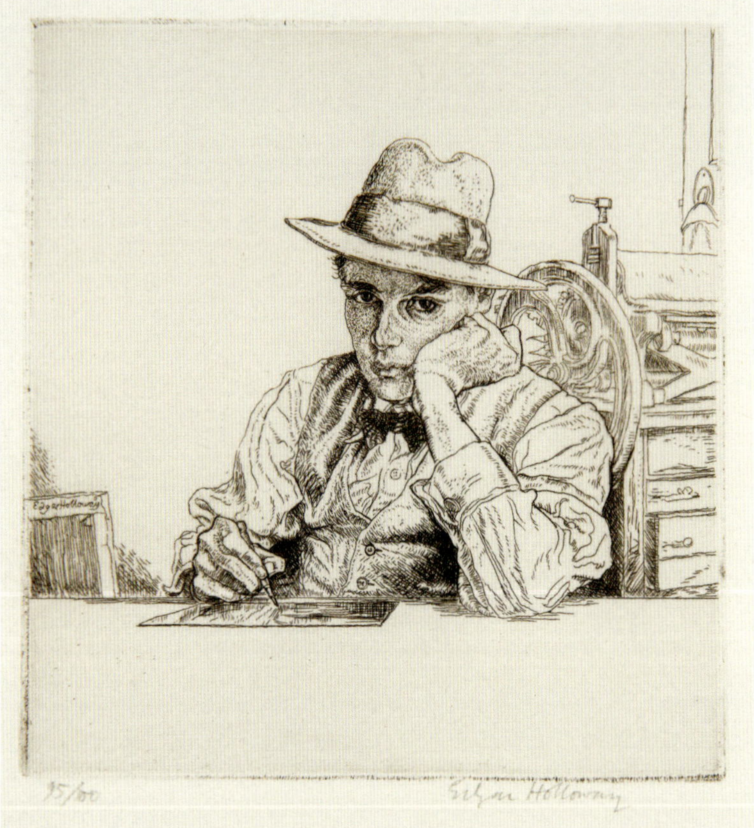

287

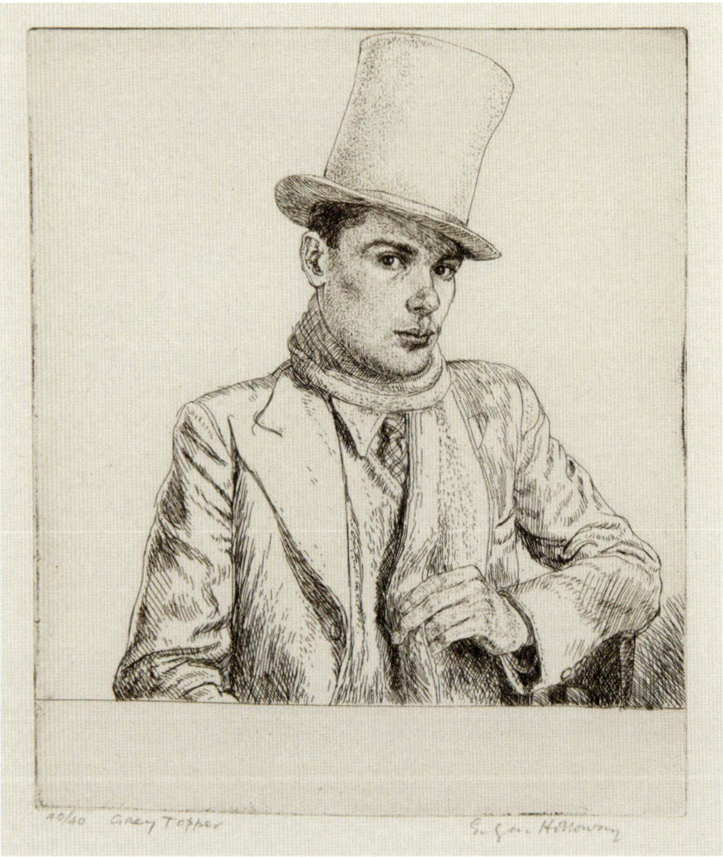

Edgar Holloway (1914-2008),

**287** *The Etcher III*, 1932, signed in the plate,
signed and numbered by the artist
reprinted by the artist in 1996
etching on paper, 10 x 10 in. (25.4 x 25.4 cm).

**288** *The Grey Topper*, 1937, signed,
etching on paper, 15 x 10 in. (38.1 x 25.4 cm).

**289** *Self-portrait (No. 6)*, 1932, signed;
etching on paper,
8 ¾ x 6 ¼ in. (22.3 x 15.9 cm).

The most widely reproduced of his self-portraits, *Self-portrait (No. 6)* (1932) demonstrates his early technical virtuosity. In common with his other prints it is based on an original drawing from life. This etching first appeared in *Studio* magazine in 1934 and was shown at the Royal Academy Summer Exhibition in the same year.

288

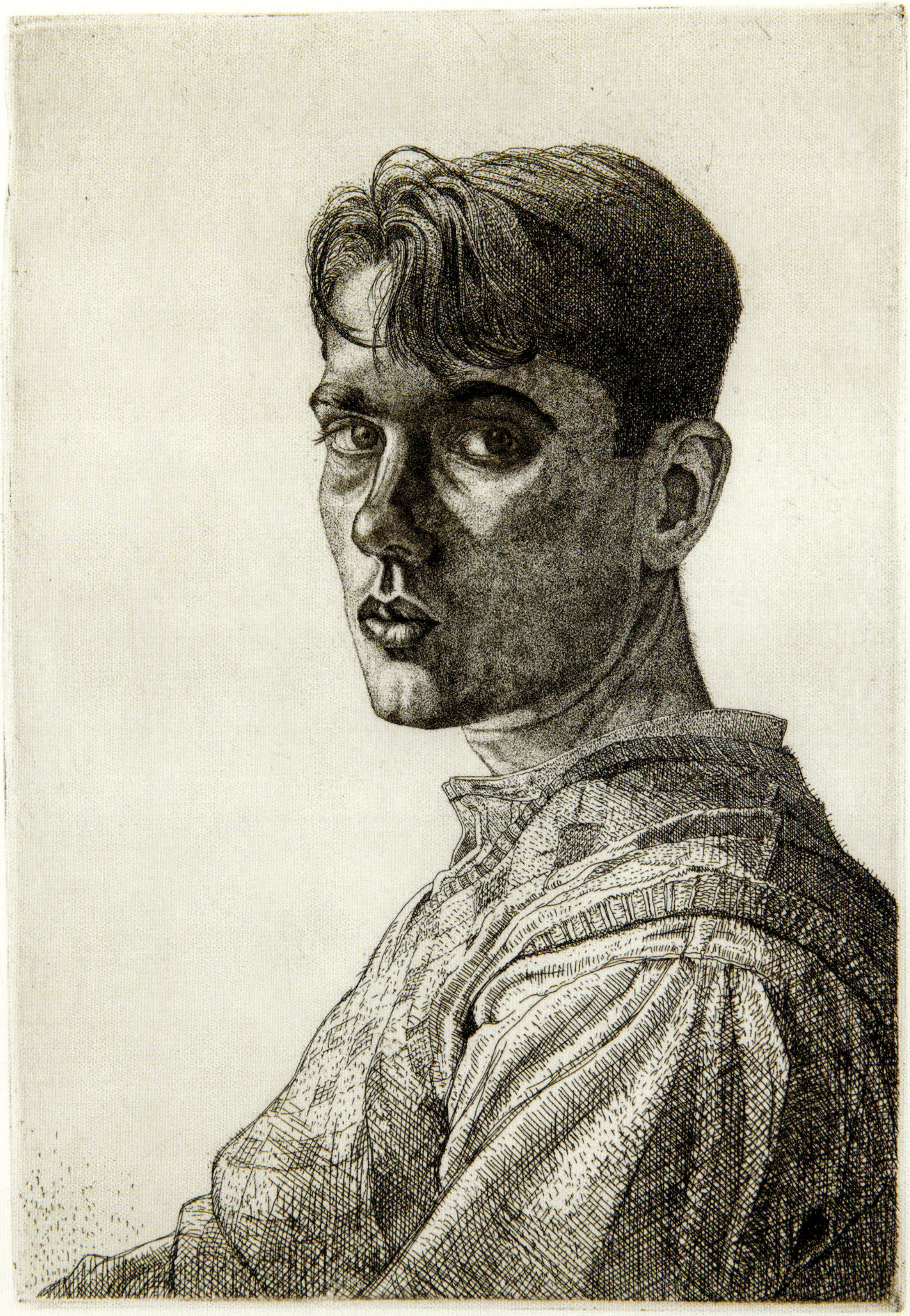

289

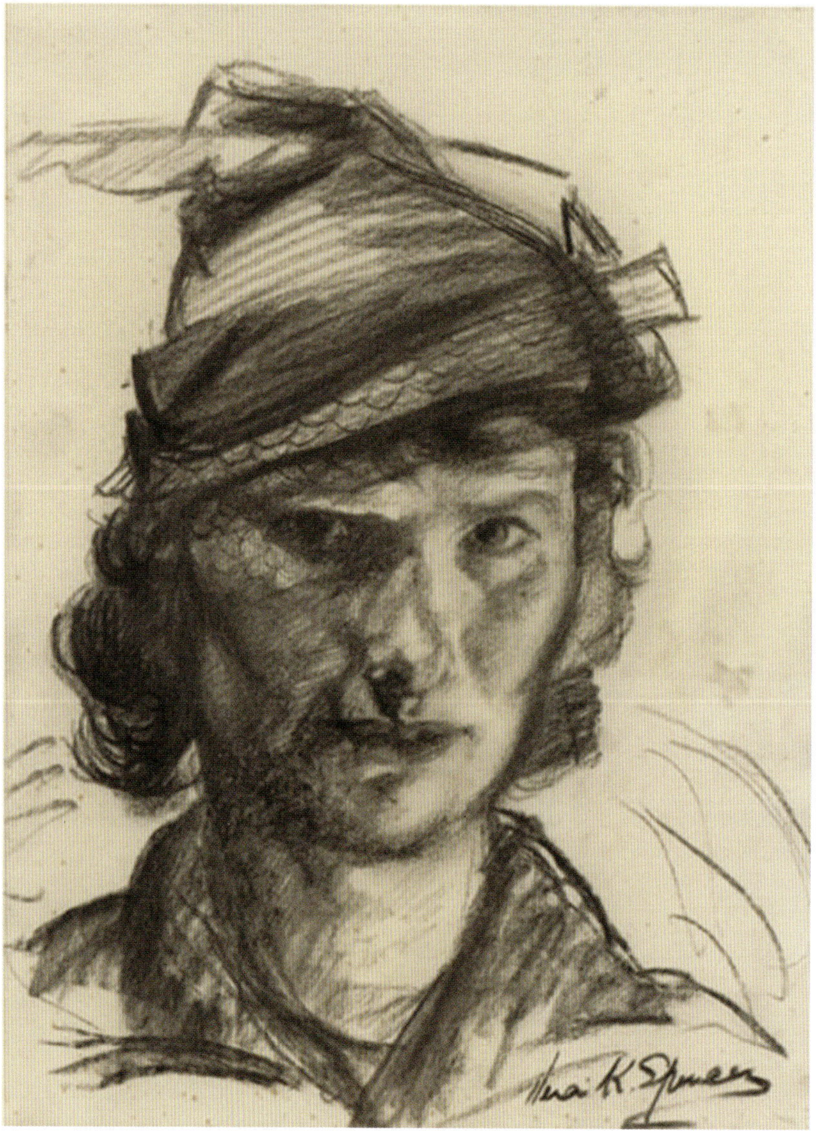

**290 Vera Spencer** (1926-2021), *Self-portrait*, c.1940, signed, black chalk on paper, 14 x 10 ½ in. (36 x 26.5 cm).

Vera Spencer was a painter and designer, born in Prague, Czechoslovakia, who arrived in England aged 10 and studied at Slade School of Fine Art and Central School of Textile Design. Spencer had solo shows at Galerie Apollinaire, and Galerie Arnaud in Paris (1948 and 1952) and at Conran Furniture in London (1953).

**291 Richard Eurich** (1903-1992), *The Green Shirt* (Self-portrait), 1932, signed and dated, oil on canvas, 9 ½ x 8 in. (24.5 x 20.3 cm). Photo by Paul Carter © Richard Eurich Paintings.

'In this small but commanding self-portrait of 1932 Eurich achieves new freedom. Having absorbed what he needed from the old masters, he has confidently developed a style identifiably his own. If there is a single outside influence it is that of the lately deceased Christopher Wood, whom he had met at the Goupil Gallery in 1929.' Peyton Skipwith, *Richard Eurich, Visionary Artist,* Paul Holberton Publishing, 2002.

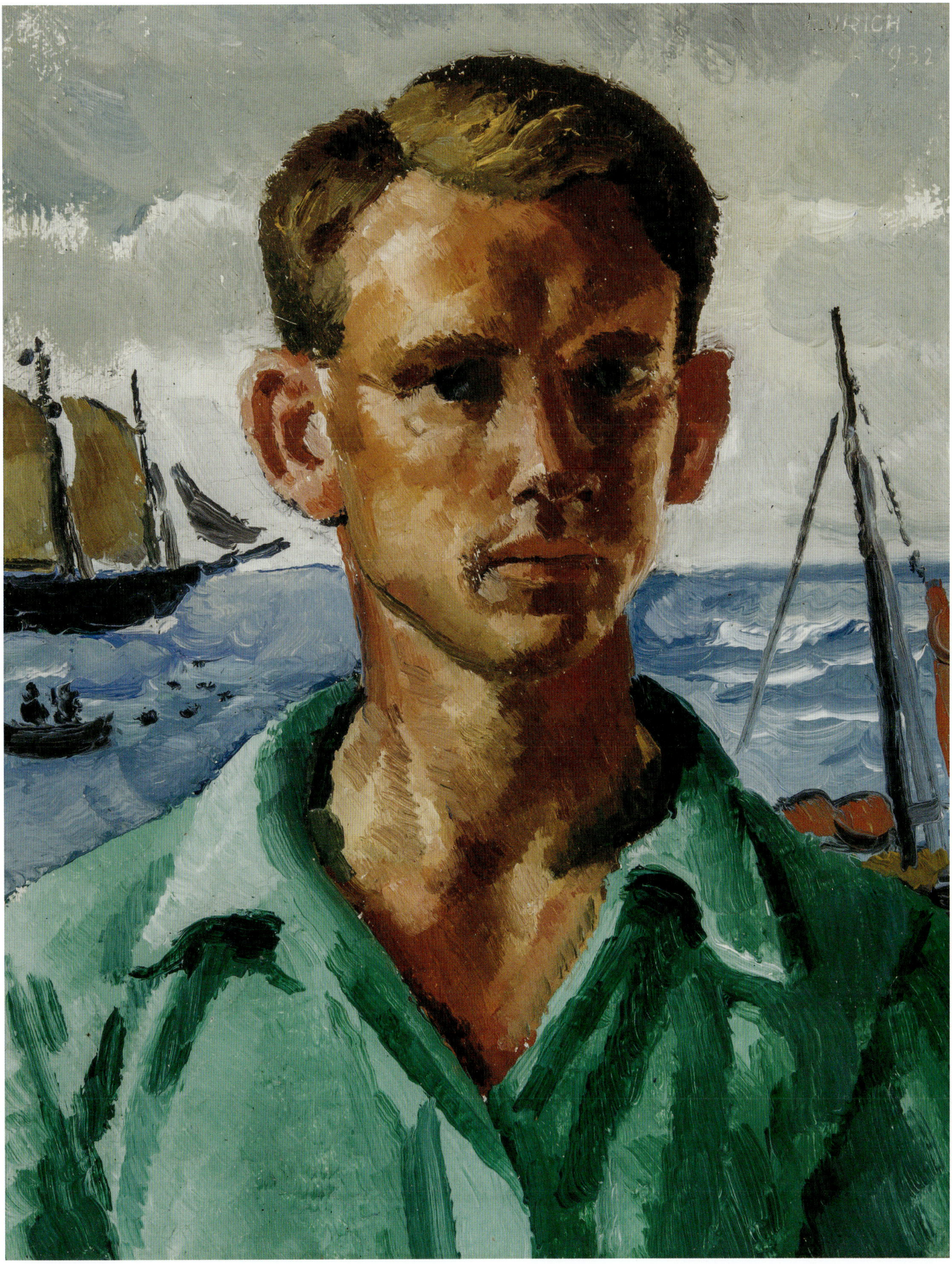

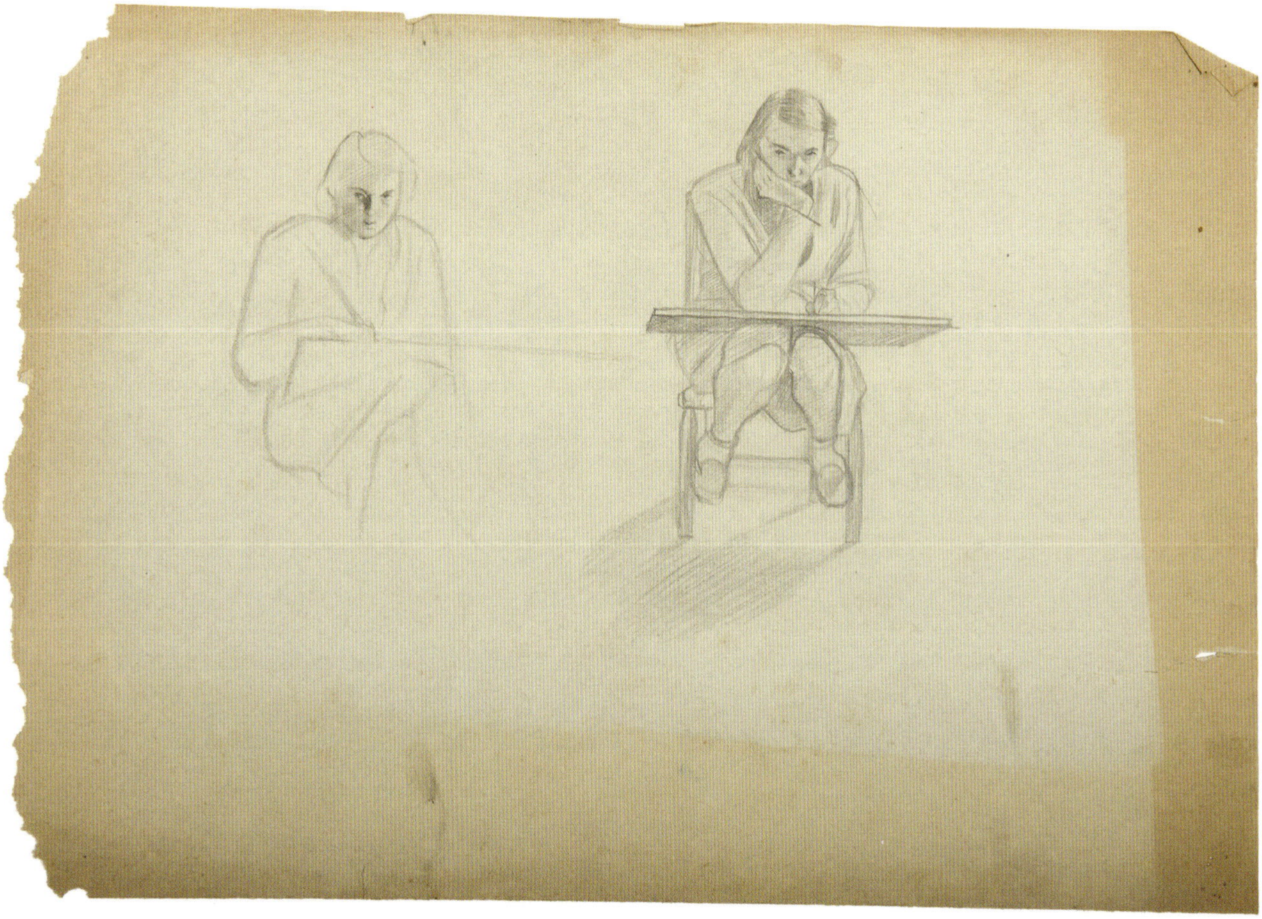

**292 Evelyn Dunbar** (1906-1960), *The Artist at Her Drawing Board*, mid-1920s, pencil on paper, 14 ¾ x 22 in. (37.6 x 55.5 cm).

This self-portrait shows Evelyn Dunbar as a 15 or 16 year old dreaming of becoming a professional artist and having a proper studio of her own. Several versions of this composition exist, one of which is in the Ashmolean Museum.

**293 Evelyn Dunbar** (1906-1960), *Self-portrait*, c.1927, oil on canvas board, 18 x 12 in. (45.7 x 30.5 cm).

This self-portrait shows Evelyn Dunbar in her early twenties, at her easel, carefully observing herself in a mirror. As a consequence she appears left- rather than right-handed. Her floppy hat adds a hint of Bohemian style to her otherwise earnest expression. As the artist Tom Phillips noted 'if self-portraits have a tendency to look glum it should not be surprising. As Rembrandt discovered, it is difficult to laugh and paint at the same time. The laugh or smile is acted and the eyes fail to join in, being themselves otherwise engaged. The other dilemma is (since a mirror is usually involved) that the image an artist makes is the wrong way round.'

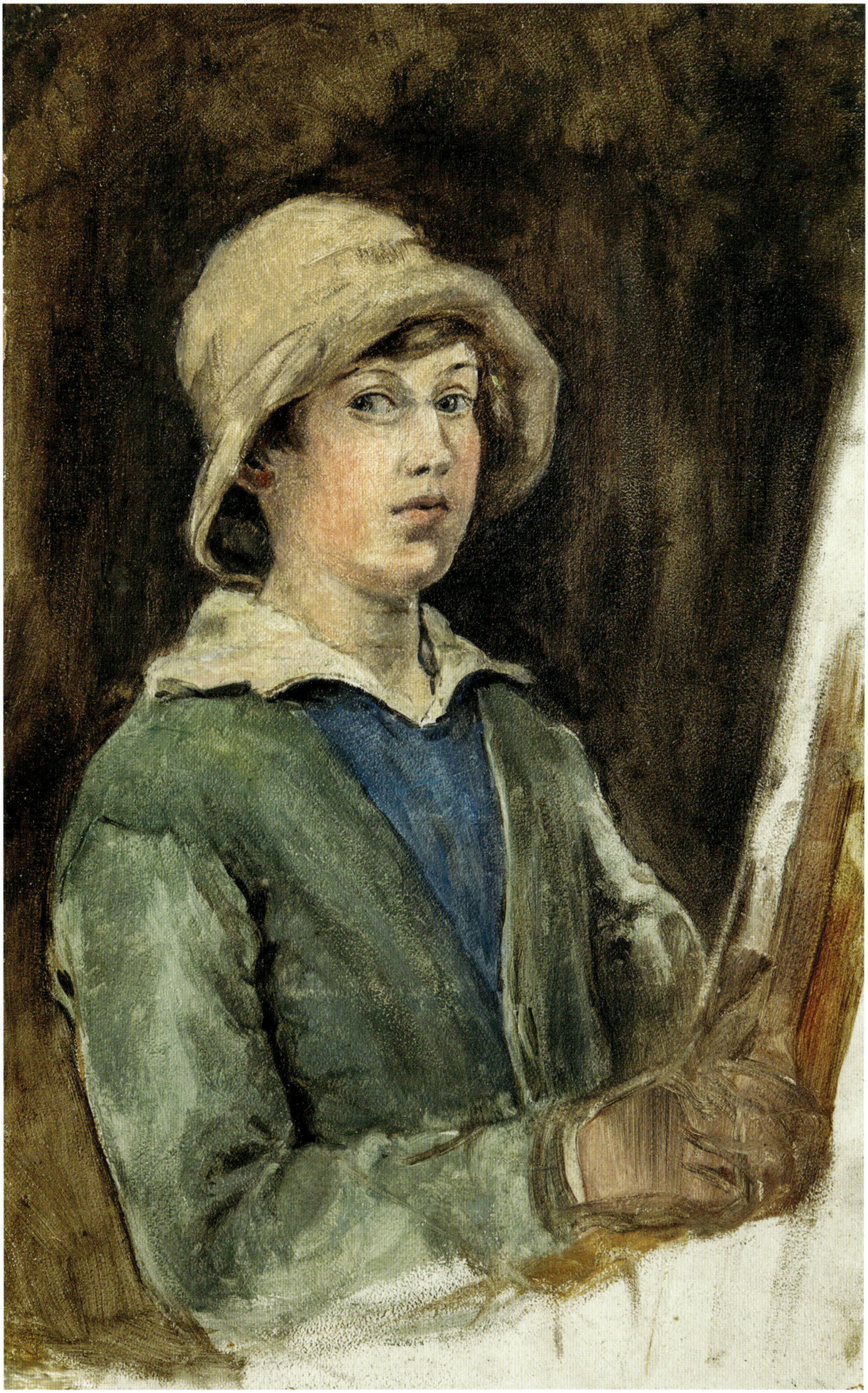

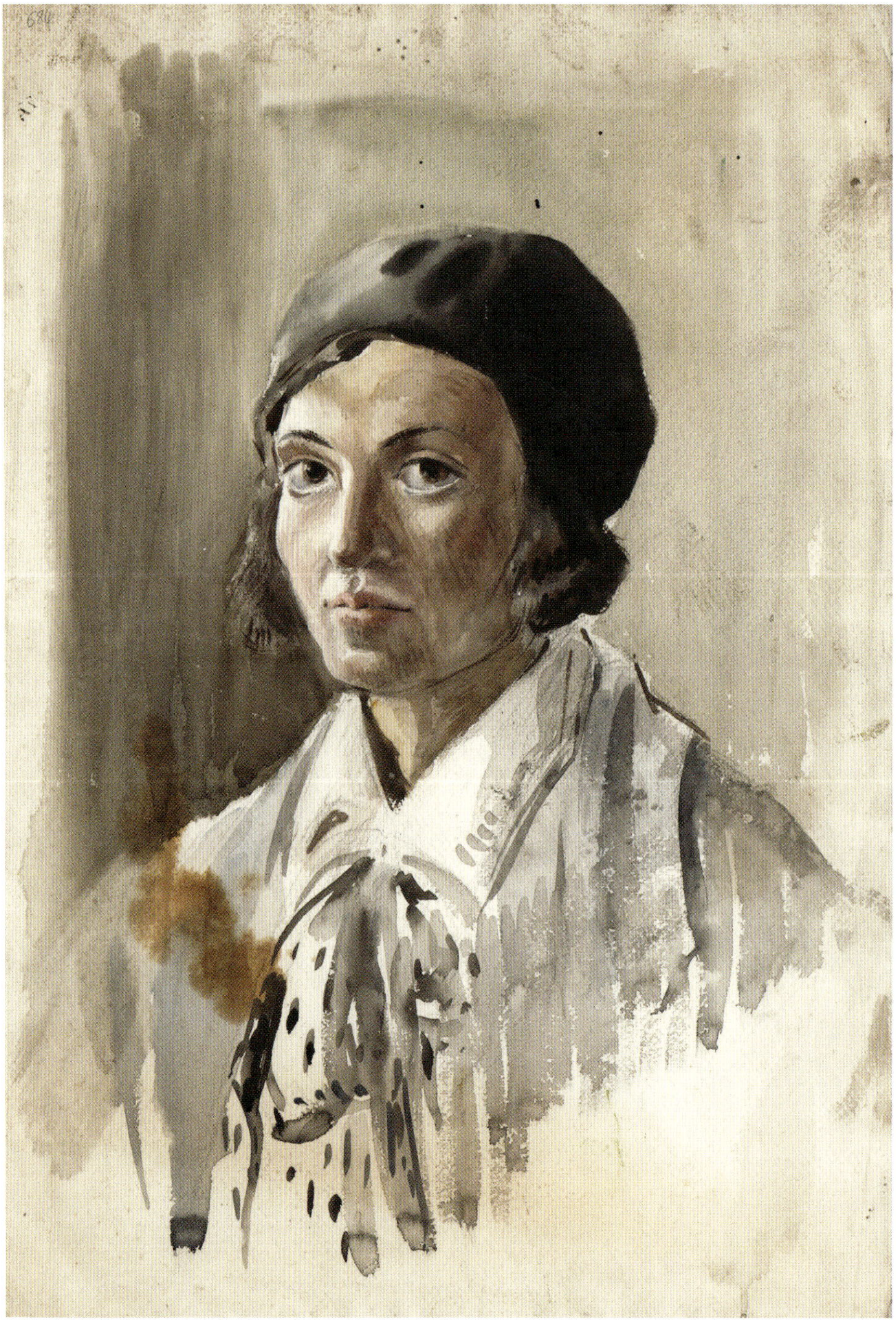

**294 Evelyn Dunbar** (1906-1960), *Self-portrait* [HMO 684], c.1930, pencil and watercolour on paper. 22 x 15 in. (56 x 38.1 cm).

This self-portrait was probably one of a student portfolio of six watercolours submitted for exhibition at the Royal College of Art, December 1930.

**295 Evelyn Dunbar** (1906-1960), *Nude Self-portrait*, 1928, pencil and watercolour on paper, 15 x 10 ½ in. (38 x 27 cm).

In the summer of 1928, not having found satisfaction in the art college courses she had attended and abandoned, Evelyn Dunbar was living at home, writing and illustrating children's books. In the absence of life classes, in the comfort of her own bedroom, using a full length mirror, she made this life study/self-portrait.

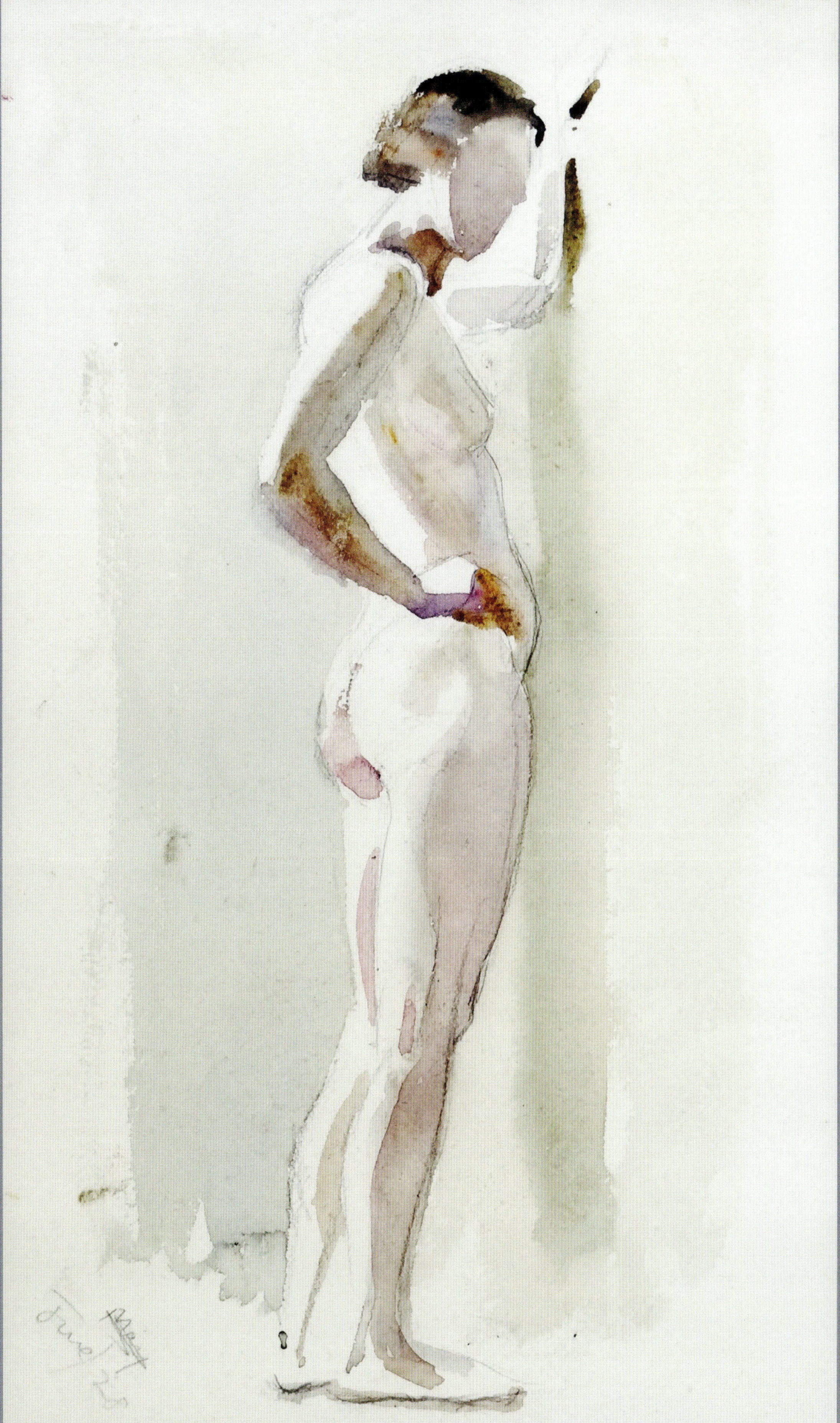

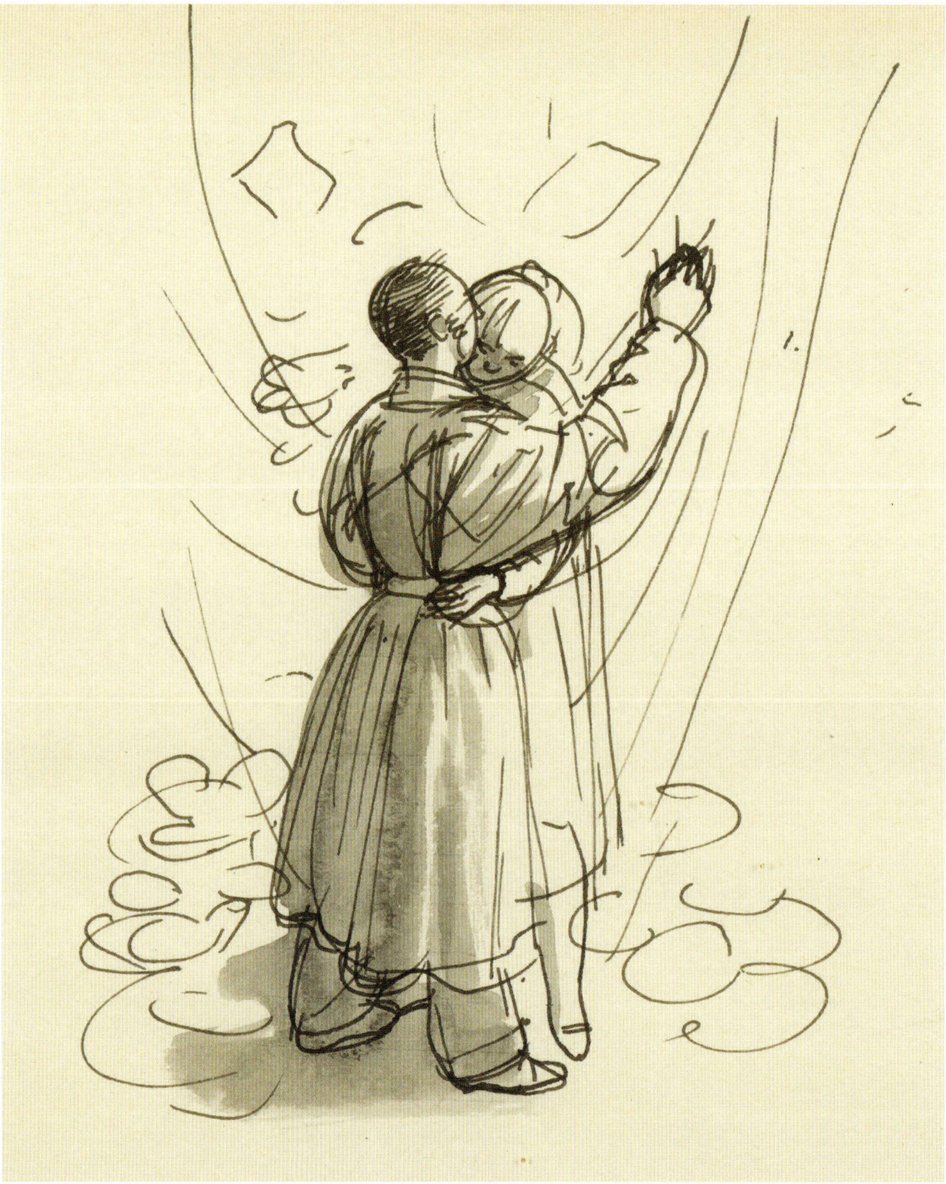

**296 Charles Mahoney** (1903-1968), *Adam and Eve Dancing*, c.1934, ink on paper, 8 ½ x 7 in. (21.5 x 18 cm).

'Adam and Eve' was the nickname given to Mahoney and Dunbar by certain members of what Anne Ullmann, Eric Ravilious' daughter, called 'the Bardfield gang'. This nickname, dating to the mid-1930s, reflects both their relationship at the time and their shared passion for plants and gardening. (**367**)

**297 Evelyn Dunbar** (1906-1960), *Self-portrait*, [HMO 766], 1958, signed and dated, oil on canvas, 20 x 12 in. (49.5 x 29.4 cm).

Painted in her studio at Staple Farm, near Wye, Kent, aged 52, (two years before she died), this was the last self-portrait undertaken by Eveyln Dunbar.

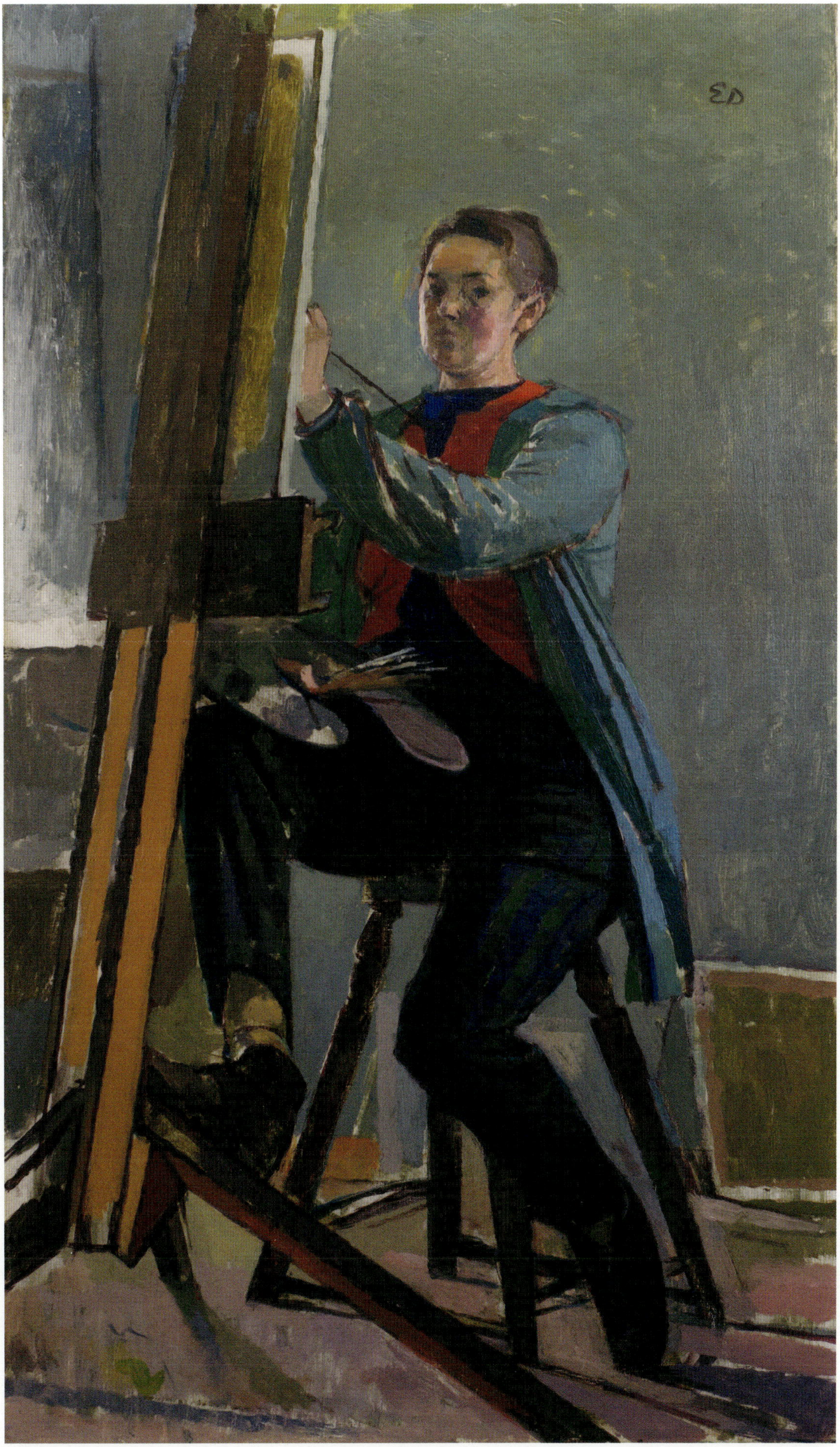
ED

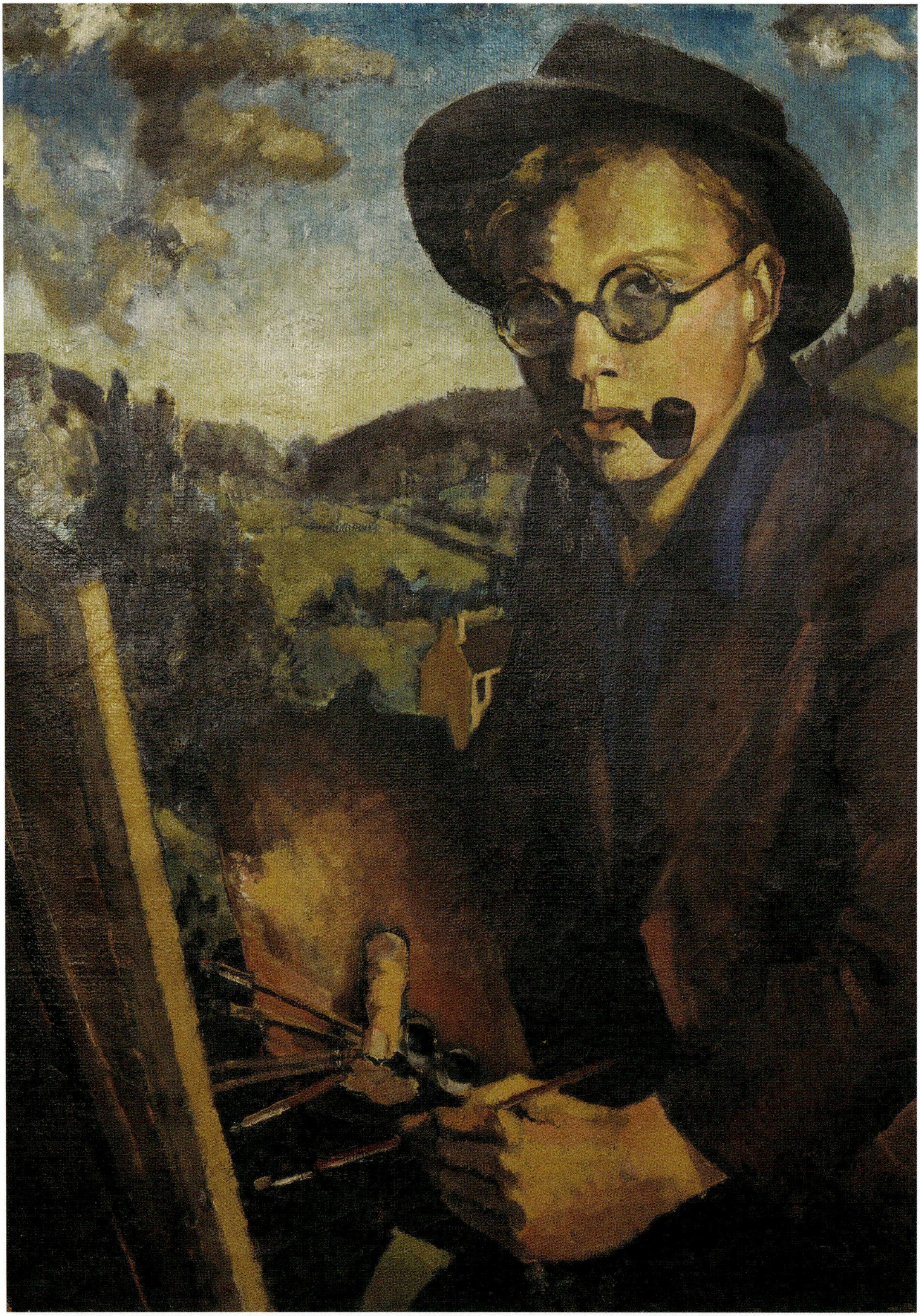

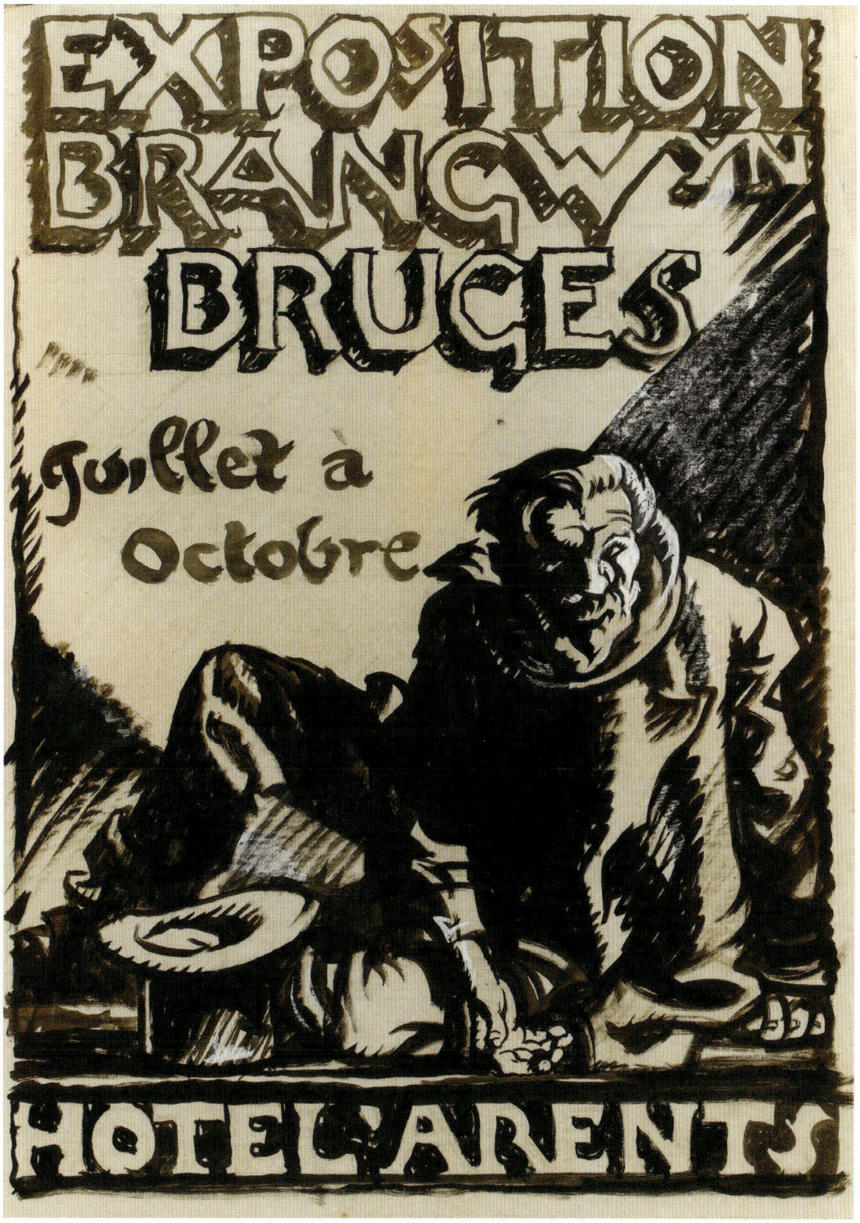


**299 Frank Brangwyn** (1867-1956), *Exposition Brangwyn Bruges*, 1936,
ink and white highlights on tracing paper, 29 x 19 ¾ in. (74 x 50.4 cm).

Typical of both the artist's humour and inventiveness this design proposal, to announce the Brangwyn exhibition held in the Arents House, Bruges in 1936, contains a self-portrait in which Brangwyn is depicted begging for alms. It was rejected in favour of a design showing a monk leafing through a portfolio. After this 1936 exhibition Brangwyn bequeathed the exhibited works to the city of Bruges as a permanent gift, resulting in what is today sometimes referred to as the Brangwyn Museum (Arentshuis). (**173**, **174**)

**298 Kenneth Rowntree** (1915-1997), *Self-portrait Aged 18*, 1933,
oil on canvas 29 ½ x 21 ¾ in. (75 x 55 cm).

This self-portrait shows the young Rowntree when he was studying at Ruskin School of Drawing, Oxford, under Albert Rutherston (1930-34), a year before he started at The Slade School of Fine Art, under Randolph Schwabe (1934-35). It was painted at Levisham in the Vale of Pickering where his aunt had a house that Rowntree and his family would visit regularly for summer holidays.

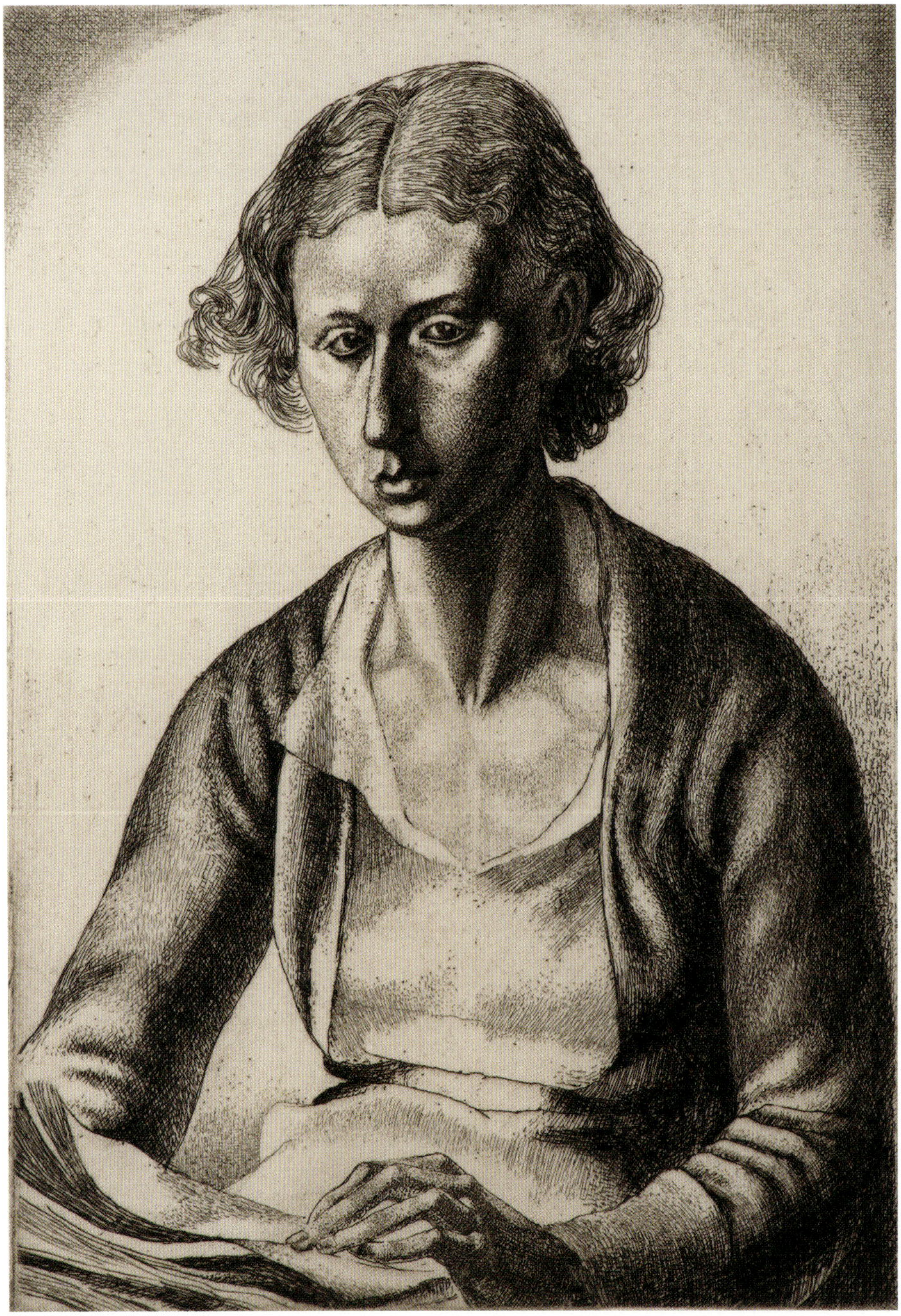

**300 Phyllis Ginger** (1907-2005), *Self-portrait*, c.1937, etching, plate size 7 x 5 in. (17.8 x 12.7 cm).

This harshly honest etched image can be dated to Phyllis Ginger's time at The Central School, (c.1937), where she studied under the tutelage of William P Robins. She had cut her long dark auburn hair after having recently left her civil service clerking job.

**301 Edward Irvine Halliday** (1902-1984), *Self-portrait in Colet Gardens Studio*, 1937, signed and dated, oil on canvas, 43 ¼ x 20 in. (110 x 50.7 cm).

This self-portrait shows the artist Edward Halliday in his studio at Colet Gardens, Hammersmith, where he lived and worked from 1934 until WW2. Halliday painted many self-portraits during the course of his life, and through them most of the important developments in his career are recorded, whether as muralist, broadcaster, designer or portrait painter.

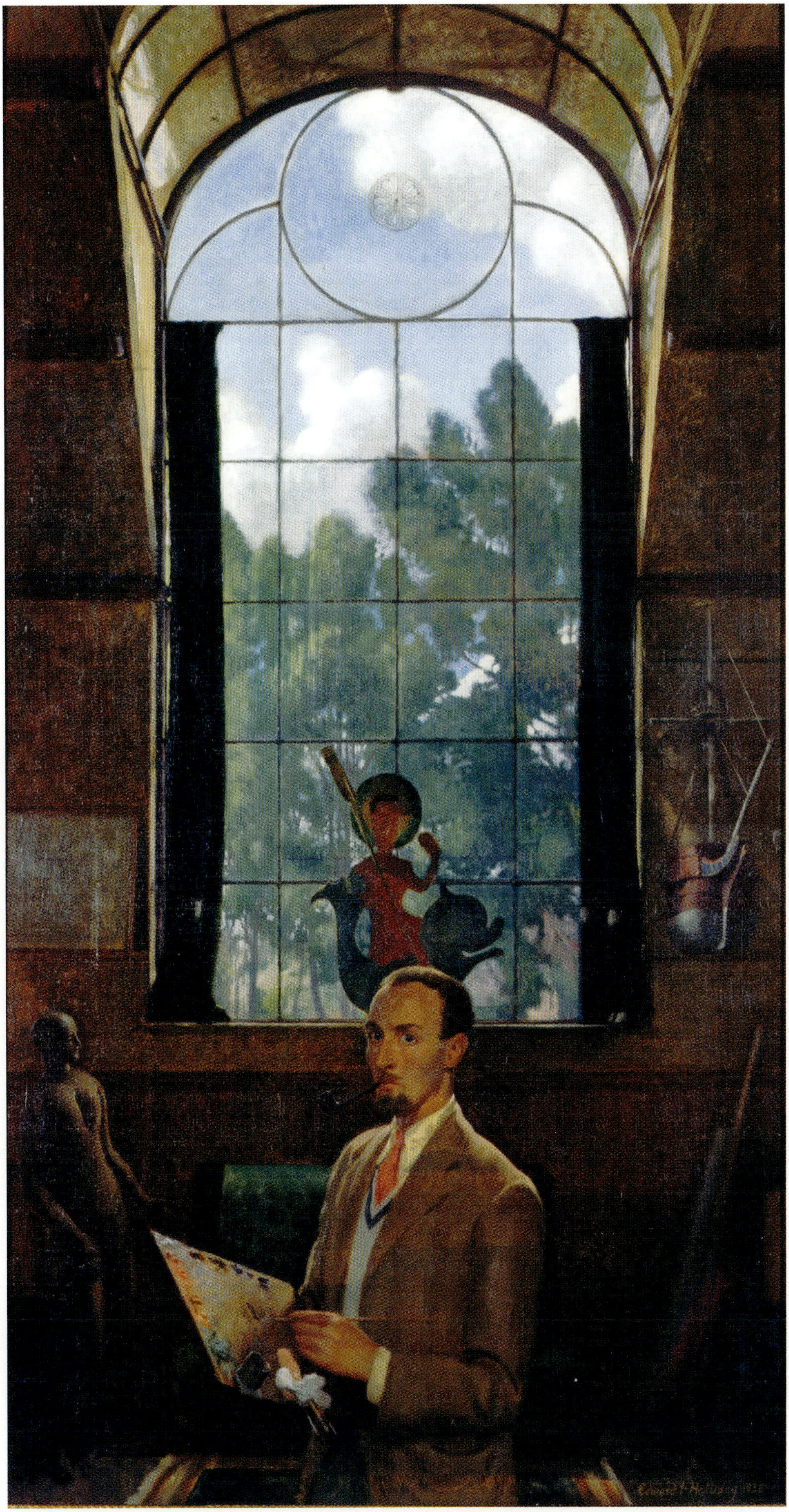

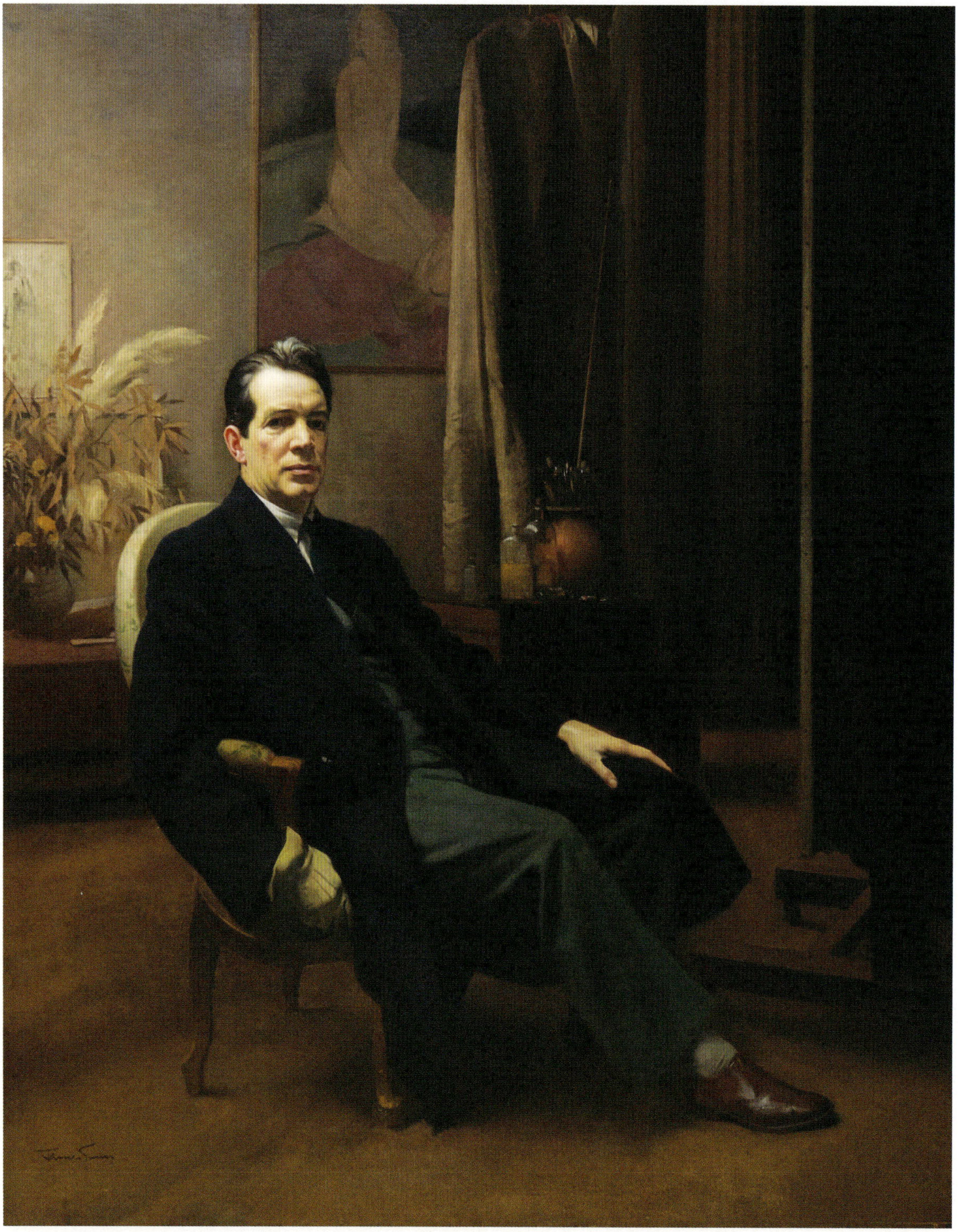

**302 Sir Herbert James Gunn** (1893-1964), *Self-portrait in Studio at Pembroke Walk*, c 1940, signed, oil on canvas, 58 x 48 cm (147.5 x 122 cm).

Self-portraits by Gunn are rare, and this work is far grander in style and execution than in earlier known examples painted in the mid-20s. The painting shows Gunn at his studio-home in Pembroke Walk, Kensington, during World War 2. Gunn portrays himself as an artist languishing in Stygian gloom – a consequence of London's wartime blackouts – striking a pose between melancholia and and heroic patriotism. His distinguished sitters included Queen Elizabeth, Prince Philip and the Queen Mother, as well as a plethora of prime ministers, field marshals, judges, dons, bankers and actors. (**17**)

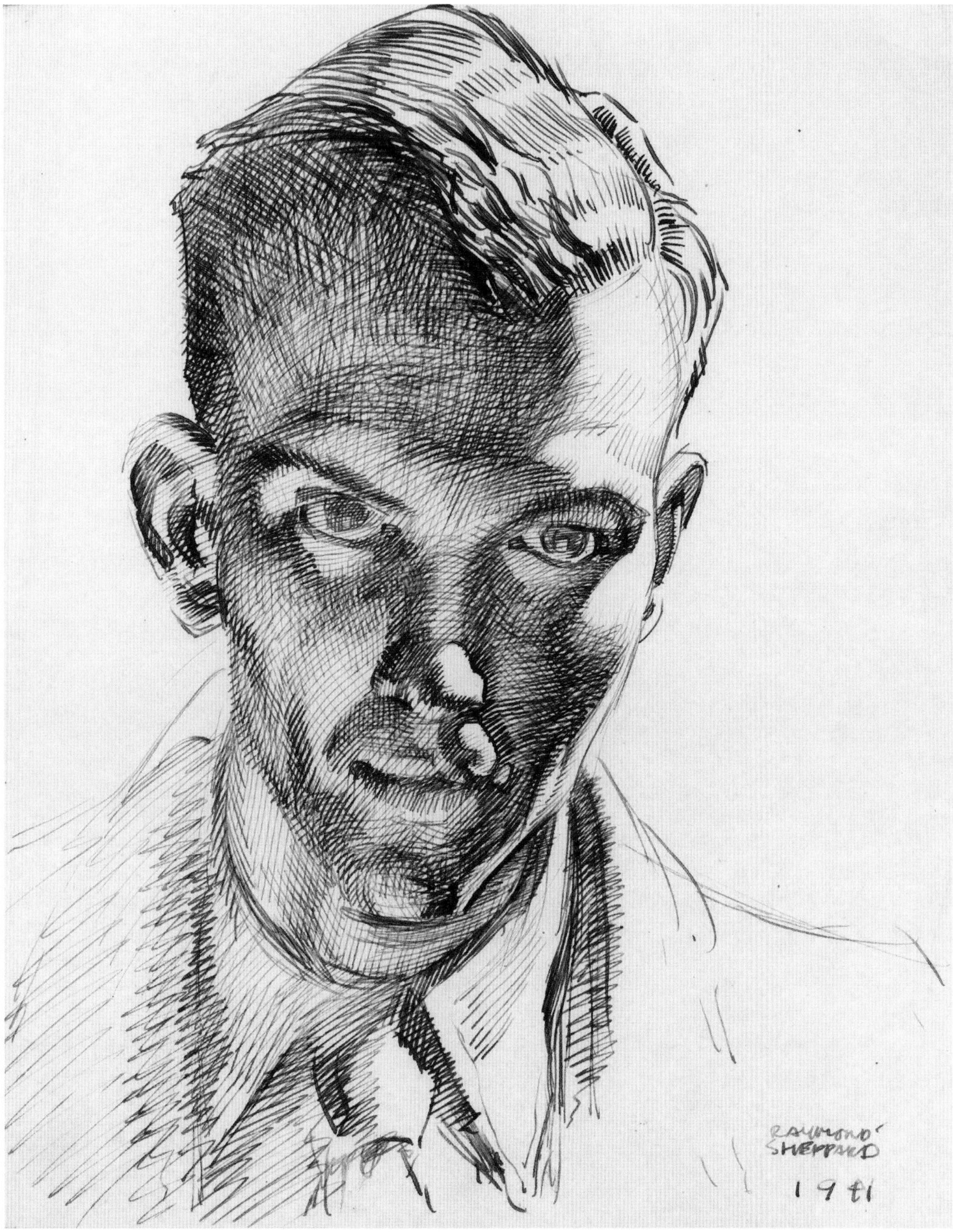


**303 Raymond Sheppard** (1913-1958), *Self-portrait*, 1941, signed and dated, pen and ink on paper, 10 ½ x 8 ¾ in. (26.7 x 22.5 cm).

Raymond Sheppard's stated aim in art was to express his inner emotion: 'that peculiar, unexplainable tightening inside that makes you want to laugh sometimes, sometimes to sing and dance for joy, and sometimes just a little sad'. This self-portrait was done during the time that Sheppard was training at the RAF School of Photography at Farnborough. In the same year he married Iris Gale. (**145**, **146**)

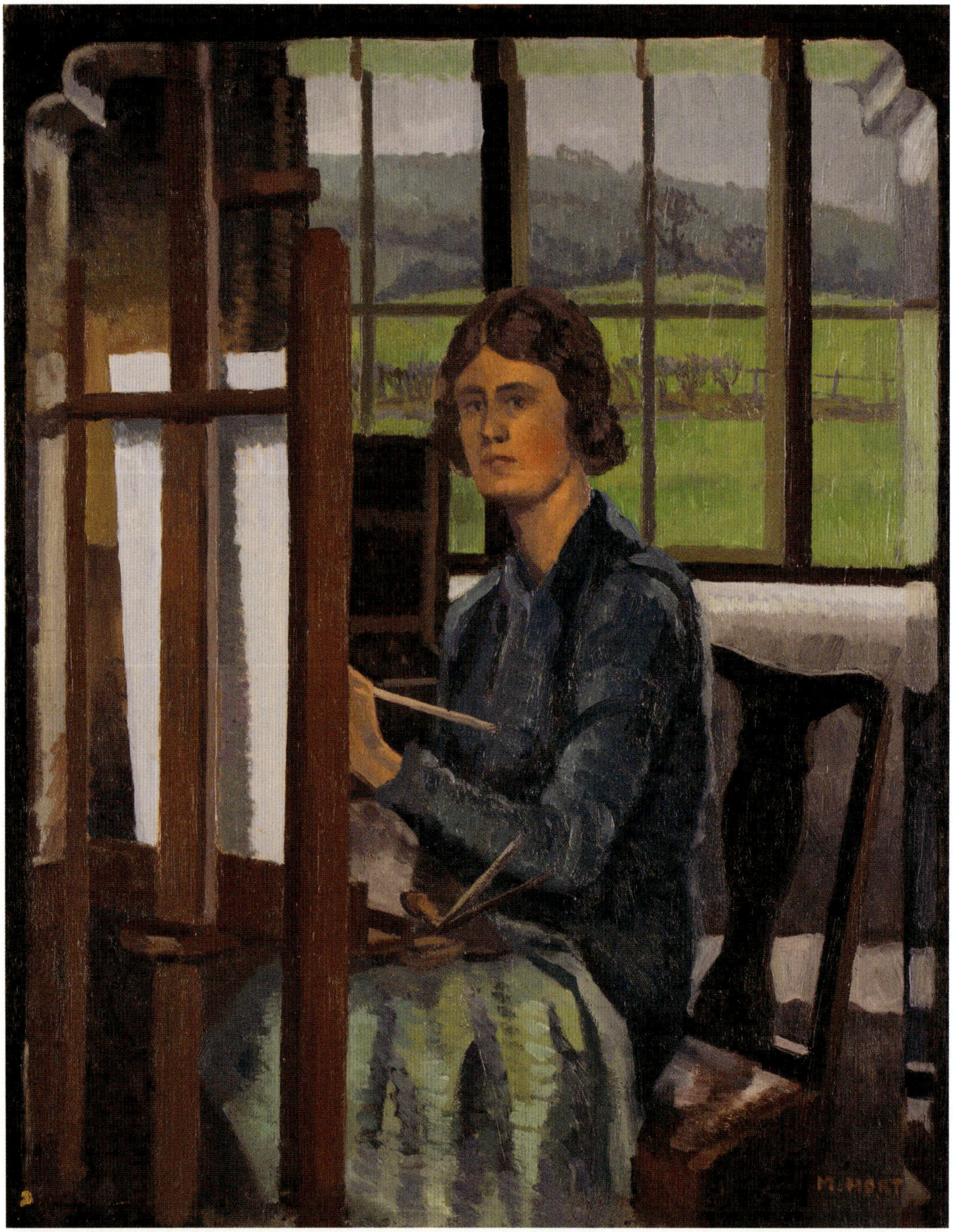


**304 Marjorie Mort** (1906-1988), *Self-portrait*, 1940, signed, titled and dated to reverse, oil on panel, 20 x 16 in. (50.8 x 40.6 cm).

Having trained in Manchester and London Mort moved to Cornwall in 1938 until the outbreak of WW2 when she went to Stockport to teach. This self-portrait, aged 34, is likely to have been undertaken shortly before leaving Cornwall, and according to the address on the reverse was probably painted in her studio at The Willows, Cornwall Terrace, Penzance. She is also recorded as having lived before the war at Keigwin Place in Mousehole. After the war she returned to Cornwall and established, with Eric Hiller and Charles Breaker, the Newlyn Holiday Sketching Group.

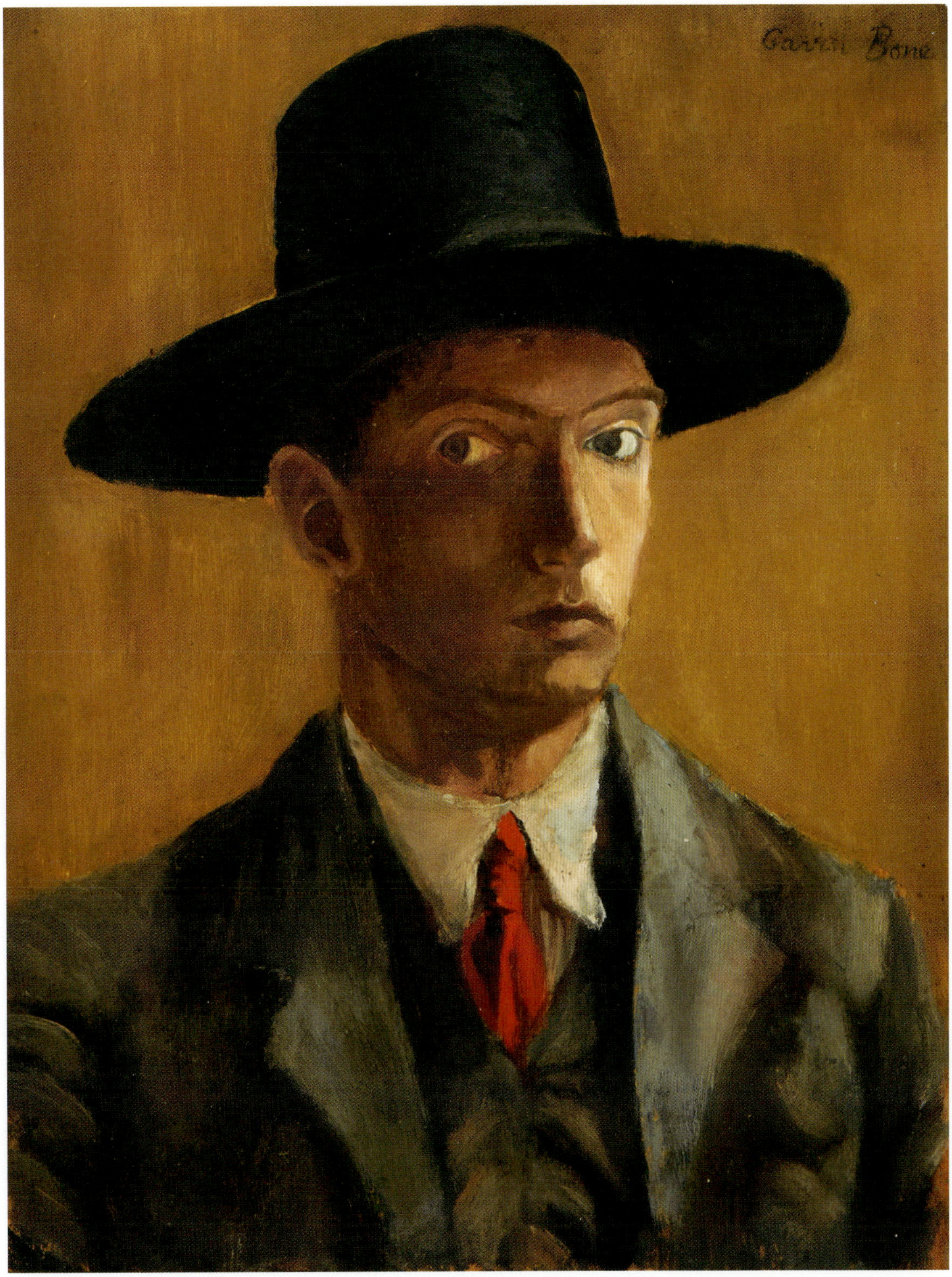


**305 Gavin Bone** (1903-1942), *Gavin David Bone, by Himself*, signed, 1920s,
inscribed to reverse "Gavin David Bone by Himself (Painted on his return from 1? visit to Spain in a Cordoba hat bought there. M.. Bone) 61",
oil on board, 13 ½ x 10 ½ in. (34.3 x 26.6 cm).

Gavin Bone (1903-1942) was a poet, artist and Fellow of St John's College, Oxford who specialised in Medieval English Language and Literature. Whilst there is a general recognition of his talents unfortunately he has been little studied and largely forgotten due to a number of factors, not least the sombre conditions of the posthumous publications of his works.

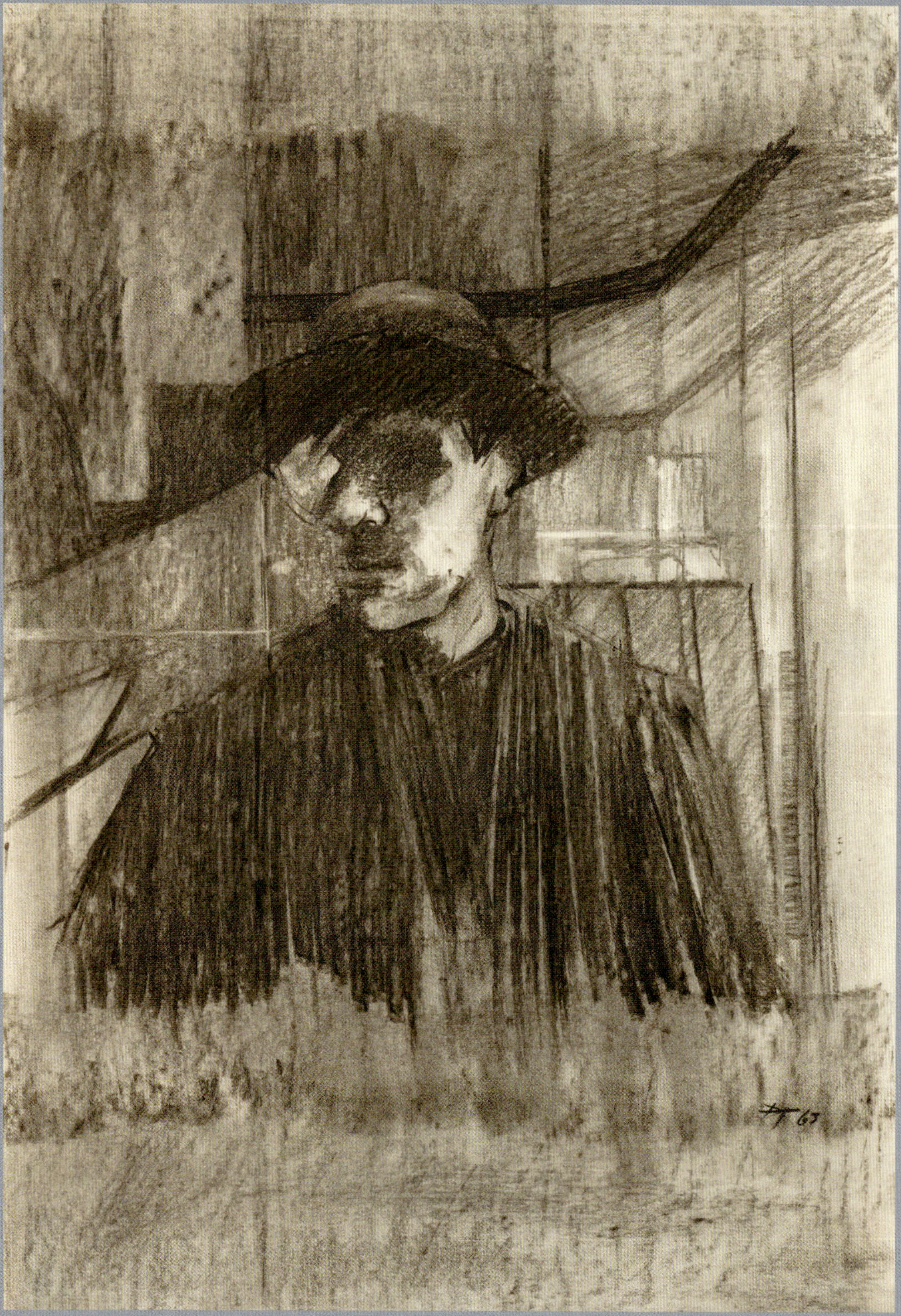

**306 David Tindle** (b. 1932), *Self-portrait in a Mirror*, signed and dated, charcoal on paper, 22 x 12 in. (55.9 x 30.5 cm).

This composition has similarities with Tindle's National Portrait Gallery self-portrait in which he explained '… the spectacles and the one eye obscured seem to hold back further inspection', adding that '… the diagonal light lines and the edge at the bottom of the picture and the general boxing-in of the composition makes it a self-contained experience.' (**71**)

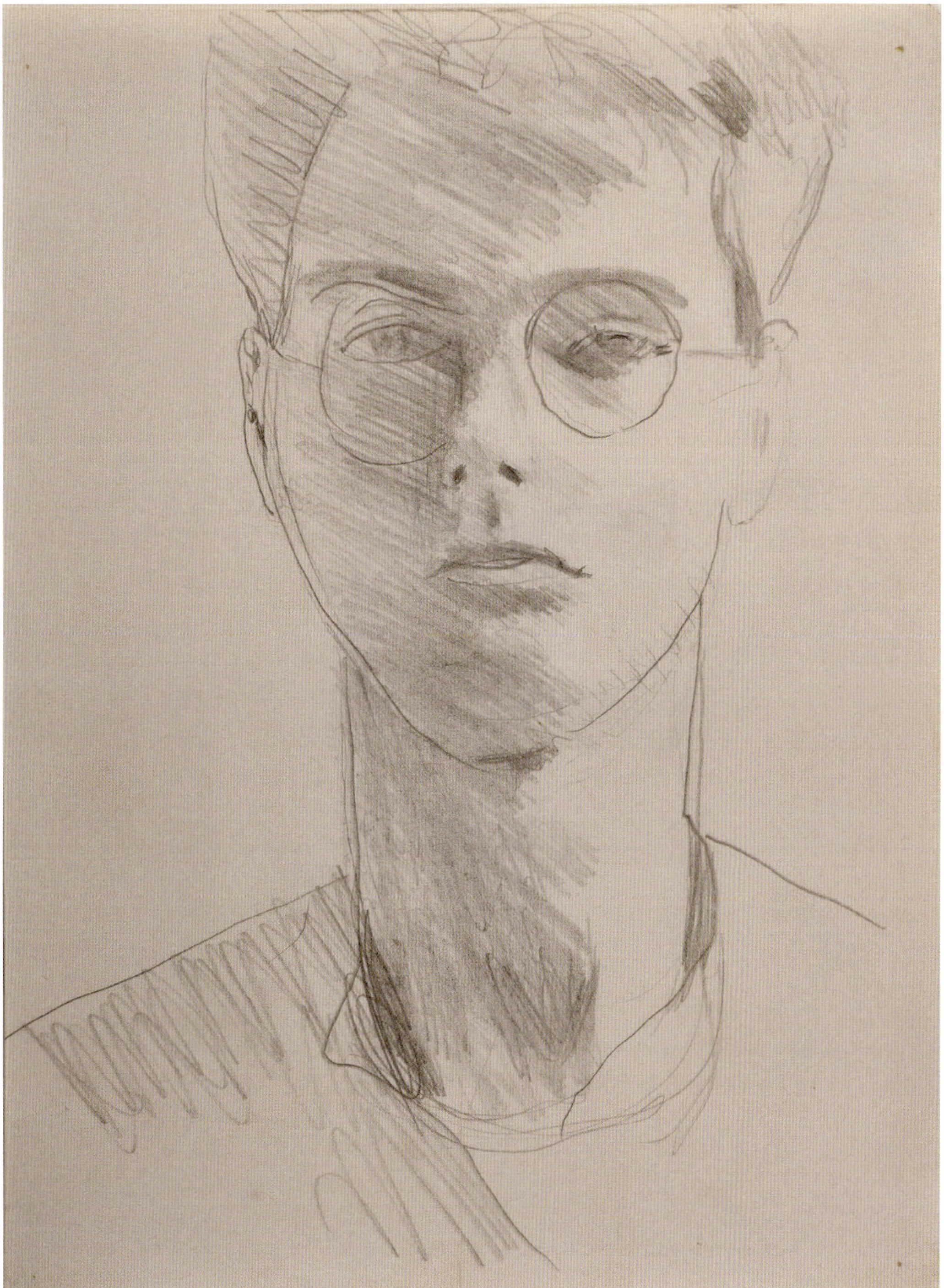

**307 Roger Hilton** (1911-1975), *Self-portrait*, 1930s,
pencil on paper, 10 ½ x 8 ¼ in. (26.7 x 20.8 cm).

This portrait was probably made during Roger Hilton's stay in Paris during the 1930s, a flamboyant time during which artists such as Picasso, Modigliani, Ernst, Magritte, Chagall and many other pioneers dominated the Parisian art scene. This self-portrait, which is clearly from a sketch book, can be compared to a slightly later version in the collection of the National Portrait Gallery.

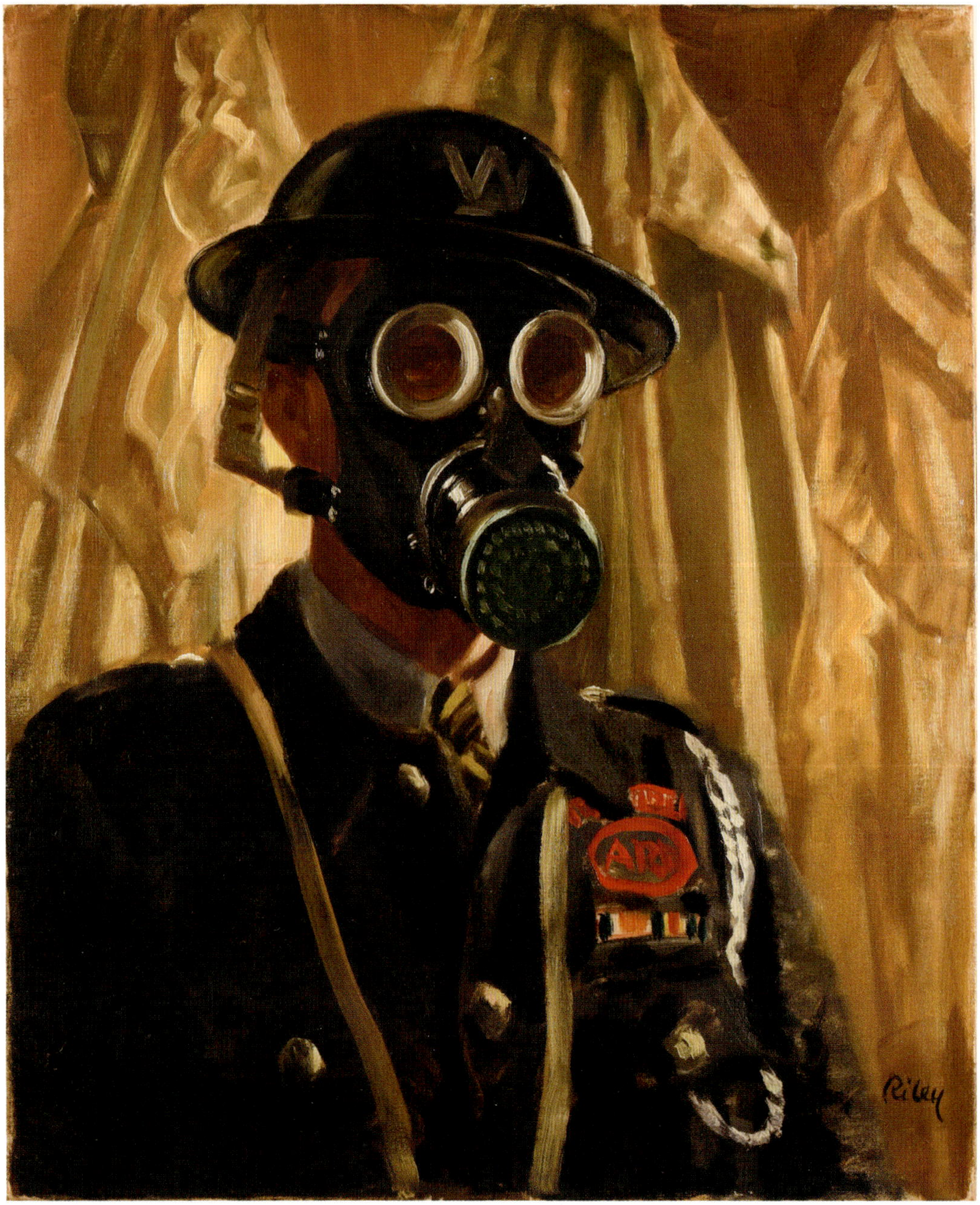


**308 Henry Arthur Riley** (1895-1966), *Me*, 1940-42, signed, inscribed with title and date on the stretcher, oil on canvas, 24 x 20 in. (61 x 51 cm).

This striking self-portrait shows Harold Riley in his ARP (Air Raid Precautions) uniform. Three anti-gas coats, worn by ARP volunteers, form the backdrop. Although Riley saw active service during WW1, when WW2 broke out he was in his mid 40s and therefore not called up. (**320**)

**309 Percy Shakespeare** (1906-1943), *Self-portrait – Morning Exercise*, c.1934, oil on canvas, 30 x 25 in. (76.2 x 63.5 cm).

Having achieved success at the 1933 Royal Academy Percy Shakespeare again set his sights on the Summer Exhibition, painting a dramatic self-portrait entitled *Morning Exercise*. Accepted for the Summer Show in 1934 Shakespeare must been disappointed when it was crowded out in the hang. *The Express* and *Star* however reviewed it favourably stating that it was 'His best work.... a finely painted and lively portrait of a young man in underclothes performing his daily dozen. The setting was the artist's bedroom at Wren's Nest, Dudley, which also doubled as his studio (**36**).

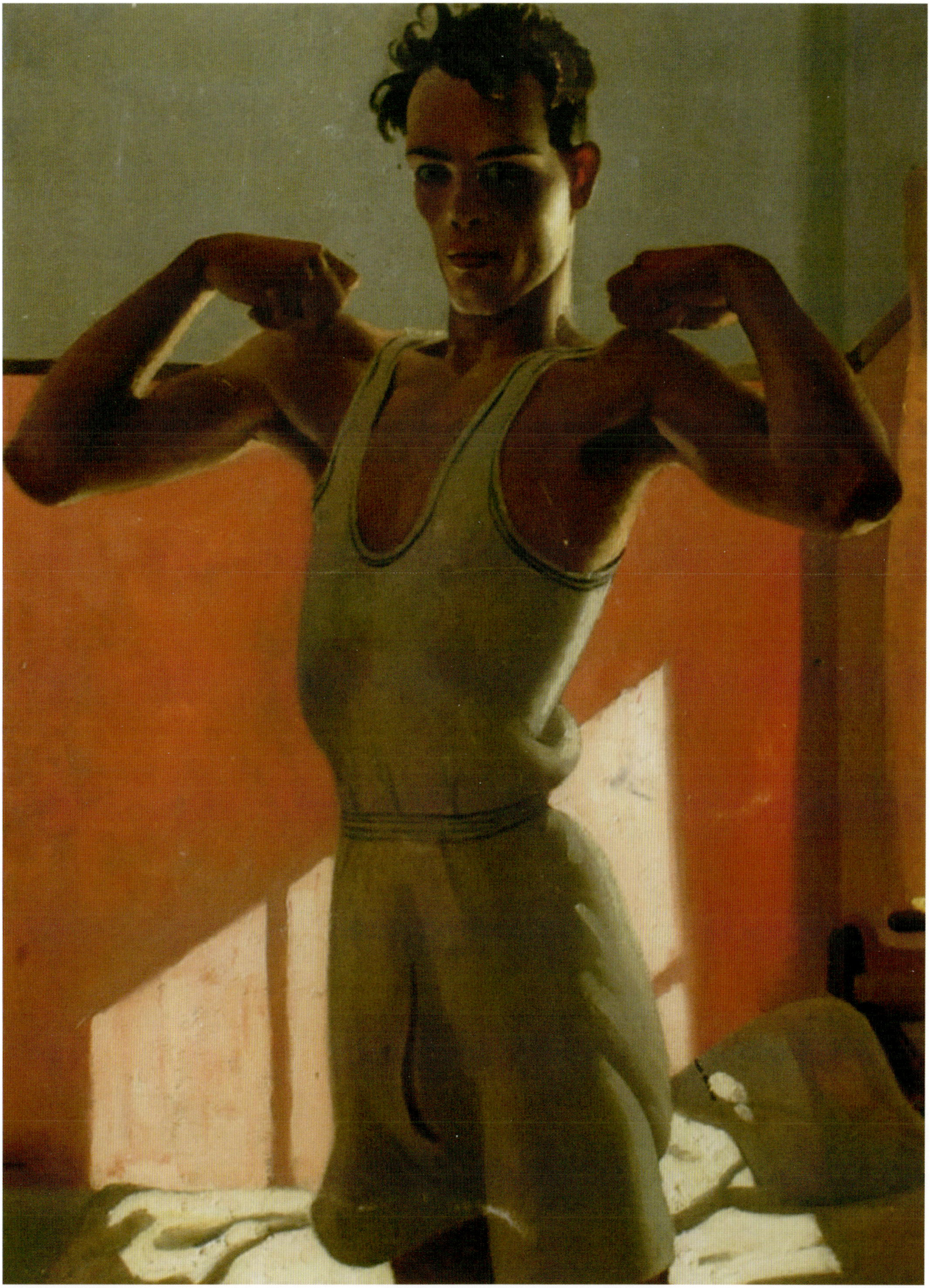

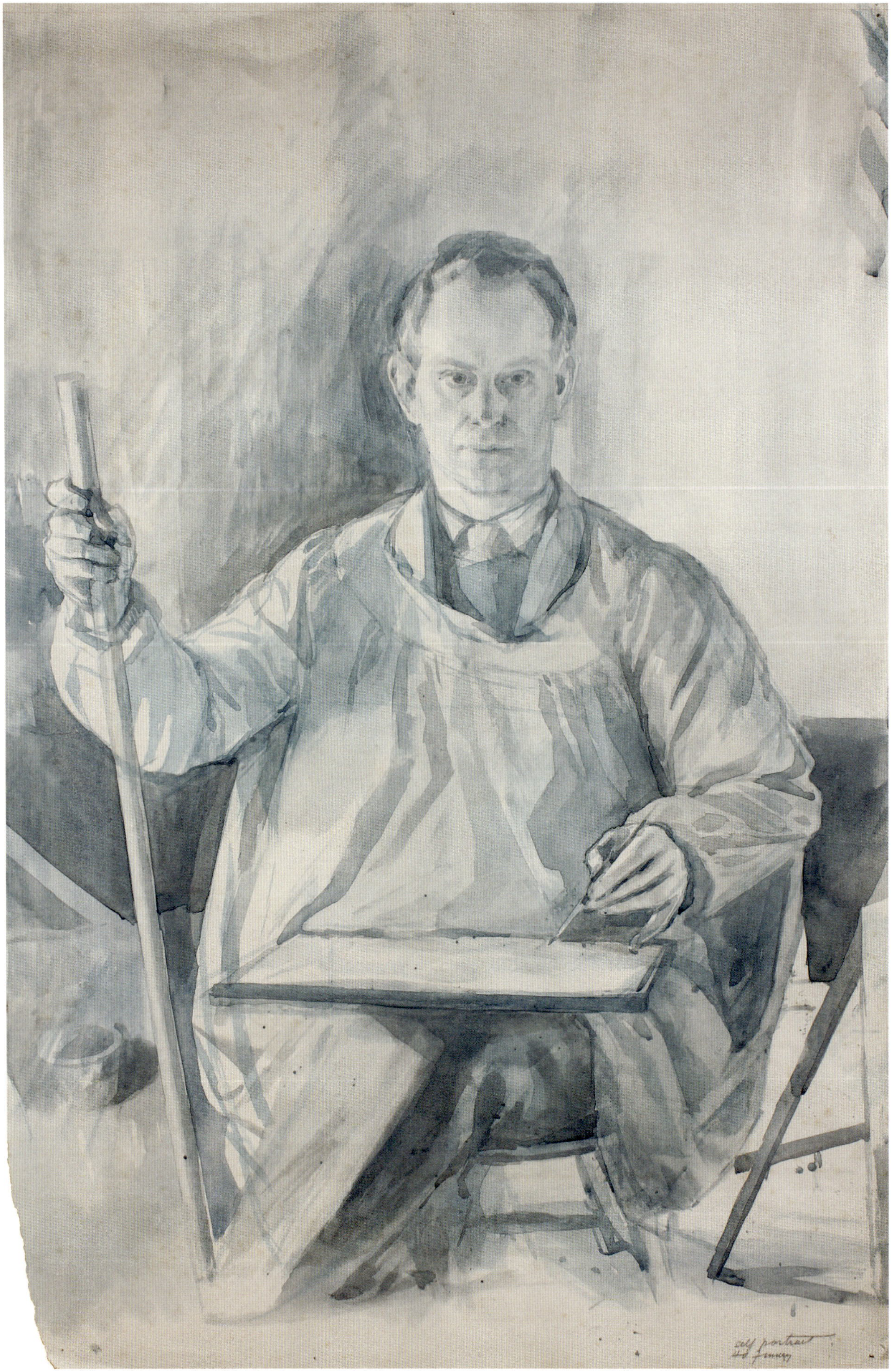
self portrait

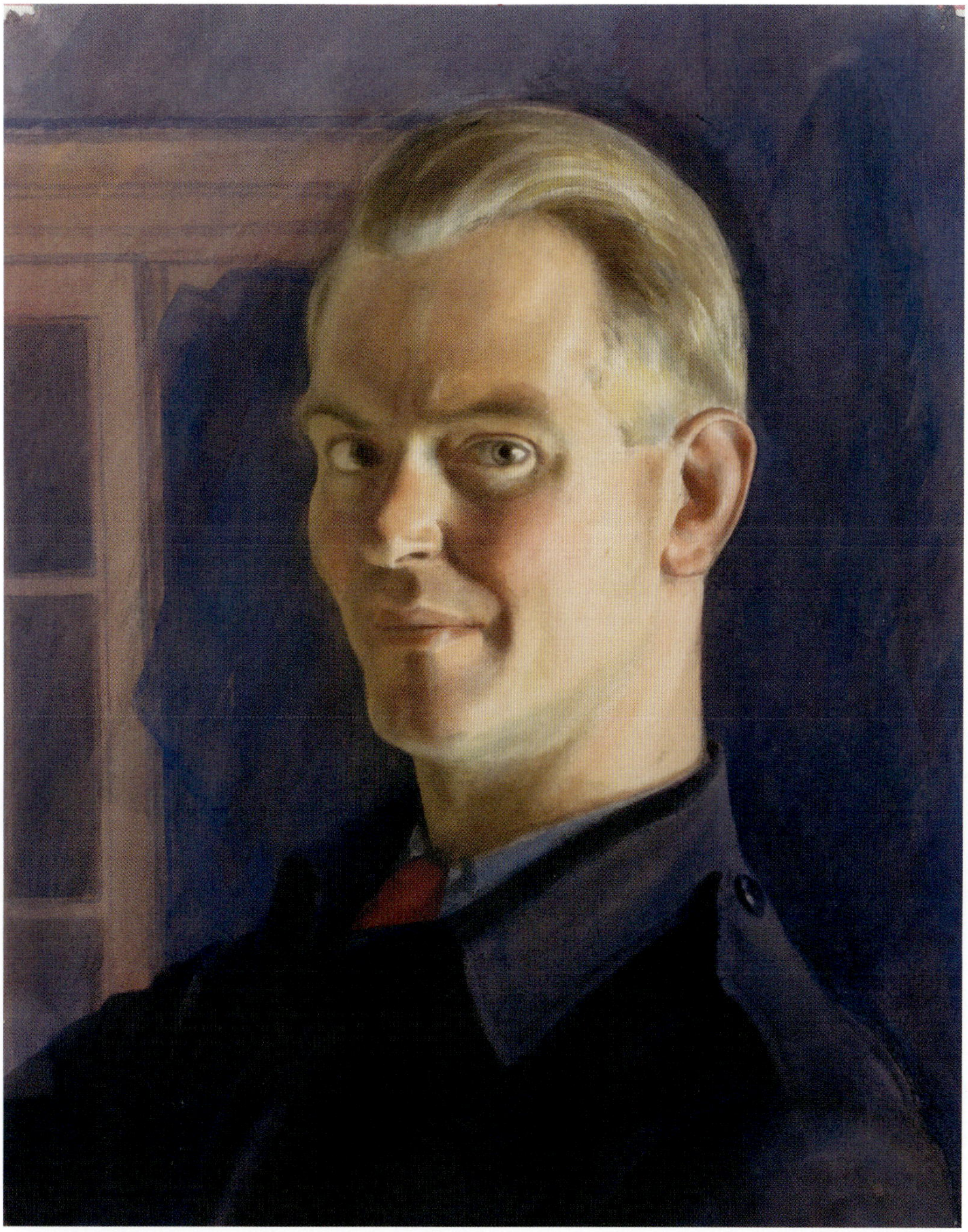

**311 Hubert Arthur Finney** (1905-1991), *Self-portrait*, 1945,
pastel on paper, 17 ½ x 14 ¼ in. (45 x 36 cm).

During WW2 Finney served in the Ambulance Crews of the Air Raid Precautions Service. Finney wears a red tie, suggesting that it dates to 1945, when he was convalescing. Red ties were worn to show that the wearer was ill or wounded and that he was a serviceman. In his unpublished autobiography Finney records: 'My health was beginning to show signs of breaking and I was sent to a Civil Defence Convalescent house…. I never ceased to draw and paint … and held a drawing class one evening a week for the Ambulance and Rescue Service Personnel.' After a period in Rome thanks to a Travelling Scholarship (1929), Finney returned to London where he obtained a part-time teaching post at Chelsea School of Art under P. H. Jowett (1882-1955). Henry Moore (1898-1986) was in charge of the sculpture department and Graham Sutherland (1903-1980) of the department of design.

**310 Hubert Arthur Finney** (1905-1991), *Self-portrait*, signed and inscribed 'self portrait', mid-1930s,
blue wash on paper, 22 x 14 ¾ in. (56 x 37.5 cm).

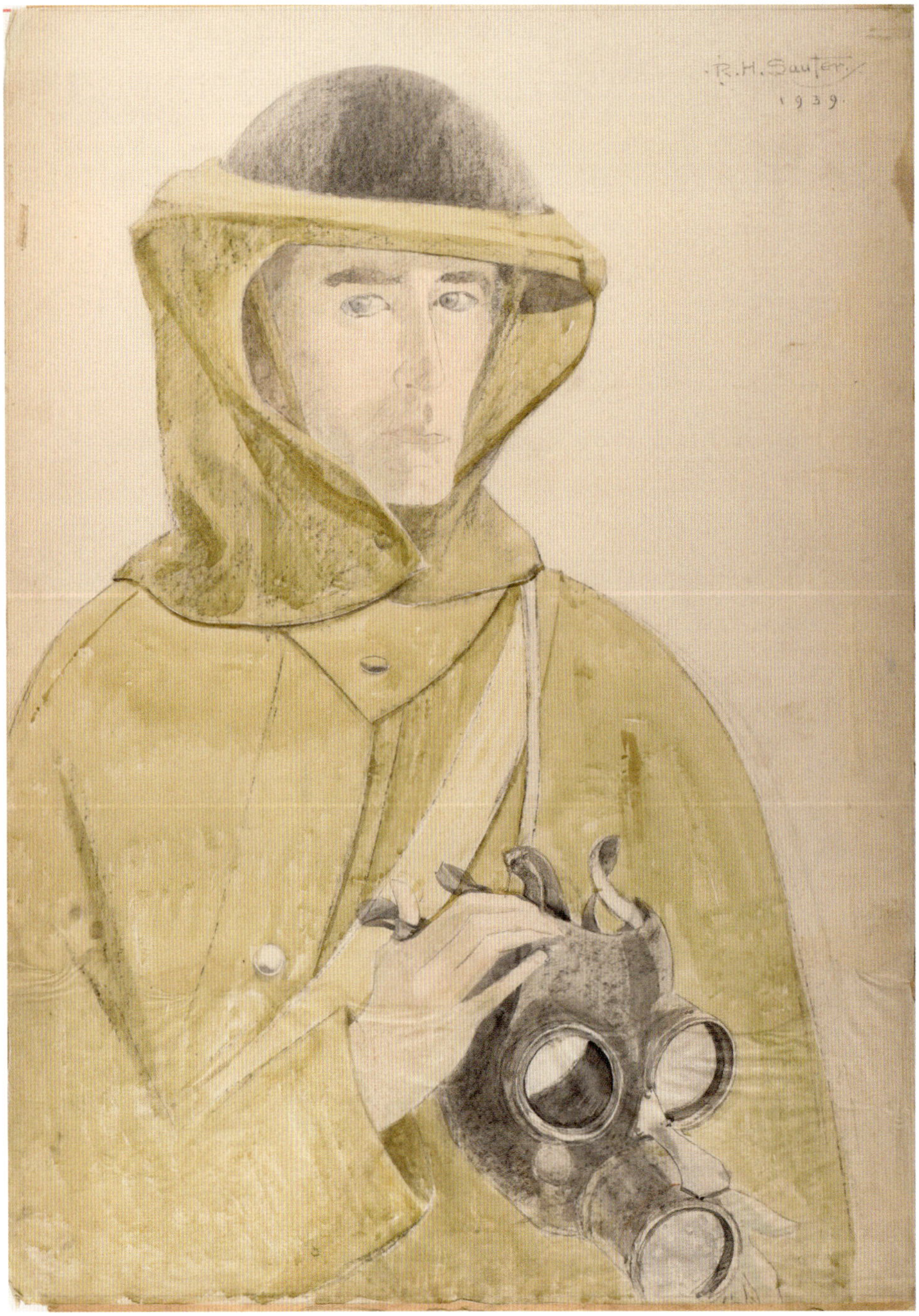


**312 Rudolf Sauter** (1895-1977), *Soldier Holding a Gas Mask* (believed to be a self-portrait), 1939, signed and dated,
pencil and watercolour on paper, 31 x 22 ¼ in. (78.5 x 56.5 cm).

**313 Rudolf Sauter** (1895-1977), *Soldier* (believed to be a self-portrait), 1939, signed;
charcoal on light brown paper, 30 ¼ x 22 in. (76.8 x 55.9 cm).

Sauter, a German-born artist, poet, cultural observer and nephew of the famed novelist John Galworthy, was interned as an 'enemy alien' in London's Alexandra Palace and Surrey's Frith Hill Camp, from March 1918 until August 1919. After the war, he became a naturalized British citizen, and during WWII he enlisted as a Local Army Welfare Officer in the Eastern Command, covering East Anglia and the Central Midland Counties. His duties across this region allowed him to continue painting. His resulting work, which focused on a variety of subjects symbolizing the realities and physical force of the nation at war, stood in stark contrast to the images of captivity he created during the previous war. Although he was never an official war artist, Rudolf documented Britain at war as accurately and meaningfully as his contemporaries.

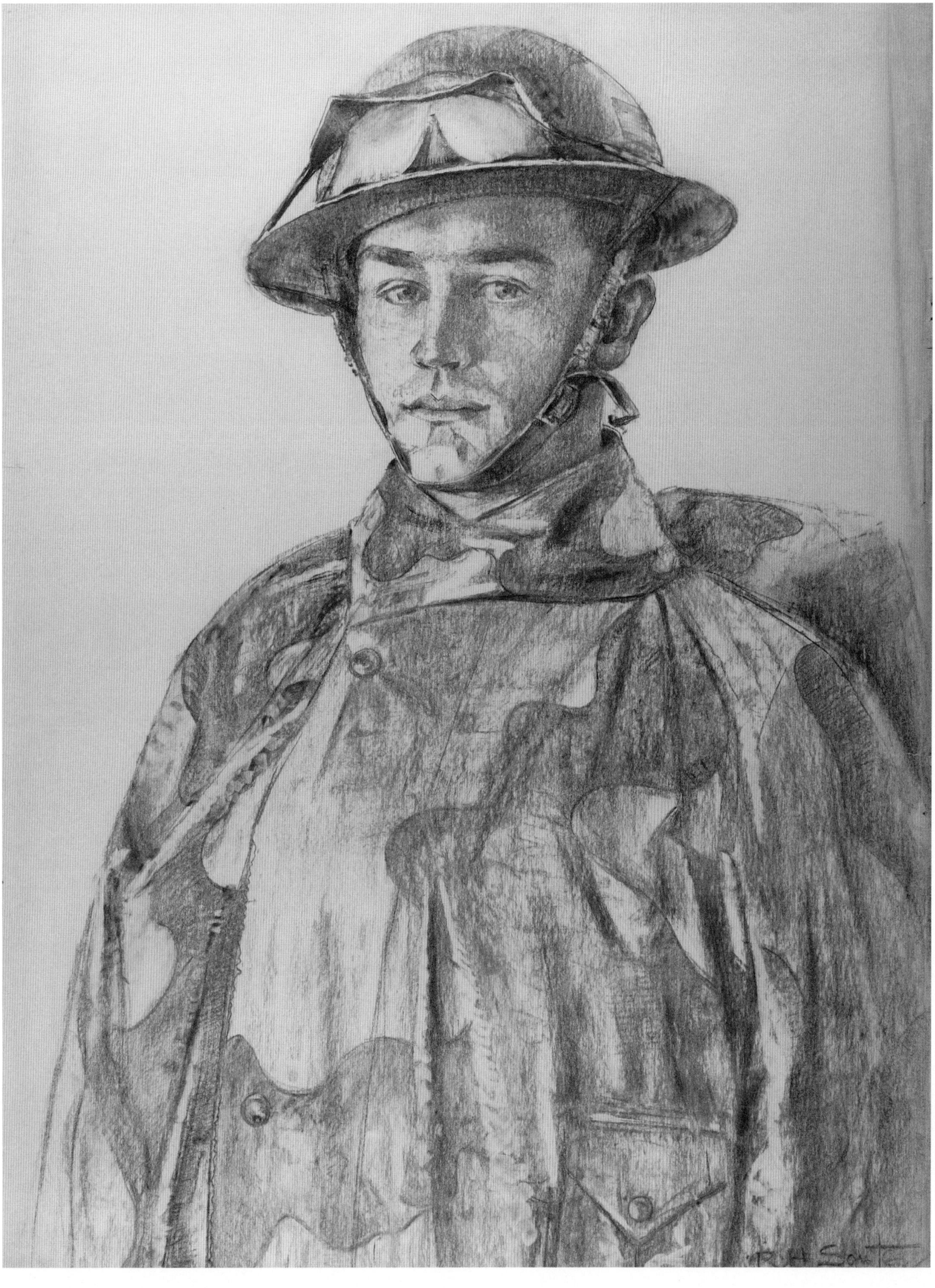

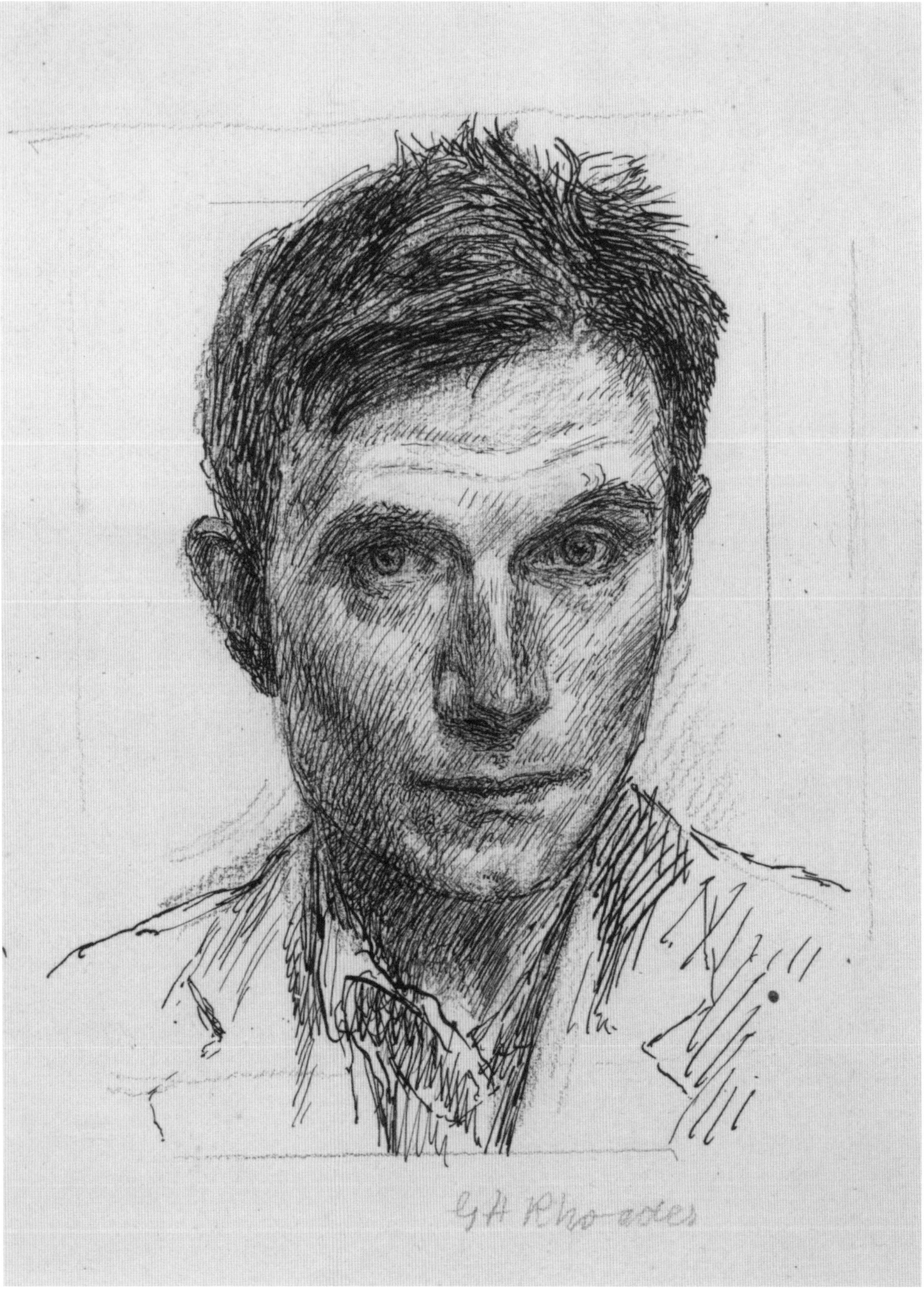


314

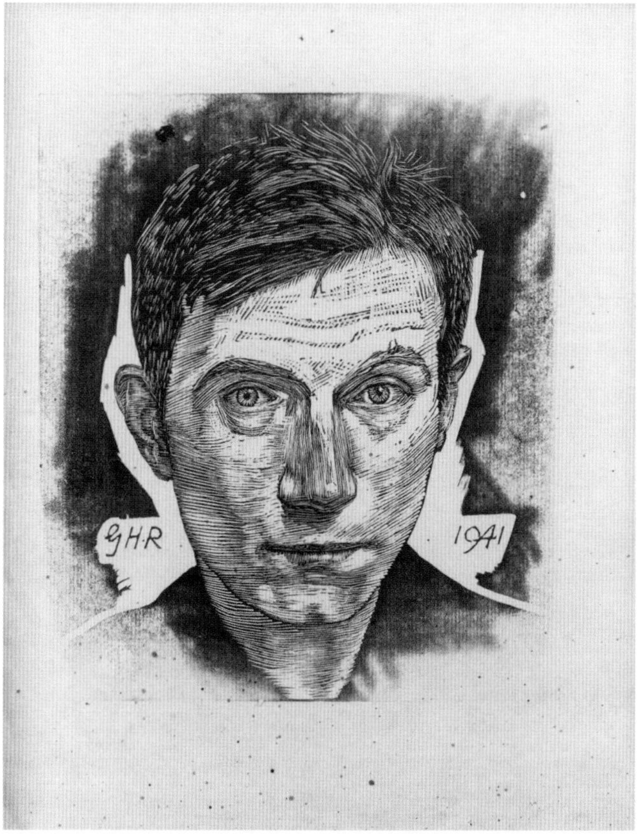


315

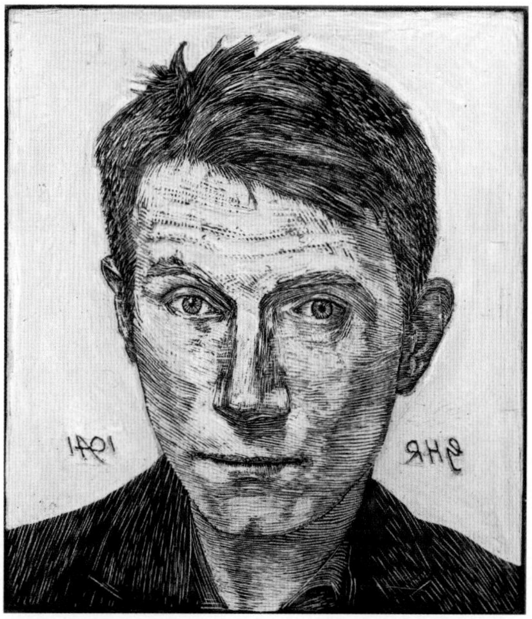

316

**Geoffrey Hamilton Rhoades** (1898-1980),

**314** *Self-portrait*, 1941, signed in pencil,
pencil and pen & ink on paper, 7 ½ x 5 ½ in. (9 x 14 cm).

**315** *Self-portrait*, 1941,
signed with initials, dated,
woodcut, un-numbered proof, 4 ¾ x 4 ¼ in. ( 12 x 10.8 cm ).

**316** *Self-portrait*, 1941, signed with initials and dated
original woodblock, 5 x 4 ½ in. (12.8 x 11.5 cm).

When Geoffrey Rhoades left the Slade Tonks said: "You've something I haven't – imagination." Rhoades had a successful career as a teacher and most notably at the Ruskin School of Drawing, Oxford, 1953-72. This wood engraving dates to WW2 when Rhoades moved with his family to Bran End, in Essex. (**218**)

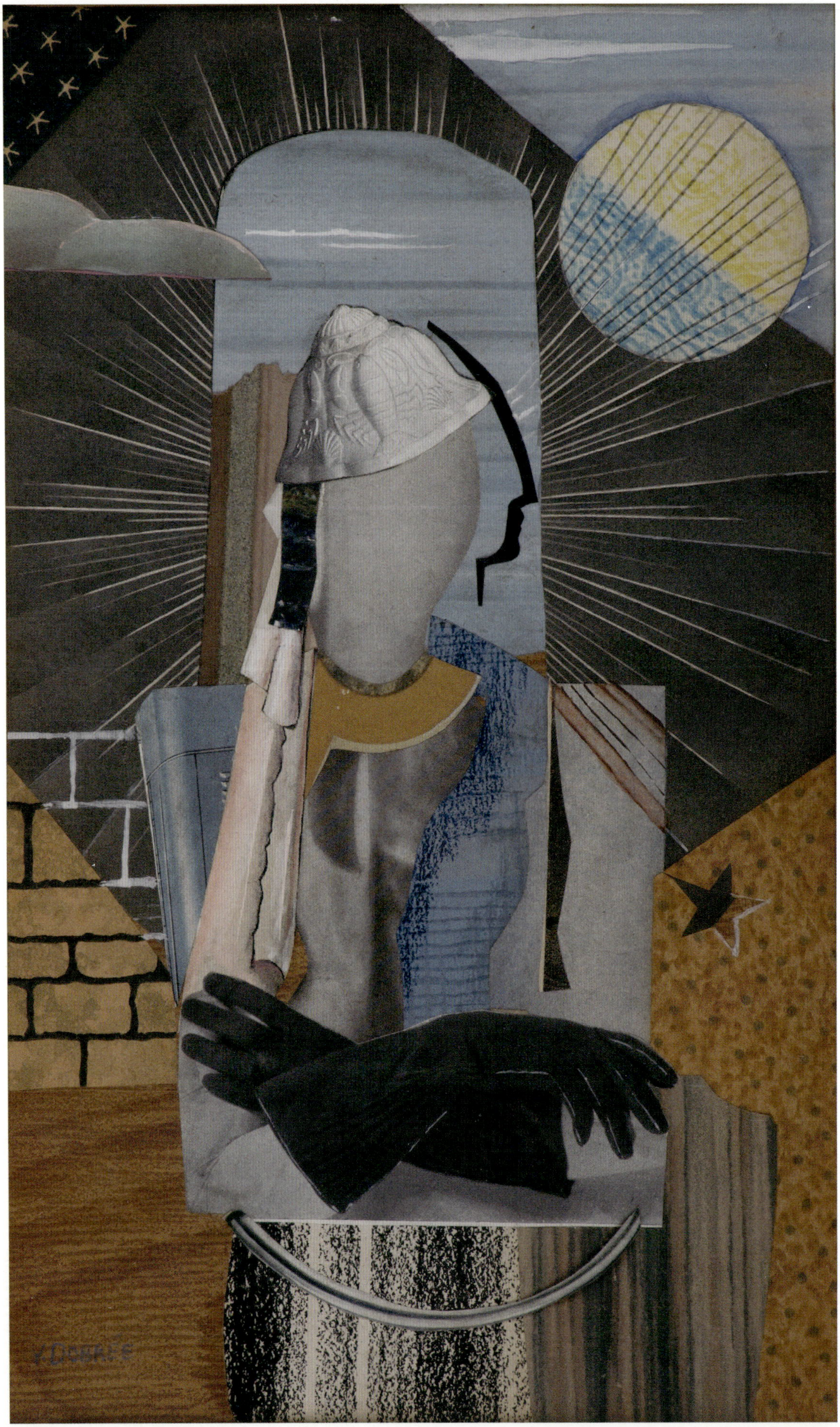

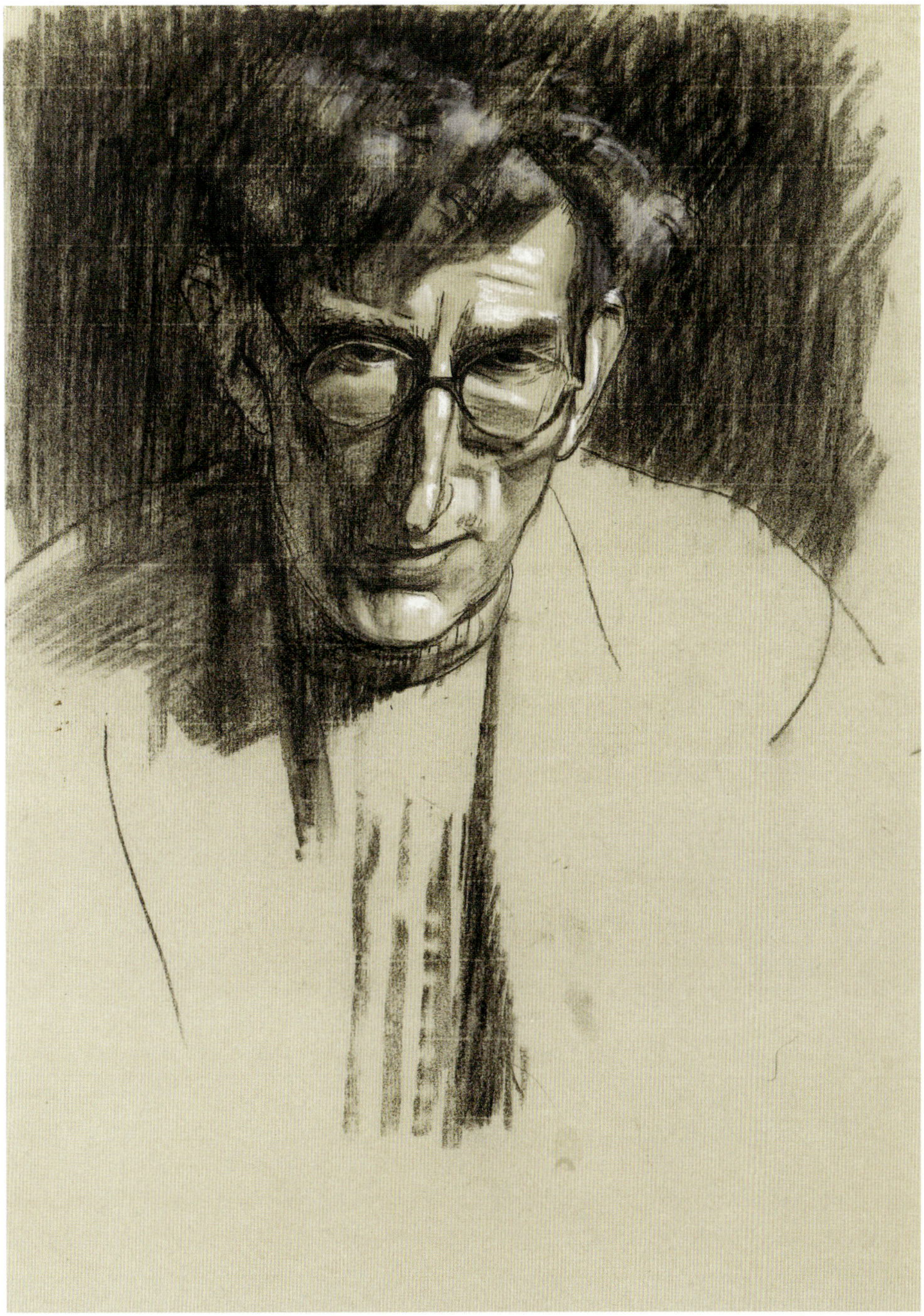

**318 Charles Mahoney** (1903-1968), *Self-portrait*, late 1950s,
charcoal, highlights in white chalk on paper, 19 x 12 ¾ in. (48.2 x 32.3 cm).

Tirzah Garwood recalled of Cyril Mahoney (known as Charlie to friends): 'Charlie had a glass eye but I thought that on the whole it improved his appearance, giving an interesting and piratical look to a face that as nature intended it, might have belonged to a Sunday School superintendent or a postman'. (**157**, **231**)

**317 Valentine Dobrée** (1894-1974), *Black Gloves*, c.1930, signed, titled to reverse,
mixed media, collage, 10 ¼ x 6 ¼ in. (26 x 16.3 cm).

'She has given so much of herself to the world, lived so fiercely it is splendid…' So wrote fellow artist Dora Carrington of her friend Valentine Dobrée, the beautiful, aristocratic yet volatile daughter of an English diplomat who lived her life variously as novelist, poet and artist.

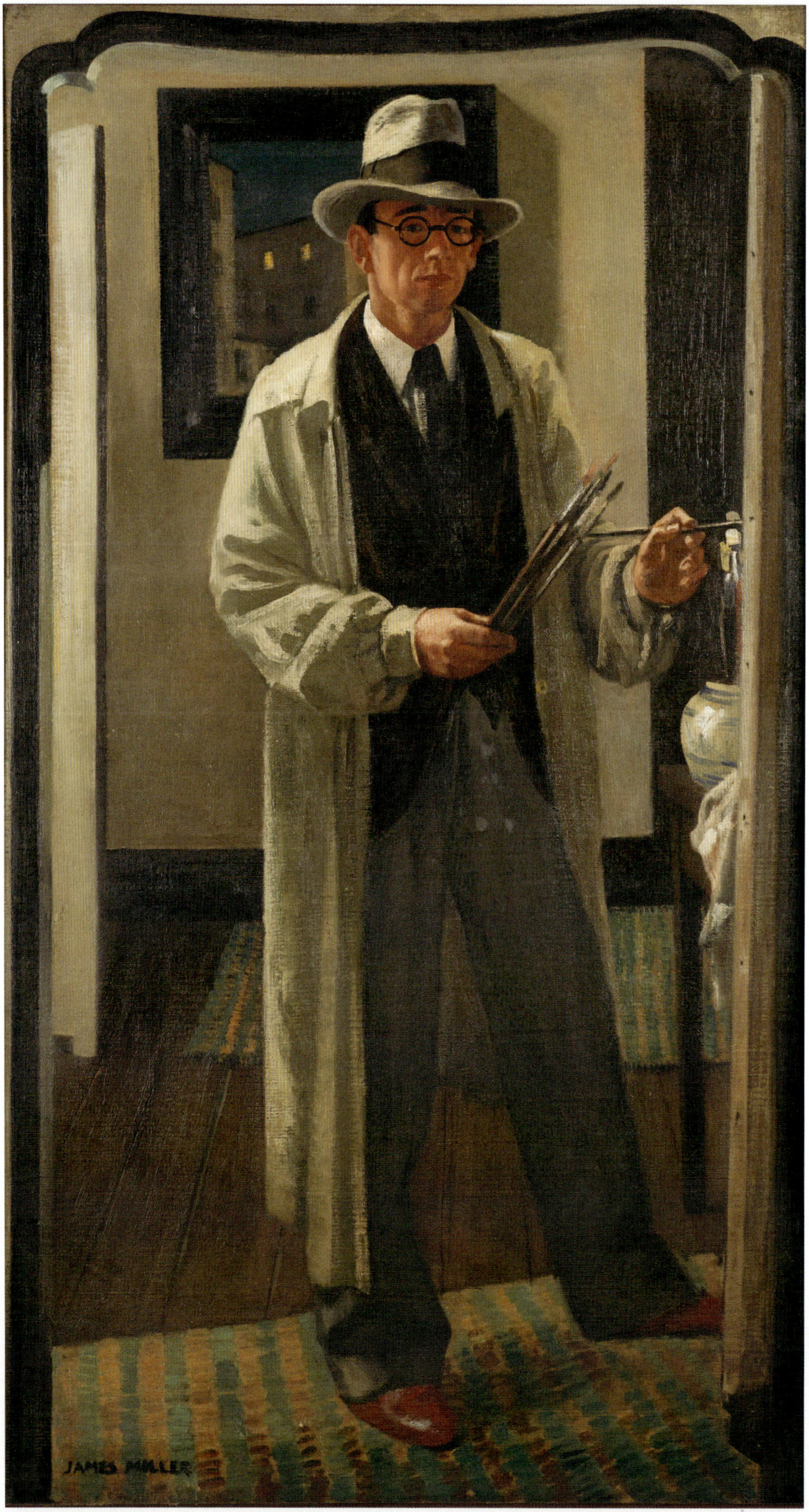
JAMES MILLER

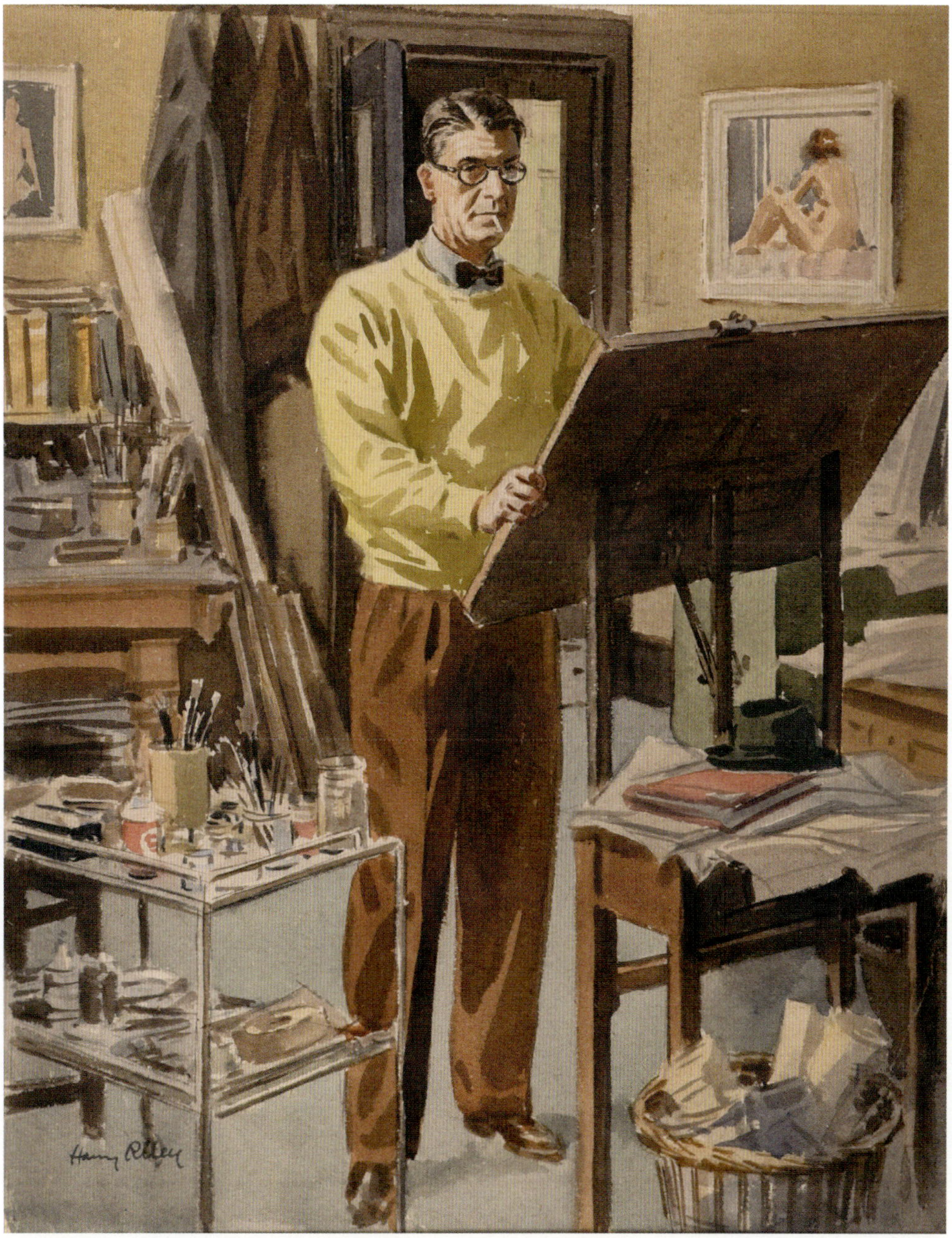

**320 Henry Arthur Riley** (1895-1966), *Harold Riley in His Studio*, c.1950, signed, inscribed on the back with instructions to the printer, gouache on buff coloured paper, 16 ¾ x 13 ¼ in. (42.5 x 33.6 cm).

By the 1950s Henry Arthur Riley had achieved a successful career, exhibiting regularly at the Royal Academy, Royal Society of British Artists and the Royal Institute of Oil Painters. His work as a cartoon illustrator was regularly published in *Reynolds News*, *London Opinion*, *Blighty*, *Humourist* and the *Sunday Chronicle*, as well as *Punch* and other influential newspapers and magazines. (**308**)

**319 James Miller** (1893-1987), *Self-portrait*, c.1940, signed lower left, oil on canvas, 49 x 27 ½ in. (125 x 70 cm).

Viewed in a mirror, glancing up momentarily to acknowledge the viewer, James Miller is posed confidently in front of the full-length canvas on which he is engaged in painting his self-portrait. The artist, in his mid- forties, was at the height of his powers, his body language self-assured, his head foiled by one of his own paintings, a nocturne, hanging behind.

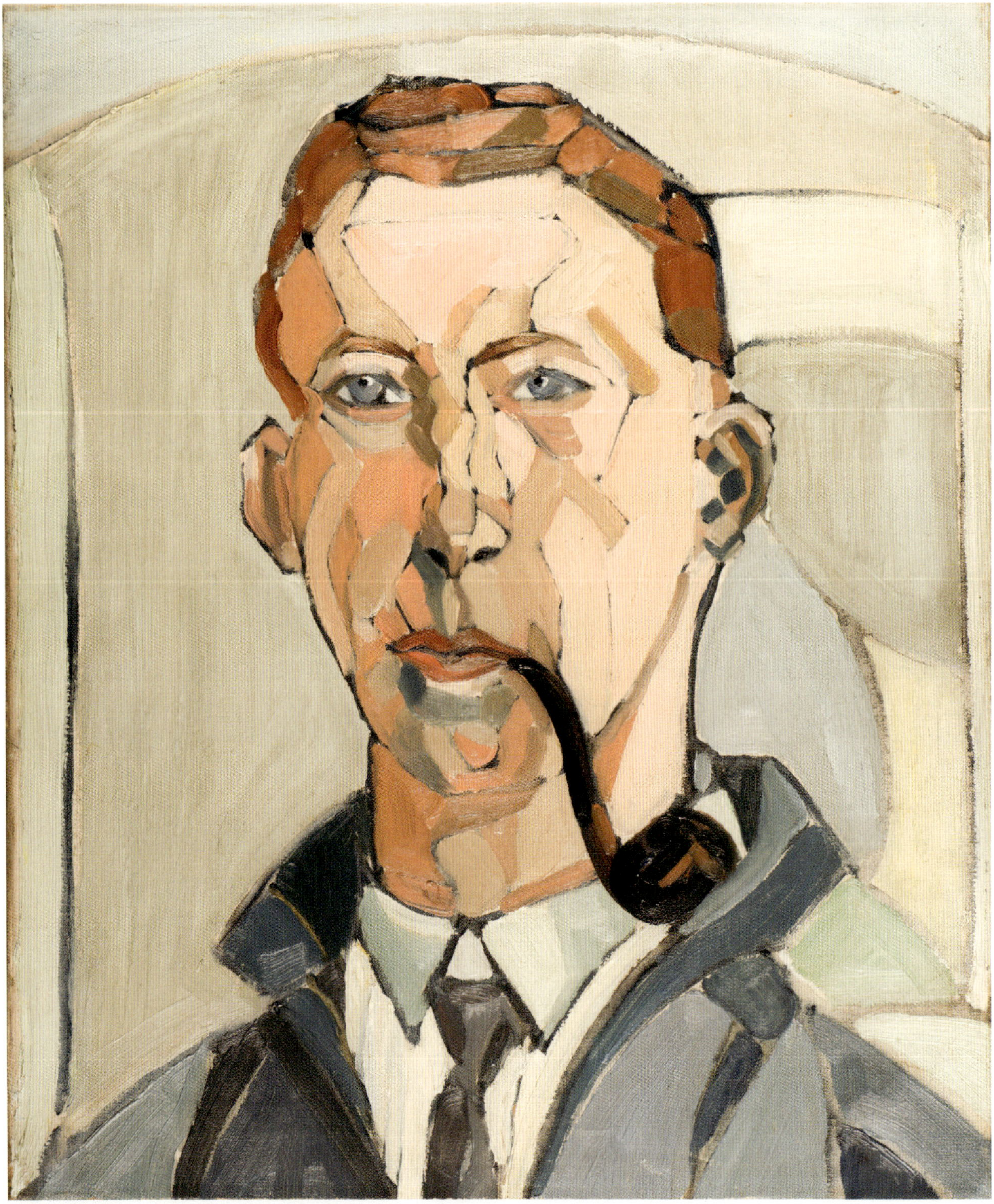

321

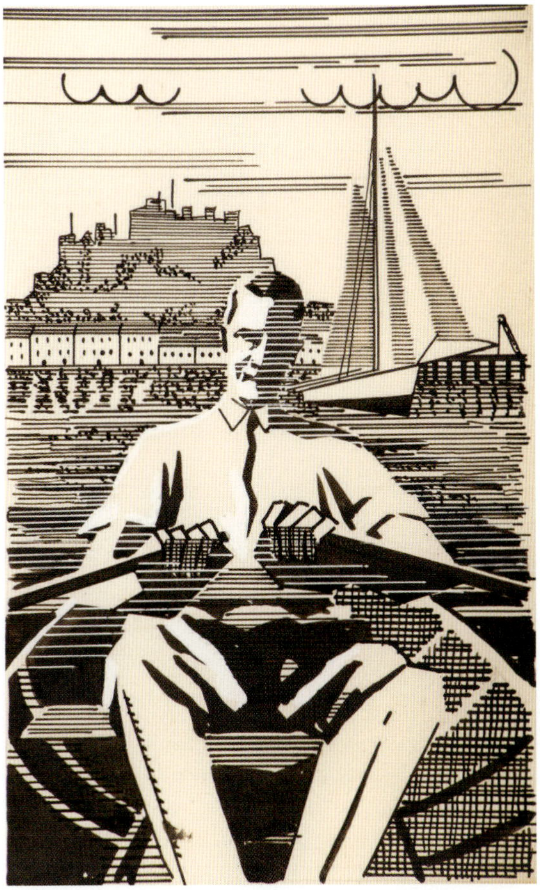

322

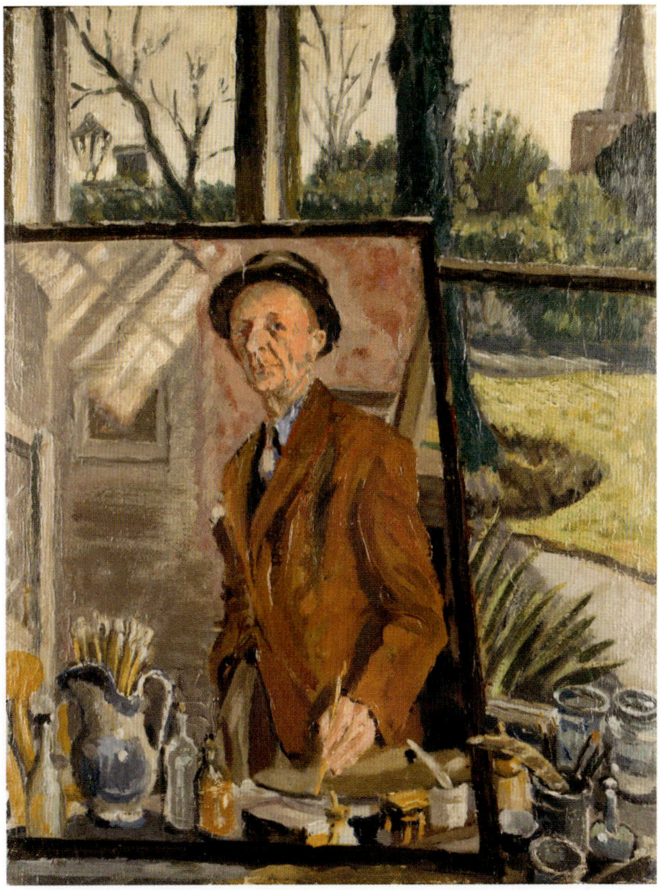

323

**Karl Hagedorn** (1889-1969),

**321** *Self-portrait with Pipe*, c.1915,
oil on canvas laid down on board, 21 x 18 in. (53.5 x 46 cm).

**322** *Design: A Self-portrait Rowing*, inscribed with title, mid-1920s,
ink, white highlights in gouache, 12 x 7 in. (30 x 17.8 cm).

**323** *Self-portrait and Mirror*, mid-1930s,
oil on panel, 18 x 14 in. (45.7 x 35.6 cm).

This self-portrait (**321**) might well have been inspired by Derain's portrait of portrait of Matisse, an artist that Hagedorn much admired and with whom he had contact when he moved to Paris in 1912. The composition is likely to be set in the artist's pre-war London home in Belsize Park.

Hagedorn was a successful graphic artist during the interwar period, producing a wide variety of commercial designs for posters, advertisements and illustrations.

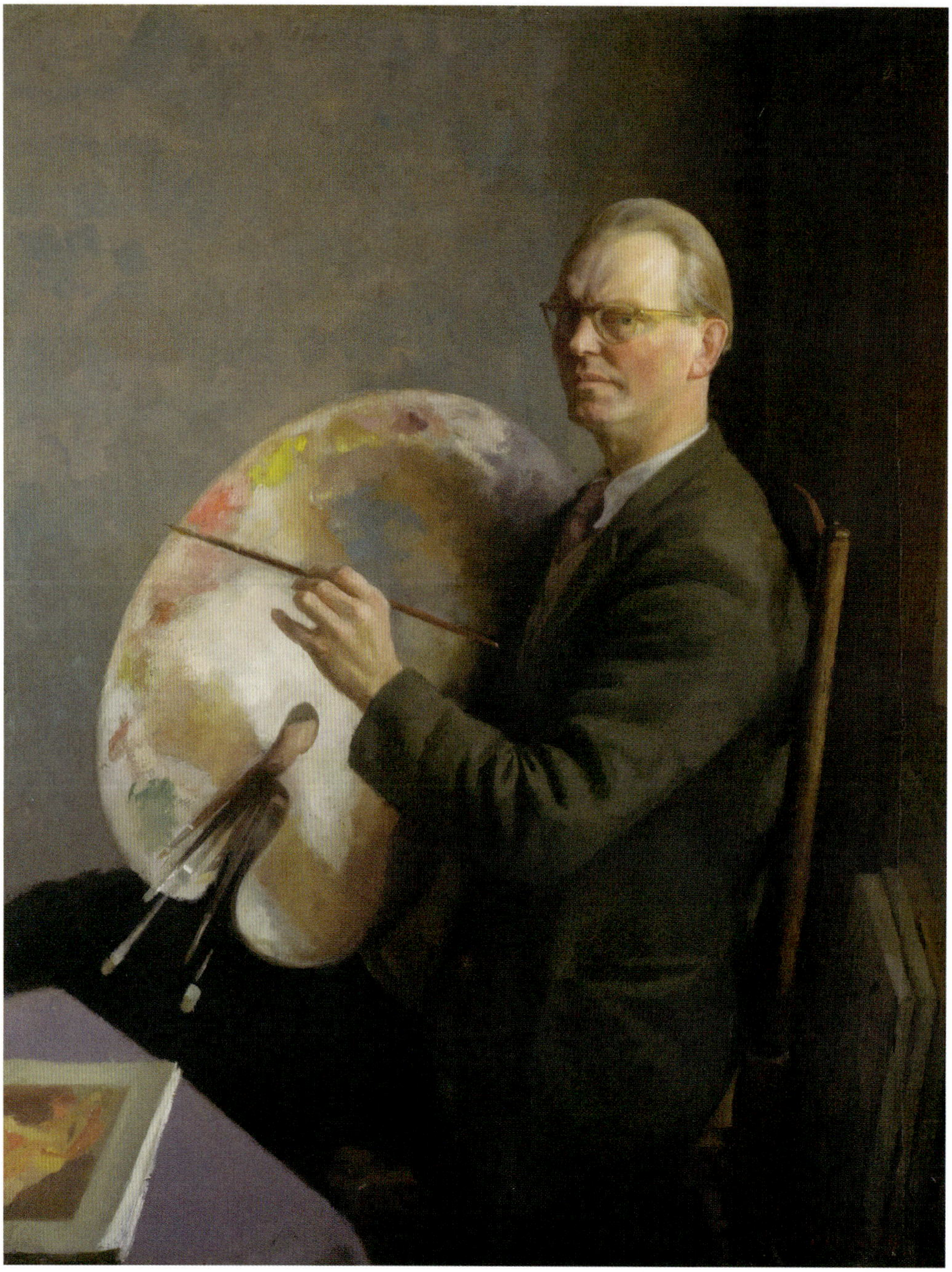

**324 Hubert Arthur Finney** (1905-1991), *Self-portrait*, 1960s, signed, titled to reverse, oil on board, 26 ½ x 21 in. (67.3 x 53.4 cm).

Painted in the 1960s, towards the end of Hugh Arthur Finney's career, when he was in charge of life drawing at the Fine Art Department of Reading University, this painting is one of his most ambitious attempts at self-portraiture. (**310**, **311**) For the composition he might have had in mind self-portraits of a similar format by Rembrandt and Gérard Dou.

**325 Gilbert Spencer** (1892-1979), *Late Self-portrait*, signed and dated January 1971, inscribed 'for Cash and later Gillian', pencil on paper, 15 x 10 in. (38 x 26 cm).

Having temporarily resigned his membership of the Royal Academy in 1968, Gilbert Spencer rejoined in 1971, the year of this self-portrait. In the same year, having lived most of the previous four decades in Berkshire, he moved to Walsham-le-Willows, Suffolk. He died in Braintree, Essex, eight years later, in 1979. (**67**, **128**, **152**,**153**, **155**)

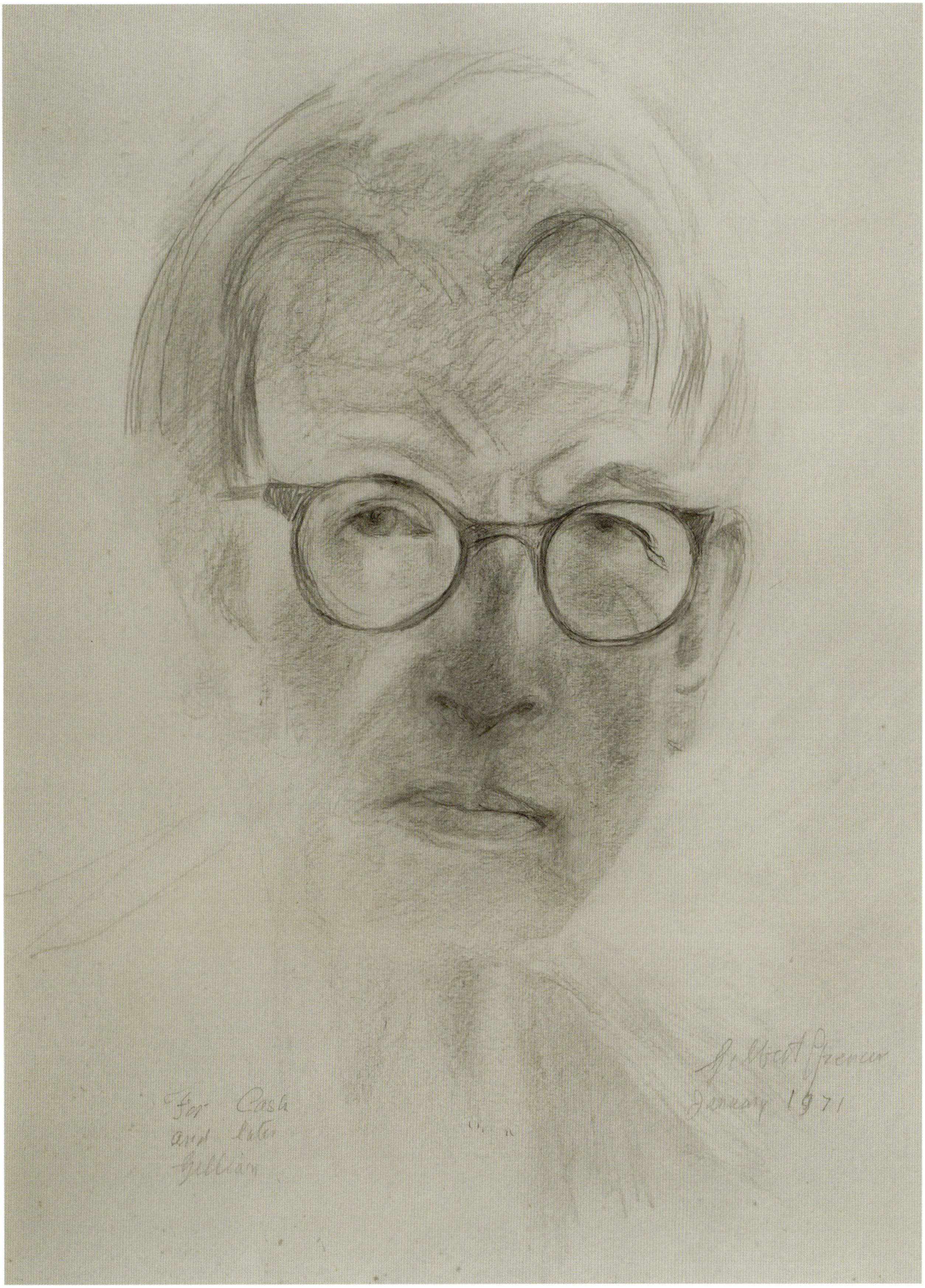
For Cosh
and later
Gillian
Gilbert Spencer
January 1971

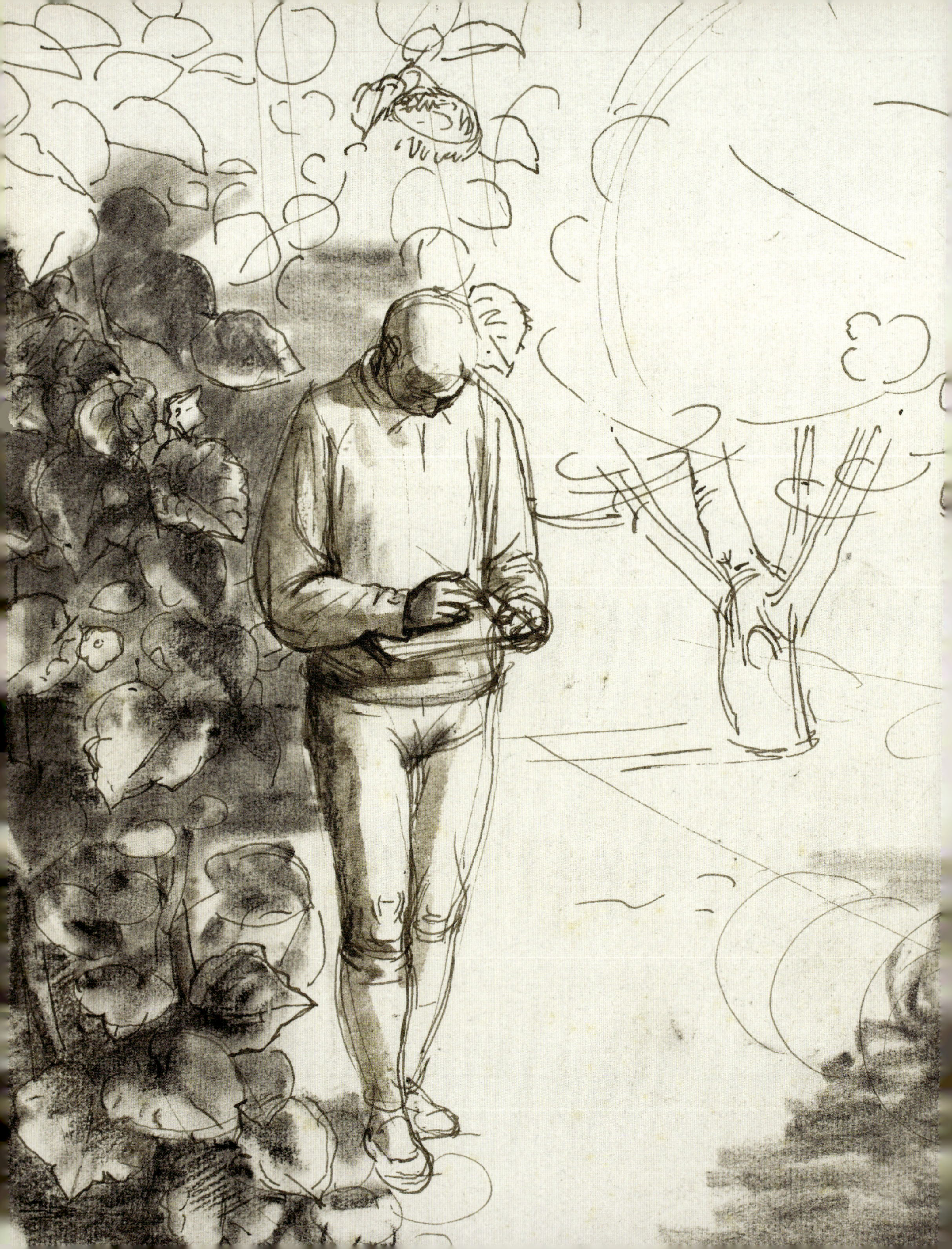

# ALLEGORIES OF CREATION

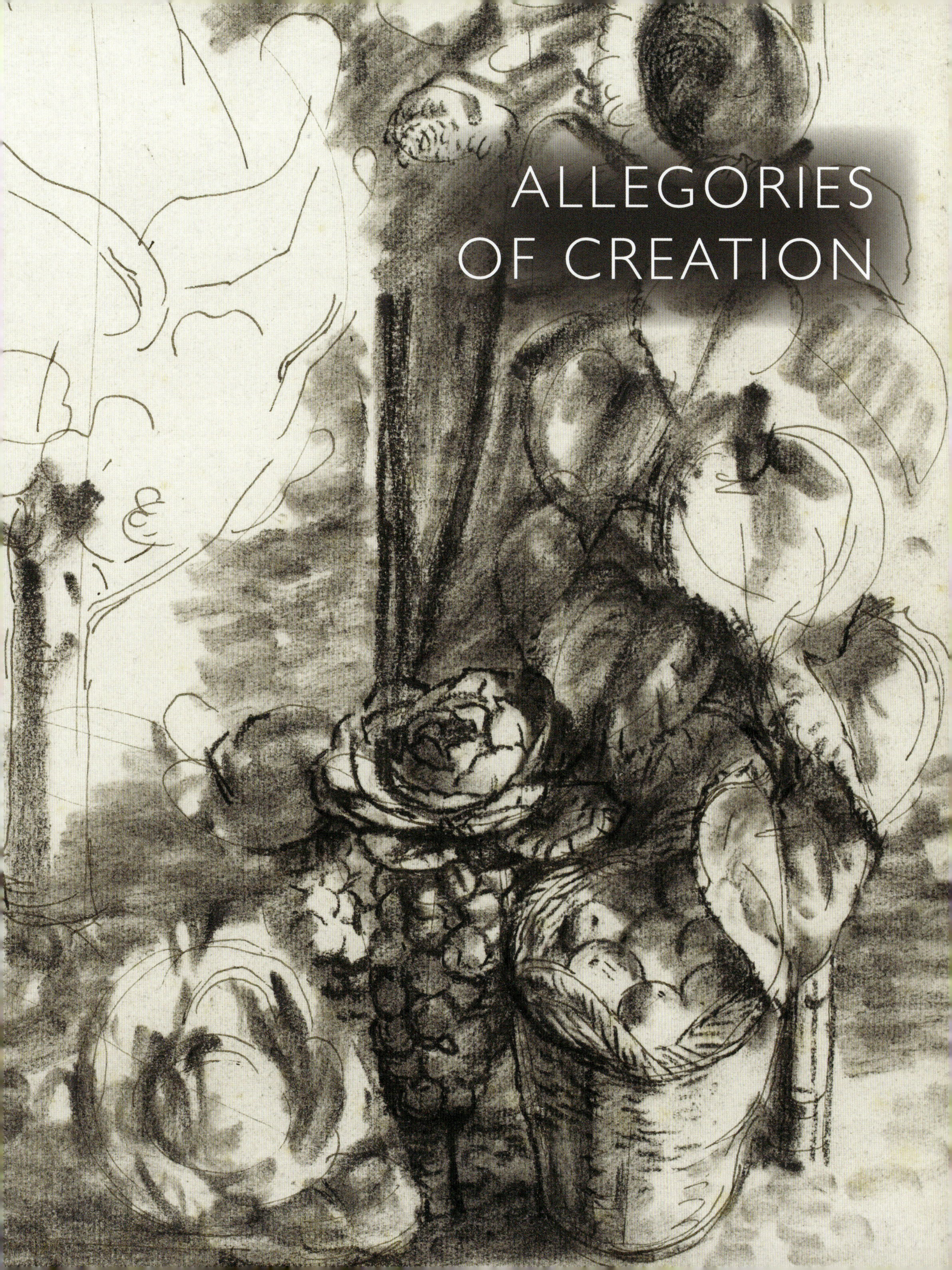

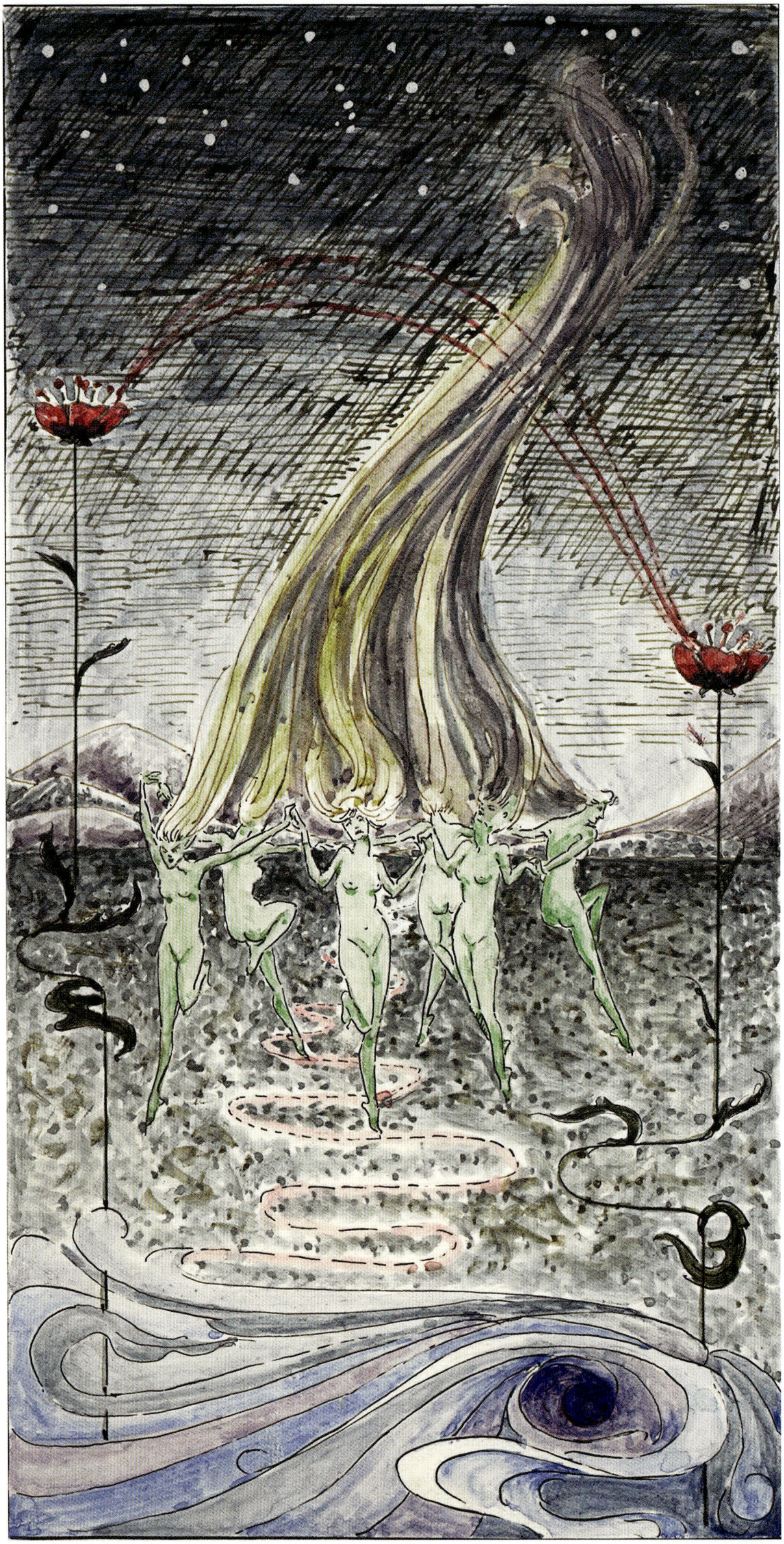

# Allegories of Creation

*'So God created man in his own image; he created him in the image of God; he created them male and female.'* Genesis 1:27

If God created men and women in his own image (or indeed if they created God in their own image) then self-portraiture is at the very heart of creation and the origin of life. This idea seems to have preoccupied a great number of artists. William Taylor, Clare Leighton, Francis Plummer, Percy Horton, Barbara Jones, Charles Mahoney, Evelyn Dunbar, Alan Sorrell, Thomas Monnington, Winifred Knights and Gladys Hynes continuously explored their own relationship to nature – and ultimately God – through art. Artists' hands, and all-seeing eyes, are recurrent motifs and there is an obvious correlation between the hand of God, and the hand of the artist, in works such as Charles Sims' *My Pain Beneath your Sheltering Hand.* Works like this inevitably touch on the artist's role in society and the existential questions that flow from this. Mahoney portrayed himself as a figure in the company of muses and delighted in recreating different episodes in the narrative of The Garden of Eden. Nature crowns Barbara Jones's personification of 'A Century of Technical and Social Progress'. Evelyn Dunbar, in both formative sketches such as her *Allegory of Creation* or personifications of Mother Earth, affirms that Nature is her ultimate source of inspiration. Likewise Sorrell's memorable image of *The Artist in the Campagna*. The numerous large scale Allegories that during the 1920s were the go-to subject of the Rome Scholars, express this same sentiment – what Monnington, talking of his *Allegory*, described as 'an attempt to express in pictorial form my attitude to life – almost my faith'. This chimes with Houthuesen's remark about his early magnum opus *The Supper at Emmaus*: 'When one talks about philosophy in relation for instance to a picture like this, I think that every picture you make, every drawing you make, is a self-portrait. If they have anything in them at all, anything real, they must reflect something that comes from within.'

It is striking how often artists served as their own models: Stanley Lewis lies languidly in the middle of Hyde Park, Gladys Hynes is the Venus emerging from the sea, Frank Potter is a fire watcher-cum-gatekeeper to St Paul's, Archibald Ziegler is Christ on the Cross, Winifred Knights battles through *The Deluge*, Frank Brangwyn helps Christ carry his cross, Alan Sorrell is one of the several artists 'Seeking Wisdom', whilst Tom Monnington oversees an allegory of *Winter* and a brow-beaten Claude Francis Barry walks with a heavy heart through a field of Crosses. What better way to explore a sense of self than by embracing ones alter-ego and becoming the main protagonist of one's own narrative?

**326 Winifred Knights** (1899-1947), Illustration to Algernon Blackwood's *The Centaur*, 1915, pen & ink and watercolour on paper, 9 ¾ x 7 ¼ in. (24.7 x 18.4 cm).

In 1915, Winifred Knights produced an illustration to Algernon Blackwood's visionary novel, *The Centaur*, published in 1911, the story of a journalist of mystical temperament who rejects the pace of the modern world for a lifestyle that is closer to nature. Often presenting herself as the central protagonist, and selecting models from her inner circle, Knights was greatly drawn to themes showing female independence, strength and courage. The conflict between female self-empowerment and subjugation was a recurrent theme, explored through women's relationship to the natural world.

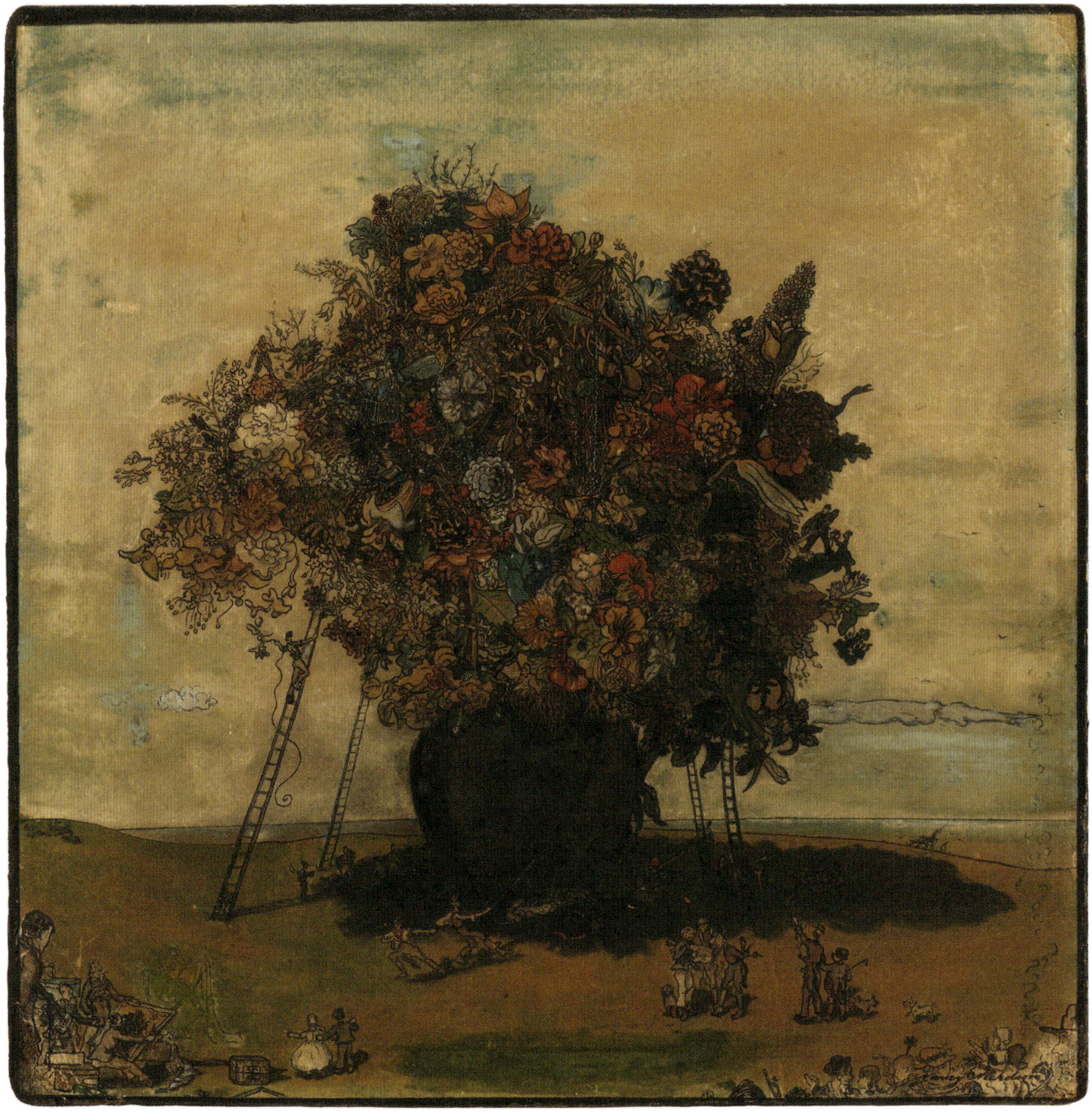

**327** **Nancy Nicholson** (1899-1977), *William Nicholson at Work*, 1918, signed, gouache on card, 14 ½ x 14 ½ in. (37 x 37 cm).

In his book *Flower and Still Life Painting* (1928), Charles Holme considered that 'William Nicholson's popular reputation is that of a flower-painter above all' and that 'his work in this direction lies along the great line of tradition'. It is hardly surprising, therefore, that Nancy Nicholson has depicted her distinguished father, with her characteristic humour, painting a still life of flowers in a vase, any hint of spontaneity negated by the group of diminutive men on ladders carefully arranging the stems. In the corner, Nancy's husband Robert Graves, newly demobilized from the army, towers above the scene.

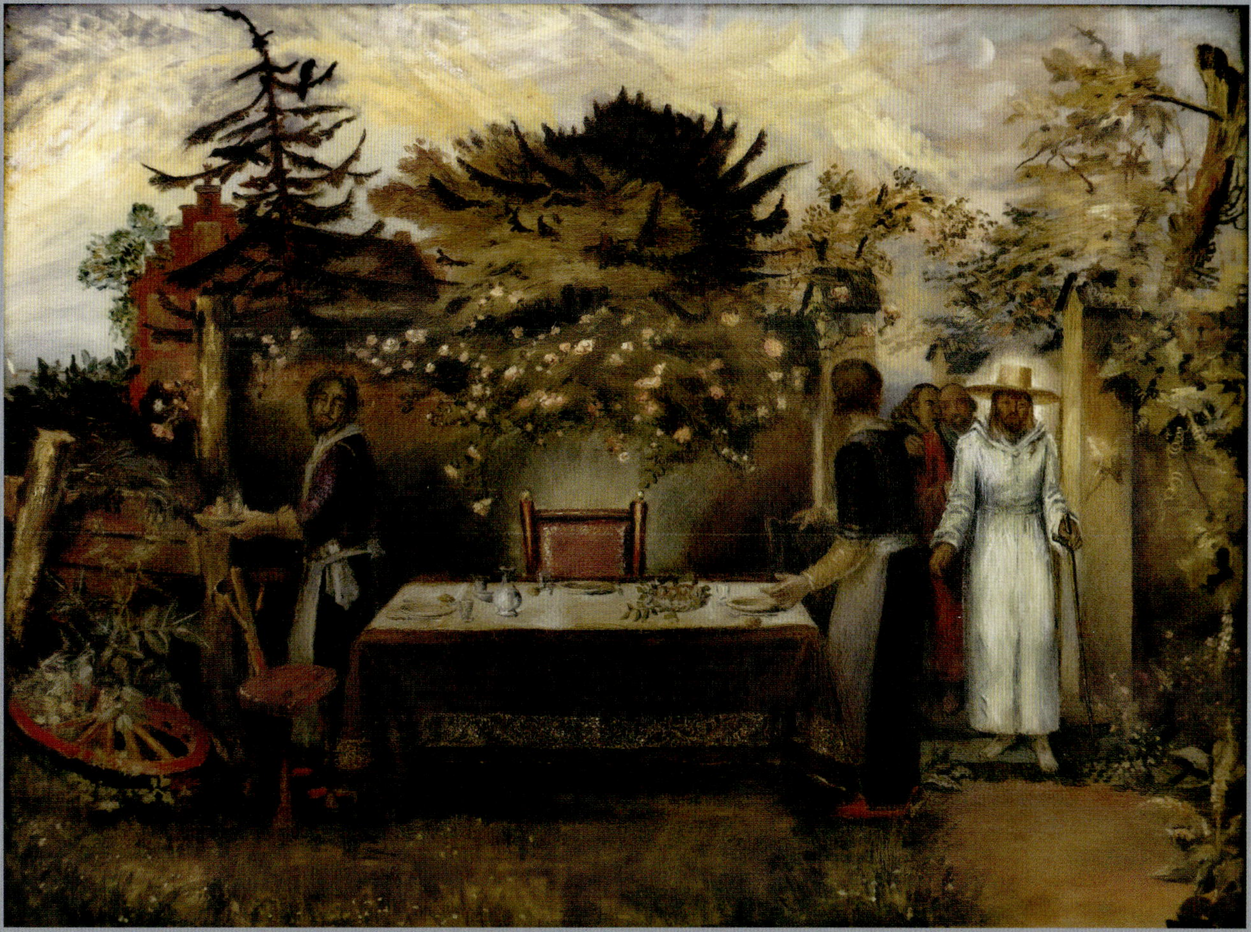

**328 Albert Anthony Houthuesen** (1903-1979), *The Supper at Emmaus*, 1927,
oil on a muslin-wrapped wooden board 30 x 41 ½ in. (76.2 x 105.3 cm).

Of this only surviving major work from his student days at The Royal College of Art, Albert Houthuesen recalled:
'I'm only sorry I couldn't have purchased a decent canvas for myself. It was poor quality board and cheap student paints. But one tried to make something of it.....This mysterious walk back from the grave is an amazing subject. I couldn't have imagined a more marvelous subject. At that time everyone spoke always of colour; and through sheer perversity, I used browns instead of greens, although I know this was painted in summer time. I started painting straight away on this panel. I didn't draw anything. I didn't make studies. I didn't square anything up. You see the thing and you paint it. It isn't in any sense a literal translation. I didn't think about Jerusalem or the Walk to Emmaus. This is Keats's Grove which by then had all become overgrown. These are the walls and trees that I saw there. The Dutch house, the sea that I knew. These three are going to sit at this table. And whilst I was painting, I thought 'This chair knows it is going to receive Christ and so it glows with a halo'. I don't really like talking about it but I think that this is filled with the idea of a man who has come back from the grave. If you think of the immense robustness of some of the Italian paintings, this man has been crushed and he feels his way, just as these two discuss whether it can be the Master. And this table suggests an alter. When one talks about philosophy in relation for instance to a picture like this, I think that every picture you make, every drawing you make, is a self-portrait. If they have anything in them at all, anything real, they must reflect something that comes from within.' (**158**)

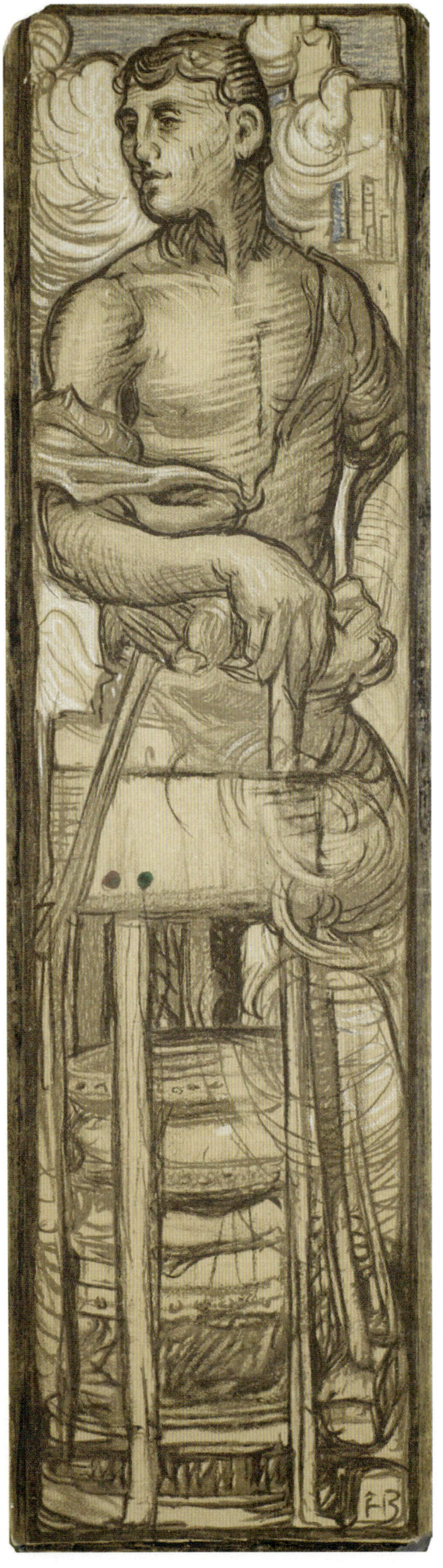

329

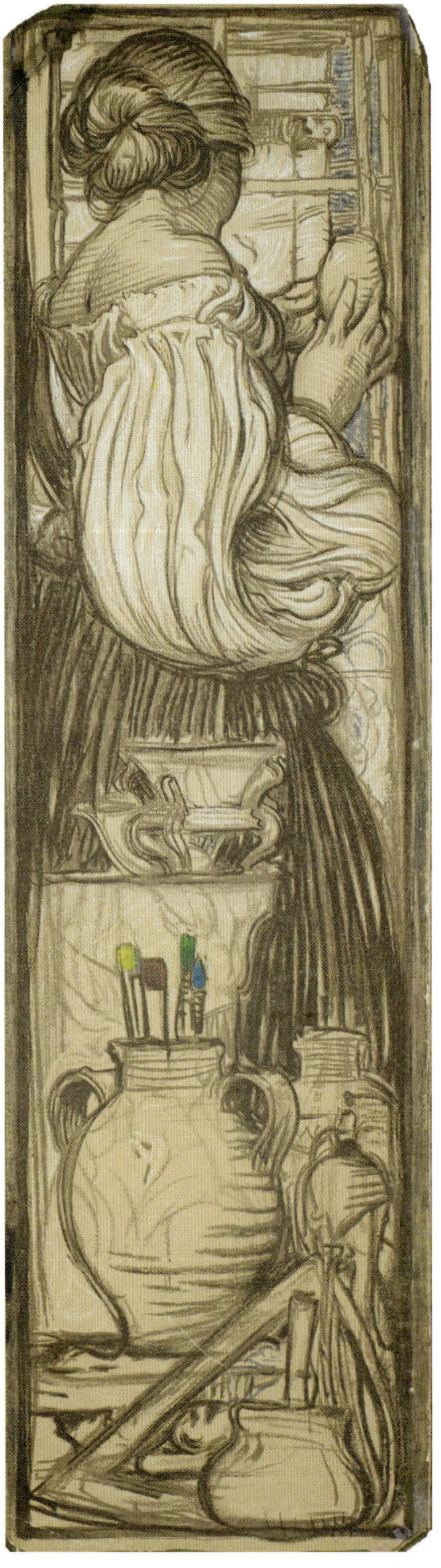

330

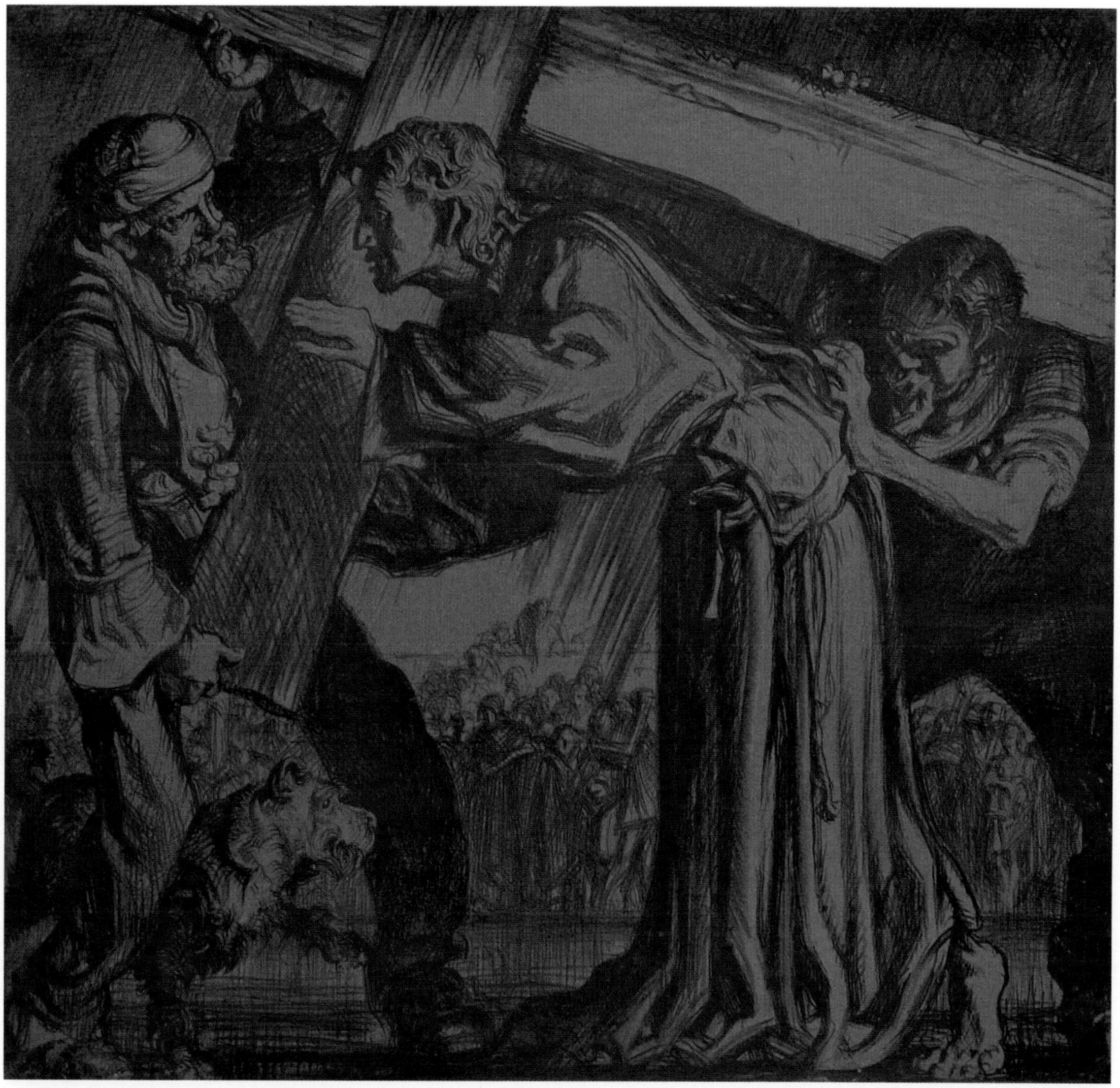

**331 Frank Brangwyn** (1867-1956), *The 2nd Station: Jesus Carries His Cross*, c.1934, signed with monogram, original zinc lithographic plate, 30 x 32 in. (76.2 x 81.3 cm).

The Stations of the Cross were described by Brangwyn as 'a subject I've had at the back of my mind all my life. . . . I've always wanted to do this, and have thought about it for years'. As G.K. Chesterton observed of Brangwyn's *Stations*: 'Every face is vigorous, with an ugly energy that is more attractive than vulgar beauty.' Brangwyn frequently included himself in his compositions and here he is seen supporting Christ and taking the weight of the cross on his back. And for good measure, on the left hand side, Brangwyn has included his dog Roger.

**Frank Brangwyn** (1867-1956),

**329** An Allegorical Figure of a Potter, from the right hand side of a calendar for 1901,
**330** An Allegorical Figure of Painting, from the left hand side of a calendar for 1901,
signed with initials in the plate, lithographic print with hand colouring, each: 18 x 5 in. (46 x 13 cm).

These proofs were commissioned by *The Studio* magazine for their 1901 Almanac.

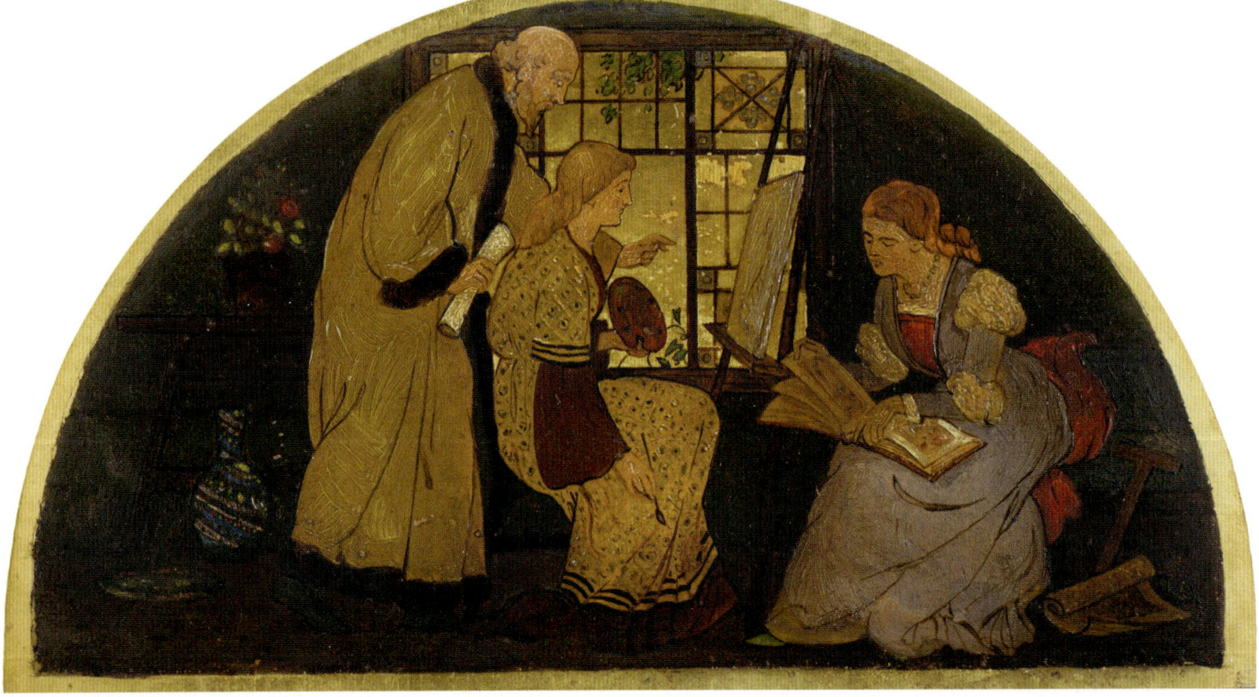

**332 English School**, *Allegory of Painting*, c.1880,
oil on a guilded ground, 5 ¼ x 9 ½ in. (13.3 x 24.1 cm).

Traditionally allegories of painting show the main protagonists as women, sometimes overseen by the figure of a wise old man, perhaps to reinforce patriarchal norms. One of the best-known allegories of painting is Artemisia Gentileschi's (1593-c.1656) self-portrait *La Pittura*, also known as *Autoritratto in veste di Pittura*.

**English School**

**333** *Hearing*, c.1880,
pencil and ink on paper,
11 ½ x 13 in. (29.2 x 33 cm).

**334** *Feeling*, c.1880,
pencil and watercolour on paper,
9 x 10 ½ in. (22.8 x 26.7 cm).

**335** *Seeing*, c.1880,
pencil and watercolour on paper,
12 x 11 in. (30.5 x 28 cm).

The allegorical representation of the five senses as female figures dates back to the 16th century, the collaborative cycle of paintings by Jan Brueghel the Elder and Peter Paul Rubens being the best known. Sight was considered the most important of the senses from the time of Aristotle, a view that artists, naturally, perpetuated, for which reason themes such *The Healing of the Blind Man*, and other secular and religious narratives, in which sight plays a central role are common subjects.

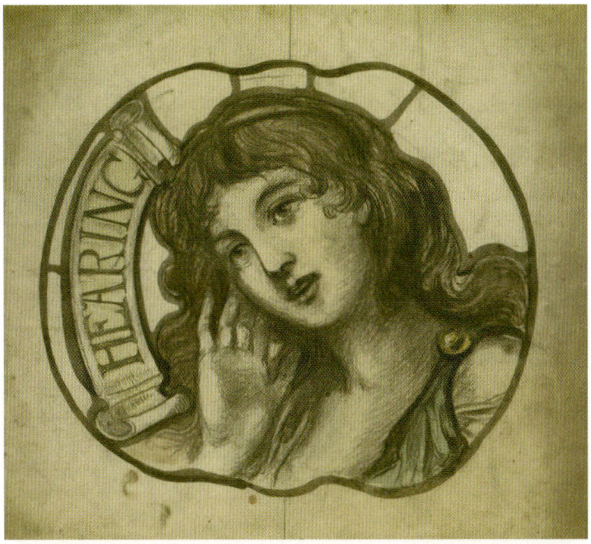


333

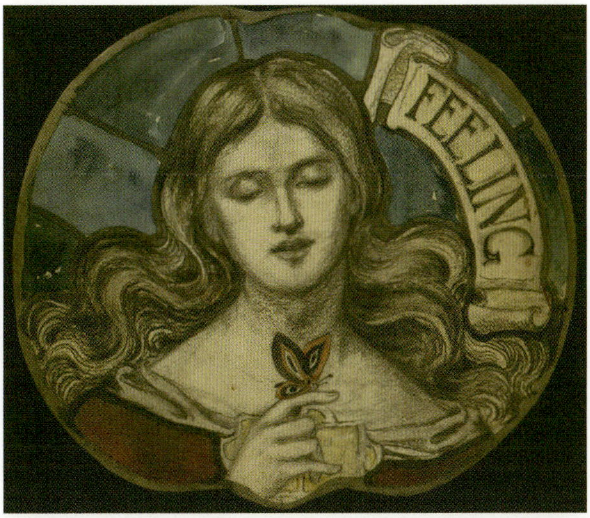


334

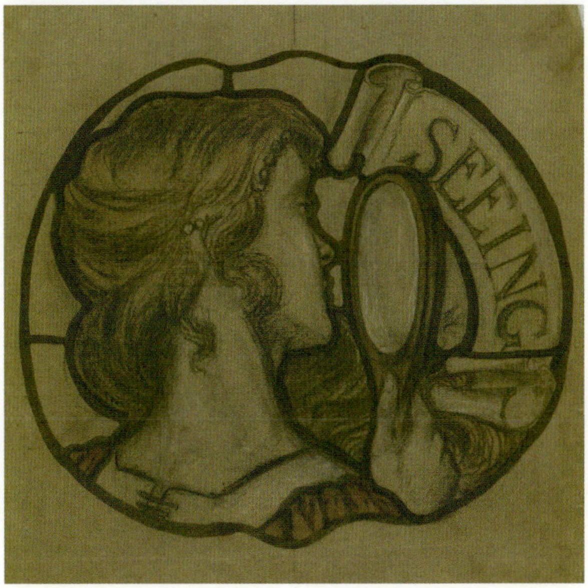


335

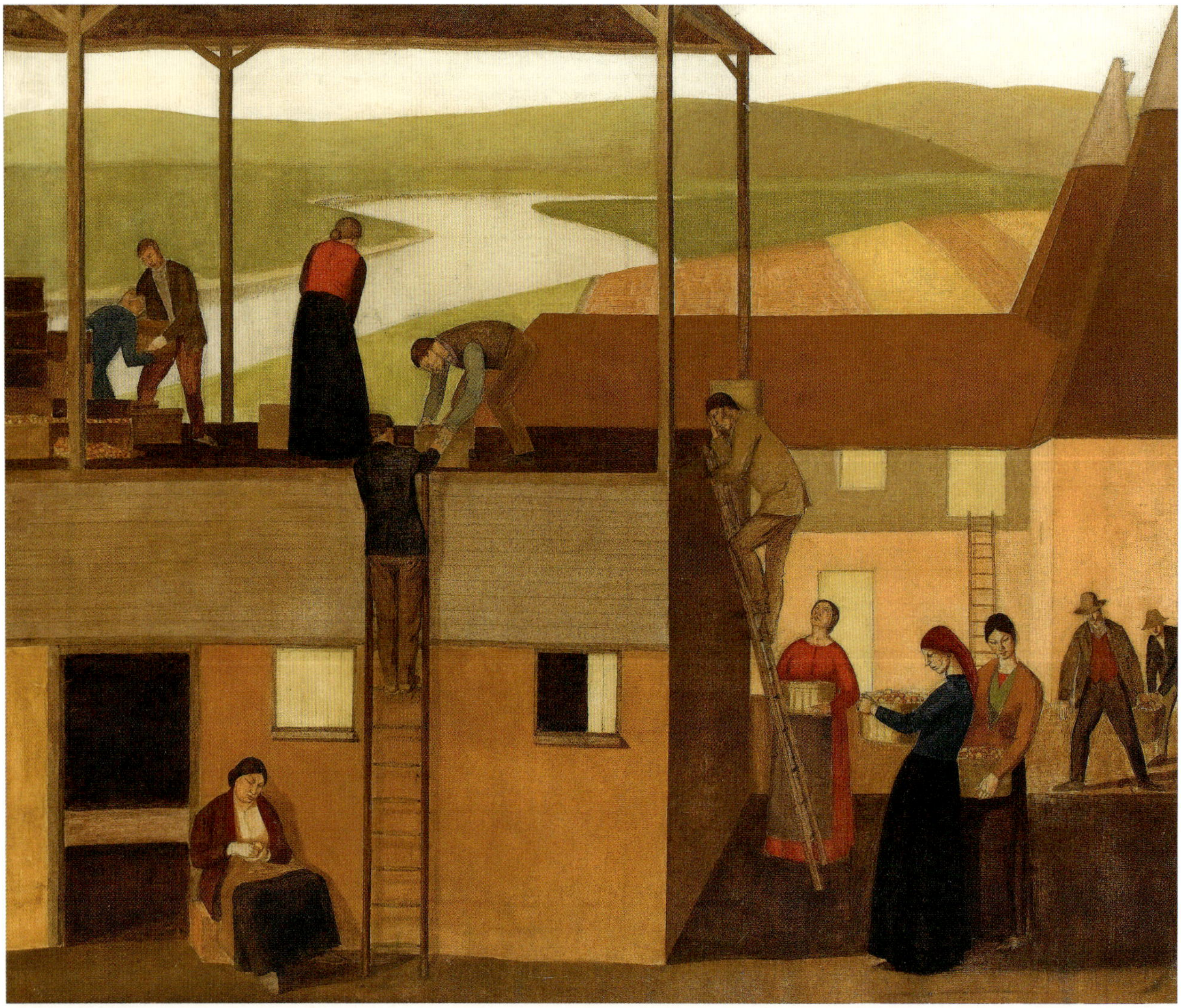

**336 Winifred Knights** (1899-1947), *Design for Wall Decoration*, c.1918, signed on the reverse, and titled (on a War Service Economy Label), oil on canvas (Artist's Colorman), 25 x 30 in. (61 x 76.2 cm).

*Design for Wall Decoration*, the Slade Sketch Club Special Figure Subject for January 1918, was conceived while Knights was at Lineholt Farm in Worcestershire, between October 1917 and October 1918, during a year of convalescence. The composition includes a portrait of Knights and various members of her family. Inspired by Edward Carpenter and his book *Socialism and Agriculture* (1908), Knights felt an affinity with his utopian aspirations in which art, nature and mankind would achieve an ideal balance. (**261**)

**Percy Horton** (1897-1970),

**337** Study for *Kensington Gardens*, 1923,
watercolour on paper, squared in pencil, 5 ½ x 9 ½ in. (14.3 x 24 cm).

**338** Study for *Kensington Gardens*, 1923,
pencil and wash on paper, squared, 8 x 11 ½ in. (20 x 29 cm).

Percy Horton was a student at The Royal College of Art between 1922 and 1924. (**281**) This study was for the main composition of his second year. Set in the nearby Kensington Gardens, Horton is shown doffing his top hat. The other figures, fellow students, have yet to be identified.

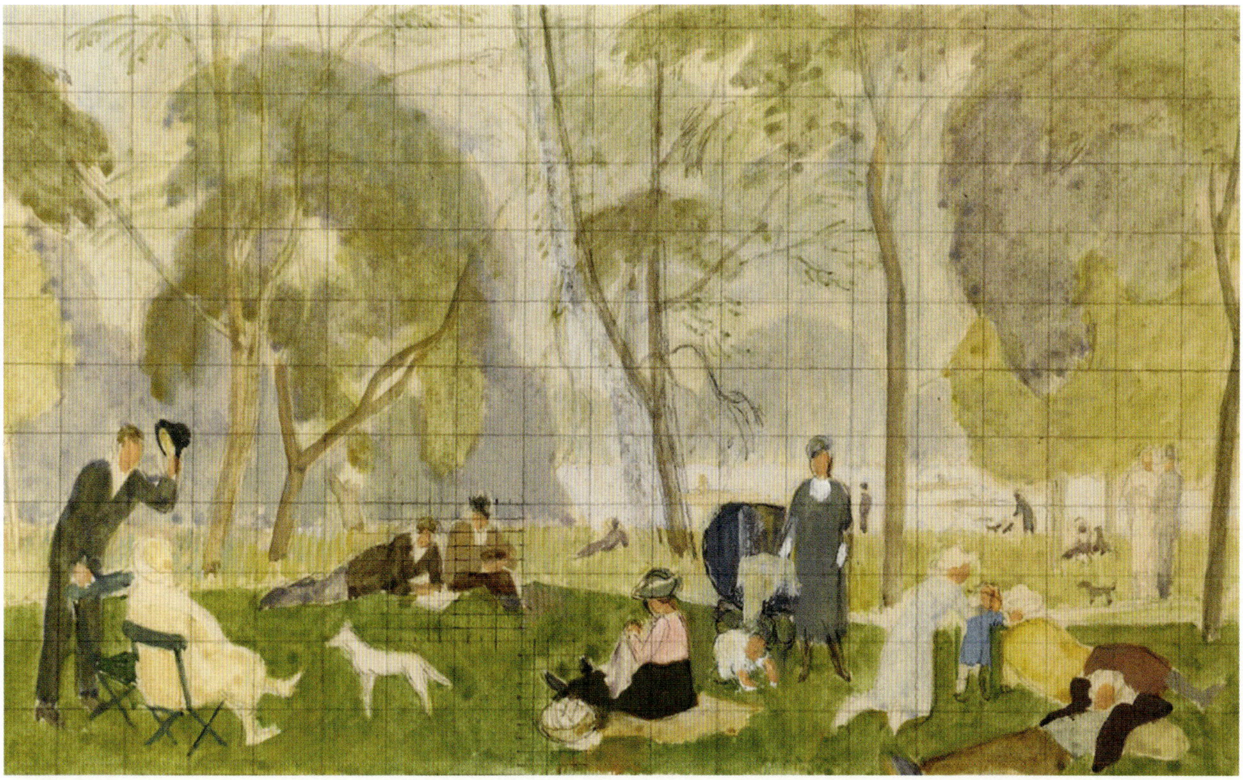

337

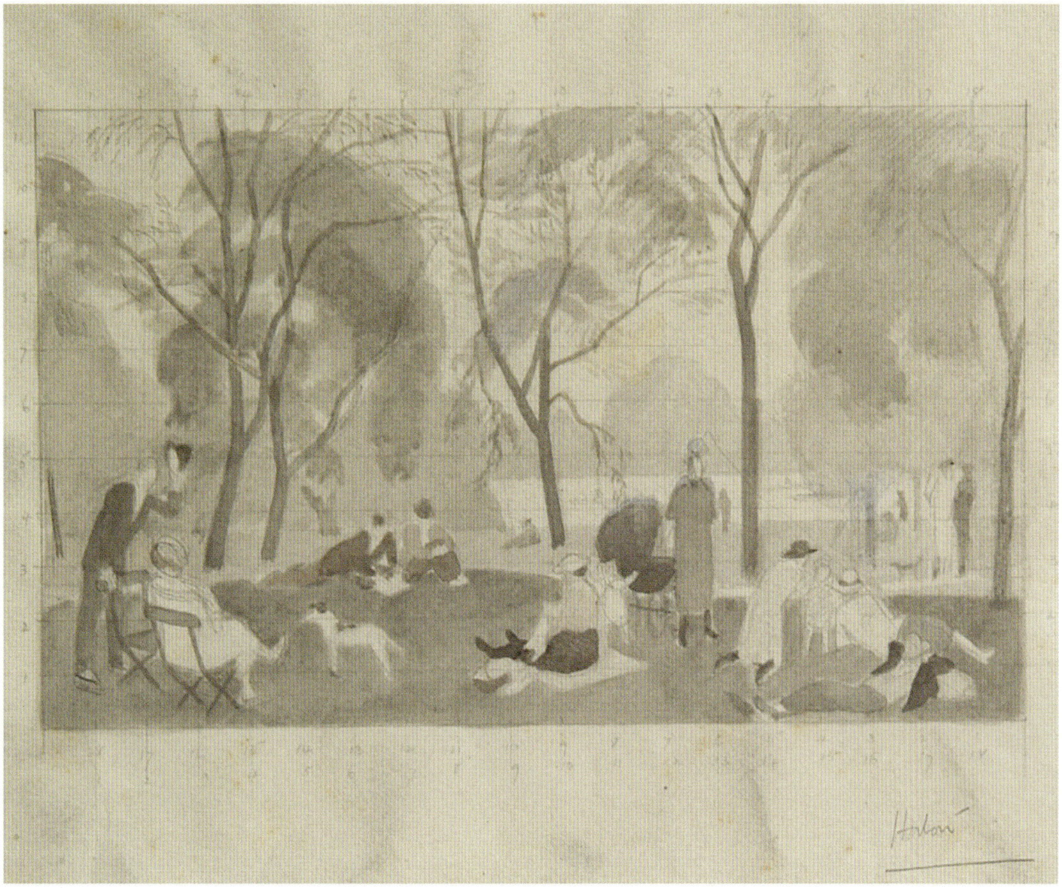

338

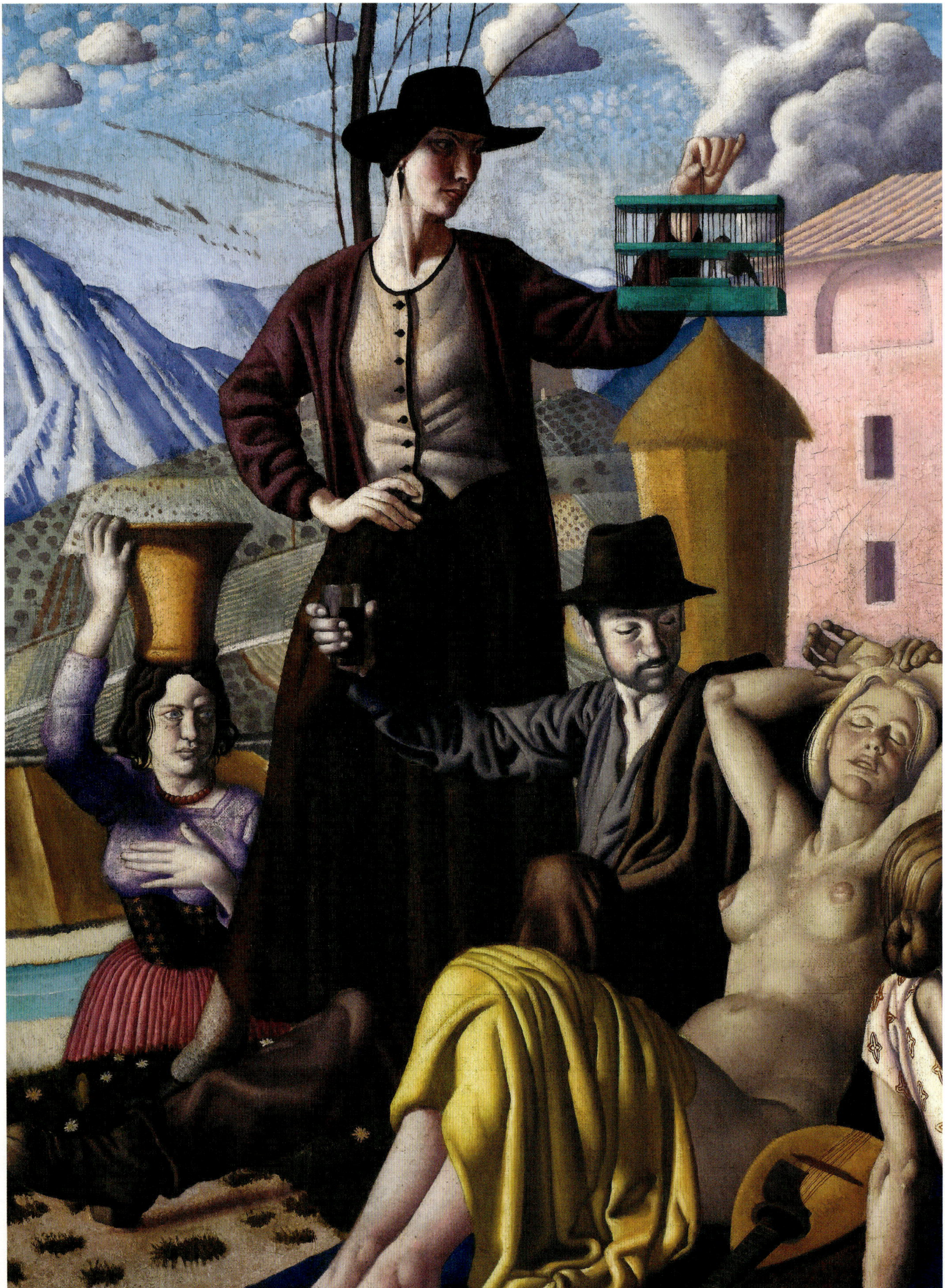

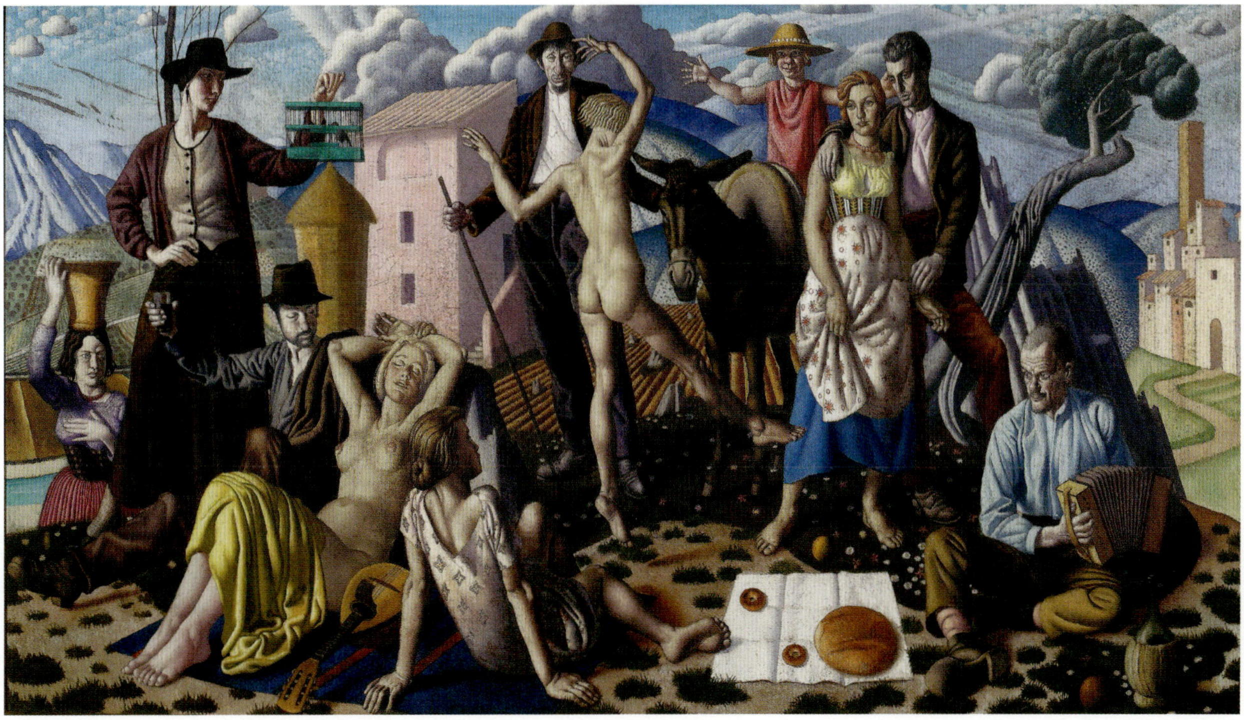

**339 Colin Gill** (1892-1940), *Allegory*, 1920-1921, signed and dated, oil on canvas, 46 x 90 in. (117 x 228.5 cm).

Colin Gill was the first artist to win a scholarship to The British School at Rome and *Allegory* was the major painting produced during his stay at the school. The composition includes portraits of Gill's fellow Rome Scholars, the sculptor Alfred Hardiman (and his wife), J M Benson (and his future wife Maria Rosa Toppi) and Winifred Knights. Knights – the first woman to win a scholarship to the British School at Rome – arrived at the end of 1920, just as Gill was completing the canvas. The two fell in love (love Sonnets by Gill include the line 'You hold my heart like a bird in a cage') and Gill painted Knights' portrait into the composition, replacing an earlier Calvary. (**163**)

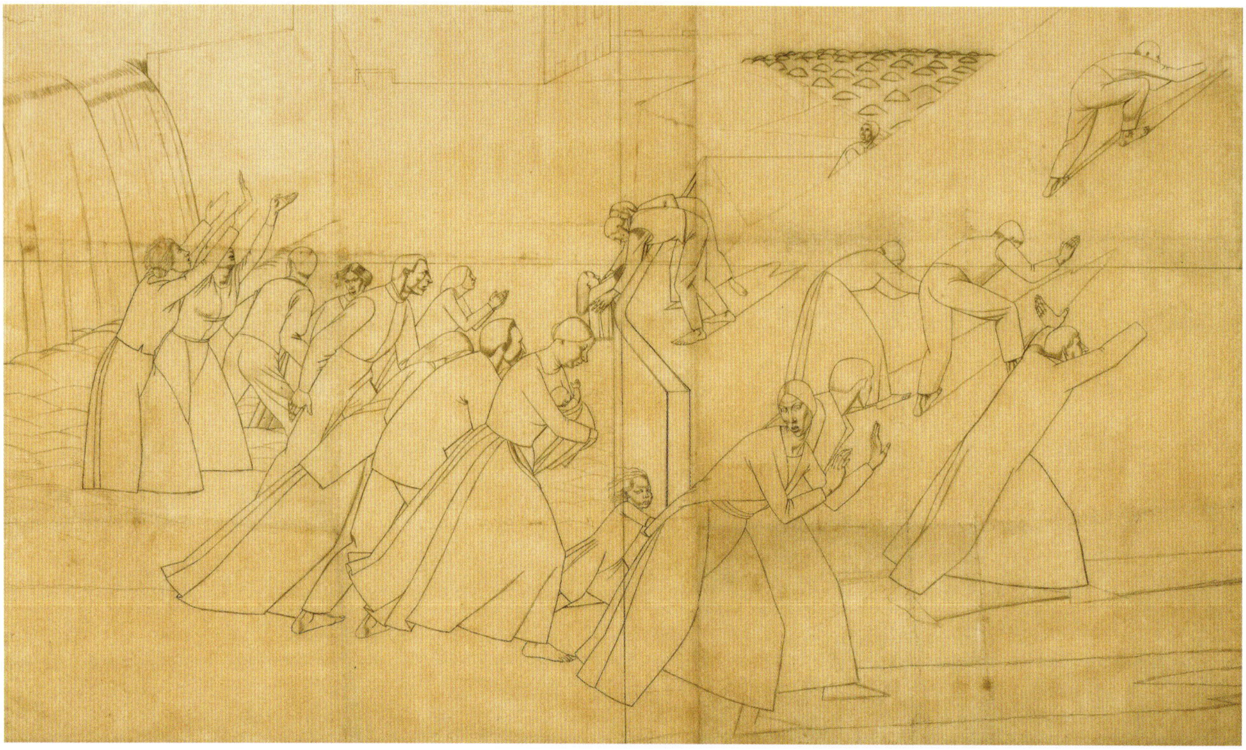

**340 Winifred Knights** (1899-1947), The original cartoon for *The Deluge*, 1920, pencil on tracing paper, 60 x 72 in. (152.4 x 183 cm).

*The Deluge* was Winifred Knights' winning entry for the Prix de Rome in 1920. On this full-size cartoon, the lines are heavily scored into the tracing paper so that the outline could be transferred on to the same size canvas – now one of the prize possessions of Tate Britain. Knights includes herself as the central protagonist with her mother, sister and Arnold Mason amongst the models. (**164**)

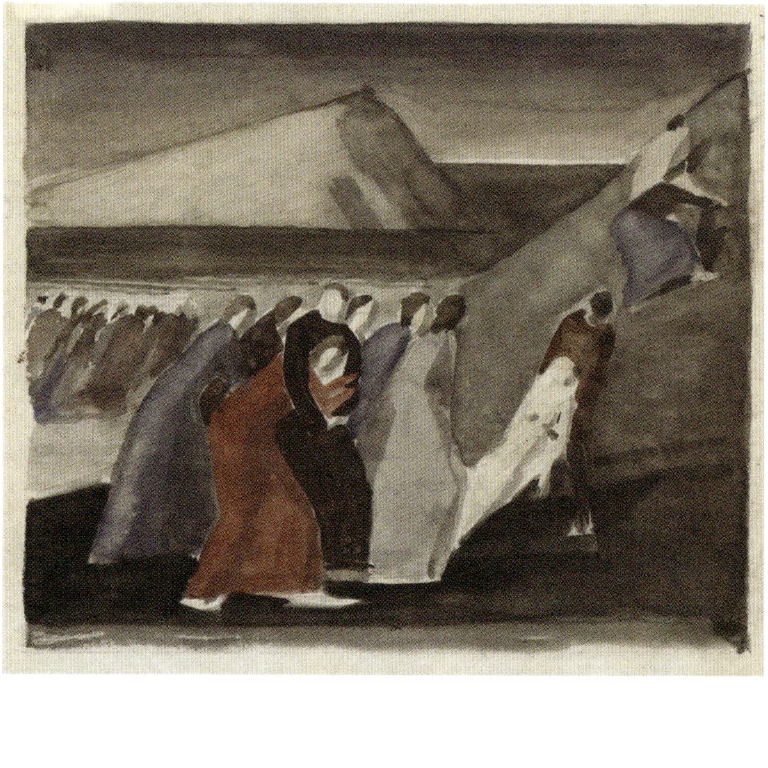

**341 Winifred Knights** (1899-1947), Early compositional study for *The Deluge*, 1920, watercolour on paper, 5 x 7 ½ in. (12.5 x 19 cm).

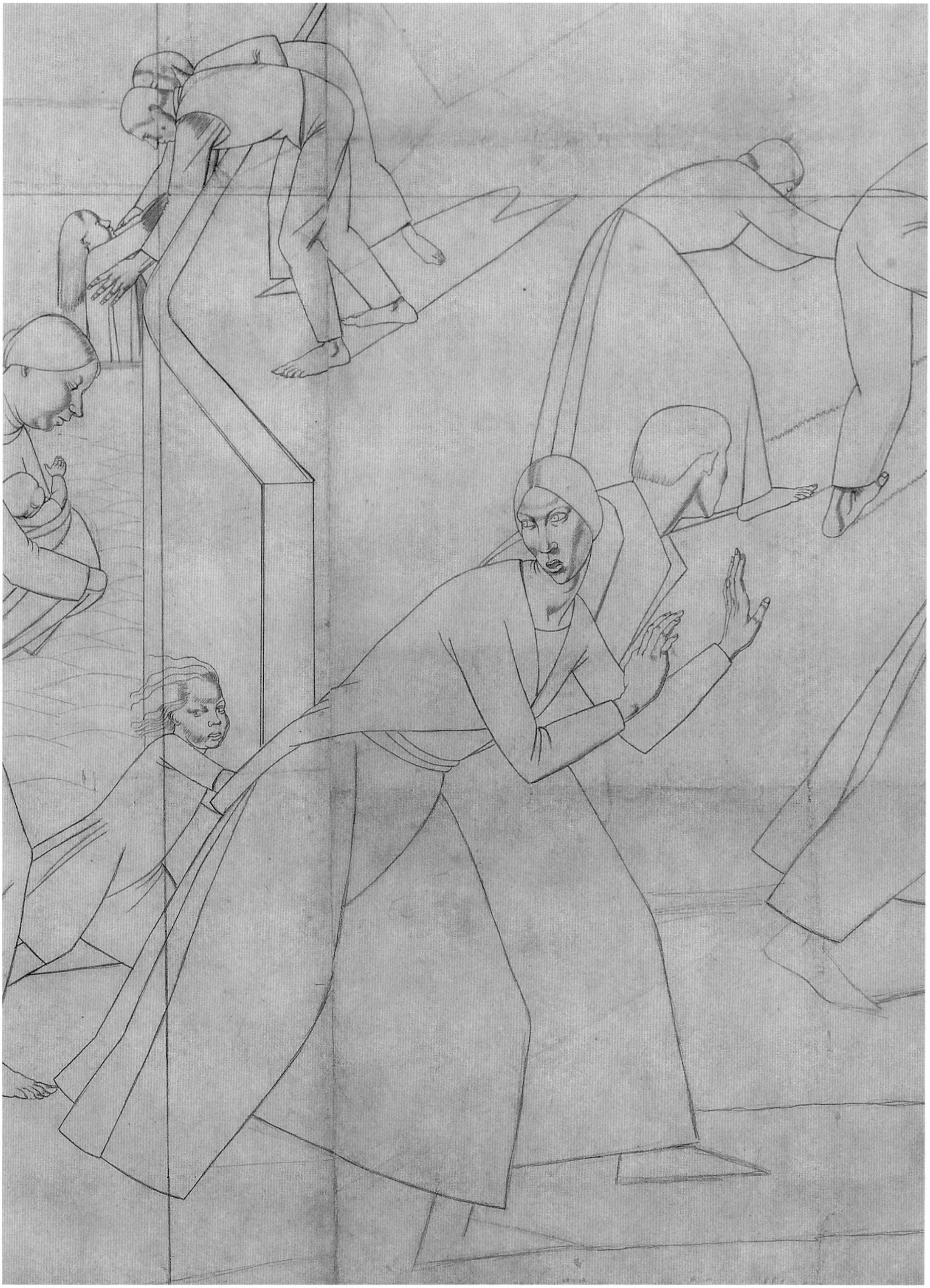

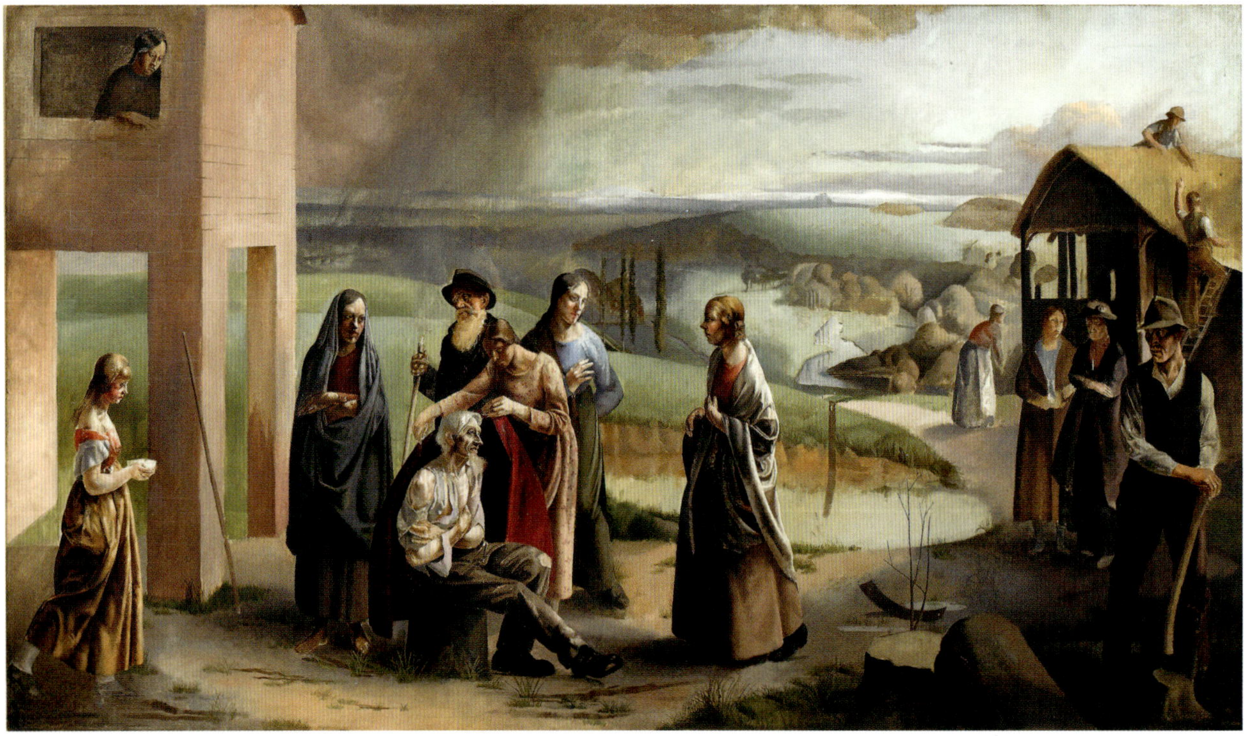

**342 Thomas Monnington** (1902-1976), *Winter*, 1922,
oil on canvas, 48 x 85 in. (122 x 216 cm).

*Winter* was Thomas Monnington's winning submission for the British School at Rome's scholarship in Decorative Painting. It comprises fourteen figures, of which the central group of art school models are supplemented on the right-hand side of the painting by Monnington, his mother and his aunt. The critic P.G.Konody, writing in *The Observer* (22 February 1922), praised Monnington's painting for being 'steeped in the best traditions of the Italian Renaissance. His colour is dull, but there is a marked sense of style in his design'.

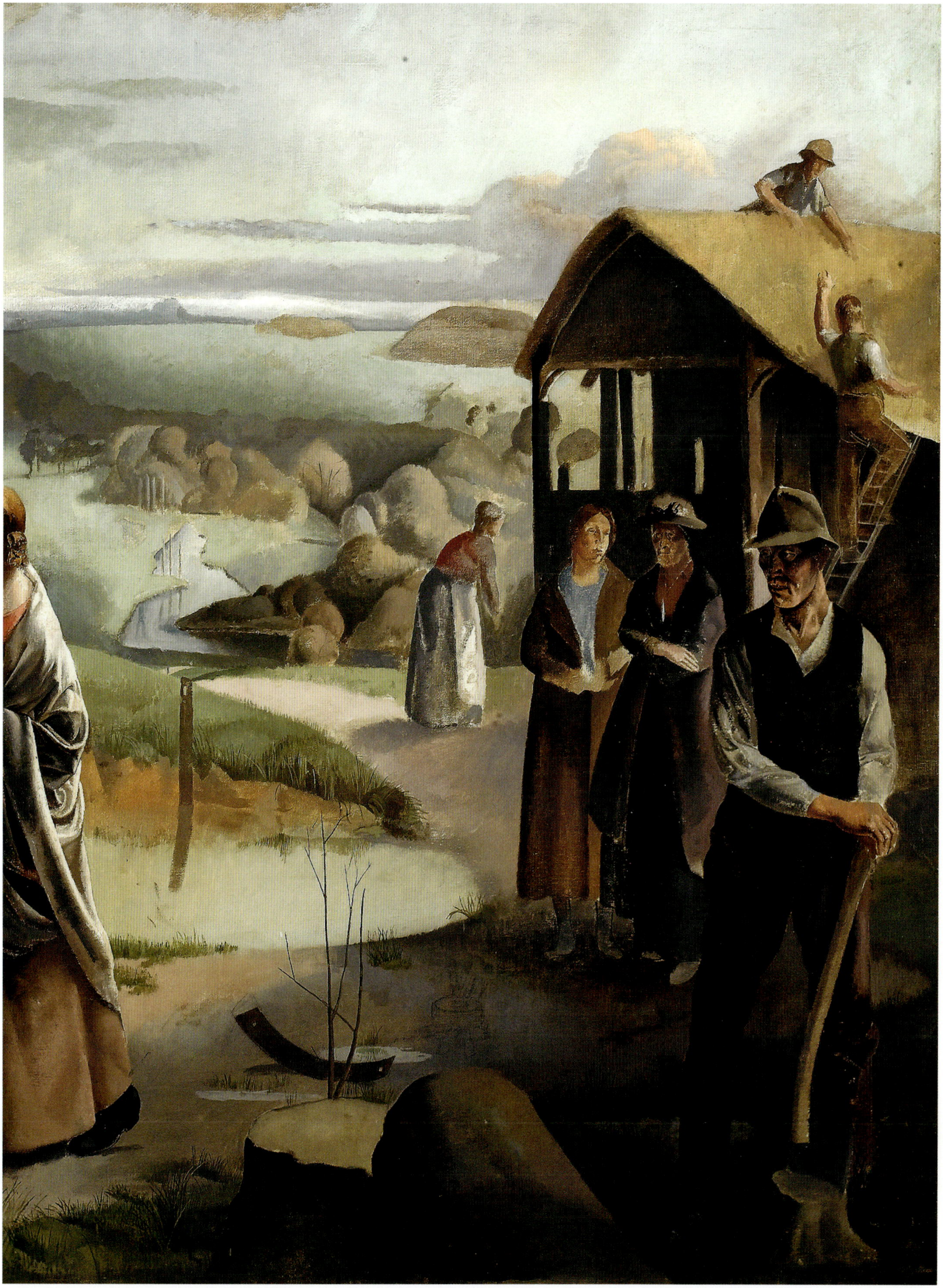

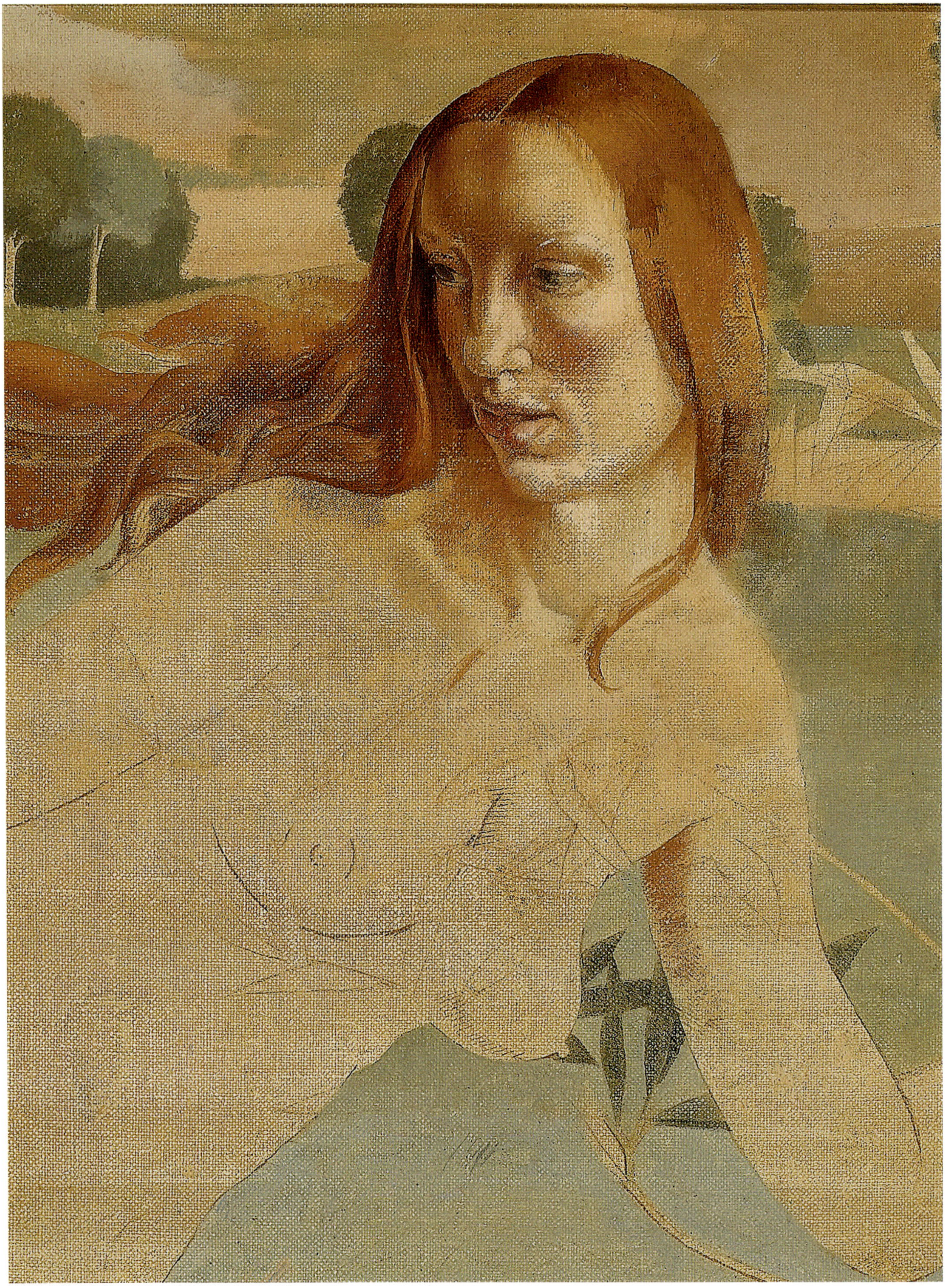

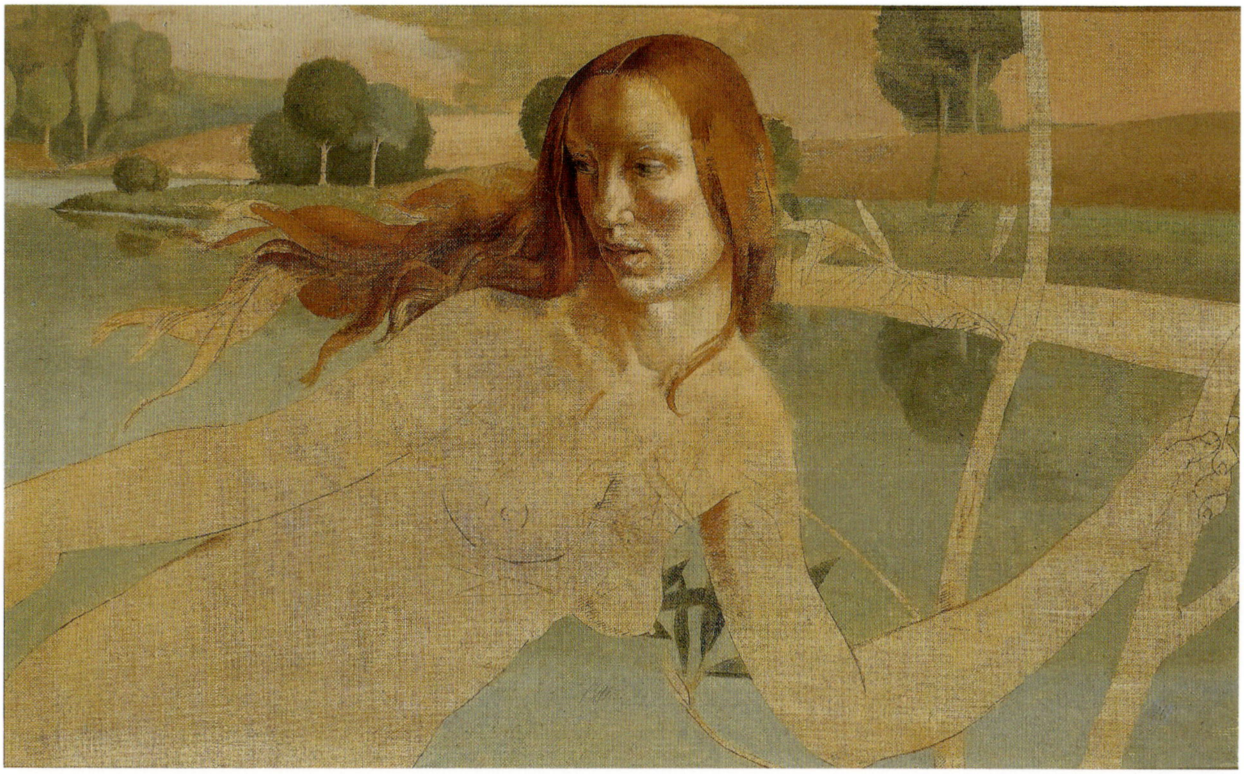

**343 Thomas Monnington** (1902-1976), Study for *Allegory*, c.1924,
oil on canvas, 11 x 19 in. (28 x 48.2 cm).

*Allegory* was the product of Tom Monnington's third and final year at The British School at Rome. It was purchased by Jim Ede for the Contemporary Art Society before it was completed, and was presented to the Tate Gallery in 1939. Winifred Knights – whom Monnington had married in Rome in April 1924 – appears several times in the composition and the background was based on studies undertaken whilst the couple were on their honeymoon at Lake Piedeluco. Invited by the Tate to explain *Allegory's* meaning, Monnington replied 'The idea is a bit complex and was based on the story of the Garden of Eden, but rather a personal interpretation of it.' (letter of 17 May 1953). When pressed a few years later to elaborate, he answered, 'I don't think this picture has anything to do with the Garden of Eden story, but I am no more able to explain its exact meaning now than I was at the time I painted it. The whole design certainly had a very particular meaning and purpose and was an attempt to express in pictorial form my attitude to life – almost my faith.' (2 April 1957). Having to be content with this, the Tate Gallery retitled the picture *Allegory*, despite Monnington having always referred to it simply by the title *Decoration*. Iconographically it contains elements of several myths but most obviously The Garden of Love.

OVERLEAF:
**344 Thomas Monnington** (1902-1976), Study for *Allegory*, c.1924,
oil on tracing paper, laid on board, squared for transfer, 12 ½ x 22 ½ in. (31.7 x 57.2 cm).

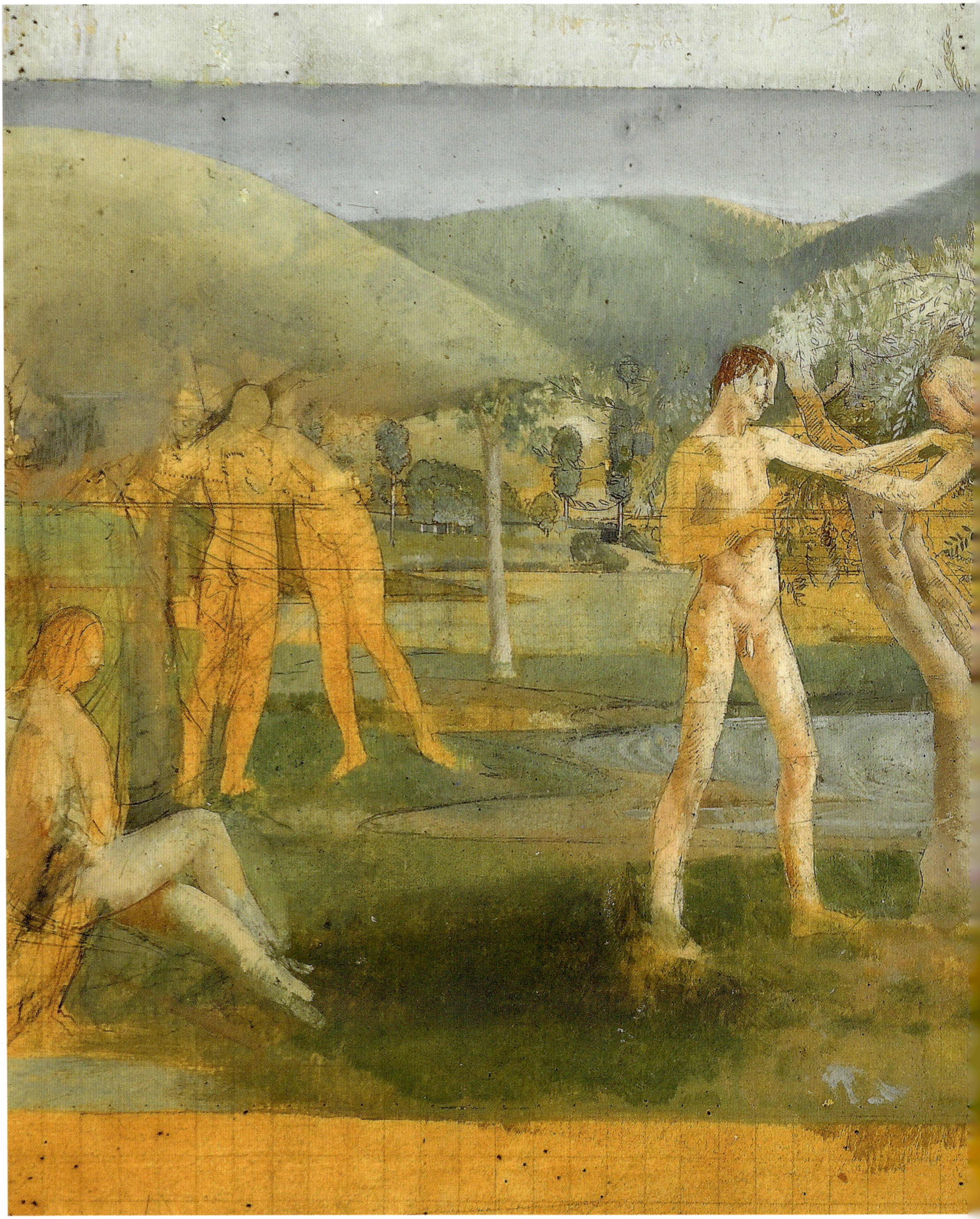

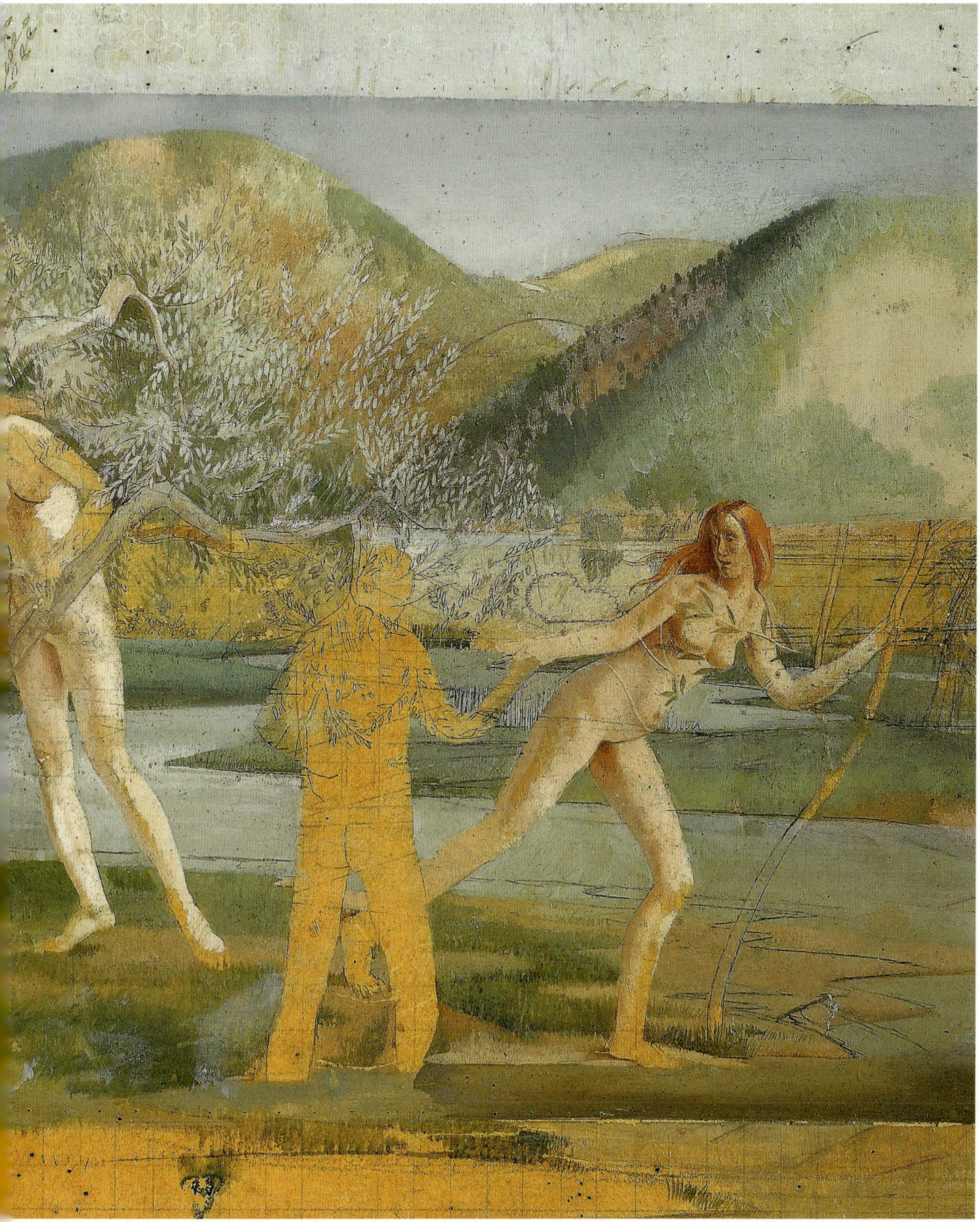

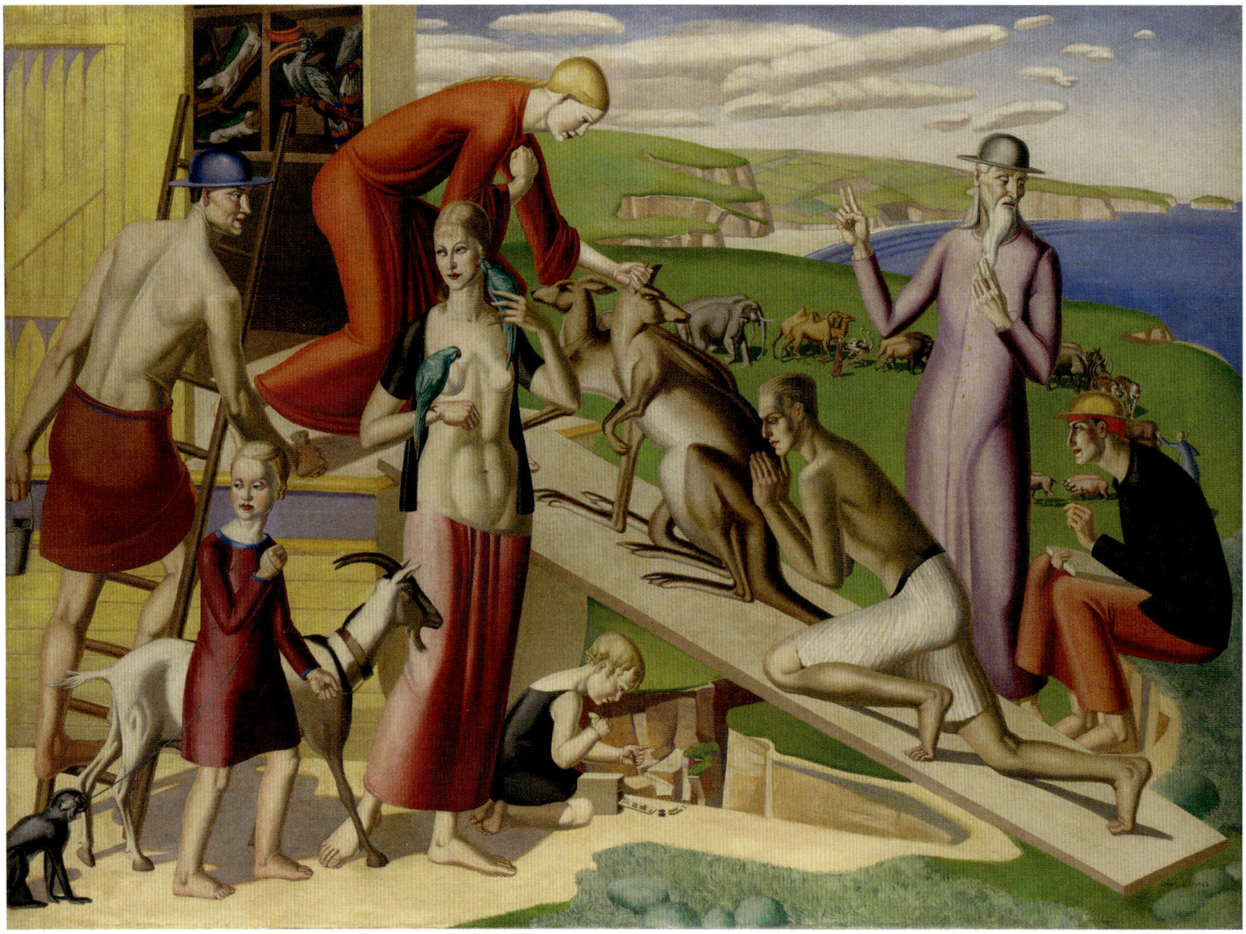

**345 Gladys Hynes** (1888-1958), *Noah's Ark*, 1919, signed and dated, oil on canvas, 39 ½ x 59 in. (100 x 150 cm).

The colourful and highly original composition of *Noah's Ark*, with its well defined outlines, clearly delineated areas of bold and vigorous colour and hard-edged imagery, shows the influence of Vorticism. Hynes was friends with Ezra Pound, the American poet and critic who gave the name Vorticism to the movement in 1913. Hynes, an impassioned campaigner for women's rights, often challenging the social construction of gender and sexuality in her work, shows herself as the central protagonist, semi-naked, holding an exotic bird.

*The Observer's* Italophile critic P. G. Konody also saw the influence of the Italian Renaissance in Hynes' work, writing in 1922, 'her assumed naivety, backed by consummate draughtsmanship, is perfectly delightful, her sense of humour probably unique among women artists'.

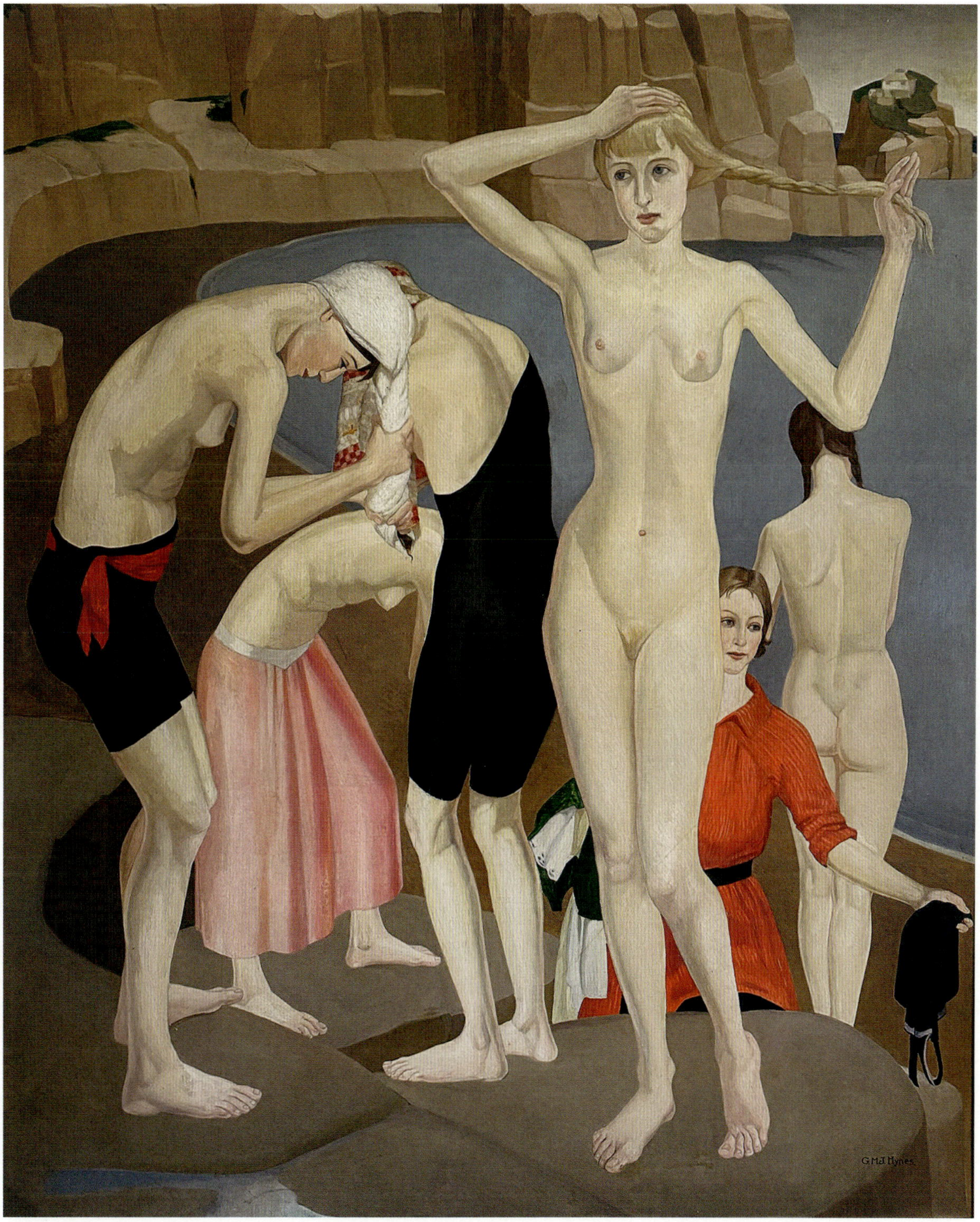


**346 Gladys Hynes** (1888-1958), *Morning*, c.1915, signed,
oil on panel, 46 x 38 ½ in. (117 x 98 cm).

Set in Lamorna Cove (West Cornwall) a favourite haunt of the Newlyn artists, Hynes recalled how she loved to lie on the cliffs all day looking out to sea, which was 'as smooth and glittering as a dancing floor… and lovely as a dream'. For her models, in addition to posing herself as the main figure, Hynes called on her artist friends. The figure drying her hair is possibly a portrait of Gluck, who who also lived in Newlyn, while the fully clothed figure in orange is Nina Hamnett, with whom Hynes had developed a deep friendship when they were students at Brangwyn's London School of Art.

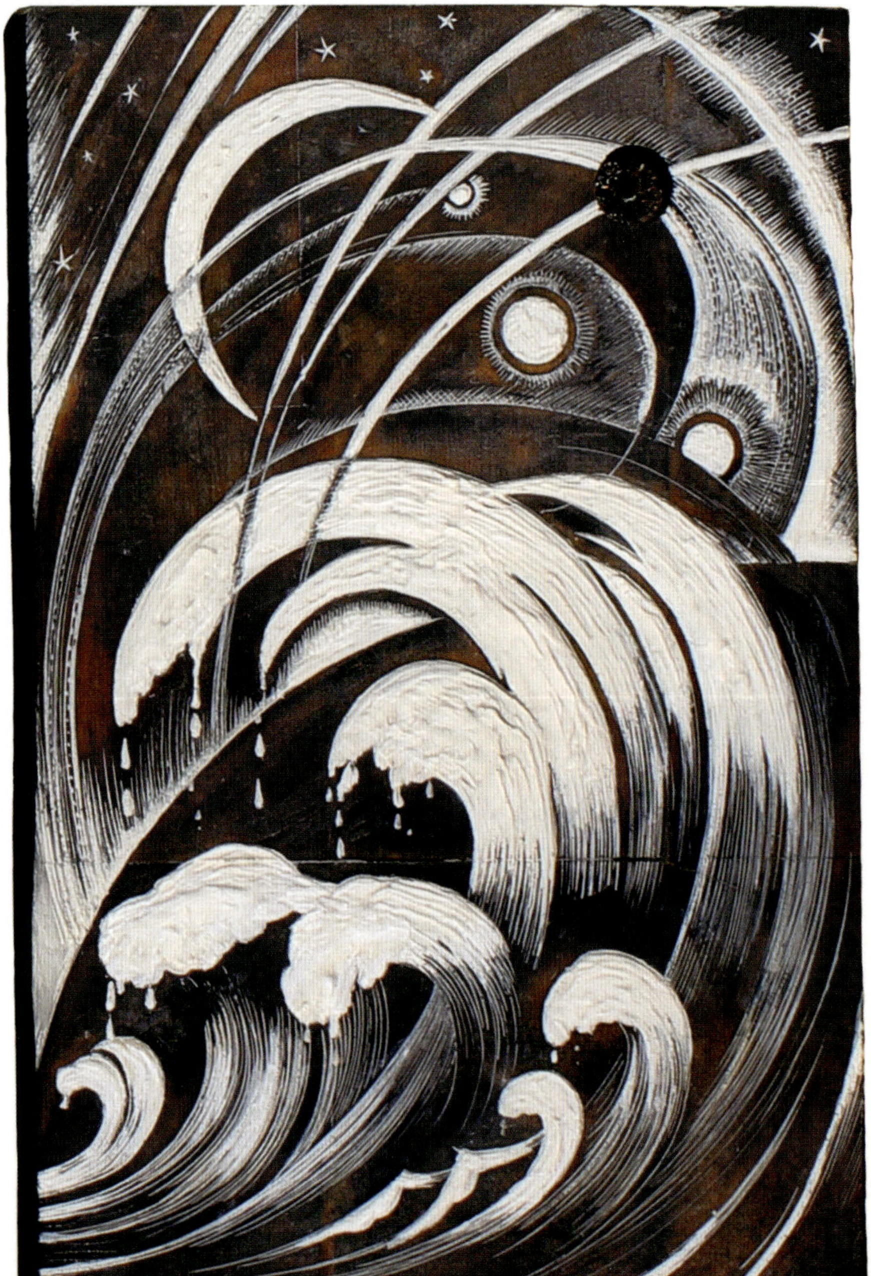

**347 Clare Leighton** (1898-1989), *In the Beginning* (BPL 716), 1955, original woodblock, cancelled, 6 x 4 in. (15.6 x 10.3 cm).

Clare Leighton attended the Brighton School of Art (1915), the Slade School of Fine Art (1921-23) and the Central School of Arts and Crafts. Despite her childhood nickname 'the Bystander', she became a hugely visible artist on both sides of the Atlantic, and her vast oeuvre includes engravings, paintings, bookplates, illustrations and stained glass.

*In the Beginning* was originally printed in an edition of 50 as part of Helen Plotz's *Imagination's Other Place: Poems of Science and Mathematics*, (New York, Thomas Y. Crowell, 1955).

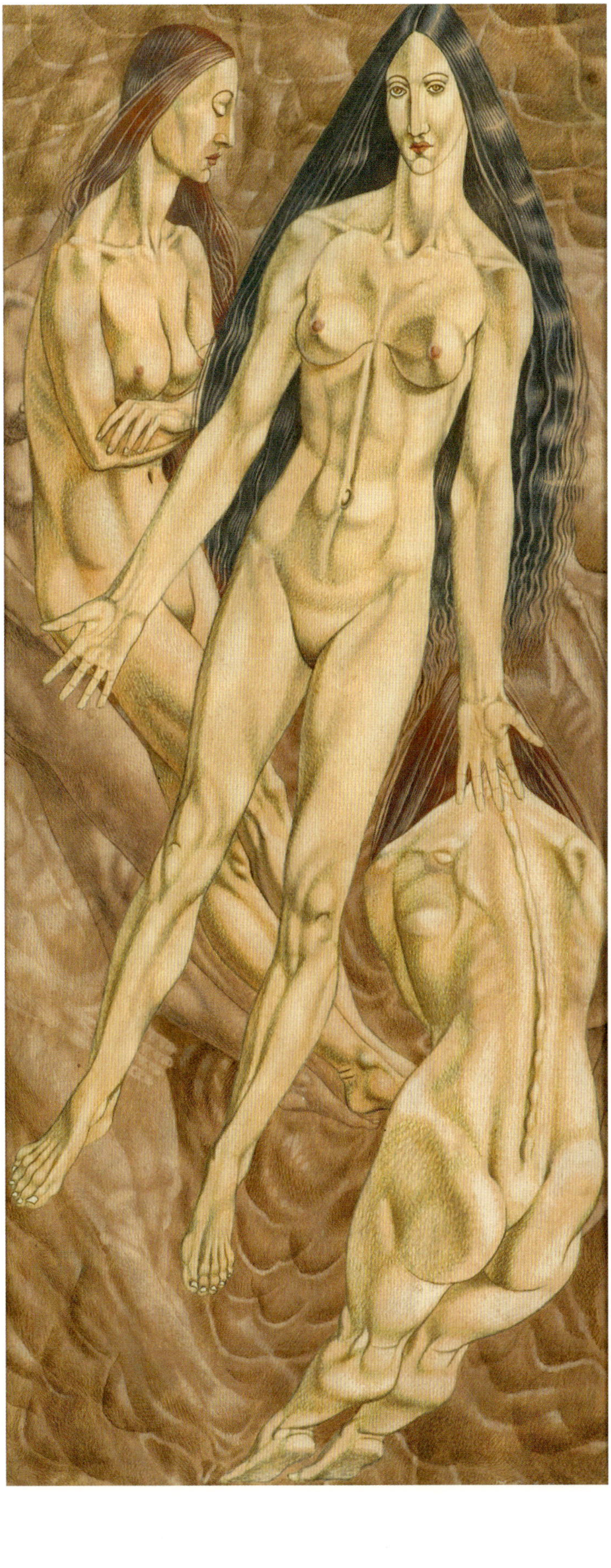

**348 Francis Plummer** (1930-2019),
*Three Muses*, c.1953,
tempera on panel
7 ½ x 17 ¾ in. (19 x 45 cm).

In a Pathé documentary made about Francis Plummer, his style was described as 'a logical development of William Blake', preoccupied with harmonies and shapes developed from the human form.

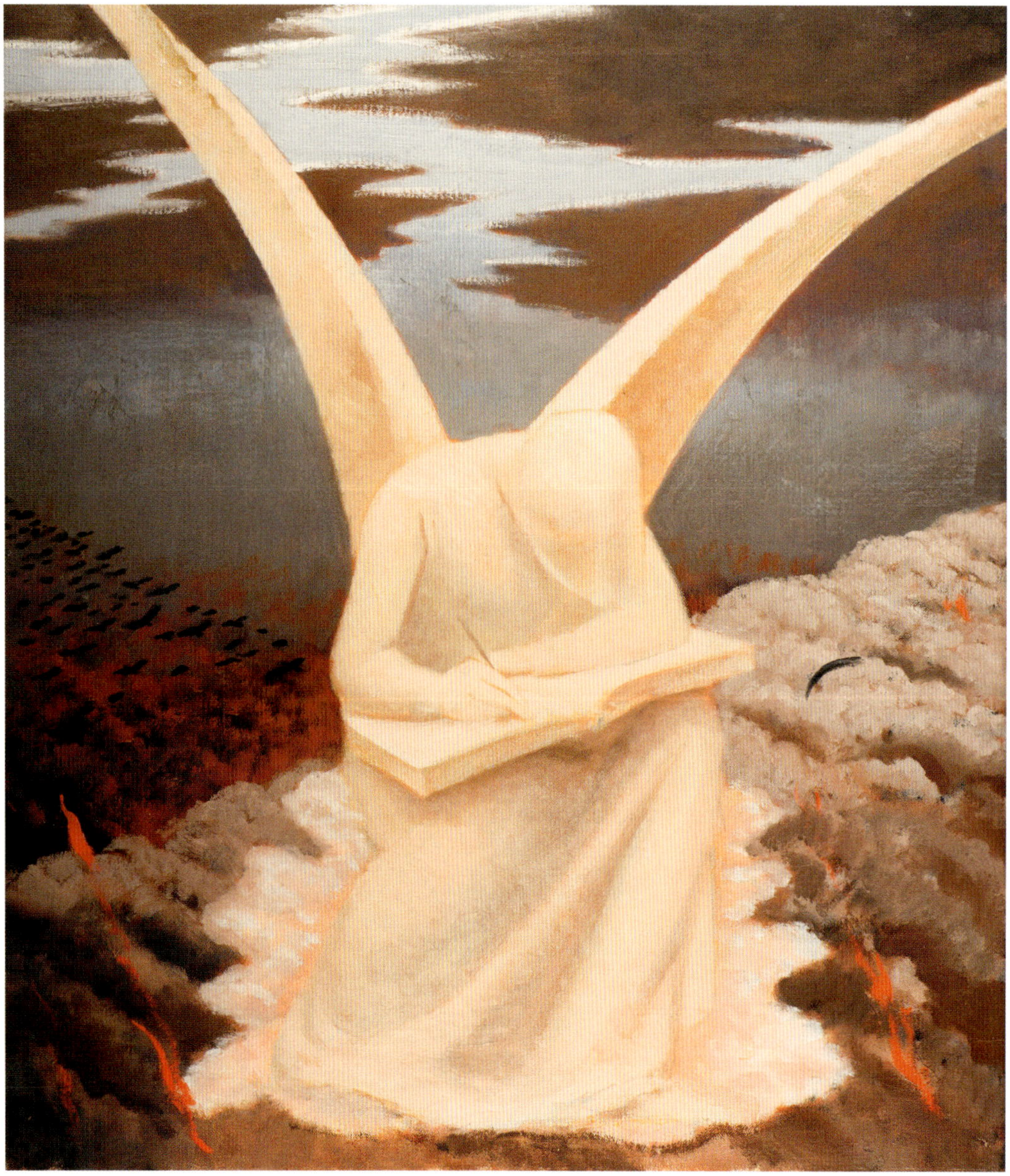

**349 Dorothea Frances MacLagan** (1895-1982), *The Angel of Revelation*, c.1925,
oil on canvas, 17 ¾ x 11 ¾ in. (45 x 29.8 cm).

Dorothea MacLagan emerged from her training at the Byam Shaw school with a style based on symbolism, and an interest in religion and myth where the line is deliberately blurred. This striking image is likely to show the Archangel Gabriel – known as the angel of revelation or announcement in Christianity, Islam, Judaism and many other faiths, was considered as a messenger for God.

**350 Dorothea Frances MacLagan** (1895-1982),
*An Allegory: Truth and Beauty Comforting Each Other*, c.1920,
oil on canvas, 17 ¾ x 11 ¾ in. (45 x 29.8 cm).

In her allegory, with its dystopian backdrop, Truth and Beauty are shown to comfort each other in the face of the terrifyingly bleak industrial cityscape behind.

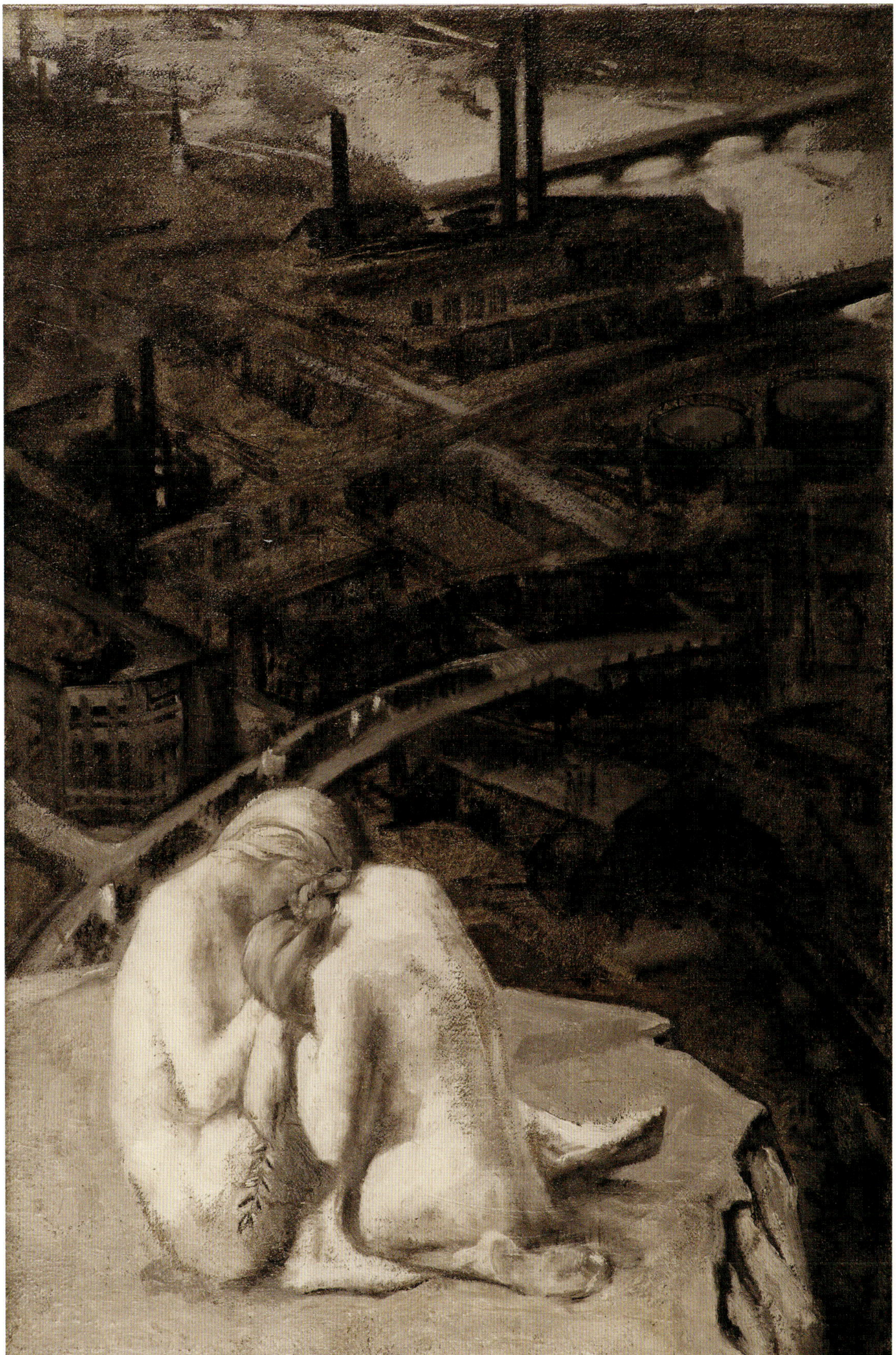

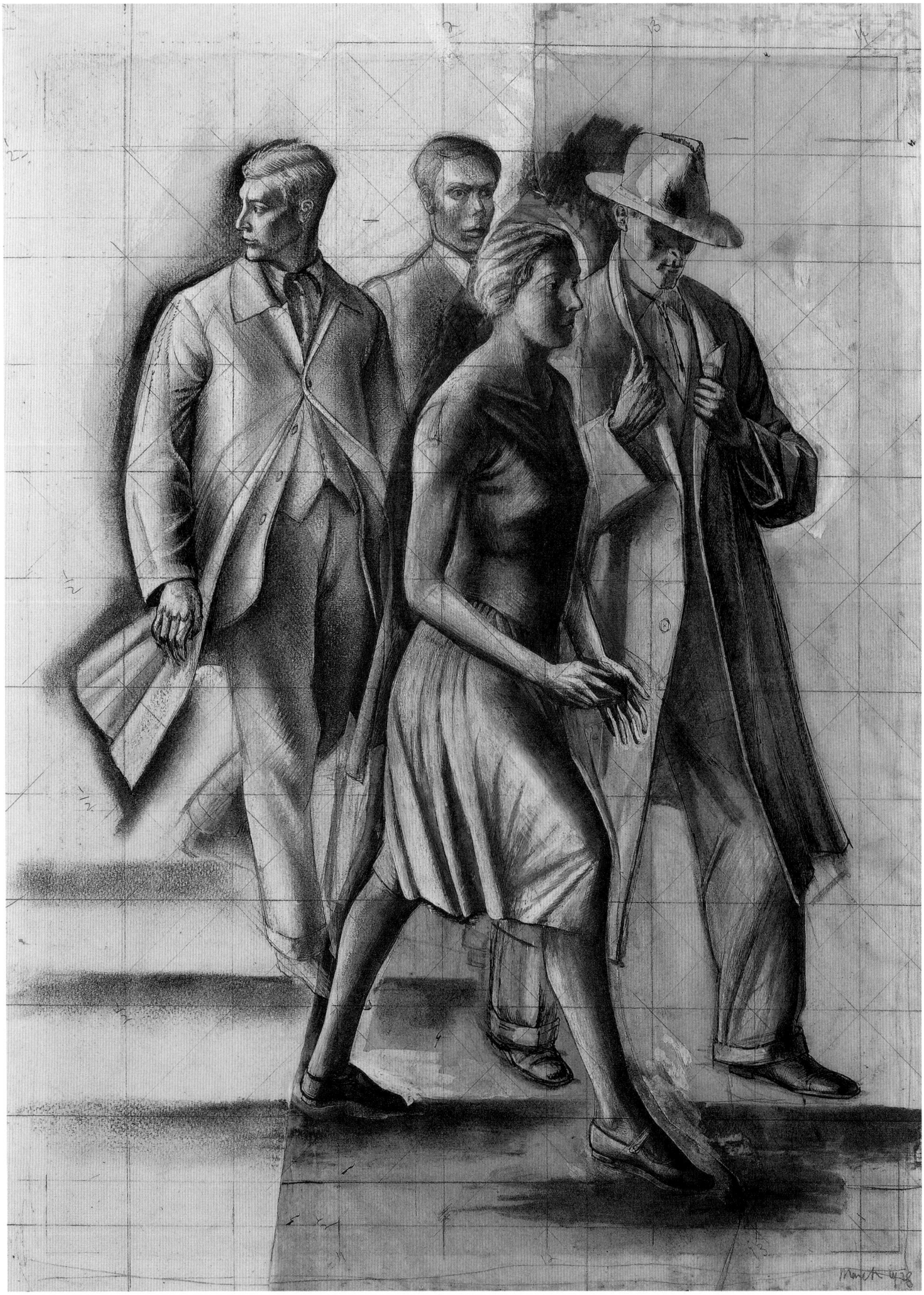

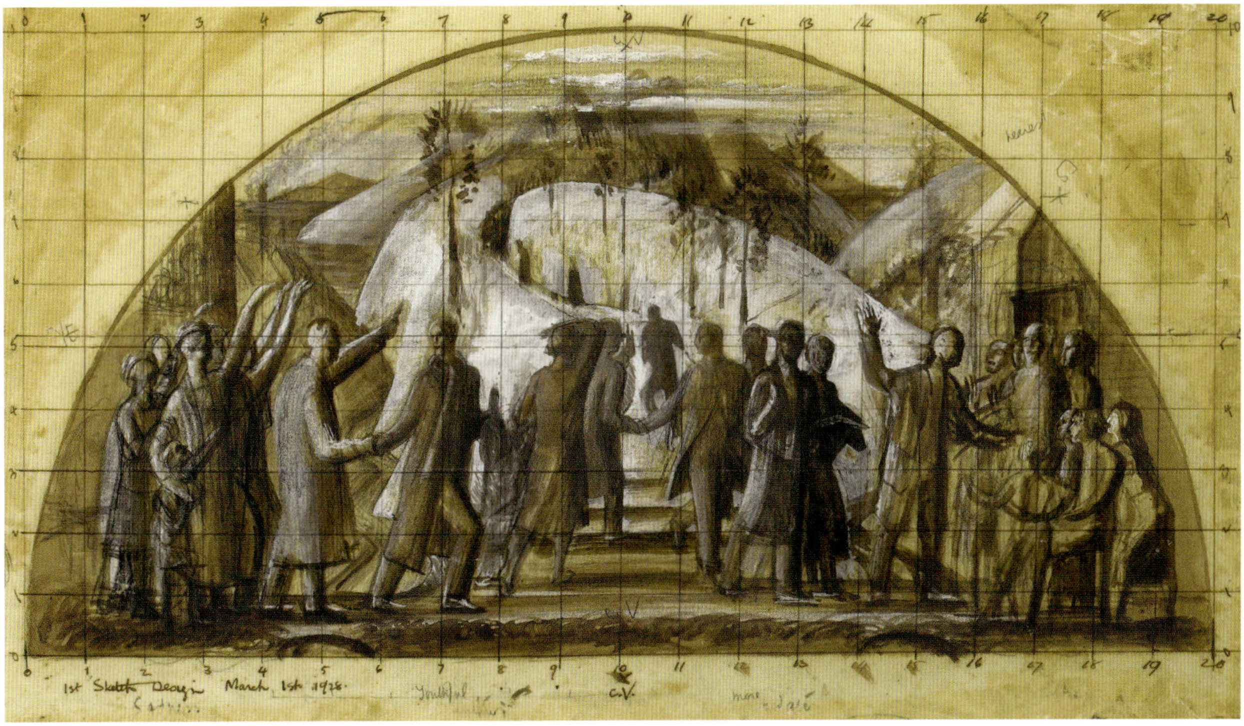

**352** **Alan Sorrell** (1904-1974), Sketch for examination competition *People Seeking After Wisdom*, March 1, 1928, pencil, ink and gouache on tracing paper, squared, 33 x 51 cm (13 x 20 in).

**351** **Alan Sorrell** (1904-1974), Study for *People Seeking After Wisdom*, dated March1928, pencil, gouache and black chalk on paper / tracing paper, 19 ½ x 15 in. (49.5 x 38 cm).

When asked to produce a 'Decoration for the Lunette in the Library of the British School at Rome' Sorrell chose as his subject *People Seeking after Wisdom*. The figure at the back of the group, staring out at the viewer, is a self-portrait, and the woman in the front is Evelyn Gibbs (**275**) who won a Rome Scholarship (in Engraving) one year after Sorrell had won his for Decorative Painting. While the Bible contains many references to the attainment of knowledge as a pre-requisite of enlightenment, the motif of blindfolded figures is equally reminiscent of the harrowing images of bandaged soldiers from the Great War, such as John Singer Sargent's *Gassed*, 1919.

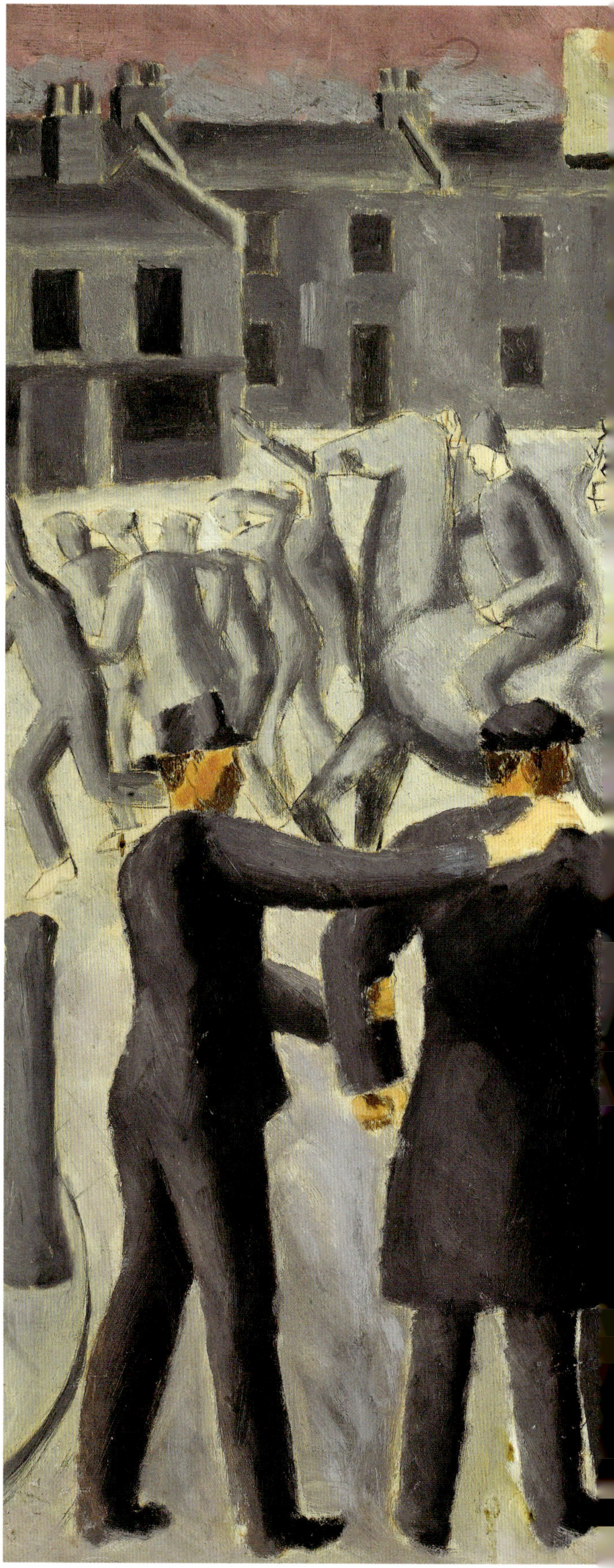

**353 Archibald Ziegler** (1903-1971),
*An Allegory of Social Strife*, late 1920s,
oil on panel over pencil and red crayon,
21 x 26 ½ in. (53.5 x 67.7 cm).

In this striking composition Zeiglar depicts himself on the cross taking a central role in his allegory about the sacrifice of the working man at the altar of the ruling classes. He is flanked on the left by pugnacious workers' leaders (a reference to Socialism) and on the right men in formal attire representing the Establishment (a reference to Capitalism) whilst brow-beaten workers, under attack, fill the background. A soldier stands guard to the Establishment figures, amongst which is a macabre, frock-coated figure whose pose and dog-collar alludes possibly to the Church.

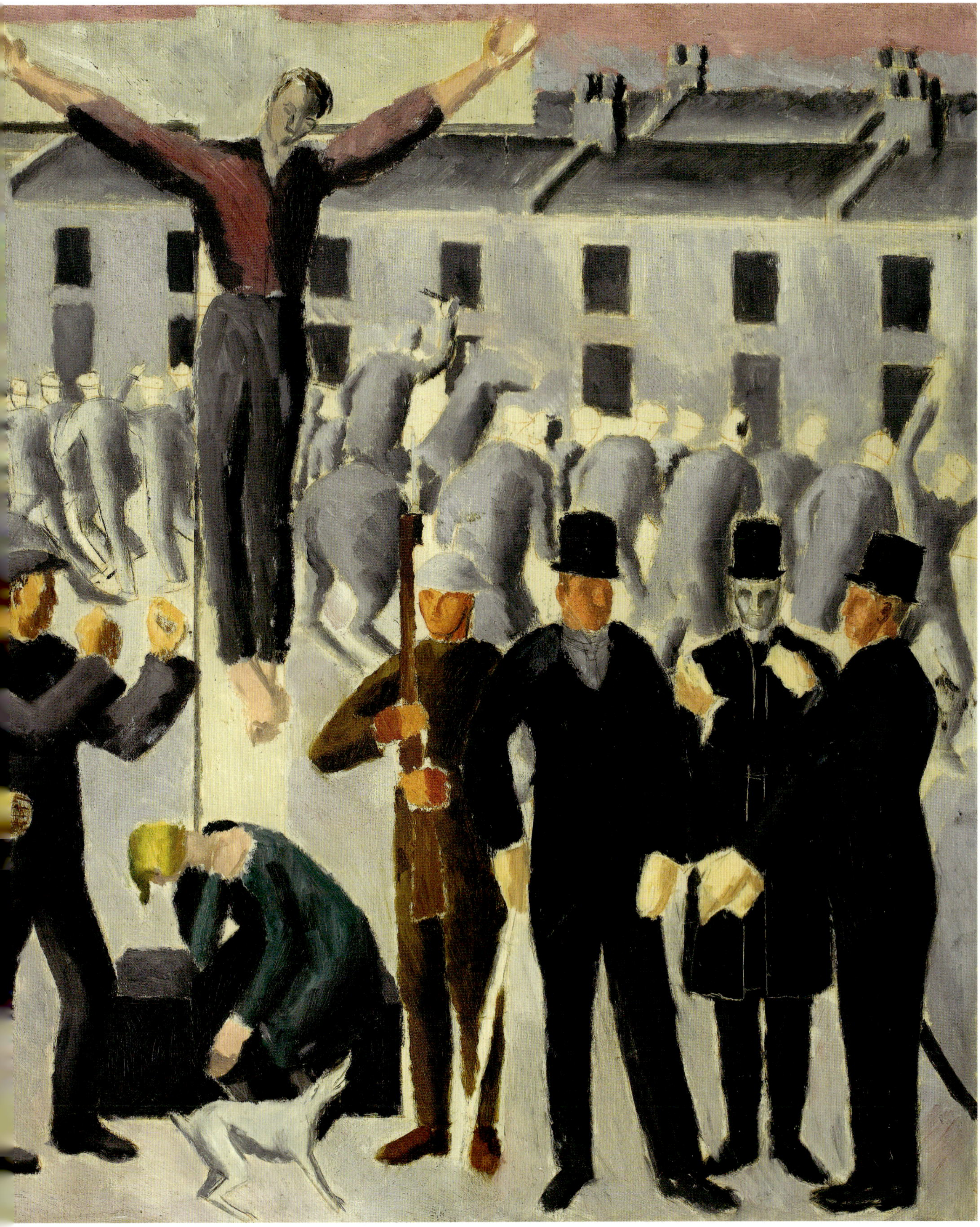

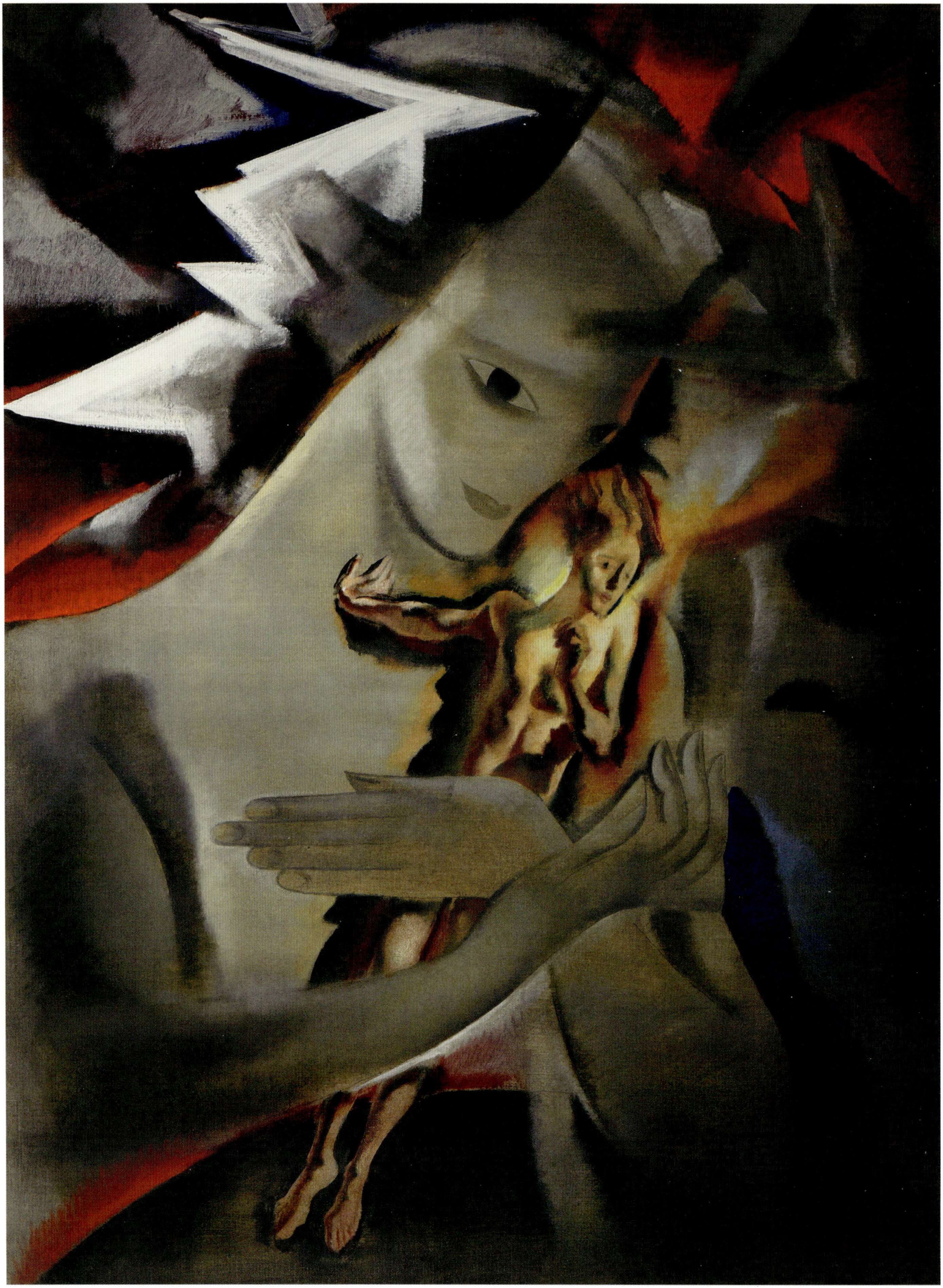

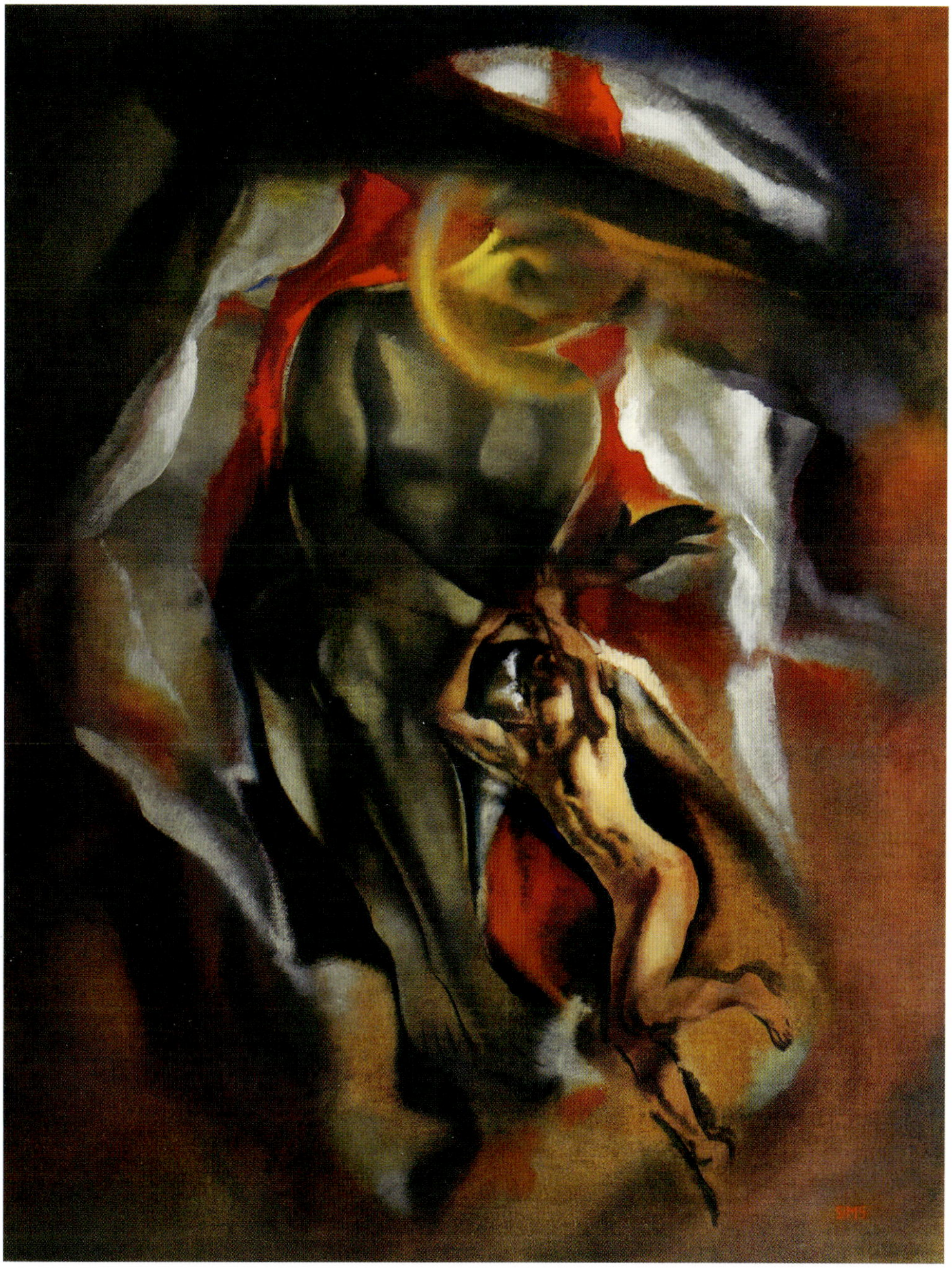

**355 Charles Sims** (1873-1928), *My Pain Beneath Your Sheltering Hand*, c.1928,
tempera on canvas, 36 x 27 in. (91 x 68.6 cm).

*My Pain Beneath Your Sheltering Hand* and *Man's Last Pretence of Consummation in Indifference* belong to a small series of works that Charles Sims called his 'Spiritual Ideas'. Tragically, the artist committed suicide just weeks after completing them, having submitted six for inclusion at the Royal Academy Summer Exhibition of 1928. Grouped together in Gallery XI, 'the paintings struck a deeper and a more intense note than anything else at the Academy' (*The Times*, 5 May 1928). The critic from the *Western Mail* called them the 'sensation of the year' (5 May, 1928), whilst another noted that 'In life, Sims' work was mainly on scholarly but orthodox lines. In his death he has left the world in his last pictures a problem which no one but himself can solve' (*The Mail*, 5 May 1928).

**354 Charles Sims** (1873-1928), *Man's Last Pretence of Consummation in Indifference*, c.1928,
tempera on canvas 36 x 27 in. (91.4 x 68.6 cm).

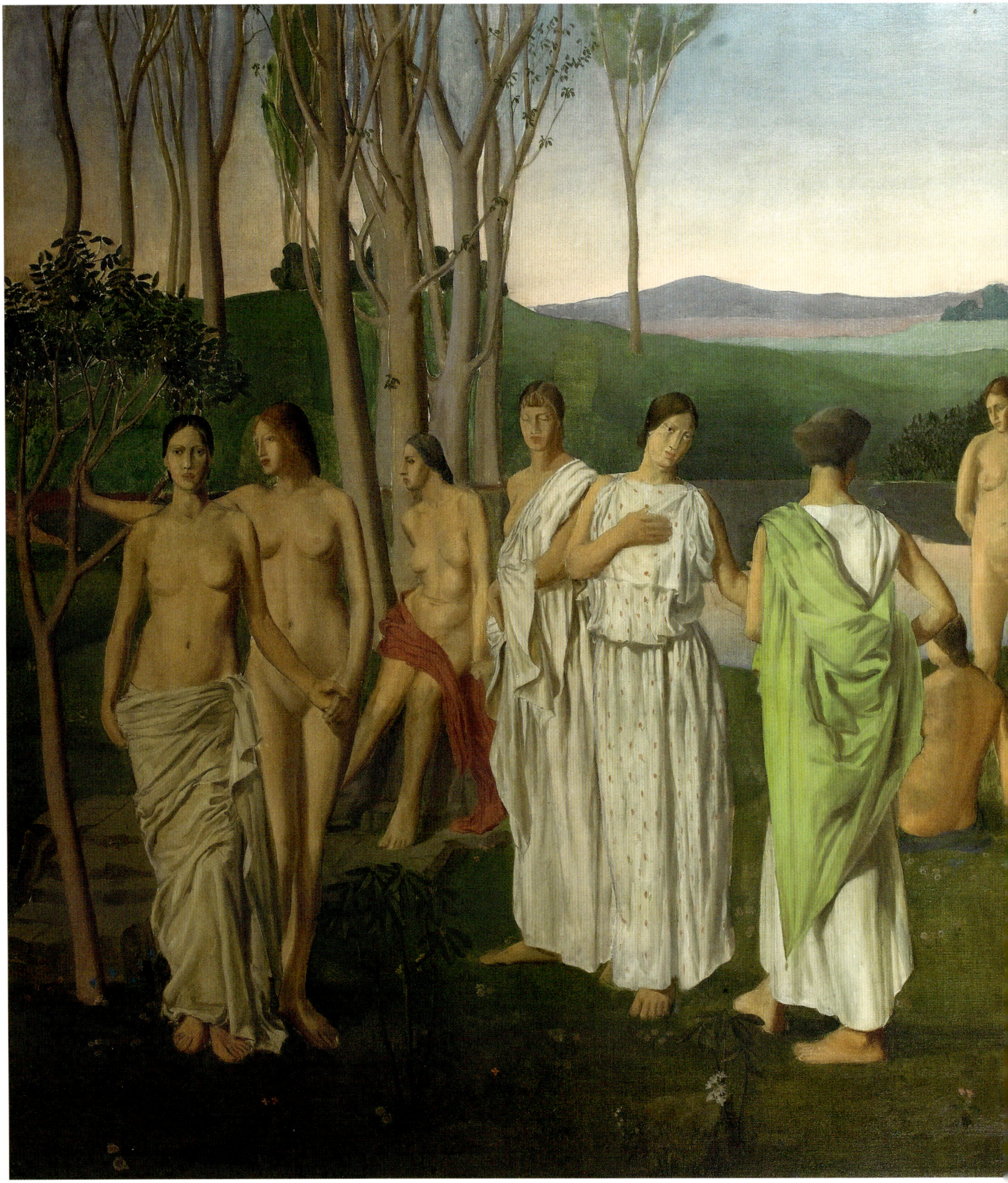

**356 Ian Grant** (1904-1993), *Figures by a Lake*, c.1928, signed and inscribed on the reverse, oil on canvas, 47 x 83 in. (119.4 x 211 cm).

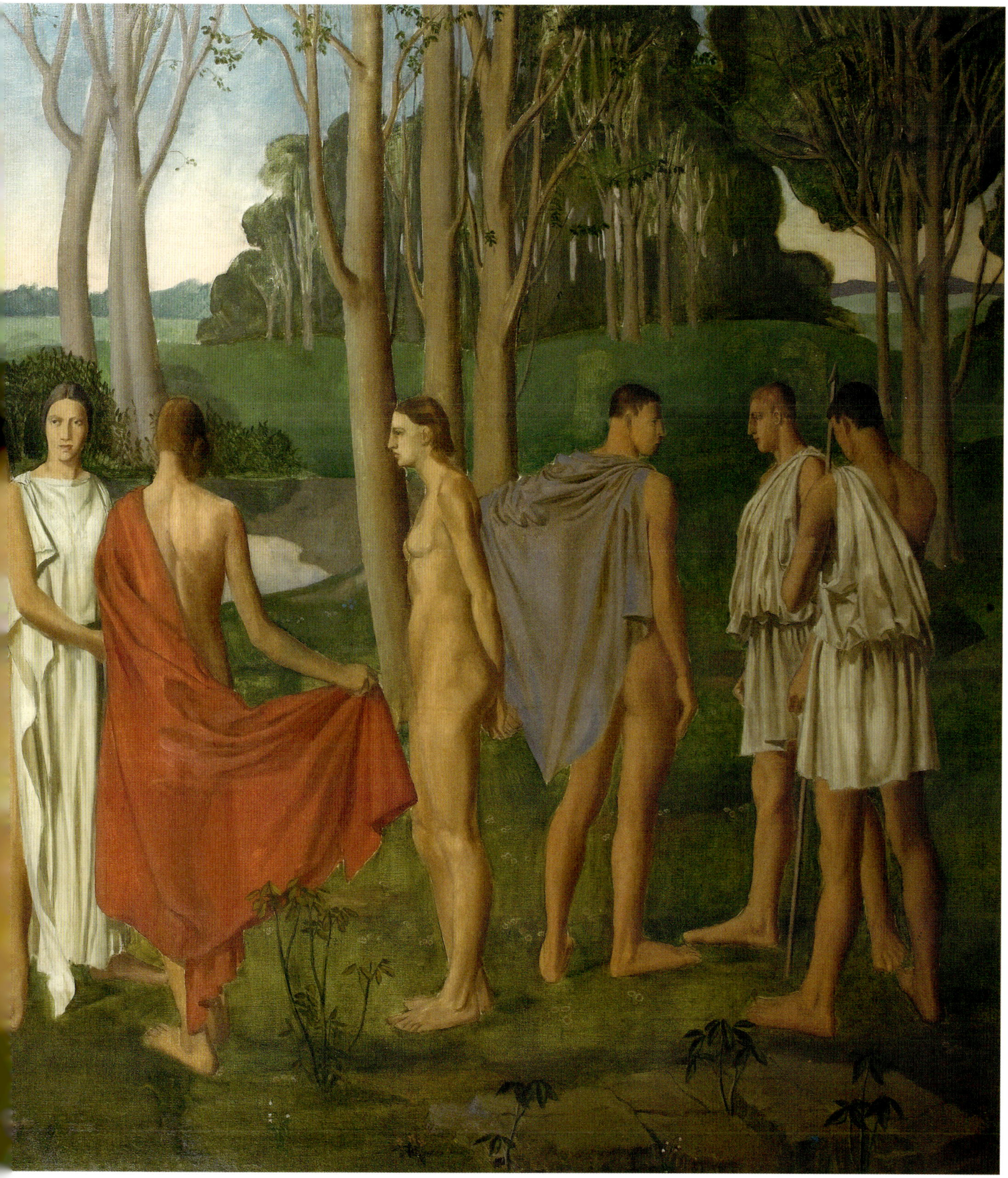

Of his education at the Royal College of Art, Ian Grant recalled: 'The great high priest of drawing was Ingres and you were told to study Piero della Francesca as a Painter.' Painted in his Diploma year, *Figures by a Lake* was Grant's entry for the 1929 Scholarship to the British School at Rome, for which he received second prize.

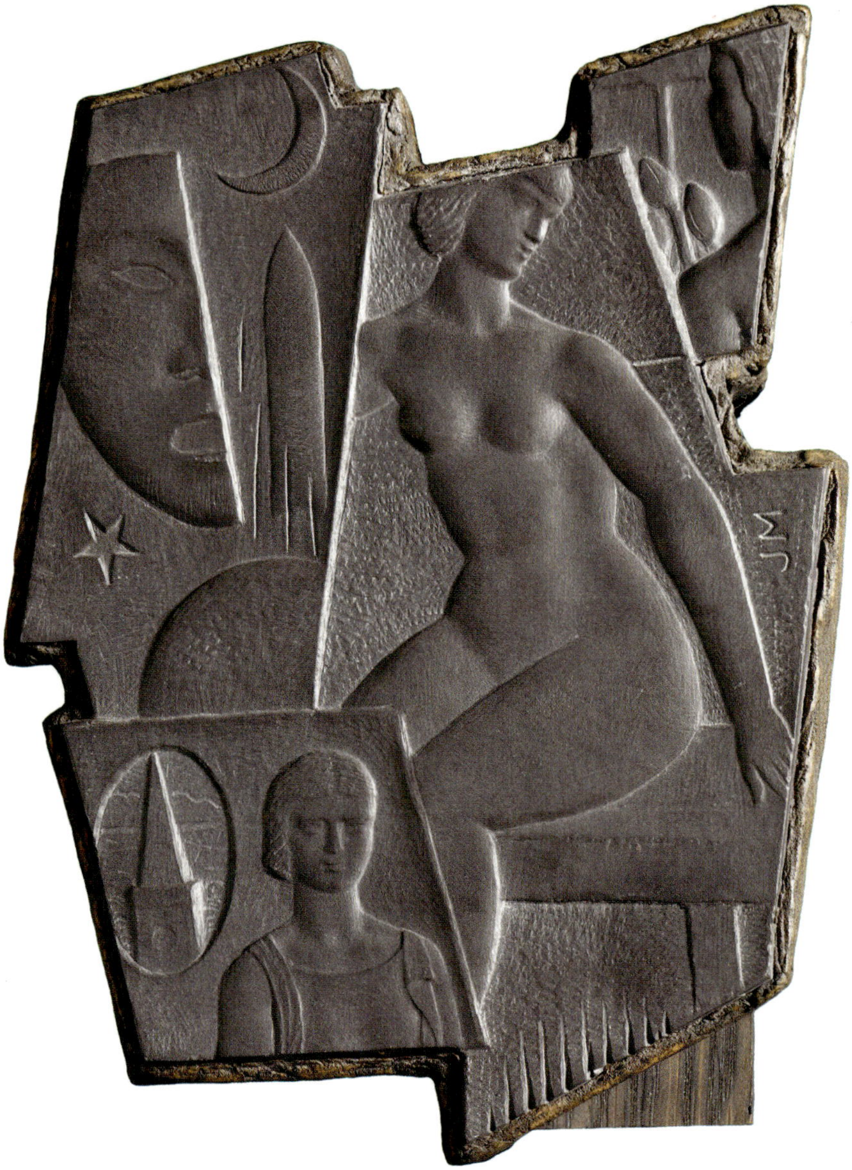

**357 John McKenzie** (1897-1972), *Moonshot*, 1940s, signed with initials, inscribed with title on reverse, Welsh slate, asymmetrical, carved in high relief, 7 ½ x 5 in. (17.5 x 12.5 cm).

By day a charge-hand mess-man on HMS Condor (and later a railwayman), the reclusive John McKenzie indulged his passion for carving by night, producing no more than a handful of slates a year. Inspired by his own system of recurrent motifs, he found it entirely natural to mix together ancient with contemporary subjects. A rich symbolism imbues his work, complemented by lyrical titles such as 'Lightsome Interlude', 'Fruitful Tree' or 'Moon Shot'

**358 Stanley Lewis** (1905-2009), Study for the Central Group of *Allegory*, c. 1929, oil on canvas, 117 x 57 in. (287x 144.8 cm).

Of this painting Stanley Lewis (**276**) commented 'The theme of this painting is man and nature – symbolized by the man holding the hedgehog – living in harmony.... The hedgehog represents the extraordinary life in the countryside. The picture's theme is a celebration of simple country, country life and animals big and small.' Lewis completed the painting whilst staying with his Aunt Joan in Westgate Terrace, London. Here he found the model for the central figure – a road sweeper who happened to be passing. 'I looked out of the window and saw a tall man cleaning the street so I got him to pose for a few minutes just so I could get the hang of it.' Sally's daughter Joan, Stanley's cousin, modelled for the girl with the apple.

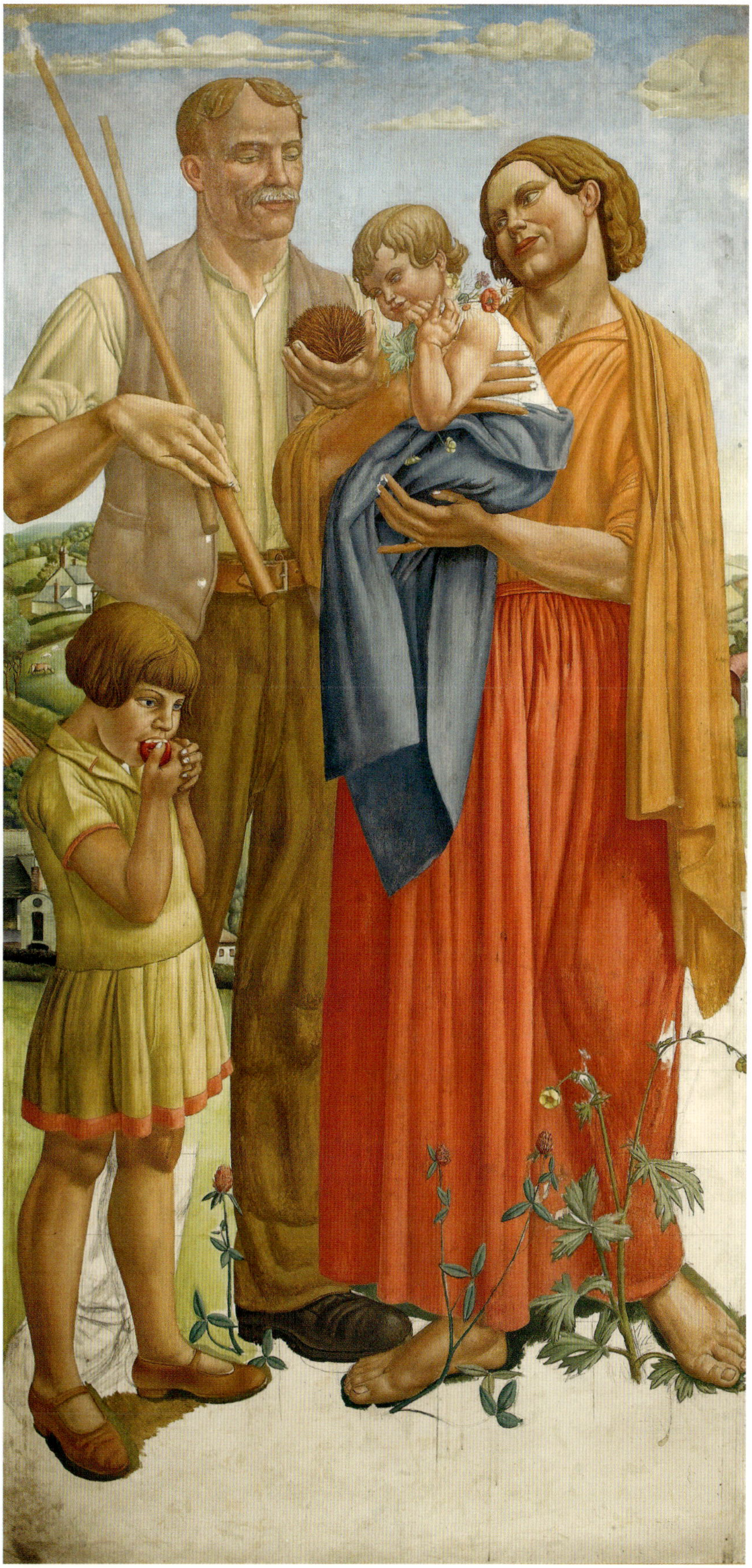

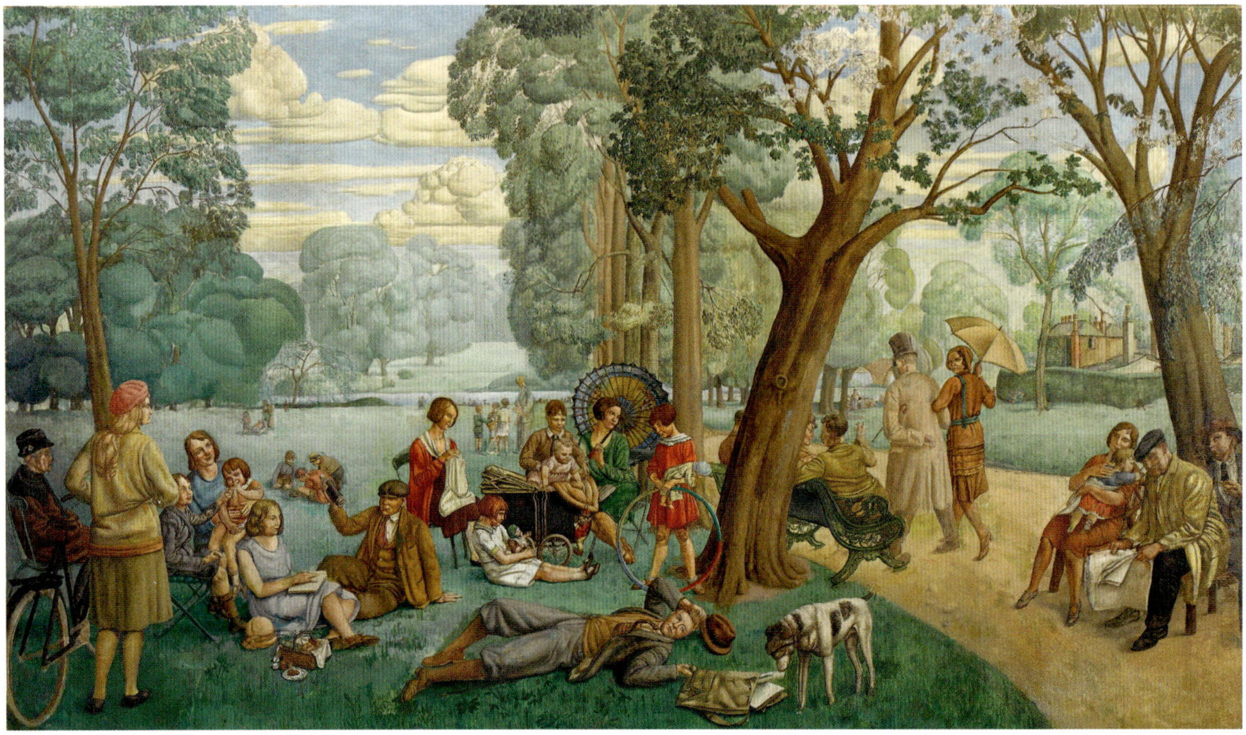

**359 Stanley Lewis** (1905-2009), *Hyde Park in Summer,* 1931,
oil on canvas, 48 x 86 ¾ in. (122 x 220.2 cm).

Stanley Lewis (**276**) portrays himself centre stage, reclining, in Hyde Park. The man seated on the far right, reading, was Lewis' father. The old lady seated in profile on the left was a Royal College of Art model. The fashionable lady holding an umbrella arm in arm with a gentleman in a top hat was Muriel Pemberton, later head of fashion at St. Martins. Lewis was courting her – she glances back coquettishly towards him. Pemberton also served as the model for the seated central figure with the Chinese parasol, which Lewis recalled going to Woolworth's to buy as a compositional device to add colour. The figure in a red beret holding Lewis' bicycle is his sister Margaret. His young cousin Joan, daughter of aunt Sally, is playing with a hoop. She was also the model for the girl eating an apple in *Allegory*. Lewis resisted criticism from Pemberton, who interfered with the painting insisting he should be more modern in his approach. Similar pressure was applied by Lewis' landlady and aunt, Sally Taylor, herself a painter whose art, as Lewis later recalled, 'took you beyond the normal world – abstract and expressionism and so on. "Stan, you might as well be a camera," she said sniffily, when she saw my studies of the painting. And that is it, really. I felt an inner force burning to capture my world around exactly as I saw it in the reality that it was.'

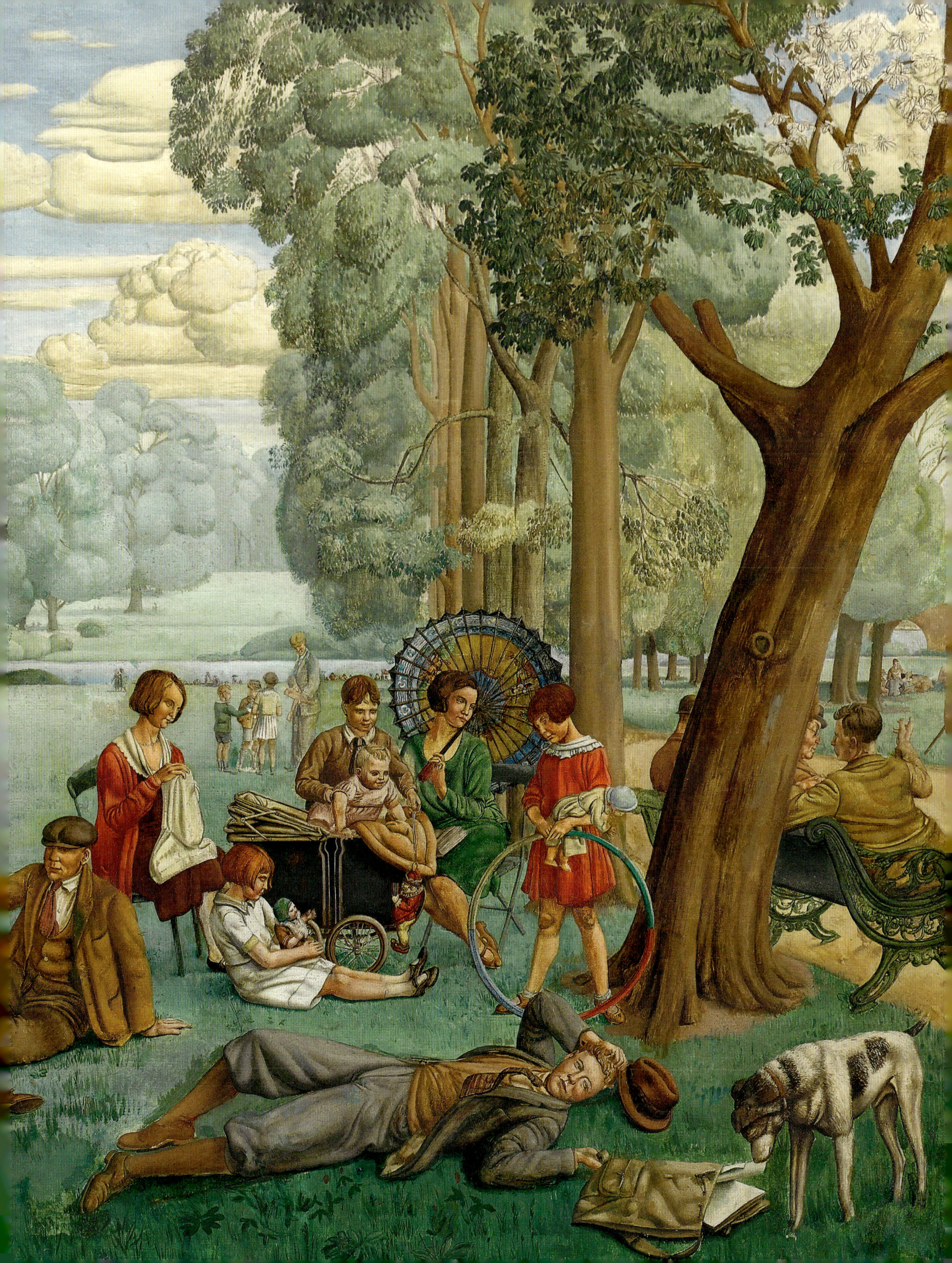

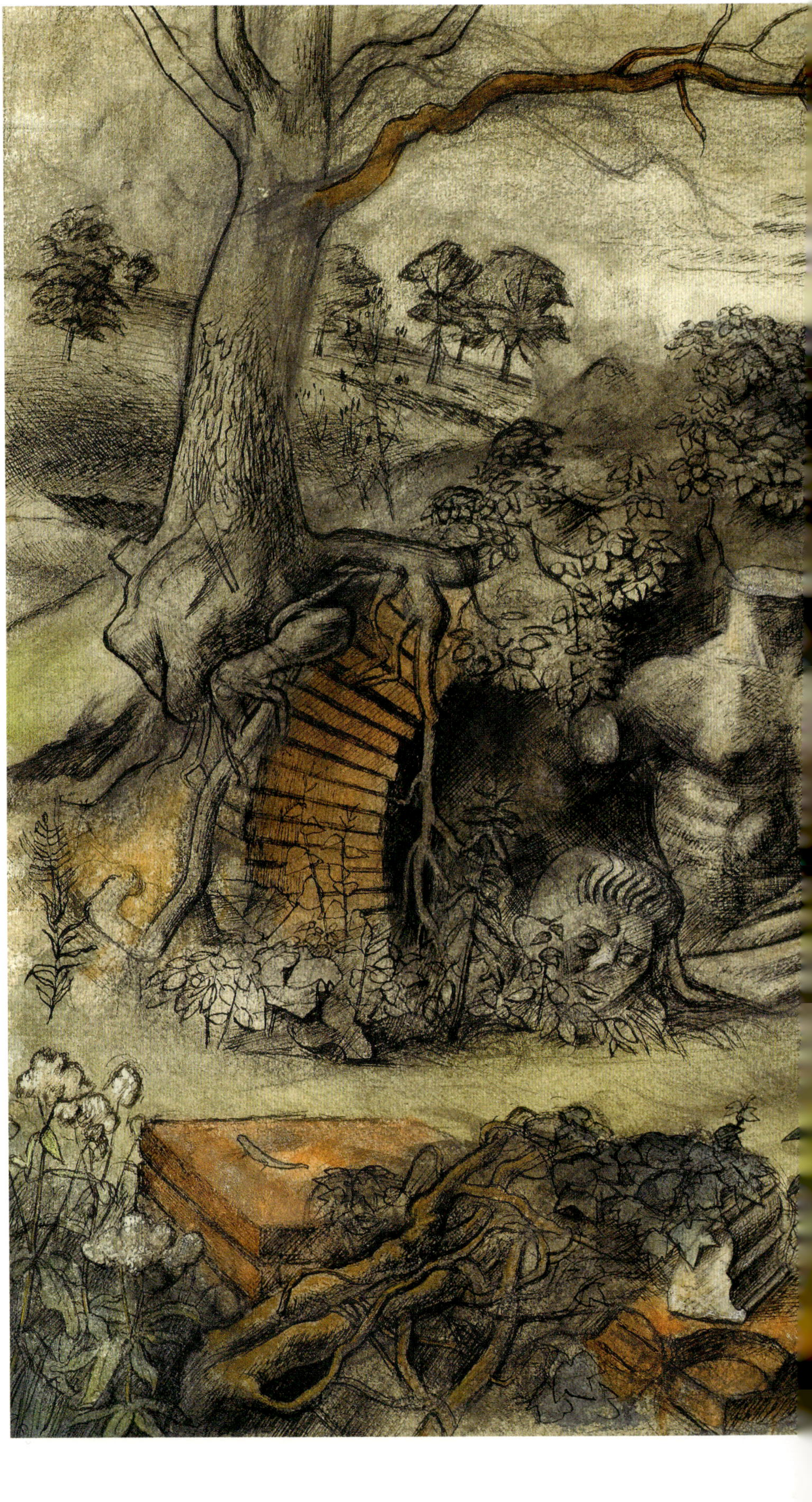

**360 Alan Sorrell** (1904-1974),
*The Artist in the Campagna,* c.1931,
pencil, ink and watercolour on paper,
15 ½ x 22 ½ in. (39.5 x 57 cm).

Drawn when Alan Sorrell (**267**) was a Scholar in Decorative Painting at The British School at Rome, this composition shows the artist standing between the invented and observed worlds. The small mound composed of collapsing classical remains is a recurring theme in Sorrell's work. The distant hill on the right is taken from a direct drawing of Lake Albano and Monte Cavo to the south of Rome.

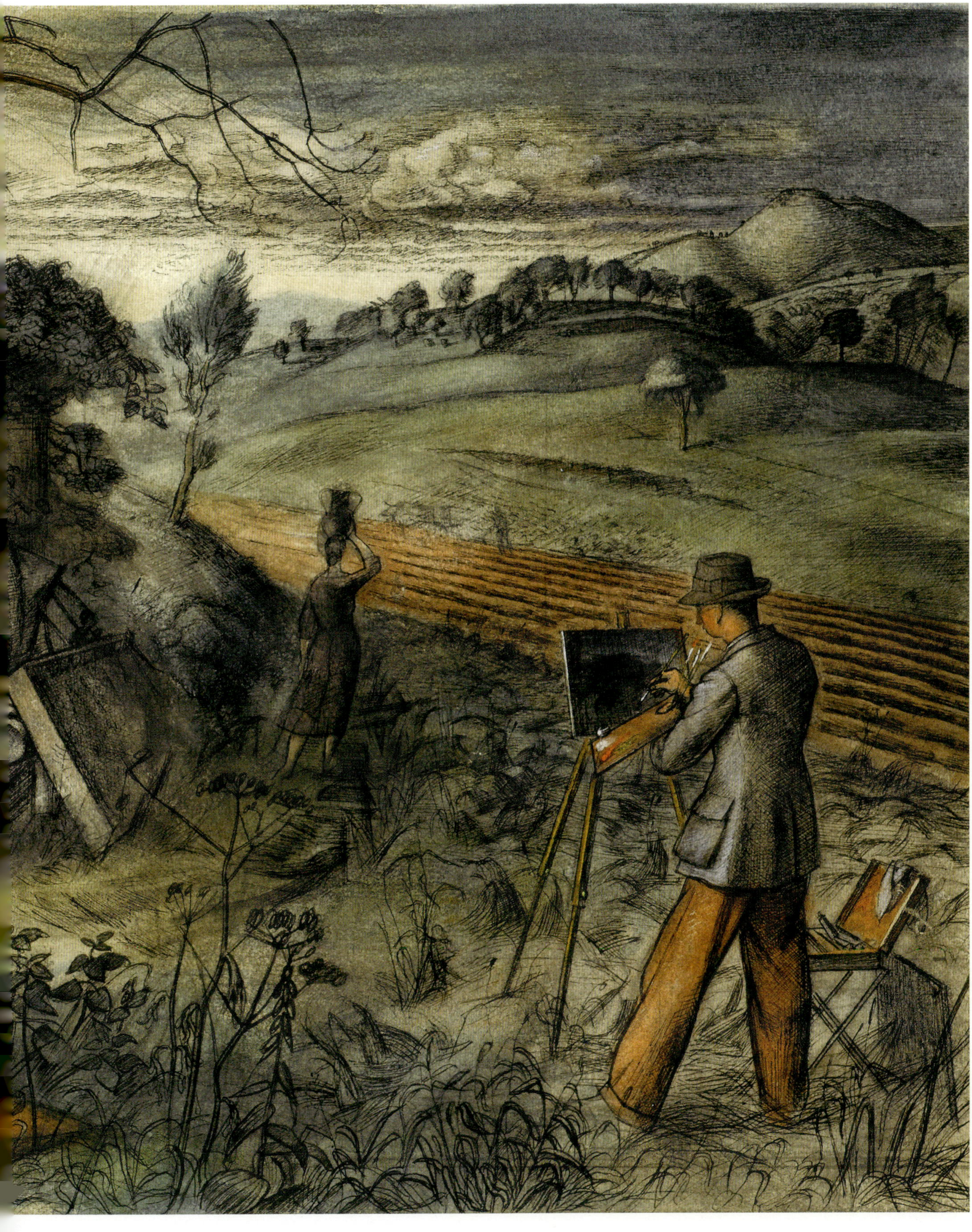

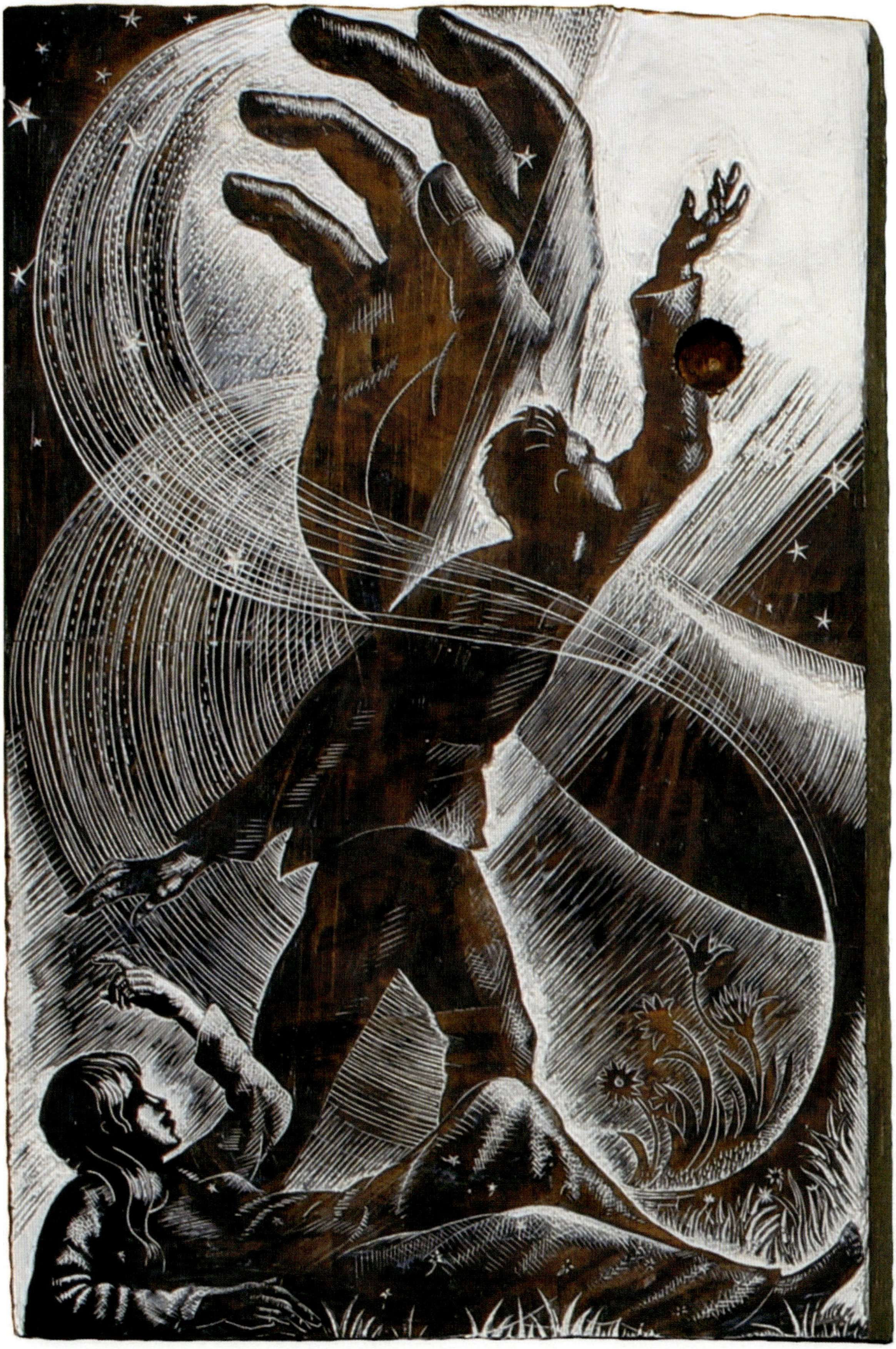

361

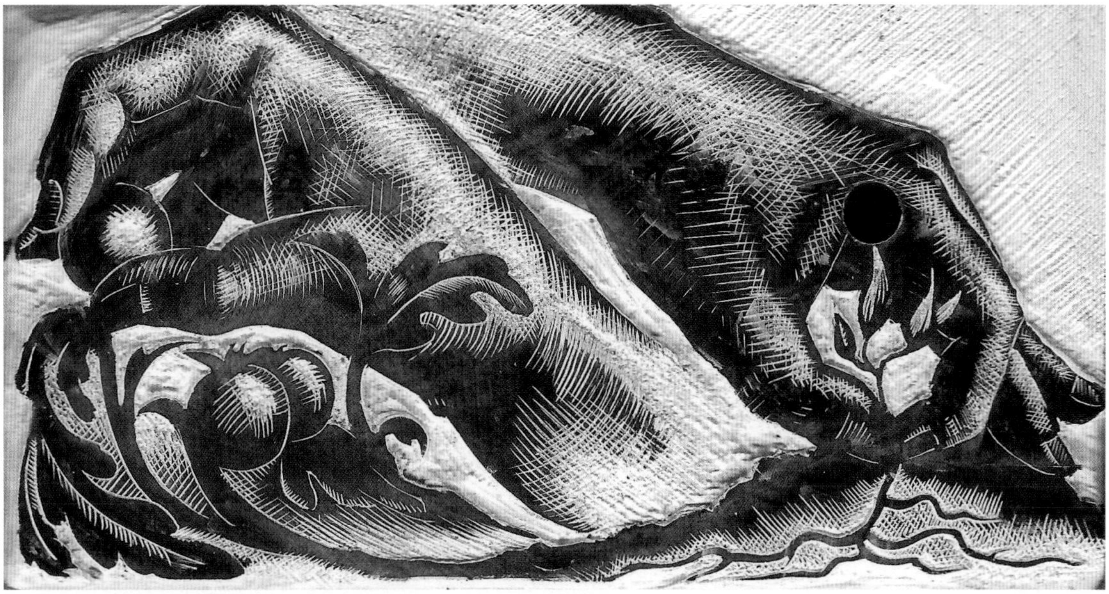

362

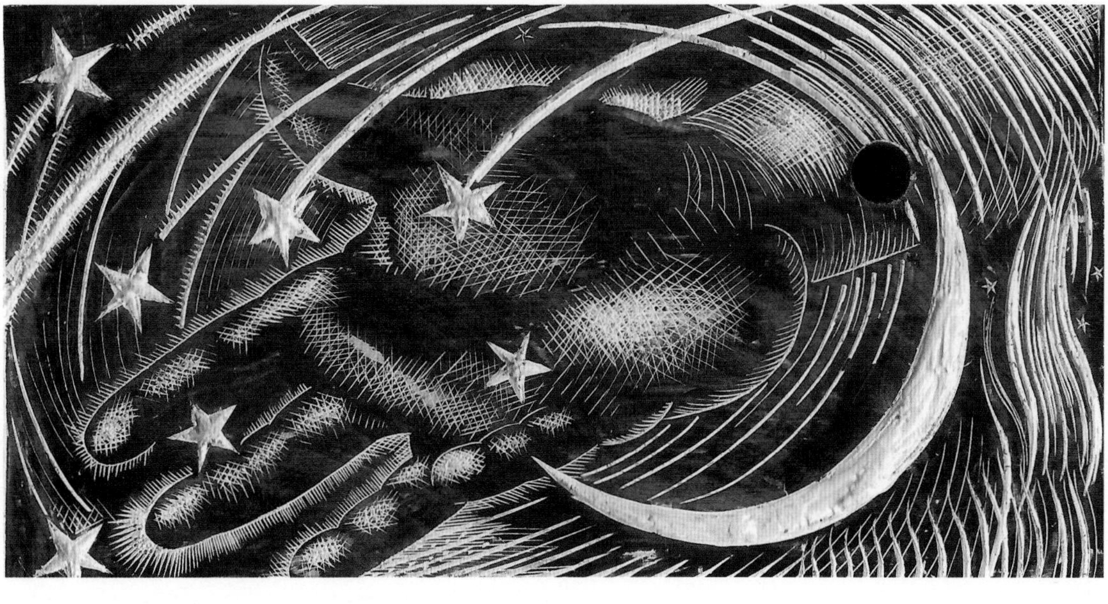

363

**Clare Leighton** (1898-1989),

**361** *Lopping, The Book of Proverbs* (BPL 210), 1933
original woodblock, cancelled, 6 x 4 in. (15.1 x 10.1 cm).

**362** *To Everything There Is a Season, Psalms* (BPL 670), 1952,
original woodblock, cancelled, 2 x 4 in. (5.3 x 10 cm).

**363** *When I Consider the Heavens, Psalms* (BPL 644), 1952,
original woodblock, cancelled, 2 x 4 in. (5.3 x 10 cm).

*When I Consider the Heavens* and *To Everything There Is a Season* were published in the 1952 Doubleday Co. Inc (New York) edition of *The Book of Psalms*, the *First Psalm of David*, the *Book of Proverbs* and *The Book of Ecclesiastes*, King James' Version. Leighton would typically take several days to produce a wood engraving, painstakingly carving the image with special tools strong enough to incise into the end grain of the block, made of boxwood, sufficiently hard to allow for a number of prints to be made before any loss of sharpness.

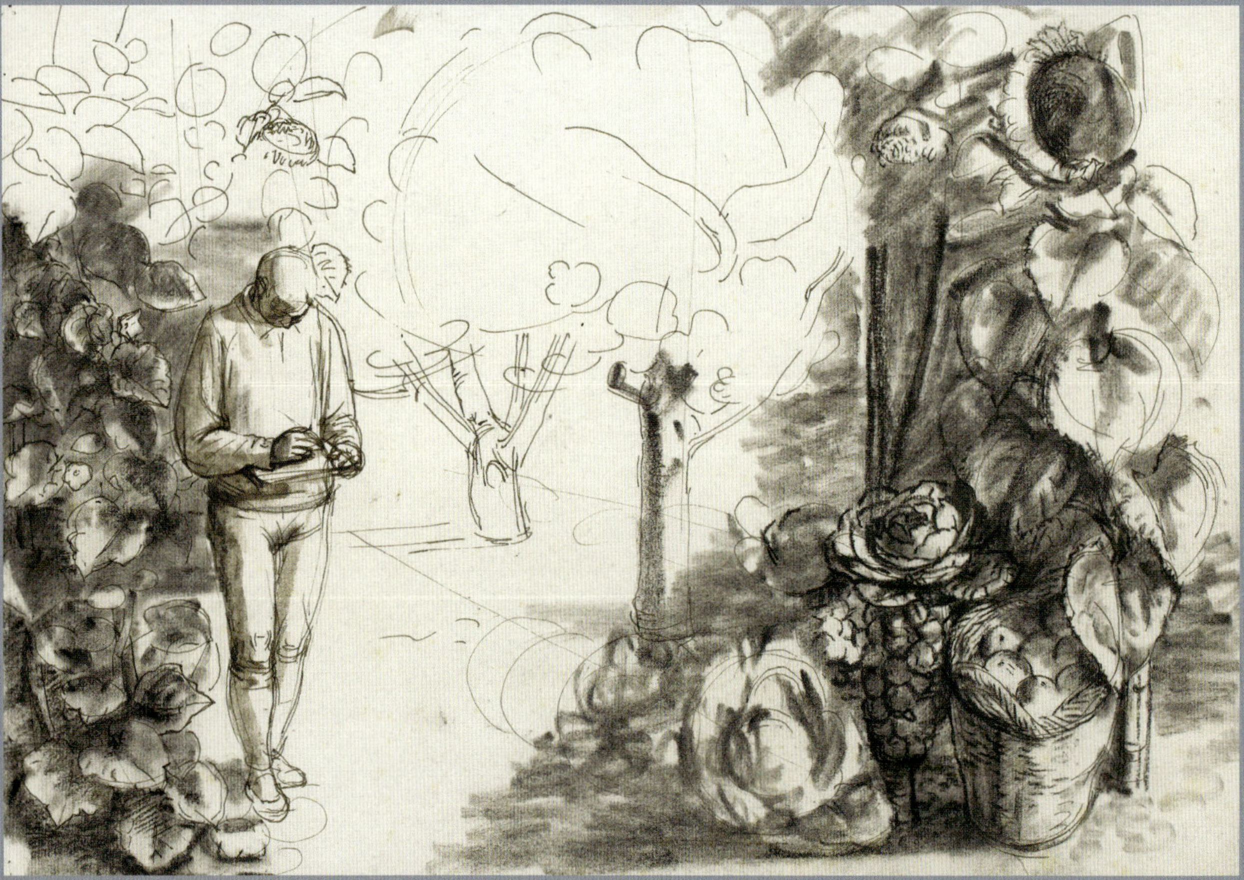

**364 Charles Mahoney** (1903-1968), *The Artist and his Muse*, c.1950,
pen & ink and wash on paper, 9 ¼ x 13 in. (23.5 x 33 cm).

First used as a series of allegorical figures in his Morley College mural of the late 1920s, Charles Mahoney returned to the theme of muses throughout his oeuvre. They represented the spiritual and creative values that he strove to express, both in his life and art and bear testament to his aspiration to create a perfect harmony between man and nature. The image of the youthful artist working undisturbed in a Garden of Paradise is a recurrent motif. In a similar vein *Bathsheba* (**368**) was a theme that Mahoney was especially drawn to and which he explored in a series of paintings in 1950s. As with his paintings and drawings of Adam and Eve (**367**), he found in his depiction of the Muses the opportunity to explore further the relationship between man and nature.

**Charles Mahoney** (1903-1968),

**365** *The Artist and his Muses*, c 1950,
wash over pen & ink on paper, 9 ¼ x 13 in. (23.5 x 33 cm).

**366** *The Artist and his Muses*, c 1961,
wash over pen & ink on paper, squared, 8 ¾ x 11 ¾ in. (22.5 x 29.8 cm).

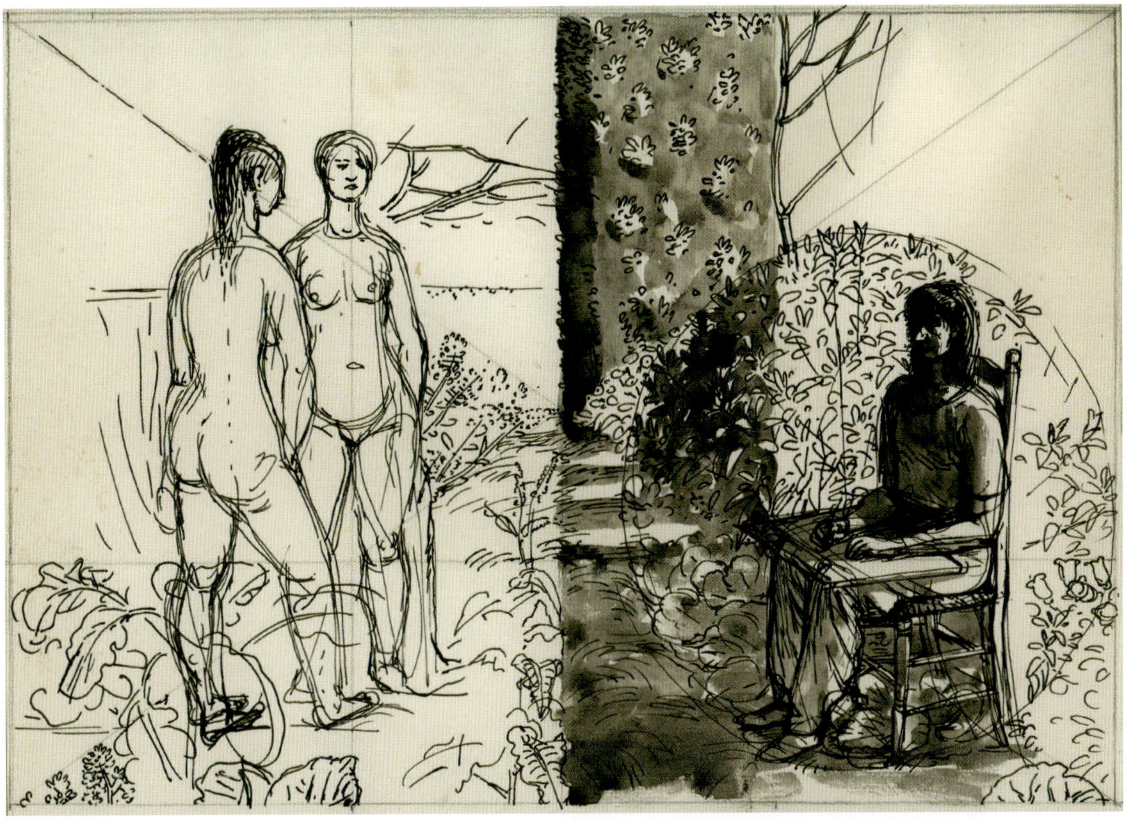

365

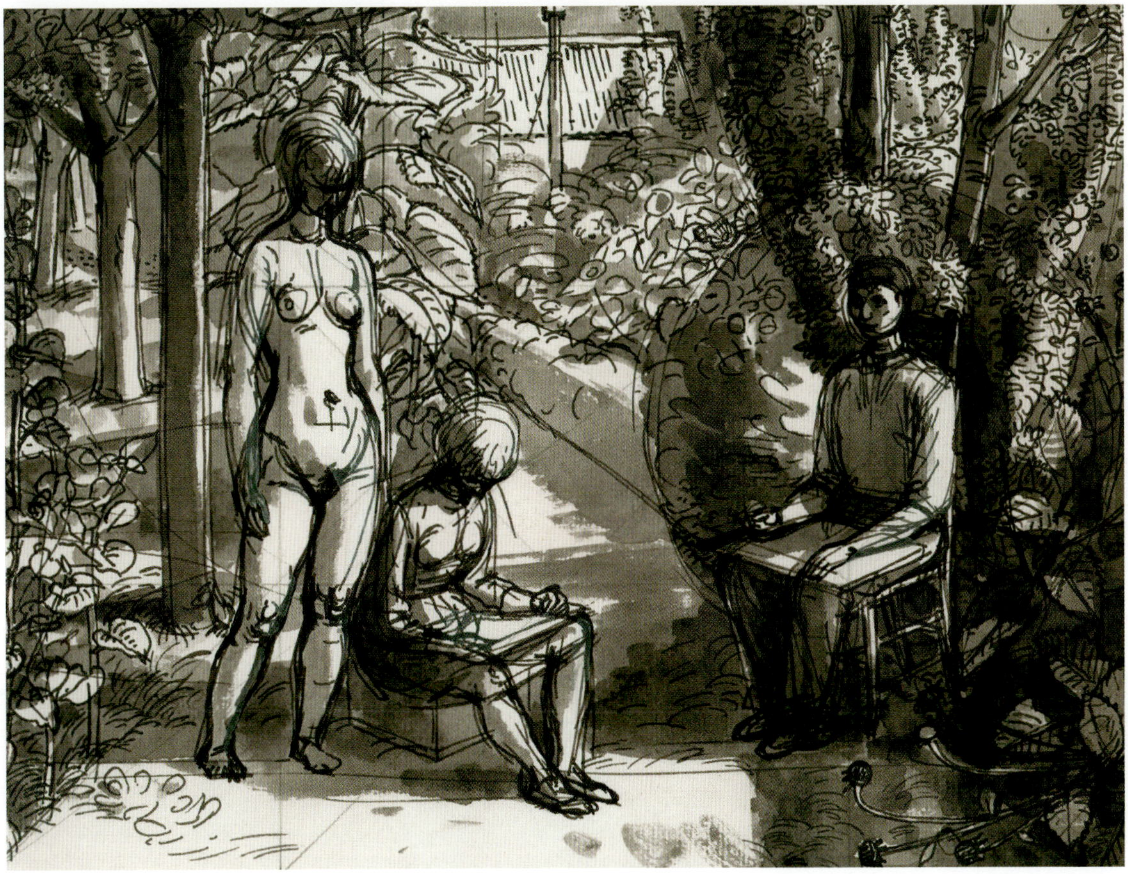

366

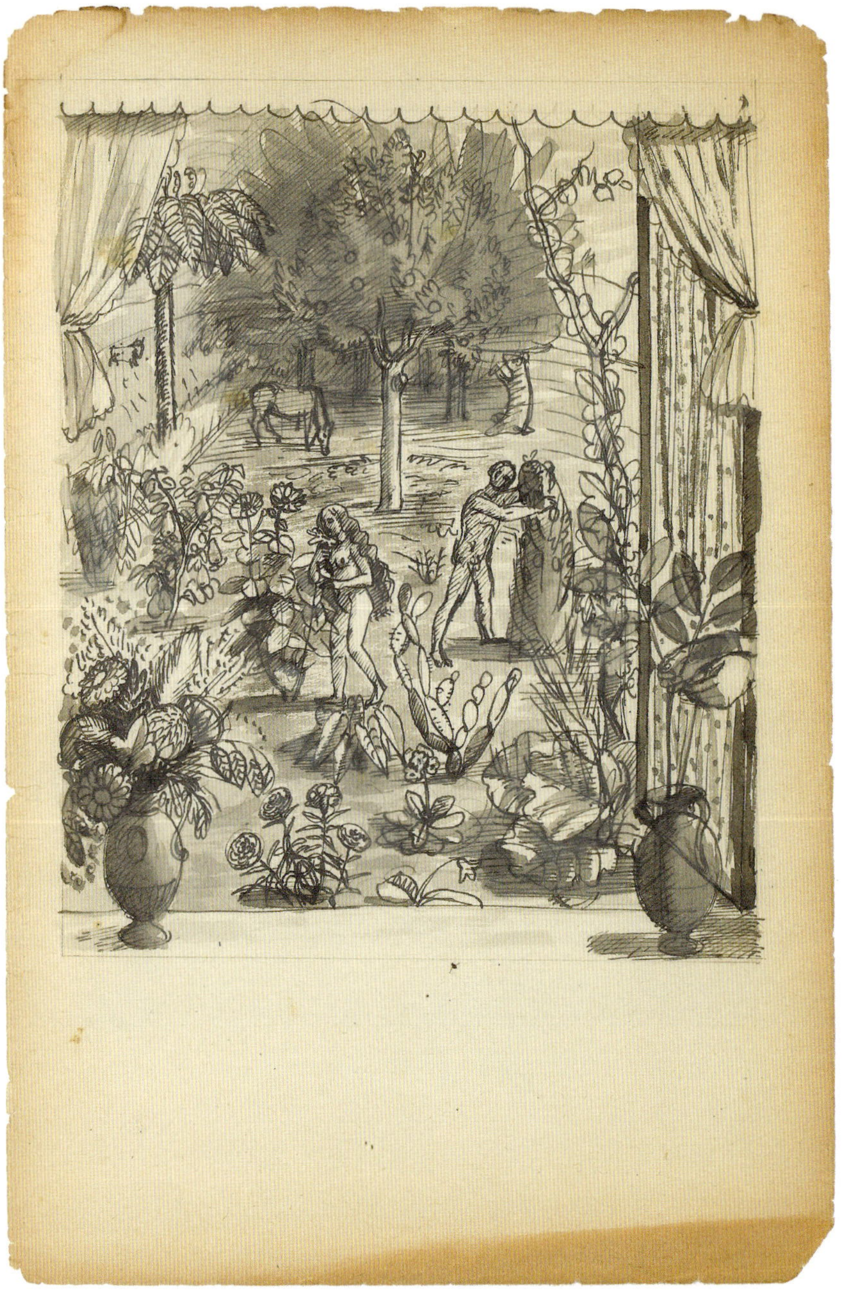

**367 Charles Mahoney** (1903-1968), *Adam and Eve Seen through a Window*, mid-1930s, pen & ink with highlights in watercolour on buff paper, 16 x 10 ¾ in. (40.8 x 27.4 cm).

This is an early study for the 1936 painting of Adam and Eve, acquired by the Tate in 1942. The Garden of Eden is presented as a horticultural fantasy, glimpsed from a domestic interior. Mahoney's first depiction of Adam and Eve appears to date to the beginning of his relationship with Evelyn Dunbar in the mid-1930s, with frequent allusions to the subject in their correspondence.

**368 Charles Mahoney** (1903-1968), *Bathsheba*, late 1940s, oil on paper, 11 ½ x 8 in. (29.2 x 20.3 cm).

The setting for this composition was inspired by the lily ponds at Kew Gardens. Mahoney's admiration for "Douanier" Rousseau is also apparent in the simplified treatment of form and choice of palette.

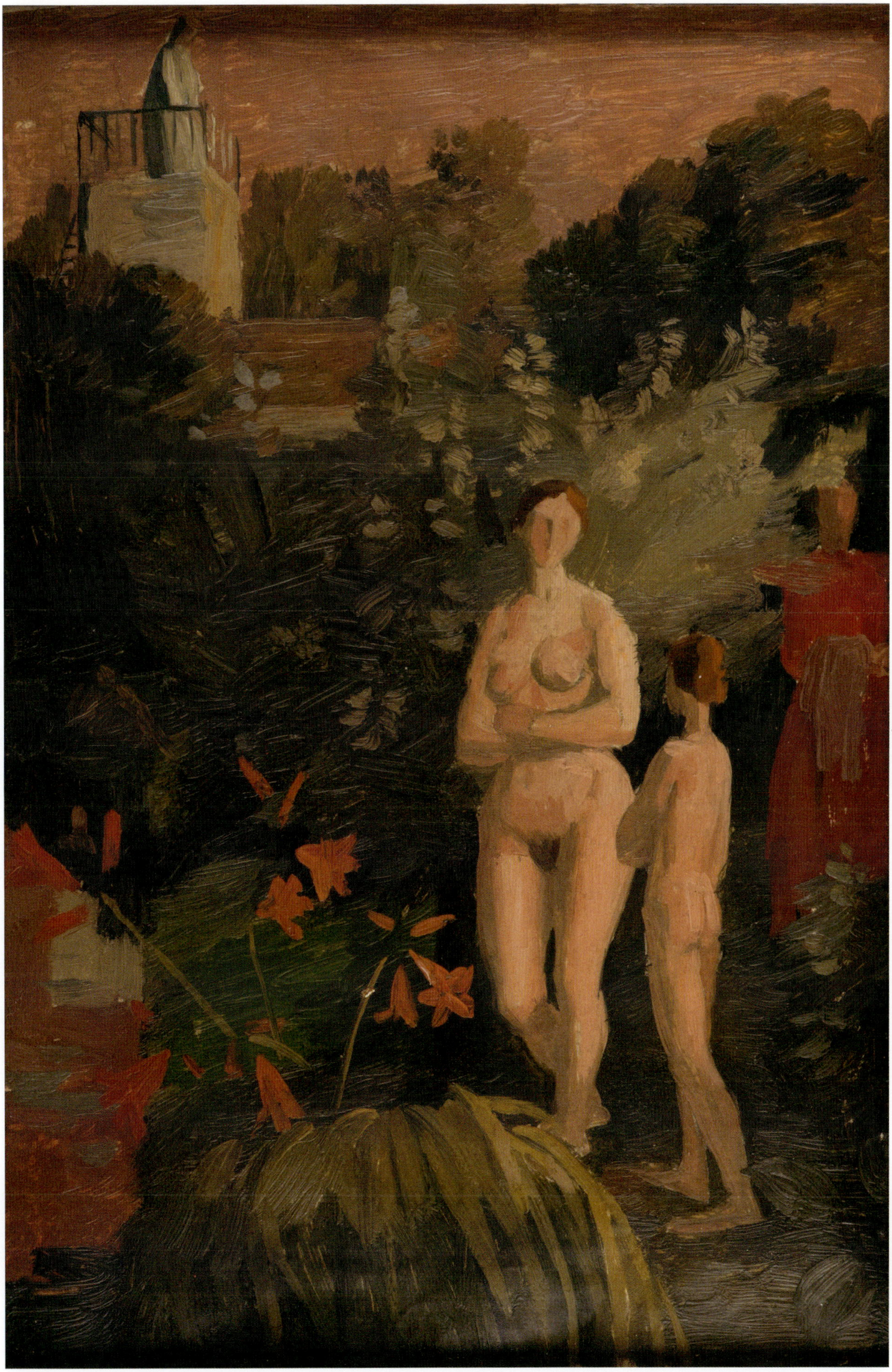

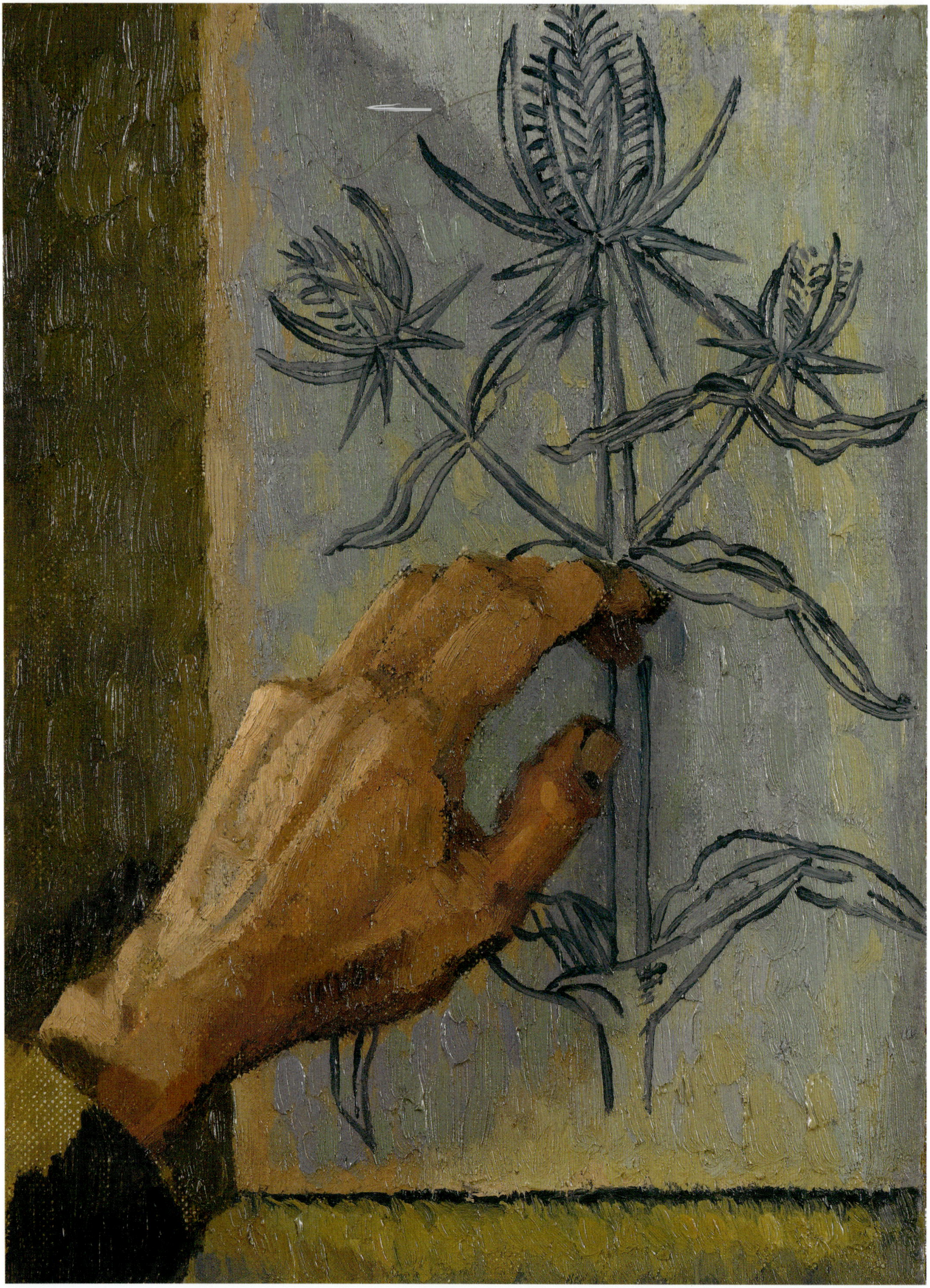

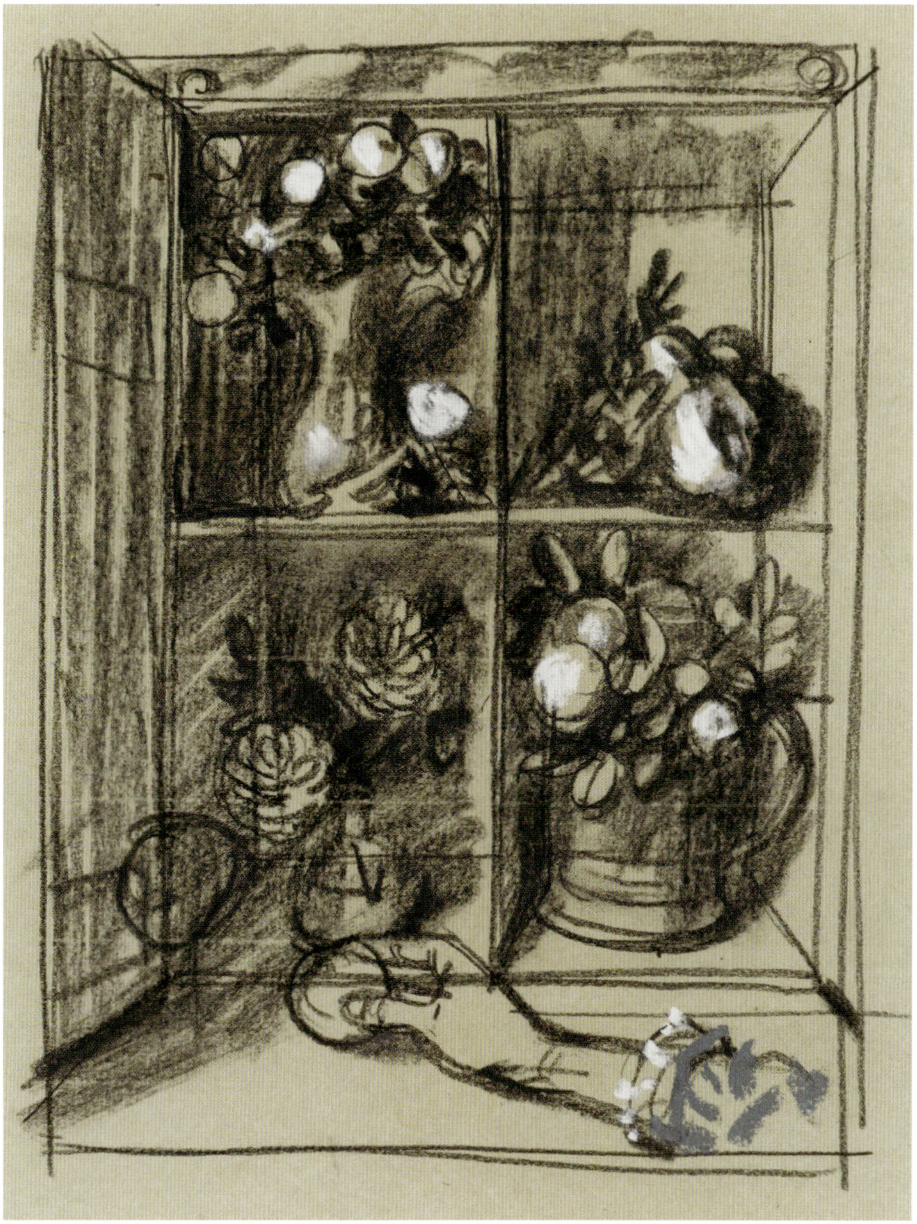

**370 Charles Mahoney** (1903-1968), *Still Life with Orange Box and Hand,* c.1940, black and white chalk and some pastel on paper, 9 ¾ x 7 ¾ in. (25 x 19.5 cm).

Still lifes arranged in orange boxes were something of hallmark of Mahoney. Hands (that of the artist or higher force) often feature in these compositions, dramatically cut by the frame as if their presence is only transitory.

**369 Charles Mahoney** (1903-1968), *The Artist's Hand,* c.1950, oil on canvas, 9 x 7 in. (22.9 x 17.8 cm).

In this composition Charles Mahoney (**318**) artfully explores several of the themes with which artists are preoccupied daily – the artist as creator and the relationship between nature and artifice. The thistle that Mahoney paints himself reaching out for is in fact one of his own paintings, not a thistle; and his hand is also a painted hand, painted by the hand of the artist that we cannot see here because it is engaged on creating this very work.

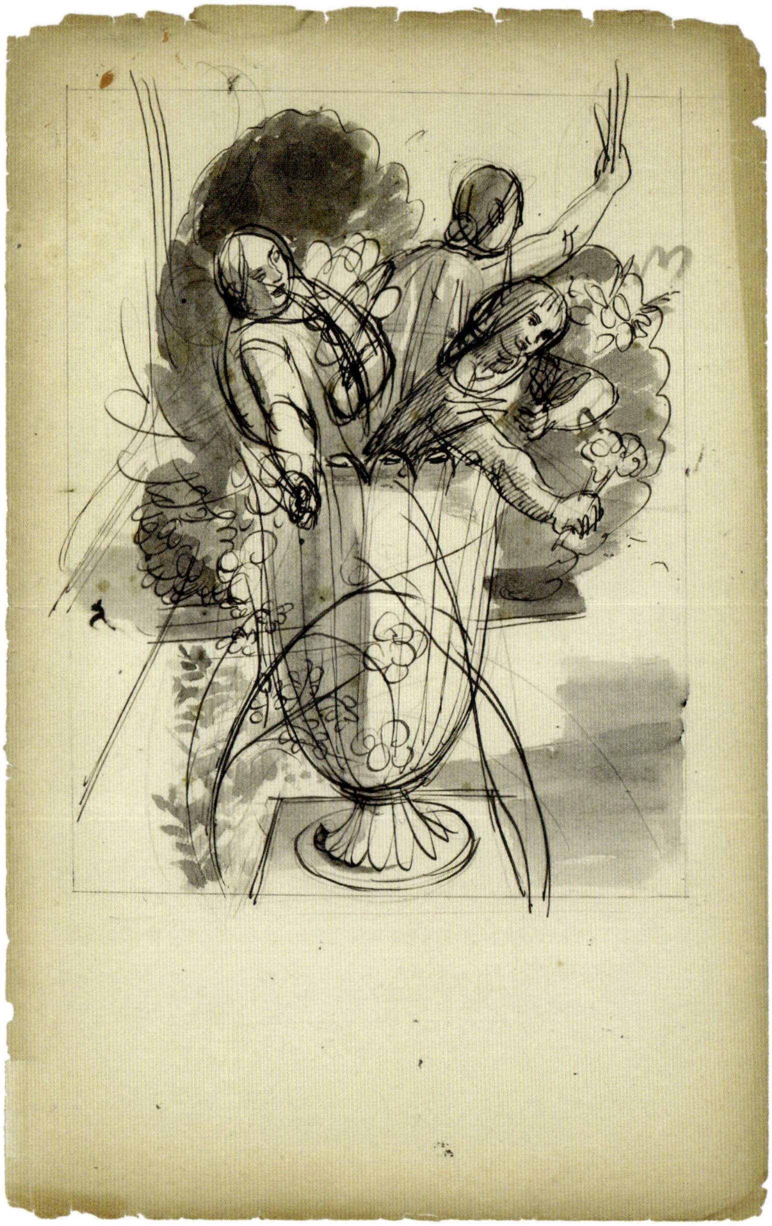

**371 Charles Mahoney** (1903-1968), *Three Women in a Vase, Handing out Flowers*, pen & ink and wash on buff paper, 16 × 10 ¾ in. (40.8 × 27.4 cm).

The tales of the Brothers Grimm were among Mahoney's favourite stories. Dreams and nightmares were a recurrent theme in his œuvre, and from the 1930s onwards he was intrigued by the advent of surrealism. These factors combined to create a sense of surprise in what might otherwise have been a predictable narrative. His vivid imagination found a natural outlet firstly in the form of illustration, especially in correspondence with friends like Edward Bawden, and secondly his keen interest in mural and theatre design, particularly after meeting Geoffrey Rhoades in 1924. (**218**, **319**)

**372 Frederick Austin** (1902-1990), *The Artist Dreaming*, unique working proof; etching with additions in black chalk, plate size 6 ¼ x 4 in. (16 × 10 cm).

The plate for this remarkable evocative dream-like self-portrait was never editioned. It pre-dates Robert Austin's *Self and Jackdaw*, 1943, which, sharing a similar hallucinogenic quality, was possibly made in response. (**257**)

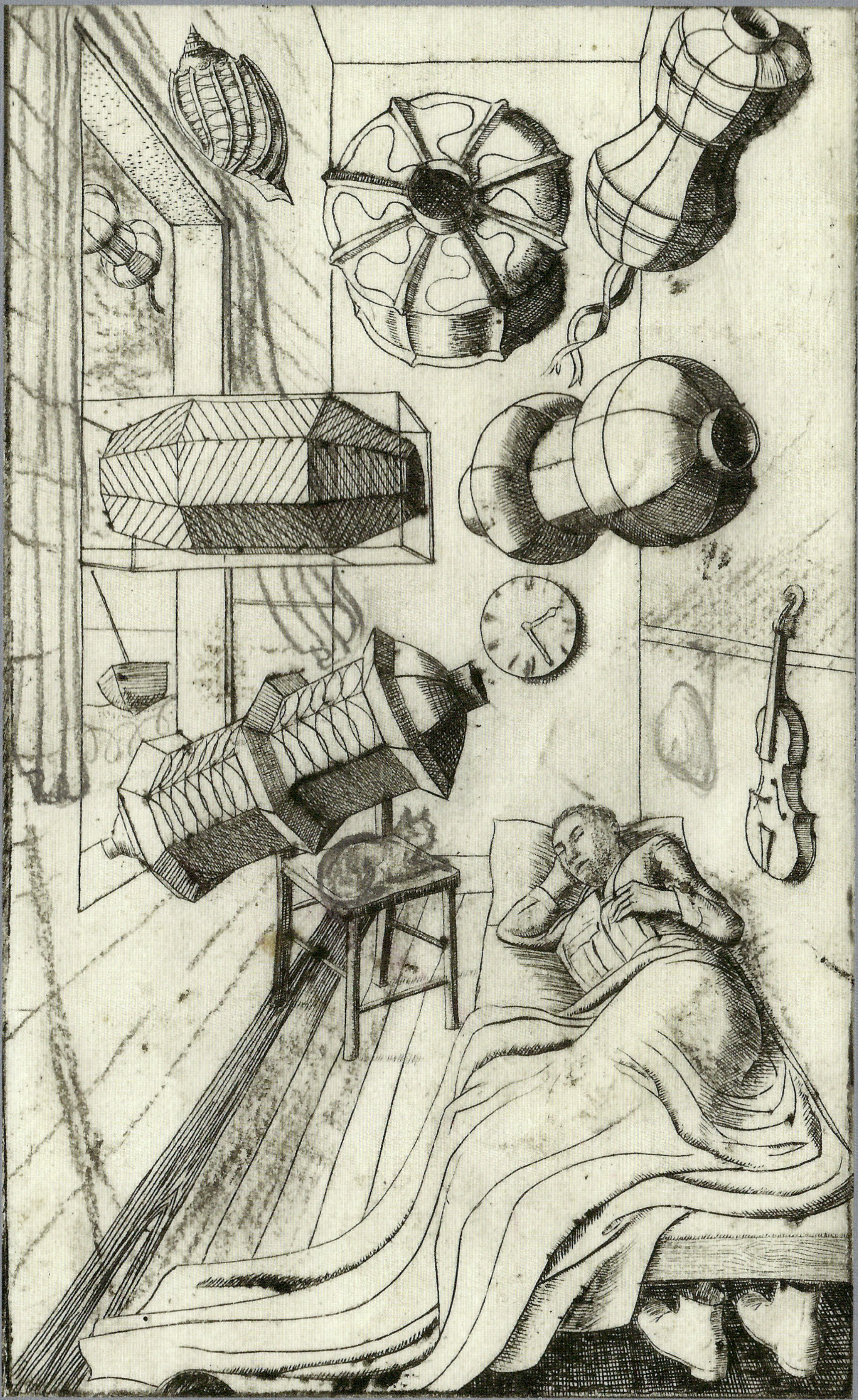

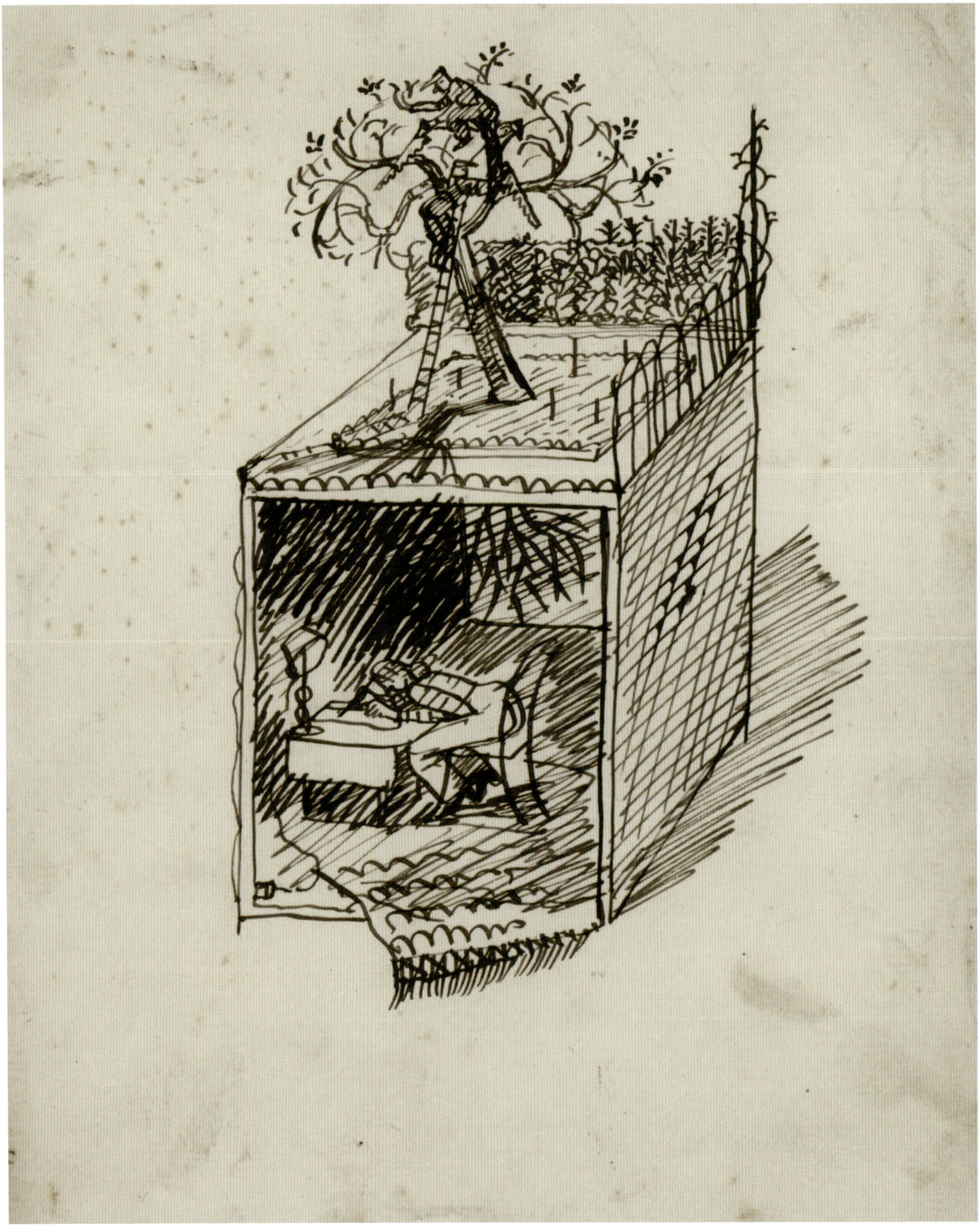

**373 Evelyn Dunbar** (1906-1960), *An Allegory of the Nature of Creation* (HMO 223), 1940s, pen & ink on paper, 9 x 6 ¾ in. (22.8 x 17.5 cm).

*An Allegory of the Nature of Creation* opens up a view on to the enduringly powerful universe that occupied Dunbar's mind in which the artist and nature are inextricably bound together. (**376**)

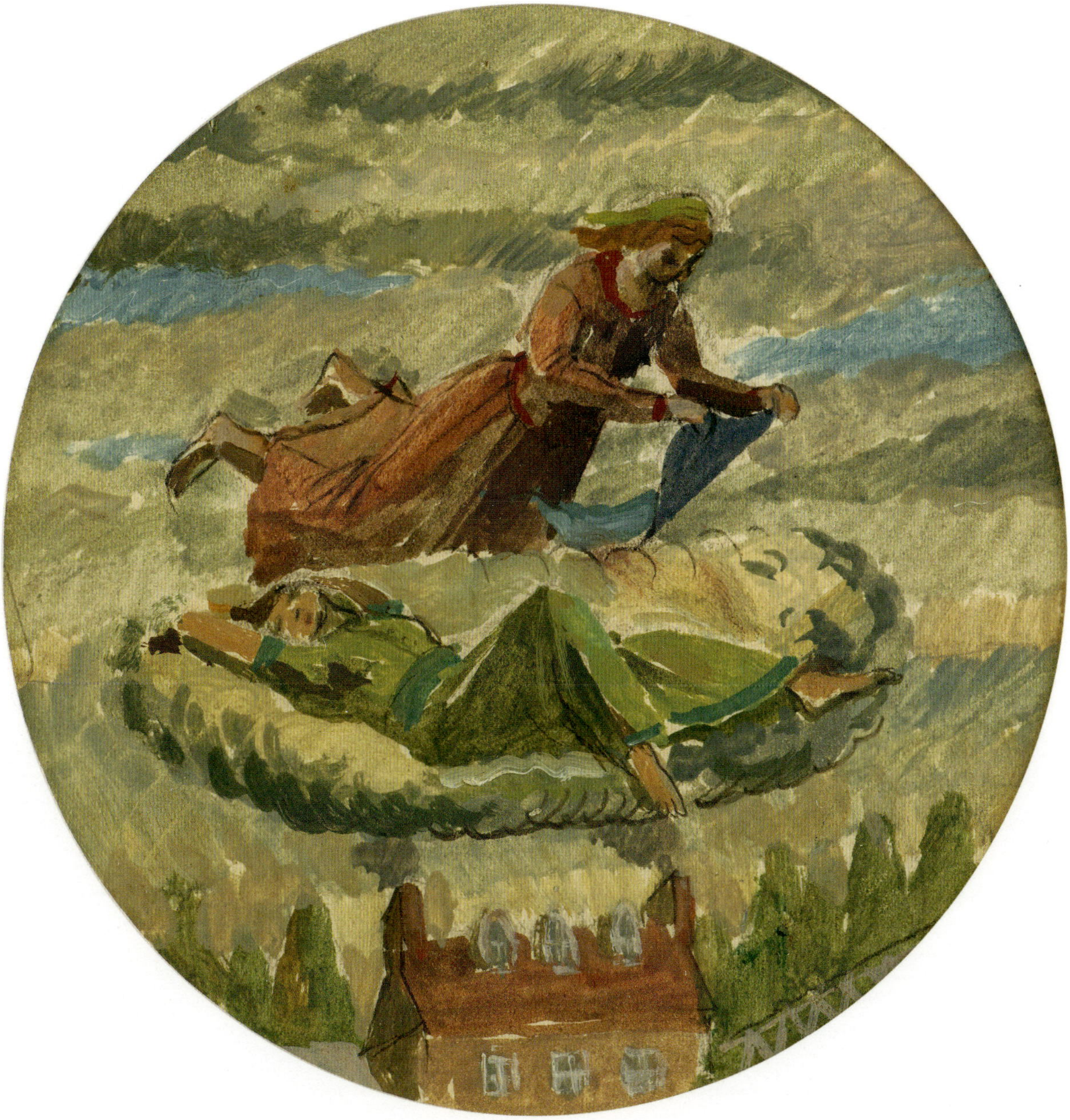

**374 Evelyn Dunbar** (1906-1960), *Industry and Sloth*, c.1932, oil on paper 6 x 6 in. (15.2 x 15.2 cm).

This was one of the proposed designs for the four ceiling roundels that were part of the mural scheme at Brockley School for Boys (now Prendergast - Hilly Fields 6th Form Centre, Lewisham.) The roundels show the classical deities Juno and Minerva rubbing shoulders with personifications of firstly the trio of Genius, Virtue and Reputation, and secondly – as in Dunbar's sketch – with Industry and Sloth. The design evolved over time from the sketch to the finished version, but in both Sloth is asleep while Industry gets on with things.

OVERLEAF:
**375 Evelyn Dunbar** (1906-1960), *Seven Days*, signed and dated, 1938, signed and dated, inscribed on stretcher 'Design for mural', oil on canvas. 18 x 30 in. (45.8 x 76.2 cm).

Loosely based on the nursery rhyme *Monday's child is fair of face, Tuesday's child is full of grace, Wednesday's child is full of woe, Thursday's child has far to go…*, *Seven Days* is an enigmatic image. As an allegory it explores the relationship of man to nature and the passing of time. It also contains a deeply autobiographical narrative alluding to what Dunbar termed her 'crisis' years and the breakdown of her relationship with Charles Mahoney.

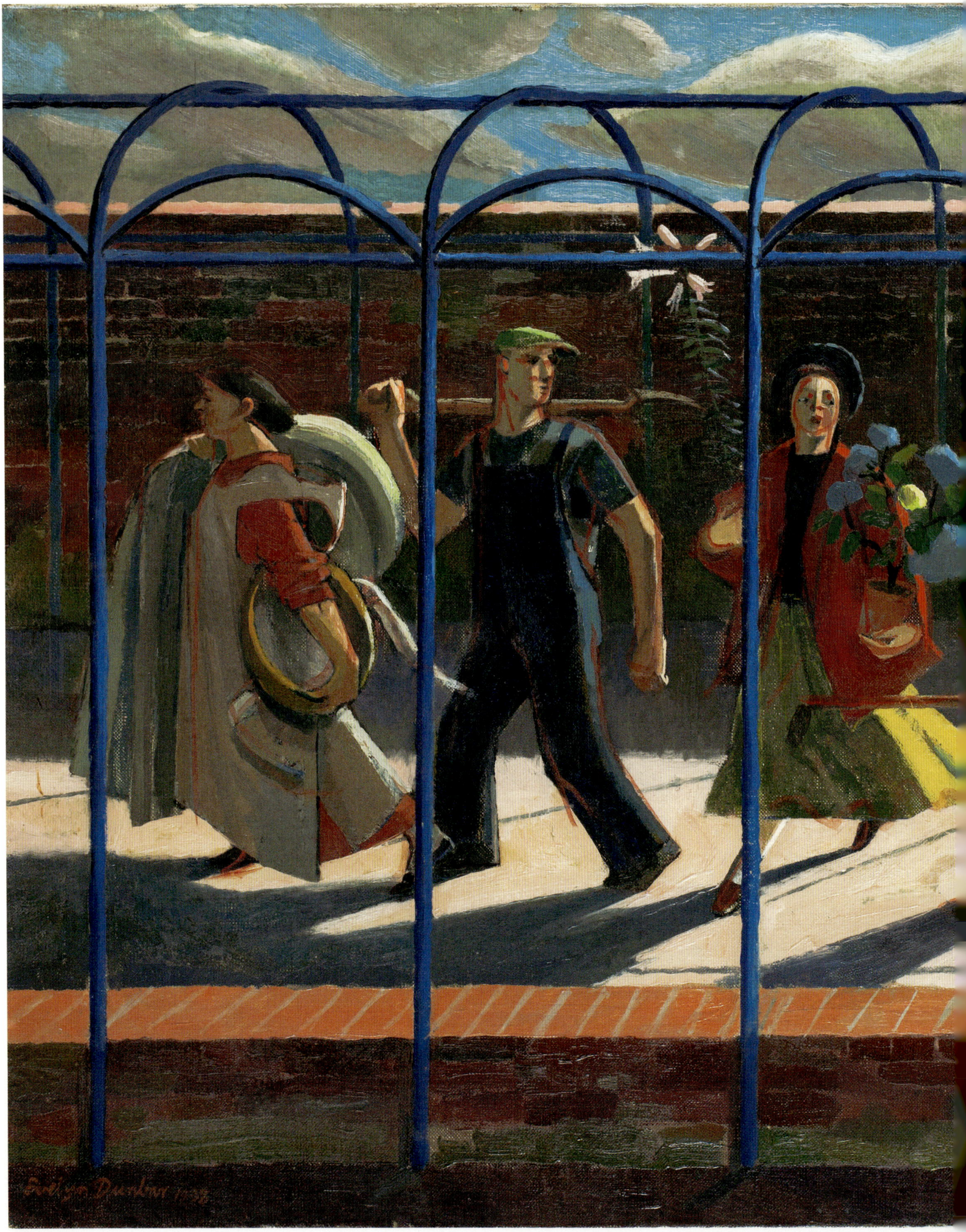
Evelyn Dunbar 1938

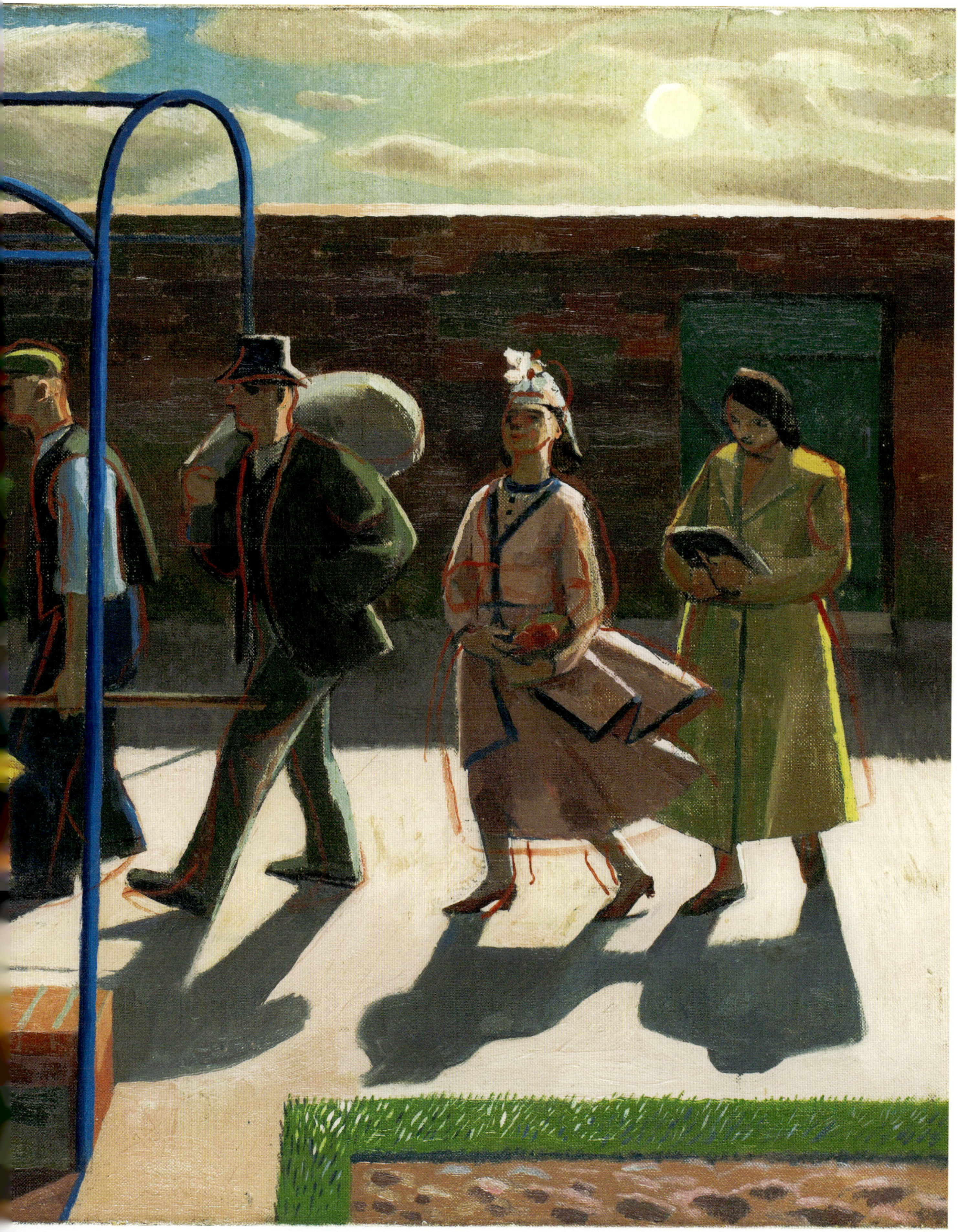

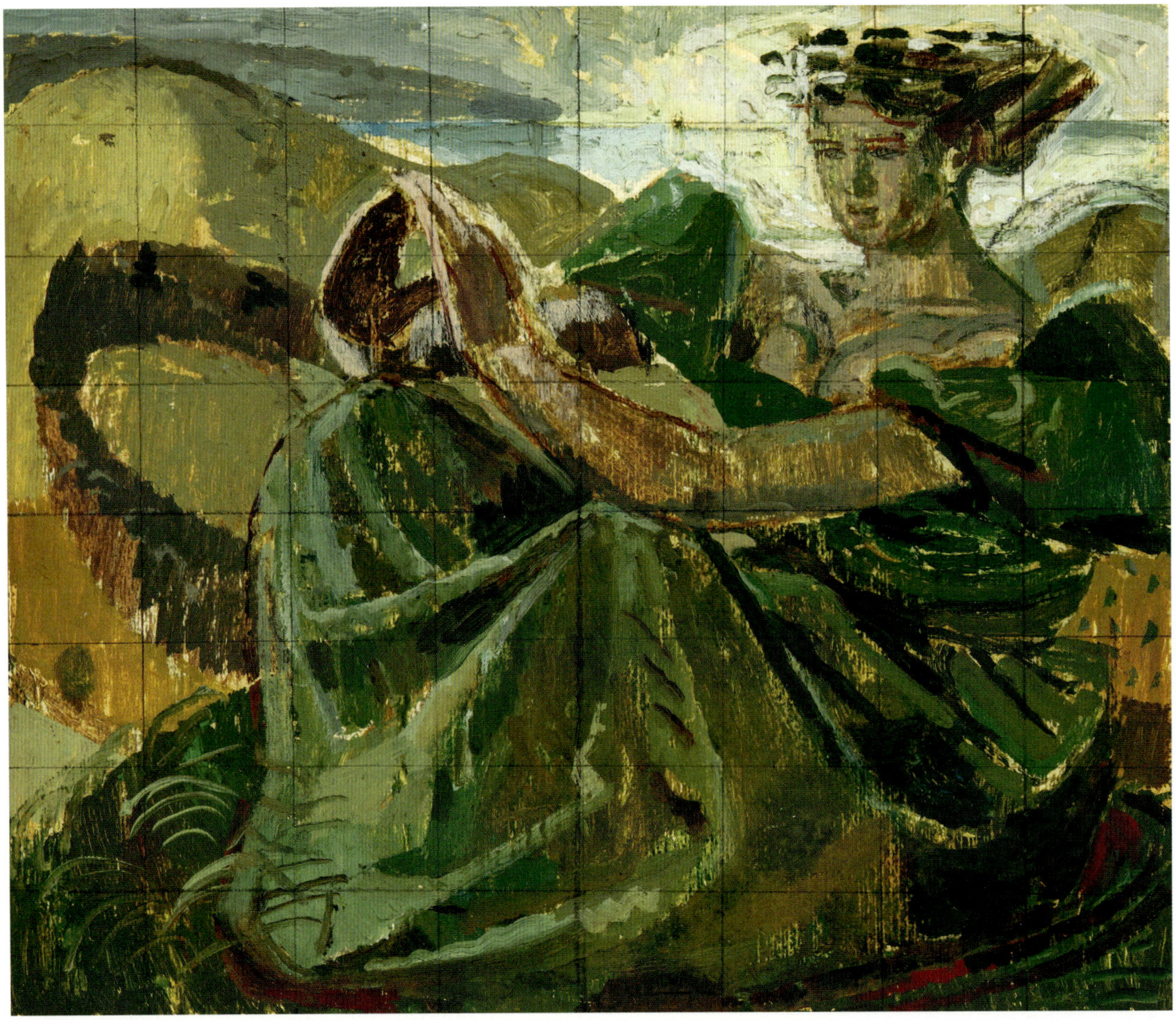

**376 Evelyn Dunbar** (1906-1960), *Dorset*, late 1940s,
oil on board 13 ½ x 16 in. (34.3 x 40.6 cm).

*Dorset* belongs to the most productive period – in terms of quality – of Dunbar's life. When her employment as a war artist finished at the end of WW2 in 1945, she went to live in the south Midlands with her husband, the horticultural economist Roger Folley. Various images, mainly allegorical, pent up during the war years, now found their expression, among them *Dorset*.

**377 Frank Potter** (1885-1958), *Self-portrait as an Auxiliary Fireman*, c.1941
oil on canvas, 62 ¼ x 40 in. (158 x 102 cm).

This painting shows the artist as an Auxiliary Fireman, his plastron-fronted tunic buttoning on the right side and his fireman's hatchet in a holder attached to his belt. Potter, who had served in WW1, enlisting in 1916 at the age of 29, was too old to fight in WW2, but served on the home front as an Auxiliary Fireman assisting in the clean-up of bomb damage to the capital.

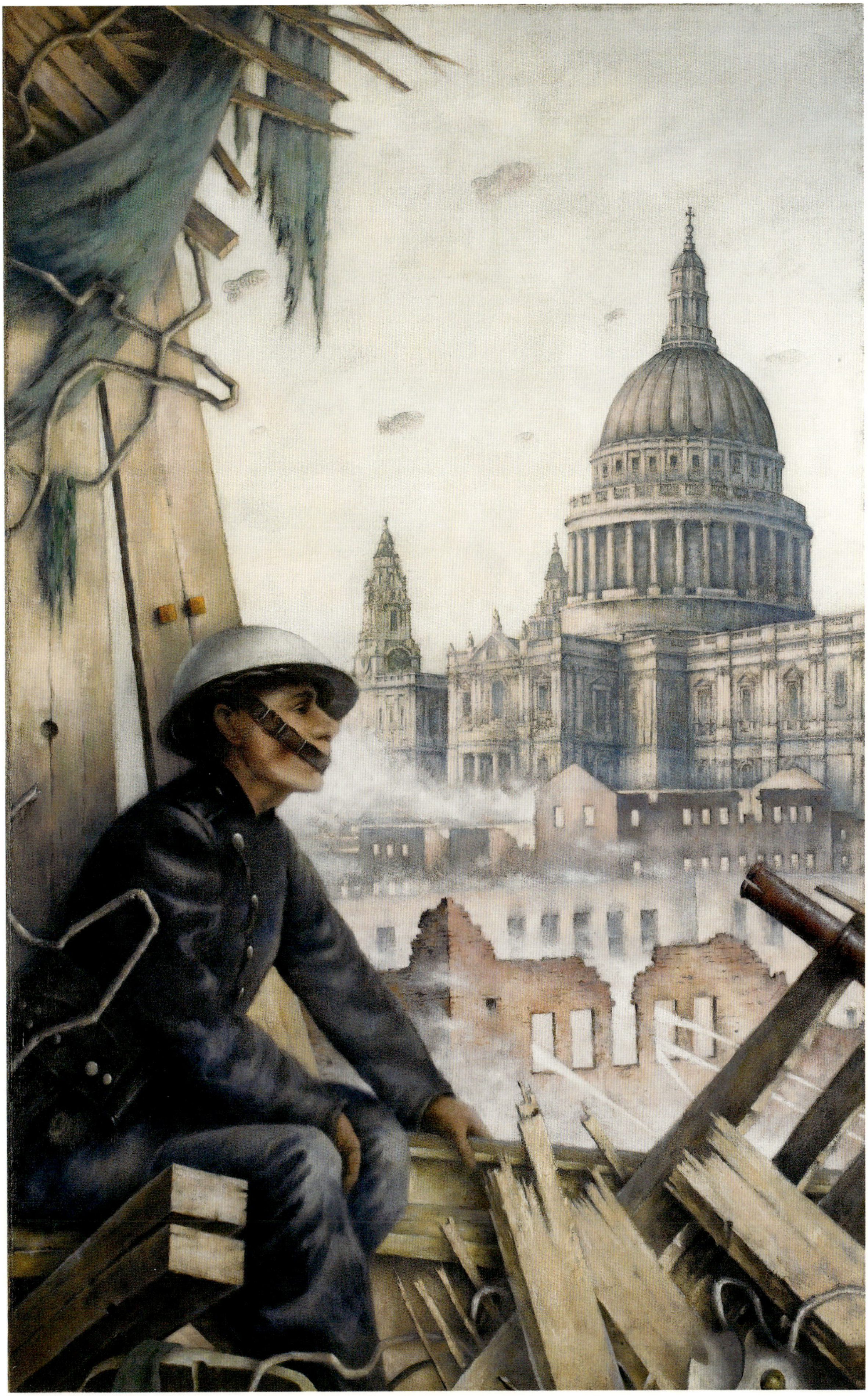

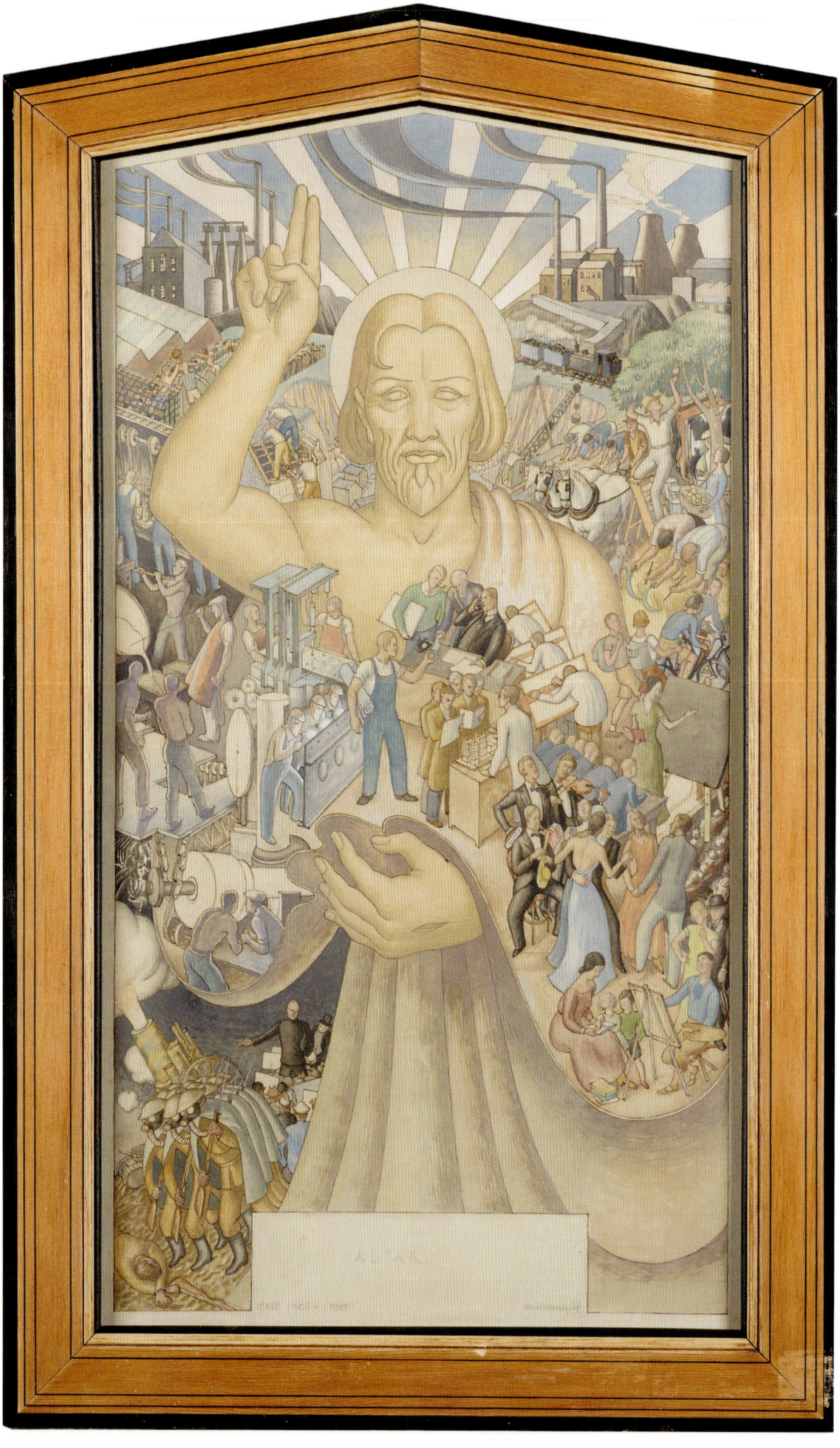
ALTAR

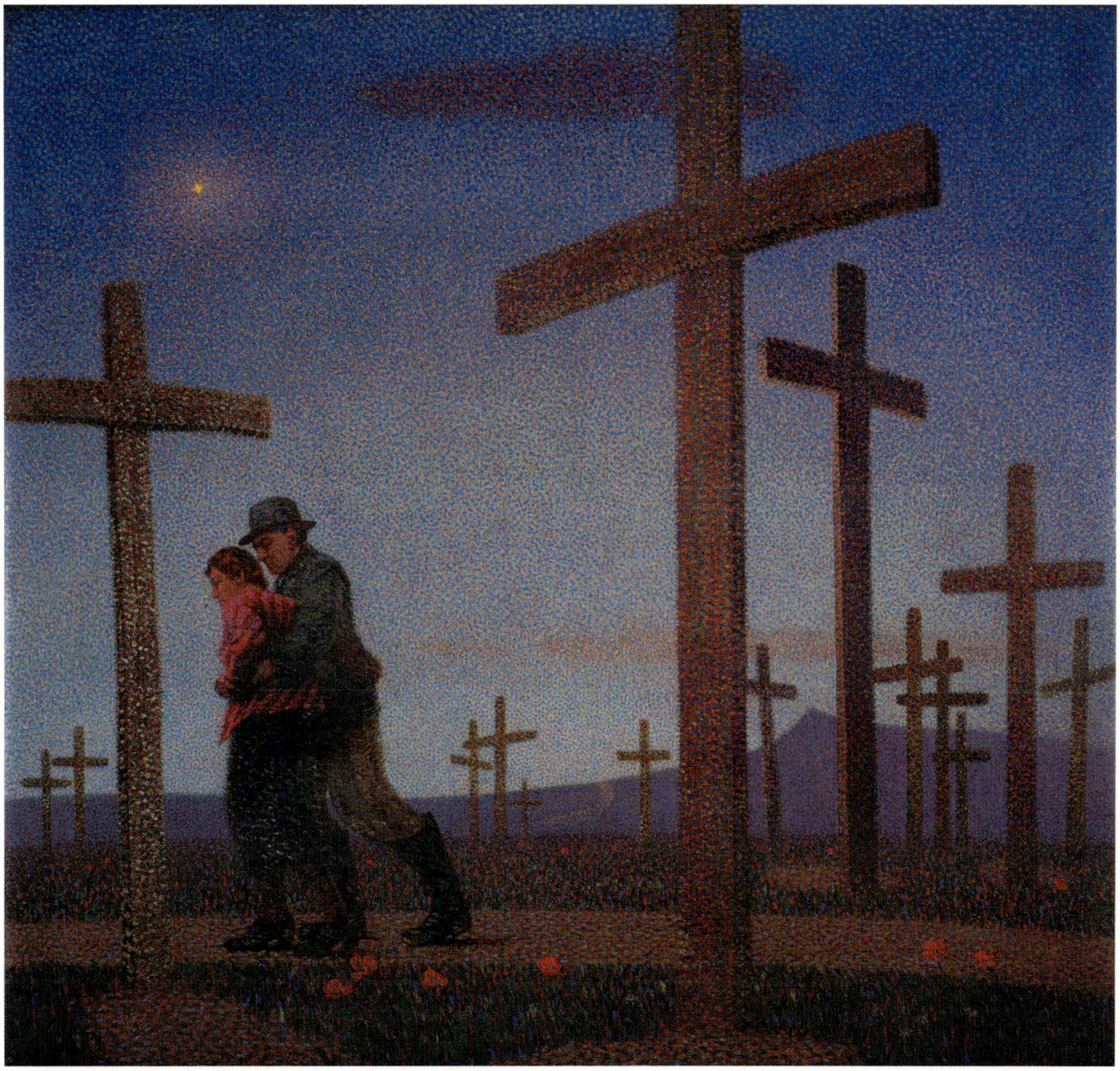

**379 Claude Francis Barry** (1883-1970), *We Shall Remember Them*, c.1945, oil on canvas, 63 x 68 in. (160 x 172.7 cm).

Some of Claude Francis Barry's wartime works reveal an uncharacteristic bleakness: the withered trees, the barren landscapes and leaning crosses supposedly of Monte Cassino (an especially murderous WW2 battle in Italy) suggests a sense of despair. In the conclusion of his treatise on painting, Barry, a life-long pacifist, declared: 'The last fifty years are the most terrible of which history has any record and many of those, myself included, who have lived through them have often wished that they had never been born'. Barry had a particular fondness for Italy – it was only with reluctance that, at the start of WW2, he abandoned his studio in Milan and moved back to England to return to St Ives. The figures in this allegorical imaginative composition, dwarfed by the crucifixes, are of Barry and his wife .

**378 Edward Irvine Halliday** (1902-1984), *Altar (War and Peace)*, 1939, signed and dated, inscribed Altar and 'I inch to a foot', ink and gouache on paper, 30 x 17 in. (76.2 x 43.2 cm).

During the war Halliday worked as an air traffic controller for the RAF and later was transferred to Intelligence and worked on intercepting German radio signals. *Altar* offers a deeply personal and kaleidoscopic vision of war and peace. Conceived in 1939 for an unidentified (and presumably never completed) altar, the dominance of the disproportionately large central figure of Christ recalls that of *Hypnos in Evening on the Roman Campagna*, which though painted in 1928, was exhibited at the Royal Academy in the same year that this composition was conceived.

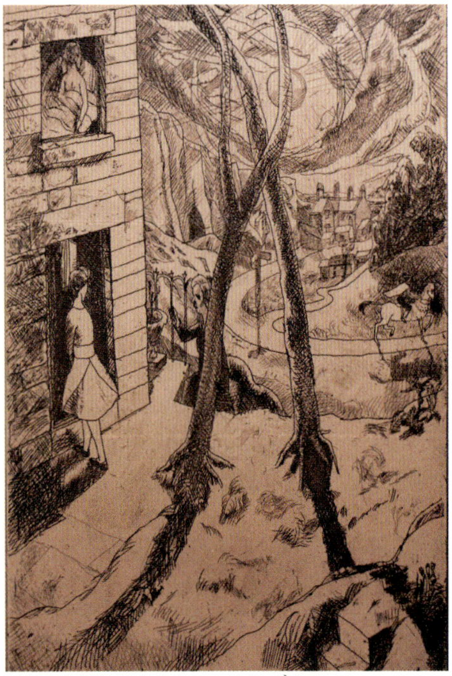

380

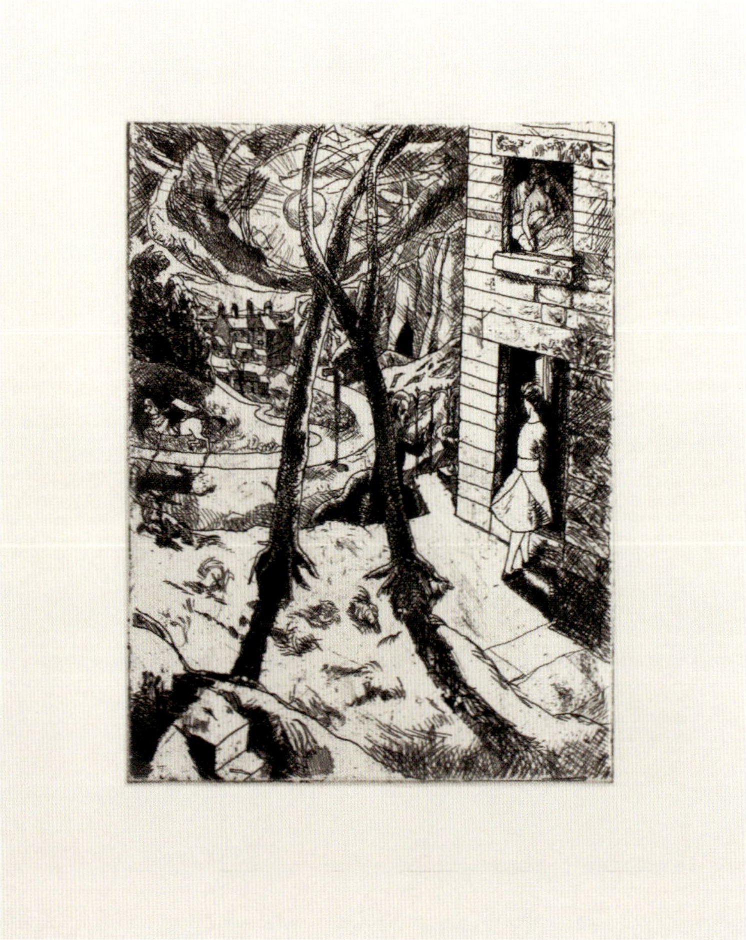

381

**William S Taylor** (1920-2010),

*The Sunne Rising*, c.1953,

**380** original copper plate, 8 x 6 in. (20.2 x 15.1 cm).

**381** etching on paper, image size: 8 x 6 in. (20.2 x 15.1 cm) / print: 12 ¼ x 9 ¾ in. (31.2 x 25.1 cm).

Taylor's pictures combine figure and landscape with strong Neo-Romantic overtones and are saturated with lyricism and a sense of longing. His compositions are frequently set in the artist's Devonshire garden and usually include portraits of his wife, Audrey, (as in this etching), who was a fellow artist.

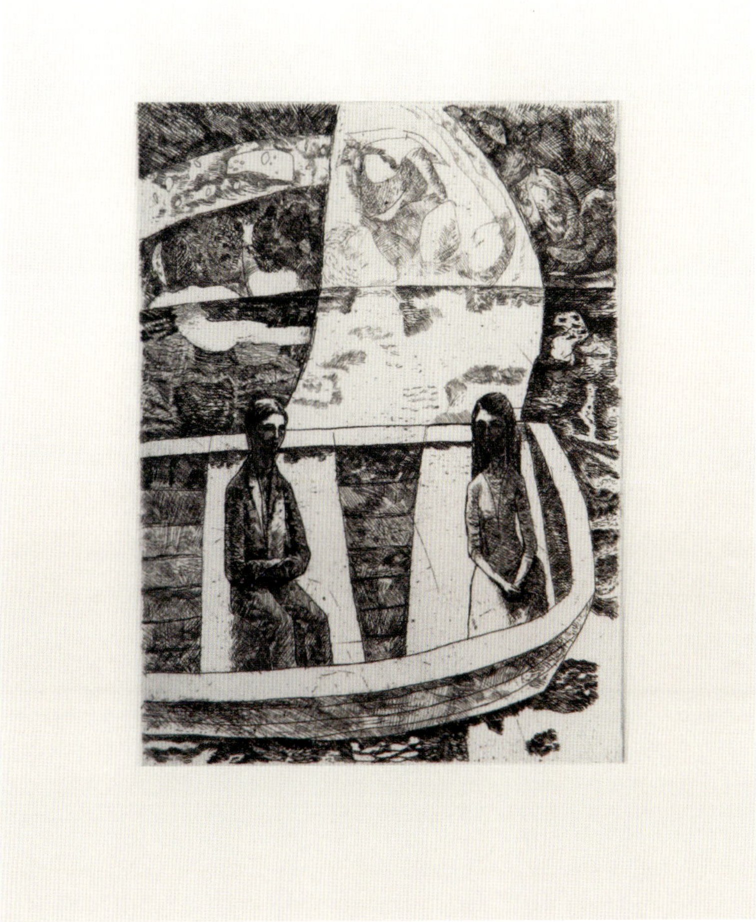

382

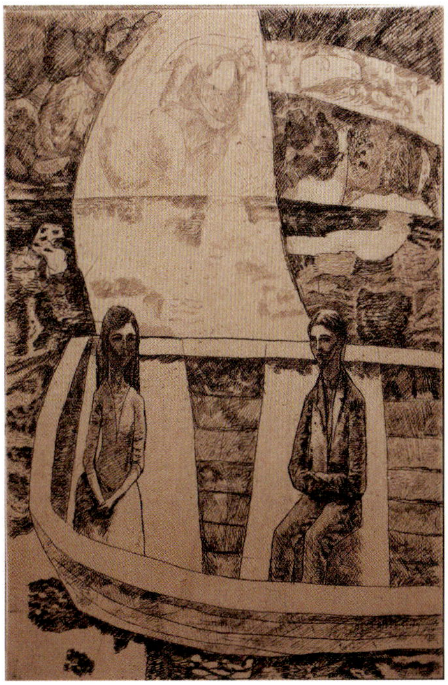

383

William S Taylor (1920-2010),

*Two Figures in a Boat*, c.1953,

382 etching on paper, image size: 8 × 6 in. (20.2 × 15.1 cm) / print: 12 ¼ × 9 ¾ in. (31.2 × 25.1 cm).

383 original copper plate, 8 × 6 in. (20.2 × 15.1 cm).

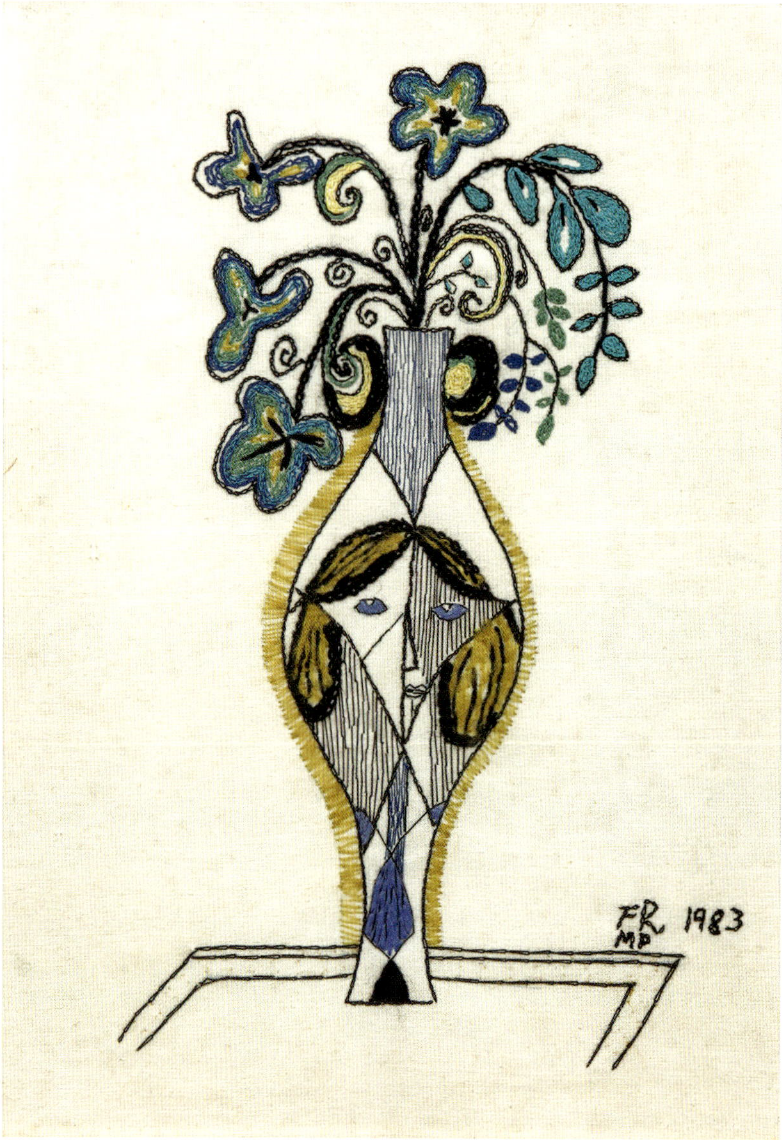


**384** **Frances Richards** (1903-1985), *Vase of Flowers*, signed with initials, and dated 1983, embroidery, 13 ¾ x 8 ¼ in. (35 x 21 cm).

From 1928 to 1939 Frances Richards worked as a teacher in the textile department at the Camberwell School of Art. Throughout her life she experimented with embroidery amongst other media. This portrait head is richly evocative of the artist's relationship with the realms of imagination and nature.

**385** **Barbara Jones** (1912-1978), *Man at Work – A Century of Technical and Social Progress*, 1961, Mural for the International Labour Exhibition of 1961, Central Office of Information, Turin, Italy, two panels, oil on board, overall 168 ¾ x 120 ¼ in. (428.6 x 305.4 cm).

*Man at Work – a Century of Technical and Social Progress* – shows Barbara Jones at what seems to have been her most capricious. A close inspection shows that at least some of the figures have a tenuous connection to the title: a board meeting, some agricultural scenes, coal miners with lamps and canaries, and, in the right ear of the head, a dentist with his patient! However, these few scenes are completely overwhelmed by a plethora of Jones's preferred subjects – a coffin, two couples embracing, a skeleton, a tiger atop a crocodile, and, her very favourite, an owl.

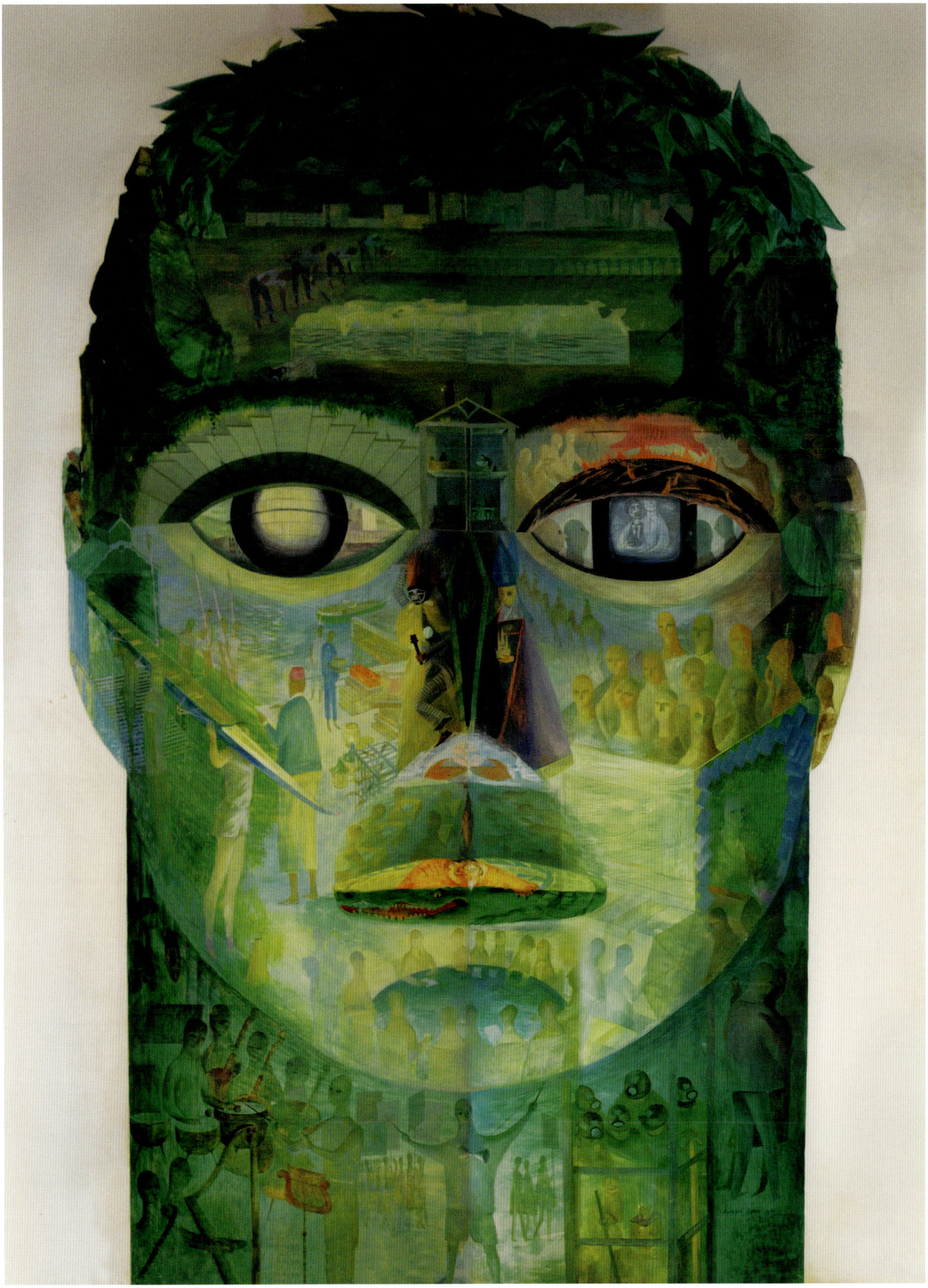

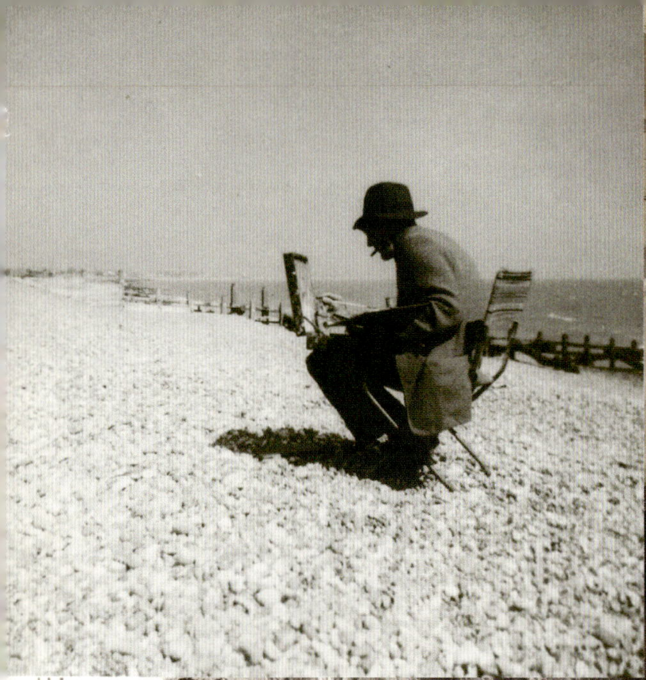
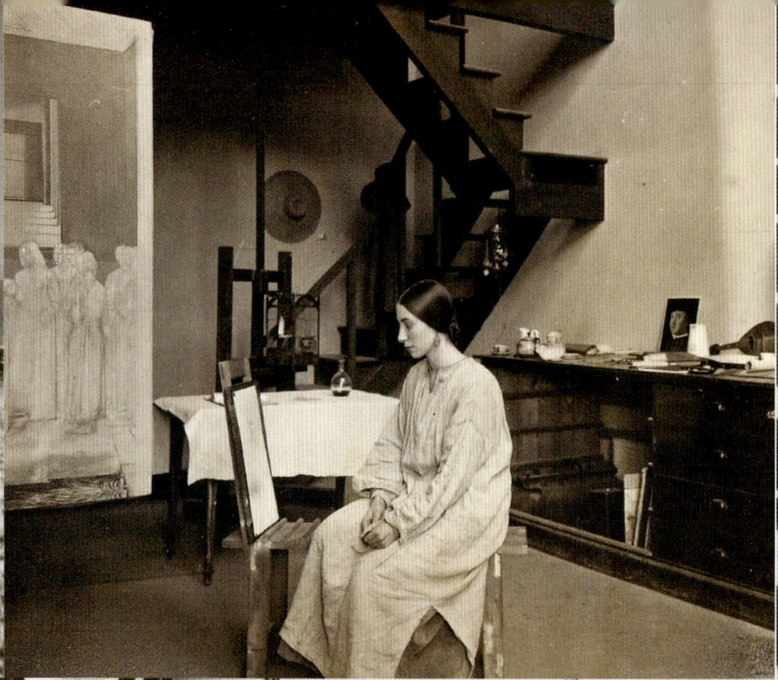
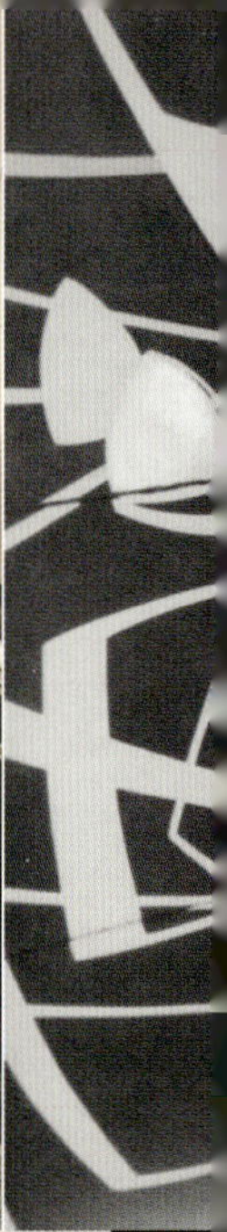
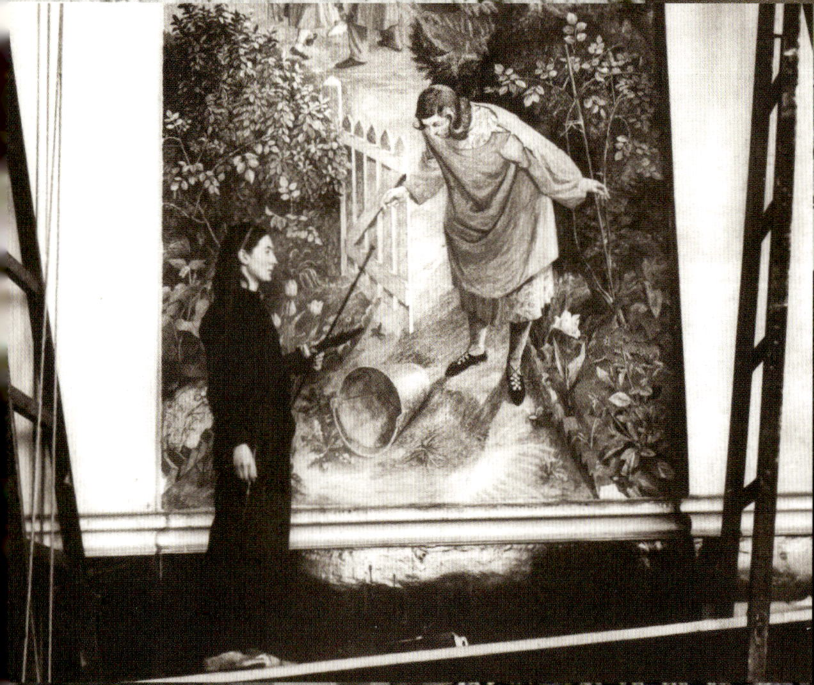
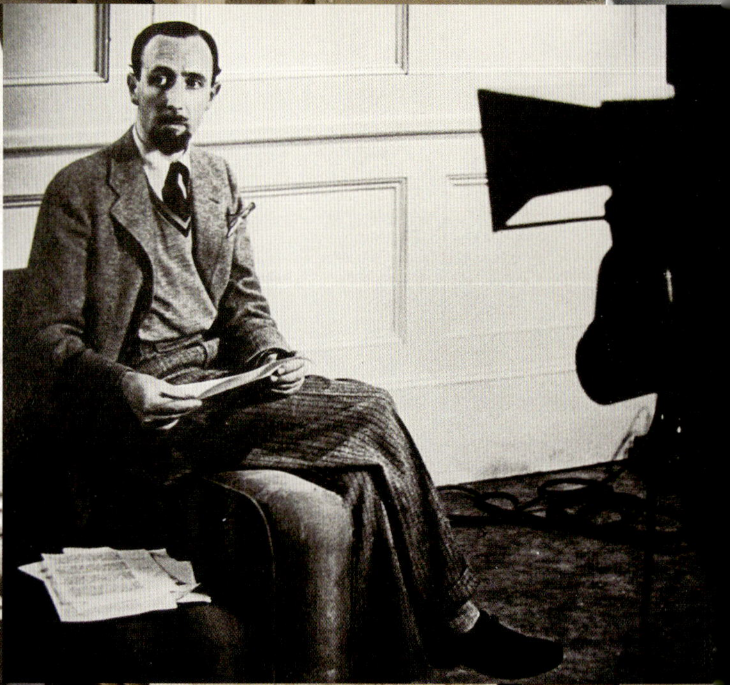
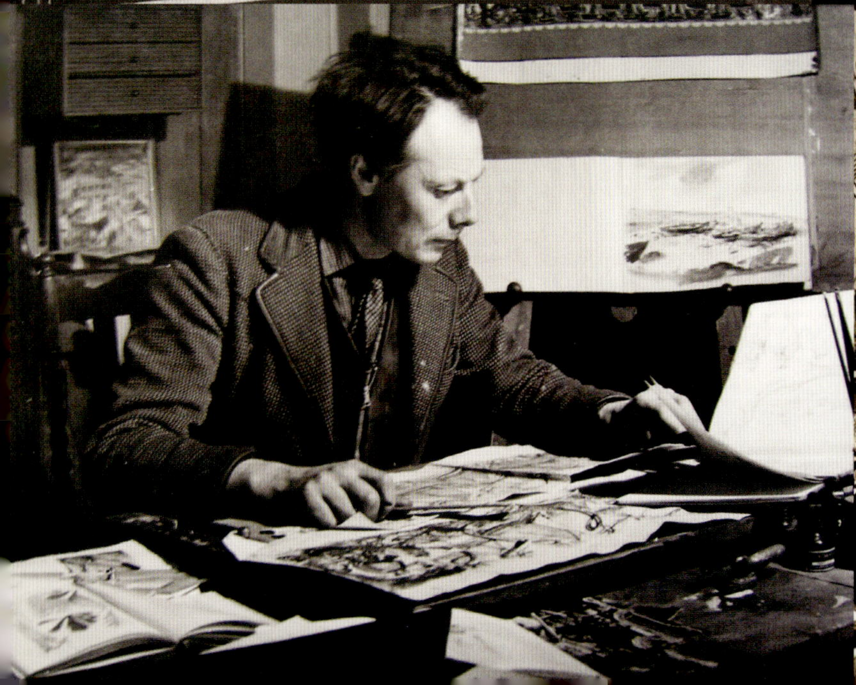
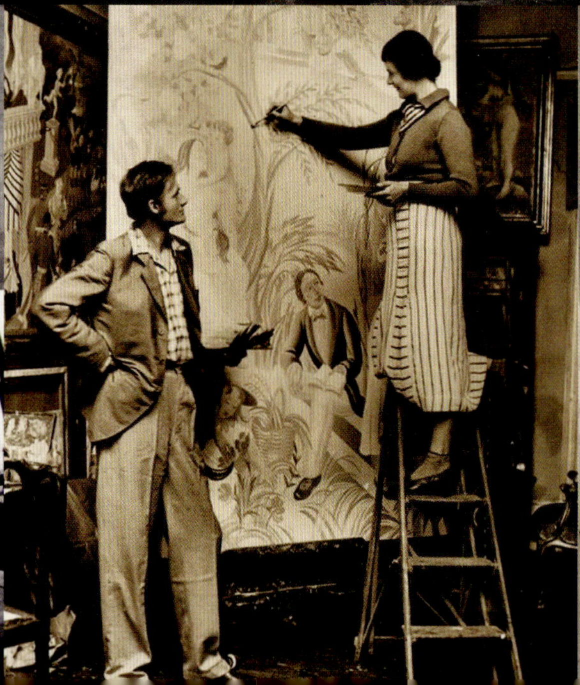
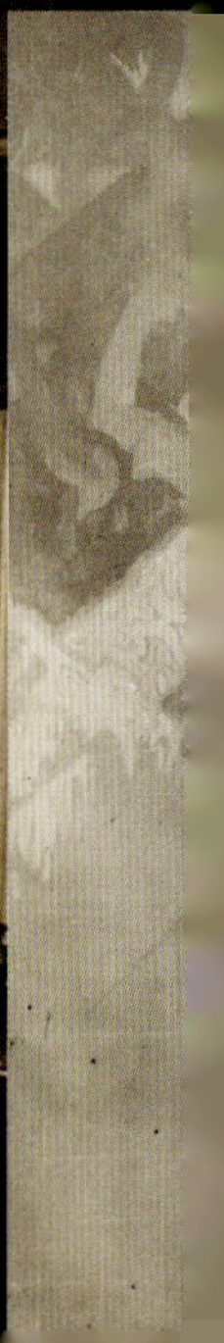

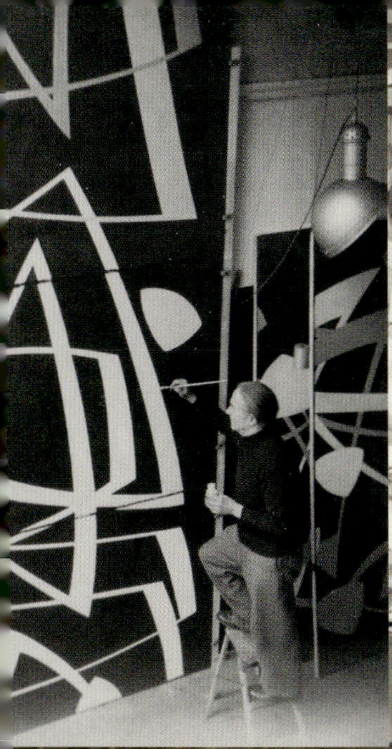

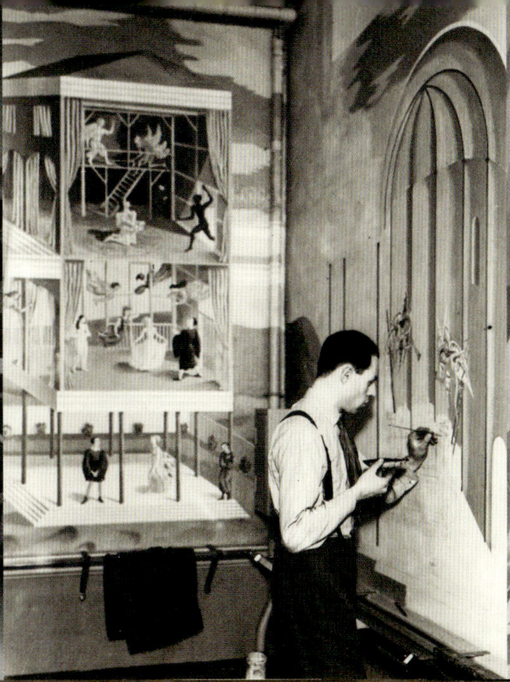

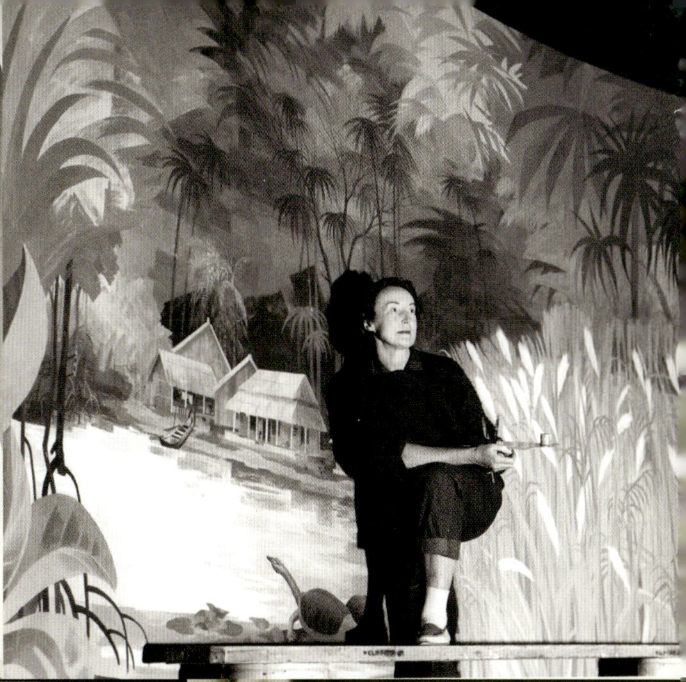

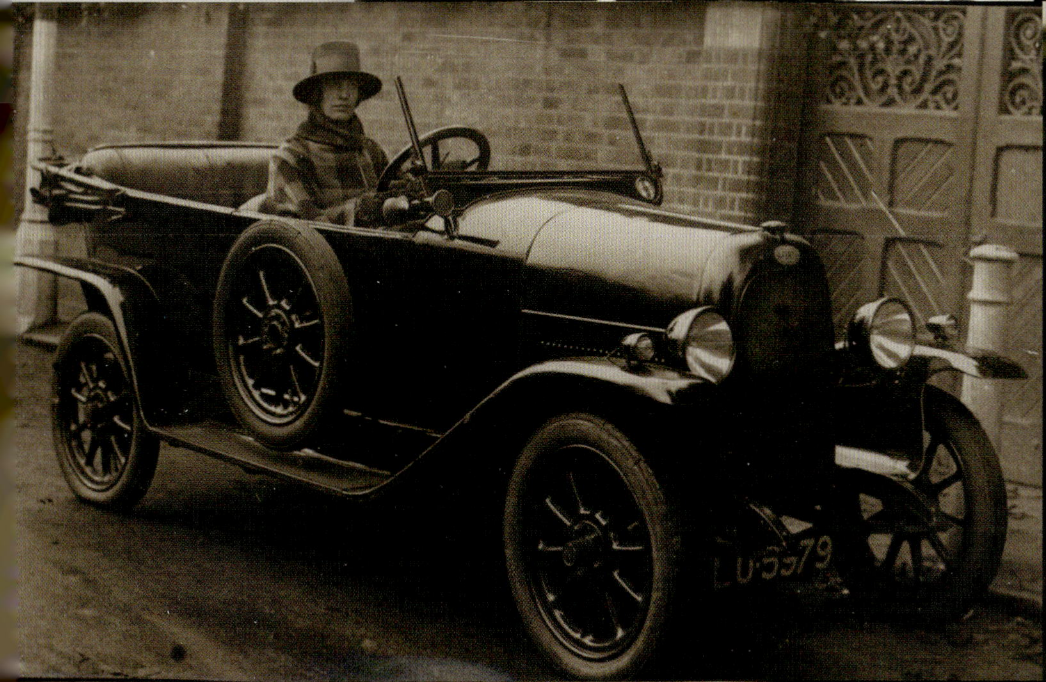

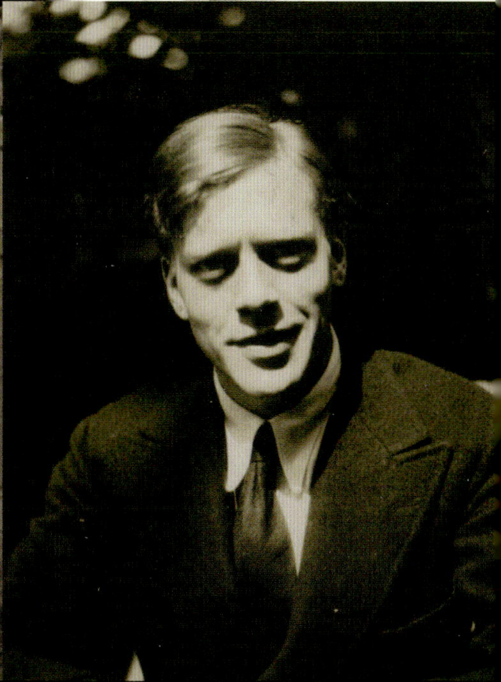

# ARTISTS INDEX

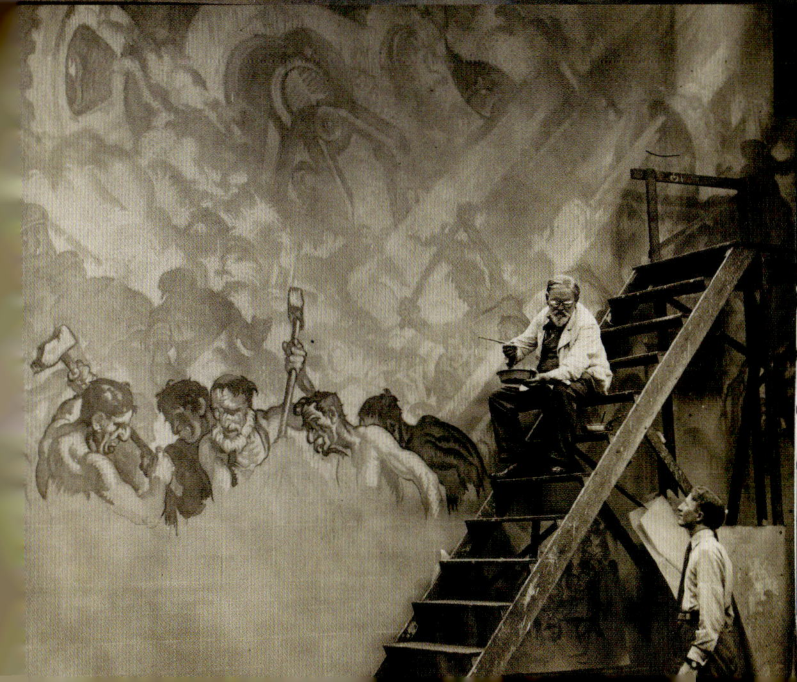

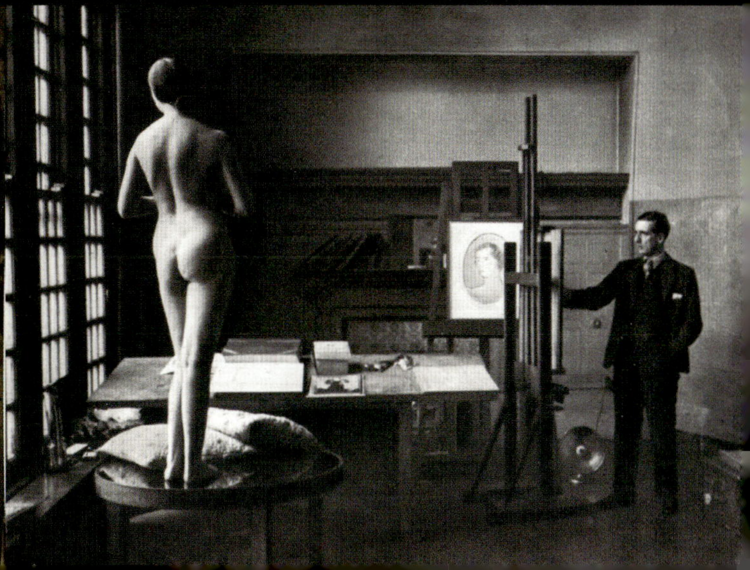

The number which follows each work listed below refers to the page where it can be found.

Audrey Weber (1898-1981)
*The Artist Painting in her Studio* (possibly a self-portrait), 284